The Exegetical Guide to the Greek New Testament

Volumes Available

Matthew	Charles L. Quarles
Mark	Joel F. Williams
Luke	Alan J. Thompson
John	Murray J. Harris
Acts	L. Scott Kellum
Romans	John D. Harvey
2 Corinthians	Colin G. Kruse
Ephesians	Benjamin L. Merkle
Philippians	Joseph H. Hellerman
Colossians, Philemon	Murray J. Harris
Hebrews	Dana M. Harris
James	Chris A. Vlachos
1 Peter	Greg W. Forbes
Revelation	Alexander E. Stewart

Forthcoming Volumes

1 Corinthians	Jay E. Smith
Galatians	Matthew S. Harmon
1–2 Thessalonians	David W. Chapman
1–2 Timothy, Titus	Ray Van Neste
2 Peter, Jude	Terry L. Wilder
1–3 John	Robert L. Plummer

"Stewart's volume on Revelation is a worthy contribution to the excellent EGGNT series. It offers a wealth of information in compact form to aid interpretation, providing concise analysis of features of the Greek text, well-informed insights on the imagery and structure of the book, suggestions about how to preach or teach individual portions, and excellent bibliographies of publications worth pursuing for further study. Most valuable are its reflections on how Revelation draws on the Old Testament as well as extra-canonical Jewish and Christian literature. Highly recommended for those with only a little Greek as well as those with more advanced knowledge who want seasoned guidance on the text and message of Revelation."

—Buist M. Fanning, senior professor emeritus of New Testament studies, Dallas Theological Seminary

"This is a valuable contribution to study of the book of Revelation for a number of reasons: it is a one-stop compendium of exegetical insights on the text of Revelation. It provides comment on all the significant grammar and reasonable solutions to Revelation's well-known grammatical 'irregularities.' It contains an up-to-date bibliography for further personal study and addresses the Old Testament usage in Revelation in a way that demonstrates its interpretive significance. Stewart's work will be a trustworthy exegetical guide through what many consider the most daunting book in the New Testament. The serious student of Revelation will want to have this book close at hand."

—David Mathewson, associate professor of New Testament, Denver Seminary

"Alex Stewart has produced a helpful guide to the Greek text of Revelation. Not only does this volume discuss the Greek text and its significance, list related topical reading, and provide relevant homiletical outlines; it also gives special attention to the use of the Old Testament in Revelation as separate breakout sections. This work is beneficial on so many levels and therefore will no doubt be a valuable resource."

—Benjamin L. Merkle, research professor of New Testament and Greek, Southeastern Baptist Theological Seminary

"For those who are investigating the Greek text of Revelation for the first time or for those wishing to probe deeper into the contents and argument of the book, Stewart's volume on Revelation will be of great benefit. In addition to a clear and concise guide to the syntax and style of the Greek text, readers of this EGGNT volume will also find a very helpful guide to relevant Old Testament texts and wider theological concerns. I hope this volume will encourage many to explore more deeply the contents and language of this important New Testament book."

—Michael Naylor, professor of Bible, Columbia International University

"The grammar in the book of Revelation, not to mention its interpretation, is challenging and in some cases quite controversial. We recognize that there will not be universal agreement on how to interpret Revelation before the return of Jesus Christ. Still, Alex Stewart provides a useful and informative guide to the grammar of this famous book. He also provides interpretive help in unlocking the meaning of the apocalypse. Both students and professors will find this to be a helpful tool in unpacking the grammar of Revelation."

—Thomas R. Schreiner, James Buchanan Harrison Professor of New Testament Interpretation and associate dean, The Southern Baptist Theological Seminary

"Interpreting Revelation is no easy task, often not because of the ambiguity of Greek but because of the canonical and genre-related concerns. Alex Stewart is a helpful guide and conversation partner to navigate the Greek and selected interpretive issues in this book. Being quite conversant with primary and secondary sources, Stewart helpfully guides readers through text-critical, grammatical, theological issues, and homiletical tips for the apocalypse. Irrespective of one's theological commitments about Revelation, Stewart's research will serve and help scholars and teachers of this book."

—Shawn J. Wilhite, associate professor of New Testament, California Baptist University

"Alexander Stewart has done readers of Revelation a great service by carefully explicating its Greek text. A detailed and informed discussion of its grammar and vocabulary is presented throughout. Organized into structural units, the volume also examines Revelation's language as it relates intertextually with the Old Testament. Recommendations for further study direct readers to more detailed discussions of the related verses. Homiletical suggestions highlight significant themes to help with sermon preparation. Scholars, students, and pastors will greatly benefit from this exegetical guide as they study John's apocalypse."

—Mark Wilson, director, Asia Minor Research Center, Antalya, Turkey, and professor extraordinary of New Testament, Stellenbosch University

EXEGETICAL
GUIDE TO THE GREEK
NEW TESTAMENT

REVELATION

Alexander E. Stewart

EXEGETICAL GUIDE TO THE GREEK NEW TESTAMENT

REVELATION

Andreas J. Köstenberger
Robert W. Yarbrough
GENERAL EDITORS

B&H ACADEMIC
Nashville, Tennessee

Exegetical Guide to the Greek New Testament: Revelation

Published by B&H Academic
Brentwood, Tennessee

ISBN: 978-1-4336-7631-4

Dewey Decimal Classification: 228

Subject Heading: BIBLE. N.T. REVELATION—STUDY AND TEACHING \ BIBLE. N.T. REVELATION—CRITICISM

Cover design by B&H Academic.

Printed in the United States of America

29 28 27 26 25 24 VP 1 2 3 4 5 6 7 8

To the faithful pastors who have shepherded and mentored me throughout my life: Mark Castro, Jay Leroux, Andre Rogers, Karl McCallister, Chris Bower, Patrick Womack, Tab Whitley, Al James, Dan Beaulieu, Alexis Wadman, and Alex Barrett.

Contents

REVELATION

Publisher's Preface

It is with great excitement that we publish this volume of the Exegetical Guide to the Greek New Testament series. When the founding editor, Dr. Murray J. Harris, came to us seeking a new publishing partner, we gratefully accepted the offer. With the help of the coeditor, Andreas J. Köstenberger, we spent several years working together to acquire all of the authors we needed to complete the series. By God's grace we succeeded and contracted the last author in 2011. Originally working with another publishing house, Murray's efforts spanned more than twenty years. As God would have it, shortly after the final author was contracted, Murray decided God wanted him to withdraw as coeditor of the series. God made clear to him that he must devote his full attention to taking care of his wife, who faces the daily challenges caused by multiple sclerosis.

Over the course of many years, God has used Murray to teach his students how to properly exegete the Scriptures. He is an exceptional scholar and professor. But even more important, Murray is a man dedicated to serving Christ. His greatest joy is to respond in faithful obedience when his Master calls. "There can be no higher and more ennobling privilege than to have the Lord of the universe as one's Owner and Master and to be his accredited representative on earth."[1] Murray has once again heeded the call of his Master.

It is our privilege to dedicate the Exegetical Guide to the Greek New Testament series to Dr. Murray J. Harris. We pray that our readers will continue the work he started.

1. Murray J. Harris, *Slave of Christ: A New Testament Metaphor for Total Devotion to Christ* (Downers Grove, IL: InterVarsity Press, 1999), 155.

Acknowledgments

No book of this nature is created in a vacuum, and I have many people to thank. I first began exploring Revelation under the guidance of Dr. David Alan Black during my doctoral studies; known by some as a confessionally faithful contrarian, he never ceased to encourage me to pursue the truth with courage regardless of the weight of scholarly consensus or popular pressure. He also significantly deepened my fascination with Greek.

My students at Tyndale Theological Seminary in the Netherlands carefully walked through the text of Revelation with me many times over the years in our morning Greek reading group and Exegesis of Revelation class, and Mark Garavaglia, the president of Tyndale at the time, encouraged my research and writing alongside teaching and administrative tasks.

I am thankful for God's direction to Gateway Seminary, where President Jeff Iorg also encourages and promotes continued academic research. Jesse Harris provided capable research assistance for parsing and definitions along with repeated proofreadings; there are lots of small details in what follows! Thanks are due to Dr. Andreas Köstenberger for guiding me in some early publishing opportunities and inviting me to contribute this volume to the series. Readers of an early draft prevented what would have been several embarrassing errors; thanks here go to Robert Yarbrough, Blake Jurgens, and Mike Naylor.

I am indebted beyond what words could express to my beloved wife, Jenny; twenty-one years ago we never could have guessed where the road would take us, and I dare not even contemplate what life would have been like without you. God's faithfulness is the foundation for my life, and I pray that this book brings him honor; may God's people clearly hear what the Spirit continues to speak to the churches.

Alexander E. Stewart

General Introduction to the EGGNT Series

Studying the New Testament in the original Greek has become easier in recent years. Beginning students will work their way through an introductory grammar or other text, but then what? Grappling with difficult verb forms, rare vocabulary, and grammatical irregularities remains a formidable task for those who would advance beyond the initial stages of learning Greek to master the interpretive process. Intermediate grammars and grammatical analyses can help, but such tools, for all their value, still often operate at a distance from the Greek text itself, and analyses are often too brief to be genuinely helpful.

The Exegetical Guide to the Greek New Testament (EGGNT) aims to close the gap between the Greek text and the available tools. Each EGGNT volume aims to provide all the necessary information for understanding the Greek text and, in addition, includes homiletical helps and suggestions for further study. The EGGNT is not a full-scale commentary. Nevertheless, these guides will make interpreting a given New Testament book easier, in particular for those who are hard-pressed for time and yet want to preach or teach with accuracy and authority.

In terms of layout, each volume begins with a brief introduction to the particular book (including such matters as authorship, date, etc.), a basic outline, and a list of recommended commentaries. At the end of each volume, you will find a comprehensive exegetical outline of the book. The body of each volume is devoted to paragraph-by-paragraph exegesis of the text. The treatment of each paragraph includes:

1. The Greek text of the passage, phrase by phrase, from the fifth edition of the United Bible Societies' *Greek New Testament* (UBS^5).
2. A structural analysis of the passage. Typically, verbal discussion of the structure of a given unit is followed by a diagram, whereby the verbal discussion serves to explain the diagram and the diagram serves to provide a visual aid illumining the structural discussion. While there is no one correct or standard way to diagram Greek sentences, the following format is typically followed in EGGNT volumes:

a. The original Greek word order is maintained.
b. When Greek words are omitted, this is indicated by ellipses (. . .).
c. The diagramming method, moving from left to right, is predicated on the following. In clauses with a finite verb, the default order is typically verb-subject-object. In verbless clauses or clauses with nonfinite verb forms, the default order is typically subject-(verb)-object. Departures from these default orders are understood to be pragmatically motivated (e.g., contrast, emphasis, etc.).
d. Indents are used to indicate subordination (e.g., in the case of dependent clauses).
e. Retaining original word order, modifiers are centered above or below the word they modify (e.g., a prepositional phrase in relation to the verb).
f. Where a given sentence or clause spans multiple lines of text, drawn lines are used, such as where a relative pronoun introduces a relative clause (often shifting emphasis).
g. Underline is used to indicate imperatives; dotted underline is used to indicate repetition (the same word or cognate used multiple times in a given unit); the symbol ⁝ may be used where an article is separated from a noun or participle by interjected material (such as a prepositional phrase).
h. In shorter letters diagrams are normally provided for every unit; in longer letters and Revelation, ellipses may be used to show less detail in diagramming (keeping larger blocks together on the same line) in order to focus primarily on the larger structure of a given unit; in the Gospels and Acts, detailed diagrams will usually not be provided, though less detailed diagrams may be used to illustrate important or more complex structural aspects of a given passage.

3. A discussion of each phrase of the passage with discussion of relevant vocabulary, significant textual variants, and detailed grammatical analysis, including parsing. When more than one solution is given for a particular exegetical issue, the author's own preference is indicated by an asterisk (*). When no preference is expressed, the options are judged to be evenly balanced, or it is assumed that the text is intentionally ambiguous. When a particular verb form may be parsed in more than one way, only the parsing appropriate in the specific context is supplied; but where there is difference of opinion among grammarians or commentators, both possibilities are given and the matter is discussed.
4. Various translations of significant words or phrases.
5. A list of suggested topics for further study with bibliography for each topic. An asterisk (*) in one of the "For Further Study" bibliographies draws attention to a discussion of the particular topic that is recommended as a useful introduction to the issues involved.
6. Homiletical suggestions designed to help the preacher or teacher move from the Greek text to a sermon outline that reflects careful exegesis. The first

> suggestion for a particular paragraph of the text is always more exegetical than homiletical and consists of an outline of the entire paragraph. These detailed outlines of each paragraph build on the general outline proposed for the whole book and, if placed side by side, form a comprehensive exegetical outline of the book. All outlines are intended to serve as a basis for sermon preparation and should be adapted to the needs of a particular audience.[1]

The EGGNT volumes will serve a variety of readers. Those reading the Greek text for the first time may be content with the assistance with vocabulary, parsing, and translation. Readers with some experience in Greek may want to skip or skim these sections and focus attention on the discussions of grammar. More advanced students may choose to pursue the topics and references to technical works under "For Further Study," while pastors may be more interested in the movement from grammatical analysis to sermon outline. Teachers may appreciate having a resource that frees them to focus on exegetical details and theological matters.

The editors are pleased to present you with the individual installments of the EGGNT. We are grateful for each of the contributors who has labored long and hard over each phrase in the Greek New Testament. Together we share the conviction that "all Scripture is inspired by God and is profitable for teaching, for rebuking, for correcting, for training in righteousness" (2 Tim 3:16 CSB) and echo Paul's words to Timothy: "Be diligent to present yourself to God as one approved, a worker who doesn't need to be ashamed, correctly teaching the word of truth" (2 Tim 2:15).

Andreas J. Köstenberger
Robert W. Yarbrough

1. As a Bible publisher, B&H Publishing follows the "Colorado Springs Guidelines for Translation of Gender-Related Language in Scripture." As an academic book publisher, B&H Academic asks that authors conform their manuscripts (including EGGNT exegetical outlines in English) to the B&H Academic style guide, which affirms the use of singular "he/his/him" as generic examples encompassing both genders. However, in their discussion of the Greek text, EGGNT authors have the freedom to analyze the text and reach their own conclusions regarding whether specific Greek words are gender specific or gender inclusive.

Abbreviations

For abbreviations used in discussion of text-critical matters, the reader should refer to the abbreviations listed in the Introduction to the United Bible Societies' *Greek New Testament*.

*	Indicates the reading of the original hand of a manuscript as opposed to subsequent correctors of the manuscript; *or* indicates the writer's own preference when more than one solution is given for a particular exegetical problem; *or* indicates a discussion of the particular topic that is recommended as a useful introduction to the issues involved in the "For Further Study" bibliographies.

Books of the Old Testament

Gen	Genesis	Song	Song of Songs (Canticles)
Exod	Exodus	Isa	Isaiah
Lev	Leviticus	Jer	Jeremiah
Num	Numbers	Lam	Lamentations
Deut	Deuteronomy	Ezek	Ezekiel
Josh	Joshua	Dan	Daniel
Judg	Judges	Hos	Hosea
Ruth	Ruth	Joel	Joel
1–2 Sam	1–2 Samuel	Amos	Amos
[1–2 Kgdms]	[1–2 Kingdoms] LXX	Obad	Obadiah
1–2 Kgs	1–2 Kings	Jonah	Jonah
[3–4 Kgdms]	[3–4 Kingdoms] LXX	Mic	Micah
1–2 Chr	1–2 Chronicles	Nah	Nahum
Ezra	Ezra	Hab	Habakkuk

Neh	Nehemiah	Zeph	Zephaniah
Esth	Esther	Hag	Haggai
Job	Job	Zech	Zechariah
Ps(s)	Psalm(s)	Mal	Malachi
Prov	Proverbs		
Eccl	Ecclesiastes		

Books of the New Testament

Matt	Matthew	1–2 Thess	1–2 Thessalonians
Mark	Mark	1–2 Tim	1–2 Timothy
Luke	Luke	Titus	Titus
John	John	Phlm	Philemon
Acts	Acts	Heb	Hebrews
Rom	Romans	Jas	James
1–2 Cor	1–2 Corinthians	1–2 Pet	1–2 Peter
Gal	Galatians	1–3 John	1–3 John
Eph	Ephesians	Jude	Jude
Phil	Philippians	Rev	Revelation
Col	Colossians		

Apocrypha, Pseudepigrapha, Dead Sea Scrolls, and Apostolic Fathers

1QH[a]	Thanksgiving Hymns (Hodayot)
As. Mos.	Assumption of Moses
Bar	Baruch
Barn.	Barnabas
2 Bar.	2 Baruch
Did.	Didache
1 En.	1 Enoch
1–2 Esd	1–2 Esdras
4 Ezra	4 Ezra
1–4 Macc	1–4 Maccabees
Mart. Ascen. Isa.	Martyrdom and Ascension of Isaiah
Pss. Sol.	Psalms of Solomon
Sir	Sirach/Ecclesiasticus
Tob	Tobit
T. Benj.	Testament of Benjamin
T. Jos.	Testament of Joseph

T. Sol.	Testament of Solomon
Wis	Wisdom of Solomon

Grammatical, Syntactical, and Textual Abbreviations

abs.	absolute(ly)
acc(s).	accusative(s)
act.	active
AD	*anno Domini* (in the year of our Lord)
adj(s).	adjective(s)
adv.	adverb(ial)
anar.	anarthrous
ant(s).	antecedent(s)
aor.	aorist
apod.	apodosis
appos.	apposition, appositional
Aram.	Aramaic
art.	(definite) article, articular
attrib.	attributive, attributively
cl(s).	clause(s)
comp.	comparative, comparison
compl.	complement
cond.	condition(al)
conj.	conjunctive, conjunction
coord.	coordinating
dat(s).	dative(s)
def.	definite
demonst.	demonstrative
dep.	deponent
dir.	direct
Eng.	English
epex.	epexegetic, epexegetical(ly)
emph.	emphatic, emphasis
esp.	especially
fem.	feminine
fut.	future
gen(s).	genitive(s)
Gk.	Greek

Heb.	Hebrew, Hebraism
impers.	impersonal
impf.	imperfect (tense)
impv(s).	imperative(s) (mood), imperatival(ly)
indef.	indefinite
indic.	indicative (mood)
indir.	indirect
inf(s).	infinitive(s)
instr.	instrument, instrumental(ly)
interj.	interjection
interr.	interrogative
iter.	iterative
lit.	literal(ly)
loc.	locative
LXX	Septuagint (Greek Old Testament)
masc.	masculine
mid.	middle
ms(s)	manuscript(s)
MT	Masoretic Text (Hebrew/Aramaic Old Testament)
neg.	negative, negation
neut.	neuter
nom(s).	nominative(s)
NT	New Testament
obj(s).	object(s), object(ive)
OT	Old Testament
part.	partitive
pass.	passive
periph.	periphrastic
pers.	person(al)
pf.	perfect
plpf.	pluperfect
pl(s).	plural(s)
poss.	possessive, possession
pred.	predicate, predicative
pref.	prefix
prep.	preposition(al)

pres.	present
prob.	probably
pron(s).	pronoun(s)
prot.	protasis
ptc(s).	participle(s), participial(ly)
refl.	reflexive
rel.	relative
sg.	singular
subj(s).	subject(s), subject(ive)
subjunc(s).	subjunctive(s)
subord.	subordinate, subordination
subst.	substantive, substantival(ly)
superl.	superlative
syn.	synonym
temp.	temporal(ly)
Theod.	Theodotion
TR	Textus Receptus
vb(s).	verb(s)
voc.	vocative

Secondary Sources Abbreviations

AB	Anchor Bible
ABG	Arbeiten zur Bibel und ihrer Geschichte
Aune[a, b, c]	D. E. Aune, *Revelation*, 3 vols., WBC 52 (Waco: Word; Nashville: Nelson, 1997–1998)
AUSDDS	Andrews University Seminary Doctoral Dissertation Series
AUSS	Andrews University Seminary Studies
Bauckham	R. J. Bauckham, *The Climax of Prophecy: Studies in the Book of Revelation* (Edinburgh: T&T Clark, 1993)
BBR	*Bulletin for Biblical Research*
Beale	G. K. Beale, *The Book of Revelation*, NIGTC (Grand Rapids: Eerdmans, 1999)
BECNT	Baker Exegetical Commentary on the New Testament
BETL	Bibliotheca Ephemeridum Theologicarum Lovaniensium
BDAG	*A Greek-English Lexicon of the New Testament and Other Early Christian Literature*, rev. and ed. F. W. Danker (Chicago: University of Chicago, 2000)
Bib	*Biblica*

BibInt	Biblical Interpretation Series
BR	*Biblical Research*
Brill	F. Montanari, *The Brill Dictionary of Ancient Greek*, ed. Madeleine Goh and Chad Schroeder (Leiden: Brill, 2015)
BTB	*Biblical Theology Bulletin*
BZNW	Beihefte zur Zeitschrift für die neutestamentliche Wissenschaft
CBQ	*Catholic Biblical Quarterly*
Charles	R. H. Charles, *A Critical and Exegetical Commentary on the Revelation of St. John*, 2 vols., ICC (Edinburgh: Clark, 1920)
CTJ	*Calvin Theological Journal*
CTR	*Criswell Theological Review*
CurBR	*Currents in Biblical Research*
EVV	English versions of the Bible
Fanning	B. M. Fanning, *Revelation*, Zondervan Exegetical Commentary on the New Testament (Grand Rapids: Zondervan Academic, 2020)
GDNTG	A. J. Köstenberger, B. L. Merkle, and R. L. Plummer, *Going Deeper with New Testament Greek: An Intermediate Study of the Grammar and Syntax of the New Testament* (Nashville: B&H Academic, 2016)
Harris	M. J. Harris, *Prepositions and Theology in the Greek New Testament: An Essential Reference Resource for Exegesis* (Grand Rapids: Zondervan, 2012)
HBT	*Horizons in Biblical Theology*
HTR	*Harvard Theological Review*
ICC	International Critical Commentary
JBL	*Journal of Biblical Literature*
JETS	*Journal of the Evangelical Theological Society*
JSNT	*Journal for the Study of the New Testament*
JSNTSup	Journal for the Study of the New Testament Supplement Series
JSOT	*Journal for the Study of the Old Testament*
Koester	C. R. Koester, *Revelation: A New Translation with Introduction and Commentary*, AB 38A (New Haven: Yale University Press, 2014)
L&N	J. P. Louw and E. A. Nida, eds., *Introduction and Domains*, vol. 1 of *Greek-English Lexicon of the New Testament Based on Semantic Domains* (New York: United Bible Societies, 1988)
LNTS	The Library of New Testament Studies
Math	D. L. Mathewson, *Revelation: A Handbook on the Greek Text* (Waco: Baylor University Press, 2016)

Moţ	L. F. Moţ, *Morphological and Syntactical Irregularities in the Book of Revelation: A Greek Hypothesis*, Linguistic Biblical Studies 11 (Leiden: Brill, 2015)
Metzger	B. M. Metzger, *A Textual Commentary on the Greek New Testament*, 2nd ed. (New York: United Bible Societies, 1994)
Neot	*Neotestamentica*
NIGTC	The New International Greek Testament Commentary
NovT	*Novum Testamentum*
NovTSup	Supplements to Novum Testamentum
NTS	*New Testament Studies*
OHR	C. R. Koester, ed., *The Oxford Handbook of the Book of Revelation* (Oxford: Oxford University Press, 2020)
Osborne	G. R. Osborne, *Revelation*, BECNT (Grand Rapids: Baker Academic, 2002)
Runge	S. E. Runge, *Discourse Grammar of the Greek New Testament: A Practical Introduction for Teaching and Exegesis* (Peabody, MA: Hendrickson, 2010)
S&B	A. E. Stewart, and A. Bandy, eds., *The Apocalypse of John among Its Critics* (Bellingham, WA: Lexham, 2023)
SBL	Society of Biblical Literature
SNTSMS	Society for New Testament Studies Monograph Series
StABH	Studies in American Biblical Hermeneutics
StBibLit	Studies in Biblical Literature (Lang)
Thomas	R. L. Thomas, *Revelation: An Exegetical Commentary*, 2 vols. (Chicago: Moody, 1992, 1995)
TJ	*Trinity Journal*
Thompson	S. Thompson, *The Apocalypse and Semitic Syntax*, SNTSMS 52 (Cambridge: Cambridge University Press, 1985)
TynBul	*Tyndale Bulletin*
Wallace	D. B. Wallace, *Greek Grammar Beyond the Basics: An Exegetical Syntax of the New Testament* (Grand Rapids: Zondervan, 1996). This is the source for the main grammatical and syntactical labels used throughout.
WBC	Word Biblical Commentary
WTJ	*Westminster Theological Journal*
WUNT	Wissenschaftliche Untersuchungen zum Neuen Testament
ZNW	Zeitschrift für die neutestamentliche Wissenschaft und die Kunde der älteren Kirche

REVELATION

Introduction

Exegesis of Revelation differs in several ways from that of the Gospels or NT Epistles. The reader will quickly realize that most of the popular debates and disagreements regarding the interpretation of Revelation do not hinge on a careful analysis of the Greek text but depend instead upon much larger interpretive discussions of the relation of OT prophecy to NT fulfillment. This should not discourage careful engagement with the Greek text of Revelation, but it is important to have proper expectations of what kind of answers the Greek text can and cannot provide. Revelation, perhaps more than other NT books, requires careful attention to both intratextual connections within the text of Revelation itself and intertextual connections to the OT and other Second Temple Jewish texts. Although space constraints preclude structural outlines and require a limited discussion of many important points, this guide gives special attention to the use of the OT in Revelation alongside the more traditional discussions of grammar, syntax, lexicography, and textual criticism. The use of the OT is perhaps the most important contribution a careful study of the Greek text of Revelation can make to the broader interpretive questions that continue to divide Christians. Revelation can make a significant contribution to the spiritual health and sanctification of God's people, if it is clearly proclaimed by faithful pastors.

AUTHORSHIP

The author is clearly John (Rev 1:1, 4, 9; 22:8), and based on the external evidence it is possible, if not probable, that he was the same John who wrote the Gospel and Johannine Letters (Justin, *Dialogue with Trypho* 81.4; Irenaeus, *Against Heresies* 4.14.1; 4.20.11; 5.26.1; Clement of Alexandria, *Salvation of the Rich* 42; *Miscellanies* 6.106; *Christ the Educator* 2.108, 119; Hippolytus, *De antichristo* 36–42; Eusebius, *Ecclesiastical History* 3.18.1). Internal evidence is inconclusive, and many interpreters do not make a firm decision on the identity of the author (for detailed discussion, see Aune[a] xlvii–lvi; Beale 34–36; Koester 65–69; Fanning 24–28).

DATE

Most scholars today support a date during the reign of Domitian (AD 81–96), with either Nero's (AD 54–68) or Galba's reign (AD 68–69) also a possibility (Wilson,

"Problem of the Domitianic Date"). Craig Koester rightly argues that many of the relevant factors could apply anytime during the final decades of the first century (*OHR* 3). Exegetes should be suspicious of interpretations that place too much weight on a specific date (for detailed discussion, see Aune[a] lvi–lxx; Beale 4–27; Koester 71–80).

GENRE

The definition of an apocalypse proposed by John J. Collins has been widely accepted: "'Apocalypse' is a genre of revelatory literature with a narrative framework, in which a revelation is mediated by an otherworldly being to a human recipient, disclosing a transcendent reality which is both temporal, insofar as it envisages eschatological salvation, and spatial insofar as it involves another, supernatural world" (J. J. Collins, "Morphology of a Genre," 9). This was later helpfully revised to include a statement of function: "intended to interpret present, earthly circumstances in light of the supernatural world and of the future, and to influence both the understanding and the behavior of the audience by means of divine authority" (A. Y. Collins, "Early Christian Apocalypticism," 7). This definition of the apocalyptic genre matches Revelation quite well and would suggest that Revelation is an apocalypse. Revelation, however, played an important role in the scholarly formulation of the definition, and the line between prophecy and apocalypse is notoriously blurry. Revelation is also introduced as a letter. Different scholars place different emphases on each of these three generic identifications, but most interpreters realize that Revelation is a mixed genre with similarities to other apocalypses, prophecies, and letters.

Genre identification greatly impacts interpretation. Comparison with other apocalypses leads a reader to expect Revelation to include a claim to divine authority for a revelation of heavenly realities through heavily symbolic visions in a narrative framework intended to instruct and motivate hearers. Comparison of John's use of symbols with other Jewish and Christian apocalypses often sheds light on John's intended meaning.

Seeing Revelation as a prophecy highlights the motivational element of the text in how it calls God's people to repentance and perseverance through warnings of judgment and promises of salvation. It also alerts readers to the way that John explicitly sought to model his message on the Hebrew writing prophets. Many of his visions become clear when seen as parallel to or as specific interpretations of visions in prior biblical prophecy.

Revelation's epistolary framework stresses the interpretive importance of John's original historical and sociological context. Revelation was written by a specific individual to other specific individuals about specific issues at a specific time and specific place. This historical context matters for evaluating proposed interpretations, and greater weight should be given to interpretations that would have been intelligible and meaningful to Christians at the end of the first century.

STRUCTURE

Revelation can be outlined in various ways, but the basic transitions are generally easy to identify. The approach taken here is to identify major transitions based on the repetition of the phrase "in the Spirit" in 1:10; 4:2; 17:3; 21:10 with subdivisions based on transitions from one vision and topic to another. Most outlines identify similar divisions, although different labels are used to describe the contents. Apart from an outline, the interpretation of the meaning of the structure of the Apocalypse is a highly debated point. There has been growing support for a forward-moving spiral with visions both overlapping and progressing (Koester 112–15) or what is more traditionally discussed as a symbolic progressive recapitulation interpretation of the seven seals, trumpets, and bowls (Beale 121–44). However, there is no consensus. Aune argues that the author "intends the visions themselves to constitute *a single chronological narrative of the eschatological events that will soon begin to unfold*" (Aune[a] xciii; italics original) while Fanning argues for chronological progression with a telescoping of the seals, trumpets, and bowls (Fanning 61–63).

Some form of progressive repetition or forward-moving spiraling seems likely based on the following examples of intratextual repetition (cf. Beale 121–41). First, there are repeated similar and apparently parallel scenes of final judgment and salvation throughout the book. Second, the conclusions of the seals (Rev 8:5), trumpets (11:19), and bowls (16:18–21) sections each contain a repetition of the same phrase from Exod 19:16–19 (sounds, lightning flashes, earthquake). Third, the repetition of three and a half years of persecution in Rev 11:2, 3; 12:6, 14; 13:5 suggests that the visions in Revelation 11, 12, and 13 do not follow one another chronologically but rather cover the same period of time. Fourth, the repetition of the phrase "gather them together for war" in Rev 16:14; 19:19; 20:8 could suggest that Rev 15:1–16:21; 17:1–19:10; 19:11–21:8 refer to the same time and episode and not to multiple final battles. Most interpreters acknowledge overlap in 16:14 and 19:19 with more disagreement on how to connect 20:8. Fifth, the refrain about the fall of Babylon in Rev 14:8; 16:19; 17:16; 18:2, 10, 17, 19–21; 19:2–3 does not point to separate events, but the same visionary event. Sixth, Revelation is heavily influenced by Daniel. Daniel's five visions all evidence recapitulation—pointing to the same period of time and the same events from different perspectives and with different degrees of detail and specificity (Daniel 2; 7; 8; 9; 10–12). Isaiah and Ezekiel also contain significant instances of recapitulation in their prophecies; visionary and oracular repetition is a normal literary feature of the Hebrew writing prophets. These instances of intratextual repetition will be discussed at the appropriate points below and are explained in various ways by the different interpretive approaches.

THE GREEK TEXT

Three hundred ten Greek mss are known to exist for Revelation: seven papyri, twelve majuscules, and 291 minuscules; the second- and third-century mss are fragmentary, with the earliest mss of the entire text being Sinaiticus and Alexandrinus (Hernández, "Greek Text of Revelation," 344). The TR is particularly problematic for Revelation with Rev 22:16–21 having been translated from the Latin Vulgate by Erasmus (Metzger 690). There is wide consensus that Alexandrinus and Ephraemi are the most important witnesses in relation to the *Urtext* although all the surviving mss preserve the *Urtext* to some extent.

GRAMMATICAL AND SYNTACTICAL IRREGULARITIES

A *solecism* is a grammatical mistake involving a phrase or multiple words (syntax) while a *barbarism* is a mistake limited to one word (morphological irregularity). Both terms are derived from ancient Greek discussions of mistakes in syntax, grammar, and morphology. Ancient Greek and Latin authors highlight the significance of intentionality; both barbarisms and solecisms were generally allowable for intentional practical, artistic, or rhetorical purposes (Moţ 69–73). Unintentional mistakes were recognized and viewed negatively in antiquity. Possible barbarisms in Revelation include irregular spellings in case and verb endings and reduplications and the use of –ω terminations for –μι verbs. Moţ is correct to conclude that in Revelation there "exist morphologically irregular words but none of them deserve the label of barbarism" (Moţ 107). The possible examples fall within legitimate first-century Greek usage and reflect gradual changes taking place within the language. Hebraisms and Aramaicisms are irregularities in Greek grammar caused by influence from their respective languages (a Semitism is similar but does not explicitly designate the original language). This influence could come from literal translation, unintentional influence upon second language Greek users, or intentional attempts to mirror the Semitic language for rhetorical effect. It is evident that John was bilingual (Rev 9:11). Septuagintalisms result from following Septuagintal translation styles.

Many argue John's irregular grammar can be attributed to Hebrew and Aramaic syntax (Ozanne, "Language of the Apocalypse"; Mussies, *Morphology of Koine Greek*; Thompson, *Apocalypse and Semitic Syntax*). This could be attributed to bilingualism or an intentional effort by John to sound biblical and increase the perceived authority of his message (Ozanne, "Language of the Apocalypse"). Beale argues that instances of irregular Greek normally signal an allusion to the OT (Beale, "Solecisms in the Apocalypse"). Some explain John's irregular grammar as an intentional form of protest against Greco-Roman culture and power (Callahan, "Language of the Apocalypse"). It is also possible to explain most of the irregularities as acceptable examples of first-century Greek with minimal Semitic influence (Porter, "Language of the Apocalypse"; Moţ). Whiteley argues that as long as John communicated effectively it is not legitimate to distinguish between good and bad Greek (Whiteley, "Explanation for the Anacoloutha"). Osborne is likely correct when he concludes that "the solecisms of Revelation are due more to Septuagintal influence but also betray some Semitic features at times; though they fall within the parameters of vulgar Greek, they more often than not highlight allusions to OT texts and critical truths" (Osborne 24–25).

Solecisms or syntactic irregularities can be grouped into five categories: (1) disagreements in case, gender, and number; (2) irregularities of tense, voice, and mood; (3) irregularities with prepositional phrases; (4) omissions; and (5) additions or redundancy (Moţ 107). These will be discussed below as they occur. Some general observations can be made here. Since John elsewhere clearly demonstrates competence in using the proper case, it is likely that the use of the nom. for oblique cases can be explained via John's idiolect as an intentional choice to place emph. on the word in the nom. (Moţ 133–34). Solecisms involving misuse of the nom. seem to be John's way of underlining, highlighting, or putting a word in italics for emph. In addition to emph., the use of the nom. for oblique cases often signals a title, quotation, or allusion to the LXX via imitation (Wallace 62).

VERBAL ASPECT

Mathewson is correct that John's use of verb tenses can be fully understood as first-century Greek and is not irregular, confusing, or Semitically governed (*Verbal Aspect* 174). Fanning notes the importance of distinguishing between the different genre types that are often intermingled ("Greek Tenses in John's Apocalypse"): the narrative of the reception of visions (primarily aorist), the narration of the visionary content (primarily aorists, imperfects, historical presents), description of visionary content (primarily presents, nom. cls.), and prophecy of future events (primarily future tenses). In general, this is not incompatible with Mathewson's observation that the imperfect tense is generally used to indicate supplemental and background information, the present tense generally indicates foreground information, and the perfect tense often signals prominence (*Verbal Aspect* xxvi–xxvii). Verbal aspect, although a fertile ground for scholarly debate, does not decisively impact many interpretive decisions in Revelation.

USE OF THE OLD TESTAMENT

Although Revelation never explicitly quotes the OT, allusions or more distant echoes can be heard in almost every verse. Although some of these allusions were likely unconscious, many seem dependent upon conscious intentionality. John uses allusions to present his message as in continuity with the message of the OT. The rhetorical result is that John appears to be something like a Christian OT prophet with the corresponding level of authority.

Various scholars of the past century argued that Revelation exclusively uses the LXX (Swete) or the Hebrew text (Charles), while more recent scholarship is much more open to its use of both (Allen, "Scriptural Allusions"). It is almost impossible to pin down the text form behind many allusions because of the multiplicity of LXX and MT textual traditions and John's free adaptation of the allusions. The LXX is the focus of this guide because most readers can be presumed to have growing competence in Greek and will benefit from considering the allusions in the LXX, although it will be noted where it seems more likely that John is drawing from the Hebrew.

Although John alludes to almost every OT book, he is most influenced by Ezekiel, Daniel, Isaiah, Psalms, and Zechariah. He draws imagery (exodus plagues, trumpets, bowls), themes (creation, covenant, redemption, judgment), and larger structural sections (Ezek 37–48 in Rev 20–22) from the OT, and fulfillment can be seen directly (e.g., Zech 12:10 in Rev 1:7), typologically, analogically, through expansion or universalization (e.g., Rev 2:26–28; 7:9–17), or through ironic or inverted uses (e.g., Rev 3:9; Beale and McDonough, "Revelation," 1085–86). The original OT context of an allusion often, although not always, provides some significant contribution to understanding John's usage. There is widespread evidence of continuity and intentionality. Revelation provides a unique window into how many OT passages were being interpreted and applied in Christian circles in western Asia Minor near the end of the first century. Because there are so many allusions or echoes (up to 1,000 by some counts) it is impossible to discuss each one in this guide. Attention will be given to allusions that have the most exegetical significance. The reader is encouraged to work through the Greek of the LXX allusions. This will reveal the extent of the allusions and will hopefully inspire a love for the Septuagint. The translations of the LXX throughout are original with the goal of providing wooden translations to aid beginning students.

PREACHING REVELATION

Most pastors who dare to preach from Revelation typically focus on chapters 1–5 or 21–22. A proper understanding of the visions in chapters 6–20 is not easy to communicate in a weekly expositional sermon series. The difficulty is compounded since it cannot be assumed a given hearer was present for the prior sermons in the series, in which necessary and pertinent elements of prior visions were discussed. While preaching Revelation is encouraged, the central chapters are perhaps better approached exegetically through a weekly Bible study with consistent attendees and ample time for questions and discussion. Nevertheless, brief sermon outlines are provided for each major section to provide examples for how the visions could be proclaimed via the sermon genre. The message of Revelation is vitally important for Christians to hear today, but significant effort is needed to continuously push against widespread misconceptions regarding the message and meaning of the book.

CONCLUSION

The Greek text of Revelation included below is the same in both the 28th edition of Nestle Aland (NA 28) and the fifth edition of the United Bible Society (UBS 5) while the LXX is Rahlfs's edition (1979). All translations, unless otherwise noted, are original. The following verse-by-verse discussion will provide a gloss for words not generally memorized by a first-year Greek student. This guide makes no attempt to list all the commentators who support various positions but will normally cite one representative commentator for a given argument or conclusion. Fanning is a compelling advocate for a premillennial approach to the book, while Beale is foundational for an amillennial perspective. Aune remains unmatched for historical parallels, and Koester provides a wide range of insights. It is not possible to cite every possible exegetical detail in the discussion that follows; much more could be written about each verse than is written here. It is hoped that the reader will benefit from what is included and forgive what is omitted.

FOR FURTHER STUDY

1. Genre

Barr, D. L. "Beyond Genre: The Expectations of Apocalypse." Pages 71–89 in *The Reality of Apocalypse: Rhetoric and Politics in the Book of Revelation*. Edited by D. L. Barr. Atlanta: Society of Biblical Literature, 2006.

Fletcher, M. "Apocalypse Noir: How Revelation Defined and Defied a Genre." Pages 115–34 in *The Book of Revelation: Currents in British Research on the Apocalypse*. Edited by G. V. Allen, I. Paul, and S. P. Woodman. Tübingen: Mohr Siebeck, 2015.

Hellholm, D. "The Problem of Apocalyptic Genre and the Apocalypse of John." *Semeia* 36 (1986): 13–64.
Mathewson, D. "Revelation in Recent Genre Criticism: Some Implications for Interpretation." *TrinJ* 13 (1992): 193–213.
Paul, I., "The Genre of Revelation." Pages 36–50 in S&B.
*Reddish, M. G. "The Genre of the Book of Revelation." Pages 21–36 in *OHR*.

2. Structure

Bandy, A. "The Layers of the Apocalypse: A Holistic Approach to Revelation's Structure." *JSNT* 31 (2009): 469–99.
Giblin, C. H. "Recapitulation and John's Apocalypse." *CBQ* 56 (1994): 81–95.
DeSilva, D. A. "X Marks the Spot? A Critique of the Use of Chiasm in Macro-Structural Analyses of Revelation." *JSNT* 30 (2007): 343–71.

3. The Greek Text

Allen, G. V. *Manuscripts of the Book of Revelation: New Philology, Paratexts, Reception*. Oxford: Oxford University Press, 2020.
*Hernández, J., Jr. "The Greek Text of Revelation." Pages 343–60 in *OHR*.
Schmid, J. *Studies in the History of the Greek Text of the Apocalypse: The Ancient Stems*. Edited and translated by J. Hernández Jr., G. V. Allen, and D. Müller. Atlanta: Society of Biblical Literature, 2018.

4. Grammatical and Syntactical Irregularities

Beale, G. K. "Solecisms in the Apocalypse as Signals for the Presence of Old Testament Allusions: A Selective Analysis of Revelation 1–22." Pages 421–46 in *Early Christian Interpretation of the Scriptures of Israel*. Edited by C. A. Evens. JSNTSup 148. Sheffield: Sheffield Academic Press, 1997.
Callahan, A. D. "The Language of Apocalypse." *HTR* 88 (1995): 453–70
Dougherty, E. C. A. "The Syntax of the Apocalypse." PhD diss., Catholic University of America, 1990.
Mathewson, D. L. "Revelation's Use of the Greek Language." Pages 101–14 in *OHR*.
*Moţ, L. F. *Morphological and Syntactical Irregularities in the Book of Revelation: A Greek Hypothesis*. Linguistic Biblical Studies 11. Leiden: Brill, 2015.
Mussies, G. *The Morphology of Koine Greek as Used in the Apocalypse of John: A Study in Bilingualism*. NovTSup 27. Leiden: Brill, 1971.
Ozanne, C. G. "The Language of the Apocalypse." *Tyndale House Bulletin* 16 (1965): 3–9.
Porter, S. E. "The Language of the Apocalypse in Recent Discussion." *NTS* 35 (1989): 582–603.
Rand, J. A. du. "A Socio-Psychological View of the Effect of the Language (Parole) of the Apocalypse of John." *Neot* 24 (1990): 351–65.
Schmidt, D. D. "Semitisms and Septuagintalisms in the Book of Revelation." *NTS* 37 (1991): 592–603.
Thompson, S. *The Apocalypse and Semitic Syntax*. SNTSMS 52. Cambridge: Cambridge University Press, 1985.
Whiteley, I. M. "An Explanation for the Anacoloutha in the Book of Revelation." *Filologia-Neotestamentaria* 20 (2007): 33–50.

5. *Verbal Aspect*

Fanning, B. "Greek Tenses in John's Apocalypse: Issues in Verbal Aspect, Discourse Analysis, and Diachronic Change." Pages 328–53 in *The Language and Literature of the New Testament: Essays in Honor of Stanley E. Porter's 60th Birthday*. Edited by L. F. Dow, C. A. Evans, and A. W. Pitts. BibInt 150. Leiden: Brill, 2017.

Mathewson, D. *Verbal Aspect in the Book of Revelation: The Function of Greek Verb Tenses in John's Apocalypse*. Linguistic Biblical Studies 4. Leiden: Brill, 2010.

6. *Use of the Old Testament*

Allen, G. V. "Scriptural Allusions in the Book of Revelation and the Contours of Textual Research 1900–2014: Retrospect and Prospect." *CurBR* 14 (2016): 319–39.

Beale, G. K. *John's Use of the Old Testament in Revelation*. JSNTSup 166. Sheffield: Sheffield Academic Press, 1998.

*———. "Thirty-Five Years of Research on John's Use of the Old Testament in Revelation." Pages 188–246 in S&B.

Beale, G. K., and S. M. McDonough. "Revelation." Pages 1081–158 in *Commentary on the New Testament Use of the Old Testament*. Edited by G. K. Beale and D. A. Carson. Grand Rapids: Baker Academic, 2007.

Hernández, J., Jr. "Recensional Activity and the Transmission of the Septuagint in John's Apocalypse." Pages 84–98 in *Die Johannesoffenbarung: Ihr Text und ihre Auslegung*. Edited by M. Labahn and M. Karrer. ABG 38. Leipzig: Evangelische Verlagsanstalt, 2012.

Moyise, S. *The Old Testament in the Book of Revelation*. JSNTSup 115. Sheffield: Sheffield Academic Press, 1995.

———. "The Old Testament in the Book of Revelation." Pages 85–100 in *OHR*.

Mathewson, D. *A New Heaven and a New Earth: The Meaning and Function of the Old Testament in Revelation 21:1–22:5*. JSNTSup 238. Sheffield: Sheffield Academic Press, 2001.

Paul, I. "The Use of the Old Testament in Revelation 12." Pages 256–76 in *The Old Testament in the New Testament: Essays in Honour of J. L. North*. JSNTSup 189. Sheffield: Sheffield Academic Press, 2000.

Paulien, J. *Decoding Revelation's Trumpets: Literary Allusions and the Interpretation of Revelation 8:7–12*. AUSDDS 11. Berrien Springs, MI: Andrews University Press, 1987.

———. "Dreading the Whirlwind: Intertextuality and the Use of the Old Testament in Revelation." *AUSS* 39 (2001): 5–22.

Stewart, A. E. "The Future of Israel, Early Christian Hermeneutics, and the Apocalypse of John." *JETS* 61 (2018): 563–76.

Tõniste, K. *The Ending of the Canon: A Canonical and Intertextual Reading of Revelation 21–22*. LNTS 526. London: T&T Clark, 2016.

RECOMMENDED COMMENTARIES

Aune, D. E. *Revelation*. 3 vols. WBC 52. Waco: Word; Nashville: Nelson, 1997–1998.

Beale, G. K. *The Book of Revelation*. NIGTC. Grand Rapids: Eerdmans, 1999.

Beasley-Murray, G. R. *The Book of Revelation*. Rev. ed. New Century Bible Commentary. London: Marshall, Morgan & Scott, 1978.

Blount, B. K. *Revelation: A Commentary*. NTL. Louisville: Westminster John Knox, 2009.

Boring, E. M. *Revelation*. Interpretation. Louisville: Knox, 1989.

Caird, G. B. *A Commentary on the Revelation of Saint John the Divine*. New York: Harper & Row, 1966.

Charles, R. H. *The Revelation of St. John*. 2 vols. ICC. New York: Scribner's Sons, 1920.

DeSilva, D. A. *Discovering Revelation: Content, Interpretation, Reception*. London: SPCK, 2021.

Fanning, B. M. *Revelation*. Zondervan Exegetical Commentary on the New Testament. Grand Rapids: Zondervan Academic, 2020.

Keener, C. S. *Revelation*. The NIV Application Commentary. Grand Rapids: Zondervan, 2000.

Kistemaker, S. J. *Revelation*. New Testament Commentary. Grand Rapids: Baker Academic, 2001.

Koester, C. R. *Revelation: A New Translation with Introduction and Commentary*. AB 38A. New Haven: Yale University Press, 2014.

Mounce, R. H. *The Book of Revelation*. NICNT. Grand Rapids: Eerdmans, 1977.

Osborne, G. R. *Revelation*. BECNT. Grand Rapids: Baker Academic, 2002.

Smalley, S. S. *The Revelation to John: A Commentary on the Greek Text of the Apocalypse*. Downers Grove, IL: InterVarsity, 2005.

Swete, H. B. *Commentary on Revelation*. 3rd ed. London: Macmillan, 1911; repr. Grand Rapids: Kregel, 1977.

Sweet, J. P. M. *Revelation*. London: SCM, 1979.

Thomas, R. L. *Revelation: An Exegetical Commentary*. 2 vols. Chicago: Moody, 1992, 1995.

Witherington, B., III. *Revelation*. New Cambridge Bible Commentary. Cambridge: Cambridge University Press, 2003.

ADDITIONAL SOURCES CITED

Aune, D. E. "The Influence of Roman Imperial Court Ceremonial on the Apocalypse of John." *BR* 28 (1983): 5–26.

Bauckham, R. J. "The List of the Tribes in Revelation 7 Again." *JSNT* 42 (1991): 99–115.

Collins, A. Y. "Introduction: Early Christian Apocalypticism." *Semeia* 36 (1986): 1–12.

Collins, J. J. "Introduction: Towards the Morphology of a Genre." *Semeia* 14 (1979): 1–20.

Dixon, S. S. U. *The Testimony of the Exalted Jesus in the Book of Revelation*. LNTS 570. London: Bloomsbury, 2017.

Ford, J. M. *Revelation*. AB 38. Garden City, NY: Doubleday, 1975.

Gulaker, C. *Satan, the Heavenly Adversary of Man: A Narrative Analysis of the Function of Satan in the Book of Revelation*. LNTS 638. London: Bloomsbury, 2021.

Hirschberg, P. "Jewish Believers in Asia Minor according to the Book of Revelation and the Gospel of John." Pages 217–38 in *Jewish Believers in Jesus: The Early Centuries*. Edited by O. Skarsaune and R. Hvalvik. Peabody, MA: Hendrickson, 2007.

Johns, L. J. *The Lamb Christology of the Apocalypse of John: An Investigation into Its Origins and Rhetorical Force*. WUNT 2.167. Tübingen: Mohr Siebeck, 2003.

Koester, C. R. "The Message to Laodicea and the Problem of Its Local Context: A Study of the Imagery in Rev 3.14–22." *NTS* 49 (2003): 407–24.

Mathewson, D. "Verbal Aspect in the Apocalypse of John: An Analysis of Revelation 5." *NovT* 50, no. 1 (2008): 58–77.

Porter, Stanley E. *Verbal Aspect in the Greek of the New Testament with Reference to Tense and Mood*. Studies in Biblical Greek 1. New York: Peter Lang, 1989.

Stewart, Alexander E. "The Future of Israel, Early Christian Hermeneutics, and the Apocalypse of John." *JETS* 61 (2018): 563–76.

———. "The Temporary Messianic Kingdom in Second Temple Judaism and the Delay of the Parousia: Psalm 110:1 and the Development of Early Christian Inaugurated Eschatology." *JETS* 59 (2016): 255–70

Wilson, C. "The Problem of the Domitianic Date of Revelation." *NTS* 39 (1993): 587–605.

I. Prologue (1:1–8)

A. TITLE AND BLESSING (1:1–3)

1:1 Ἀποκάλυψις (nom. abs. title of the book; a nom. abs. is grammatically independent and is commonly used in titles [Wallace 51], ant. of ἥν) **Ἰησοῦ Χριστοῦ** (obj. gen. "revelation *about* Jesus" or more likely subj. gen./gen. of source, Jesus as the one revealing, "*from* Jesus"; possibly a plenary gen. [an intentionally ambiguous combination of subj. and obj.], however, the appeal to a plenary gen. should be dismissed because ambiguity is contextual [semantics] and not grammatical [cf. Math 1; contra Wallace 120–21]. The fact that God has Jesus mediate this revelation to his servants favors the gen. of source. John is thus claiming authority for the revelation; it came from Jesus) **ἥν** (dir. obj. of ἔδωκεν) **ἔδωκεν** (3rd sg. aor. act. ind. of δίδωμι) **αὐτῷ** (indir. obj.) **ὁ θεός** (subj. nom.) **δεῖξαι** (aor. act. inf. of δείκνυμι, "show," purpose) **τοῖς δούλοις** (indir. obj.) **αὐτοῦ** (poss.) **ἅ** (headless rel. pron.; the rel. cl. functions as the dir. obj. of δεῖξαι) **δεῖ γενέσθαι** (aor. mid. inf., compl. inf., "necessary to happen") **ἐν τάχει** (τάχος, -ους, τό, "quickness," lit. "with speed"; i.e., a short time, soon; temp. dat.), **καὶ ἐσήμανεν** (3rd sg. aor. act. ind. of σημαίνω, "report, tell, communicate by symbols, signify") **ἀποστείλας** (nom. sg. masc. of aor. act. ptc. of ἀποστέλλω, means, "by sending") **διὰ τοῦ ἀγγέλου** (intermediate agency) **αὐτοῦ** (poss.) **τῷ δούλῳ** (indir. obj.) **αὐτοῦ** (poss.) **Ἰωάννῃ** (appos., ant. of ὅς in 1:2),

The verbless cl. containing the title of the book is expanded with a rel. cl. containing two vbs. It is the Ἀποκάλυψις that God gave (ἔδωκεν) and signified (ἐσήμανεν). He *gave* it to show to his servants what was necessary to happen soon, and he *signified* it by sending it through his angel to his servant John. However, the chain of revelatory communication indicated by the context suggests that Jesus is the subject of ἐσήμανεν: God gave it to Jesus, and he (Jesus) communicated it. The coord. conj. καί naturally implies that God is the subj.: God gave *and* God communicated. Aune attempts to solve this problem by suggesting that καί functions here as a rel. pron. (cf. Mark 2:14) and he notes several other instances in Revelation where an indir. obj. is used as the subj. of a vb. in the following cl. (Aune[a] 6; cf. 2:21; 12:14; 14:4, which involve a subord. cl. instead of a coord. cl.). Although the use of καί as a rel. pron. is very uncommon, Aune's second observation supports taking Jesus as the subject of ἐσήμανεν.

Ἀποκάλυψις is not yet an indication of genre but suggests that the book will reveal or uncover heavenly mysteries. Δοῦλος should be translated "slave" but is often translated in EVV as "servant" because to be God's slave paradoxically combines a term for low status with the reality of high status. John characteristically describes God's people as slaves (1:1; 2:20; 6:11; 7:3; 10:7; 11:18; 19:2, 5; 22:3, 6; used of an angel in 19:10; 22:9). Although some of these references refer to prophets or martyrs, δοῦλος is not a technical term for either group in Revelation and more broadly describes all Christians (note the reference to the churches in 1:4). Ἐν τάχει could be understood to mean that all the visions would be fulfilled very soon, but the motif of imminence or nearness (1:1, 3; 2:16; 3:11; 6:11; 22:6, 7, 10, 12, 20) more likely points to how the visions describe things that were beginning to take place within John's generation and would continue to intensify until the end. John and the first Christians were convinced that they were in the end times or latter days, and the visions in Revelation describe things already beginning to take place. The theme of imminence intensifies the rhetorical force of the book and elicits a response of constant expectation—judgment and salvation were near! Although it was also used to indicate ordinary communication, when *σημαίνω* (cognate noun: *σημεῖον*) is used in revelatory literature it commonly points to the presence of deeper, symbolic, or allegorical meaning (Beale 51–52; cf. John 12:33; 18:32; 21:19). The choice of this lexeme alerts the reader to expect symbolic visionary material. Ἀγγέλος in Revelation indicates an angelic messenger. This points forward to the use of angels to communicate to John throughout Revelation. John identifies himself as God's (*αὐτοῦ*) slave and the recipient of this divine revelation.

Use of the OT: Beale notes that "the whole of Rev 1:1 is patterned after the broad structure of Dan 2:28–30, 45–47 (cf. LXX, Theod.), where the vb. *ἀποκαλύπτω* ("reveal") appears five times (cf. also 2:19, 22 in Theod.), the phase *ἃ δεῖ γενέσθαι* ("What must come to pass") appears three times (see Theod.), and *σημαίνω* ("signify") appears twice (LXX; cf. also 2:23 LXX)" (Beale 181). He further notes that John replaces Daniel's *ἃ δεῖ γενέσθαι ἐπ' ἐσχάτων τῶν ἡμερῶν* (Dan 2:28) with *ἃ δεῖ γενέσθαι ἐν τάχει* (Rev 1:1; Beale 181). This observation supports the discussion of imminence above: John viewed Daniel's "last days" as being fulfilled in his present and immediate future. Parallels to Rev 1:1–20 can be seen in Jer 1:1–4; Ezek 1:1–3; Hag 1:1; and Zech 1:1, which provide descriptions of the prophets' works as "the word of the Lord" and of the circumstances surrounding the reception of their vision (Fanning 73).

1:2 **ὃς** (subj. nom.) **ἐμαρτύρησεν** (3rd sg. aor. act. ind. of *μαρτυρέω*, "testify, bear witness," epistolary aor.) **τὸν λόγον** (dir. obj.) **τοῦ θεοῦ** (gen. of source or subj. gen.) **καὶ** (epex., "even," BDAG 495c) **τὴν μαρτυρίαν** (dir. obj.) **Ἰησοῦ Χριστοῦ** (possibly obj. gen., "the testimony about Jesus," but more likely subj. gen., "the testimony from Jesus" because of the chain of revelatory communication from God to Jesus through an angel to John for the churches) **ὅσα εἶδεν** (3rd sg. aor. act. ind. of *ὁράω*, "as much as he saw;" the rel. cl. summarizes the prior two acc.).

Sarah Dixon argues that "the testimony of Jesus" is a moniker for the book of Revelation and that John uses the expression as a consistent internal self-reference to the book's own message which can be applied to those who hear and embrace or hold to the message of the book (Dixon, *Testimony of the Exalted Jesus*). There is no consensus, however, regarding whether "the testimony of Jesus" can be taken as a technical description of the book in every occurrence (1:2, 9; 12:17; 19:10; 20:4).

1:3 **Μακάριος** (*μακάριος, -ία, -ιον*, "blessed, happy," pred. adj. of verbless cl.; often indicating the "privileged recipient of divine favor" [BDAG 611a]; this is the first of seven pronouncements of blessing, Rev 14:13; 16:15; 19:9; 20:6; 22:7, 14) **ὁ ἀναγινώσκων** (nom. sg. masc. of pres. act. ptc. of *ἀναγινώσκω*, "read aloud," subst., subj. nom. of verbless cl.) **καὶ οἱ ἀκούοντες** (nom. pl. masc. of pres. act. ptc. of *ἀκούω*, subst., coord. subj. nom.) **τοὺς λόγους** (dir. obj.) **τῆς** (deictic, "this" [Wallace 221]) **προφητείας** (attrib. gen., "prophetic words," or epex. gen., "words, that is, the prophecy;" this is a self-reference to the book of Revelation) **καὶ τηροῦντες** (nom. pl. masc. of pres. act. ptc. of τηρέω, subst., coord. subj. nom.) **τὰ** (goes with the ptc.) **ἐν αὐτῇ** (loc.) **γεγραμμένα** (acc. pl. neut. of pf. pass. ptc. of γράφω, subst., dir. obj.), **ὁ** (likely the "well-known" use of the art., "*the* time" [Wallace 225; Fanning 78]) **γὰρ** (causal; the ones who keep are blessed *because* the nearness of the time) **καιρὸς** (subj. nom. of verbless cl.) **ἐγγύς** (adv., "near," adv. pred. of verbless cl.).

The three coordinated subst. ptcs. are the nom. subjs. of the verbless cl.; they indicate a sg. reader and a group who both hear and keep (one art. governs both later ptcs.). This blessing forms a literary inclusio with the blessing pronounced in 22:7. There the reader and hearers are omitted, and the blessing focuses on the individual who keeps the words of the prophecy of this book. The inclusio heightens the rhetorical force of the blessing as a call for each individual hearer to respond to the message of Revelation with appropriate action. Revelation describes itself as a prophecy in 1:3; 10:11; 22:7, 9, 10, 18, 19.

FOR FURTHER STUDY

7. Use of Daniel in Revelation

Beale, G. K. *The Use of Daniel in Jewish Apocalyptic Literature and in the Revelation of St John*. London: University Press of America, 1984.

———. "A Reconsideration of the Text of Daniel in the Apocalypse." *Bib* 67 (1986): 539–43.

8. Declarations of Blessing

Nwachukwu, O. O. *Beyond Vengeance and Protest: A Reflection on the Macarisms in Revelation*. StBibLit 71. New York: Lang, 2005.

Cruz, V. P. "The Beatitudes of the Apocalypse: Eschatology and Ethics." Pages 269–83 in *Perspectives on Christology: Essays in Honor of Paul K. Jewett*. Edited by M. Shuster and R. Muller. Grand Rapids: Zondervan, 1991.

9. Imagery and Symbolism

Beale, G. K. "The Purpose of Symbolism in the Book of Revelation." *CTJ* 41 (2006): 53–66.

Huber, K. "Imagery in the Book of Revelation." Pages 53–68 in *OHR*.

*Kuykendall, M. *Lions, Locusts, and the Lamb: Interpreting Key Images in the Book of Revelation*. Eugene, OR: Wipf & Stock, 2019.

Paul, I. "The Book of Revelation: Image, Symbol and Metaphor." Pages 131–47 in *Studies in the Book of Revelation*. Edited by S. Moyise. Edinburgh: T&T Clark, 2001.

Villiers, P. G. R. de. "The Lord was Crucified in Sodom and Egypt: Symbols in the Apocalypse of John." *Neot* 22 (1988): 125–38.

10. Immanence

Barr, D. L. "Waiting for the End That Never Comes: The Narrative Logic of John's Story." Pages 101–12 in *Studies in the Book of Revelation*. Edited by S. Moyise. Edinburgh: T&T Clark, 2001.

*Mathewson, D. "Revelation and the Future: Was John a False Prophet?" Pages 150–61 in S&B.

B. EPISTOLARY PRESCRIPT (1:4–5c)

1:4 Ἰωάννης (The use of a nom. abs. followed by a dat. of recipient in a verbless cl. is characteristic of epistolary introductions in general as evident in Pauline practice: sender *to* recipient *in* city/geographical location) **ταῖς ἑπτὰ** ("seven," attrib.) **ἐκκλησίαις** (dat. of recipient) **ταῖς** (adjectivizer which links the prep. phrase to ἐκκλησίαις; this is a common use of the art. with prep. phrases which is often translated with the rel. pron. who/which: "to the seven churches which are in Asia") **ἐν τῇ Ἀσίᾳ** ("Asia," loc.)· **χάρις** (subj. nom. of verbless cl.) **ὑμῖν** (dat. of advantage) **καὶ εἰρήνη** (coord. subj. nom.) **ἀπὸ ὁ ὢν** (nom. sg. masc. of pres. act. ptc. of εἰμί, subst. ptc. functioning as a gen. of source; see below on the use of a nom. with ἀπό) **καὶ ὁ** (substantivizer) **ἦν** (3rd sg. impf. act. ind. of εἰμί; see below on the use of an art. with a finite vb.) **καὶ ὁ ἐρχόμενος** (nom. sg. masc. of pres. mid. ptc. of ἔρχομαι, subst.) **καὶ ἀπὸ τῶν ἑπτὰ** (attrib.) **πνευμάτων** (gen. of source, ant. of ἅ) **ἃ** (subj. nom. of verbless cl.) **ἐνώπιον** (improper prep., "in the presence of, before") **τοῦ** (cataphoric to 4:2) **θρόνου** (loc.) **αὐτοῦ** (poss.)

This epistolary address and salutation could reflect Pauline influence on early Christian epistolary customs, but it is not distinctive enough to draw firm conclusions. The mismatch of the prep. and its obj. reflected in ἀπὸ ὁ ὢν is the most famous and obvious example of a solecism in Revelation. John uses the nom. case for the obj. of the prep. ἀπό instead of the gen. case. Since John uses the proper case with ἀπό thirty-two other times it must be an intentional choice and not an example of incompetence (Wallace 63). Most interpreters recognize the irregular grammar as an allusion to Exod 3:14 (ἐγώ εἰμι ὁ ὤν). This demonstrates that John does indeed signal some allusions to the OT by maintaining the grammar from the original context even though it complicates his own grammar. This allusion-alerting function explains some but not all possible solecisms in Revelation. The expression καὶ ὁ ἦν is also grammatically awkward. The connection of an art. to a finite vb. instead of a ptc. is unusual (lit. "the he was") but could be explained by the lack of impf. or aor. ptc. forms for εἰμί. John thus improvised within the constraints of the Greek language. The use of an art. instead of an expected rel. pron. with ἦν preserves the titular parallelism, and although a past tense ptc. of γίνομαι could have been used it would have given the wrong impression that God had come into being (Harris 67). John distinctively uses καὶ ὁ ἐρχόμενος instead of ἐσόμενος to stress, not that God will always exist, but that he is coming to his creation. The phrase ὁ ὢν καὶ ὁ ἦν occurs in 1:4, 8, 11, 17; 16:5. The ἑπτὰ πνευμάτων indicates either the Holy Spirit in a trinitarian greeting or seven angelic beings (Aune[a] 34–35). The Holy Spirit is probably in view because of how the references to the seven spirits throughout Revelation place them alongside or in close relationship to God and Jesus (particularly their inclusion between God and Jesus here; cf. 3:1; 4:5; 5:6) and the number seven would be symbolic, indicating completion and fullness although the seven spirits could also point to the seven well-known angels in Second Temple Judaism (Koester 216).

Use of the OT: John's seven spirits could be an allusion to the seven lamps in Zech 4:1–10 or the seven attributes of the Spirit in Isa 11:2 (seven requires the inclusion of τοῦ θεοῦ). Isaiah describes God as both first and existing with the last things: ἐγὼ θεὸς πρῶτος, καὶ εἰς τὰ ἐπερχόμενα ἐγώ εἰμι (Isa 41:4). There are also prophetic declarations of the coming of God such as Isa 40:10 (ἰδοὺ κύριος μετὰ ἰσχύος ἔρχεται). On Exod 3:14, see above.

1:5a καὶ ἀπὸ Ἰησοῦ Χριστοῦ (gen. of source), **ὁ μάρτυς** (μάρτυς, -υρος, ὁ, "witness," appos.), **ὁ πιστός** (subst. in appos., "faithful one," or attrib., "faithful witness"; the use of πιστός to describe Antipas as a "faithful one" in 2:13 and the fact that the rider in Rev 19:11 is also called πιστός would support taking this as a subst. adj. while the combination of ὁ πιστὸς καὶ ἀληθινός in Rev 3:14 and John's preference for groups of three [Aune[a] 25] would suggest attrib. adj.) **ὁ πρωτότοκος** (πρωτότοκος, -ον, "first-born," appos.) **τῶν νεκρῶν** (gen. of separation or part.) **καὶ ὁ ἄρχων** (ἄρχων, -οντος, ὁ, "ruler," appos.) **τῶν βασιλέων** (gen. of subord.) **τῆς γῆς** (gen. of subord.).

The string of noms. are in appos. to the gen. Ἰησοῦ Χριστοῦ and should thus be in the gen. case. The lack of agreement likely indicates that the noms. are titles or quotations functioning as if they were proper names. The discord places emph. on the noms. (Wallace 62). Paul's references to Jesus as πρωτότοκος πάσης κτίσεως (Col 1:15) and πρωτότοκος ἐκ τῶν νεκρῶν (Col 1:18) are significant parallels.

Use of the OT: It is possible that the irregular grammar signals an allusion to Ps 88:38 LXX (καὶ ὁ μάρτυς ἐν οὐρανῷ πιστός [Ps 89:37 EVV]). More clearly, in Ps 88:28 LXX (Ps 89:27 EVV) God promises to make David a firstborn and high beyond the kings on earth: κἀγὼ πρωτότοκον θήσομαι αὐτόν, ὑψηλὸν παρὰ τοῖς βασιλεῦσιν τῆς γῆς. Jesus, as the descendent of David, fulfills this promise and is God's answer to the lament of nonfulfillment in Ps 88 LXX (Ps 89 EVV).

FOR FURTHER STUDY

11. God

*Bauckham, R. *The Theology of the Book of Revelation*. Cambridge: Cambridge University Press, 1993.

Karrer, M. "God in the Book of Revelation." Pages 205–22 in *OHR*.

12. The Spirit

Kuykendall, M. "An Expanded Role for the Spirit in the Book of Revelation." *JETS* 64 (2022): 527–44.

Thomas, J. C. "The Spirit in the Book of Revelation." Pages 241–256 in *OHR*.

Wilson, M. "The Spirit in Revelation: Explorations in Imagery and Metaphor." *CTR* 17 (2019): 83–96.

13. Christology

Allen, G. V. "The Son of God in the Book of Revelation and Apocalyptic Literature." Pages 53–71 in *Son of God: Divine Sonship in Jewish and Christian Antiquity*. Edited by G. V. Allen et. al. University Park, PA: Eisenbrauns, 2019.

Boring, M. E. "Narrative Christology in the Apocalypse." *CBQ* 54 (1992): 702–23.

Johns, L. "Jesus in the Book of Revelation." Pages 223–40 in *OHR*.

———. *The Lamb Christology of the Apocalypse of John: An Investigation into Its Origins and Rhetorical Force*. WUNT 2.167. Tübingen: Mohr Siebeck, 2003.

C. DOXOLOGY (1:5d–6)

1:5b Τῷ ἀγαπῶντι (dat. sg. masc. of pres. act. ptc. of ἀγαπάω, subst., dat. of poss. [Wallace 149–50], "to the one who loves") **ἡμᾶς** (dir. obj.; missing in some mss.) **καὶ λύσαντι** (dat. sg. masc. of aor. act. ptc. of λύω, "set free," subst., coord. dat. of poss.) **ἡμᾶς** (dir. obj.) **ἐκ τῶν ἁμαρτιῶν** (separation, "from") **ἡμῶν** (poss.) **ἐν τῷ αἵματι** (means) **αὐτοῦ** (poss.),

The nom. subjs. come in the next verse: "Glory and strength be to/belong to (dat. of poss.) the one who loves and loosed and made." The dat. ptcs. are fronted for emph. The change in tense is possibly noteworthy between the ptcs. with the aor. pointing back to conversion-initiation and the pres. pointing to ongoing activity ("To the one who loves us and loosed us"). The shift could also be more mundanely explained by the fact that ἀγαπάω is an atelic vb. while λύω is a telic vb. "[T]elic verbs tend to prefer the perfective aspect (aor. tense-form) whereas atelic verbs prefer the imperfective aspect (present or imperfect)" (*GDNTG*, 237). Many late mss (*Byz*) read λούσαντι ("to the one who washed"), making this a reference to baptism, but λύσαντι has better external support (𝔓[18] ℵ A C et al.) and suggests a metaphor of untying, loosing, or freeing from sin understood as bondage of some kind. The allusion to the Exodus in the following verse also supports λύσαντι. "Here, as in Hebrews, Christ is portrayed as both priest and sacrifice" (Beale 191). The blood of Jesus is connected with salvation through a variety of images throughout the NT (Acts 20:28; Rom 3:25; 5:9; Eph 2:13; 1 Pet 1:19; 1 John 1:7; Rev 5:9; 7:14; 12:11).

Use of the OT: The prohibition against eating blood is grounded in Lev 17:11 by linking the blood with atonement (ἡ γὰρ ψυχὴ πάσης σαρκὸς αἷμα αὐτοῦ ἐστιν, καὶ ἐγὼ δέδωκα αὐτὸ ὑμῖν ἐπὶ τοῦ θυσιαστηρίου ἐξιλάσκεσθαι περὶ τῶν ψυχῶν ὑμῶν, τὸ γὰρ αἷμα αὐτοῦ ἀντὶ τῆς ψυχῆς ἐξιλάσεται). Although using different words to translate the Heb., there could be an allusion to Ps 129:8 LXX (καὶ αὐτὸς λυτρώσεται τὸν Ισραηλ ἐκ πασῶν τῶν ἀνομιῶν αὐτοῦ [Ps 130:8 EVV]). Matching lexemes are found in the comfort expressed regarding Jerusalem in Isa 40:2 that λέλυται αὐτῆς ἡ ἁμαρτία. What Isaiah declares as completed in the exile, John attributes to the work of Jesus.

1:6 καὶ ἐποίησεν (3rd sg. aor. act. ind. of ποιέω) **ἡμᾶς** (dir. obj.) **βασιλείαν** (obj.-compl. double acc., "he made us to be a kingdom"), **ἱερεῖς** (ἱερεύς, -έως, ὁ, "priest," acc. pl. masc., appos. to βασιλείαν) **τῷ θεῷ** (dat. of advantage) **καὶ** (epex., "even") **πατρὶ** (dat. of advantage) **αὐτοῦ** (gen. of relationship, i.e., Jesus's father), **αὐτῷ** (dat. of poss. recalling the dat. ptcs. in the prior verse) **ἡ δόξα** ("glory," subj. nom.) **καὶ τὸ κράτος** (κράτος, -ους, τό, "strength," coord. subj. nom.) **εἰς τοὺς αἰῶνας** ("ages," measure) [**τῶν αἰώνων**] (missing in 𝔓[18] A P 2050 cop[bo]; it was prob. added by later scribes because of its presence in the same expression elsewhere in Rev)· **ἀμήν**.

The coordination of a finite vb. with two ptcs. is grammatically awkward (lit.: "To the one who loves and who loosed and he made") but not unparalleled elsewhere in antiquity. It has been explained as a Hebraism but could also be understood as a parenthetical construction: "To the one who freed us from our sins by his blood—indeed [καί], he made us a kingdom, priests to his God and Father—to him be the glory" (Math 6). Some later scribes "fixed" the problem by changing the finite vb. to a ptc. (ποιήσαντι; Beale 192). Similar NT doxologies include Rom 11:36; Phil 4:20; 1 Pet 4:11; Jude v. 25.

Use of the OT: There is a clear allusion here and in Rev 5:10 to God's promise in Exod 19:6 to make his people a *βασίλειον ἱεράτευμα*. The application of the promise from Exod 19:6 to the multiethnic Christian community formed by Jesus is paralleled in 1 Pet 2:9. A future nation of priests was mentioned in Isa 61:6 (ὑμεῖς δὲ ἱερεῖς κυρίου κληθήσεσθε) and 66:21 (καὶ ἀπ' αὐτῶν λήμψομαι ἐμοὶ ἱερεῖς καὶ Λευίτας, εἶπεν κύριος). Through Christ's perfect priestly work, the nation under his rule could finally fulfill the OT expectation by "mediating Yahweh's light of salvific revelation" (Beale 193) to the world (e.g., Isa 42:1–9; 43:10–13; 49:5–7). This is a clear example of John's tendency to apply OT promises and passages originally focused on ethnic Israel to the multiethnic people of God constituted by allegiance to the Messiah.

FOR FURTHER STUDY

14. Blood

Decock, P. "The Symbol of Blood in the Apocalypse of John." *Neot* 38 (2004): 157–82.

D. PROPHETIC ORACLES (1:7–8)

1:7 Ἰδοὺ (interj. for emph.; common in Revelation; "Behold!," "See!," or "Indeed!" [L&N 91.10, 13]) **ἔρχεται** (3rd sg. pres. mid. ind. of ἔρχομαι; likely a futuristic pres. "he is coming" which indicates either immediacy or certainty [Wallace 535–37]) **μετὰ τῶν νεφελῶν** (νεφέλη, -ης, ἡ, "cloud," association), **καὶ ὄψεται** (3rd sg. fut. mid. ind. of ὁράω) **αὐτὸν** (dir. obj.) **πᾶς** (attrib.) **ὀφθαλμὸς** (subj. nom.) **καὶ** (ascensive, "even," [Wallace 670]) **οἵτινες** (subj. nom., headless rel. pron.) **αὐτὸν** (dir. ob.) **ἐξεκέντησαν** (3rd pl. aor. act. ind. of ἐκκεντέω, "pierce"), **καὶ κόψονται** (3rd pl. fut. mid. ind. of κόπτω, "beat, cut," in the mid., κόπτω means to beat one's breast as an expression of mourning [BDAG 559b]) **ἐπ' αὐτὸν** (when ἐπί follows vbs. that express emotion or opinion it can indicate direction, "at" or "over," or cause, "because" [BDAG 365a; 366c]; the causal meaning seems to fit here) **πᾶσαι** (attrib.) **αἱ φυλαὶ** (φυλή, -ῆς, ἡ, "tribe," subj. nom.) **τῆς γῆς** (gen. of place). **ναί, ἀμήν** (the combination of both ναί and ἀμήν indicates emph. affirmation).

John transitions abruptly from a doxology to prophetic oracles. The juxtaposition of the pres. with the fut. tenses implies the certainty or nearness of the fut. event of Christ's coming. This compound sentence coordinates different subjects: He is coming . . . *and* every eye will see (even those who pierced), *and* all the tribes will mourn. In Revelation, the language of "coming" is applied to both Jesus (2:5, 16; 3:3 [ἥκω], 11, 20; 16:15; 22:7, 12, 20) and God (1:4, 8; 4:8). The significance of mourning is unclear and could suggest a mourning of repentance leading to salvation or mourning amid judgment. An allusion to the Abrahamic promise in Gen 12:3; 28:14 that all the tribes of the earth (πᾶσαι αἱ φυλαὶ τῆς γῆς) would be blessed in Abraham could suggest a positive interpretation (Fanning 86–87; note also that the context of Zech 12:10 would suggest a repentant mourning), but it is also evident throughout Revelation that many people do not repent (6:15–17; 9:20–21; 16:9, 11, 21).

Use of the OT: John's words parallel both a prophecy by Daniel concerning the "Son of Man" (Dan 7:13) and Zechariah concerning a postexilic event involving Jerusalem (Zech 12:10; John 19:37). The imagery of "coming with the clouds" may allude to the angelic pronouncement of Jesus's return (Acts 1:9–11) in addition to the messianic vision in Dan 7:13 (ἐπὶ [John uses μετά as in Theod.] τῶν νεφελῶν τοῦ οὐρανοῦ ὡς υἱὸς ἀνθρώπου ἤρχετο [impf.]). Daniel 7:13 alludes to the messianic enthronement motif, Christ's authority, and his role in a future kingdom. Zechariah 12:10 reads καὶ ἐκχεῶ ἐπὶ τὸν οἶκον Δαυιδ καὶ ἐπὶ τοὺς κατοικοῦντας Ιερουσαλημ πνεῦμα χάριτος καὶ οἰκτιρμοῦ, καὶ ἐπιβλέψονται πρός με ἀνθ' ὧν κατωρχήσαντο καὶ κόψονται ἐπ' αὐτὸν κοπετὸν ὡς ἐπ' ἀγαπητὸν καὶ ὀδυνηθήσονται ὀδύνην ὡς ἐπὶ πρωτοτόκῳ. Zechariah has ἐπιβλέπω instead of John's ὁράω and uses κατορχέομαι in 12:10 "to dance in mockery before" (Brill) instead of John's ἐκκεντέω (cf. Isa 53:5). The MT uses דקר "pierce," which aligns in meaning with Rev 1:7 and John 19:37. Both LXX/MT of Zech 12:10 include ἀγαπητός ("beloved") // יָחִיד ("only-child") and πρωτότοκος ("firstborn")

//בְּכוֹר ("firstborn"). The term beloved (only-child) is used of Isaac (Gen 22), Israel (Amos 8:10, Jer 6:26), and Jesus (Matt 3:17; 12:18; 17:5). The NT use of "firstborn" is a central christological term (Rom 8:29; Col 1:15, 18; Heb 1:6; Rev 1:5; cf. Exod 4:22). Similar terminology for mourning (πένθος ἀγαπητοῦ) is used in Amos 8:10 and Jer 6:26, which are preexilic prophecies of Israel's coming destruction and exile. These prophecies in Amos, Jeremiah, and Zechariah were originally for the house of David and Jerusalem but are extended in Rev 1:7d to "all the tribes of the earth" (Zech 12:3 [John's expansion is already anticipated in Zech 14:16–17 and introduced into early Christianity by Jesus in Matt 24:30]; cf. Gen 12:3; 28:14; Ps 72:17). A similar yet different combination of Dan 7:13 and Zech 12:10 is found in Matt 24:30 and Did. 16:8, which suggests that these verses were regularly combined in early Christianity to refer to Jesus's second coming. It is evident in various OT passages that riding in/with the clouds was a divine prerogative (Pss 68:4; 104:3–4; Isa 19:1; Jer 4:13; Nah 1:3; see Fanning 84–85).

1:8 Ἐγώ (subj. nom.) **εἰμι τὸ Ἄλφα** (pred. nom.) **καὶ τὸ Ὦ** (coord. pred. nom.; the expression is a merism which highlights two extremes and everything in between), **λέγει** (3rd sg. pres. act. ind. of λέγω) **κύριος** (subj. nom.) **ὁ θεός** (appos.), **ὁ ὢν** (nom. sg. masc. of pres. act. ptc. of εἰμί, subst., appos.) **καὶ ὁ** (substantivizer) **ἦν** (3rd sg. impf. act. ind. of εἰμί) **καὶ ὁ ἐρχόμενος** (nom. sg. masc. of pres. mid. ptc. of ἔρχομαι, subst., on this threefold expression, see 1:4), **ὁ παντοκράτωρ.** (-ορος, ὁ, "all-powerful, almighty," appos.).

The shift to 1st sg. indicates a shift in prophetic oracles to direct divine speech; this is rare in Revelation and only occurs here and in 21:5–8. The phrase "Alpha and Omega" is a merism that is repeated by God in 21:6 and by Jesus in 22:13. The merism parallels Jesus's claim to be the "the first and the last" (Rev 1:17; 2:8; 21:13) and "the beginning and the end" (Rev 21:6 [of God]; 22:13 [of Jesus]). It is noteworthy that these other titular expressions refer to Jesus, who, alongside God, is declared to be the Alpha and Omega. The TR follows א* in adding ἀρχὴ καὶ τέλος, but this is likely an assimilation to the expression in 21:6 and there is no explanation for why it would be removed if original (Metzger 663). God here describes himself as παντοκράτωρ. This title is used throughout the book, generally combined with κύριος and θεός and frequently in expressions of acclamation and worship ("Lord, God Almighty" in 4:8; 11:17; 15:3; 16:7, 14; 19:6, 15; 21:22; "God Almighty" in 16:14 and 19:15).

Use of the OT: The verse begins with the common construction Ἐγώ εἰμι, often appearing in the Pentateuch in conjunction with "God" or "Lord" as either Ἐγώ εἰμι ὁ θεός or Ἐγώ εἰμι Κύριος ὁ θεὸς. In the Gospel of John, it appears often with divine or messianic implication (e.g., John 4:26; 6:20, 35; 8:12, 28; 10:7; 11:25; 14:6; 15:1; 18:5). The "first and the last" alludes to several divine claims in

Isaiah: in Isa 41:4 God claims ἐγὼ θεὸς πρῶτος, καὶ εἰς τὰ ἐπερχόμενα ἐγώ εἰμι; in Isa 44:6 he claims Ἐγὼ πρῶτος; and in Isa 48:12 he claims ἐγώ εἰμι πρῶτος, καὶ ἐγώ εἰμι εἰς τὸν αἰῶνα. Παντοκράτωρ was the standard LXX term used to translate צְבָאוֹת "hosts" in the divine title "the Lord of hosts," except in Job for שַׁדַּי "almighty." The formulaic expression κύριος ὁ θεὸς ὁ παντοκράτωρ occurs in Amos 3:13; 4:13.

FOR FURTHER STUDY

15. Use of Zechariah in Revelation

Allen, G. V. "Textual Pluriformity and Allusions in the Book of Revelation: The Text of Zechariah 4 in the Apocalypse." *ZNW* 106 (2015): 136–45.

Jauhiainen, M. *The Use of Zechariah in Revelation*. WUNT 2.199. Tübingen: Mohr Siebeck, 2005.

HOMILETICAL SUGGESTIONS

The first sermon in a series on Revelation should probably focus on interpretive guidance related to genre.

Reading Revelation Well (1:1–8)

1. As an apocalypse, Revelation unveils spiritual realities through symbolic revelation.
2. As a letter, Revelation was written to specific Christians to motivate faithful perseverance.
3. As a prophecy, Revelation calls God's people to repentance and witness in light of God's promised future.

Alternatively, it could focus on the main divine actors introduced in these verses.

Revelation: A Message from the Triune God (1:1–8)

1. A message from God, the almighty, the great "I am."
2. A message from Jesus, the ruler of kings on earth, the coming one.
3. A message from the Spirit who speaks to the churches.

II. In the Spirit on Patmos (1:9–3:22)

John refers to himself as "in/by the Spirit" four times in Revelation. Each of these references is connected to a geographical location. John is in the Spirit on Patmos (Rev 1:9–10), in the heavenly throne room (4:2), in the wilderness (17:3), and on a great and high mountain (21:10). These references provide one way to structure the text based on literary features. They also mark significant logical transitions in the content and development of the book. The first text segment "in the Spirit" contains John's inaugural vision of Jesus, his commission, and the proclamations from Jesus through John to the seven churches.

A. JOHN'S VISION AND COMMISSION (1:9–20)

This section has three main parts. First, John describes his commission to write down the visions and send them to the churches (Rev 1:9–11). Second, he describes his vision of the exalted Son of Man (Rev 1:12–16). Third, he describes his response to the vision and recounts Jesus's repetition of the commission to write (Rev 1:17–20). The repetition of the commission functions rhetorically to strengthen John's ethos as a trustworthy prophet, and the exalted vision of Jesus establishes his authority to commend, rebuke, and command the seven churches in Revelation 2–3.

1. John's Commission (1:9–11)

1:9 **Ἐγὼ** (subj. nom.; John writes here in the 1st pers.) **Ἰωάννης** (appos.), **ὁ ἀδελφὸς** (coord. appos.) **ὑμῶν** (relationship) **καὶ συγκοινωνὸς** (συγκοινωνός, -οῦ, ὁ, "participant, partner, sharer," coord. appos.) **ἐν τῇ** (the art. governs all three fem. nouns as the spheres in which John was their fellow participant) **θλίψει** (θλῖψις, -εως, ἡ, "tribulation, affliction, trouble") **καὶ βασιλείᾳ καὶ ὑπομονῇ** (ὑπομονή, -ῆς, ἡ, "endurance") **ἐν Ἰησοῦ** (likely applies to all three nouns as a metaphorical loc. [Math 9]), **ἐγενόμην** (1st sg. aor. mid. ind. of γίνομαι) **ἐν τῇ νήσῳ** (νῆσος, -ου, ἡ, "island," loc.) **τῇ καλουμένῃ** (dat. sg. fem. of pres. pass. ptc. of καλέω, "being called," attrib.) **Πάτμῳ** ("Patmos," an island in the Aegean Sea near the southwest coast of Asia Minor) **διὰ τὸν λόγον** (causal; the prep. phrase provides the reason John was on Patmos) **τοῦ θεοῦ** (gen. of source) **καὶ** (likely epex., "namely, that is") **τὴν μαρτυρίαν** (μαρτυρία, -ας, ἡ, "testimony") **Ἰησοῦ** (prob. obj. gen., "testimony about Jesus," but poss. subj. gen., see 1:2).

The gen. of relationship ὑμῶν connected to ἀδελφός functions to build ethos through a reminder of fictive kinship. It is important to note that θλῖψις is not used here in a technical way to describe a future seven-year tribulation but rather a present reality for John and his original hearers. The coexistence of both tribulation and kingdom in the present time requires a response of endurance from John and the churches. The text does not require that John was on Patmos because of persecution, although early church traditions understood it as such. The text itself only claims that he was there (willingly or unwillingly) because of the word and testimony, that is, to receive the visions contained in Revelation. Paul commends the Philippians for sharing in his tribulation in Phil 4:14 (συγκοινωνήσαντές μου τῇ θλίψει).

1:10 **ἐγενόμην** (1st sg. aor. mid. ind. of γίνομαι) **ἐν πνεύματι** (loc. or manner, cf. Ezek 43:5; the prep. phrase suggests a visionary experience) **ἐν τῇ κυριακῇ** (κυριακός, -ή, -όν, "the Lord's," attrib.) **ἡμέρᾳ** (temp. prep. phrase; "the Lord's Day" likely points to Sunday as the day of the resurrection) **καὶ ἤκουσα** (1st sg. aor. act. ind. ἀκούω, coord. with ἐγενόμην) **ὀπίσω** (improper prep., "behind") **μου** (loc. gen.) **φωνὴν** (dir. obj.) **μεγάλην** (attrib.) **ὡς** (comp., "like" or "as") **σάλπιγγος** (σάλπιγξ, -ιγγος, ἡ, "trumpet," gen. sg. fem.)

Use of the OT: Jeremiah was also commanded to write the words of divine revelation in a book (Γράψον πάντας τοὺς λόγους, οὓς ἐχρημάτισα πρός σέ, ἐπὶ βιβλίου, Jer 37:2 LXX [Jer 30:2 EVV]). Ezekiel often describes himself as being acted upon by the Spirit (Ezek 2:2: καὶ ἦλθεν ἐπ' ἐμὲ πνεῦμα καὶ ἀνέλαβέν με καὶ ἐξῆρέν με καὶ ἔστησέν με ἐπὶ τοὺς πόδας μου; 3:12: ἀνέλαβέν με πνεῦμα; 3:14: τὸ πνεῦμα ἐξῆρέν με καὶ ἀνέλαβέν με; 3:24: ἦλθεν ἐπ' ἐμὲ πνεῦμα καὶ ἔστησέν με ἐπὶ πόδας μου, καὶ ἐλάλησεν πρός με; 11:1: ἀνέλαβέν με πνεῦμα καὶ ἤγαγέν με; 43:5: ἀνέλαβέν με πνεῦμα καὶ εἰσήγαγέν με). When the Spirit takes him up, Ezekiel also hears a voice behind him (Ezek 3:12: καὶ ἤκουσα κατόπισθέν μου φωνὴν).

1:11 λεγούσης (gen. sg. fem. of pres. act. ptc. of λέγω, compl. in obj.-compl. double gen. construction following ἤκουσα, "I heard a voice speaking"), **ὃ** (the headless rel. cl. is fronted for emph. and functions as the dir. obj. of γράψον) **βλέπεις** (2nd sg. pres. act. ind. of βλέπω) **γράψον** (2nd sg. aor. act. impv. of γράφω; "The aorist here refers to the writing of the entire book" [Math 10]; cf. the command to write in 1:19; 2:1, 8, 12, 18; 3:1, 7, 14; 14:13; 19:9; 21:5) **εἰς βιβλίον** (βιβλίον, -ου, τό, "scroll, book," loc.) **καὶ πέμψον** (2nd sg. aor. act. impv. of πέμπω) **ταῖς ἑπτὰ** (attrib.) **ἐκκλησίαις** (indir. obj.), **εἰς Ἔφεσον** ("Ephesus," loc.) **καὶ εἰς Σμύρναν** ("Smyrna," loc.) **καὶ εἰς Πέργαμον** ("Pergamum," loc.) **καὶ εἰς Θυάτειρα** ("Thyatira," loc.) **καὶ εἰς Σάρδεις** ("Sardis," loc.) **καὶ εἰς Φιλαδέλφειαν** ("Philadelphia," loc.) **καὶ εἰς Λαοδίκειαν** ("Laodicea," loc.).

The ptc. λεγούσης is in grammatical agreement with the gen. σάλπιγγος in 1:10 and not the acc. φωνήν. Grammatically, this makes the trumpet and not the voice speak. John uses a similar construction in Rev 4:1; 19:1; 19:6 (ἀκούειν + φωνή + gen. qualifier of φωνή + gen. ptc. of speaking; Moţ 142). John is consistent in his idiolect, and it appears to be a *constructio ad sensum* (Moţ 142–43).

2. The Vision of Jesus (1:12–16)

1:12 Καὶ ἐπέστρεψα (1st sg. aor. act. ind. of ἐπιστρέφω, "turn") **βλέπειν** (pres. act. inf. βλέπω, purpose) **τὴν** (anaphroic to 1:10) **φωνὴν** (dir. obj., ant. of ἥτις, an example of synecdoche in which the voice represents the person [Aune[a] 88]) **ἥτις** (subj. nom.) **ἐλάλει** (3rd sg. impf. act. ind. of λαλέω) **μετ' ἐμοῦ** (association), **καὶ ἐπιστρέψας** (nom. sg. masc. of aor. act. ptc. of ἐπιστρέφω, temp. adv. ptc.) **εἶδον** (1st sg. aor. act. ind. of ὁράω) **ἑπτὰ** ("seven," attrib.) **λυχνίας** (λυχνία, -ας, ἡ, "lampstand," dir. obj.) **χρυσᾶς** (χρυσοῦς, -ῆ, -οῦν, "golden," attrib.)

Note the hearing-seeing literary dynamic that appears throughout Revelation whereby John first hears something or about something and then sees it.

1:13 καὶ (coord. the two dir. objs. of ὁράω: "I saw lampstands and a son") **ἐν μέσῳ** (loc.) **τῶν λυχνιῶν** (gen. of place) **ὅμοιον** (ὅμοιος, -οία, -οιον, "like, similar," comp. adj.) **υἱὸν** (ὅμοιος should be followed by a dat. as in A C and several minuscules; John's use of an acc. likely indicates an intentional allusion to Dan 7:13 as in 14:14 [Math 11]) **ἀνθρώπου** (gen. of relationship) **ἐνδεδυμένον** (acc. sg. masc. of pf. pass. ptc. of ἐνδύω, "dress, clothe," attrib.) **ποδήρη** (ποδήρης, -ους, ὁ, "long robe" which reaches the feet, dir. obj.; the use of the acc. with vbs. of clothing/wearing is normal Greek but in English "with" is often supplied) **καὶ περιεζωσμένον** (acc. sg. masc. of pf. pass. ptc. of περιζώννυμι, "gird, tie around," attrib.) **πρὸς τοῖς μαστοῖς** (μαστός, -οῦ, ὁ, "chest," loc.) **ζώνην** (ζώνη, -ης, ἡ, "belt, sash," dir. obj. of περιεζωσμένον) **χρυσᾶν** (χρυσοῦς, -ῆ, -οῦν, "golden," attrib.).

Χρυσᾶν could be seen as a barbarism and the acc. fem. should read χρυσῆν, but there are examples of this variant spelling in Greek authors both before and after John wrote (Moţ 97). The clustering of pf. ptcs. describes the new character being introduced, the Son of Man.

> **Use of the OT:** The one like a son of man connects this individual with the "son of man" in Dan 7:13 and builds upon the prophetic oracle in 1:7. John here has a vision of the one who will come on the clouds. The figure in Ezek 9:2, 11 is clothed with a long robe (ὁ ἐνδεδυκὼς τὸν ποδήρη) and girded with a belt (ἐζωσμένος τῇ ζώνῃ) while the figure in Dan 10:5 is clothed and girded with linen (ἐνδεδυμένος βύσσινα καὶ τὴν ὀσφὺν περιεζωσμένος βυσσίνῳ [with gold in the MT]). It is possible that ποδήρης could evoke a priestly image (cf. Exod 28:4, 31; 29:5; Zech 3:4), but it is not a technical term for the robe of a high priest (Fanning 99).

1:14 ἡ δὲ (Although a slight nuance could be suggested for the use of δέ instead of καί to indicate a shift in focus to the head and face [Math 12], John's key source texts in Dan 7:9; 10:5–6 consistently use καί, which could suggest that John is simply using δέ as a syn. for καί here.) **κεφαλὴ** (subj. nom. of verbless cl.) **αὐτοῦ** (poss.) **καὶ** (epex., "that is") **αἱ τρίχες** (θρίξ, τριχός, ἡ, "hair," coord. subj. nom.) **λευκαὶ** (λευκός, -ή, -όν, "white, bright," pred. adj.) **ὡς** (comp.) **ἔριον** (-ου, τό, "wool" either processed or unprocessed) **λευκὸν** (attrib. adj. modifying ἔριον) **ὡς** (comp.) **χιὼν** (-όνος, ἡ, "snow") **καὶ οἱ ὀφθαλμοὶ** (subj. nom. of verbless cl.) **αὐτοῦ** (poss.) **ὡς** (comp.) **φλὸξ** (φλογός, ἡ, "flame") **πυρὸς** (πῦρ, πυρός, τό, "fire," attrib. gen. "fiery flame")

The rider in Rev 19:12 has eyes like a flame of fire (ὀφθαλμοὶ αὐτοῦ [ὡς] φλὸξ πυρός); this is one of several points of similarity that suggest the same person.

> **Use of the OT:** The ancient of days in Dan 7:9 has clothing like snow and white hair like clean white wool (περιβολὴν ὡσεὶ χιόνα, καὶ τὸ τρίχωμα τῆς κεφαλῆς αὐτοῦ ὡσεὶ ἔριον λευκὸν καθαρόν) while sitting on a throne like a flame of fire (ὁ θρόνος ὡσεὶ φλὸξ πυρός). The figure in Dan 10:6 has eyes like lamps of fire (οἱ ὀφθαλμοὶ αὐτοῦ ὡσεὶ λαμπάδες πυρός).

1:15 καὶ οἱ πόδες (πούς, ποδός, ὁ, "foot," subj. nom. of verbless cl.) **αὐτοῦ** (poss.) **ὅμοιοι** (ὅμοιος, -οία, -οιον, "like, similar," comp. pred. adj.) **χαλκολιβάνῳ** (χαλκολίβανον, -ου, τό, "fine/bright bronze") **ὡς** (manner, "as") **ἐν καμίνῳ** (κάμινος, -ου, ἡ, "furnace, oven," prob. loc. but possibly means) **πεπυρωμένης** (gen. sg. fem. pf. pass. ptc. πυρόω, "burn," gen. abs. of manner without a gen. noun or pron. [see below]; the pf. tense indicates the stative result of the purification process) **καὶ ἡ φωνὴ** (subj. nom. of verbless cl.) **αὐτοῦ** (poss.) **ὡς** (comp.) **φωνὴ ὑδάτων** (ὕδωρ, ὕδατος, τό, gen. of source) **πολλῶν** (attrib.),

The gen. ptc. πεπυρωμένης, 𝔓[98vid]A, C) should be dat. to match its ant. χαλκολιβάνῳ. Some scribes solved this problem by changing it to the dat. πεπυρωμένῳ (א, 2062, 2053, 2050) while others make it nom. pl. (πεπυρωμένοι) to match οἱ πόδες (many minuscules). Aune shows that χαλκολιβάνῳ could be a fem. noun, which would relieve the problem while also suggesting it could be gen. abs. without the noun or pron. (Aune[a] 65–66). Moţ likewise suggests that John had a pron. in mind, πεπυρωέμένης αὐτῆς, but simply omitted the pron. while writing (Moţ 137). The heavenly voice in Rev 14:2 also sounds like many waters and the worship of the great crowd in 19:6 is like φωνὴν ὑδάτων πολλῶν.

Use of the OT: The figure in Dan 10:6 has feet like flashing brass (καὶ οἱ πόδες ὡσεὶ χαλκὸς ἐξαστράπτων) and a voice like an uproar (καὶ φωνὴ λαλιᾶς αὐτοῦ ὡσεὶ φωνὴ θορύβου). The sound of the living creatures' wings in Ezek 1:24 is ὡς φωνὴν ὕδατος πολλοῦ (cf. Ezek 43:2).

1:16 καὶ ἔχων (nom. sg. masc. of pres. act. ptc. of ἔχω, periph. [see below]) **ἐν τῇ δεξιᾷ** (δεξιός, -ά, -όν, "right," attrib.) **χειρὶ** (χείρ, χειρός, ἡ, "hand," loc.) **αὐτοῦ** (poss.) **ἀστέρας** (ἀστήρ, -έρος, ὁ, "star," acc., dir. obj.) **ἑπτὰ** ("seven," attrib.) **καὶ ἐκ τοῦ στόματος** (στόμα, -ατος, τό, "mouth," source) **αὐτοῦ** (poss.) **ῥομφαία** (ῥομφαία, -ας, ἡ, "sword," subj. nom.) **δίστομος** (-ον, adj., "double-edged," attrib.) **ὀξεῖα** (ὀξύς, -εῖα, -ύ, adj., "sharp, quick," attrib.) **ἐκπορευομένη** (nom. sg. fem. of pres. mid. ptc. of ἐκπορεύομαι, periph. [see below]) **καὶ ἡ ὄψις** (-εως, ἡ, "face, appearance," subj. nom. of verbless cl.) **αὐτοῦ** (poss.) **ὡς** (comp.) **ὁ ἥλιος** (-ου, ὁ, "sun") **φαίνει** (3rd sg. pres. act. ind. of φαίνω, "shine") **ἐν τῇ δυνάμει** (manner) **αὐτοῦ** (poss.).

The case of ἔχων might be expected to be gen. to match αὐτοῦ in the prior verse. Both ptcs. in this verse, however, are better understood as being periph. with an implied ἦν (Math 14). Verse 16 thus likely starts a new sentence ("And he was holding . . ."). The seven stars are mentioned again in 1:20; 2:1; 3:1. Although different words are used, the shining face seems to point to heavenly or divine glory as with Moses after encountering God (Exod 34:29; δεδόξασται ἡ ὄψις τοῦ χρώματος τοῦ προσώπου αὐτοῦ) and Jesus's transfiguration (Matt 17:2; καὶ ἔλαμψεν τὸ πρόσωπον αὐτοῦ ὡς ὁ ἥλιος).

Use of the OT: In Isa 49:2 the mouth of God's servant, Israel, is made like a sharp sword (ἔθηκεν τὸ στόμα μου ὡσεὶ μάχαιραν ὀξεῖαν). The messianic branch of Isa 11:4 will strike the earth with the word of his mouth and will destroy the ungodly with the breath of his lips (πατάξει γῆν τῷ λόγῳ τοῦ στόματος αὐτοῦ καὶ ἐν πνεύματι διὰ χειλέων ἀνελεῖ ἀσεβῆ).

---

3. John's Commission Repeated (1:17–20)

1:17 Καὶ ὅτε (temp., "when") **εἶδον** (1st sg. aor. act. ind. of ὁράω) **αὐτόν** (dir. obj.), **ἔπεσα** (1st sg. aor. act. ind. of πίπτω) **πρὸς τοὺς πόδας** (loc.) **αὐτοῦ** (poss.) **ὡς** (manner) **νεκρός, καὶ ἔθηκεν** (3rd sg. aor. act. ind. of τίθημι) **τὴν δεξιὰν** (δεξιός, -ά, -όν, "right [hand]," dir. obj.) **αὐτοῦ** (poss.) **ἐπ' ἐμὲ** (loc.) **λέγων** (nom. sg. masc. of pres. act. ptc. of λέγω, possibly temp. "while saying," the pres. ptc. of λέγω introduces dir. discourse fifty-three times in Rev and, although not a Septuagintalism, John's frequent usage is prob. influenced by the almost 800 uses of λέγων in the LXX [Aune[a] 66]), **Μὴ φοβοῦ** (2nd sg. pres. mid. impv. of φοβέω, the context [not the tense] makes it clear that this prohibition is intended to stop an action in process; the pres. tense is the default for atelic impvs.). **ἐγώ εἰμι** (1st sg. pres. act. ind. of εἰμί) **ὁ πρῶτος** (pred. adj.) **καὶ ὁ ἔσχατος** (-η, -ον, "last," coord. pred. adj.)

It is significant that John is not rebuked for falling on his face before Jesus while later being rebuked for worshipping angels (19:10; 22:8–9; Fanning 103).

Use of the OT: On Jesus's claim to be the "first and last," see 1:8. Daniel 10 is alluded to several times in the above description of Jesus. Daniel responds to the vision and the voice by falling on his face on the ground (10:9: ἐγὼ ἤμην πεπτωκὼς ἐπὶ πρόσωπόν μου ἐπὶ τὴν γῆν) and is subsequently raised up by a hand upon him (10:10: καὶ ἰδοὺ χεῖρα προσήγαγέ μοι καὶ ἤγειρέ με) and commanded not to fear (καὶ εἶπεν πρός με Μὴ φοβοῦ [Dan 10:12]). Abram (Gen 17:3), Joshua (Josh 5:14), Ezekiel (Ezek 1:28), and Daniel (Dan 8:17) all fall on their faces when encountering God or a heavenly being.

1:18 καὶ ὁ ζῶν (nom. sg. masc. of pres. act. ptc. of ζάω, subst., pred. nom. "the living one"), **καὶ ἐγενόμην** (1st sg. aor. mid. ind. of γίνομαι, ingressive) **νεκρὸς** (pred. adj.) **καὶ** (likely contrastive to note an unexpected fact, "and yet, but" [BDAG 495b]) **ἰδοὺ** (emph. interj.) **ζῶν** (either periph., "I am living," or subst. ptc., pred. nom. in parallel with ὁ ζῶν at the opening of the verse, "I am the living one") **εἰμι** (1st sg. pres. act. ind., provides a deliberate contrast with the aor. ἐγενόμην) **εἰς τοὺς αἰῶνας** (measure) **τῶν αἰώνων** (the repetition of αἰών is emph. and common in doxologies [L&N 67.95]) **καὶ ἔχω** (1st sg. pres. act. ind. of ἔχω) **τὰς κλεῖς** (κλείς, κλειδός, ἡ, "key," dir. obj.) **τοῦ θανάτου** (possibly poss. gen. with death and Hades personified but more likely obj. gen with death and Hades understood spatially, "key to death and Hades"; against personification, Aune notes that "[d]eath is never described in ancient texts as possessing keys" [Aune[a] 103]) **καὶ τοῦ ᾅδου** (ᾅδης, -ου, ὁ, "Hades, abode of the dead," obj. gen.).

Aune assembles many examples from the OT, early Jewish literature, and pagan religious literature to argue that the description of Jesus as ὁ ζῶν is a double entendre referring both to the resurrection and a traditional Jewish designation for God: "the living God" (Aune[a] 101–2). Jesus's victory and authority over death is celebrated elsewhere in the NT (1 Cor 15:26, 54–57; Heb 2:14–15).

1:19 γράψον (2nd sg. aor. act. impv. of γράφω) **οὖν** (inferential) **ἃ** (subj. nom. of headless rel. cl.) **εἶδες** (2nd sg. aor. act. ind. of ὁράω, epistolary aor.; from the perspective of the reader it could be translated "you saw" but from John's perspective it could be translated "you will see") **καὶ** (epex., "even, that is") **ἃ** (subj. nom. of headless rel. cl.) **εἰσὶν** (3rd pl. pres. act. ind. of εἰμί) **καὶ ἃ** (subj. nom. of headless rel. cl.) **μέλλει** (3rd sg. pres. act. ind. of μέλλω) **γενέσθαι** (aor. mid. inf. of γίνομαι, compl. inf.) **μετὰ** (temp. "after") **ταῦτα** (the ant. of ταῦτα is the prior rel. cl. ἃ εἰσὶν).

It is possible to see the three rel. cls. as coord. dir. objs. of the command to write. If the first καί is epex., however, there is one dir. obj.: "what you saw" (Aune[a] 106; Koester 248). The following two rel. cls. then would further expand on what he saw: "even/that is, the things which are and which are about to happen after these things." John's visions encompass the present and future but this verse does not provide a structural outline for the book. Jesus here reissues the command to write from 1:11.

Use of the OT: In Isa 48:6 God declares to the house of Jacob that he will announce new things that are about to happen (τὰ καινὰ ἀπὸ τοῦ νῦν, ἃ μέλλει γίνεσθαι). The phrase ἃ μέλλει γενέσθαι μετὰ ταῦτα is drawn from Dan 2:28–29a, 45–47. Μετὰ ταῦτα and ἐπ' ἐσχάτων τῶν ἡμερῶν ("in the last days") are roughly synonymous in Daniel 2 (cf. Peter's change of μετὰ ταῦτα from Joel 3:1 to ἐν ταῖς ἐσχάταις ἡμέραις in Acts 2:17). "The Dan 2 references treat μετὰ ταῦτα as synonymous with ἐπ' ἐσχάτων τῶν ἡμερῶν, both referring to the general era of the end times (the LXX has the latter in vv. 28, 29, and 45, but Theod. has μετὰ ταῦτα in vv. 29 and 45 and ἐπ' ἐσχάτων τῶν ἡμερῶν in v. 28)" (Beale 155). Beale rightly observes that "[a] large portion of NT references to 'the latter days', 'end times', and synonymous expressions refer not exclusively to the future but to the end-time period as having begun, as continuing, and as being consummated at some future point (e.g., Mark 1:15; Acts 2:17; Gal 4:4; 1 Cor 10:11; 2 Cor 6:2; 1 Tim 4:1; 2 Tim 3:1; 1 Pet 1:20; 2 Pet 3:3; Heb 1:2; 9:26; Jas 5:3; 1 John 2:18; Jude 18)" (Beale 140).

1:20 τὸ μυστήριον (μυστήριον, -ου, τό, "mystery, secret," nom. or acc., see below) **τῶν** (anaphoric to 1:16) **ἑπτὰ** ("seven," attrib.) **ἀστέρων** (ἀστήρ, -έρος, ὁ, "star," epex. gen., "the mystery, that is, the seven stars," ant. of οὕς) **οὓς** (dir. obj.) **εἶδες** (2nd sg. aor. act. ind. of ὁράω) **ἐπὶ τῆς δεξιᾶς** (δεξιός, -ά, -όν, "right [hand]," subst. adj., loc.) **μου**

(poss.) **καὶ τὰς ἑπτὰ** (attrib.) **λυχνίας** (λυχνία, -ας, ἡ, "lampstand," see below) **τὰς χρυσᾶς** (χρυσοῦς, -ῆ, -οῦν, "golden," attrib.)· **οἱ ἑπτὰ ἀστέρες** (subj. nom.) **ἄγγελοι** (pred. nom.) **τῶν ἑπτὰ ἐκκλησιῶν** (gen. of subord., "over") **εἰσιν** (3rd pl. pres. act. ind. of εἰμί) **καὶ αἱ λυχνίαι** (subj. nom.) **αἱ ἑπτὰ ἑπτὰ ἐκκλησίαι** (pred. nom.) **εἰσίν**.

The general meaning of the verse is clear but the grammar can be explained various ways. The acc. λυχνίας should be gen. since it seems to be coordinated with ἀστέρων. This could be seen as a solecism due to authorial error and Moţ suggests that Rev 1:20 "either contains a syntactical ambiguity or lacks discourse coherence" (Moţ 154). Other options exist. It could work to take μυστήριον as an acc. dir. obj. coordinated with λυχνίας. This requires there to be an implied vb. such as "I will explain" (Math 17). Both accs. could also be respect or reference although this is a rare use of the acc. (Wallace 203–4; Fanning 106). It seems most natural to take μυστήριον as a nom. abs. but this would not explain the solecism beyond noting that λυχνίας is attracted to the acc. case of οὕς (Aune[a] 68).

Most interpreters agree that in Revelation ἄγγελος is consistently used to describe heavenly or supernatural beings so 1:20 seems to point to some representative relationship between angels and Christian communities. Although explicit instruction is lacking, there are hints in this direction elsewhere in Scripture and Second Temple Judaism (Deut 32:8; Dan 10:13, 20, 21; 12:1; Matt 18:10; Acts 12:15; Tob 12:12–15; Sir 17:17). Because the Scriptures are not as explicit as we would like on this point, caution should be exercised in drawing additional conclusions from this observation.

Use of the OT: In light of the pattern of allusions to Daniel noted in 1:1, 19, the use of μυστήριον should be seen as an allusion to Dan 2:29 (σύ, βασιλεῦ, . . . ἑώρακας πάντα, ὅσα δεῖ γενέσθαι ἐπ' ἐσχάτων τῶν ἡμερῶν, καὶ ὁ ἀνακαλύπτων μυστήρια ἐδήλωσέ σοι ἃ δεῖ γενέσθαι) or 2:47 (ἐστὶν ὁ θεὸς ὑμῶν . . . ὁ ἐκφαίνων μυστήρια κρυπτὰ μόνος, ὅτι ἐδυνάσθης δηλῶσαι τὸ μυστήριον τοῦτο). God revealed mysteries to both Daniel and John regarding what was necessary to happen in the last days.

HOMILETICAL SUGGESTIONS

Jesus Is with His Suffering People (1:9–20)

1. God's people share with John in tribulation, the kingdom, and perseverance (1:9).
2. Despite tribulation, Jesus is present among the churches as the exalted king and priest who conquered death (1:10–16).
3. Jesus's power and victory over death enables his followers to overcome fear (1:17–20).

B. PROCLAMATIONS TO SEVEN CHURCHES (2:1–3:22)

The structural similarities in the seven proclamations are widely recognized. The seven proclamations each follow a similar format.

1. Each one is addressed to the angel of a particular church with a stereotypical expression: Τῷ ἀγγέλῳ τῆς ἐν X (dat. loc. of the church) ἐκκλησίας γράψον.
2. The speaker, Jesus, is then identified, generally with a reference back to John's vision of Jesus in Rev 1:12–16.
3. Jesus tells them something he knows about that particular church, whether good or bad.
4. This statement about Jesus's knowledge of the situation is followed up by encouragement or warnings depending upon the needs of the church.
5. The proclamation concludes with a call for spiritual discernment and a promise to the one who overcomes (the order of these two elements reverses in the fourth proclamation).

The churches are arranged chiastically. The first and last are in grave danger of losing their identity as Christian churches. The second and sixth are parallel to each other and are not rebuked. The middle three contain mixed messages targeted at a mixed membership (some compromising and some faithful). The middle church contains a phrase clarifying that the content of each proclamation was meant for the instruction of all: καὶ γνώσονται πᾶσαι αἱ ἐκκλησίαι (2:23). Most of the vbs. referring to the churches in Revelation 2–3 are sg. because these proclamations are addressed τῷ ἀγγέλῳ of each church. The proclamations resemble both imperial and royal edicts as well as prophetic judgment and salvation oracles, the latter of which focus on the covenant lawsuit. John, as a Christian prophet in line with OT prophets, is calling both Jewish and gentile believers in Jesus to covenant faithfulness with accompanying blessings and curses.

FOR FURTHER STUDY

16. The Seven Proclamations (2:1–3:22)

*Aune, D. E. "The Form and Function of the Proclamations to the Seven Churches (Revelation 2–3)." *NTS* 36 (1990): 182–204.

Hemer, C. J. *The Letters to the Seven Churches of Asia in Their Local Setting*. Sheffield, UK: JSOT Press, 1986.

Kirby, J. T. "The Rhetorical Situations of Revelation 1–3." *NTS* 34 (1988): 197–207.

Ramsey, W. M. *The Letters to the Seven Churches in Asia*. Rev. ed. Peabody, MA: Hendrickson, 1994.

Scobie, C. H. "Local References in the Letters to the Seven Churches." *NTS* 39 (1993): 606–24.

17. Rhetoric

*DeSilva, D. A. "Rhetorical Features in the Book of Revelation." Pages 69–84 in *OHR*.

———. *Seeing Things John's Way: The Rhetoric of the Book of Revelation*. Louisville: Westminster John Knox, 2009.

———. "What Has Athens to Do with Patmos? Rhetorical Criticism of the Revelation of John (1980–2005)." *CurBR* 6 (2008): 256–89.

Kirby, J. T. "The Rhetorical Situations of Revelation 1–3." *NTS* 34 (1988): 197–207.

Rossing, B. *The Choice between Two Cities: Whore, Bride, and Empire in the Apocalypse*. Harrisburg, PA: Trinity Press International, 1999.

Smith, I. "A Rational Choice Model of the Book of Revelation." *JSNT* 85 (2002): 97–116.

18. Covenant

*Bandy, A. "Patterns of Prophetic Lawsuits in the Oracles to the Seven Churches." *Neot* 45 (2011): 178–205.

———. *The Prophetic Lawsuit in the Book of Revelation*. New Testament Monographs 29. Sheffield: Sheffield Academic Press, 2010.

Campbell, G. "Findings, Seals, Trumpets, and Bowls: Variations upon the Theme of Covenant Rupture and Restoration in the Book of Revelation." *WTJ* 66 (2004): 71–96.

Decker, T. L. "'Live Long in the Land': The Covenantal Character of the Old Testament Allusions in the Message to Laodicea (Revelation 3:14–22)." *Neot* 48 (2014): 417–46.

Shea, W. H. "The Covenantal Form of the Letters to the Seven Churches." *AUSS* 21 (1983): 71–84.

Strand, K. A. "A Further Note on the Covenantal Form in the Book of Revelation." *AUSS* 21 (1983): 251–64.

1. Proclamation to Ephesus (2:1–7)

2:1 (asyndeton, the lack of a coord. conj.) **Τῷ ἀγγέλῳ** (indir. obj.) **τῆς ἐν Ἐφέσῳ** (loc., "Ephesus") **ἐκκλησίας** (gen. of subord., "over") **γράψον** (2nd sg. aor. act. impv. of γράφω)· **Τάδε** (acc. pl. neut. demonst. pron., dir. obj., ὅδε, used in archaically stylized formal introductions to prophetic or imperial pronouncements, "Thus says . . .") **λέγει** (3rd sg. pres. act. ind. of λέγω) **ὁ κρατῶν** (nom. sg. masc. of pres. act. ptc. of κρατέω, "hold, keep," subst., subj. nom.) **τοὺς ἑπτὰ** ("seven," attrib.) **ἀστέρας** (ἀστήρ, -έρος, ὁ, "star," dir. obj.) **ἐν τῇ δεξιᾷ** (δεξιός, -ά, -όν, "right [hand]," subst., loc.) **αὐτοῦ** (poss.), **ὁ περιπατῶν** (nom. sg. masc. of pres. act. ptc. of περιπατέω, subst., nom. of appos. to κρατῶν) **ἐν μέσῳ** (loc.) **τῶν ἑπτὰ** (attrib.) **λυχνιῶν** (λυχνία, -ας, ἡ, "lampstand," gen. of place) **τῶν χρυσῶν** (χρυσοῦς, -ῆ, -οῦν, "golden," attrib.)

The description of the speaker as holding the seven stars and walking among the lampstands provides a dir. connection to John's immediately preceding vision of Jesus in 1:13, 16 (note the change to κρατέω and the additional detail περιπατῶν).

Use of the OT: Τάδε λέγει is a common introductory expression in the Hebrew prophets (over 250 times, see, for example, Τάδε λέγει κύριος in Jer 30:1). Significantly the use of this formula regarding Jesus puts him in the place/role of Yahweh. The expression also clearly signals that John viewed himself as similar to OT prophets with a prophetic message from Jesus to God's people.

2:2 Οἶδα (1st sg. pf. act. ind. of οἶδα, "know," Mathewson rightly cautions that although οἶδα is often explained as a pf. tense with pres. tense meaning, the stative force of the pf. tense remains [Math 19]) **τὰ ἔργα** (dir. obj.) **σου** (subj. gen.) **καὶ** (possibly epex., "that is" [Aune[a] 134], but likely coord. "and") **τὸν κόπον** (κόπος, -ου, ὁ, "work, trouble," coord. dir. obj.) **καὶ τὴν ὑπομονήν** (ὑπομονή, -ῆς, ἡ, "endurance," coord. dir. obj.) **σου** (subj.) **καὶ ὅτι** (content of knowledge, "I know that . . .") **οὐ** (neg.) **δύνῃ** (2nd sg. pres. mid. ind. of δύναμαι) **βαστάσαι** (aor. act. inf. of βαστάζω, "bear, endure," compl. inf.) **κακούς** (subst., "evil ones"), **καὶ ἐπείρασας** (2nd sg. aor. act. ind. of πειράζω, "test") **τοὺς λέγοντας** (acc. pl. masc. of pres. act. ptc. of λέγω, subst., dir. obj., "the ones claiming" or "calling") **ἑαυτοὺς** (dir. obj.) **ἀποστόλους** (obj.-compl. double acc., "themselves *to be* apostles") **καὶ** (contrastive, "but" [Aune[a] 134]) **οὐκ εἰσὶν** (3rd pl. pres. act. ind. of εἰμί) **καὶ εὗρες** (2nd sg. aor. act. ind. of εὑρίσκω) **αὐτοὺς** (dir. obj.) **ψευδεῖς** (ψευδής, -ές, "false," acc. pl. masc., subst., obj.-compl. double acc., "you found them *to be* liars"),

First John 4:1 commands the readers to test the spirits because of the reality of false prophets (δοκιμάζετε τὰ πνεύματα εἰ ἐκ τοῦ θεοῦ ἐστιν, ὅτι πολλοὶ ψευδοπροφῆται ἐξεληλύθασιν εἰς τὸν κόσμον.). The command to repent reappears in 2:16, 22; 3:3, 19.

2:3 καὶ ὑπομονὴν (ὑπομονή, -ῆς, ἡ, "endurance," dir. obj.) **ἔχεις** (2nd sg. pres. act. ind. of ἔχω) **καὶ ἐβάστασας** (2nd sg. aor. act. ind. of βαστάζω, "bear, endure") **διὰ τὸ ὄνομά** (causal) **μου** (poss.) **καὶ οὐ** (neg.) **κεκοπίακες** (2nd sg. pf. act. ind. of κοπιάω, "grow weary, toil").

Κεκοπίακες could be seen as a barbarism and the 2nd sg. pf. act. should read κεκοπίακας, but a similar spelling in 2:4 would suggest an explanation in John's idiolect. Other NT authors speak of suffering because of Jesus's name (Matt 10:22; Mark 13:13; John 15:21; cf. Matt 5:11) or because of righteousness (1 Pet 3:14). The necessary response to persecution is ὑπομονή.

2:4 ἀλλ' (contrastive) **ἔχω** (1st sg. pres. act. ind.) **κατὰ σοῦ** (gen. of opposition, "against") **ὅτι** (content) **τὴν ἀγάπην** (dir. obj.) **σου** (poss. or subj. gen.) **τὴν πρώτην** (attrib.) **ἀφῆκες** (2nd sg. aor. act. ind. of ἀφίημι).

Ἀφῆκες could be seen as a barbarism and the 2nd sg. aor. act. should read ἀφῆκας, but there are examples of this variant spelling in other Greek authors (Moț 99). Neither the grammar nor the context definitively indicates whether this loss of love indicates love toward God and Jesus, love toward other believers, or love toward nonbelievers.

2:5 μνημόνευε (2nd sg. pres. act. impv. of μνημονεύω, "remember") **οὖν** (inferential) **πόθεν** (interr. adv., "from where") **πέπτωκας** (2nd sg. pf. act. ind. of πίπτω) **καὶ μετανόησον** (2nd sg. aor. act. impv. of μετανοέω, "repent") **καὶ τὰ πρῶτα** (attrib.) **ἔργα** (dir. obj.) **ποίησον** (2nd sg. aor. act. impv. of ποιέω)· **εἰ δὲ μή** ("and if not, otherwise" [BDAG 278c]), **ἔρχομαί** (1st sg. pres. mid. ind. of ἔρχομαι, futuristic pres.) **σοι** (loc. "to you," perhaps dat. of disadvantage, "against you") **καὶ κινήσω** (1st sg. fut. act. ind. of κινέω, "move") **τὴν λυχνίαν** (λυχνία, -ας, ἡ, "lampstand," dir. obj.) **σου** (poss.) **ἐκ τοῦ τόπου** (τόπος, -ου, ὁ, "place," gen. of separation, "from") **αὐτῆς** (poss., fem. to match its ant. λυχνίαν), **ἐὰν μὴ** ("if not, unless") **μετανοήσῃς** (2nd sg. aor. act. subjunc. of μετανοέω).

The change in tense between the pres. impv. μνημόνευε and aor. impvs. μετανόησον and ποίησον is probably due more to conventional lexical influence than conscious choice; atelic vbs. prefer the pres. and conventionally focus on general practices while telic vbs. prefer the aor. and often focus on specific occasions (*GDNTG*, 239–41). There is perhaps significance in the repetition of the cond. apod. with a development from εἰ to ἐάν. "[T]he fulfillment of the apodosis seems stronger with εἰ δὲ μή and less strong with ἐὰν μὴ. If the church of Ephesus remains unrepentant, Jesus will surely come to her in judgment. But, at the end of the sentence, Jesus presents, as less probable, the possibility that the church of Ephesus will not repent" (Moţ 213). The concluding third-class prot. (ἐὰν μὴ) does not mute the warning with assurance since it still leaves the future open to either possibility. The repetition of μετανοέω stresses the response necessary to avoid Jesus's judgment.

In addition to 2:5, other commands addressed to the hearer of Revelation include the command to repent (2:16; 3:3, 19), to not fear coming suffering (2:10), to be faithful unto death (2:10), to wake up and strengthen what is about to die (3:2), to remember and keep what they had received and heard (3:3), to hold on to what they had (3:11), to buy from Christ gold, white garments, and eye salve (3:18), to fear God, give him glory, and worship him (14:7), to come out from Babylon (18:4), to rejoice over Babylon's judgments (18:20), to praise God (19:5), to rejoice, exult, and give God glory (19:7), and to continue in righteousness and holiness (22:11). These commands can be grouped and expanded into five broader themes representing the goal of Revelation's motivational argumentation: *Repentance*: 2:5, 16, 21, 22; 3:3, 19; 9:20, 21; 16:9, 11. *Perseverance*: persevere (1:9; 2:2, 3, 19; 3:10; 13:10; 14:12), be faithful (1:5; 2:10, 13; 3:14; 17:14), hold fast (2:13, 25; 3:11). *Obedience*: keep the commandments and do good works (1:3; 2:2, 5, 19, 26; 3:3, 8; 12:17; 14:12–13; 22:7). *Witness*: (1:2, 5, 9; 2:13; 3:14; 12:17; 19:10; 20:4; cf. 6:9; 11:1–14; 12:10–12; 20:4–6). *Worship*: (14:7; 19:5; cf. 4:1–11; 5:6–14; 7:9–17; 8:1–5; 11:15–19; 12:10–12; 14:1–5; 15:1–4; 16:1–7; 19:1–8).

Threats and warnings directed toward compromising Christians are also found in 2:16, 22; 3:3, 16, 19; 18:4. The threat of Jesus's coming in judgment here and in 2:16; 3:3 likely refers to coming in judgment to his church within history in preparation for the end, while 3:11; 16:15; 22:7, 12 seem to focus more on the final coming, although this distinction is not made explicitly by John.

2:6 ἀλλὰ (contrastive) **τοῦτο** (dir. obj.) **ἔχεις** (2nd sg. pres. act. ind. of ἔχω), **ὅτι** (epex. content cl.) **μισεῖς** (2nd sg. pres. act. ind. of μισέω, "hate") **τὰ ἔργα** (dir. obj., ant. of ἅ) **τῶν Νικολαϊτῶν** ("Nicolaitan," subj. gen.) **ἃ** (acc. pl. neut., rel. pron.) **κἀγὼ** (crasis of καί and ἐγώ, subj. nom.) **μισῶ** (1st sg. pres. act. ind. of μισέω).

Use of the OT: In Ps 138:21 LXX (139:21 EVV), David expresses hate for those who hate God (οὐχὶ τοὺς μισοῦντάς σε, κύριε, ἐμίσησα).

2:7 ὁ ἔχων (nom. sg. masc. of pres. act. ptc. of ἔχω, subst., subj. nom.) **οὖς** (οὖς, ὠτός, τό, "ear," acc. sg. neut., dir. obj.) **ἀκουσάτω** (3rd sg. aor. act. impv. of ἀκούω, "let him hear" or "he must hear") **τί** (τίς, dir. obj., interr. pron., "what") **τὸ πνεῦμα** (subj. nom.) **λέγει** (3rd sg. pres. act. ind. of λέγω) **ταῖς ἐκκλησίαις** (indir. obj.). **τῷ νικῶντι** (dat. sg. masc. of pres. act. ptc. of νικάω, "overcome, conquer," subst., indir. obj.) **δώσω** (1st sg. fut. act. ind. of δίδωμι) **αὐτῷ** (redundant/resumptive personal pron. for emph.) **φαγεῖν** (aor. act. inf. of ἐσθίω, subst., dir. obj.) **ἐκ τοῦ ξύλου** (ξύλον, -ου, τό, "tree," gen. of source, ant. of the following ὅ) **τῆς ζωῆς** (gen. of product, "which produces"), **ὅ** (nom. sg. neut., rel. pron.) **ἐστιν** (3rd sg. pres. act. ind. of εἰμί) **ἐν τῷ παραδείσῳ** (παράδεισος, -ου, ὁ, "paradise," loc.) **τοῦ θεοῦ** (poss.).

Byz along with some versions and church fathers that were likely influenced by 3:2, 12 add μου at the end of the verse ("my God"), but it is missing in A C P in addition to some minuscules (Metzger 664). The promises to the "one who overcomes" in the seven churches point forward to resurrection life in God's new creation (21:7). The language of conquering is also used to describe Jesus's victory (3:21; 5:5–6) and the beast's temporary victory over the saints (11:7; 13:7). The phrase, "He who has an ear, let him hear what the Spirit says to the churches" (cf. 13:9–10), echoes Jesus's use of the same expression throughout the Gospels as a formulaic command to understand his symbolic parables. The parallel with Jesus's parables suggests that the visions of Revelation contain a deeper meaning that will be veiled to outsiders but understandable to those with ears to hear what the Spirit is speaking.

Use of the OT: The tree of life and paradise of God are clear allusions to Gen 2:8 (ἐφύτευσεν κύριος ὁ θεὸς παράδεισον ἐν Εδεμ), 2:9 (τὸ ξύλον τῆς ζωῆς ἐν μέσῳ τῷ παραδείσῳ); 3:22 (καὶ νῦν μήποτε ἐκτείνῃ τὴν χεῖρα καὶ λάβῃ τοῦ ξύλου τῆς ζωῆς καὶ φάγῃ καὶ ζήσεται εἰς τὸν αἰῶνα), 3:24 (the cherubim were positioned φυλάσσειν τὴν ὁδὸν τοῦ ξύλου τῆς ζωῆς) along with Ezek 28:13 (the king of Tyre ἐν τῇ τρυφῇ τοῦ παραδείσου τοῦ θεοῦ ἐγενήθης). Ezekiel 31:8, 9 refers to the paradise of God in its description of the glory (and subsequent judgment) of Assyria (κυπάρισσοι τοιαῦται οὐκ ἐγενήθησαν ἐν τῷ παραδείσῳ τοῦ θεοῦ . . . πᾶν ξύλον ἐν τῷ παραδείσῳ τοῦ θεοῦ οὐχ ὡμοιώθη αὐτῷ . . . καὶ ἐζήλωσεν αὐτὸν τὰ ξύλα τοῦ παραδείσου τῆς τρυφῆς τοῦ θεοῦ). The Genesis allusions are significant in connecting God's promised new creation with his original intent for creating humanity. Adam was prevented from eating of the tree of life because of his sin but overcomers will have access to it.

FOR FURTHER STUDY

19. Emotions

*DeSilva, D. A. "The Strategic Arousal of Emotions in the Apocalypse of John: A Rhetorical-Critical Investigation of the Oracles to the Seven Churches." *NTS* 54 (2008): 90–114.

Stewart, A. E. "The Ethics of Fear Appeals and the Apocalypse of John." *CTR* 17 (2019): 53–66.

———. "The Role of Fear and Hope in Drawing and Transcending Boundaries in the Apocalypse of John." Pages 85–97 in *Drawing and Transcending Boundaries in the New Testament and Early Christianity*. Edited by J. Kok et al. Beiträge zum Verstehen der Bibel 38. Berlin: LIT Verlag, 2019.

20. Victory

Aune, D. E. "Following the Lamb: Discipleship in the Apocalypse." Pages 269–84 in *Patterns of Discipleship in the New Testament*. Edited by R. N. Longenecker. Grand Rapids: Eerdmans, 1996.

Den Dulk, M. "The Promises to the Conquerors in the Book of Revelation." *Bib* 87 (2006): 516–22.

Homcy, S. L. "'To Him Who Overcomes': A Fresh Look at What 'Victory' Means for the Believer According to the Book of Revelation." *JETS* 38 (1995): 193–201.

Shin, E. C. "More Than Conquerors: The Conqueror (NIKAΩ) Motif in the Book of Revelation." PhD diss., Pretoria University, 2006.

2. Proclamation to Smyrna (2:8–11)

2:8 Καὶ τῷ ἀγγέλῳ (indir. obj.) **τῆς ἐν Σμύρνῃ** (loc., "Smyrna") **ἐκκλησίας** (gen. of subord., "over") **γράψον** (2nd sg. aor. act. impv. of γράφω)· **Τάδε** (see on 2:1) **λέγει** (3rd sg. pres. act. ind. of λέγω) **ὁ πρῶτος** (subst., subj. nom.) **καὶ ὁ ἔσχατος** (ἔσχατος, -η, -ον, "last," subst., coord. subj. nom., ant. of ὅς), **ὃς** (subj. nom.) **ἐγένετο** (3rd sg. aor. mid. ind. of γίνομαι, ingressive) **νεκρὸς** (pred. adj., "dead") **καὶ ἔζησεν** (3rd sg. aor. act. ind. of ζάω, prob. ingressive aor., "came to life," [Wallace 559])

The description of Jesus refers back to the inaugural vision in 1:17, 18.

Use of the OT: On ὁ πρῶτος καὶ ὁ ἔσχατος, see 1:8.

2:9 Οἶδά (1st sg. pf. act. ind. of οἶδα) **σου** (fronted for prominence and connected to both the following nouns, poss.) **τὴν θλῖψιν** (θλῖψις, -εως, ἡ, "tribulation, affliction, trouble," dir. obj.) **καὶ τὴν πτωχείαν** (πτωχεία, -ας, ἡ, "poverty," coord. dir. obj.), **ἀλλὰ** (contrastive) **πλούσιος** (πλούσιος, -ία, -ιον, "rich, wealthy," pred. adj.) **εἶ** (2nd sg. pres. act. ind. of εἰμί), **καὶ τὴν βλασφημίαν** (βλασφημία, -ας, ἡ, "slander," but "blasphemy" when directed against God, coord. dir. obj. of οἶδα) **ἐκ τῶν λεγόντων** (gen. pl. masc. of pres. act. ptc. of λέγω, subst., source, introduces indir. discourse) **Ἰουδαίους** (pred. acc., "Jews") **εἶναι** (pres. act. inf. of εἰμί) **ἑαυτοὺς** (acc. subj. of inf.) **καὶ οὐκ εἰσὶν** (3rd pl. pres. act. ind. of εἰμί) **ἀλλὰ** (contrastive) **συναγωγὴ** (συναγωγή, -ῆς, ἡ, "synagogue, assembly," pred. nom. of assumed εἰσίν) **τοῦ Σατανᾶ** (σατανᾶς, -ᾶ, ὁ, "Satan, enemy, adversary," traditionally a title in the MT, but increasingly in the NT a proper name, poss.).

Their present experience is described as tribulation and poverty, yet the spiritual reality is that they were rich. This is an example of how Jesus's knowledge of the true state of things, reality from God's perspective, is a direct reversal of the apparent situation. James 2:5 claims similarly that God selected the poor to be rich in faith and heirs of the kingdom (οὐχ ὁ θεὸς ἐξελέξατο τοὺς πτωχοὺς τῷ κόσμῳ πλουσίους ἐν πίστει καὶ κληρονόμους τῆς βασιλείας ἧς ἐπηγγείλατο τοῖς ἀγαπῶσιν αὐτόν). The characterization of the Jews as a synagogue of Satan parallels the inter-Jewish polemic of the Qumran sectarians who called apostate Jews "a congregation of Belial" (1QH[a] 2.22 [Beale 241]). Some of the ethnic Jews in Smyrna lost their right to the name "Jew" because of their opposition (evidenced by slander) to Jesus and his people (both Jew and gentile); this would suggest that allegiance to Israel's Messiah was viewed by John as more determinative than ethnic descent for inclusion in God's promised restoration of Israel.

2:10 **μηδὲν** (acc. sg. neut., likely dir. obj., "nothing," lit. "not one thing") **φοβοῦ** (2nd sg. pres. mid. impv. of φοβέω) **ἃ** (acc. pl. neut., does not match its ant. μηδὲν in number; alternatively, Mathewson suggests that μηδέν be taken as an adv. acc., "not at all" or "in no way"; if so, the headless rel. cl. introduced by ἅ becomes the acc. dir. obj. of φοβοῦ [Math 25]) **μέλλεις** (2nd sg. pres. act. ind. of μέλλω, "about to") **πάσχειν** (pres. act. inf. of πάσχω, "suffer," compl. inf.). **ἰδοὺ** (emph. interj., here perhaps better translated rhetorically as "beware" or "indeed" [Fanning 129]) **μέλλει** (3rd sg. pres. act. ind. of μέλλω) **βάλλειν** (pres. act. inf. of βάλλω, compl. inf.) **ὁ διάβολος** (διάβολος, -ον, "slanderer, adversary, devil," nom. subj.) **ἐξ ὑμῶν** (part., τίνας is implied; note how the pl. indicates that even though the proclamation is formally addressed to the sg. angel, the contents of each proclamation are directed toward the Christians in the church; this switch to the pl. happens also in 2:13, 23–25) **εἰς φυλακὴν** (φυλακή, -ῆς, ἡ, "prison," loc.) **ἵνα** (purpose) **πειρασθῆτε** (2nd pl. aor. pass. subjunc. of πειράζω, "test") **καὶ** (coordinates μέλλει with ἕξετε, "the devil is about to cast . . . and you will have") **ἕξετε** (2nd pl. fut. act. ind. of ἔχω) **θλῖψιν** (θλῖψις, -εως, ἡ, "tribulation, affliction, trouble," dir. obj.) **ἡμερῶν** (gen. of time) **δέκα** ("ten," attrib.). **γίνου** (2nd sg. pres. mid. impv. of γίνομαι) **πιστὸς** (pred. adj. "faithful") **ἄχρι** ("until") **θανάτου** (gen. of time), **καὶ δώσω** (1st sg. fut. act. ind. of δίδωμι) **σοι** (indir. obj.) **τὸν στέφανον** (στέφανος, -ου, ὁ, "wreath, crown, prize," in particular one "made from foliage or designed to resemble foliage and worn by one of high status or held in high regard" [BDAG 943d], διάδημα suggests royalty while στέφανος suggests victory [Fanning 130], dir. obj.) **τῆς ζωῆς** (epex. gen., "that is, even").

James 1:12 also references the "wreath/crown of life" as an eschatological promise (Μακάριος ἀνὴρ ὃς ὑπομένει πειρασμόν, ὅτι δόκιμος γενόμενος λήμψεται τὸν στέφανον τῆς ζωῆς). First Peter 5:4 refers to the unfading crown of glory (τῆς δόξης στέφανον). The second death is referred to again in Rev 20:14; 21:8 and indicates the lake of fire. There is no indication that "ten days" refers to a literal period of time; it is likely a symbolic time period drawn from the period of testing endured by Daniel (see below). Note that tribulation in 2:9, 10 is a present and not future reality (cf. 1:9); θλῖψις is not a technical term in Revelation for a specific period of future time but describes the default experience of God's people until Jesus's return.

Use of the OT: Daniel and his companions are tested ten days in order to avoid being defiled by the king's food (Dan 1:12: Πείρασον δὴ τοὺς παῖδάς σου ἐφ' ἡμέρας δέκα; 1:15: μετὰ δὲ τὰς δέκα ἡμέρας).

2:11 **ὁ ἔχων** (nom. sg. masc. of pres. act. ptc. of ἔχω, subst.) **οὖς** (οὖς, ὠτός, τό, "ear," acc. sg. neut., dir. obj.) **ἀκουσάτω** (3rd sg. aor. act. impv. of ἀκούω) **τί** (τίς, dir. obj., interr. pron., "what") **τὸ πνεῦμα** (subj. nom.) **λέγει** (3rd sg. pres. act. ind. of λέγω) **ταῖς ἐκκλησίαις** (indir. obj.). **ὁ νικῶν** (nom. sg. masc. of pres. act. ptc. of νικάω, "overcome, conquer," subst., subj. nom.) **οὐ μὴ** (double neg. for emph., "will certainly not") **ἀδικηθῇ** (3rd sg. aor. pass. subjunc. of ἀδικέω, "harm, damage") **ἐκ τοῦ θανάτου** (means, "by death," or agency if death is personified) **τοῦ δευτέρου** (attrib.).

FOR FURTHER STUDY

21. Wealth

Mathews, M. D. *Riches, Poverty, and the Faithful: Perspectives on Wealth in the Second Temple Period and the Apocalypse of John*. SNTSMS 154. Cambridge: Cambridge University Press, 2013.

22. The Jews (2:9; 3:9)

Cromhout, M. "Israelite Ethnic Identity Responding to the Roman Imperium in Revelation." Pages 527–50 in *T&T Clark Handbook to Social Identity in the New Testament*. Edited by J. B. Tucker and C. A. Baker. London: T&T Clark, 2014.

Dalrymple, R. "Was John Antisemitic?" Pages 128–49 in S&B.

Mayo, P. L. *"Those Who Call Themselves Jews": The Church and Judaism in the Apocalypse of John*. Princeton Theological Monograph Series. Eugene, OR: Pickwick, 2006.

Tellbe, M. "Relationships among Christ-Believers and Jewish Communities in First-Century Asia Minor," Pages 153–68 in *OHR*.

3. Proclamation to Pergamum (2:12–17)

2:12 **Καὶ τῷ ἀγγέλῳ** (indir. obj.) **τῆς ἐν Περγάμῳ** (loc.) **ἐκκλησίας** (gen. of subord.) **γράψον** (2nd sg. aor. act. impv. of γράφω)· **Τάδε** (see on 2:1) **λέγει** (3rd sg. pres. act. ind. of λέγω) **ὁ ἔχων** (nom. sg. masc. of pres. act. ptc. of ἔχω, subst.) **τὴν** (anaphoric, referring to *the* sword in 1:16) **ῥομφαίαν** (ῥομφαία, -ας, ἡ, "sword," dir. obj.) **τὴν δίστομον** (δίστομος, -ον, "double-edged," attrib.) **τὴν ὀξεῖαν** (ὀξύς, -εῖα, -ύ, "sharp, quick," attrib.)

The description of Jesus refers back to 1:16.

2:13 **Οἶδα** (1st sg. pf. act. ind. of οἶδα) **ποῦ** (adv. of place, "where," introduces a cl. which functions as the dir. obj. of Οἶδα) **κατοικεῖς** (2nd sg. pres. act. ind. of κατοικέω, "dwell"), **ὅπου** (adv. of place, "where," introduces verbless cl. in appos. to the prior ποῦ cl.) **ὁ θρόνος** (subj. nom.) **τοῦ Σατανᾶ** (σατανᾶς, -ᾶ, ὁ, "Satan, enemy, adversary," poss., on Satan, see 2:9), **καὶ** (prob. contrastive) **κρατεῖς** (2nd sg. pres. act. ind., "hold") **τὸ ὄνομά** (dir. obj.) **μου** (poss.) **καὶ οὐκ ἠρνήσω** (2nd sg. aor. mid. ind. of ἀρνέομαι, "deny") **τὴν πίστιν μου** (obj. gen., "faith in me"), **καὶ** (ascensive for emph., "even") **ἐν ταῖς ἡμέραις** (temp. dat.) **Ἀντιπᾶς** (gen., see below on the case and function, ant. of ὃς) **ὁ μάρτυς** (μάρτυς, -υρος, ὁ, "witness," nom. of appellation, cf. 1:5) **μου** (this and the following μου are likely obj. gen., "the one who witnesses to me, the one who is faithful to me") **ὁ πιστός** (nom. of appellation, the repetition of μου with both πιστός and μάρτυς prob. suggests that this is a subst. adj., "my faithful one," and not attrib. adj., "my faithful witness," although the lack of a conj. leads many EVV to leave the second μου untranslated and take πιστός as attrib.) **μου, ὃς** (subj. nom.) **ἀπεκτάνθη** (3rd sg. aor. pass. ind. of ἀποκτείνω) **παρ' ὑμῖν** (loc., "among"), **ὅπου** (adv. of place) **ὁ Σατανᾶς** (subj. nom.) **κατοικεῖ** (3rd sg. pres. act. ind. of κατοικέω).

Although thrones in Revelation are generally connected to God and Jesus (1:4; 3:1; 4:2–6, 9–10; 5:1, 6–7, 11, 13; 6:16; 7:9–11, 15, 17; 8:3; 12:5; 14:3; 16:17; 19:4–5; 20:11–12; 21:3, 5; 22:1, 3), heavenly beings (4:4; 11:16), and possibly victorious believers (20:4) as an indication of rightful rule and authority, God's rule is currently contested on earth by the existence of Satan's throne, which he gives to the beast in order to oppose God's people (13:2; 16:10).

A possible solecism exists in the way that John has Ἀντιπᾶς (nom.) instead of Ἀντιπᾶ (gen.) and multiple variants attest to scribal attempts to fix this problem. It is likely that John treats Ἀντιπᾶς as indeclinable and functioning as a gen., and, if so, then the following nom. nouns in appos. are functioning as noms. of appellation and the lack of concord with the gen. puts emph. on the titles as in 1:5. Beale explains the nom. in appos. to a gen. as indicating an allusion to Ps 88:38 LXX (Ps 89:37 EVV: ὁ μάρτυς ἐν οὐρανῷ πιστός [Beale 247]). Antipas's death is significant for assessing the level of active opposition experienced by these Christian communities. Some of the churches were evidently not facing any persecution and were well-off financially while others, such as Pergamum, experienced deadly opposition. The various letters address a wide spectrum of Christian experience of integration with or opposition from the surrounding culture and political institutions.

2:14 ἀλλ' (contrastive) **ἔχω** (1st sg. pres. act. ind.) **κατὰ σοῦ** (gen. of opposition, "against") **ὀλίγα** (ὀλίγος, -η, -ον, "small, short, few," subst., dir. obj., "a few things") **ὅτι** (content, "that," epex. to indicate the content of the "few things") **ἔχεις** (2nd sg. pres. act. ind. of ἔχω) **ἐκεῖ** (adv. of place, "there") **κρατοῦντας** (acc. pl. masc. of pres. act. ptc. of κρατέω, "hold, keep," subst.) **τὴν διδαχὴν** (διδαχή, -ῆς, ἡ, "teaching, instruction," dir. obj.) **Βαλαάμ** ("Balaam," subj. gen., ant. of ὅς), **ὃς** (subj. nom.) **ἐδίδασκεν** (3rd sg. imp. act. ind. of διδάσκω) **τῷ Βαλὰκ** ("Balak," indir. obj., the use of the dat. instead of the acc. following διδάσκω is rare but not unparalleled in later Koine Greek [MoT 147]) **βαλεῖν** (aor. act. inf. of βάλλω, subst. inf., dir. obj. of ἐδίδασκεν) **σκάνδαλον** (σκάνδαλον, -ου, τό, "trap, temptation, stumbling-block," dir. obj. of βαλεῖν) **ἐνώπιον** (improper prep., "before") **τῶν υἱῶν** (gen. of place) **Ἰσραὴλ** (gen. of relationship) **φαγεῖν** (aor. act. inf. of ἐσθίω, subst. inf., appos. to σκάνδαλον) **εἰδωλόθυτα** (εἰδωλόθυτος, -ον, "something offered to an idol" [BDAG 280b], subst., acc. dir. obj.) **καὶ πορνεῦσαι** (aor. act. inf. of πορνεύω, "commit sexual immorality"; broadly and generically understood, the context could provide specificity if particular acts are intended, subst. inf., appos. to *σκάνδαλον*).

If εἰδωλόθυτος refers to sacrificial meat sold in the marketplace, Jesus through John could be opposing Pauline guidance regarding idol meat (1 Cor 8:1–13; 10:23–30), but the term εἰδωλόθυτος is not that specific and John likely refers to eating meat in the idol's presence or as part of idolatrous worship, something Paul forbids (1 Cor 10:1–22 [Beale 248]). Committing sexual immorality could be understood literally or metaphorically for idolatry; John's reference to the ones who commit adultery with Jezebel in Rev 2:22 suggests that the broader use of sexual immorality and sexual purity language in Revelation is figurative. It is not likely that Jezebel's followers in Thyatira were physically committing adultery with her; they were following her teaching into idolatrous compromise. Jude v. 11 also references the deception of Balaam (*καὶ τῇ πλάνῃ τοῦ Βαλαὰμ μισθοῦ ἐξεχύθησαν*).

Use of the OT: In Shittim, the people of God were defiled by committing sexual immorality with the daughters of Moab (Num 25:1: *καὶ ἐβεβηλώθη ὁ λαὸς ἐκπορνεῦσαι εἰς τὰς θυγατέρας Μωαβ*) who invited them to participate in sacrifices to idols (25:2: *καὶ ἐκάλεσαν αὐτοὺς ἐπὶ ταῖς θυσίαις τῶν εἰδώλων αὐτῶν*). This narrative demonstrates a close connection between idolatry and literal sexual immorality; God's anger was averted by Phineas's violent actions. In Num 31:16 Moses rebukes the soldiers who did not kill the women of Midian who, on Balaam's instruction (*κατὰ τὸ ῥῆμα Βαλααμ*), caused God's people to transgress.

2:15 οὕτως (adv. of manner, "thus, in this way") **ἔχεις** (2nd sg. pres. act. ind. of ἔχω) **καὶ** (ascensive, "also," this does not suggest a second group but rather strengthens the typological connection between false teachers in Israel's history and false teachers in the church [Fanning 139]) **σὺ** (subj. nom.) **κρατοῦντας** (acc. pl. masc. of pres. act. ptc. of κρατέω, "hold, keep," subst., dir. obj.) **τὴν διδαχὴν** (διδαχή, -ῆς, ἡ, "teaching, instruction," dir. obj.) [τῶν] **Νικολαϊτῶν** ("Nicolaitan," subj. gen.) **ὁμοίως** (adv., "likewise," seems to naturally draw a comparison to the reference to the Nicolaitans in Ephesus in 2:6 [Aune[a] 188], but Fanning makes a cogent case that οὕτως and ὁμοίως bracket 2:15 to draw a typological connection between the false teaching of Balaam in Israel's history discussed in 2:14 and what some of the Christians were doing in the present: "They [did] . . . so likewise some among you [do]" [Fanning 138]).

2:16 μετανόησον (2nd sg. aor. act. impv. of μετανοέω, "repent") **οὖν** (inferential, absent in א P and most minuscules but present in A C and some minuscules and versions; the omission is prob. a transcriptional oversight due to -σον [Metzger 664])· **εἰ δὲ μή** ("and if not"), **ἔρχομαί** (1st sg. pres. mid. ind. of ἔρχομαι, futuristic pres.) **σοι** (loc., "to you," possibly dat. of disadvantage, "against you") **ταχὺ** (ταχύς, -εῖα, -ύ, "soon, quickly," temp. adv.) **καὶ πολεμήσω** (1st sg. fut. act. ind. of πολεμέω, "fight, make war," coord.)

μετ' αὐτῶν (association, "with") **ἐν τῇ ῥομφαίᾳ** (dat.) **τοῦ στόματός** (gen. of source) **μου** (poss.).

The promise to come "soon" (ταχύς) is also found in 3:11; 22:7, 12, 20 and in the proclamations to the churches; it is not always clear whether they point to a coming in judgment within history in anticipation of the final coming or the final coming itself. The prons. here are instructive: Jesus commands the church to repent (2nd sg.) or he would come to you (2nd sg.) to war with them (pl.). The whole church is called to repentance, but Jesus would only war against those who do not repent; Jesus differentiates between two groups in the church.

2:17 ὁ ἔχων (nom. sg. masc. of pres. act. ptc. of ἔχω, subst., subj. nom.) **οὖς** (οὖς, ὠτός, τό, "ear," acc. sg. neut., dir. obj.) **ἀκουσάτω** (3rd sg. aor. act. impv. ἀκούω) **τί** (τίς, acc. dir. obj., interr. pron., "what") **τὸ πνεῦμα** (subj. nom.) **λέγει** (3rd sg. pres. act. ind. of λέγω) **ταῖς ἐκκλησίαις** (indir. obj.). **τῷ νικῶντι** (dat. sg. masc. of pres. act. ptc. of νικάω, "overcome, conquer," subst., indir. obj.) **δώσω** (1st sg. fut. act. ind. of δίδωμι) **αὐτῷ** (indir. obj., redundant/resumptive personal pron. for emph.) **τοῦ μάννα** ("manna," part. gen., assumes τινας) **τοῦ κεκρυμμένου** (gen. sg. neut. of pf. pass. ptc. of κρύπτω, "hide," attrib.) **καὶ δώσω** (1st sg. fut. act. ind. of δίδωμι) **αὐτῷ** (indir. obj.) **ψῆφον** (ψῆφος, -ου, ἡ, "pebble," dir. obj.) **λευκήν** (λευκός, -ή, -όν, "white, bright," attrib.), **καὶ ἐπὶ τὴν ψῆφον** (loc.) **ὄνομα** (subj. nom. of verbless cl., ant. of ὅ) **καινὸν** ("new," attrib.) **γεγραμμένον** (acc. sg. neut. pf. pass. ptc. γράφω, attrib., "written") **ὃ** (dir. obj.) **οὐδεὶς** ("no one," subj. nom.) **οἶδεν** (3rd sg. pf. act. ind. of οἶδα, "knows") **εἰ μὴ** ("except," L&N 89.131) **ὁ λαμβάνων** (nom. sg. masc. of pres. act. ptc. of λαμβάνω, subst.).

Note the contrast between manna and idol meat. Most interpreters suggest that the white stone refers either to a vote of acquittal or to something like a ticket giving access to the new Jerusalem. All of the promises to the overcomers relate to final salvation in God's new creation, but the precise meaning of the white stone is not explicitly evident.

Use of the OT: Psalm 77:24 LXX (78:24 EVV) celebrates how God rained down manna and gave bread from heaven to his people (καὶ ἔβρεξεν αὐτοῖς μαννα φαγεῖν καὶ ἄρτον οὐρανοῦ ἔδωκεν αὐτοῖς). In Isa 62:2 God promises, as part of Jerusalem's future restoration, to give her a new name (καὶ καλέσει σε τὸ ὄνομά σου τὸ καινόν, ὃ ὁ κύριος ὀνομάσει αὐτό). Isaiah 65:15 contrasts those who forsake God for idolatry (Isa 65:11) and will be destroyed with those who remain faithful and will be called by a new name (τοῖς δὲ δουλεύουσιν αὐτῷ κληθήσεται ὄνομα καινόν). Jesus promises the overcomers in Pergamum (both Jew and gentile) that they will participate in the fulfillment of these Isaianic prophecies regarding the restoration of Jerusalem and the new creation.

FOR FURTHER STUDY

23. Satan's Throne (2:13)

Collins, A. Y. "Pergamon in Early Christian Literature." Pages 163–84 in *Pergamon: Citadel of the Gods*. Edited by H. Koester. Harrisburg, PA: Trinity Press International, 1998.

Friesen, S. J. "Satan's Throne, Imperial Cults and the Social Settings of Revelation." *JSNT* 27 (2005): 351–67.

4. Proclamation to Thyatira (2:18–29)

2:18 Καὶ τῷ ἀγγέλῳ (indir. obj.) **τῆς ἐν Θυατείροις** (loc.) **ἐκκλησίας** (gen. of subord.) **γράψον** (2nd sg. aor. act. impv. of γράφω) **Τάδε** (see 2:1) **λέγει** (3rd sg. pres. act. ind. of λέγω) **ὁ υἱὸς** (subj. nom.) **τοῦ θεοῦ** (gen. of relationship), **ὁ ἔχων** (nom. sg. masc. of pres. act. ptc. of ἔχω, subst., appos. to υἱὸς) **τοὺς ὀφθαλμοὺς** (dir. obj.) **αὐτοῦ** (poss.) **ὡς** (comp.) **φλόγα** (φλόξ, φλογός, ἡ, "flame,") **πυρὸς** (πῦρ, πυρός, τό, "fire," attrib. gen., "fiery flame") **καὶ οἱ πόδες** (πούς, ποδός, ὁ, "foot," subj. nom.) **αὐτοῦ** (poss.) **ὅμοιοι** (ὅμοιος, -οία, -οιον, "like, similar," pred. comp. adj. of verbless cl.) **χαλκολιβάνῳ** (χαλκολίβανον, -ου, τό, dat., "fine/bright bronze").

The description of Jesus refers back to 1:14, 15. The nom. πούς would be expected to be acc. to be coord. with ὀφθαλμούς ("having eyes . . . and feet"); as a nom. it is awkwardly coord. with υἱός: "The Son of God speaks thus . . . and his feet (are) like bright bronze." Although Revelation does not frequently describe Jesus as the Son of God it often refers to God as his father (1:6; 2:28; 3:5, 21; 14:1).

Use of the OT: Based on the allusion to Ps 2:9 in Rev 2:27 it would be reasonable to see an allusion to Ps 2:7 (Κύριος εἶπεν πρός με Υἱός μου εἶ σύ, ἐγὼ σήμερον γεγέννηκά σε) in the description of Jesus as the Son of God.

2:19 Οἶδά (1st sg. pf. act. ind. of οἶδα) **σου** (subj. gen., fronted for emph. and modifying each of the following accs.) **τὰ ἔργα** (dir. obj.) **καὶ** (possibly epex., "namely, that is" [BDAG 495c; Aune[a] 202]) **τὴν ἀγάπην** (dir. obj.) **καὶ τὴν πίστιν** (coord. dir. obj.) **καὶ τὴν διακονίαν** (διακονία, -ας, ἡ, "service, ministry," coord. dir. obj.) **καὶ τὴν ὑπομονήν** (ὑπομονή, -ῆς, ἡ, "endurance," coord. dir. obj.) **σου** (subj. gen., the list of dir. objs. begins and concludes with the pron. for emph.), **καὶ τὰ ἔργα** (subj. nom. of verbless cl.) **σου** (subj. gen.) **τὰ ἔσχατα** (ἔσχατος, -η, -ον, "last," attrib.) **πλείονα** (pred. adj., "much," comp. "more") **τῶν πρώτων** (subst., comp. gen. "than the first ones").

Jesus here commends the church for what they were doing well.

2:20 ἀλλ' (contrastive) **ἔχω** (1st sg. pres. act. ind. of ἔχω) **κατὰ σοῦ** (opposition, "against") **ὅτι** (content) **ἀφεῖς** (2nd sg. pres. act. ind. of ἀφίημι) **τὴν** (the art. here indicates the woman was well known to the hearers [Wallace 225]) **γυναῖκα** (dir. obj.) **Ἰεζάβελ** (acc., appos.), **ἡ λέγουσα** (nom. sg. fem of pres. act. ptc. of λέγω, subst., see below on the case) **ἑαυτὴν** (dir. obj.) **προφῆτιν** (compl. of an obj.-compl. double acc., "claiming herself to be a prophetess" or "calling herself a prophetess") **καὶ διδάσκει** (3rd sg. pres. act. ind. of διδάσκω) **καὶ πλανᾷ** (3rd sg. pres. act. ind. of πλανάω, "deceive") **τοὺς ἐμοὺς** (emph. poss. adj., "my") **δούλους** (dir. obj.) **πορνεῦσαι** (aor. act. inf. of πορνεύω, "commit sexual immorality," inf. of result) **καὶ φαγεῖν** (aor. act. inf. of ἐσθίω, coord. inf. of result) **εἰδωλόθυτα** (εἰδωλόθυτος, -ον, "something offered to an idol" [BDAG 280b], subst., dir. obj.).

Jezebel's teaching (πορνεῦσαι and φαγεῖν εἰδωλόθυτα) corresponds to that of Balaam in 2:14. The use of the vb. πλανάω connects Jezebel to the other demonic antagonists in Revelation who deceive (12:9; 13:14; 18:23; 19:20; 20:3, 8, 10). This presents Jezebel as being on the same team as the dragon, beast, false prophet, and Babylon. Jezebel is the physical false teacher in the church accomplishing the evil goals of these later supernatural or otherworldly antagonists in the visions.

A and *Byz* among other mss have σου after γυναῖκα, suggesting that Jezebel was the wife of the ἄγγελος, but the absence of σου in א C P and others speaks against its inclusion. The nom. ptc. ἡ λέγουσα should be in the acc. case to match τὴν γυναῖκα Ἰεζάβελ. Some scribes attempted to solve the problem by writing the art. ἡ as the rel. pron. (ἥ, *Byz*) or using the proper acc. case (τὴν λέγουσαν, 1773, 1854, א[2] [Moţ 129]). The explanation that this is an example of anacoluthon and John intended the ptc. to start a new cl. seems to be complicated by the use of καί to join λέγουσα to διδάσκει. The καί pulls the vbs. (διδάσκει καὶ πλανᾷ) into the expanded subj. of a cl. with no main vb. It is best to explain this solecism as an example of the common and likely intentional (mis)use of the nom. for emph. in John's idiolect. It may signal an allusion to 1 Kgdms 20:5, 7 (1 Sam 20:5, 7 EVV [Beale 263]). The nom. puts emph. on Jezebel's self-attested claim to be a prophetess.

Use of the OT: Third Kingdoms 16:31 (1 Kgs 16:31 EVV) records how Ahab married Jezebel and served and worshipped Baal (καὶ ἐδούλευσεν τῷ Βααλ καὶ προσεκύνησεν αὐτῷ). Fourth Kingdoms 9:22 (2 Kgs 9:22 EVV) records Jehu's words to Joram regarding the sexual immorality and sorcery of his mother, Jezebel (ἔτι αἱ πορνεῖαι Ιεζαβελ τῆς μητρός σου καὶ τὰ φάρμακα αὐτῆς τὰ πολλά). John's labeling of the rival prophetess, "Jezebel," seeks to discredit her teaching by connecting her to the historical Jezebel, who promoted idolatry and persecuted true prophets.

2:21 καὶ ἔδωκα (1st sg. aor. act. ind. of δίδωμι) **αὐτῇ** (ind. ob.) **χρόνον** (dir. obj.) **ἵνα** (Fanning rightly notes that this is not a purpose cl. but rather an explanation of the time period: "time for repenting" [Fanning 151]) **μετανοήσῃ** (3rd sg. aor. act. subjunc. of μετανοέω, "repent"), **καὶ** (contrastive, "but") **οὐ θέλει** (3rd sg. pres. act. ind. of θέλω, progressive pres.) **μετανοῆσαι** (aor. act. inf. of μετανοέω, compl. inf.) **ἐκ τῆς πορνείας** (πορνεία, -ας, ἡ, "sexual immorality," separation) **αὐτῆς** (subj. gen.).

The description of Jezebel's sexual immorality (τῆς πορνείας αὐτῆς) further connects her with Babylon in later visions (14:8; 17:2, 4; 18:3). This rhetorically discredits the prophetess for supporting the activity of Babylon.

2:22 ἰδοὺ (emph. interj.) **βάλλω** (1st sg. pres. act. ind. of βάλλω, futuristic pres.) **αὐτὴν** (dir. obj.) **εἰς κλίνην** (κλίνη, -ης, ἡ, "bed," the context of punishment suggests "sick-bed," loc.) **καὶ τοὺς μοιχεύοντας** (acc. pl. masc. of pres. act. ptc. of μοιχεύω, "commit adultery," subst., dir. obj.) **μετ' αὐτῆς** (association) **εἰς θλῖψιν** (θλῖψις, -εως, ἡ, "tribulation, affliction," loc. acc.) **μεγάλην** (attrib.), **ἐὰν μὴ** ("unless, if not," prot. of 3rd class cond. cl.) **μετανοήσωσιν** (3rd pl. aor. act. subjunc. of μετανοέω, "repent") **ἐκ τῶν ἔργων** (separation) **αὐτῆς** (subj. gen., the TR following A reads αὐτῶν to make the repentance be for their own works [Metzger 665]),

It is not likely that church members were literally committing adultery with Jezebel. This suggests that the critique of sexual immorality throughout Revelation (2:14, 20, 21; 14:8; 17:2, 4; 18:3, 9; 19:2) primarily points to religious purity and the rejection of idolatry, although John would also be opposed to literal sexual immorality (9:21; 21:8; 22:15; likely 21:27).

2:23 καὶ τὰ τέκνα (dir. obj.) **αὐτῆς** (gen. of relationship) **ἀποκτενῶ** (1st sg. fut. act. ind. of ἀποκτείνω) **ἐν θανάτῳ** (conceptual cognate dat. for emph. or instr. to indicate the manner of death: "fatal illness, pestilence" [BDAG 443d]). **καὶ** (result: "and so" [BDAG 495a]) **γνώσονται** (3rd pl. fut. mid. ind. of γινώσκω) **πᾶσαι** (attrib.) **αἱ ἐκκλησίαι** (subj. nom.) **ὅτι** (content, "that") **ἐγώ** (subj. nom.) **εἰμι ὁ ἐραυνῶν** (nom. sg. masc. of pres. act. ptc. of ἐραυνάω, "attempt to learn something by careful investigation or searching" [L&N 27.34], subst., pred. nom.) **νεφροὺς** (νεφρός, -οῦ, ὁ, "kidney," connotative use for "the psychological faculty of desire, intent, and feeling" [L&N 26.11], pl. dir. obj.) **καὶ καρδίας** (acc. pl. fem., coord. dir. obj.), **καὶ δώσω** (1st sg. fut. act. ind. of δίδωμι) **ὑμῖν** (indir. obj.) **ἑκάστῳ** (indir. obj.) **κατὰ τὰ ἔργα** (reference) **ὑμῶν** (subj. gen.).

Jesus indicates that all of these messages are for all the churches when he writes "and all the churches will know that I am he who searches mind and heart." Four times κατά in the Apocalypse signals "the norm according to which a judgment is rendered, or rewards or punishments are given" (BDAG 512d; Rev 2:23; 18:6; 20:12, 13). "Oft. the norm is at the same time the reason, so that *in accordance with* and *because of* are merged . . . Instead of 'in accordance w.' κ. can also mean simply *because of, as a result of, on the basis of*" (BDAG 512d–513a; italics original). Interpreters should be hesitant to draw fine theological distinctions based on the different semantics of "according to" and "on the basis of" in English since these distinctions are not clearly evident in the Greek expression. Judgment κατὰ τὰ ἔργα is true of the churches (Rev 2:23; cf. Rev 14:13; 22:12), Babylon (Rev 18:6), and all of humanity (Rev 20:12, 13). A similar idea is expressed in 22:12 (ὡς τὸ ἔργον ἐστὶν αὐτοῦ) and widely held in Second Temple Judaism and early Christianity (2 Chr 6:23; Job 34:11; Pss 28:4; 62:12; Prov 24:12; Jer 17:10; Ezek 18:30; 24:14; 33:20; Hos 12:2; Matt 16:27; Rom 2:6–11; 2 Cor 11:15; 2 Tim 4:14; 1 Pet 1:17; Sir 16:12, 14; 1 En. 41:1–2; 4 Ezra 8:33; Pss. Sol. 2:16; 17:8).

Use of the OT: The threat to kill Jezebel's children parallels the fate of Jezebel's children prophesied in 2 Kgs 9:7–8 and carried out in 2 Kgs 10:7. Psalm 7:10 LXX (Ps 7:9 EVV) describes God as the one testing hearts and kidneys (ἐτάζων καρδίας καὶ νεφροὺς ὁ θεός). Proverbs 24:12 combines God's knowledge of all hearts with his ability to give to each according to one's works (κύριος καρδίας πάντων γινώσκει . . . ὃς ἀποδίδωσιν ἑκάστῳ κατὰ τὰ ἔργα αὐτοῦ). The same connection of God's knowledge with judgment is evident in Jer 17:10 (ἐγὼ κύριος ἐτάζων καρδίας καὶ δοκιμάζων νεφροὺς τοῦ δοῦναι ἑκάστῳ κατὰ τὰς ὁδοὺς αὐτοῦ καὶ κατὰ τοὺς καρποὺς τῶν ἐπιτηδευμάτων αὐτοῦ). Jeremiah elsewhere appeals to God's knowledge of hearts and kidneys in a prayer for justice/vengeance (Jer 11:20: κύριε κρίνων δίκαια δοκιμάζων νεφροὺς καὶ καρδίας, ἴδοιμι τὴν παρὰ σοῦ ἐκδίκησιν ἐξ αὐτῶν). Revelation similarly looks to God's complete knowledge as the basis for confidence in the justice of God's judgments.

2:24 ὑμῖν (indir. obj., fronted for emph.) **δὲ** (indicates a development in the discourse or argument [Runge 31]) **λέγω** (1st sg. pres. act. ind. of λέγω) **τοῖς λοιποῖς** (appos. to ὑμῖν) **τοῖς** (adjectivizer) **ἐν Θυατείροις** ("Thyatira," loc.), **ὅσοι** (correlative rel. pron., "as many as") **οὐκ ἔχουσιν** (3rd pl. pres. act. ind. of ἔχω) **τὴν διδαχὴν** (διδαχή, -ῆς, ἡ, "teaching, instruction," dir. obj.) **ταύτην** (attrib.), **οἵτινες** (indef. rel. pron., "whoever") **οὐκ ἔγνωσαν** (3rd pl. aor. act. ind. of γινώσκω, prob. ingressive) **τὰ βαθέα** (βαθύς, -εῖα, -ύ, "deep," subst., "deep things," dir. obj.) **τοῦ Σατανᾶ** (σατανᾶς, ᾶ, ὁ, "Satan, enemy, adversary," gen. of source) **ὡς** (manner) **λέγουσιν** (3rd pl. pres. act. ind. of λέγω). **οὐ βάλλω** (1st sg. pres. act. ind. of βάλλω) **ἐφ' ὑμᾶς** (loc. acc.) **ἄλλο** (attrib., "other") **βάρος** (βάρος, -ους, τό, "burden, weight," dir. obj.),

The transition to a 2nd pl. pron. stands out from the normal address to the sg. ἄγγελος; this reveals the intended audience of the commands, warnings, and encouragements of these proclamations. The language of not casting another burden on the disciples has some parallels with the decree of the apostolic council in Acts 15:28 (ἔδοξεν γὰρ τῷ πνεύματι τῷ ἁγίῳ καὶ ἡμῖν μηδὲν πλέον ἐπιτίθεσθαι ὑμῖν βάρος πλὴν τούτων τῶν ἐπάναγκες) but the echo is too faint for strong conclucions.

2:25 πλὴν (contrastive, "but, except, only" [BDAG 826d]) **ὃ** (rel. pron., introduces headless rel. cl. functioning as dir. obj. of κρατήσατε) **ἔχετε** (2nd pl. pres. act. ind. of ἔχω) **κρατήσατε** (2nd pl. aor. act. impv. of κρατέω, "hold, keep") **ἄχρι[ς]** (temp. prep., "until") **οὗ** (the entire rel. cl. functions as the temp. obj. of the prep., "when") **ἂν** (introduces contingency or indefiniteness, "-ever," i.e., "whenever") **ἥξω** (1st sg. aor. act. subjunc. of ἥκω, "come," subjunc. because of the contingency introduced by ἄν).

The uncertain contingency communicated by οὗ ἂν ἥξω does not relate to whether or not Jesus would come but when he would come. Revelation leaves no doubt that he will come. Those who are not compromised with Jezebel's teaching and practice are simply commanded to endure/hold fast.

2:26 καὶ ὁ νικῶν (nom. sg. masc. of pres. act. ptc. of νικάω, "overcome, conquer," subst., pendent/hanging nom. which is "the logical rather than syntactical subject at the beginning of a sentence, followed by a sentence in which this subject is now replaced by a pron. in the case required by the syntax" [Wallace 51]) **καὶ ὁ τηρῶν** (nom. sg. masc. of pres. act. ptc. of τηρέω, subst., hanging nom.) **ἄχρι** (temp.) **τέλους** (τέλος, -ους, τό, obj. of prep.) **τὰ ἔργα** (dir. obj. of τηρῶν) **μου** (subj. gen.), **δώσω** (1st sg. fut. act. ind. of δίδωμι) **αὐτῷ** (indir. obj.) **ἐξουσίαν** (dir. obj.) **ἐπὶ τῶν ἐθνῶν** (subord., "over")

The true subject is the 1st sg. "I" in δώσω. Syntactically, the two ptcs. connect to the indir. obj. αὐτῷ. It is not evident that the hanging nom. is a Semitism (Moţ 120–21).

2:27 καὶ ποιμανεῖ (3rd sg. fut. act. ind. of ποιμαίνω, "shepherd, rule") **αὐτοὺς** (dir. obj.) **ἐν ῥάβδῳ** (ῥάβδος, -ου, ἡ, "rod, staff, scepter," means, "with") **σιδηρᾷ** (σιδηροῦς, -ᾶ, -οῦν, "made of iron," attrib.) **ὡς** (comp.) **τὰ σκεύη** (σκεῦος, -ους, τό, "object, vessel," pl. subj. nom.) **τὰ κεραμικὰ** (κεραμικός, -ή, -όν, "made of clay," attrib.) **συντρίβεται** (3rd sg. pres. pass. ind. of συντρίβω, "break, shatter," sg. vb. with neut. pl. subj., gnomic pres.),

---

Use of the OT: It is said of the future Messiah in Ps 2:9 that ποιμανεῖς αὐτοὺς ἐν ῥάβδῳ σιδηρᾷ, ὡς σκεῦος κεραμέως συντρίψεις αὐτούς. It is significant that Jesus extends the fulfillment of this messianic prophecy to the one who overcomes; they will share in his rule of the nations (although the "reigning" in Rev 20:5–6 and 22:5 does not indicate that anyone is being ruled). This prophecy from Ps 2:9 is applied to the Messiah in Rev 12:5.

2:28 ὡς (comp.) **κἀγὼ** (crasis of καί and ἐγώ, nom. subj., "I also") **εἴληφα** (1st sg. pf. act. ind. of λαμβάνω, possibly aoristic pf., but the stative force of the pf. tense remains and highlights a state of affairs [Math 75]) **παρὰ τοῦ πατρός** (source) **μου** (gen. of relationship), **καὶ δώσω** (1st sg. fut. act. ind. of δίδωμι) **αὐτῷ** (indir. obj.) **τὸν ἀστέρα** (ἀστήρ, -έρος, ὁ, "star," dir. obj.) **τὸν πρωϊνόν** (πρωϊνός, -ή, -όν, "morning," attrib.).

The morning star in 22:16 is identified as Jesus; the overcomer is here promised a share in Jesus's final victory.

Use of the OT: Balaam's messianic prophecy in Num 24:17 speaks of a star that will rise out of Jacob (ἀνατελεῖ ἄστρον ἐξ Ιακωβ).

2:29 ὁ ἔχων (nom. sg. masc. of pres. act. ptc. of ἔχω, subst., subj. nom.) **οὖς** (οὖς, ὠτός, τό, "ear," acc. sg. neut., dir. obj.) **ἀκουσάτω** (3rd sg. aor. act. impv. of ἀκούω) **τί** (τίς, acc. dir. obj., interr. pron., "what") **τὸ πνεῦμα** (subj. nom.) **λέγει** (3rd sg. pres. act. ind. of λέγω) **ταῖς ἐκκλησίαις** (indir. obj.).

FOR FURTHER STUDY

24. Good Works

Decock, P. "The Works of God, of Christ, and of the Faithful in the Apocalypse of John." *Neot* 41 (2007): 37–66.

25. Rival Christian Prophets (2:20)

Carey, G. *Elusive Apocalypse: Reading Authority in the Revelation to John*. Studies in American Biblical Hermeneutics 15. Macon, GA: Mercer University Press, 1999.

Collins, A. Y. "Vilification and Self-Definition in the Book of Revelation." *HTR* 79 (1986): 308–20.

Duff, P. B. *Who Rides the Beast? Prophetic Rivalry and the Rhetoric of Crisis in the Churches of the Apocalypse*. Oxford: Oxford University Press, 2001.

*Stewart, A. E. "Authority and Motivation in the Apocalypse of John." *BBR* 23 (2013): 547–63.

5. Proclamation to Sardis (3:1–6)

3:1 Καὶ τῷ ἀγγέλῳ (indir. obj.) **τῆς ἐν Σάρδεσιν** (loc., "Sardis") **ἐκκλησίας** (gen. of subord.) **γράψον** (2nd sg. aor. act. impv. of γράφω)· **Τάδε** (see on 2:1) **λέγει** (3rd sg. pres. act. ind. of λέγω) **ὁ ἔχων** (nom. sg. masc. of pres. act. ptc. of ἔχω, subst.) **τὰ ἑπτὰ** ("seven," attrib.) **πνεύματα** (dir. obj.) **τοῦ θεοῦ** (poss. or source) **καὶ τοὺς** (anaphoric to 1:16) **ἑπτὰ** (attrib.) **ἀστέρας** (ἀστήρ, -έρος, ὁ, "star," dir. obj.) **Οἶδά** (1st sg. pf. act. ind. of οἶδα) **σου** (subj. gen., fronted for emph.) **τὰ ἔργα** (dir. obj.) **ὅτι** (content, epex. to ἔργα) **ὄνομα** (dir. obj.; here "reputation" [BDAG 714c]) **ἔχεις** (2nd sg. pres. act. ind. of ἔχω) **ὅτι** (content, epex. to ὄνομα) **ζῇς** (2nd sg. pres. act. ind. of ζάω), **καὶ** (contrastive, "but") **νεκρὸς** (pred. adj.) **εἶ** (2nd sg. pres. act. ind. of εἰμί).

The description of Jesus holding seven stars refers back to 1:16, 20; 2:1, and the seven spirits appear in 1:4; 4:5; 5:6. Jesus's insight pierces the reputation to reveal the real state of the church. There is a dramatic difference between opinions based on appearances and the inward reality which only God can see.

3:2 γίνου (2nd sg. pres. mid. impv. of γίνομαι) **γρηγορῶν** (nom. sg. masc. of pres. act. ptc. of γρηγορέω, "be awake, be alert," periph.) **καὶ στήρισον** (2nd sg. aor. act. impv. of στηρίζω, "strengthen, establish") **τὰ λοιπὰ** (subst., "the remaining things," dir. obj., ant. of ἅ) **ἃ** (rel. pron. subj. nom.) **ἔμελλον** (3rd pl. impf. act. ind. of μέλλω; the impf. with a compl. inf. often does not refer to past time [Math 40]) **ἀποθανεῖν** (aor. act. inf. of ἀποθνήσκω, compl. inf.), **οὐ γὰρ** (explanatory) **εὕρηκά** (1st sg. pf. act. ind. of εὑρίσκω, can indicate "the result of a judicial investigation" [BDAG 412a]) **σου** (subj. gen.) **τὰ ἔργα** (dir. obj.) **πεπληρωμένα** (acc. pl. neut. of pf. pass. ptc. of πληρόω, compl. in an obj.-compl. double acc., "I have not found your works *to be* fulfilled") **ἐνώπιον** ("before, in the sight of") **τοῦ θεοῦ** (loc. with figurative extension, "in the view/opinion of" [L&N 90.20]) **μου** (in light of the claim to be the Son of God in 2:18 and the gen. of relationship in 3:5, this could be described as a gen. of relationship; Mathewson identifies it as a gen. of subord. [Math 40]).

The command to become or remain awake is common in early Christian teaching; the command is often given in light of the unexpectedness of the second coming and is sometimes linked with the need to remain sober (γρηγορεῖτε οὖν, ὅτι οὐκ οἴδατε ποίᾳ ἡμέρᾳ ὁ κύριος ὑμῶν ἔρχεται [Matt 24:42]; γρηγορεῖτε οὖν [Mark 13:35]; γρηγορεῖτε [Mark 13:37]; μακάριοι οἱ δοῦλοι ἐκεῖνοι, οὓς ἐλθὼν ὁ κύριος εὑρήσει γρηγοροῦντας [Luke 12:37]; Γρηγορεῖτε [1 Cor 16:13]; ἄρα οὖν μὴ καθεύδωμεν ὡς οἱ λοιποὶ ἀλλὰ γρηγορῶμεν καὶ νήφωμεν [1 Thess 5:6]; Νήψατε, γρηγορήσατε [1 Pet 5:8]).

Wakefulness/alertness is a moral stance of active engagement in doing God's will. The call to wake up in 3:2 involves the need to fulfill the works that would be pleasing to God. John's use of a periph. construction could perhaps be seen as more emph. than the impv. alone (Fanning 163).

3:3 μνημόνευε (2nd sg. pres. act. impv. of μνημονεύω, "remember") **οὖν** (inferential) **πῶς** (interr. adv. of manner, "how") **εἴληφας** (2nd sg. pf. act. ind. of λαμβάνω; εἴληφας is foregrounded both by its order in the sentence and the pf. tense [Math 41]) **καὶ ἤκουσας** (2nd sg. aor. act. ind. of ἀκούω) **καὶ** (coord. with μνημόνευε) **τήρει** (2nd sg. pres. act. impv. of τηρέω, the telic aor. impv. μετανόησον is coord. with the atelic progressive pres. impv. τήρει) **καὶ μετανόησον** (2nd sg. aor. act. impv. of μετανοέω, "repent"; logically, repentance precedes keeping but τήρει is fronted for emph.). **ἐὰν** (prot. of 3rd class cond. cl.) **οὖν** (inferential or, because the vb. is repeated from 3:2, the conj. here could "resume a subject once more after an interruption" [BDAG 736d]) **μὴ γρηγορήσῃς** (2nd sg. aor. act. subjunc. of γρηγορέω, "be awake, be alert," subjunc. because of ἐὰν), **ἥξω** (1st sg. fut. act. ind. of ἥκω, "come") **ὡς** (comp., "like") **κλέπτης** (κλέπτης, -ου, ὁ, "thief"), **καὶ οὐ μὴ** (emph. double neg.) **γνῷς** (2nd sg. aor. act. subjunc. of γινώσκω) **ποίαν** (attrib., "which") **ὥραν** ("hour," dir. obj., temp. acc.) **ἥξω** (1st sg. fut. act. ind. of ἥκω) **ἐπὶ σέ** (opposition, "against").

The command to repent occurs in 2:5, 16, 22; 3:19. The motif of Jesus coming like a thief echoes Jesus's words in the Gospels (Matt 24:43–44; Luke 12:39–40) and is referred to by both Paul (1 Thess 5:2: ἡμέρα κυρίου ὡς κλέπτης ἐν νυκτὶ οὕτως ἔρχεται) and Peter (2 Pet 3:10: Ἥξει δὲ ἡμέρα κυρίου ὡς κλέπτης). It was evidently a well-known Jesus saying and occurs again in 16:15. The thief motif stresses the unexpected and unknown timing of the coming and is motivationally linked with the need to stay alert (γρηγορέω) and morally vigilant.

3:4 ἀλλ' (contrastive) **ἔχεις** (2nd sg. pres. act. ind. of ἔχω) **ὀλίγα** (attrib., "few") **ὀνόματα** (dir. obj., the "names" refer to individuals, ant. of ἅ) **ἐν Σάρδεσιν** (loc., "Sardis") **ἃ** (rel. pron., subj. nom.) **οὐκ ἐμόλυναν** (3rd pl. aor. act. ind. of μολύνω, "defile, make dirty," a sg. vb. is expected with a neut. pl. subj., but the pl. is used here prob. because ὀνόματα refers to persons and the subj. is thus personal) **τὰ ἱμάτια** (dir. obj.) **αὐτῶν** (poss.), **καὶ περιπατήσουσιν** (3rd pl. fut. act. ind. of περιπατέω) **μετ' ἐμοῦ** (gen. of association, "with") **ἐν λευκοῖς** (λευκός, -ή, -όν, "white, bright," adv. dat. of manner), **ὅτι** (causal) **ἄξιοί** (ἄξιος, -ία, -ον, "worthy," pred. adj.) **εἰσιν** (3rd pl. pres. act. ind. of εἰμί).

The motif of defiled garments also occurs in Jude 23 (μισοῦντες καὶ τὸν ἀπὸ τῆς σαρκὸς ἐσπιλωμένον χιτῶνα). The bride in Rev 19:7–8 is given to wear bright and clean linen, which is interpreted as the righteous deeds of the saints. Jesus again distinguishes between those in the church who were faithful and those who were compromised.

3:5 ὁ νικῶν (nom. sg. masc. of pres. act. ptc. of νικάω, "overcome, conquer," subst., pendent/hanging nom) **οὕτως** (manner, "thus, in this way," the majority of mss read οὗτος ["the one who overcomes, this one will . . ."], but οὕτως has slightly better ancient support with א* (A) C 1006 2344 it[gig, ar] vg syr[ph, h] cop[sa, bo] arm (eth) *al* [Metzger 665]) **περιβαλεῖται** (3rd sg. fut. mid. ind. of περιβάλλω, "wrap, clothe") **ἐν ἱματίοις** ("clothing" or more specifically, "cloak," dat. of manner) **λευκοῖς** (λευκός, -ή, -όν, "white, bright," attrib.) **καὶ οὐ μὴ** (emph. double neg.) **ἐξαλείψω** (1st sg. fut. act. ind., of ἐξαλείφω, "wipe away") **τὸ ὄνομα** (dir. obj.) **αὐτοῦ** (poss.) **ἐκ τῆς βίβλου** (βίβλος, -ου, ἡ, "scroll," separation) **τῆς ζωῆς** (descriptive gen.) **καὶ ὁμολογήσω** (1st sg. fut. act. ind. of ὁμολογέω, "declare, confess") **τὸ ὄνομα** (dir. obj.) **αὐτοῦ** (poss.) **ἐνώπιον** ("before, in the sight of") **τοῦ πατρός** (loc.) **μου** (gen. of relationship) **καὶ ἐνώπιον τῶν ἀγγέλων** (loc.) **αὐτοῦ** (poss.).

White garments are used throughout Revelation to portray purity and victory (3:18; 4:4; 6:11; 7:9, 13; 19:14). The book of life appears again in 13:8; 17:8; 20:12, 15; 21:27 and is referred to by Paul in Phil 4:3 to describe coworkers (ὧν τὰ ὀνόματα ἐν βίβλῳ ζωῆς). The promise to confess the name of the overcomers before God and his angels echoes Jesus's words in Matt 10:32 (ὁμολογήσω κἀγὼ ἐν αὐτῷ ἔμπροσθεν τοῦ πατρός μου τοῦ ἐν [τοῖς] οὐρανοῖς) and Luke 12:8 (ὁ υἱὸς τοῦ ἀνθρώπου ὁμολογήσει ἐν αὐτῷ ἔμπροσθεν τῶν ἀγγέλων τοῦ θεοῦ). The promise not to blot out the name of the overcomer from the book of life is an emphatic positive promise of reward and not a threat. Jesus does, however, elsewhere directly threaten judgment on those who are compromised within the churches (2:5, 16; 3:3); the seven proclamations blend promise and threat to maximize the rhetorical persuasive force of the message. Although not a formal threat, this promise of not erasing names does contain an implicit warning to those within the churches who choose not to overcome. Discussions of eternal security often prematurely undermine Revelation's motivational force by confusing assurance of salvation with eternal security. Compromising Christians are more in need of threats than of false assurance, and repentant and believing Christians are more in need of assurance than threats. Both are necessary parts of Christian proclamation to hearers who may need to hear one message (threat) or the other (assurance). The final day of judgment will fully, finally, and publically distinguish between true believers who overcome and false believers who do not. The rhetorical strategies employed in the seven proclamations make it clear that threats, warnings, and assurances of God's forgiveness, presence, and support are all equally necessary to enable God's people to persevere and overcome.

Use of the OT: Moses asks God to blot his name from the book if he does not forgive the people's sin (Exod 32:32: ἐξάλειψόν με ἐκ τῆς βίβλου σου). God responds that the one who sins will be blotted out (32:33: Εἴ τις ἡμάρτηκεν ἐνώπιόν μου, ἐξαλείψω αὐτὸν ἐκ τῆς βίβλου μου). In Ps 68:29 LXX (69:28 EVV) David prays that his enemies would be blotted from the book of life (ἐξαλειφθήτωσαν ἐκ βίβλου ζώντων καὶ μετὰ δικαίων μὴ γραφήτωσαν). Daniel 12:1 describes God's people who will be delivered as those written in the book (ὃς ἂν εὑρεθῇ ἐγγεγραμμένος ἐν τῷ βιβλίῳ).

3:6 ὁ ἔχων (nom. sg. masc. of pres. act. ptc. of ἔχω, subst.) **οὖς** (οὖς, ὠτός, τό, "ear," acc. sg. neut., dir. obj.) **ἀκουσάτω** (3rd sg. aor. act. impv. of ἀκούω) **τί** (τίς, dir. obj., interr. pron., "what") **τὸ πνεῦμα** (subj. nom.) **λέγει** (3rd sg. pres. act. ind. of λέγω) **ταῖς ἐκκλησίαις** (indir. obj.).

6. Proclamation to Philadelphia (3:7–13)

3:7 Καὶ τῷ ἀγγέλῳ (indir. obj.) **τῆς ἐν Φιλαδελφείᾳ** (loc., "Philadelphia") **ἐκκλησίας** (gen. of subord.) **γράψον** (2nd sg. aor. act. impv. of γράφω) **Τάδε** (see on 2:1) **λέγει** (3rd sg. pres. act. ind. of λέγω) **ὁ ἅγιος** (subst., subj. nom.), **ὁ ἀληθινός** (subst., "the true one," appos. to ἅγιος), **ὁ ἔχων** (nom. sg. masc. of pres. act. ptc. of ἔχω, subst., appos. to ἅγιος) **τὴν κλεῖν** (κλείς, κλειδός, ἡ, "key," dir. obj.) **Δαυίδ** (poss. gen. or obj. gen., "key to David," i.e., "the key to the Davidic or messianic kingdom" [Aune[a] 235]), **ὁ ἀνοίγων** (nom. sg. masc. of pres. act. ptc. of ἀνοίγω, "open," subst., appos. to ἅγιος) **καὶ οὐδεὶς** (subj. nom.) **κλείσει** (3rd sg. fut. act. ind. of κλείω, "shut") **καὶ κλείων** (nom. sg. masc. of pres. act. ptc. of κλείω, subst., coord. with ἀνοίγων and sharing the art.) **καὶ οὐδεὶς** (subj. nom.) **ἀνοίγει** (3rd sg. pres. act. ind. of ἀνοίγω).

This description of Jesus stands out for not referring back to John's inaugural vision of Jesus. It highlights Jesus's authority over final salvation/judgment and presents him as the one who will determine who has access to the new Jerusalem. God is described as ὁ ἅγιος καὶ ἀληθινός in Rev 6:10. Jesus is described as the holy one in the Gospels (ὁ ἅγιος τοῦ θεοῦ [Mark 1:24]; ὁ ἅγιος τοῦ θεοῦ [Luke 4:34]; ἐγνώκαμεν ὅτι σὺ εἶ ὁ ἅγιος τοῦ θεοῦ [John 6:69]).

Use of the OT: God is often described as the holy one (e.g., ὁ ἅγιος [Isa 40:25]; ἐγὼ κύριος ὁ θεὸς ὁ ἅγιος ὑμῶν [Isa 43:15]). The description of Jesus parallels words spoken concerning Eliakim that he will be a father to the inhabitants of Jerusalem and will possess the key of the house of David to shut and open with authority (Isa 22:22 MT and some Greek mss). Job describes God as one who has the power to irreversibly shut against a man (Job 12:14: ἐὰν κλείσῃ κατὰ ἀνθρώπων, τίς ἀνοίξει;).

3:8 Οἶδά (1st sg. pf. act. ind. of οἶδα) **σου** (subj. gen., fronted for emph.) **τὰ ἔργα** (dir. obj., unlike in 3:1, 15, there is no description here of their works and ἔργα should prob. be followed by a period and not a comma), **ἰδοὺ** (emph. interj.) **δέδωκα** (1st sg. pf. act. ind. of δίδωμι, the intensive pf. tense here and in the following ptc. emphasizes the resultant state of affairs) **ἐνώπιόν** (loc. "before") **σου** (loc.) **θύραν** (dir. obj., ant. of ἥν) **ἠνεῳγμένην** (acc. sg. fem. of pf. pass. ptc. of ἀνοίγω, attrib.), **ἣν** (rel. pron. dir. obj.) **οὐδεὶς** (subj. nom.) **δύναται** (3rd sg. pres. mid. ind. of δύναμαι) **κλεῖσαι** (aor. act. inf. of κλείω, "shut," compl. inf.) **αὐτήν** (redundant pron. for emph., cf. 7:2, 9; 12:6, 14; 13:8, 12; 17:9; 19:9; 20:8; appos. to ἥν), **ὅτι** (causal) **μικρὰν** ("little," attrib. adj. fronted for emph. but modifying δύναμιν) **ἔχεις** (2nd sg. pres. act. ind. of ἔχω) **δύναμιν** (dir.

obj.) **καὶ** ("and yet"; "emphasizing a fact as surprising or unexpected or noteworthy" [BDAG 495b]) **ἐτήρησάς** (2nd sg. aor. act. ind. of τηρέω) **μου** (gen. of source, "from me"; obj. gen. "about me"; or subj. gen., "my word," fronted for emph.) **τὸν λόγον** (dir. obj.) **καὶ οὐκ ἠρνήσω** (2nd sg. aor. mid. ind. of ἀρνέομαι, "deny") **τὸ ὄνομά** (dir. obj.) **μου** (poss.).

Although Paul uses the image of an open door to describe effective opportunities for evangelism (1 Cor 16:9; 2 Cor 2:12; Col 4:3), the allusion to Isa 22:22 in 3:8 and the broader network of promises in the seven proclamations, which point forward to the new creation, would suggest that the open door promise in 3:8 guarantees access to the new Jerusalem provided by Jesus, who now holds the key of David (Fanning 173; Aune[a] 236).

3:9 ἰδοὺ (emph. interj.) **διδῶ** (1st sg. pres. act. ind. of δίδωμι, this form reflects the transition from -μι vbs. to -ω vbs. [Math 47], futuristic pres.; Aune suggests this is a Hebraism with the connotation "make" [Aune[a] 230] although Louw and Nida suggest δίδωμι can indicate cause without any reference to the Hebrew [L&N 90.51]) **ἐκ τῆς συναγωγῆς** (the prep. phrase functions as obj. of the vb.; part. [Aune[a] 230] likely with an assumed τίνας, "some out of the synagogue"; without an assumed τίνας the prep. phrase would presumably include all from the synagogue) **τοῦ Σατανᾶ** (σατανᾶς, -ᾶ, ὁ, "Satan, enemy, adversary," poss.) **τῶν λεγόντων** (gen. pl. masc. of pres. act. ptc. of λέγω, subst., appos. to συναγωγῆς) **ἑαυτοὺς** (acc. subj. of inf.) **Ἰουδαίους** (pred. acc.) **εἶναι** (pres. act. inf. of εἰμί), **καὶ** (contrastive) **οὐκ εἰσὶν** (3rd pl. pres. act. ind. of εἰμί) **ἀλλὰ** (contrastive) **ψεύδονται** (3rd pl. pres. mid. ind. of ψεύδομαι, "lie"). **ἰδοὺ** (emph. interj., Fanning suggests that the repetition of this interj. in 3:9 is "evidence of lively speech in written form" [Fanning 174]) **ποιήσω** (1st sg. fut. act. ind. of ποιέω) **αὐτοὺς** (dir. obj.) **ἵνα** (substituting for an inf. to indicate purpose or result [Aune[a] 230]; the idiomatic combination of ποιέω + ἵνα has been described as expressing causation, "make [to] cause [someone] to," or "bring it about that," cf. 13:12, 16 [BDAG 840b–c]) **ἥξουσιν** (3rd pl. fut. act. ind. of ἥκω, "come") **καὶ προσκυνήσουσιν** (3rd pl. fut. act. ind. of προσκυνέω, "worship, kneel down before") **ἐνώπιον τῶν ποδῶν** (loc.) **σου** (poss.) **καὶ γνῶσιν** (3rd pl. aor. act. subjunc. of γινώσκω) **ὅτι** (content) **ἐγὼ** (subj. nom.) **ἠγάπησά** (1st sg. aor. act. ind. of ἀγαπάω, prob. gnomic aor., "I love") **σε** (dir. obj.).

John coordinates three vbs. with mixed moods following ἵνα: two fut. ind. (ἥξουσιν and προσκυνήσουσιν) and one subjunc. (γνῶσιν). This likely reflects a growing practice in Koine Greek to mix the fut. and subjunc. due to their similar form and meaning. John elsewhere uses a fut. in place of a subjunc. with ἵνα in 3:9; 6:4, 11; 8:3; 9:4, 5, 20; 13:12; 14:13; 22:14 (Math 48).

Use of the OT: Isaiah 45:14; 49:23; 60:14 all develop a motif of the gentiles bowing down before the feet of God's people Israel in a time of restoration. John's use of this motif is significant because the synagogue of Satan is presented as the outsiders while the church, made up of both Jews and gentiles, is honored. Some interpreters see a note of hope for the synagogue of Satan because the gentile outsiders in Isaiah take part to some degree in Israel's restoration. The affirmation of God's love for the church echoes language of God's love for Israel in Isa 43:4 (κἀγώ σε ἠγάπησα).

3:10 **ὅτι** (causal, the causal cl. is fronted for emph.) **ἐτήρησας** (2nd sg. aor. act. ind. of τηρέω) **τὸν λόγον** (dir. obj.) **τῆς ὑπομονῆς** (ὑπομονή, -ῆς, ἡ, "endurance," obj. gen.) **μου** (subj. gen., likely connects to λόγον, "my word about endurance," cf. 3:8 [Math 49]), **κἀγώ** (crasis of καί and ἐγώ, nom. subj.) **σε** (dir. obj., fronted for emph.) **τηρήσω** (1st sg. fut. act. ind. of τηρέω) **ἐκ τῆς** (the art. here indicates the hour was well-known to the hearers [Wallace 225]) **ὥρας** (separation) **τοῦ πειρασμοῦ** (πειρασμός, -οῦ, ὁ, "testing, temptation," descriptive gen.) **τῆς μελλούσης** (gen. sg. fem. of pres. act. ptc. of μέλλω, "about to," attrib.) **ἔρχεσθαι** (pres. mid. inf. of ἔρχομαι, compl. inf.) **ἐπὶ τῆς οἰκουμένης** (prob. loc.; possibly opposition, "against") **ὅλης** (attrib.) **πειράσαι** (aor. act. inf. of πειράζω, "test," purpose) **τοὺς κατοικοῦντας** (acc. pl. masc. of pres. act. ptc. of κατοικέω, "dwell," subst., dir. obj.) **ἐπὶ τῆς γῆς** (loc.).

The parallel grammar in John 17:15 (ἵνα τηρήσης αὐτοὺς ἐκ τοῦ πονηροῦ) suggests that τηρέω + ἐκ should be understood as protection (and not removal) from the source of danger (Beale 290–91). God's people are thus promised spiritual protection through the time of testing. This argument is strengthened by noting that the visions do not indicate that God's people will be kept out of future tribulation (6:2–11; 7:14; 11:7; 12:17; 13:7; 14:13; 17:6; 18:24) even though they will be protected from demonic opposition (9:4) and there is no indication they experience God's wrath. The grammar, however, is not determinative, and Fanning points to the thematic parallel in 2 Pet 2:6–9 to argue that Rev 3:10 contains a promise to keep the Christians "'from' the period of severe worldwide 'trial' by taking them away from the earthly scene entirely" (Fanning 177). This illustrates the point that grammar and syntax alone are often not determinative, and interpretive conclusions often involve one's understanding of the book as a whole and how individual verses relate to more comprehensive or systematic eschatological scenarios. This promise in Rev 3:10 is generally a central point in the debate between pre- and post-tribulation positions. Aune's conclusion seems correct that the promise does not mean "they will be physically absent but rather that they will not be touched by that which touches others" (Aune[a] 240). He is wrong, however, in suggesting that the promise only applied to the original Philadelphian Christians (Aune[a] 240); the seven proclamations function rhetorically as a unified whole which provide warnings and promises meant to be read and applied by every Christian hearer.

The focus on endurance recalls the teaching of Jesus in Luke 21:19 (ἐν τῇ ὑπομονῇ ὑμῶν κτήσασθε τὰς ψυχὰς ὑμῶν), Matt 24:13 (ὁ δὲ ὑπομείνας εἰς τέλος οὗτος σωθήσεται) along with early Christian teachings such as 2 Tim 2:12 (εἰ ὑπομένομεν, καὶ συμβασιλεύσομεν) and Heb 10:36 (ὑπομονῆς γὰρ ἔχετε χρείαν ἵνα τὸ θέλημα τοῦ θεοῦ ποιήσαντες κομίσησθε τὴν ἐπαγγελίαν). The "hour" does not match other time periods in Revelation and symbolically communicates that the time is bounded and set by God; it will not go on forever and is not under the control of the enemy.

John consistently refers to "the ones dwelling on the earth" (here acc. with ἐπί: τοὺς κατοικοῦντας ἐπὶ τῆς γῆς) in a negative way to describe those who refuse to repent and will experience God's judgment (6:10; 8:13; 11:10; 13:8, 12, 14; 17:2, 8). The expression does not require the reader to think of a deterministically fixed group but is rather the way John's narrative describes those who are ultimately judged. In the present time the boundaries are porous and there is still time to repent in response to the faithful witness of God's people (see 5:9).

3:11 ἔρχομαι (1st sg. pres. mid. ind. of ἔρχομαι) **ταχύ** (ταχύς, -εῖα, -ύ, "soon, quickly," temp. adv.). **κράτει** (2nd sg. pres. act. impv. of κρατέω, "hold, keep," progressive pres.) **ὃ** (dir. obj. of ἔχεις, introduces headless rel. cl. which functions as dir. obj. of κράτει) **ἔχεις** (2nd sg. pres. act. ind. of ἔχω), **ἵνα** (purpose) **μηδεὶς** (subj. nom.) **λάβῃ** (3rd sg. aor. act. subjunc. of λαμβάνω) **τὸν στέφανόν** (στέφανος, -ου, ὁ, "wreath, crown, prize," dir. obj.) **σου** (poss.).

3:12 ὁ νικῶν (nom. sg. masc. of pres. act. ptc. of νικάω, "overcome, conquer," subst., pendent/hanging nom, logical but not syntactical subj.) **ποιήσω** (1st sg. fut. act. ind. of ποιέω) **αὐτὸν** (dir. obj.) **στῦλον** (στῦλος, -ου, ὁ, "pillar," compl. in obj.-compl. double acc.) **ἐν τῷ ναῷ** (loc.) **τοῦ θεοῦ** (poss.) **μου** (gen. of relationship), **καὶ ἔξω** (adv. of place, "outside") **οὐ μὴ** (emph. double neg.) **ἐξέλθῃ** (3rd sg. aor. act. subjunc. of ἐξέρχομαι) **ἔτι** (temp. adv.) **καὶ γράψω** (1st sg. fut. act. ind. of γράφω) **ἐπ' αὐτὸν** (loc.) **τὸ ὄνομα** (dir. obj.) **τοῦ θεοῦ** (poss.) **μου** (gen. of relationship), **καὶ τὸ ὄνομα** (dir. obj.) **τῆς πόλεως** (poss.) **τοῦ θεοῦ** (poss.) **μου** (gen. of relationship) **τῆς καινῆς** (attrib.) **Ἰερουσαλὴμ** (appos. to πόλεως) **ἡ καταβαίνουσα** (nom. sg. fem. of pres. act. ptc. of καταβαίνω, prob. incongruous attrib. ptc., but possibly subst. ptc. if taken as starting a parenthetical cl. [Math 51]) **ἐκ τοῦ οὐρανοῦ** (gen. of source) **ἀπὸ τοῦ θεοῦ** (gen. of source; ἀπό and ἐκ similarly express source, but ἀπό more naturally communicates the "originator of the action" [BDAG 106d]) **μου** (gen. of relationship) **καὶ τὸ ὄνομά** (dir. obj.) **μου** (poss.) **τὸ καινόν** (attrib.).

In 14:1, the 144,000 have both the name of Jesus and God written on their forehead while in 22:4 all the saved will have God's name written on their foreheads. The parallel with 14:1, in particular, suggests that the divine seal of 7:2–8 is the divine name and is found on all overcomers. The promise of the descent of the new Jerusalem points forward to 21:2. To have the name of new Jerusalem written on the overcomers intimately connects them, both Jew and gentile, with God's promised future restoration of his creation. Believing gentiles also fully belong to the restored Jerusalem. The nom. ptc. ἡ καταβαίνουσα should be in the gen. case (τῆς καταβαίνουσης) to match the gen. Ἰερουσαλὴμ (indeclinable in Revelation). Although some later scribes correct the grammar, there is no obvious explanation for this beyond John's tendency to use the nom. to modify indeclinable nouns (Moț 117).

Use of the OT: The phrase τὸ ὄνομα τῆς πόλεως is found in the final verse of Ezekiel in regard to the new Jerusalem (Ezek 48:35). In Isa 62:2 God promises to give Jerusalem a new name (καὶ καλέσει σε τὸ ὄνομά σου τὸ καινόν, ὃ ὁ κύριος ὀνομάσει αὐτό) and in Isa 65:15 he promises to call his servants a new name (τοῖς δὲ δουλεύουσιν αὐτῷ κληθήσεται ὄνομα καινόν).

3:13 **ὁ ἔχων** (nom. sg. masc. of pres. act. ptc. of ἔχω, subst.) **οὖς** (οὖς, ὠτός, τό, "ear," acc. sg. neut., dir. obj.) **ἀκουσάτω** (3rd sg. aor. act. impv. of ἀκούω) **τί** (τίς, acc. dir. obj., interr. pron., "what") **τὸ πνεῦμα** (subj. nom.) **λέγει** (3rd sg. pres. act. ind. of λέγω) **ταῖς ἐκκλησίαις** (indir. obj.).

7. Proclamation to Laodicea (3:14–22)

3:14 **Καὶ τῷ ἀγγέλῳ** (indir. obj.) **τῆς ἐν Λαοδικείᾳ** (loc., "Laodicea") **ἐκκλησίας** (gen. of subord.) **γράψον** (2nd sg. aor. act. impv. of γράφω)· **Τάδε** (see on 2:1) **λέγει** (3rd sg. pres. act. ind. of λέγω) **ὁ Ἀμήν** (subj. nom., indeclinable but nominalized by the art., transliterated from Hebrew) **ὁ μάρτυς** (μάρτυς, -υρος, ὁ, "witness"; not yet a technical term for "martyr," subj. nom. appos. to Ἀμήν) **ὁ πιστὸς** (attrib.) **καὶ ἀληθινός** (ἀληθινός, -ή, -όν, "true," attrib. shares the art. with πιστός), **ἡ ἀρχὴ** (ἀρχή, -ῆς, ἡ, "beginning, ruler," subj. nom., appos. to Ἀμήν) **τῆς κτίσεως** (κτίσις, -εως, ἡ, "creature, creation," gen. of subord., "ruler over the creation" or obj. gen, "origin of the creation") **τοῦ θεοῦ** (subj. gen. or poss.)

The description of Jesus as ὁ μάρτυς ὁ πιστὸς καὶ ἀληθινός refers back to 1:5 (ὁ μάρτυς ὁ πιστός) and forward to 19:11 (πιστὸς καὶ ἀληθινός). As a faithful and true witness, Jesus's assessment of the church is accurate. The description of Jesus as ἡ ἀρχὴ τῆς κτίσεως finds a parallel in Col 1:15 (πρωτότοκος πάσης κτίσεως) and Jesus is connected closely with creation in John 1:3 (πάντα δι' αὐτοῦ ἐγένετο) and Heb 1:2 (δι' οὗ καὶ ἐποίησεν τοὺς αἰῶνας). Revelation, however, does not elsewhere describe Jesus as active in the creation of the world (this is ascribed to God in 4:11; 10:6; 14:7; 21:5) and instead presents him as the ruler of the kings of the world (1:5; 17:14; 19:16). This would suggest that ἡ ἀρχὴ τῆς κτίσεως describes Jesus as "the ruler over God's creation" (Koester 336; Fanning 185). Fanning astutely notes that the description of both Jesus and God as the beginning and end (ἡ ἀρχὴ καὶ τὸ τέλος [21:6; 22:13]) establishes Jesus's existence prior to creation which undermines the argument that he is the "first part" or "first created" being (Fanning 185).

Use of the OT: The allusion to Isa 65:15 in Rev 3:12 is followed immediately by an allusion to Isa 65:16 in 3:14. In Isa 65:16 God describes himself as "the God, the Amen," (בֵּאלֹהֵי אָמֵן; translated as "the true God" in the LXX: τὸν θεὸν τὸν ἀληθινόν). This is an example of applying an original description of God to Jesus. Proverbs 8:22 describes wisdom as the beginning of God's ways into his works (ἀρχὴν ὁδῶν αὐτοῦ εἰς ἔργα αὐτοῦ).

3:15 **Οἶδά** (1st sg. pf. act. ind. of οἶδα) **σου** (subj. gen., fronted for emph.) **τὰ ἔργα** (dir. obj.) **ὅτι** (content, epex.) **οὔτε** (adv. functioning as neg. correlative conj., "neither . . . nor") **ψυχρὸς** (ψυχρός, -ά, -όν, "cold," pred. adj.) **εἶ** (2nd sg. pres. act. ind. of εἰμί) **οὔτε ζεστός** (ζεστός, -ή, -όν, "hot," pred. adj.). **ὄφελον** (interj. of unfulfilled wish, "that which ought to be if one only had one's wish—'would that.'" [L&N 71.28]) **ψυχρὸς** (pred. adj.) **ἦς** (2nd sg. pres. act. impf. of εἰμί) **ἢ** (disjunctive) **ζεστός** (pred. adj.).

Many interpreters compare Jesus's imagery with a hypothetical historical reconstruction of the local water supply at Laodicea, but the ancient evidence does not support this approach and the imagery is better interpreted against broader attitudes toward drinking water in the ancient world, in which both hot and cold water were valued depending upon the purpose and climate (Koester 337; Koester, "Message to Laodicea").

3:16 οὕτως (inferential [Math 53]) **ὅτι** (causal, the causal cl. is fronted for emph.) **χλιαρὸς** (χλιαρός, -ά, -όν, "lukewarm," pred. adj.) **εἶ** (2nd sg. pres. act. ind. of εἰμί) **καὶ οὔτε** (adv. functioning as neg. correlative conj., "neither . . . nor") **ζεστὸς** (ζεστός, -ή, -όν, "hot," pred. adj.) **οὔτε ψυχρός** (ψυχρός, -ά, -όν, "cold," pred. adj.), **μέλλω** (1st sg. pres. act. ind. of μέλλω) **σε** (dir. obj.) **ἐμέσαι** (aor. act. inf. of ἐμέω, "vomit," compl. inf.) **ἐκ τοῦ στόματός** (source or separation) **μου** (poss.).

3:17 ὅτι (causal, the causal cl. is fronted for emph.) **λέγεις** (2nd sg. pres. act. ind. of λέγω) **ὅτι** (content, introduces dir. speech) **πλούσιός** (πλούσιος, -ία, -ιον, "rich, wealthy," pred. adj.) **εἰμι** (1st sg. pres. act. ind. of εἰμί) **καὶ πεπλούτηκα** (1st sg. pf. act. ind. of πλουτέω, "prosper, be wealthy," intensive pf.) **καὶ οὐδὲν** (attrib.) **χρείαν** ("need," dir. obj.) **ἔχω** (1st sg. pres. act. ind. of ἔχω), **καὶ** (contrastive) **οὐκ οἶδας** (2nd sg. pf. act. ind. of οἶδα) **ὅτι** (content) **σὺ** (subj. nom.) **εἶ** (2nd sg. pres. act. ind. of εἰμί) **ὁ ταλαίπωρος** (-ον, "wretched," pred. adj.) **καὶ ἐλεεινὸς** (-ή, -όν, "pitiable," pred. adj.) **καὶ πτωχὸς** (-ή, -όν, "poor," pred. adj.) **καὶ τυφλὸς** (-ή, -όν, "blind," pred. adj.) **καὶ γυμνός** ("naked," pred. adj.),

The Laodiceans likely viewed prosperity as a sign of God's blessing; Jesus reveals the reality of their spiritual poverty.

Use of the OT: Similar to Laodicea, in Hos 12:9 Ephraim boasts of becoming wealthy (Πλὴν πεπλούτηκα [12:8 EVV]) with innocence, but Hos 12:7 clarifies that they attained wealth through deception and oppression.

3:18 συμβουλεύω (1st sg. pres. act. ind. of συμβουλεύω, "plot, advise") **σοι** (dat. dir. obj.) **ἀγοράσαι** (aor. act. inf. of ἀγοράζω, "buy," indir. speech) **παρ' ἐμοῦ** (source) **χρυσίον** (χρυσίον, -ου, τό, "gold," dir. obj.) **πεπυρωμένον** (acc. sg. neut. of pf. pass. ptc. of πυρόω, "burn, refine," attrib.) **ἐκ πυρὸς** (cognate gen., means) **ἵνα** (purpose) **πλουτήσῃς** (2nd sg. aor. act. subjunc. of πλουτέω, "prosper, be wealthy"), **καὶ ἱμάτια** (coord. dir. obj.) **λευκὰ** (λευκός, -ή, -όν, "white, bright," attrib.) **ἵνα** (purpose) **περιβάλῃ** (2nd sg. aor. mid. subjunc. of περιβάλλω, "wrap, clothe") **καὶ μὴ φανερωθῇ** (3rd sg. aor. pass. subjunc. of φανερόω, "reveal") **ἡ αἰσχύνη** (αἰσχύνη, -ης, ἡ, "shame," subj. nom.) **τῆς γυμνότητός** (γυμνότης, -ητος, ἡ, "nakedness," attributed gen., "shameful nakedness," or gen. of source, "shame from nakedness") **σου** (poss.), **καὶ κολλ[ο]ύριον** (κολλούριον, -ου, τό, medicinal "eye salve," coord. dir. obj.) **ἐγχρῖσαι** (aor. act. inf. of ἐγχρίω, "anoint," purpose) **τοὺς ὀφθαλμούς** (dir. obj.) **σου** (poss.) **ἵνα** (purpose) **βλέπῃς** (2nd sg. pres. act. subjunc. of βλέπω).

On white garments, see 3:5. Revelation 16:15 pronounces a blessing on the one who keeps his garments so that the he might not walk naked and they might see his shame (ἵνα μὴ γυμνὸς περιπατῇ καὶ βλέπωσιν τὴν ἀσχημοσύνην αὐτοῦ).

Use of the OT: Isaiah 55:1 invites everyone who thirsts to buy without money and without price (ἀγοράσατε καὶ πίετε ἄνευ ἀργυρίου καὶ τιμῆς). In both Isaiah and Revelation, the hearers have no money or means to purchase what is needed; the currency is repentance (Isa 55:7; Rev 3:19) and God's grace will freely give all that is needed. The uselessness of physical money to gain God's favor is rhetorically highlighted by the first item in Rev 3:18; what currency could possibly be used to buy purified gold (the most valuable coin in the Roman Empire)?

3:19 ἐγὼ (subj. nom.) **ὅσους** (correlative pron., dir. obj. of φιλῶ, "as many as," the correlative cl. functions as dir. obj. of ἐλέγχω) **ἐὰν** (adds element of indefiniteness to ὅσους, "whoever," lit., "as many as if I love") **φιλῶ** (1st sg. pres. act. subjunc. of φιλέω, "love") **ἐλέγχω** (1st sg. pres. act. ind. of ἐλέγχω, "rebuke, expose") **καὶ παιδεύω** (1st sg. pres. act. ind. of παιδεύω, "discipline, instruct," coord.). **ζήλευε** (2nd sg. pres. act. impv. of ζηλεύω, "be eager, be zealous") **οὖν** (inferential) **καὶ μετανόησον** (2nd sg. aor. act. impv. of μετανοέω, "repent," coord.).

God's discipline was a topic of early Christian teaching, as evident in 1 Cor 11:32 (κρινόμενοι δὲ ὑπὸ [τοῦ] κυρίου παιδευόμεθα, ἵνα μὴ σὺν τῷ κόσμῳ κατακριθῶμεν) and Heb 12:6 (ὃν γὰρ ἀγαπᾷ κύριος παιδεύει). The impvs. in Rev 3:19 reveal how one buys from Jesus in 3:18: be zealous and repent! Revelation 3:19 is important for revealing the motive of love behind God's discipline.

Use of the OT: Proverbs 3:12 declares that Lord disciplines the one he loves (ὃν γὰρ ἀγαπᾷ κύριος παιδεύει).

3:20 ἰδοὺ (emph. interj.) **ἕστηκα** (1st sg. pf. act. ind. of ἵστημι, intensive pf.) **ἐπὶ τὴν θύραν** (loc., "at") **καὶ κρούω** (1st sg. pres. act. ind. of κρούω, "knock," progressive pres.)· **ἐάν** (prot. of 3rd class cond. cl.) **τις** (subj. nom., indef. pron., "anyone, someone") **ἀκούσῃ** (3rd sg. aor. act. subjunc. of ἀκούω) **τῆς φωνῆς** (gen. dir. obj.; John uses both the acc. and gen. cases for the dir. obj. following ἀκούω with no evident difference in meaning) **μου** (poss.) **καὶ ἀνοίξῃ** (3rd sg. aor. act. subjunc. of ἀνοίγω) **τὴν θύραν** (dir. obj.), **[καὶ] εἰσελεύσομαι** (1st sg. fut. mid. ind. of εἰσέρχομαι) **πρὸς αὐτὸν** (relationship)

καὶ δειπνήσω (1st sg. fut. act. ind. δειπνέω, "eat") **μετ' αὐτοῦ** (association) **καὶ αὐτὸς** (subj. nom.) **μετ' ἐμοῦ** (association).

The use of *καί* to introduce an apod. could be due to MT/LXX influence (BDAG 494d). Jesus's promise to enter in to eat with the one who hears and opens the door echoes Jesus's promise in John 14:23 to the one who loves him and keeps his word (πρὸς αὐτὸν ἐλευσόμεθα καὶ μονὴν παρ' αὐτῷ ποιησόμεθα). The imagery of Jesus knocking on the door is not used here evangelistically but as a call to the Christians to repent.

3:21 ὁ νικῶν (nom. sg. masc. of pres. act. ptc. of νικάω, "overcome, conquer," subst. ptc., pendent/hanging nom) **δώσω** (1st sg. fut. act. ind. of δίδωμι) **αὐτῷ** (indir. obj.) **καθίσαι** (aor. act. inf. of καθίζω, "sit," subst. inf., dir. obj.) **μετ' ἐμοῦ** (association) **ἐν τῷ θρόνῳ** (loc.) **μου** (poss.), **ὡς** (comp.) **κἀγὼ** (crasis of καί and ἐγώ, subj. nom., "I also") **ἐνίκησα** (1st sg. aor. act. ind. of νικάω) **καὶ ἐκάθισα** (1st sg. aor. act. ind. of καθίζω, "sit") **μετὰ τοῦ πατρός** (association) **μου** (gen. of relationship) **ἐν τῷ** (cataphoric to 4:2) **θρόνῳ** (loc.) **αὐτοῦ** (poss.).

The parallel with Jesus suggests that overcomers overcome in the same way as Jesus through faithfulness to death. Victory is expected to come as a result of painful suffering at the hands of adversaries. The reference to God's throne anticipates the transition to the throne-room vision of Revelation 4.

Use of the OT: The promise to the overcomers to share the throne builds on God's promise to the Messiah in Ps 109:1 LXX (Κάθου ἐκ δεξιῶν μου, ἕως ἂν θῶ τοὺς ἐχθρούς σου ὑποπόδιον τῶν ποδῶν σου [Ps 110:1 EVV]).

3:22 ὁ ἔχων (nom. sg. masc. of pres. act. ptc. of ἔχω, subst.) **οὖς** (οὖς, ὠτός, τό, "ear," acc. sg. neut., dir. obj.) **ἀκουσάτω** (3rd sg. aor. act. impv. of ἀκούω) **τί** (τίς, acc. dir. obj., interr. pron., "what") **τὸ πνεῦμα** (subj. nom.) **λέγει** (3rd sg. pres. act. ind. of λέγω) **ταῖς ἐκκλησίαις** (indir. obj.).

HOMILETICAL SUGGESTIONS

These seven proclamations are often viewed as the easiest sections to preach. Sermons on individual churches should seek to follow the consistent and shared structure noted above in the introduction to 2:1–3:22 with variation based on the content of each proclamation. Often, the churches have a different view of themselves than Christ. Compromise with the world leads to ease and comfort while faithful witness to Christ leads to persecution and difficulty. Application, for John's original hearers and hearers today, should focus on the need to repent, obey, witness, worship, and persevere depending upon the needs of the audience and individuals. The letters alternate between severe warnings and strong assurance and each ends with a call to discern what the Spirit is speaking and respond appropriately. Neither the warning nor the assurance should be downplayed, and each side of this apparent dichotomy will be necessary to different hearers in different life situations.

The Spirit Is Speaking to You (2:1–3:22)

1. Jesus knows your specific situation, the good and the bad.
2. Jesus calls you to repent if necessary and persevere.
3. Jesus promises that the cost of overcoming discipleship is worth it!

III. In the Spirit in Heaven (4:1–16:21)

A. THE DIVINE THRONE ROOM (4:1–5:14)

In Revelation 4–5 John sees the divine throne room. Chapter 4 descriptively sets the stage in a static way with a large number of verbless clauses and participles while chapter 5 employs more indicative verbs to move the narrative forward (Math 58–59). "Thus the main focus in this section is Rev 5 since it is where all the action takes place" (Math 59). The model of heavenly worship in Revelation 4–5 is meant to inform and shape the church's earthly worship.

1. Worship of God (4:1–11)

4:1 Μετὰ (temp., "after") **ταῦτα** (demon. pron., "these things," the ant. is 1:9–3:21) **εἶδον** (1st sg. aor. act. ind. of ὁράω), **καὶ ἰδοὺ** (prompts attention to something new or unusual [BDAG 468b]) **θύρα** (subj. nom., "door") **ἠνεῳγμένη** (nom. sg. fem. of pf. pass. ptc. of ἀνοίγω, attrib.) **ἐν τῷ οὐρανῷ** (loc.), **καὶ ἡ φωνὴ** (subj. nom., ant. of ἥν) **ἡ πρώτη** (attrib., this first or earlier voice appears in 1:10) **ἣν** (dir. obj. of ἤκουσα) **ἤκουσα** (1st sg. aor. act. ind. of ἀκούω) **ὡς** (comp.) **σάλπιγγος** (comp. gen.) **λαλούσης** (gen. sg. fem. of pres. act. ptc. of λαλέω, attrib., on the case, see 1:11) **μετ' ἐμοῦ** (association) **λέγων** (nom. sg. masc. of pres. act. ptc. of λέγω, introduces dir. speech; the masc. gender is incongruous with the fem. φωνή but was likely changed to reflect the gender of the speaker, Jesus, as a *constructio ad sensum*), **Ἀνάβα** (2nd sg. aor. act. impv. of ἀναβαίνω) **ὧδε** (adv. of place, "here"), **καὶ δείξω** (1st sg. fut. act. ind. of δείκνυμι, "show") **σοι** (indir. obj.) **ἃ** (acc. subj. of inf.; the headless rel. cl. functions as dir. obj. of δείξω) **δεῖ** (3rd sg. pres. act. ind., "it is necessary, must") **γενέσθαι** (aor. mid. inf. of γίνομαι, compl. inf.) **μετὰ** (temp.) **ταῦτα** (subst., "after these things").

The coord. and temp. connections between visions in Revelation (here indicated by Μετὰ ταῦτα) indicate visionary sequence, not the historical or chronological order of fulfillment. There is no indication here of the rapture of the church. John reports on his own visionary movement to the divine throne room. The closing expression, ἃ δεῖ γενέσθαι μετὰ ταῦτα, parallels the expression ἃ μέλλει γενέσθαι μετὰ ταῦτα in Rev 1:19 as a way to refer to the end times or latter days, which were beginning to be fulfilled in John's day. The scene of Revelation 4–5 thus parallels John's present historical time—Jesus has ascended and is enthroned in the divine throne room (3:21; 5:6), and God's end-time judgments had not yet been poured out. John's ascent to the heavenly throne room is described differently, but it is probably similar to Paul's experience in 2 Cor 12:2–4. Paul expresses genuine uncertainty regarding the bodily nature of the heavenly journey. An opened heaven elsewhere provides visual access to God or access to heavenly revelation (καὶ ἠνοίχθησαν οἱ οὐρανοί, καὶ εἶδον ὁράσεις θεοῦ [Ezek 1:1]; ὄψεσθε τὸν οὐρανὸν ἀνεῳγότα [John 1:51]; Ἰδοὺ θεωρῶ τοὺς οὐρανοὺς διηνοιγμένους καὶ τὸν υἱὸν τοῦ ἀνθρώπου ἐκ δεξιῶν ἑστῶτα τοῦ θεοῦ [Acts 7:56]; καὶ θεωρεῖ τὸν οὐρανὸν ἀνεῳγμένον καὶ καταβααῖνον σκεῦός τι [Acts 10:11]).

An opened heaven is also used to describe instances where God intervenes in earthly affairs through manna (Ps 77:23 [78:23 EVV]: καὶ θύρας οὐρανοῦ ἀνέῳξεν) or the descent of the Spirit on Jesus (Matt 3:16: καὶ ἰδοὺ ἠνεῴχθησαν οἱ οὐρανοί).

Use of the OT: Similar language is used to describe how Moses went up to meet with God at Sinai (καὶ ἐκάλεσεν κύριος Μωυσῆν . . . καὶ ἀνέβη Μωυσῆς [Exod 19:20]; ἀνάβηθι σὺ καὶ Ααρων μετὰ σοῦ [Exod 19:24]). On the allusion to Dan 2:28, 29, 45 see 1:1, 19.

4:2 εὐθέως (temp. adv., "immediately") **ἐγενόμην** (1st sg. aor. mid. ind. of γίνομαι) **ἐν πνεύματι** (loc. or manner, cf. Ezek 43:5; the prep. phrase suggests a visionary experience, see 1:10), **καὶ ἰδοὺ** (emph. interj. introducing something new [BDAG 468b]) **θρόνος** (subj. nom.) **ἔκειτο** (3rd sg. impf. mid./pass. ind. of κεῖμαι, "recline, be set, be appointed," in the sense here of "a throne was set") **ἐν τῷ οὐρανῷ** (loc.), **καὶ ἐπὶ τὸν** (anaphoric art.) **θρόνον** (loc.) **καθήμενος** (nom. sg. masc. of pres. mid. ptc. of κάθημαι, subst. ptc., "[there was] one sitting"),

The image of God on his throne significantly anchors future visions; all that happens does so under the authority of God (4:9; 5:1, 7, 13; 6:16; 7:10, 15; 19:4; 21:5).

Use of the OT: The image of God sitting on his throne occurs throughout the OT. In 3 Kgdms 22:19 [1 Kgs 22:19 EVV] the prophet Micaiah εἶδον τὸν κύριον θεὸν Ισραηλ καθήμενον ἐπὶ θρόνου αὐτοῦ (cf. 2 Chr 18:18). Psalms 46:9 LXX (47:8 EVV) claims that God sits on his holy throne (ὁ θεὸς κάθηται ἐπὶ θρόνου ἁγίου αὐτοῦ). Isaiah saw God on his throne (6:1: εἶδον τὸν κύριον καθήμενον ἐπὶ θρόνου ὑψηλοῦ καὶ ἐπηρμένου). Ezekiel saw the likeness of a sapphire throne with the likeness of a man on it (1:26: ὡς ὅρασις λίθου σαπφείρου ὁμοίωμα θρόνου ἐπ' αὐτοῦ, καὶ ἐπὶ τοῦ ὁμοιώματος τοῦ θρόνου ὁμοίωμα ὡς εἶδος ἀνθρώπου ἄνωθεν). Sirach 1:8 describes God as one who is wise, exceedingly fearful, and sitting on his throne (εἷς ἐστιν σοφός, φοβερὸς σφόδρα, καθήμενος ἐπὶ τοῦ θρόνου αὐτοῦ).

4:3 καὶ ὁ (anaphoric to 4:2) **καθήμενος** (nom. sg. masc. of pres. mid. ptc. of κάθημαι, subst., subj. of verbless cl.) **ὅμοιος** (ὅμοιος, -οία, -οιον, "like, similar," comp. pred. adj. "[was] like") **ὁράσει** (ὅρασις, -εως, ἡ, "appearance, vision," dat. of reference, "was like a stone with regard to appearance") **λίθῳ** (comp., the dat. often follows adj. of "likeness" [Wallace 174]) **ἰάσπιδι** (ἴασπις, -ιδος, ἡ, "jasper," the word could denote an opaque precious stone of any color and does not correspond directly to modern understandings of jasper [BDAG 465c], attrib.) **καὶ σαρδίῳ** (σάρδιον, -ου, τό, "sardius, a reddish precious stone" [BDAG 913d], attrib.), **καὶ ἶρις** (ἶρις, -ιδος, ἡ, "a band of light, rainbow," subj. nom. of verbless cl.) **κυκλόθεν** (improper prep., "around") **τοῦ** (anaphoric to 4:2) **θρόνου** (loc.) **ὅμοιος** (comp. pred. adj.) **ὁράσει** (dat. of reference) **σμαραγδίνῳ** (σμαράγδινος, -η, -ον, "emerald, a bright green transparent precious stone" [BDAG 933b–c], subst.).

The stones point to and express God's glory and are also part of God's new creation (21:10–11, 18–23).

Use of the OT: Ezekiel's throne vision in Ezek 1:28 also notes a rainbow (ὡς ὅρασις τόξου, ὅταν ᾖ ἐν τῇ νεφέλῃ ἐν ἡμέρᾳ ὑετοῦ). It is possible that the rainbow recalls God's covenant with Noah, but the Ezek 1:28 allusion more likely explains the presence of the rainbow.

4:4 καὶ κυκλόθεν (improper prep., "around") **τοῦ** (anaphoric to 4:2) **θρόνου** (loc.) **θρόνους** (dir. obj. of implied εἶδον) **εἴκοσι** ("twenty") **τέσσαρες** ("four"), **καὶ ἐπὶ τοὺς θρόνους** (loc.) **εἴκοσι τέσσαρας πρεσβυτέρους** (coord. dir. obj. of implied εἶδον) **καθημένους** (acc. pl. masc. of pres. mid. ptc. of κάθημαι, attrib. ptc.) **περιβεβλημένους** (acc. pl. masc. of pf. pass. ptc. of περιβάλλω, "wrap, clothe," attrib.) **ἐν ἱματίοις** (manner) **λευκοῖς** (λευκός, -ή, -όν, "white, bright," attrib.) **καὶ ἐπὶ τὰς κεφαλὰς** (loc.) **αὐτῶν** (poss.) **στεφάνους** (στέφανος, -ου, ὁ, "wreath, crown, prize," dir. obj.) **χρυσοῦς** (χρυσοῦς, -ῆ, -οῦν, "golden," attrib.).

The switch from nom. to acc. nouns in 4:4 seems abrupt but makes sense if we assume an unwritten εἶδον (perhaps implied from 4:1 [Moţ 151]). The nom. nouns in 4:1–3 are required by ἰδού while εἶδον requires acc. dir. objects. The numeral τέσσαρες is nom. in form but there are many contemporary examples of this nom. functioning as an acc. as it does here (Moţ 151). The description and activity of the elders in this vision of the divine counsel indicates that they are either "heavenly representatives of God's people" (Koester 360) or "a council of heavenly beings who surround God's throne" (Fanning 200–201).

Use of the OT: Isaiah 24:23 describes how God will be glorified before the elders (ὅτι βασιλεύσει κύριος ἐν Σιων καὶ ἐν Ιερουσαλημ καὶ ἐνώπιον τῶν πρεσβυτέρων δοξασθήσεται). The number twenty-four can be explained as an allusion to the union of the twelve tribes of Israel with the twelve apostles, the orders of priests (1 Chr 24:4), the Levitical worship leaders (1 Chr 25:9–31), or the Levitical gatekeepers (1 Chr 26:17–18).

4:5 καὶ ἐκ τοῦ (anaphoric to 4:2) **θρόνου** (source) **ἐκπορεύονται** (3rd pl. pres. mid. ind. of ἐκπορεύομαι, narrative pres.) **ἀστραπαὶ** (ἀστραπή, -ῆς, ἡ, "lightning," subj. nom.) **καὶ φωναὶ** (φωνή, -ῆς, ἡ, coord. subj. nom.) **καὶ βρονταί** (βροντή, -ῆς, ἡ, "thunder," coord. subj. nom.), **καὶ ἑπτὰ** ("seven," attrib.) **λαμπάδες** (λαμπάς, -άδος, ἡ, "torch, lamp," subj. nom. of verbless cl., ant. of ἅ) **πυρὸς** (attrib.) **καιόμεναι** (nom. pl. fem. of pres. pass. ptc. of καίω, "burn, light," attrib.) **ἐνώπιον τοῦ** (anaphoric to 4:2) **θρόνου** (loc.), **ἅ** (subj. nom. rel. pron., should be fem. to match λαμπάδες but was prob. written by John as neut. to match πνεύματα) **εἰσιν** (3rd pl. pres. act. ind. of εἰμί) **τὰ ἑπτὰ** (attrib.) **πνεύματα** (pred. nom.) **τοῦ θεοῦ** (gen. of source or poss.),

The lightning, sounds, and thunder alluding to Exod 19:16 occur at the end of each series of seven judgments (8:5; 11:19; 16:18); this connection links each of those series of judgments to the divine throne.

Use of the OT: When God descends on Sinai in Exod 19:16 there are sounds and lightning along with a dark cloud and the sound of a trumpet (καὶ ἐγίνοντο φωναὶ καὶ ἀστραπαὶ καὶ νεφέλη γνοφώδης ἐπ' ὄρους Σινα, φωνὴ τῆς σάλπιγγος ἤχει μέγα). Descriptions of theophanies often feature earthquakes, thunder, lightning, and dark clouds (Judg 5:4–5; Pss 18:7–15; 68:7–9; 77:17–18; Isa 13:13; 64:1–3; Jer 10:10; Hag 2:6–7, 21). Descriptions of theophanies accompanied by cosmic upheaval generally draw from the Sinai account and often occur in prophetic descriptions of future judgment. Ezekiel sees burning coals of fire like the appearance of lamps in the midst of the four living creatures (1:13: καὶ ἐν μέσῳ τῶν ζῴων ὅρασις ὡς ἀνθράκων πυρὸς καιομένων, ὡς ὄψις λαμπάδων; the MT, in contrast, describes the living creatures as the coals of fire like lamps). In Zech 4:2 the Spirit is connected with a lampstand with seven lamps (καὶ ἑπτὰ λύχνοι ἐπάνω αὐτῆς).

4:6 καὶ ἐνώπιον τοῦ (anaphoric to 4:2) **θρόνου** (loc.) **ὡς** (comp.) **θάλασσα** (the comp. cl. functions as subj. of a verbless cl.) **ὑαλίνη** (ὑάλινος, -η, -ον, "made of glass," attrib.) **ὁμοία** (ὅμοιος, -οία, -οιον, "like, similar," comp.) **κρυστάλλῳ** (κρύσταλλος, -ου, ὁ, "crystal"). **Καὶ ἐν μέσῳ** (loc.) **τοῦ** (anaphoric to 4:2) **θρόνου** (loc.) **καὶ κύκλῳ** (improper prep., "around") **τοῦ** (anaphoric to 4:2) **θρόνου** (loc.) **τέσσαρα** ("four," attrib.) **ζῷα** (ζῷον, -ου, τό, "animal, living thing," subj. nom. of verbless cl.) **γέμοντα** (nom. pl. neut. of pres. act. ptc. of γέμω, "be full," attrib. ptc.) **ὀφθαλμῶν** (gen. of content) **ἔμπροσθεν** (adv., "front, before") **καὶ ὄπισθεν** (adv., "back, behind").

The floor of the divine throne room appeared to John like a glass sea. The seemingly paradoxical combination of ἐν μέσῳ τοῦ θρόνου καὶ κύκλῳ τοῦ θρόνου suggests close proximity to the throne (see below on many OT descriptions of God being enthroned above the cherubim). Some interpreters draw various significances from the number four, but it is highly likely that the number is simply derived here from Ezek 1:4–14 (see below) and no further significance should be sought. The number explicitly links these angelic throne creatures with those in Ezekiel.

Use of the OT: Ezekiel 1:22 describes the expanse above the living creatures supporting God's throne ὡς ὅρασις κρυστάλλου. Solomon's temple also had a metal sea (3 Kgdms 7:10 [1 Kgs 7:23 EVV]: ἐποίησεν τὴν θάλασσαν). There are many similarities and differences between the four living beings in Revelation and those in Ezek 1:5–10; 10:14 and the seraphim in Isa 6:1–6. In Ezekiel, each living being (ὡς ὁμοίωμα τεσσάρων ζῴων) has four faces (man, lion, ox [cherub in 10:14], eagle) and four wings (Ezek 1:6) and their hands and wings are full of eyes all around (10:12: πλήρεις ὀφθαλμῶν κυκλόθεν; cf. the wheels in Ezek 1:18). In Isaiah the unnumbered seraphim have six wings (Isa 6:2). The living beings in Revelation have characteristics from both Ezekiel's cherubim (Ezek 10:1–20; 11:22) and Isaiah's seraphim (Isa 6:2) suggesting the same or similar angelic beings were in mind; in each case they are closely connected with God's throne. The cherubim were a central feature of both the tabernacle (Exod 25:18–22; 37:7–9; Num 7:89) and the temple (1 Kgs 6:23–28; 8:6–7; 1 Chr 28:18; 2 Chr 3:10–11, 13; 5:7–8) with embroidery of cherubim in the curtains and veil of the tabernacle (Exod 26:1, 31; 36:8, 35) and engravings and embroidery of cherubim around all the walls, doors, and veil of the temple (1 Kgs 6:29, 32, 35; 7:29, 36; 2 Chr 3:7, 14). God is described as being enthroned above the cherubim (1 Sam 4:4; 2 Sam 6:2; 2 Kgs 19:15; 1 Chr 13:6; Pss 80:1; 99:1; Isa 37:16). This close connection of cherubim with the ark, tabernacle, temple, and God's throne supports the identification of God's throne room as the heavenly temple in Revelation.

4:7 καὶ τὸ ζῷον (ζῷον, -ου, τό, "animal, living thing," each occurrence of ζῷον in this verse is subj. nom. of verbless cl.) **τὸ πρῶτον** (attrib.) **ὅμοιον** (ὅμοιος, -οία, -οιον, "like, similar," pred. adj., comp., "[was] like") **λέοντι** (λέων, -οντος, ὁ, "lion") **καὶ τὸ δεύτερον** (attrib., "second") **ζῷον ὅμοιον μόσχῳ** (μόσχος, -ου, ὁ, "calf") **καὶ τὸ τρίτον** (attrib., "third") **ζῷον ἔχων** (nom. sg. masc. of pres. act. ptc. of ἔχω, ptc. functioning as finite vb., the masc. ptc. does not match the neut. noun ζῷον, perhaps as a *constructio ad sensum* because John viewed the living being as personal) **τὸ πρόσωπον** (dir. obj.) **ὡς** (comp.) **ἀνθρώπου καὶ τὸ τέταρτον** (attrib., "fourth") **ζῷον ὅμοιον ἀετῷ** (ἀετός, -οῦ, ὁ, "eagle, vulture") **πετομένῳ** (dat. sg. masc. of mid. act. ptc. of πέτομαι, "fly," attrib.).

The four faces represent human beings, wild animals, domesticated animals, and flying animals. Although not exhaustive, this collection seems to reflect God's creation.

Use of the OT: See 4:6.

4:8 καὶ τὰ (anaphoric to 4:6) **τέσσαρα** ("four," attrib.) **ζῷα** (ζῷον, -ου, τό, "animal, living thing," subj. nom.), **ἓν καθ' ἓν** (idiomatic distributive expression for "each one" [BDAG 58a]) **αὐτῶν** (part. gen.) **ἔχων** (nom. sg. masc. of pres. act. ptc. of ἔχω, functioning as finite vb., the masc. ptc. does not match the neut. noun ζῷον, perhaps because John viewed the living being as personal, see 4:7) **ἀνὰ** (redundant distributive adv., "each")

πτέρυγας (πτέρυξ, -υγος, ἡ, "wing," dir. obj.) **ἓξ** ("six," attrib.), **κυκλόθεν** (adv. of place, "around") **καὶ ἔσωθεν** (adv., "inside") **γέμουσιν** (3rd pl. pres. act. ind. of γέμω, "be full") **ὀφθαλμῶν** (gen. of content), **καὶ ἀνάπαυσιν** (ἀνάπαυσις, -εως, ἡ, "rest," dir. obj.) **οὐκ ἔχουσιν** (3rd pl. pres. act. ind. of ἔχω) **ἡμέρας** (gen. of time) **καὶ νυκτὸς** (gen. of time) **λέγοντες** (nom. pl. masc. of pres. act. ptc. of λέγω; seems to express the cause or reason that they do not have rest although Wallace notes that a causal ptc. normally precedes the vb. [Wallace 631]; Mathewson identifies it as manner which answers "how" they do not have rest [Math 65]; introduces dir. speech)· **Ἅγιος** (pred. adj.) **ἅγιος ἅγιος κύριος** (subj. nom. of verbless cl.) **ὁ θεὸς** (appos. to κύριος) **ὁ παντοκράτωρ** (appos. to κύριος, "almighty"), **ὁ** (substantivizer) **ἦν** (3rd sg. impf. act. ind. of εἰμί; appos. to κύριος; on this expression, see 1:4) **καὶ ὁ ὢν** (nom. sg. masc. of pres. act. ptc. of εἰμί, appos. to κύριος) **καὶ ὁ ἐρχόμενος** (nom. sg. masc. of pres. mid. ptc. of ἔρχομαι, appos. to κύριος).

Use of the OT: The seraphim in Isa 6:3 call out Ἅγιος ἅγιος ἅγιος κύριος σαβαωθ, πλήρης πᾶσα ἡ γῆ τῆς δόξης αὐτοῦ. Amos 3:13 and 4:13 describe God as κύριος ὁ θεὸς ὁ παντοκράτωρ. For Isa 41:4 and Exod 3:14, see 1:4.

4:9 καὶ ὅταν (temp. indef. conj., "whenever") **δώσουσιν** (3rd pl. fut. act. ind. of δίδωμι, John uses the fut. instead of the expected subjunc.; see 3:9) **τὰ** (anaphoric to 4:6) **ζῷα** (ζῷον, -ου, τό, "animal, living thing," subj. nom.) **δόξαν** (dir. obj.) **καὶ τιμὴν** (τιμή, -ῆς, ἡ, "honor," coord. dir. obj.) **καὶ εὐχαριστίαν** (εὐχαριστία, -ας, ἡ, "thanksgiving," coord. dir. obj.) **τῷ** (anaphoric to 4:2) **καθημένῳ** (dat. sg. masc. of pres. mid. ptc. of κάθημαι, subst., indir. obj.) **ἐπὶ τῷ** (anaphoric to 4:2) **θρόνῳ** (loc.) **τῷ ζῶντι** (dat. sg. masc. of pres. act. ptc. of ζάω, subst. ptc. in appos. to καθημένῳ or attrib. ptc.) **εἰς τοὺς αἰῶνας** (temp. acc. of measure) **τῶν αἰώνων** (emph. repetition of αἰών),

Mathewson suggests that since ὅταν in Revelation normally refers to "something specific in the context (8:1, 10:7, 11:7, 12:4, 17:10, 18:9, 20:7)" it probably refers to the worship recounted in 5:13–14 (Math 66). It is also possible that it refers implicitly to scenes of worship throughout Revelation.

Use of the OT: Daniel 12:7 describes God as the one who lives into the age (τὸν ζῶντα εἰς τὸν αἰῶνα θεὸν; cf. Dan 4:34 MT; 6:27 LXX [6:26 EVV]).

4:10 πεσοῦνται (3rd pl. fut. mid. ind. of πίπτω) **οἱ** (anaphoric to 4:4) **εἴκοσιν** ("twenty") **τέσσαρες** ("four") **πρεσβύτεροι** (subj. nom.) **ἐνώπιον** (improper prep., loc., "before") **τοῦ** (anaphoric to 4:2) **καθημένου** (gen. sg. masc. of pres. mid. ptc. of κάθημαι, subst.) **ἐπὶ τοῦ** (anaphoric to 4:2) **θρόνου** (loc.) **καὶ προσκυνήσουσιν** (3rd pl. fut. act. ind. of προσκυνέω) **τῷ ζῶντι** (dat. sg. masc. of pres. act. ptc. of ζάω, subst., dat. dir. obj.) **εἰς τοὺς αἰῶνας**

(measure) **τῶν αἰώνων** (emph. repetition of αἰών) **καὶ βαλοῦσιν** (3rd pl. fut. act. ind. of βάλλω, normally glossed as "throw" but could also mean "put" or "place" depending upon the context [BDAG 163d]) **τοὺς στεφάνους** (στέφανος, -ου, ὁ, "wreath, crown, prize," dir. obj.) **αὐτῶν** (poss.) **ἐνώπιον τοῦ** (anaphoric to 4:2) **θρόνου** (loc.) **λέγοντες** (nom. pl. masc. of pres. act. ptc. of λέγω, adv. ptc. of manner, introduces dir. speech), **4:11 Ἄξιος** (ἄξιος, -ία, -ον "worthy," pred. adj.) **εἶ** (2nd sg. pres. act. ind. of εἰμί), **ὁ κύριος** (nom. for voc. [Wallace 56–59]) **καὶ ὁ θεὸς** (coord. nom. for voc.) **ἡμῶν** (subord.), **λαβεῖν** (aor. act. inf. of λαμβάνω, epex. inf. [Math 68]) **τὴν δόξαν** (dir. obj.) **καὶ τὴν τιμὴν** (τιμή, -ῆς, ἡ, "honor," coord. dir. obj.) **καὶ τὴν δύναμιν** (coord. dir. obj.), **ὅτι** (causal) **σὺ** (emph. subj. nom.) **ἔκτισας** (2nd sg. aor. act. ind. of κτίζω, "create") **τὰ πάντα** (dir. obj.) **καὶ διὰ τὸ θέλημά** (causal) **σου** (subj. gen.) **ἦσαν** (3rd pl. impf. act. ind. of εἰμί) **καὶ ἐκτίσθησαν** (3rd pl. aor. pass. ind. of κτίζω).

The logical difficulty of having ἦσαν before ἐκτίσθησαν "was alleviated in several witnesses either by reading οὐκ ἦσαν or by omitting ἦσαν καί" (Metzger 665). The final hymn of Revelation 4 affirms God's worthiness to receive worship because he was the one who created it all. This affirmation of God as the creator is significant throughout Revelation (3:14; 10:6; 14:7) because the seals, trumpets, and bowls narrate a de-creation, while Revelation 21–22 narrate God's new creation of a new heaven and earth. The affirmation of God's role in original creation affirms our belief that he is indeed powerful and able enough to recreate (21:5). The acclamation ὁ κύριος καὶ ὁ θεὸς ἡμῶν is in contrast to the acclamation, *dominus et deus noster*, which was used to address the emperor Domitian (Suetonius, *Domitian*, 13).

FOR FURTHER STUDY

26. The Throne Room (4:1–11)

*Aune, D. E. "The Influence of Roman Imperial Court Ceremonial on the Apocalypse of John." *BR* 28 (1983): 5–26.

Gallusz, L. *The Throne Motif in the Book of Revelation*. LNTS 487. London: T&T Clark, 2014.

Morton, R. S. *One upon the Throne and the Lamb: A Tradition Historical/Theological Analysis of Revelation 4–5*. StBibLit 110. New York: Lang, 2007.

———. "Glory to God and to the Lamb: John's Use of Jewish and Hellenistic Roman Themes in Formatting his Theology in Revelation 4–5." *JSNT* 83 (2001): 89–109.

27. Worship

Bauckham, R. "Creation's Praise of God in the Book of Revelation." *BTB* 38 (2008): 55–63.

Grabiner, S. *Revelation's Hymns: Commentary on the Cosmic Conflict*. LNTS 511. London: T&T Clark, 2015.

Massyngberde, F. J. "The Christological Function of the Hymns in the Apocalypse of John." *AUSS* 36 (1998): 207–29.

O'Rourke, J. J. "The Hymns of the Apocalypse." *CBQ* 30 (1968): 400–422.

Rand, J. A. du. "'Now the Salvation of Our God Has Come . . .' A Narrative Perspective on the Hymns in Revelation 12–15." *Neot* 27 (1993): 313–30.

Schedtler, J. J. *A Heavenly Chorus: The Dramatic Function of Revelation's Hymns*. WUNT 2.381. Tübingen: Mohr Siebeck, 2014.

———. "Praising Christ the King: Royal Discourse and Ideology in Revelation 5." *NovT* 60 (2018): 162–82.

Schimanowski, G. "Connecting Heaven and Earth: The Function of the Hymns in Revelation 4–5." Pages 67–84 in *Heavenly Realms and Earthly Realities in Late Antique Religions*. Edited by R. S. Boustan and A. Y. Reed. Cambridge: Cambridge University Press, 2004.

28. Numbers

Collins, A. Y. "Numerical Symbolism in Jewish and Early Christian Apocalyptic Literature." Pages 1221–87 in *Aufstieg und Niedergang der römischen Welt* II.21.2. Edited by W. Haase. Berlin: de Gruyter, 1984.

Resseguie, J. L. "Narrative Features of the Book of Revelation." Pages 37–52 in *OHR*.

HOMILETICAL SUGGESTIONS

Chapter 4 focuses on God enthroned. This would be an ideal point in the sermon series to discuss the different occurrences of the throne in Revelation; it is a key image in the visions for God's rule and reign. Both judicial and saving acts flow from the authority of the one sitting on the throne. John's vision provides a true picture of God's rule, which is stable, secure, and universal even though we experience chaos and danger in our day-to-day lives because God's rule is currently contested on earth (2:13) and rejected by many in the present time.

God, the True Ruler of the Universe (4:1–11)

1. God is ruling (4:1–6a).
2. God is holy (4:6b–8).
3. God is worthy (4:9–11).

2. Enthronement of the Lamb (5:1–14)

5:1 Καὶ εἶδον (1st sg. aor. act. ind. of ὁράω; καὶ εἶδον introduces a new vision, scene, figure, or activity [Aune[a] 338]) **ἐπὶ τὴν δεξιὰν** (δεξιός, -ά, -όν, "right [hand]," subst., loc.) **τοῦ** (anaphoric to 4:2) **καθημένου** (gen. sg. masc. of pres. mid. ptc. of κάθημαι, subst., poss.) **ἐπὶ τοῦ** (anaphoric to 4:2) **θρόνου** (loc.) **βιβλίον** (βιβλίον, -ου, τό, "scroll," dir. obj. of εἶδον) **γεγραμμένον** (acc. sg. neut. of pf. pass. ptc. of γράφω, attrib.) **ἔσωθεν** (adv. of place, "inside") **καὶ ὄπισθεν** (adv. of place, "back, behind") **κατεσφραγισμένον** (acc. sg. neut. of pf. pass. ptc. of κατασφραγίζω, "seal," attrib.) **σφραγῖσιν** (σφραγίς, ῖδος, ἡ, "seal," cognate dat. of means, "with") **ἑπτά** ("seven," attrib.).

This chapter can be structured by four occurrences of the phrase καὶ εἶδον: John saw a scroll (5:1), a mighty angel (5:2), a lamb (5:6), and a worshipping multitude (5:11 [Fanning 211]).

The scroll seems to contain the unfolding of God's plan for human history set in motion by Jesus's death, resurrection, ascension, and enthronement. If it could not be opened, God's plan would not be able to proceed. Having seven seals, the scroll is completely secured and the writing on both sides is modeled on Ezek 2:10 (see below) and probably indicates comprehensiveness.

Use of the OT: Isaiah describes his vision as a scroll that has been sealed (οἱ λόγοι τοῦ βιβλίου τοῦ ἐσφραγισμένου τούτου) and cannot be read (Isa 29:11). The scroll that Ezekiel is commanded to eat was written on the front and on the back (2:10: καὶ ἐν αὐτῇ γεγραμμένα ἦν τὰ ὄπισθεν καὶ τὰ ἔμπροσθεν). Daniel is commanded to seal the scroll until the time of completion (12:4: κάλυψον τὰ προστάγματα καὶ σφράγισαι τὸ βιβλίον ἕως καιροῦ συντελείας [cf. Dan 12:9]). In Isaiah, Ezekiel, and Daniel the sealed scroll seems to relate to the content of their prophetic activity regarding God's future actions to bring judgment and salvation. The breaking of the seals in Revelation would suggest that the time of completion had come with the enthronement of the Messiah.

5:2 καὶ εἶδον (1st sg. aor. act. ind. of ὁράω; καὶ εἶδον introduces a new vision, scene, figure, or activity [Aune[a] 338]) **ἄγγελον** (dir. obj.) **ἰσχυρὸν** (ἰσχυρός, -ά, -όν, "strong," attrib.) **κηρύσσοντα** (acc. sg. masc. of pres. act. ptc. of κηρύσσω, attrib.) **ἐν φωνῇ** (means) **μεγάλῃ** (attrib.), **Τίς** (interr. pron.) **ἄξιος** (ἄξιος, -ία, -ον, "worthy," pred. adj. of verbless cl.) **ἀνοῖξαι** (aor. act. inf. of ἀνοίγω, epex. inf.) **τὸ** (anaphoric to 5:1) **βιβλίον** (βιβλίον, -ου, τό, "scroll," dir. obj.) **καὶ** (epex., "that is" [Aune[a] 322]) **λῦσαι** (aor. act. inf. of λύω, coord. epex. inf.) **τὰς** (anaphoric to 5:1) **σφραγῖδας** (σφραγίς, -ῖδος, ἡ, "seal," dir. obj.) **αὐτοῦ** (poss.);

The opening of the scroll is stated before the breaking of the seals for emph. (Math 70). The use of questions in contexts featuring the divine council function to move the narrative forward (1 Kgs 22:20–21; Isa 6:8), while questions in visionary experiences clarify the significance or meaning of what has been visually seen (Dan 8:13–14; 10:20; 12:5–13; Zech 4–5 [Fanning 214–15]).

5:3 καὶ οὐδεὶς (subj. nom.) **ἐδύνατο** (3rd sg. impf. mid. ind. of δύναμαι, the use of the impf. in narratives normally provides information offline from the main storyline [Math 70]) **ἐν τῷ οὐρανῷ** (loc.) **οὐδὲ** (neg. disjunctive conj., "neither . . . nor") **ἐπὶ τῆς γῆς** (loc.) **οὐδὲ ὑποκάτω** (improper prep., "under") **τῆς γῆς** (loc.) **ἀνοῖξαι** (aor. act. inf. of ἀνοίγω, compl. inf. with ἐδύνατο) **τὸ** (anaphoric to 5:1) **βιβλίον** (βιβλίον, -ου, τό, "scroll," dir. obj.) **οὔτε** (neg. disjunctive conj., "nor") **βλέπειν** (pres. act. inf. of βλέπω, compl. inf.) **αὐτό** (dir. obj.).

The tripartite division of the universe is a traditional way to describe the totality of God's creation, although the elements are normally heaven, the earth, and the sea (Exod 20:11; Ps 146:6; Acts 4:24; 14:15). Similarly, John normally prefers to include the sea instead of "under the earth" as the third element (10:6; 12:12; 14:7 [adds the springs of water as a fourth element]; 21:1; note the inclusion of all four elements in 5:13 and Job 11:8–9 through two sets of contrasts). Deuteronomy mentions the third element as the waters under the earth (5:8: ὅσα ἐν τοῖς ὕδασιν ὑποκάτω τῆς γῆς); this probably led to the variation in the third element observed in later authors. Paul's tripartite description in Phil 2:10 parallels Rev 5:3.

5:4 καὶ (result: "and so" [BDAG 495a]) **ἔκλαιον** (1st sg. impf. act. ind. of κλαίω, "weep," the context suggests an inceptive impf.) **πολύ** (adv. use of the adj. to express manner), **ὅτι** (causal) **οὐδεὶς** (subj. nom.) **ἄξιος** (ἄξιος, -ία, -ον, "worthy," pred. adj. in a double nom. construction: "no one was found *to be* worthy" [cf. Math 71]) **εὑρέθη** (3rd sg. aor. pass. ind. of εὑρίσκω) **ἀνοῖξαι** (aor. act. inf. of ἀνοίγω, epex. inf.) **τὸ** (anaphoric to 5:1) **βιβλίον** (βιβλίον, -ου, τό, "scroll," dir. obj.) **οὔτε** (neg. disjunctive conj., "nor") **βλέπειν** (pres. act. inf. of βλέπω, epex. inf.) **αὐτό** (dir. obj.).

5:5 καὶ εἷς ("one," subst., subj. nom.) **ἐκ τῶν** (anaphoric to 4:4) **πρεσβυτέρων** (part.) **λέγει** (3rd sg. pres. act. ind. of λέγω, narrative pres.; Fanning suggests the historical present is generally anticipatory or cataphoric and highlights the following event or statement [Fanning 216]) **μοι** (indir. obj.), **Μὴ κλαῖε** (2nd sg. pres. act. impv. of κλαίω, "weep," the context indicates that this is a prohibition of an action in progress), **ἰδοὺ** (emph. interj.) **ἐνίκησεν** (3rd sg. aor. act. ind. of νικάω, "overcome, conquer," consummative [Wallace 560], fronted for emph.) **ὁ λέων** (λέων, -οντος, ὁ, "lion," subj. nom.) **ὁ** (adjectivizer; the following prep. phrase functions as attrib. adj.) **ἐκ τῆς φυλῆς** (φυλή, -ῆς, ἡ, "tribe, nation," gen. of source) **Ἰούδα** (epex. to φυλῆς), **ἡ ῥίζα** (ῥίζα, -ης, ἡ, "root," used as imagery for "descendent" [BDAG 906a], appos. to λέων) **Δαυίδ** (gen. of source, "David"), **ἀνοῖξαι** (aor. act. inf. of ἀνοίγω, inf. of result) **τὸ βιβλίον** (βιβλίον, -ου, τό, "scroll," dir. obj.) **καὶ τὰς** (anaphoric to 5:1) **ἑπτὰ** ("seven," attrib.) **σφραγῖδας** (σφραγίς, -ῖδος, ἡ, "seal," coord. dir. obj.) **αὐτοῦ** (poss.).

In Rev 22:16 Jesus describes himself as ἡ ῥίζα καὶ τὸ γένος Δαυίδ. Note the difference between what John hears with his ears (5:5) and sees with his eyes (5:6). He hears a description that would fit expectations of a political and militaristic Jewish messianic conqueror, and he sees a slain lamb. What he sees interprets what he hears and vice versa, but the juxtaposition of what he sees and hears is unexpected, paradoxical, or seemingly contradictory. This hearing-seeing literary technique is used at key points in 1:12; 5:5–6; 7:2–9; 21:9–10. The lamb does not replace the lion; both are appropriate images for Jesus. The conquering lion helps us recognize this figure as the Messiah promised throughout the Old Testament and affirms that God's Messiah has conquered evil. The slain lamb shows us how he conquered evil.

Use of the OT: In Gen 49:9, Jacob prophesies concerning Judah that he is the cub of a lion (σκύμνος λέοντος Ιουδα), which is interpreted as future rule (Gen 49:10). Isaiah 11:1 prophesies that a staff will come out of the root of Jesse and a bloom will come up out of the root (Καὶ ἐξελεύσεται ῥάβδος ἐκ τῆς ῥίζης Ιεσσαι, καὶ ἄνθος ἐκ τῆς ῥίζης ἀναβήσεται). Isaiah 11:10 prophesies that in that day the root of Jesse will rise up to rule the nations and the nations will hope in him (Καὶ ἔσται ἐν τῇ ἡμέρᾳ ἐκείνῃ ἡ ῥίζα τοῦ Ιεσσαι καὶ ὁ ἀνιστάμενος ἄρχειν ἐθνῶν, ἐπ' αὐτῷ ἔθνη ἐλπιοῦσιν). The introduction of the lamb in Rev 5:6 presents him as the fulfillment of Gen 49:9 and Isa 11:1, 10.

5:6 Καὶ εἶδον (1st sg. aor. act. ind. of ὁράω; καὶ εἶδον introduces a new vision, scene, figure, or activity [Aune[a] 338]) **ἐν μέσῳ** (loc., "among" [BDAG 635b–c]) **τοῦ** (anaphoric to 4:2) **θρόνου** (loc.) **καὶ τῶν** (anaphoric to 4:6) **τεσσάρων** (τέσσαρες, "four," attrib.) **ζῴων** (ζῷον, -ου, τό, "animal, living thing," loc.) **καὶ ἐν μέσῳ** (loc.) **τῶν** (anaphoric to 4:4) **πρεσβυτέρων** (loc.) **ἀρνίον** (ἀρνίον, -ου, τό, "lamb," dir. obj. of εἶδον) **ἑστηκὸς** (acc. sg. neut. of pf. act. ptc. of ἵστημι, compl. in double acc. construction, "I saw a lamb *to be* standing") **ὡς** (comp.) **ἐσφαγμένον** (acc. sg. neut. of pf. pass. ptc. of σφάζω, "slaughter" or kill with violence [BDAG 979d], subst.) **ἔχων** (nom. sg. masc. of pres. act. ptc. of ἔχω) **κέρατα** (κέρας, -ατος, τό, "horn," dir. obj.) **ἑπτὰ** ("seven," attrib.) **καὶ ὀφθαλμοὺς** (dir. obj., ant. of οἵ) **ἑπτὰ** (attrib.) **οἵ** (subj. nom., rel. pron.) **εἰσιν** (3rd pl. pres. act. ind. of εἰμί) **τὰ [ἑπτὰ]** (the brackets indicate that the external and internal evidence is evenly split; it may have been omitted accidently because of the prior two occurrences of ἑπτά in 5:6 or added because of 1:4; 3:1; 4:5 [Metzger 666]) **πνεύματα** (pred. nom.) **τοῦ θεοῦ** (gen. of source or poss.) **ἀπεσταλμένοι** (nom. pl. masc. of pf. pass. ptc., of ἀποστέλλω, attrib., should be neut. to match πνεύματα but is masc. as a *constructio ad sensum* reflecting John's choice to present the πνεύματα as personal beings) **εἰς πᾶσαν** (attrib.) **τὴν γῆν** (loc.).

The location of the lamb ἐν μέσῳ τοῦ θρόνου may seem ambiguous but it indicates being seated "on the center of the throne" (BDAG 635b–c; cf. 3:21; 7:17). The lamb is on God's throne at the center of the concentric circles of the divine council. Horns are symbolically associated in Hebrew poetry with strength, the ability to overcome, authority, or an authority figure (2 Sam 22:3; Pss 18:2; 89:17, 24; 92:10; 112:9; 132:17). The nom. sg. ptc. ἔχων should be acc. to match its ant. ἀρνίον ἑστηκὸς ὡς ἐσφαγμένον. This could be explained by taking ἀρνίον ἑστηκὸς ὡς ἐσφαγμένον as nom. instead of acc. neut. This solution requires εἶδον to be intransitive but the intransitive use of εἶδον in Revelation is normally paired with καὶ ἰδοὺ (6:2, 5, 8; 14:1, 14; Moţ 123–24). It is better to see the mismatch as part of John's idiolect to put emph. upon the ptc. ἔχων.

The use of lamb imagery to interpret Jesus's death as sacrificial or salvific is common in early Christianity, but the terminology is not consistent (ἀμνός: John 1:29, 36; Acts 8:32; 1 Pet 1:19; πρόβατον: Acts 8:32, more commonly used to refer to Christians and not Christ; πάσχα: 1 Cor 5:7). "Lamb" (ἀρνίον; twenty-nine occurrences) is the most prominent christological title in the Apocalypse but its meaning is hotly debated. Interpreters suggest it is a militaristic/messianic symbol of power (Ford, *Revelation*, 88–89; T. Jos. 19:8; T. Benj. 3:8; 1 En. 89–90), a symbol of vulnerability and nonviolent resistance (Johns, *Lamb Christology*), or some form of sacrificial metaphor (Beasley-Murray, *Book of Revelation*, 125; cf. Lev 17:11). Aune wisely notes, "The major issue is whether the image of the lamb centers on its sacrificial associations (in which case John has expanded this to include other functions) or on its apocalyptic and messianic associations (in which case John has expanded this to include sacrificial imagery). However, it is not necessary to choose between these two possibilities, for it seems clear that the author of Revelation has fused *both* of these associations together in the single figure of the Lamb" (Aune[a] 368; italics original; cf. Beale 351). The Gospel of John declares that Jesus is ὁ ἀμνὸς τοῦ θεοῦ ὁ αἴρων τὴν ἁμαρτίαν τοῦ κόσμου

(John 1:29; cf. John 1:36). Paul describes Jesus in 1 Cor 5:7 as the Passover lamb who was sacrificed (καὶ γὰρ τὸ πάσχα ἡμῶν ἐτύθη Χριστός).

Use of the OT: Exodus 12:1–28 narrates the institution of the Passover in which the unblemished male lamb was slaughtered to avert God's judgment. Isaiah 53:7 speaks of the suffering servant as a sheep being led to slaughter and a silent lamb (ὡς πρόβατον ἐπὶ σφαγὴν ἤχθη καὶ ὡς ἀμνὸς . . . ἄφωνος). Zechariah 4:10 speaks of the seven eyes of the Lord looking upon all the land (ἑπτὰ οὗτοι ὀφθαλμοὶ κυρίου εἰσὶν οἱ ἐπιβλέποντες ἐπὶ πᾶσαν τὴν γῆν). Horns often express the power to conquer (Deut 33:17; 1 Kgs 22:11).

5:7 καὶ ἦλθεν (3rd sg. aor. act. ind. of ἔρχομαι) **καὶ εἴληφεν** (3rd sg. pf. act. ind. of λαμβάνω, aoristic pf., see below) **ἐκ τῆς δεξιᾶς** (δεξιός, -ά, -όν, "right [hand]," subst., gen. of separation) **τοῦ** (anaphoric to 4:2) **καθημένου** (gen. sg. masc. of pres. mid. ptc. of κάθημαι, subst., poss.) **ἐπὶ τοῦ** (anaphoric to 4:2) **θρόνου** (loc.).

Εἴληφεν is an aor. use of the pf. in narratives (see similar narratival uses of the pf. in 7:14; 8:5; 19:3). Mathewson ("Verbal Aspect in the Apocalypse," 71–74) argues that the pf. marks prominence (i.e., frontground) but Fanning argues that although the action of taking the scroll does have prominence in the narrative, it is not clear that this prominence is caused by the use of the pf.; the pf. in these four examples is rather functioning like an aor. and simply moves the mainline of the narrative along (i.e., foreground; Fanning, "Greek Tenses in John's Apocalypse," 347–48).

5:8 καὶ ὅτε (temp. conj., "when") **ἔλαβεν** (3rd sg. aor. act. ind. of λαμβάνω; the repetition of λαμβάνω from 5:7 slows down the narrative to provide emph. in what can be called "tail-head linkage" [Fanning 221]) **τὸ** (anaphoric to 5:1) **βιβλίον** (βιβλίον, -ου, τό, "scroll," dir. obj.), **τὰ** (anaphoric to 4:6) **τέσσαρα** (τέσσαρες, "four," attrib.) **ζῷα** (ζῷον, -ου, τό, "animal, living thing," subj. nom.) **καὶ οἱ** (anaphoric to 4:4) **εἴκοσι** ("twenty") **τέσσαρες** ("four") **πρεσβύτεροι** (coord. subj. nom.) **ἔπεσαν** (3rd pl. aor. act. ind. of πίπτω) **ἐνώπιον τοῦ ἀρνίου** (ἀρνίον, -ου, τό, "lamb," loc.) **ἔχοντες** (nom. pl. masc. of pres. act. ptc. of ἔχω, manner with ἔπεσαν, or attrib. with ἕκαστος) **ἕκαστος** (subj. nom., the unusual use of a sg. subj. with pl. ptc. is prob. explainable by the distributive sense of ἕκαστος [BDAG 298c]) **κιθάραν** (κιθάρα, -ας, ἡ, "lyre," dir. obj.) **καὶ φιάλας** (φιάλη, -ης, ἡ, "bowl," dir. obj., the switch from the sg. κιθάραν to the pl. φιάλας prob. indicates each one had a lyre and a bowl) **χρυσᾶς** (χρυσοῦς, -ῆ, -οῦν, "golden," attrib.) **γεμούσας** (acc. pl. fem. of pres. act. ptc. of γέμω, "be full," attrib.) **θυμιαμάτων** (θυμίαμα, -ατος, το, "incense," gen. of content, ant. of αἵ), **αἵ** (subj. nom., matches προσευχαὶ instead of its ant. in gender) **εἰσιν** (3rd pl. pres. act. ind. of εἰμί) **αἱ προσευχαὶ** (προσευχή, -ῆς, ἡ, "prayer," pred. nom.) **τῶν ἁγίων** (subst., subj. gen.),

The prayers of the saints ascend to God in 8:4 and are verbalized in 6:9–11 as a prayer for divine justice. Paul regularly describes Christians as "saints." The physical posture of worship directed toward the lamb parallels the worship of God in 4:10 (πίπτω + ἐνώπιον).

Use of the OT: Although often translated "harp," the κιθάρα was more like a lyre and was traditionally associated with praise of God (Ps 32:2 LXX [33:2 EVV]: ἐξομολογεῖσθε τῷ κυρίῳ ἐν κιθάρᾳ; Ps 97:5 LXX [98:5 EVV]: ψάλατε τῷ κυρίῳ ἐν κιθάρᾳ, ἐν κιθάρᾳ καὶ φωνῇ ψαλμοῦ; cf. 2 Chr 9:11; Pss 43:4; 57:8; 71:22; 81:2; 92:3; 108:2; 147:7; 150:3). Incense was associated with both sacrifice and prayer, and in Ps 140:2 LXX (141:2 EVV) David pleads with God to allow his prayer to be counted as incense (κατευθυνθήτω ἡ προσευχή μου ὡς θυμίαμα ἐνώπιόν σου).

5:9 καὶ ᾄδουσιν (3rd pl. pres. act. ind. of ᾄδω, "sing," narrative pres.) **ᾠδὴν** (ᾠδή, -ῆς, ἡ, "song," dir. obj., cognate acc.) **καινὴν** (attrib.) **λέγοντες** (nom. pl. masc. of pres. act. ptc. of λέγω, manner, introduces dir. speech), **Ἄξιος** (ἄξιος, -ία, -ον, "worthy," pred. adj.) **εἶ** (2nd sg. pres. act. ind. of εἰμί) **λαβεῖν** (aor. act. inf. of λαμβάνω, epex. inf.) **τὸ** (anaphoric to 5:1) **βιβλίον** (βιβλίον, -ου, τό, "scroll," dir. ob.) **καὶ ἀνοῖξαι** (aor. act. inf. of ἀνοίγω, epex. inf.) **τὰς** (anaphoric to 5:1) **σφραγῖδας** (σφραγίς, -ῖδος, ἡ, "seal," dir. obj.) **αὐτοῦ** (poss.), **ὅτι** (causal) **ἐσφάγης** (2nd sg. aor. pass. ind. of σφάζω, "slay") **καὶ ἠγόρασας** (2nd sg. aor. act. ind. of ἀγοράζω, "buy") **τῷ θεῷ** (dat. of advantage, "for") **ἐν τῷ αἵματί** (dat. of means) **σου** (poss.) **ἐκ πάσης φυλῆς** (φυλή, -ῆς, ἡ, "tribe," part. with an assumed dir. obj. τίνας, "you bought *some* out of," the same for the following three gen. nouns) **καὶ γλώσσης** (γλῶσσα, -ης, ἡ, "tongue, language") **καὶ λαοῦ καὶ ἔθνους**.

The 144,000 in 14:3 also sing a new song. New songs indicate a creative response of praise to God for deliverance or intervention (see below). Only two mss read τῷ θεῷ (A eth), but this reading best explains the others: the replacement of τῷ θεῷ with ἡμᾶς and the addition of ἡμᾶς to τῷ θεῷ (Metzger 666). The addition of ἡμᾶς helpfully provides a dir. obj. to ἠγόρασας but it contradicts αὐτούς in 5:10.

The causal cl. is theologically central; the lamb is worthy to open the scroll because he had been slain and had purchased human beings for God by his blood. The metaphor of purchase here mentions the cost (by your blood) but says nothing about to whom the price was paid; such a detail is either assumed to be known or assumed to be irrelevant to the celebration of redemption. A similar dat. of means is used in 1:5 to describe how Jesus λύσαντι ἡμᾶς ἐκ τῶν ἁμαρτιῶν ἡμῶν ἐν τῷ αἵματι αὐτοῦ. First Peter 1:18–19 describes how Christians were ransomed (λυτρόω) by the valuable blood of a lamb (τιμίῳ αἵματι ὡς ἀμνοῦ). In Rom 5:9, Paul describes how we are justified by his blood (δικαιωθέντες νῦν ἐν τῷ αἵματι αὐτοῦ) and Rom 3:25 links propitiation to his blood (ὃν προέθετο ὁ θεὸς ἱλαστήριον διὰ [τῆς] πίστεως ἐν τῷ αὐτοῦ αἵματι). Blood is generally seen as a metonymy for Jesus's death particularly well suited to sacrificial interpretation and was widely utilized in early Christianity to explain the saving benefits of Jesus's death as redemption, justification, and propitiation.

The fourfold description φυλῆς καὶ γλώσσης καὶ λαοῦ καὶ ἔθνους occurs with variation in word order seven times in Revelation (5:9; 7:9; 10:11 [βασιλεῦσιν instead of φυλή]; 11:9; 13:7; 14:6; 17:15 [ὄχλοι instead of φυλή]). The phrase describes the groups out of which Jesus purchased people for God (5:9), which comprise the uncountable multitude of the victorious before the throne (7:9), over which John is commissioned to prophesy (10:11), which view and refuse burial to the corpses of God's two witnesses (11:9), over which the beast has authority for forty-two months (13:7), to which the eternal Gospel is proclaimed (14:6), and which are under the authority or influence of the great prostitute (17:15). Unlike the expression "inhabitants of the earth," which is consistently used negatively to describe unrepentant humanity (see 3:10), this fourfold expression is used to describe all of humanity as those who are under the authority and deception of the beast and prostitute, but who hear the Gospel and must respond. Their destiny is not fixed and their response to the Gospel will determine whether they become overcomers who will be saved or inhabitants of the earth who will experience God's judgment. The fourfold expression in Revelation communicates the universality of humanity's brokenness and the inclusivity of God's salvation. No tribe, language, people, or nation is excluded; all are called upon to overcome and participate in God's new creation. This fourfold expression contributes to the missionary emph. of Revelation; a vision of people from every possible identity group being saved motivates the mission of God's people to make that future vision a present reality. Visualization of the future ideal of unity among groups that would normally be in conflict invites hearers in the present to actualize that ideal in the present time. The universal scope of God's mission is evident throughout both the OT and the NT and is succinctly expressed in the Great Commission in Matt 28:19–20.

Use of the OT: The psalmist exhorts the righteous to sing a new song to God (Ps 32:3 LXX [33:3 EVV]: ᾄσατε αὐτῷ ᾆσμα καινόν). David declares in Ps 39:4 LXX (40:3 EVV) that God put a new song in his mouth (καὶ ἐνέβαλεν εἰς τὸ στόμα μου ᾆσμα καινόν). Exhortations to sing a new song of praise occur in Pss 95:1 LXX (96:1 EVV) and 97:1 LXX (98:1 EVV) (Ἄισατε τῷ κυρίῳ ᾆσμα καινόν; cf. Pss 143:9 LXX [144:9 EVV]; 149:1; Isa 42:10). Daniel employs a threefold or fourfold expression to describe the universality of humanity (Dan 3:4: ἔθνη καὶ χῶραι, λαοὶ καὶ γλῶσσαι; cf. Dan 3:7, 96 LXX [3:29 EVV]; 4:1; 5:19; 6:26 LXX [6:25 EVV]; 7:14).

5:10 καὶ ἐποίησας (2nd sg. aor. act. ind. of ποιέω) **αὐτοὺς** (dir. obj., αὐτούς has overwhelming mss support although the TR follows it[ar, gig] vg[cl] cop[sa] in reading ἡμᾶς) **τῷ θεῷ** (dat. of advantage) **ἡμῶν** (gen. of relationship or subord.) **βασιλείαν** (compl. in obj.-compl. double acc., "made them *to be* a kingdom") **καὶ ἱερεῖς** (ἱερεύς, -έως, ὁ, "priest," coord. compl.), **καὶ βασιλεύσουσιν** (3rd pl. fut. act. ind. of βασιλεύω, "rule") **ἐπὶ τῆς γῆς** (gen of subord.).

The ms evidence is inconclusive in support of the fut. βασιλεύσουσιν (א P 1 94 1854 2053 2344 it[gig] vg syr[ph] cop[sa, bo] arm *al*) and the pres. βασιλεύουσιν (A 046 1006 1611 it[61] syr[h] *al*). The fact that A also has pres. tense βασιλεύουσιν in 20:6, a context that seems to require the fut. tense, leads most interpreters to argue for the fut. here. Revelation has an inaugurated kingdom theology with both present (note the pres. presence of the kingdom in 1:6, 9; 5:10) and future elements, so both the pres. and fut. make theological and intratextual sense here.

Use of the OT: On Exod 19:6 and Isa 61:6, see Rev 1:6.

5:11 Καὶ εἶδον (1st sg. aor. act. ind. of ὁράω), **καὶ ἤκουσα** (1st sg. aor. act. ind. of ἀκούω) **φωνὴν** (dir. obj.) **ἀγγέλων** (gen. of source) **πολλῶν** (attrib.) **κύκλῳ** (improper prep., "around") **τοῦ** (anaphoric to 4:2) **θρόνου** (loc.) **καὶ τῶν** (anaphoric to 4:6) **ζῴων** (ζῷον, -ου, τό, "animal, living thing," coord. gen. of source) **καὶ τῶν** (anaphoric to 4:4) **πρεσβυτέρων** (coord. gen. of source), **καὶ ἦν** (3rd sg. impf. act. ind. of εἰμί) **ὁ ἀριθμὸς** (ἀριθμός, -οῦ, ὁ, "number," subj. nom.) **αὐτῶν** (obj. gen.) **μυριάδες** (μυριάς, -άδος, ἡ, pred. nom., when a specific number is in mind it is 10,000, but it is regularly used figuratively for a large unnumbered or countless number [BDAG 661b]) **μυριάδων** (the gen. is often taken here to suggest multiplication, the pl. suggests an indefinite uncountable number, "ten thousands times ten thousands") **καὶ χιλιάδες** (χιλιάς, -άδος, ἡ, "thousand," pred. nom.) **χιλιάδων** (see on μυριάδων)

The picture seems to be of concentric circles of attendants joining in worship; the uncountable multitude of angels is a new addition to the scene at this point. Hebrews 12:22 speaks of μυριάσιν ἀγγέλων.

Use of the OT: Daniel 7:10 describes the number of God's attendants around the divine throne in the divine council: χίλιαι χιλιάδες ἐθεράπευον αὐτὸν καὶ μύριαι μυριάδες παρειστήκεισαν αὐτῷ (cf. 1 En. 14:22). Psalm 67:18 (68:17 EVV) declares that God's chariots are ten-thousandfold (μυριοπλάσιος) while Deut 33:2 describes how Yahweh came from Sinai with ten thousands of holy ones (note how the LXX simply transliterates the Heb. for holy ones: σὺν μυριάσιν Καδης).

5:12 λέγοντες (nom. pl. masc. of pres. act. ptc. of λέγω, manner, introduces dir. speech) **φωνῇ** (dat. of means, conceptually cognate dat.) **μεγάλῃ** (attrib.), **Ἄξιόν** (ἄξιος, -ία, -ον, "worthy," pred. adj.) **ἐστιν** (3rd sg. pres. act. ind. of εἰμί) **τὸ ἀρνίον** (ἀρνίον, -ου, τό, "lamb," subj. nom.) **τὸ ἐσφαγμένον** (nom. sg. neut. of pf. pass. ptc. of σφάζω, "slay," attrib.) **λαβεῖν** (aor. act. inf. of λαμβάνω, epex. inf.) **τὴν** (the single art. with seven coord. objs.

suggests they are united yet distinct [Wallace 286]) **δύναμιν καὶ πλοῦτον** (πλοῦτος, -ου, ὁ, "riches") **καὶ σοφίαν** (σοφία, -ας, ἡ, "wisdom") **καὶ ἰσχὺν** (ἰσχύς, -ύος, ἡ, "power") **καὶ τιμὴν** (τιμή, -ῆς, ἡ, "honor") **καὶ δόξαν καὶ εὐλογίαν** (εὐλογία, -ας, ἡ, "praise, blessing").

Since the nom. ptc. λέγοντες modifies ἀγγέλων it should be in the gen. case (λεγόντων). Its occurrence in the nom. case is likely influenced by the comment about their number being μυριάδες (nom.; Moŧ 117). John's interest in seven would suggest that he intentionally listed seven dir. objs. with λαβεῖν for emph. Fanning helpfully describes the pattern of worship in Rev 4–5: "(1) acclamation of worthiness for their person and work (4:11; 5:9, 12); (2) chanting or singing of praise hymns to them (4:8, 11; 5:9, 12–13); and (3) ascription of glory, honor, power, and other virtues to them (4:9, 11; 5:12–13)" (Fanning 221). The attributes listed in 5:12 belong to God but can be bestowed on a king by God (Aune[a] 365; see below). Δύναμις is ascribed to God (4:11; 7:12; 11:17; 19:1) along with ἰσχύς (7:12) although neither are elsewhere ascribed to Jesus; πλοῦτος is not attributed to God or Jesus elsewhere; σοφία is ascribed to God in 7:12; τιμή is ascribed to God in 4:11 and 7:12 and to both God and the lamb in 5:13; δόξα is ascribed to God in 4:11; 7:12; 19:1 and God and the lamb together in 5:13; εὐλογία is ascribed to God in 7:12 and to God and the lamb in 5:13 (Aune[a] 365). The lamb is worthy to be ascribed these attributes because he is God's rightfully appointed king.

Use of the OT: In 1 Chr 29:11 David prays σοί, κύριε, ἡ μεγαλωσύνη καὶ ἡ δύναμις καὶ τὸ καύχημα καὶ ἡ νίκη καὶ ἡ ἰσχύς. This language of prayer to God provides a model for worship of the Lamb in 5:12. Daniel begins to interpret Nebuchadnezzar's dream in Dan 2:37 by noting that God had given to him primacy, the kingdom, power, honor, and glory (ὁ κύριος τοῦ οὐρανοῦ τὴν ἀρχὴν καὶ τὴν βασιλείαν καὶ τὴν ἰσχὺν καὶ τὴν τιμὴν καὶ τὴν δόξαν ἔδωκεν). These characteristics ultimately belong to God but are shared by God with kings.

5:13 καὶ πᾶν (attrib.) **κτίσμα** (κτίσμα, -ατος, τό, "creature," dir. obj. of ἤκουσα below, ant. of ὅ) **ὃ** (subj. nom. of verbless rel. cl.) **ἐν τῷ οὐρανῷ** (loc.) **καὶ ἐπὶ τῆς γῆς** (coord. loc.) **καὶ ὑποκάτω** (improper prep., "under") **τῆς γῆς** (coord. loc.) **καὶ ἐπὶ τῆς θαλάσσης** (coord. loc.) **καὶ** (several mss provide a vb. here for the rel. cl. [ἐστίν, καί; ἅ ἐστιν, καί; ὅσα ἐστίν, καί] but καί by itself likely explains these variant readings [Metzger 667]) **τὰ** (goes with πάντα to bracket the prep. phrase) **ἐν αὐτοῖς** (loc.) **πάντα** (dir. obj.) **ἤκουσα** (1st sg. aor. act. ind. of ἀκούω) **λέγοντας** (acc. pl. masc. of pres. act. ptc. of λέγω, compl. in obj.-compl. double acc., "I heard all things speaking," the masc. gen. of the ptc. does not match the neut. gender of πάντα but is a *constructio ad sensum*, introduces dir. speech), **Τῷ** (anaphoric to 4:2) **καθημένῳ** (dat. sg. masc. of pres. mid. ptc. of κάθημαι, subst., dat. of poss.) **ἐπὶ τῷ** (anaphoric to 4:2) **θρόνῳ** (loc.) **καὶ τῷ** (anaphoric to 5:6) **ἀρνίῳ** (ἀρνίον, -ου, τό, "lamb," dat. of poss.) **ἡ εὐλογία** (εὐλογία, -ας, ἡ, "praise, blessing," this and the following nom. nouns are subj. nom. to a verbless cl., "blessing . . . *be* to . . .") **καὶ ἡ τιμὴ** (τιμή, -ῆς, ἡ, "honor") **καὶ ἡ δόξα καὶ τὸ κράτος** (κράτος, -ους, τό, "power") **εἰς τοὺς αἰῶνας** (acc. of measure, temp.) **τῶν αἰώνων** (emph. repetition of αἰών).

The concentric circles of worship now expand beyond an uncountable angelic host to include all of creation (see 5:3 on the universality of this fourfold description of the created universe). This inclusion of all of creation suggests that this is a proleptic vision of future universal acclamation because God's reign is currently contested on earth. Revelation 5:13 provide a picture of how things should and one day will be when all of creation rightfully recognizes and worships its creator and ruler. Rhetorically, the universality of the worship invokes the *argumentum e consensus omnium* (argument from universal consent), a key element in validating and legitimating an emperor's assumption of power (Aune, "Roman Imperial Court Ceremonial," esp. 18–20).

The inclusion of the lamb in the worship directed toward God is theologically significant; this excludes any kind of angel Christology because John clearly indicates that angels must not be worshipped (19:10; 22:9). The universal worship described here parallels Phil 2:10–11. Here is a summary of other ways that Revelation closely connects Jesus with God without either losing their distinct identities. Jesus alone shares God's throne (3:21; 22:1, 3). The day of the Lord from the OT is transformed in Revelation into the day of the Lord and the lamb (6:16–17). Salvation belongs to both God and the lamb (7:10). "Thus says the Lord" is used throughout the OT prophets to introduce divine speech but in Revelation it introduces Jesus's speech (2:1, 8, 12, 18; 3:1, 7, 14). God's seal is the name of both God and the lamb (14:1). The 144,000 are firstfruits for both God and the lamb (14:4). Both God and the lamb replace the temple in the new Jerusalem (21:22) and both fill it with light (21:23). In 1:8 God describes himself as the "Alpha and the Omega," and Jesus also describes himself as "the Alpha and the Omega, the first and the last, the beginning and the end" (22:13).

The Holy Spirit is also quite active in Revelation: John sends greetings to the churches from God, Jesus, and the Spirit (1:4–5; cf. 4:5), the Holy Spirit is intimately connected with Jesus as the lamb's seven eyes (Rev 5:6), and everything that Jesus says to the churches in Revelation 2–3 is also described as what the Spirit is saying to the churches (Rev 2:7, 11, 17, 29; 3:6, 13, 22). Revelation does not use the language for Trinity developed by later church councils, but it does provide the exegetical foundation for later developments.

5:14 καὶ τὰ (anaphoric to 4:6) **τέσσαρα** (τέσσαρες, "four," attrib.) **ζῷα** (ζῷον, -ου, τό, "animal, living thing," subj. nom.) **ἔλεγον** (3rd pl. impf. act. ind. of λέγω, a pl. vb. with a neut. pl. subj. is unusual but not infrequent in Rev when the subj. is living beings; the impf. does not move the narrative forward but provides offline information [Math 81]), **Ἀμήν** (indeclinable interj. of affirmation from Heb., "truly," dir. obj.). **καὶ οἱ** (anaphoric to 4:4) **πρεσβύτεροι** (subj. nom.) **ἔπεσαν** (3rd pl. aor. act. ind. of πίπτω, the aor. tense moves the narrative forward) **καὶ προσεκύνησαν** (3rd pl. aor. act. ind. of προσκυνέω, coord.).

HOMILETICAL SUGGESTIONS

Chapter 5 introduces Jesus as the slain but living lamb who will implement God's plans for judgment and salvation within history. The lamb rules on God's throne and is the proper recipient of divine worship alongside God.

The Lamb and God's Plan (5:1–14)

1. God has a plan to bring salvation and judgment: The sealed scroll (5:1–4).
2. The lion-lamb will accomplish God's plan (5:5–7).
3. Jesus is worthy of divine worship and we are invited to participate (5:8–14).

B. OPENING THE SEVEN SEALS (6:1–8:5)

1. The First Four Seals (6:1–8)

The OT background seems to include the vision of four chariots in Zech 6:1–8 led by horses of different colors: red (ἵπποι πυρροί), black (ἵπποι μέλανες), white (ἵπποι λευκοί), and dappled (ἵπποι ποικίλοι ψαροί). The MT states that they are going out to the four winds while the LXX states that the four chariots are the four winds (Zech 6:5: Ταῦτά ἐστιν οἱ τέσσαρες ἄνεμοι τοῦ οὐρανοῦ). The chariots are sent out to patrol the earth as God's agents.

Textual variants reflect a perceived problem with how God seems to summon these causes of chaos and harm in 6:1–8. Several mss add καὶ ἴδε (א 046 about 120 minuscules it[gig] syr[ph] eth *al*) or καὶ βλέπε (296 2049 and TR) to direct the command "come" to John ("come and see") and not to the horseman in 6:1, 3, 5, 7 (Metzger 667). The command to come directed to the horsemen has better external support (A C P 1 1006 1611 1854 2053 vg cop[sa] *al*); this makes it clear that even evil and rebellious forces are under God's sovereignty and command (this is reinforced by the aor. pass. ἐδόθη in 6:2, 4, 8). The first horseman represents human warfare and conquest, the second civil unrest and civil wars, the third famine (the prices listed are eight to sixteen times the average; Cicero, *In Verrem* 3.81), and the fourth functions as a summary of the all four: death. Death is presented chiastically in the narrative as both the first and final adversary to be defeated and judged (Rev 1:18; 20:14). Death, as the fourth horseman, is under God's direction and control.

6:1 Καὶ εἶδον (1st sg. aor. act. ind. of ὁράω; καὶ εἶδον introduces a new vision, scene, figure, or activity [Aune[a] 338]) **ὅτε** (temp. subord. conj., "when") **ἤνοιξεν** (3rd sg. aor. act. ind. of ἀνοίγω) **τὸ** (anaphoric to 5:6) **ἀρνίον** (ἀρνίον, -ου, τό, "lamb," subj. nom.) **μίαν** (subst., dir. obj.) **ἐκ τῶν ἑπτὰ** ("seven," attrib.) **σφραγίδων** (σφραγίς, -ῖδος, ἡ, "seal," part. gen.), **καὶ ἤκουσα** (1st sg. aor. act. ind. of ἀκούω) **ἑνὸς** (subst., gen. dir. obj.) **ἐκ τῶν** (anaphoric to 4:6) **τεσσάρων** (τέσσαρες, "four," attrib.) **ζῴων** (ζῷον, -ου, τό, "animal, living thing," part. gen.) **λέγοντος** (gen. sg. neut. of pres. act. ptc. of λέγω, compl. in obj.-compl. double gen. construction [Math 82], "I heard one . . . speaking," introduces dir. speech) **ὡς** (manner) **φωνὴ** (normally a dat. follows ὡς; cf. 16:13) **βροντῆς** (βροντή, -ῆς, ἡ, "thunder," attrib. gen.), **Ἔρχου** (2nd sg. pres. mid. impv. of ἔρχομαι).

John uses the nom. φωνὴ after the comp. ὡς instead of the usual dat. (φωνῇ). This is likely not a Semitism but rather characteristic of John's elliptical style with comparisons (leaving out something like καὶ ἡ φωνὴ αὐτοῦ before ὡς; Moţ 122–23).

6:2 καὶ εἶδον (1st sg. aor. act. ind. of ὁράω; καὶ εἶδον introduces a new vision, scene, figure, or activity [Aune[a] 338]), **καὶ ἰδοὺ** (emph. interj.) **ἵππος** (ἵππος, -ου, ὁ, "horse," subj. nom. of verbless cl.) **λευκός** (λευκός, -ή, -όν, "white, bright," attrib.), **καὶ ὁ καθήμενος** (nom. sg. masc. of pres. mid. ptc. of κάθημαι, subst., subj. nom.) **ἐπ' αὐτὸν** (loc.) **ἔχων** (nom. sg. masc. of pres. act. ptc. of ἔχω, functions as finite vb.) **τόξον** (τόξον, -ου, τό, "bow," dir. obj.) **καὶ ἐδόθη** (3rd sg. aor. pass. ind. of δίδωμι) **αὐτῷ** (indir. obj.) **στέφανος** (στέφανος, -ου, ὁ, "wreath, crown," subj. nom.) **καὶ ἐξῆλθεν** (3rd sg. aor. act. ind. of ἐξέρχομαι) **νικῶν** (nom. sg. masc. of pres. act. ptc. of νικάω, "overcome, conquer," manner) **καὶ ἵνα** (purpose) **νικήσῃ** (3rd sg. aor. act. subjunc. of νικάω, the expression repeats νικάω for emph.).

The rider in Rev 19:11 is also on a ἵππος λευκὸς, but these riders should not be identified because the four horsemen here function as a unified group. The four horsemen are often understood to represent the warfare, chaos, and suffering that takes place throughout history in line with Jesus's teaching in the Olivet Discourse regarding wars, rumors of wars, famines, and earthquakes that would come before the end (Matt 24:6–8; Mark 13:7–9; Luke 21:9–12). Just as Rom 1:18–32 presents the active outpouring of God's wrath as consisting in God handing humanity over to the consequences of its own choices and rejection of him, the four horsemen likely represent God's active judgment that plays out in history as humans engage in warfare and civil unrest, which produces famine and death. The first readers could have identified points of fulfillment already in the first century as Roman conquests led to civil unrest (particularly in AD 69) and famine (particularly in AD 92).

The passive ἐδόθη, like many passives in Revelation that do not specify the agent (i.e., 6:4, 8, 11), can be described as a divine passive. This is an interpretive theological designation and is not grammatical or syntactical. It is based on the context and indicates the interpretive conclusion that God is the one allowing or permitting or accomplishing the stated action. Although grammatically, the passive voice draws attention to the passive subject and not the active agent, the passive was used intentionally at times in the LXX to avoid directly referring to God or the divine name, so it should not be assumed that it is inappropriate to draw interpretive attention to the unstated divine agent.

6:3 Καὶ ὅτε (temp. subord. conj., "when") **ἤνοιξεν** (3rd sg. aor. act. ind. ἀνοίγω) **τὴν σφραγῖδα** (σφραγίς, -ῖδος, ἡ, "seal," dir. obj.) **τὴν δευτέραν** (δεύτερος, -α, -ον, "second," attrib.), **ἤκουσα** (1st sg. aor. act. ind. ἀκούω) **τοῦ** (anaphoric to 4:7) **δευτέρου** ("second," attrib.) **ζῴου** (ζῷον, -ου, τό, "animal, living thing," gen. of dir. obj.) **λέγοντος** (gen. sg. neut. pres. act. ptc. λέγω, compl. in obj.-compl. double gen. construction, introduces dir. speech), **Ἔρχου** (2nd sg. pres. mid. impv. ἔρχομαι).

6:4 καὶ ἐξῆλθεν (3rd sg. aor. act. ind. of ἐξέρχομαι) **ἄλλος** (attrib.) **ἵππος** (ἵππος, -ου, ὁ, "horse," subj. nom.) **πυρρός** (πυρρός, -ά, -όν, "fiery red," attrib.), **καὶ τῷ καθημένῳ** (dat. sg. masc. of pres. act. ptc. of κάθημαι, subst., indir. obj.) **ἐπ' αὐτὸν** (loc.) **ἐδόθη** (3rd sg. aor. pass. ind. of δίδωμι) **αὐτῷ** (redundant indir. obj. for clarity) **λαβεῖν** (aor. act. inf. of λαμβάνω, subst. inf., subj. of ἐδόθη) **τὴν εἰρήνην** (dir. obj.) **ἐκ τῆς γῆς** (gen. of separation) **καὶ ἵνα** (Mathewson cites Smalley who suggests ἵνα functions like the inf. λαβεῖν as the coord. subject of ἐδόθη [Math 84]; this would explain καί as coord., but the conj. could function as an intensifier, "even" [BDAG 495d]) **ἀλλήλους** (reciprocal pron., dir. obj.) **σφάξουσιν** (3rd pl. fut. act. ind. of σφάζω, "slaughter," fut. in place of the expected subjunc., the subj. is left implicit) **καὶ ἐδόθη** (3rd sg. aor. pass. ind. of δίδωμι) **αὐτῷ** (indir. obj.) **μάχαιρα** (μάχαιρα, -ης, ἡ, "sword," subj. nom.) **μεγάλη** (attrib.).

6:5 Καὶ ὅτε (temp. subord. conj., "when") **ἤνοιξεν** (3rd sg. aor. act. ind. of ἀνοίγω) **τὴν σφραγῖδα** (σφραγίς, -ῖδος, ἡ, "seal," dir. obj.) **τὴν τρίτην** ("third," attrib.), **ἤκουσα** (1st sg. aor. act. ind. of ἀκούω) **τοῦ** (anaphoric to 4:7) **τρίτου** (attrib.) **ζῴου** (ζῷον, -ου, τό, "animal, living thing," gen. dir. obj.) **λέγοντος** (gen. sg. neut. of pres. act. ptc. of λέγω, compl. in obj.-compl. double gen. construction, introduces dir. speech), **Ἔρχου** (2nd sg. pres. mid. impv. of ἔρχομαι). **καὶ εἶδον** (1st sg. aor. act. ind. of ὁράω), **καὶ**

ἰδοὺ (emph. interj.) **ἵππος** (ἵππος, -ου, ὁ, "horse," subj. nom.) **μέλας** (μέλας, -αινα, -αν, "black," attrib.), **καὶ ὁ καθήμενος** (nom. sg. masc. of pres. mid. ptc. of κάθημαι, subst., subj. nom.) **ἐπ' αὐτὸν** (loc.) **ἔχων** (nom. sg. masc. of pres. act. ptc. of ἔχω, ptc. functions as finite vb.) **ζυγὸν** (ζυγός, -οῦ, ὁ, "scale," dir. obj.) **ἐν τῇ χειρὶ** (loc.) **αὐτοῦ** (poss.).
6:6 καὶ ἤκουσα (1st sg. aor. act. ind. of ἀκούω) **ὡς** (comp., the entire cl. functions as dir. obj. of ἤκουσα) **φωνὴν ἐν μέσῳ** (loc.) **τῶν** (anaphoric to 4:6) **τεσσάρων** (τέσσαρες, "four," attrib.) **ζῴων** (ζῷον, -ου, τό, "animal, living thing," loc.) **λέγουσαν** (acc. sg. fem. of pres. act. ptc. of λέγω, compl. in an obj.-compl. double acc. construction, "I heard a voice speaking," introduces dir. speech), **Χοῖνιξ** (χοῖνιξ, -ικος, ἡ, "quart, liter," subj. nom. of verbless cl.) **σίτου** (σῖτος, -ου, ὁ, "wheat," gen. of measure) **δηναρίου** (δηνάριον, -ου, τό, "denarius," gen. of price) **καὶ τρεῖς** ("three," attrib.) **χοίνικες** (χοῖνιξ, -ικος, ἡ, "quart, liter," subj. nom.) **κριθῶν** (κριθή, -ῆς, ἡ, "barley," gen. of content) **δηναρίου** (δηνάριον, -ου, τό, "denarius," gen. of price) **καὶ τὸ ἔλαιον** (ἔλαιον, -ου, τό, "olive oil," dir. obj.) **καὶ τὸν οἶνον** (οἶνος, -ου, ὁ, "wine," coord. dir. obj.) **μὴ ἀδικήσῃς** (2nd sg. aor. act. subjunc. of ἀδικέω, "harm, damage," preventive prohibition [Math 86]).

Use of the OT: Joel 1:10–11 brings together these four products to describe severe famine: the grain is destroyed (τεταλαιπώρηκεν σῖτος), the wine is dried up (ἐξηράνθη οἶνος), and the oil is diminished (ὠλιγώθη ἔλαιον), therefore, wail for the wheat and barley because the harvest from the field is destroyed (θρηνεῖτε . . . ὑπὲρ πυροῦ καὶ κριθῆς, ὅτι ἀπόλωλεν τρυγητὸς ἐξ ἀγροῦ).

6:7 Καὶ ὅτε (temp. subord. conj., "when") **ἤνοιξεν** (3rd sg. aor. act. ind. of ἀνοίγω) **τὴν σφραγῖδα** (σφραγίς, -ῖδος, ἡ, "seal," dir. obj.) **τὴν τετάρτην** (τέταρτος, -η, -ον, "fourth," attrib.), **ἤκουσα** (1st sg. aor. act. ind. of ἀκούω) **φωνὴν** (dir. obj.) **τοῦ** (anaphoric to 4:7) **τετάρτου** (τέταρτος, -η, -ον, "fourth," attrib.) **ζῴου** (ζῷον, -ου, τό, "animal, living thing," gen. of source) **λέγοντος** (gen. sg. neut. pres. act. ptc. of λέγω, compl. in obj.-compl. double gen. [with ζῴου] construction; the ptc. should be acc. to match φωνὴν but is attracted to the case of the one speaking, introduces dir. speech), **Ἔρχου** (2nd sg. pres. mid. impv. of ἔρχομαι).
6:8 καὶ εἶδον (1st sg. aor. act. ind. of ὁράω; καὶ εἶδον introduces a new vision, scene, figure, or activity [Aune[a] 338]), **καὶ ἰδοὺ** (emph. interj.) **ἵππος** (ἵππος, -ου, ὁ, "horse," subj. nom.) **χλωρός** (χλωρός, -ά, -ό, "pale greenish-gray, sickly or deathly color," attrib.), **καὶ ὁ καθήμενος** (nom. sg. masc. of pres. mid. ptc. of κάθημαι, subst., hanging nom. that functions as the logical rather than the syntactical subject of the sentence [Koester 59]; the true subject is ὄνομα; syntactically, the ptc. connects to the indir. obj. αὐτῷ) **ἐπάνω** (improper prep., "above, over") **αὐτοῦ** (loc.) **ὄνομα** (subj. nom.) **αὐτῷ** (poss. dat., although examples exist elsewhere, this way of introducing names is unique in the NT to John's Gospel and Revelation [John 1:6; 3:1; Rev 6:8; 9:11]) **[ὁ] Θάνατος** (if the art. is original, this is the subj. nom. of a verbless cl. and ὄνομα is the pred. nom., "Death is his name"), **καὶ ὁ ᾅδης** (ᾅδης, -ου, ὁ, "Hades," subj. nom.) **ἠκολούθει** (3rd sg. impf. act.

ind. of ἀκολουθέω, impf. provides offline information) **μετ' αὐτοῦ** (gen. of association) **καὶ ἐδόθη** (3rd sg. aor. pass. ind. of δίδωμι) **αὐτοῖς** (indir. obj. likely referring to death and Hades and not all four horsemen) **ἐξουσία** (subj. nom.) **ἐπὶ τὸ τέταρτον** (τέταρτος, -η, -ον, "fourth," subst., acc. of subord. with ἐπί) **τῆς γῆς** (part. gen.) **ἀποκτεῖναι** (aor. act. inf. of ἀποκτείνω, epex. with ἐξουσία) **ἐν ῥομφαίᾳ** (ῥομφαία, -ας, ἡ, "sword," dat. of means) **καὶ ἐν λιμῷ** (λιμός, -οῦ, ὁ/ἡ, "hunger, famine," coord. dat. of means) **καὶ ἐν θανάτῳ** (coord. dat. of means) **καὶ ὑπὸ τῶν θηρίων** (θηρίον, -ου, τό, "animal, beast," gen. of agency) **τῆς γῆς** (attrib. gen., or gen. of place).

Use of the OT: Several passages in Jeremiah and Ezekiel describe God's judgment as consisting of sword, famine, wild animals, and disease (Jer 14:12; 15:3; Ezek 5:12, 17; 14:21; 33:27). Ezekiel 5:1–12 EVV describes judgments which will each impact a third of the inhabitants of the city: (1) famine and disease; (2) a sword in the city; and (3) a sword in exile. The LXX describes judgments in fourths instead of thirds: (1) disease [ἐν θανάτῳ]; (2) famine; (3) exile; and (4) sword. The LXX expansion to fourths is probably influenced by Ezek 14:21, where God promises to send upon Jerusalem four evil judgments (τὰς τέσσαρας ἐκδικήσεις μου τὰς πονηράς: ῥομφαίαν καὶ λιμὸν καὶ θηρία πονηρὰ καὶ θάνατον).

FOR FURTHER STUDY

29. Narrative Approaches

Barr, D. L. *Tales of the End: A Narrative Commentary on the Book of Revelation*. 2nd ed. Salem, MA: Polebridge, 2012.

Morales, J. *Christ, Shepherd of the Nations: The Nations as Narrative Character and Audience in John's Apocalypse*. LNTS 577. London: Bloomsbury, 2017.

Resseguie, J. L. *The Revelation of John: A Narrative Commentary*. Grand Rapids: Baker Academic, 2009.

Ureña, L. G. *Narrative and Drama in the Book of Revelation: A Literary Approach*. SNTSMS 175. Cambridge: Cambridge University Press, 2019.

2. The Fifth Seal (6:9–11)

6:9 Καὶ ὅτε (temp. subord. conj., "when") **ἤνοιξεν** (3rd sg. aor. act. ind. of ἀνοίγω) **τὴν πέμπτην** (πέμπτος, -η, -ον, "fifth," attrib.) **σφραγῖδα** (σφραγίς, -ῖδος, ἡ, "seal," dir. obj.), **εἶδον** (1st sg. aor. act. ind. of ὁράω) **ὑποκάτω** (improper prep., "under") **τοῦ θυσιαστηρίου** (θυσιαστήριον, -ου, τό, "altar," loc., the first reference to the θυσιαστήριον is articular suggesting the "well-known" use of the art., "*the* altar" [Wallace 225]) **τὰς ψυχὰς** (dir. obj.) **τῶν ἐσφαγμένων** (gen. pl. masc. of pf. pass. ptc. of σφάζω, "slay," subst., poss.) **διὰ τὸν λόγον** (causal) **τοῦ θεοῦ** (obj. gen. "word about God," or subj. gen. "word from

God") **καὶ διὰ τὴν μαρτυρίαν** (causal, ant. of ἥν) **ἣν** (dir. obj. of εἶχον) **εἶχον** (3rd pl. impf. act. ind. of ἔχω).

It is unclear whether the altar is meant to be the sacrificial altar or the altar of incense; the connection with prayer and its proximity to the divine throne suggests the latter (8:3, 5). It could seem that faithfulness required martyrdom in Revelation, but in early Christianity faithful discipleship is often connected with death (literal or figurative; Matt 10:38–39; 16:24–26; Rom 8:35–39; 12:1–2; Phil 2:17) and Rev 13:10 seems to confirm that John knows that not every overcomer will be slain. The souls under the altar were slaughtered (σφάζω) just as the lamb had been (5:6); they had overcome the same way that he had (3:21). The fifth seal visualizes disembodied souls as alert and active in the presence of God in the intermediate state prior to future resurrection.

6:10 καὶ ἔκραξαν (3rd pl. aor. act. ind. of κράζω) **φωνῇ** (dat. of means) **μεγάλῃ** (attrib.) **λέγοντες** (nom. pl. masc. of pres. act. ptc. of λέγω, manner, introduces dir. speech, the masc. ptc. is incongruous with the fem. ant. ψυχὰς but reflects the sense of the speakers as noted in the masc. ptc. ἐσφαγμένων [Moţ 163]), **Ἕως** (improper prep., "until") **πότε** (interr. adv. of time, "when," i.e., "how long"), **ὁ δεσπότης** (δεσπότης, -ου, ὁ, "master," nom. for voc.) **ὁ ἅγιος** (attrib. adj. or subst. adj. in appos.) **καὶ ἀληθινός** (ἀληθινός, -ή, -όν, "true," attrib. adj. or subst. adj. in appos.), **οὐ κρίνεις** (2nd sg. pres. act. ind. of κρίνω) **καὶ ἐκδικεῖς** (2nd sg. pres. act. ind. of ἐκδικέω, "avenge, give justice") **τὸ αἷμα** (dir. obj.) **ἡμῶν** (poss.) **ἐκ τῶν κατοικούντων** (gen. pl. masc. of pres. act. ptc. of κατοικέω, "dwell," subst., possibly indicating the source of the shedding of the blood [Aune[b] 384; Math 89, who cites the parallel in 19:2], but more likely indicating the "the pers. on whom vengeance is taken" [BDAG 301a]; see 3:10 on the κατοικούντων) **ἐπὶ τῆς γῆς** (loc.);

Δεσπότης is a nom. of address, the use of a nom. in place of a voc. This is common in biblical and nonbiblical Greek. It is possible that the nom. of address here indicates "distance and discretion towards the Judge" (Moţ 132). This lament of "how long" and prayer for God to avenge their blood is celebrated as having been answered in 19:2 through God's judgment of Babylon. "Vengeance" as a gloss for ἐκδικέω could be misleading because of the connotations of the English word; it is not about paying someone back from a motive of rage, bitterness, or resentment, but rather a concern for justice. The range of meaning includes: "1. to procure justice for someone, *grant justice* . . . 2. to inflict appropriate penalty for wrong done, . . . *punish, take vengeance for* . . . 3. to carry out one's obligations in a worthy manner, *do justice to*" (BDAG 300d–301a, italics original).

Use of the OT: The question "how long" is common in Psalms of lament in response to unjust suffering. The Song of Moses concludes by calling the heavens to rejoice (εὐφράνθητε, οὐρανοί) because God avenges the blood of his sons and will avenge and repay justice to the enemies and will repay the ones hating (Deut 32:43: ὅτι τὸ αἷμα τῶν υἱῶν αὐτοῦ ἐκδικᾶται, καὶ ἐκδικήσει καὶ ἀνταποδώσει δίκην τοῖς ἐχθροῖς καὶ τοῖς μισοῦσιν ἀνταποδώσει). On a side note, Deut 32:43 LXX notably expands the call to worship and celebrate to the gentiles, a universal expansion that is evident in Revelation (προσκυνησάτωσαν αὐτῷ πάντες υἱοὶ θεοῦ, εὐφράνθητε, ἔθνη, μετὰ τοῦ λαοῦ αὐτοῦ). In 4 Kgdms 9:7 (2 Kgs 9:7 EVV) Jehu is anointed to avenge the blood of God's servants the prophets and the blood of all the Lord's servants (καὶ ἐκδικήσεις τὰ αἵματα τῶν δούλων μου τῶν προφητῶν καὶ τὰ αἵματα πάντων τῶν δούλων κυρίου ἐκ χειρὸς Ιεζαβελ). In Ps 78:10 LXX (79:10 EVV) Asaph prays that the vengeance of the blood of God's servants that was poured out would be known among the nations (καὶ γνωσθήτω ἐν τοῖς ἔθνεσιν ἐνώπιον τῶν ὀφθαλμῶν ἡμῶν ἡ ἐκδίκησις τοῦ αἵματος τῶν δούλων σου τοῦ ἐκκεχυμένου). Nahum 1:2 expresses the conviction that God is an avenging lord (Θεὸς ζηλωτὴς καὶ ἐκδικῶν κύριος, ἐκδικῶν κύριος μετὰ θυμοῦ ἐκδικῶν κύριος τοὺς ὑπεναντίους αὐτοῦ, καὶ ἐξαίρων αὐτὸς τοὺς ἐχθροὺς αὐτοῦ).

6:11 καὶ ἐδόθη (3rd sg. aor. pass. ind. of δίδωμι) **αὐτοῖς** (indir. obj.) **ἑκάστῳ** (subst. adj., indir. obj., distributive pron., redundant for specificity and emph., "to them, to each one") **στολὴ** (στολή, -ῆς, ἡ, "robe," subj. nom., distributive sg.) **λευκὴ** (λευκός, -ή, -όν, "white, bright" attrib.) **καὶ ἐρρέθη** (3rd sg. aor. pass. ind. of εἶπον) **αὐτοῖς** (indir. obj.) **ἵνα** (content, introduces indir. speech) **ἀναπαύσονται** (3rd pl. fut. mid. ind. of ἀναπαύω, "rest," fut. in place of subjunc.) **ἔτι** (temp. adv., "still, yet") **χρόνον** (adv. acc. of time) **μικρόν** (attrib.), **ἕως** (subord. temp. conj., "until") **πληρωθῶσιν** (3rd pl. aor. pass. subjunc. of πληρόω) **καὶ οἱ σύνδουλοι** (σύνδουλος, -ου, ὁ, "fellow-servant," prob. subj. nom. of πληρωθῶσιν) **αὐτῶν** (gen. of relationship) **καὶ** (prob. epex. to further describe a single group but possibly coord. to distinguish two groups) **οἱ ἀδελφοὶ** (subj. nom.) **αὐτῶν** (gen. of relationship) **οἱ μέλλοντες** (nom. pl. masc. of pres. act. ptc. of μέλλω, "about to," attrib.) **ἀποκτέννεσθαι** (pres. pass. inf. of ἀποκτείνω, compl. inf.) **ὡς** (manner) **καὶ** (ascensive, "also") **αὐτοί** (subj. nom. of verbless cl. which assumes ἀποκτείνω).

Parallel visions of believers in rest or victory appear throughout Revelation: 6:9–11; 7:9–17; 11:15–18; 14:1–5, 13; 15:2–4; 19:1–9; 20:4–6; 21:1–22:5. There is an idea expressed elsewhere in Second Temple Jewish writings that a certain number of righteous needed to be born, exist, or be killed before the end (1 En. 47:1–4; 4 Ezra 4:33–37; 2 Bar. 21:19–23; 23:4–7). 1 Enoch 47:1–4 provides a particularly close parallel to the fifth seal. For a different reading, Koester points to the use of πληρόω in 3:2 to argue that it is the work or witness of the faithful that would be fulfilled before the end, not a specific number of deaths (Koester 401).

FOR FURTHER STUDY

30. Martyrdom

Lee, M. V. "A Call to Martyrdom: Function as Method and Message in Revelation." *NovT* 40 (1998): 164–94.

Middleton, P. *The Violence of the Lamb: Martyrs as Agents of Divine Judgment in the Book of Revelation*. LNTS 586. London: T&T Clark, 2018.

Rand, J. A. du. "The Ethical Response of an Alternative Community in a Critical Situation: Marturia and Martyrdom in the Apocalypse of John." Pages 565–96 in *Identity, Ethics, and Ethos in the New Testament*. Edited by J. G. van der Watt. Berlin: de Gruyter, 2006.

Trites, A. A. "Μάρτυς and Martyrdom in the Apocalypse: A Semantic Study." *NovT* 15 (1973): 72–80.

Van Henten, J. W. "The Concept of Martyrdom in Revelation." Pages 587–618 in *Die Johannesapokalypse: Kontexte-Konzepte-Rezeption*. Edited by J. Frey, J. A. Kelhoffer, and F. Tóth. WUNT 287. Tübingen: Mohr Siebeck, 2012.

31. Theodicy

Kallas, J. "The Apocalypse—An Apocalyptic Book?" *JBL* 86 (1967): 68–80.

O'Leary, S. D. *Arguing the Apocalypse: A Theory of Millennial Rhetoric*. Oxford: Oxford University Press, 1994.

*Osborne, G. "Theodicy in the Apocalypse." *TJ* 14 (1993): 63–77.

Tonstad, S. K. *Saving God's Reputation: The Theological Function of Pistis Iesou in the Cosmic Narratives of Revelation*. LNTS 337. London: T&T Clark, 2006.

3. The Sixth Seal (6:12–17)

6:12 Καὶ εἶδον (1st sg. aor. act. ind. of ὁράω; καὶ εἶδον introduces a new vision, scene, figure, or activity [Aune[a] 338]) **ὅτε** (temp. subord. conj., "when") **ἤνοιξεν** (3rd sg. aor. act. ind. of ἀνοίγω) **τὴν σφραγῖδα** (σφραγίς, -ῖδος, ἡ, "seal," dir. obj.) **τὴν ἕκτην** (ἕκτος, -η, -ον, "sixth," attrib.), **καὶ σεισμὸς** (σεισμός, -οῦ, ὁ, "earthquake," subj. nom.) **μέγας** (attrib.) **ἐγένετο** (3rd sg. aor. mid. ind. of γίνομαι) **καὶ ὁ ἥλιος** (ἥλιος, -ου, ὁ, "sun," subj. nom.) **ἐγένετο** (3rd sg. aor. mid. ind. of γίνομαι) **μέλας** (μέλας, -αινα, -αν, "black," pred. adj.) **ὡς** (comp.) **σάκκος** (σάκκος, -ου, ὁ, "sackcloth") **τρίχινος** (τρίχινος, -η, -ον, "made of hair," attrib. gen.) **καὶ ἡ σελήνη** (σελήνη, -ης, ἡ, "moon," subj. nom.) **ὅλη** (attrib.) **ἐγένετο** (3rd sg. aor. mid. ind. of γίνομαι) **ὡς** (comp. cl. functions as pred. nom.) **αἷμα**.

The language of cosmic upheaval draws from the same OT prophecies as Jesus's teaching about the coming of the Son of Man in Matt 24:9; Mark 13:24–25; Luke 21:25. The similar language of cosmic upheaval in the Olivet Discourse is connected with the second coming. In the fourth trumpet judgment of 8:12 a third of cosmic light is darkened.

Use of the OT: Joel 3:4 LXX (2:31 EVV) prophesies that the sun would be turned to darkness and the moon to blood before the great day of the Lord (ὁ ἥλιος μεταστραφήσεται εἰς σκότος καὶ ἡ σελήνη εἰς αἷμα πρὶν ἐλθεῖν ἡμέραν κυρίου τὴν μεγάλην καὶ ἐπιφανῆ). Joel 4:15 LXX (3:15 EVV) likewise states ὁ ἥλιος καὶ ἡ σελήνη συσκοτάσουσιν, καὶ οἱ ἀστέρες δύσουσιν φέγγος αὐτῶν at the day of the Lord. Joel 2:10 describes an army at the day of the Lord before whom heaven will be shaken, the sun and moon will be darkened, and the stars will diminish their light (σεισθήσεται ὁ οὐρανός, ὁ ἥλιος καὶ ἡ σελήνη συσκοτάσουσιν, καὶ τὰ ἄστρα δύσουσιν τὸ φέγγος αὐτῶν). In Isaiah's oracle about the day of the Lord against Babylon he declares that the stars of heaven will not give light, the rising sun will be darkened, and the moon will not give its light (13:10: οἱ γὰρ ἀστέρες τοῦ οὐρανοῦ . . . τὸ φῶς οὐ δώσουσιν, καὶ σκοτισθήσεται τοῦ ἡλίου ἀνατέλλοντος, καὶ ἡ σελήνη οὐ δώσει τὸ φῶς αὐτῆς). Ezekiel 32:7–8 contains a prophetic pronouncement against Egypt in which God threatens that when he extinguishes Pharaoh he will cover heaven, darken its stars, and cover the sun with a cloud and the moon will not shine its light (καὶ κατακαλύψω ἐν τῷ σβεσθῆναί σε οὐρανὸν καὶ συσκοτάσω τὰ ἄστρα αὐτοῦ, ἥλιον ἐν νεφέλῃ καλύψω, καὶ σελήνη οὐ μὴ φάνῃ τὸ φῶς αὐτῆς). The Hebrew prophets associated cosmic upheaval with the day of the Lord and applied such descriptions to both divine judgments throughout history and to the final day of the Lord. The language of cosmic upheaval from Isa 13:10 and Ezek 32:7–8 was fulfilled figuratively (prophetic hyperbole) by human armies in the destruction of Babylon and Egypt, so it is not certain that the language of cosmic upheaval in the Olivet Discourse and Revelation should be interpreted literally, although the connection of this language with Rev 21:2 could suggest it literally describes a decreation followed by recreation at the end. The diminishment of cosmic light accompanying prophecies of God's arrival and judgment in the Hebrew prophets is grounded historically in the Sinai theophany.

6:13 καὶ οἱ ἀστέρες (ἀστήρ, -έρος, ὁ, "star," subj. nom.) **τοῦ οὐρανοῦ** (attrib. gen. or gen. of place) **ἔπεσαν** (3rd pl. aor. act. ind. of πίπτω) **εἰς τὴν γῆν** (loc.), **ὡς** (comp.) **συκῆ** (συκῆ, -ῆς, ἡ, "fig tree," subj. nom.) **βάλλει** (3rd sg. pres. act. ind. of βάλλω, customary pres.) **τοὺς ὀλύνθους** (ὄλυνθος, -ου, ὁ, "unripe fig," dir. obj.) **αὐτῆς** (poss.) **ὑπὸ ἀνέμου** (ἄνεμος, -ου, ὁ, "wind," means) **μεγάλου** (attrib.) **σειομένη** (nom. sg. fem. of pres. pass. ptc. of σείω, "shake," temp., "when being shaken by a great wind"),

---

Use of the OT: See 6:12. In the prophecy of the judgment of the nations in Isa 34:4 it says that the sky/heaven will be rolled up as a scroll and all the stars will fall as leaves from a vine and fig tree (καὶ ἑλιγήσεται ὁ οὐρανὸς ὡς βιβλίον, καὶ πάντα τὰ ἄστρα πεσεῖται ὡς φύλλα ἐξ ἀμπέλου καὶ ὡς πίπτει φύλλα ἀπὸ συκῆς). This example of prophetic hyperbole related to cosmic upheaval associated with divine judgment was fulfilled historically in the destruction of Edom.

6:14 καὶ ὁ οὐρανὸς (subj. nom.) **ἀπεχωρίσθη** (3rd sg. aor. pass. ind. of ἀποχωρίζω, "recede, separate") **ὡς** (comp.) **βιβλίον** (βιβλίον, -ου, τό, "scroll") **ἑλισσόμενον** (nom. sg. neut. of pres. pass. ptc. of ἑλίσσω, "roll up," attrib.) **καὶ πᾶν** (attrib.) **ὄρος** (subj. nom.) **καὶ νῆσος** (νῆσος, -ου, ἡ, "island," coord. subj. nom.) **ἐκ τῶν τόπων** (gen. of separation) **αὐτῶν** (poss.) **ἐκινήθησαν** (3rd pl. aor. pass. ind. of κινέω, "move").

Revelation 16:20 describes how every island fled and mountains were not found in the judgment of the seventh bowl (καὶ πᾶσα νῆσος ἔφυγεν καὶ ὄρη οὐχ εὑρέθησαν). In 20:11 the earth and heaven flee from the face of the one sitting on the throne. This intratextual feature may not require that the events be identified, but it does seem to support some degree of repetition in the visions.

6:15 καὶ οἱ βασιλεῖς (subj. nom.) **τῆς γῆς** (gen. of subord. or gen. of place) **καὶ οἱ μεγιστᾶνες** (μεγιστάν, -ᾶνος, ὁ, "important person," coord. subj. nom.) **καὶ οἱ χιλίαρχοι** (χιλίαρχος, -ου, ὁ, "military unit, commander," coord. subj. nom.) **καὶ οἱ πλούσιοι** (πλούσιος, -ία, -ιον, "rich, wealthy," subst., coord. subj. nom.) **καὶ οἱ ἰσχυροὶ** (ἰσχυρός, -ά, -όν, "strong," subst., coord. subj. nom.) **καὶ πᾶς** (attrib.) **δοῦλος** (coord. subj. nom.) **καὶ ἐλεύθερος** (ἐλεύθερος, -έρα, -ον, "free," subst., coord. subj. nom.) **ἔκρυψαν** (3rd pl. aor. act. ind. of κρύπτω, "hide") **ἑαυτοὺς** (dir. obj., refl. pron.) **εἰς τὰ σπήλαια** (σπήλαιον, -ου, τό, "cave," loc.) **καὶ εἰς τὰς πέτρας** (coord. loc.) **τῶν ὀρέων** (gen. of place)

John's interest in the number seven could explain why there are seven nom. subjects. The list demonstrates how all humanity will be subject to God's judgment; both high and low status individuals will give an account and high social or economic status will provide no protection. Similar inclusive and comprehensive lists of humanity are utilized in 13:16 to describe those who receive the beast's mark and in 19:18 to describe the slain armies of the beast.

Use of the OT: Isaiah 2:10 gives a command to enter into the rocks and hide in the earth from the face of the fear of the Lord and from the glory of his strength when he arises to shatter the earth (καὶ νῦν εἰσέλθετε εἰς τὰς πέτρας καὶ κρύπτεσθε εἰς τὴν γῆν ἀπὸ προσώπου τοῦ φόβου κυρίου καὶ ἀπὸ τῆς δόξης τῆς ἰσχύος αὐτοῦ, ὅταν ἀναστῇ θραῦσαι τὴν γῆν). Isaiah 2:19, 21 describes how people enter caves and holes in the ground from the terror of the Lord. Jeremiah 4:29 LXX describes people hiding in caves (εἰσέδυσαν εἰς τὰ σπήλαια) and among rocks (καὶ ἐπὶ τὰς πέτρας ἀνέβησαν) in the day of judgment.

6:16 καὶ λέγουσιν (3rd pl. pres. act. ind. of λέγω, narrative pres., introduces dir. speech) **τοῖς ὄρεσιν** (indir. obj.) **καὶ ταῖς πέτραις** (coord. indir. obj.), **πέσετε** (2nd pl. aor. act. impv. of πίπτω) **ἐφ' ἡμᾶς** (loc.) **καὶ κρύψατε** (2nd pl. aor. act. impv. of κρύπτω, "hide," coord. impv.) **ἡμᾶς** (dir. obj.) **ἀπὸ προσώπου** (gen. of separation) **τοῦ** (anaphoric to 4:2) **καθημένου** (gen. sg. masc. pres. mid. ptc. of κάθημαι, subst., poss.) **ἐπὶ τοῦ** (anaphoric to 4:2) **θρόνου** (loc.) **καὶ ἀπὸ τῆς ὀργῆς** (ὀργή, ῆς, ἡ, "anger, wrath," coord. gen. of separation) **τοῦ** (anaphoric to 5:6) **ἀρνίου** (ἀρνίον, -ου, τό, "lamb," subj. gen.),

When Jesus is being led away to be crucified, he prophecies concerning a future day when ἄρξονται λέγειν τοῖς ὄρεσιν· πέσετε ἐφ' ἡμᾶς, καὶ τοῖς βουνοῖς· καλύψατε ἡμᾶς (Luke 23:30).

Use of the OT: Hosea 10:8 describes people's prayer in judgment for the mountains to cover and the hills to fall on them (καὶ ἐροῦσιν τοῖς ὄρεσιν Καλύψατε ἡμᾶς, καὶ τοῖς βουνοῖς Πέσατε ἐφ' ἡμᾶς).

6:17 ὅτι (causal) **ἦλθεν** (3rd sg. aor. act. ind. of ἔρχομαι, immediate past aor.) **ἡ ἡμέρα** (subj. nom.) **ἡ μεγάλη** (attrib.) **τῆς ὀργῆς** (ὀργή, -ῆς, ἡ, "anger, wrath," attrib. gen. or, as Mathewson suggests, something like a gen. of time, "the day when their wrath occurs" [Math 93]) **αὐτῶν** (subj. gen., many mss [A and most minuscules] read αὐτοῦ to single out God or the lamb while ℵ C 1611 1854 2329 2053 2344 it[ar, gig] vg syr[ph, h] Fulgentius support the arguably harder reading αὐτῶν [Metzger 668]), **καὶ τίς** (interr. pron., subj. nom.) **δύναται** (3rd sg. pres. mid. ind. of δύναμαι) **σταθῆναι** (aor. pass. [for mid.] inf. of ἵστημι, compl. inf.);

The day of the Lord is a common motif in the Hebrew prophets but here it is expanded to include the lamb. The lamb is not collapsed into God (they remain distinct persons) but the lamb is intimately connected to God in a way that is qualitatively different from every created being, angelic or human.

Use of the OT: Joel 2:11 asks who will be sufficient in the great day of the Lord (διότι μεγάλη ἡ ἡμέρα τοῦ κυρίου, μεγάλη καὶ ἐπιφανὴς σφόδρα, καὶ τίς ἔσται ἱκανὸς αὐτῇ). Nahum 1:6 asks who can withstand the face of God's wrath and stand against the fury of his wrath because his wrath melts powers (ἀρχάς) and shatters rocks (ἀπὸ προσώπου ὀργῆς αὐτοῦ τίς ὑποστήσεται; καὶ τίς ἀντιστήσεται ἐν ὀργῇ θυμοῦ αὐτοῦ; ὁ θυμὸς αὐτοῦ τήκει ἀρχάς, καὶ αἱ πέτραι διεθρύβησαν ἀπ' αὐτοῦ). Malachi 3:2 rhetorically asks who can endure the day of God's coming and who can stand in his appearance (καὶ τίς ὑπομενεῖ ἡμέραν εἰσόδου αὐτοῦ; ἢ τίς ὑποστήσεται ἐν τῇ ὀπτασίᾳ αὐτοῦ).

---

4. The Sealing of 144,000 (7:1–8)

7:1 Μετὰ (temp., "after") **τοῦτο** (demon. pron., the ant. is the vision of the sixth seal; visionary sequence does not determine the historical chronology of the vision's referent) **εἶδον** (1st sg. aor. act. ind. of ὁράω) **τέσσαρας** ("four," attrib.) **ἀγγέλους** (dir. obj.) **ἑστῶτας** (acc. pl. masc. of pf. act. ptc. of ἵστημι, compl. in obj.-compl. double acc., "I saw angels standing") **ἐπὶ τὰς τέσσαρας** (attrib.) **γωνίας** (γωνία, -ας, ἡ, "corner," loc.) **τῆς γῆς** (part. gen.), **κρατοῦντας** (acc. pl. masc. of pres. act. ptc. of κρατέω, "hold, keep," attrib., modifying ἀγγέλους) **τοὺς τέσσαρας** (attrib.) **ἀνέμους** (ἄνεμος, -ου, ὁ, "wind," dir. obj.) **τῆς γῆς** (gen. of place) **ἵνα** (purpose) **μὴ πνέῃ** (3rd sg. pres. act. subjunc. of πνέω, "blow") **ἄνεμος** (ἄνεμος, -ου, ὁ, subj. nom.) **ἐπὶ τῆς γῆς** (gen. of place) **μήτε** ("nor") **ἐπὶ**

τῆς θαλάσσης (coord. gen. of place) **μήτε ἐπὶ πᾶν** (attrib., the neg. expression with πᾶς is a Hebraism to indicate "not any" [BDAG 782b–c]) **δένδρον** (δένδρον, -ου, τό, "tree," acc. of disadvantage, "against").

Mark 13:27 references the four winds to indicate the furthest extent and totality of the world (ἐπισυνάξει τοὺς ἐκλεκτοὺς [αὐτοῦ] ἐκ τῶν τεσσάρων ἀνέμων ἀπ' ἄκρου γῆς ἕως ἄκρου οὐρανοῦ).

Use of the OT: The four corners of the earth would suggest northeast, northwest, southeast, and southwest; they are referenced elsewhere to indicate the furthest extent of the earth (Isa 11:12: ἐκ τῶν τεσσάρων πτερύγων τῆς γῆς) or the full extent of the land (Ezek 7:2: ἐπὶ τὰς τέσσαρας πτέρυγας τῆς γῆς). The four winds are mentioned in Jer 49:36 where they would scatter Elam to the four quarters of heaven (Jer 25:16 LXX). In Ezek 37:9 they bring breath in the valley of dry bones, and in Dan 7:2 they stir up the sea that produces the four beasts. They are used to describe global dispersion in Dan 11:4, where the kingdom of a mighty king will be divided toward the four winds of heaven, and in Zech 2:6 where they will be spread abroad as the four winds of heaven. None of this background seems particularly relevant to 7:1. An intriguing parallel is with Zech 6:5 LXX, which equates the four winds with the four chariots pulled by red, black, white, and dappled horses. This suggests an identification between the four winds in 7:1 with the four horsemen of 6:1–8 (Beale 406). This connection is perhaps too subtle but John is heavily dependent upon Zechariah. If this connection is correct, the sealing of the 144,000 takes place chronologically before the four horsemen are summoned to inflict harm, even though the vision is recounted later in the narrative.

7:2 καὶ εἶδον (1st sg. aor. act. ind. of ὁράω; καὶ εἶδον introduces a new vision, scene, figure, or activity [Aune[a] 338]) **ἄλλον** (attrib.) **ἄγγελον** (dir. obj.) **ἀναβαίνοντα** (acc. sg. masc. of pres. act. ptc. of ἀναβαίνω, compl. in an obj.-compl. double acc. construction) **ἀπὸ ἀνατολῆς** (ἀνατολή, -ῆς, ἡ, "rising," gen. of source) **ἡλίου** (ἥλιος, -ου, ὁ, "sun," subj. gen.) **ἔχοντα** (acc. sg. masc. of pres. act. ptc. of ἔχω, manner) **σφραγῖδα** (σφραγίς, -ῖδος, ἡ, "seal," dir. obj.) **θεοῦ** (poss.) **ζῶντος** (gen. sg. masc. of pres. act. ptc. of ζάω, attrib.), **καὶ ἔκραξεν** (3rd sg. aor. act. ind. of κράζω) **φωνῇ** (dat. of means) **μεγάλῃ** (attrib.) **τοῖς** (anaphoric to 7:1) **τέσσαρσιν** ("four," attrib.) **ἀγγέλοις** (indir. obj., ant. of οἷς) **οἷς** (indir. obj.) **ἐδόθη** (3rd sg. aor. pass. ind. of δίδωμι) **αὐτοῖς** (redundant indir. obj. for clarity) **ἀδικῆσαι** (aor. act. inf. of ἀδικέω, "harm, damage," subst. inf., subj. of ἐδόθη) **τὴν γῆν** (dir. obj.) **καὶ τὴν θάλασσαν** (coord. dir. obj.)

7:3 λέγων (nom. sg. masc. of pres. act. ptc. of λέγω, manner, introduces dir. speech, should be acc. to match ἄγγελον in 7:2), **Μὴ ἀδικήσητε** (2nd pl. aor. act. subjunc. of ἀδικέω, "harm, damage," prohibition) **τὴν γῆν** (dir. obj.) **μήτε** ("nor") **τὴν θάλασσαν** (coord. dir. obj.) **μήτε τὰ δένδρα** (δένδρον, -ου, τό, "tree," coord. dir. obj.), **ἄχρι** (temp., "until") **σφραγίσωμεν** (1st pl. aor. act. subjunc. of σφραγίζω, "seal") **τοὺς δούλους** (dir. obj.) **τοῦ θεοῦ** (poss.) **ἡμῶν** (gen. of subord.) **ἐπὶ τῶν μετώπων** (μέτωπον, -ου, τό, "forehead," loc.) **αὐτῶν** (poss.).

In early Christianity, the seal of God is normally connected with the Holy Spirit (2 Cor 1:22; Eph 1:13; 4:30), but in Revelation it is identified as God's name (14:1; 22:4), likely indicating ownership and protection (note the theme of protection in the delay in the wind harming and protection from the locusts in Rev 9:4). John characteristically describes God's people as slaves (1:1; 2:20; 6:11; 7:3; 10:7; 11:18; 19:2, 5; 22:3, 6; used of an angel in 19:10; 22:9). Although some of these references refer to prophets or martyrs, δοῦλος is not a technical term for either group in Revelation and is a more general term utilized by John to describe God's people (without any ethnic specificity elsewhere).

Use of the OT: In Ezek 9:1–7, the prophet has a vision of a man in linen who marks the foreheads of those who are faithful in Jerusalem while others come behind and slay all who do not have the mark (9:4: Δίελθε μέσην τὴν Ιερουσαλημ καὶ δὸς τὸ σημεῖον ἐπὶ τὰ μέτωπα τῶν ἀνδρῶν). God's people are marked for protection from God's judgment. Aune discusses how Pss. Sol. 15:4–9 expands upon Ezekiel 9 to highlight the divine mark of protection versus the mark of judgment: "For the *mark of God* [τὸ σημεῖον τοῦ θεοῦ] is upon the righteous for salvation. *Famine* and *sword* and *death* [λιμὸς καὶ ῥομφαία καὶ θάνατος [Rev 6:8] shall be far from the righteous, . . . But they shall pursue sinners and overtake them, . . . For the *mark of destruction* [τὸ γὰρ σημεῖον τῆς ἀπωλείας] is *upon their forehead* [ἐπὶ τοῦ μετώπου αὐτῶν] (Aune[b] 530; brackets and italics original).

7:4 καὶ ἤκουσα (1st sg. aor. act. ind. of ἀκούω) **τὸν ἀριθμὸν** (ἀριθμός, -οῦ, ὁ, "number," dir. obj.) **τῶν ἐσφραγισμένων** (gen. pl. masc. of pf. pass. ptc. of σφραγίζω, "seal," subst., obj. gen.), **ἑκατὸν** ("hundred") **τεσσεράκοντα** ("forty") **τέσσαρες** ("four," attrib.) **χιλιάδες** ("thousand," subst., subj. nom. of verbless cl., the switch to the nom. is prob. explained as a quote of what John heard [Moț 118]), **ἐσφραγισμένοι** (nom. pl. masc. of pf. pass. ptc. of σφραγίζω, subst. ptc. in appos. to 144,000 or attrib., the incongruity with the fem. χιλιάδες is a *constructio ad sensum*) **ἐκ πάσης** (attrib.) **φυλῆς** (φυλή, -ῆς, ἡ, "tribe, nation," source) **υἱῶν** (part. gen.) **Ἰσραήλ** (gen. of relationship)

Multiples of twelve are also common in the vision of the new Jerusalem in Revelation 21 and the number twelve (and multiples) in Revelation seems to point symbolically to the completed people of God. The description of the 144,000 as from every tribe of the sons of Israel clearly establishes an Israelite ethnic identity for the recipients of God's seal (see below on 7:8).

7:5 ἐκ φυλῆς (φυλή, -ῆς, ἡ, "tribe," gen. of source) **Ἰούδα** (gen. of relationship) **δώδεκα** ("twelve") **χιλιάδες** ("thousand," attrib.) **ἐσφραγισμένοι** (nom. pl. masc. of pf. pass. ptc.

of σφραγίζω, "seal," subst.), **ἐκ φυλῆς Ῥουβὴν** ("Reuben") **δώδεκα χιλιάδες** (this and the rest of the tribes in this list presuppose the ptc. ἐσφραγισμένοι), **ἐκ φυλῆς Γὰδ** ("Gad") **δώδεκα χιλιάδες,**

Judah fronts the list as the Messiah's tribe (5:5). This list of tribes is unique and has been shaped for its literary context with the fronting of Judah, inclusion of Levi and Joseph, and exclusion of Dan and Ephraim (likely because of the association of these tribes with idolatry). This shaping is important to note but should not be overemphasized since there is no standardized list of the tribes in the OT and the lists are generally shaped to fit the contextual needs of the narrative in which the list appears (Bauckham, "List of the Tribes"). The grammar and syntax of the list is identical for each tribe with the ptc. ἐσφραγισμένοι functioning as an inclusio at the start and end of the list.

Use of the OT: The numbering of the 144,000 takes the form of a census, indicating a holy army prepared for holy war (Num 1:1–46; see the phrase ἐκ τῆς φυλῆς in Num 1:21 and following [Bauckham 217–29]).

7:6 ἐκ φυλῆς Ἀσὴρ ("Asher") **δώδεκα χιλιάδες, ἐκ φυλῆς Νεφθαλὶμ** ("Naphtali") **δώδεκα χιλιάδες, ἐκ φυλῆς Μανασσῆ** ("Manasseh") **δώδεκα χιλιάδες,**
7:7 ἐκ φυλῆς Συμεὼν ("Simeon") **δώδεκα χιλιάδες, ἐκ φυλῆς Λευὶ** ("Levi") **δώδεκα χιλιάδες, ἐκ φυλῆς Ἰσσαχὰρ** ("Issachar") **δώδεκα χιλιάδες,**
7:8 ἐκ φυλῆς Ζαβουλὼν ("Zebulun") **δώδεκα χιλιάδες, ἐκ φυλῆς Ἰωσὴφ** ("Joseph") **δώδεκα χιλιάδες, ἐκ φυλῆς Βενιαμὶν** ("Benjamin") **δώδεκα χιλιάδες ἐσφραγισμένοι** (nom. pl. masc. of pf. pass. ptc. of σφραγίζω, "seal," subst.; this ptc. forms an inclusio with the first tribe in the list).

Various interpretations have been offered for the relationship between the 144,000 (Rev 7:5–8) and the innumerable multitude (Rev 7:9). The two main options are well articulated by Beale (416–26) who argues that the two visions provide different perspectives on the same group of God's redeemed people and Fanning (261–68) who builds on the explicit contrasts (numbered vs. unnumbered, Israelite vs. multiethnic, on earth vs. in heaven) between the two groups to identify the first group as Jewish Christians and the second group as gentile Christians. A decision between these two positions involves an analysis of two widely different interpretive frameworks for biblical theology and is beyond the scope of this volume. Some of Beale's key arguments can be paraphrased and expanded as follows (cf. Koester 427): this approach seems to present a more compelling and coherent interpretation of the book as a whole within broader biblical theology. First, John identifies the two groups by employing the same hearing/seeing literary device that he used to identify the lion with the lamb (5:5–6) and the bride with the city (21:9–10). In each of these three cases, John hears one thing and then sees something different yet somehow the same; it is the explicit contrasts between what he hears and sees that invites the hearer to deeper reflection and understanding (on this reading, the explicit contrasts that ground Fanning's interpretation support the opposite conclusion). Second, in 14:3–4 the 144,000 are described as οἱ ἠγορασμένοι ἀπὸ τῆς γῆς. This is parallel to the description of all the saved in 5:9 (ἠγόρασας τῷ θεῷ). The phrase ἐκ πάσης φυλῆς καὶ γλώσσης καὶ λαοῦ καὶ ἔθνους from 5:9 is used to describe the innumerable multitude in 7:9 (ἐκ παντὸς ἔθνους καὶ φυλῶν καὶ λαῶν καὶ γλωσσῶν). Third, the 144,000 are described in 7:3 as δούλους τοῦ θεοῦ and δοῦλος is used elsewhere in the Apocalypse to describe all of God's people without ethnic specificity (see 7:3). Fourth, throughout the Apocalypse, God's seal (7:3; 9:4; 14:1; 22:4) is parallel to Satan's seal/mark (13:16, 17; 14:9, 11; 16:2; 19:20; 20:4). If Satan's seal covers all his followers, this implies that God's seal does likewise. Fifth, the book elsewhere presents God's people in the present, made up of both Jew and gentile, as constituting the restored people of God in contrast to those who claim to be Jews but are not because they were opposing Israel's Messiah and the Messiah's people (Rev 2:9; 3:9; cf. Gal 6:16; Eph 2:19; Jas 1:1; 1 Pet 1:1; 2:9). This inclusion of gentiles in promises of Israel's future restoration is confirmed by the application of the words of Exod 19:6 (Israel as a kingdom of priests) to both Jewish and gentile believers in 1:6; 5:10. The main distinction seems to be temporal between God's people being sealed before tribulation in preparation for holy war (7:5–8) and God's people who have triumphantly come out of tribulation (7:9–17).

Is the interpretation recommended here, that the sealed 144,000 Israelites function as a symbolic description of God's multiethnic people, supersessionistic? It is possible to make that argument, but it is a misunderstanding of John's understanding of the relationship of Jews and gentiles in the churches. The visions of Revelation present an Israel-shaped salvation accomplished by Israel's Messiah Jesus culminating in the fulfillment of God's promises to his people Israel. This salvation and restoration is christologically determined: entrance to the new Jerusalem depends on being written in the lamb's book of life (Rev 21:27; cf. 20:15). The lamb's blood looses from sin, redeems human beings, produces white robes, and provides victory (1:5; 5:9; 7:14; 12:11). Jesus has the keys of David and determines who is allowed into the new Jerusalem (3:7–8), and those who keep the commandments of God also hold to the witness of Jesus and maintain faithfulness/allegiance to Jesus (12:17; 14:12). Gentile conversion to Christianity in the first century involved an ethnic as much as a religious conversion as gentile Christians took on Jewish ethnic identity through exclusively worshipping the Jewish God; pledging allegiance to the Jewish Messiah; adopting the sacred texts of Judaism; identifying with common ancestry (Abraham as father, see on 7:9); sharing historical memories; clinging to the same hopes for inclusion within God's promised future restoration of the city, land, and creation (a shared telos); following the same ethics and moral codes; and entering into the customs and rituals of diaspora worship. In antiquity, ethnicity was accretive (people could take on additional ethnic designations over time) and polythetic as opposed to monothetic (see For Further Study 33 [Ethnicity in Antiquity] below). That is, ethnicity consisted of a cluster of shared characteristics and not just a single characteristic such as common descent, geography, or language. Revelation reflects a situation in the latter half of the first century in which Jewish Christians were extending a form of Jewish ethnic identity to gentiles through conversion (with no mention of circumcision or food laws in Revelation). This could be understood as fictive ethnic identity (similar to the fictive kinship of ἀδελφὸς ὑμῶν in 1:9), although with an accretive and polythetic understanding of ethnic identity in antiquity it is not at all clear that "fictive" properly applies (fictive would apply with a monothetic approach to ethnicity). Revelation celebrates and anticipates the salvation of Israel, a salvation to which gentiles were being welcomed to join through submission and allegiance to Israel's Messiah Jesus. This understanding of the inclusion of gentiles in Israel's restoration in Revelation reflects the broad approach of early Christianity and is not supersessionistic (although supersessionistic ideas are evident from the second century onward).

Peter Hirschberg ("Jewish Believers in Asia Minor," 225) presents an interesting variant that attempts to bridge the two main opposing views by appealing to salvation history to argue that the 144,000 are ethnic Jews.

> This Jewish particularity [of the 144,000] stands in a clear contrast to the troop of the completed who are described in universal terms (Rev 7:9–17). If, in spite of these differences, both groups in the end have to be identical, there is actually only one given solution; the text must be read as salvation history. In 7:1–8 the Seer remains deliberately in the Jewish milieu, so that the readers associate automatically with the eschatologically renewed Israel, and from here they are led to the understanding, developed especially in 7:9–17, that with this Israel there are also Gentiles. By leading the readers in this way, the author attains the following: (1) He adheres to a priority of the salvation history of the Jewish people and differentiates between Israel and the Gentiles by letting the movement flow—in a good biblical manner—from Israel to the Gentiles. (2) He emphasizes that the true Israel is the Israel that found its completion in Christ, reckoned here as the Jewish Israel believing in Jesus. (3) This Israel, in return, has opened itself to the Gentiles and they belong now—in the soteriological sense—entirely to it, but from the point of view of salvation history they are "being added."

FOR FURTHER STUDY

32. The 144,000 (7:1–8)

Bauckham, R. "The List of the Tribes in Revelation 7 Again." *JSNT* 42 (1991): 99–115.

Hirschberg, P. "Jewish Believers in Asia Minor according to the Book of Revelation and the Gospel of John." Pages 217–38 in *Jewish Believers in Jesus: The Early Centuries*. Edited by O. Skarsaune and R. Hvalvik. Peabody, MA: Hendrickson, 2007.

Smith, C. R. "The Portrayal of the Church as the New Israel in the Names and Order of the Tribes in Revelation 7.5–8." *JSNT* 39 (1990): 111–18.

White, J. R. "The 144,000 in Revelation 7 and 14: Old Testament and Intratextual Clues to Their Identity." Pages 179–97 in *From Creation to New Creation: Biblical Theology and Exegesis*. Edited by D. M. Gurtner and B. J. Gladd. Peabody, MA: Hendrickson, 2013.

33. Ethnicity in Antiquity

Barclay, J. M. G. "Ἰουδαῖος: Ethnicity and Translation." Pages 46–58 in *Ethnicity, Race, Religion: Identities and Ideologies in Early Jewish and Christian Texts, and in Modern Biblical Interpretation*. Edited by K. M. Hockey and D. G. Horrell. London: T&T Clark, 2018.

Cromhout, M. "Israelite Ethnic Identity Responding to the Roman Imperium in Revelation." Pages 527–50 in *T&T Clark Handbook to Social Identity in the New Testament*. Edited by J. B. Tucker and C. A. Baker. London: T&T Clark, 2014.

Morgan, T. "Society, Identity, and Ethnicity in the Hellenic World." Pages 23–45 in *Ethnicity, Race, Religion: Identities and Ideologies in Early Jewish and Christian Texts, and in Modern Biblical Interpretation*. Edited by K. M. Hockey and D. G. Horrell. London: T&T Clark, 2018.

5. The Uncountable Multitude (7:9–17)

7:9 Μετὰ (temp., "after") **ταῦτα** (demon. pron., the ant. is the hearing of the numbering of the 144,000; visionary sequence does not determine the historical chronology of the vision's referent) **εἶδον** (1st sg. aor. act. ind. of ὁράω), **καὶ ἰδοὺ** (emph. interj.) **ὄχλος** (subj. nom. of verbless cl., ant. of ὅν) **πολύς** (attrib.), **ὃν** (dir. obj. of ἀριθμῆσαι) **ἀριθμῆσαι** (aor. act. inf. of ἀριθμέω, "count, number," compl. inf.) **αὐτὸν** (redundant pron. with ὅν for clarity and emph.) **οὐδεὶς** (subj. nom.) **ἐδύνατο** (3rd sg. impf. mid. ind. of δύναμαι, impf. provides offline information), **ἐκ παντὸς** (attrib.) **ἔθνους** (part. gen. of source) **καὶ φυλῶν** (φυλή, -ῆς, ἡ, "tribe, nation," coord. part. gen. of source) **καὶ λαῶν** (coord. part. gen. of source) **καὶ γλωσσῶν** (γλῶσσα, -ης, ἡ, "tongue, language," coord. part. gen. of source) **ἑστῶτες** (nom. pl. masc. of pf. act. ptc. of ἵστημι, compl. in a sub.-compl. double nom. construction, should be sg. to match ὄχλος but is prob. pl. to match the sense of the collective noun [Math 99]) **ἐνώπιον τοῦ** (anaphoric to 4:2) **θρόνου** (loc.) **καὶ ἐνώπιον τοῦ** (anaphoric to 5:6) **ἀρνίου** (ἀρνίον, -ου, τό, "lamb," coord. loc.) **περιβεβλημένους** (acc. pl. masc. of pf. pass. ptc. of περιβάλλω, "wrap, clothe," dir. obj. of εἶδον, see below on the case) **στολὰς** (στολή, -ῆς, ἡ, "robe," dir. obj.) **λευκὰς** (λευκός, -ή, -όν, "white, bright" attrib.) **καὶ φοίνικες** (φοῖνιξ, -ικος, ὁ, "palm branch," subj. nom. of verbless cl.) **ἐν ταῖς χερσὶν** (loc.) **αὐτῶν** (poss.),

The acc. ptc. περιβεβλημένους is not in accord with its nom. ant. ὄχλος (note the nom. πολύς and ἑστῶτες). Moţ suggests that this relates to John's frequent shift between εἶδον with acc. and ἰδού with nom., which changes John from a speaker to viewer and changes the reader from viewer to listener (Moţ 152). Although there is technical grammatical discord, it does not obscure the meaning. The vision of people standing before the throne answers the question that closed chapter 6 regarding who could stand in the day of the wrath of God and the lamb. The celebratory use of palm branches is best understood against broad cultural associations of palm branches with worship, prayer, and the welcome of a ruler (Koester 428).

Use of the OT: This vision of victory for God's people builds on God's promise to Abraham about having innumerable descendants but universalizes it to include those from every nation, tribe, people, and language. Compare ὃν ἀριθμῆσαι αὐτὸν οὐδεὶς ἐδύνατο in Rev 7:9 with Gen 13:16 (εἰ δύναταί τις ἐξαριθμῆσαι τὴν ἄμμον τῆς γῆς, καὶ τὸ σπέρμα σου ἐξαριθμηθήσεται), 15:5 (ἀρίθμησον τοὺς ἀστέρας, εἰ δυνήσῃ ἐξαριθμῆσαι αὐτούς. καὶ εἶπεν Οὕτως ἔσται τὸ σπέρμα σου), 32:13 (ἣ οὐκ ἀριθμηθήσεται ἀπὸ τοῦ πλήθους), and Hos 2:1 (ἦν ὁ ἀριθμὸς τῶν υἱῶν Ισραηλ ὡς ἡ ἄμμος τῆς θαλάσσης, ἣ οὐκ ἐκμετρηθήσεται οὐδὲ ἐξαριθμηθήσεται). Christian believers (both Jew and gentile) bring consummate fulfillment to God's promises to Abraham about his seed (cf. Gal 3:29; Rom 4:16).

7:10 καὶ κράζουσιν (3rd pl. pres. act. ind. of κράζω, narrative pres.) **φωνῇ** (means) **μεγάλῃ** (attrib.) **λέγοντες** (nom. pl. masc. of pres. act. ptc. of λέγω, manner, introduces dir. speech), **Ἡ σωτηρία** (subj. nom. of verbless cl.) **τῷ θεῷ** (poss. dat.) **ἡμῶν** (gen. of subord.) **τῷ** (anaphoric to 4:2) **καθημένῳ** (dat. sg. masc. of pres. mid. ptc. of κάθημαι, attrib.) **ἐπὶ τῷ** (anaphoric to 4:2) **θρόνῳ** (loc.) **καὶ τῷ** (anaphoric to 5:6) **ἀρνίῳ** (ἀρνίον, -ου, τό, "lamb," poss. dat.).

It is important to note that the lamb is worshiped alongside God. Salvation is associated with God in worship in 19:1 with a gen. instead of a dat. of poss. (ἡ σωτηρία καὶ ἡ δόξα καὶ ἡ δύναμις τοῦ θεοῦ ἡμῶν [Rev 19:1]; cf. Ps 3:9 LXX [3:8 EVV]: τοῦ κυρίου ἡ σωτηρία).

7:11 καὶ πάντες (attrib.) **οἱ** (anaphoric to 5:11) **ἄγγελοι** (subj. nom.) **εἱστήκεισαν** (3rd pl. plpf. act. ind. of ἵστημι, it is hard to determine a rationale for the only plpf. in Revelation; it could express the spatial remoteness of the angels as encircling the other groups [Math 100] but prob. simply carries a past stative meaning as common in the NT [Fanning 268]) **κύκλῳ** (improper prep., "around") **τοῦ θρόνου** (loc.) **καὶ τῶν** (anaphoric to 4:4) **πρεσβυτέρων** (loc., coord. obj. of prep. κύκλῳ) **καὶ τῶν** (anaphoric to 4:6) **τεσσάρων** ("four," attrib.) **ζῴων** (ζῷον, -ου, τό, "animal, living thing," coord. loc., obj. of prep. κύκλῳ) **καὶ ἔπεσαν** (3rd pl. aor. act. ind. of πίπτω, the subj. of this vb. is ἄγγελοι) **ἐνώπιον τοῦ** (anaphoric to 4:2) **θρόνου** (loc.) **ἐπὶ τὰ πρόσωπα** (loc.) **αὐτῶν** (poss.) **καὶ προσεκύνησαν** (3rd pl. aor. act. ind. of προσκυνέω) **τῷ θεῷ** (dat. dir. obj.)

7:12 λέγοντες (nom. pl. masc. of pres. act. ptc. of λέγω, manner, "the angels stood . . . and fell . . . saying," introduces dir. speech), **Ἀμήν** (indeclinable interj. of affirmation from Hebrew), **ἡ εὐλογία** (εὐλογία, -ας, ἡ, "praise, blessing," subj. nom. of verbless cl., this applies to the following six nouns) **καὶ ἡ δόξα καὶ ἡ σοφία καὶ ἡ εὐχαριστία** (εὐχαριστία, -ας, ἡ, "thanksgiving") **καὶ ἡ τιμὴ** (τιμή, -ῆς, ἡ, "honor") **καὶ ἡ δύναμις καὶ ἡ ἰσχὺς** (ἰσχύς, -ύος, ἡ, "power") **τῷ θεῷ** (poss. dat.) **ἡμῶν** (gen. of subord.) **εἰς τοὺς αἰῶνας** (measure) **τῶν αἰώνων** (emph.) **ἀμήν**.

As elsewhere, John uses a list of seven terms.

7:13 Καὶ ἀπεκρίθη (3rd sg. aor. mid. ind. of ἀποκρίνομαι) **εἷς** (subj. nom.) **ἐκ τῶν** (anaphoric to 4:4) **πρεσβυτέρων** (part. gen.) **λέγων** (nom. sg. masc. pres. act. ptc. of λέγω, manner, introduces dir. speech) **μοι** (indir. obj.), **Οὗτοι** (pred. nom. of εἰσὶν, fronted for emph.; a topic construction resumed by τίνες [Math 102], ant. of Οὗτοί in 7:14 and αὐτούς in 7:17) **οἱ** (anaphoric to 7:9) **περιβεβλημένοι** (nom. pl. masc. of pf. pass. ptc. of περιβάλλω, "wrap, clothe," subst. in appos. to Οὗτοι or attrib. to Οὗτοι)

τὰς (anaphoric to 7:9) **στολὰς** (στολή, -ῆς, ἡ, "robe," dir. obj.) **τὰς λευκὰς** (λευκός, -ή, -όν, "white, bright," attrib.) **τίνες** (interr. pron., subj. nom.) **εἰσὶν** (3rd pl. pres. act. ind. of εἰμί) **καὶ πόθεν** (interr. adv., "from where") **ἦλθον** (3rd pl. aor. act. ind. of ἔρχομαι); **7:14 καὶ εἴρηκα** (1st sg. pf. act. ind. of λέγω, the pf. seems to function as an aor.; Mathewson argues that the change in tense indicates intentional choice although it is not evident what that would contribute beyond subtle emph. [Math 102]; it is better understood as an aoristic pf. in light of its coordination with aorists in the context [11b, 11c, 13a, 14b; see Fanning 269]; introduces dir. speech) **αὐτῷ** (indir. obj.), **Κύριέ** (voc. of address) **μου** (gen. of subord.), **σὺ** (subj. nom.) **οἶδας** (2nd sg. pf. act. ind. of οἶδα). **καὶ εἶπέν** (3rd sg. aor. act. ind. of λέγω, introduces dir. speech) **μοι** (indir. obj.), **Οὗτοί** (subj. nom.) **εἰσιν** (3rd pl. pres. act. ind. of εἰμί) **οἱ ἐρχόμενοι** (nom. pl. masc. of pres. mid. ptc. of ἔρχομαι, subst., pred. nom., the pres. tense could suggest that this is a vision of the intermediate state during which the tribulation is still unfolding on earth or it could carry a distributive sense to refer to the repetition of various individual "comings" viewed together [Fanning 271]) **ἐκ τῆς θλίψεως** (θλῖψις, -εως, ἡ, "tribulation, affliction, trouble," separation) **τῆς μεγάλης** (attrib.) **καὶ ἔπλυναν** (3rd pl. aor. act. ind. of πλύνω, "wash," the coordination of a ptc. with finite vbs. seems awkward but occurs elsewhere in Revelation and extrabiblical Greek) **τὰς στολὰς** (στολή, -ῆς, ἡ, "robe," dir. obj.) **αὐτῶν** (poss.) **καὶ ἐλεύκαναν** (3rd pl. aor. act. ind. of λευκαίνω, "make white," coord.) **αὐτὰς** (dir. obj.) **ἐν τῷ αἵματι** (means) **τοῦ ἀρνίου** (ἀρνίον, -ου, τό, "lamb," gen. of source).

There is a paradox in the use of blood to make clothes white; this conceptually points to the use of blood for purification. Jesus's blood looses from sin, redeems human beings, produces white robes, and provides victory (Rev 1:5; 5:9; 7:14; 12:11). Revelation does not use θλῖψις as a technical term for a seven-year period of time; tribulation is instead the present reality of the churches (1:9; 2:9, 10; cf. 2:22). Some early Christians saw Daniel's prophecies (see below) as being fulfilled in Christ's first coming (Matt 21:44; Luke 20:18; John 5:24–29), and many viewed themselves as living in the final tribulational period before the end (note the present reality of θλῖψις for the early Christian community in Matt 13:21; 24:9; Mark 4:17; John 16:33; Acts 11:19; 14:22; 20:23; Rom 5:3; 8:35; 12:12; 2 Cor 1:4, 8; 4:17; 6:4; 8:2; Col 1:24; 1 Thess 1:6; 3:3; 2 Thess 1:4; Heb 10:33; Rev 1:9; 2:9, 10; cf. 2 Tim 3:12; 1 Pet 4:17). Jesus's reference to θλῖψις μεγάλη in Matt 24:21 likely refers to the time of the destruction of the Jerusalem temple in AD 70 (cf. Matt 24:1–2; Mark 13:1–2; Luke 21:5–6, 20–24). The early Christians held that the last days, end times, or latter days had already begun (Mark 1:15; Acts 2:16–17; Gal 4:4; 1 Cor 10:11; 2 Cor 6:2; 1 Tim 4:1; 2 Tim 3:1; 1 Pet 1:20; 2 Pet 3:3; Heb 1:2; 9:26; Jas 5:3; 1 John 2:18; Jude 18). The great tribulation in 7:14 is the entire period between Jesus's enthronement and return (Koester 429).

Use of the OT: Ezekiel 37:3 contains a question from God to Ezekiel regarding the vision to which Ezekiel answered εἶπα Κύριε, σὺ ἐπίστῃ ταῦτα. Jewish apocalyptic literature frequently features examples of the use of questions and answers between the angelic intermediary and the recipient of divine revelation to provide further explanation of reported visions (see Dan 7:15–27; 12:6–8; and Zech 4:2–7 for other biblical examples).

The idea of a great eschatological tribulation is drawn from Dan 12:1 where the eschatological opponent persecutes Israelites who remained faithful to the covenant (Dan 11–12). Daniel 12:1 speaks of a day of unparalleled tribulation but does not call it "great" (ἐκείνη ἡ ἡμέρα θλίψεως, οἵα οὐκ ἐγενήθη ἀφ᾽ οὗ ἐγενήθησαν ἕως τῆς ἡμέρας ἐκείνης). That intense tribulation will be followed by the exaltation of all the people who were found written in the book (ὃς ἂν εὑρεθῇ ἐγγεγραμμένος ἐν τῷ βιβλίῳ [Dan 12:1]; cf. Rev 3:5; 13:8; 17:8; 20:15) and the resurrection of many (πολλοὶ τῶν καθευδόντων ἐν τῷ πλάτει τῆς γῆς ἀναστήσονται [Dan 12:2]) into eternal life (εἰς ζωὴν αἰώνιον) or disgrace (εἰς ὀνειδισμόν), dispersion, and eternal shame (εἰς διασπορὰν καὶ αἰσχύνην αἰώνιον [Dan 12:2]; cf. Rev 20:11–15). When Daniel asks (εἶπα; note the change from 3rd sg. in the MT to 1st sg. in LXX) when the completion would be (Dan 12:6), the man clothed in linen raises his hands and swears an oath (ὤμοσε τὸν ζῶντα εἰς τὸν αἰῶνα θεὸν [Dan 12:7]; cf. Rev 10:5–6) that the shattering of the power of the holy people would last for a time, times, and half a time (Dan 12:7; cf. Rev 12:14). This time would last until many were tested and purified (ἕως ἂν πειρασθῶσι καὶ ἁγιασθῶσι πολλοί [Dan 12:9–10]; cf. Rev 2:10; 22:11). During this time, sinners will sin and not understand (ἁμάρτωσιν οἱ ἁμαρτωλοί, καὶ οὐ μὴ διανοηθῶσι πάντες οἱ ἁμαρτωλοί [Dan 12:10]; cf. Rev 22:11) while the understanding take heed (Dan 12:10: οἱ διανοούμενοι προσέξουσιν). Daniel 12:11 does not seem to be picked up by John, who does not mention the abomination of desolation (τὸ βδέλυγμα τῆς ἐρημώσεως) or the 1,290 and 1,335-day time periods (focusing instead on 1,260 days in Rev 11:3), although John does contain similar macarisms (Dan 12:12: μακάριος ὁ ἐμμένων). The cluster of allusions to Dan 12 are scattered throughout Revelation but suggest the following eschatological scenario: the time between Daniel (and John) and the end will last a time, times, and half a time and will be characterized by progressively intensifying tribulation that will test and purify God's people. This period of testing will be concluded with a resurrection to glorification or shame based upon one being written in a book. God's people are called to endure with understanding in order to gain the blessing. These parallels (both specific features and the general scenario) are spread throughout the entire book of Revelation and indicate that Daniel 12 played an important role in shaping John's thinking about the future. Daniel 11:35 (12:10 MT) refers to purification as "making white" (as in Rev 7:14) but the LXX does not use λευκαίνω; this points to the influence of the Hebrew Bible on John in this instance.

7:15 διὰ τοῦτό (causal, the ant. is the action of washing and making robes white in 7:14) **εἰσιν** (3rd pl. pres. act. ind. of εἰμί) **ἐνώπιον τοῦ** (anaphoric to 4:2) **θρόνου** (loc.) **τοῦ θεοῦ** (poss.) **καὶ λατρεύουσιν** (3rd pl. pres. act. ind. of λατρεύω, "worship, serve," futuristic pres.) **αὐτῷ** (dat. dir. obj.) **ἡμέρας** (gen. of time) **καὶ νυκτὸς** (gen. of time) **ἐν**

τῷ ναῷ (ναός, -οῦ, ὁ, "temple," loc.) **αὐτοῦ** (poss.), **καὶ ὁ** (anaphoric to 4:2) **καθήμενος** (nom. sg. masc. of pres. mid. ptc. of κάθημαι, subst., subj. nom.) **ἐπὶ τοῦ** (anaphoric to 4:2) **θρόνου** (loc.) **σκηνώσει** (3rd sg. fut. act. ind. of σκηνόω, "live in a tent, dwell") **ἐπ' αὐτούς** (loc., "pitch a tent *over* them," or "dwell *among* them").

The vb. λατρεύω points to cultic service and strengthens John's depiction of God's people as priests (note the allusion to Exod 19:6 in Rev 1:6; 5:10); here they are pictured as serving as priests in the intermediate state in God's heavenly temple/throne room prior to resurrection life in God's new creation (recall the lack of a temple in new creation in 21:22). Understanding 7:9–17 as describing the intermediate state, however, is complicated by the clear allusions to future resurrection life in God's new creation. Parallels with the future new creation include God's presence (7:15; 21:3; 22:3–4), lack of hunger and thirst (7:16; 22:1–2), protection from the sun's harm (7:16; 21:23; 22:4), access to living water (7:17; 21:6; 22:1, 17), and the wiping away of all tears (7:17; 21:4). This vision seems to move seamlessly from the intermediate state into descriptions of God's people in the new creation without any explicit distinction between the two situations. This vision of the intermediate state greatly expands upon the more concise vision in 6:9–11 and shows the overcomers as proleptically experiencing the realities of new creation, which are further detailed in 21:1–22:5. This lack of precision highlights the rhetorical purpose of visions of believers in victory and rest (whether in the intermediate or final state), which are meant to encourage and motivate believers in the present time of tribulation to persevere and overcome. The lack of precision also serves to caution readers who may want John's apocalyptic visions to be more precise, coherent, or logically consistent than they were originally intended to be.

Use of the OT: Ezekiel prophesies that in the restoration of Israel God's tent/habitation would be among them (37:27: καὶ ἔσται ἡ κατασκήνωσίς μου ἐν αὐτοῖς). Zechariah 2:14 LXX (2:10 EVV) contains God's promise to come and dwell in their midst (ἰδοὺ ἐγὼ ἔρχομαι καὶ κατασκηνώσω ἐν μέσῳ σου). The fulfillment of these OT promises to Israel are expanded in Rev 7:15 to include gentiles (recall 7:9).

7:16 οὐ πεινάσουσιν (3rd pl. fut. act. ind. of πεινάω, "hunger") **ἔτι** (temp. adv., "again, still") **οὐδὲ** (neg. disjunctive conj., "neither . . . nor") **διψήσουσιν** (3rd pl. fut. act. ind. of διψάω, "thirst") **ἔτι οὐδὲ μὴ** (double neg. for emph.) **πέσῃ** (3rd sg. aor. act. subjunc. of πίπτω) **ἐπ' αὐτοὺς** (acc. of disadvantage "against them," or loc. "upon them") **ὁ ἥλιος** (ἥλιος, -ου, ὁ, "sun," subj. nom.) **οὐδὲ πᾶν** (attrib., "any" [BDAG 782b]) **καῦμα** (καῦμα, -ατος, τό, "heat," coord. subj. nom.),

---

Use of the OT: Isaiah prophesies that in the restoration of Israel they will not hunger or thirst (49:10: οὐ πεινάσουσιν οὐδὲ διψήσουσιν).

7:17 ὅτι (causal) **τὸ** (anaphoric to 5:6) **ἀρνίον** (ἀρνίον, -ου, το, "lamb," subj. nom.) **τὸ** (adjectivizer) **ἀνὰ μέσον** (ἀνὰ μέσον means "in the midst of," here it indicates being seated "on the center of the throne" [BDAG 635a; cf. 3:21; 7:17]) **τοῦ** (anaphoric to 4:2) **θρόνου** (loc.) **ποιμανεῖ** (3rd sg. fut. act. ind. of ποιμαίνω, "shepherd, rule") **αὐτοὺς** (dir. obj.) **καὶ ὁδηγήσει** (3rd sg. fut. act. ind. of ὁδηγέω, "lead, guide") **αὐτοὺς** (dir. obj.) **ἐπὶ ζωῆς** (attrib. gen. with ὑδάτων, fronted for emph.) **πηγὰς** (πηγή, -ῆς, ἡ, "spring," loc., obj. of prep.) **ὑδάτων** (gen. of content, "full of"), **καὶ ἐξαλείψει** (3rd sg. fut. act. ind. of ἐξαλείφω, "wipe away") **ὁ θεὸς** (subj. nom.) **πᾶν** (attrib.) **δάκρυον** (δάκρυον, -ου, τό, "tear," dir. obj.) **ἐκ τῶν ὀφθαλμῶν** (separation) **αὐτῶν** (poss.).

John elsewhere has the gen. ζωῆς follow "water" (τῆς πηγῆς τοῦ ὕδατος τῆς ζωῆς in 21:6 and ὕδωρ ζωῆς in 22:17). The placement of ζωῆς here before πηγὰς ὑδάτων is unusual and emphasizes the life. In John 10:11, 14 Jesus claims to be the good shepherd (ὁ ποιμὴν ὁ καλός) who lays down his life for his sheep.

Use of the OT: Psalm 22:1–2 LXX (23:1–2 EVV) describes God as the shepherd (Κύριος ποιμαίνει με) who leads his sheep by still waters (ἐπὶ ὕδατος ἀναπαύσεως ἐξέθρεψέν με). Ezekiel 34:23 contains God's promise to raise up one shepherd over his people who would shepherd them, God's servant David (καὶ ἀναστήσω ἐπ' αὐτοὺς ποιμένα ἕνα καὶ ποιμανεῖ αὐτούς, τὸν δοῦλόν μου Δαυιδ, καὶ ἔσται αὐτῶν ποιμήν). Isaiah 49:10 prophesies that in the restoration of Israel the burning heat and sun would not fall on them (οὐδὲ πατάξει αὐτοὺς καύσων οὐδὲ ὁ ἥλιος) and that the one having mercy on them will comfort and will lead them through springs of waters (ὁ ἐλεῶν αὐτοὺς παρακαλέσει καὶ διὰ πηγῶν ὑδάτων ἄξει αὐτούς). Jeremiah confronts God's people for forsaking God, the fountain of living waters (2:13: ἐμὲ ἐγκατέλιπον, πηγὴν ὕδατος ζωῆς). Isaiah 25:8 contains the promise that God would wipe away tears from all faces (καὶ πάλιν ἀφεῖλεν ὁ θεὸς πᾶν δάκρυον ἀπὸ παντὸς προσώπου).

FOR FURTHER STUDY

34. Salvation

Rand, J. A. du. "The New Jerusalem as Pinnacle of Salvation: Text (Rev 21:1–22:5) and Intertext." *Neot* 38 (2004): 275–302.

———. "Soteriology in the Apocalypse of John." Pages 465–504 in *Salvation in the New Testament: Perspectives on Soteriology*. NovTSup 121. Edited by J. G. van der Watt. Leiden: Brill, 2005.

Rowland, C. "The Lamb and the Beast, the Sheep and the Goats: 'The Mystery of Salvation' in Revelation." Pages 181–92 in *A Vision for the Church: Studies in Early Christian Ecclesiology in Honour of J. P. M. Sweet*. Edited by M. Bockmuehl and M. B. Thompson. Edinburgh: T&T Clark, 1997.

Stewart, A. E. *Soteriology as Motivation in the Apocalypse of John*. Gorgias Biblical Studies 61. Piscataway, NJ: Gorgias, 2015.

*Talbert, C. H. "Divine Assistance and Enablement of Human Faithfulness in the Revelation of John Viewed within Its Apocalyptic Context." Pages 265–82 in *Getting "Saved": The Whole Story of Salvation in the New Testament*. Edited by C. H. Talbert and J. A. Whitlark. Grand Rapids: Eerdmans, 2011.

6. The Seventh Seal (8:1–5)

8:1 Καὶ ὅταν (temp. subord. conj., א P and most minuscules read ὅτε to match 6:1, 3, 5, 7, 9, 12 while the harder reading of ὅταν with the ind. mood is found in A C 1006 1611 1841 and finds a parallel in 4:9 [Metzger 669]) **ἤνοιξεν** (3rd sg. aor. act. ind. of ἀνοίγω, the subjunc. mood is expected because of ὅταν but the ind. mood is likely used to indicate a specific instead of indefinite event [Math 106]) **τὴν σφραγῖδα** (σφραγίς, -ῖδος, ἡ, "seal," dir. obj.) **τὴν ἑβδόμην** (ἕβδομος, -η, -ον, "seventh," attrib.), **ἐγένετο** (3rd sg. aor. mid. ind. of γίνομαι) **σιγὴ** (σιγή, -ῆς, ἡ, "silence," pred. nom., "there was silence") **ἐν τῷ οὐρανῷ** (loc.) **ὡς** (indicates approximation, "about" [L&N 78.42; BDAG 1105d]) **ἡμιώριον** (ἡμιώριον, -ου, τό, "half-hour").

The silence underscores that God is attentively listening to the prayers of his people (Koester 431). The silence is linked to incense and prayer in 8:3. There is no obvious significance to half an hour beyond being a sufficient but limited period of time set aside to ensure that God hears the prayer of his people (likely the prayer recounted in 6:10 as representative and giving voice to the prayers of God's people on earth).

8:2 καὶ εἶδον (1st sg. aor. act. ind. of ὁράω; καὶ εἶδον introduces a new vision, scene, figure, or activity [Aune[a] 338]) **τοὺς** (likely the "well-known" use of the art., "*the* seven angels" [Wallace 225] known to hearers from Jewish tradition [1 En. 20:1–8; Tob 12:15]; alternatively, but less likely, it could be anaphoric to the angels associated with the seven churches in 1:20 [anar. ἄγγελοι]; it is not likely anaphoric to the seven spirits of 1:4 [articular πνευμάτων] because of the change in noun) **ἑπτὰ** (attrib.) **ἀγγέλους** (dir. obj., ant. of οἵ) **οἳ** (subj. nom.) **ἐνώπιον τοῦ θεοῦ** (loc.) **ἑστήκασιν** (3rd pl. pf. act. ind. of ἵστημι, elsewhere in Revelation the 3rd pl. of ἵστημι ends with –καν/αν [Aune[b] 483], intensive pf. highlights the pres. state), **καὶ ἐδόθησαν** (3rd pl. aor. pass. ind. of δίδωμι) **αὐτοῖς** (indir. obj.) **ἑπτὰ** ("seven," attrib.) **σάλπιγγες** (σάλπιγξ, -ιγγος, ἡ, "trumpet," subj. nom.).

The introduction of the angels with the seven trumpets in 8:2 seems to disrupt the narration of the sixth seal in 8:1, 3–5. This interruption could indicate that the seven trumpets are contained in the seventh seal judgment in a telescoping manner, but the interruption does not require this interpretation. Instead, it should be recognized as a literary interlocking technique that John also uses when introducing the seven bowls

of judgment. John introduces the seven angels with seven bowls in 15:1 but then uses 15:2–4 to conclude the prior topic before returning to the seven bowls in 15:5. John interlocks the seal and trumpet judgments in Rev 8:1–5 in a similar way. This suggests a literary connection between the sets of seven, but it does not seem to favor telescoping over recapitulation or chronological progression. Understanding 8:3–5 as the conclusion of the seventh seal makes it evident that the seventh seal is not without content.
8:3 Καὶ ἄλλος (attrib.) **ἄγγελος** (subj. nom.) **ἦλθεν** (3rd sg. aor. act. ind. of ἔρχομαι) **καὶ ἐστάθη** (3rd sg. aor. pass. [for mid.] ind. of ἵστημι) **ἐπὶ τοῦ θυσιαστηρίου** (θυσιαστήριον, -ου, τό, "altar," loc.) **ἔχων** (nom. sg. masc. of pres. act. ptc. of ἔχω, manner) **λιβανωτὸν** (λιβανωτός, -οῦ, ὁ, "frankincense, censer," the adj. χρυσοῦν requires this to indicate the censor in which the incense burned and not the incense itself, dir. obj.) **χρυσοῦν** (χρυσοῦς, -ῆ, -οῦν, "golden," attrib.), **καὶ ἐδόθη** (3rd sg. aor. pass. ind. of δίδωμι) **αὐτῷ** (indir. obj.) **θυμιάματα** (θυμίαμα, -ατος, τό, "incense," subj. nom.) **πολλά** (attrib.), **ἵνα** (purpose) **δώσει** (3rd sg. fut. act. ind. of δίδωμι, the fut. ind. is used instead of the expected subjunc.; this is not uncommon in Revelation) **ταῖς προσευχαῖς** (dat. of association, "with the prayers," this has also been understood as a dat. of advantage, "on behalf of the prayers," or a temp. dat., "at the same time as the prayers," but association is most likely [Math 108]) **τῶν ἁγίων** (subst., subj. gen.) **πάντων** (attrib.) **ἐπὶ τὸ θυσιαστήριον** (θυσιαστήριον, -ου, τό, "altar," loc.) **τὸ χρυσοῦν** (χρυσοῦς, -ῆ, -οῦν, "golden," attrib.) **τὸ** (adjectivizer) **ἐνώπιον τοῦ** (anaphoric to 4:2) **θρόνου** (loc.).

Revelation 8:1, 3–5 likely describes God's answer to the prayer of his people articulated and expressed in 6:9; judgment was delayed but will come at last. At the sounding of the sixth trumpet in 9:13 a voice comes from the golden altar; this reference to the altar intratextually connects the judgment of 9:13 back to 8:3 and the prayers of 6:9–10. The altar is also connected with the judgment of the grape harvest in 14:18 and the third bowl judgment in 16:7. Each of these intratextual connections represents God's judgment as his response to the prayer of his people for justice.

Use of the OT: In Ps 140:2 LXX (141:2 EVV) David asks that his prayer would be guided like incense before God (κατευθυνθήτω ἡ προσευχή μου ὡς θυμίαμα ἐνώπιόν σου). Exodus 30:1–3 gives instruction for the building of the altar of incense (θυσιαστήριον θυμιάματος) overlaid with gold. There is a theme in the OT of God hearing and responding to the desperate prayer of his oppressed people by judging the oppressors: the cry of the Israelites from their works went up to God in Exod 2:23 (καὶ ἀνέβη ἡ βοὴ αὐτῶν πρὸς τὸν θεὸν ἀπὸ τῶν ἔργων), and God responded by sending Moses to enact the events of the exodus, which brought judgment to oppressors and liberation to the oppressed (Exod 3:7–10; Neh 9:9–10). The recollection of God's past acts of deliverance in response to prayer motivates fresh prayer for deliverance in the present time (Ps 106:44–47).

8:4 καὶ ἀνέβη (3rd sg. aor. act. ind. of ἀναβαίνω) **ὁ καπνὸς** (καπνός, -οῦ, ὁ, "smoke," subj. nom.) **τῶν θυμιαμάτων** (θυμίαμα, -ατος, τό, "incense," gen. of source) **ταῖς προσευχαῖς** (dat. of association) **τῶν ἁγίων** (subst., subj. gen.) **ἐκ χειρὸς** (source) **τοῦ ἀγγέλου** (poss.) **ἐνώπιον τοῦ θεοῦ** (loc.).
8:5 καὶ εἴληφεν (3rd sg. pf. act. ind. of λαμβάνω, aoristic pf.) **ὁ ἄγγελος** (subj. nom.) **τὸν λιβανωτὸν** (λιβανωτός, -οῦ, ὁ, "censer," dir. obj.) **καὶ ἐγέμισεν** (3rd sg. aor. act. ind. of γεμίζω, "fill") **αὐτὸν** (dir. obj.) **ἐκ τοῦ πυρὸς** (source, "from," possibly content, "with") **τοῦ θυσιαστηρίου** (θυσιαστήριον, -ου, τό, "altar," gen. of source) **καὶ ἔβαλεν** (3rd sg. aor. act. ind. of βάλλω) **εἰς τὴν γῆν** (loc.), **καὶ ἐγένοντο** (3rd pl. aor. mid. ind. of γίνομαι) **βρονταὶ** (βροντή, -ῆς, ἡ, "thunder," subj. nom., "thunder happened") **καὶ φωναὶ** (coord. subj. nom.) **καὶ ἀστραπαὶ** (ἀστραπή, -ῆς, ἡ, "lightning," coord. subj. nom.) **καὶ σεισμός** (σεισμός, -οῦ, ὁ, "earthquake," coord. subj. nom.).

Use of the OT: On the allusion to the Sinai theophany in Exod 19:16–19, see on 4:5. In Ezekiel's vision of the judgment of Jerusalem he saw a man in linen who was instructed to go among the wheels underneath the cherubim and the throne to receive burning coals to scatter over the city (πλῆσον τὰς δράκας σου ἀνθράκων πυρὸς ἐκ μέσου τῶν χερουβιν καὶ διασκόρπισον ἐπὶ τὴν πόλιν [Ezek 10:2]; cf. Ezek 10:7).

HOMILETICAL SUGGESTIONS

The seven seals describe the beginning of God's judgments within history, which intensify and culminate with cosmic upheaval at the day of the Lord. The fifth seal provides encouragement to God's suffering people that the delay will not be forever and that God will bring justice. The interlude in chapter 7 describes God's action to protect his people from spiritual harm (sealing) and the result of such sealing (victorious celebration and worship around God's throne in the intermediate state).

Seven Seals of Judgment Bringing Salvation (6:1–8:5)

1. God's judgments have already begun and will culminate in the second coming (6:1–8, 12–17; 8:1–5).
2. God's people will suffer but are promised vindication (6:9–11).
3. God will protect his people from spiritual harm (7:1–8).
4. God's people will experience tribulation followed by salvation (7:9–17).

C. SEVEN TRUMPET JUDGMENTS (8:6–11:19)

The seven trumpet judgments are divided into two groups. The first four trumpets are recounted in a rapid manner in 8:6–12 while the last three are discussed in more detail and grouped together as the three woes announced in 8:13. Similar to the digression in 7:1–17 between the sixth and seventh seal judgments, a digression in 10:1–11:14 separates the sixth from the seventh trumpet judgment.

1. Preparation of the Seven Trumpets (8:6)

8:6 Καὶ οἱ ἑπτὰ (attrib.) **ἄγγελοι** (subj. nom.) **οἱ ἔχοντες** (nom. pl. masc. of pres. act. ptc. of ἔχω, attrib.) **τὰς** (anaphoric to 8:2) **ἑπτὰ** (attrib.) **σάλπιγγας** (σάλπιγξ, -ιγγος, ἡ, "trumpet," dir. obj.) **ἡτοίμασαν** (3rd pl. aor. act. ind. of ἑτοιμάζω, "prepare") **αὐτοὺς** (a dir. obj. in reference to the trumpets should be fem. so this is refl. to indicate the angels, "themselves") **ἵνα** (purpose) **σαλπίσωσιν** (3rd pl. aor. act. subjunc. of σαλπίζω, "blow a trumpet").

2. The First Six Trumpet Judgments (8:7–9:21)

a. The First Trumpet (8:7)

8:7 Καὶ ὁ πρῶτος (subst., subj. nom.) **ἐσάλπισεν** (3rd sg. aor. act. ind. of σαλπίζω, "blow a trumpet")· **καὶ ἐγένετο** (3rd sg. aor. mid. ind. of γίνομαι, it is common for coord. subjects to take a sg. vb. which would match the first subj.) **χάλαζα** (χάλαζα, -ης, ἡ, "hail," subj. nom.) **καὶ πῦρ** (coord. subj. nom., "hail and fire happened") **μεμιγμένα** (nom. pl. neut. of pf. pass. ptc. of μίγνυμι, "mix," attrib., pl. according to the sense, modifying two subjects, hail and fire) **ἐν αἵματι** (association) **καὶ ἐβλήθη** (3rd sg. aor. pass. ind. of βάλλω, the sg. vb. views hail and fire as a unified subject) **εἰς τὴν γῆν** (loc.), **καὶ τὸ τρίτον** (subst.) **τῆς γῆς** (part. gen.) **κατεκάη** (3rd sg. aor. pass. ind. of κατακαίω, "burn up, consume," the prep. prefix intensifies the burning) **καὶ τὸ τρίτον** (subst.) **τῶν δένδρων** (δένδρον, -ου, τό, "tree," part. gen.) **κατεκάη** (3rd sg. aor. pass. ind. of κατακαίω) **καὶ πᾶς** (attrib.) **χόρτος** (χόρτος, -ου, ὁ, "grass," subj. nom.) **χλωρὸς** (χλωρός, -ά, -ό, "pale greenish-gray," attrib.) **κατεκάη** (3rd sg. aor. pass. ind. of κατακαίω).

The trumpet judgments draw significantly from the Exodus plague traditions and employ the imagery of ecological disaster. This could suggest God's judgment will be linked to human mismanagement of the created order as human beings suffer the consequences of the harmful exploitation of creation, but it is more likely explained by holy war traditions in the OT in which God often engages in judgment through natural phenomenon and natural judgments. The descriptions of God's use of nature in holy war is normally literal in historical narratives such as the Exodus itself but overwhelmingly figurative and symbolic in prophetic and apocalyptic texts (see Isa 13:10–13; 34:4; Ezek 32:6–8; Hab 3:6–11). The reappropriation of Exodus judgments likely suggests that in Revelation God's judgments have a liberative purpose; the goal is not simply to punish evildoers but to bring salvation to his people through judgment of the oppressors. The judgment of a third indicates a progression from the fourth impacted in the fourth seal (6:8) but is a step back from the apparent universality of the judgment of the sixth and seventh seals.

Use of the OT: The hail and fire connect with the seventh plague of Exod 9:13–35, but apart from the combination of χάλαζα and πῦρ (and perhaps the damage to βοτάνη and ξύλον in Exod 9:25) the other details do not match. Exodus does not mention blood but has "sound/thunder" (φωνή: 9:23, 28, 29, 33, 34) and rain (ὑετός: 9:29, 33, 34). Exodus also focuses on hail as the source of damage while John focuses on fire (the repetition of κατεκάη). Ezekiel 38:22 expands hail and fire to include death (disease), blood, and sulfur (καὶ κρινῶ αὐτὸν θανάτῳ καὶ αἵματι καὶ ὑετῷ κατακλύζοντι καὶ λίθοις χαλάζης, καὶ πῦρ καὶ θεῖον βρέξω ἐπ' αὐτὸν) in God's theophanic judgment of Gog and his host. Note how Wis 16:16–22, reflecting on the seventh plague, explores the unusual ability of the fire to still burn alongside rain. John perhaps avoids the potential problem by omitting reference to rain.

Ezekiel 5:1–2, 12 describes how the entirety of Jerusalem will be judged in thirds (fourths in the LXX; see on 6:8). Zechariah 13:8–9 describes a judgment which destroys two-thirds so that the remaining one-third can be refined in fire.

---

b. The Second Trumpet (8:8–9)

8:8 Καὶ ὁ δεύτερος (attrib.) **ἄγγελος** (subj. nom.) **ἐσάλπισεν** (3rd sg. aor. act. ind. of σαλπίζω, "blow a trumpet"). **καὶ ὡς** (comp., the comp. cl. functions as subj. of ἐβλήθη) **ὄρος μέγα** (attrib.) **πυρὶ** (conceptually cognate dat. of means, the redundancy perhaps explains why πυρί is missing in 046 and some minuscules [Metzger 669]) **καιόμενον** (nom. sg. neut. of pres. pass. ptc. of καίω, "burn," attrib.) **ἐβλήθη** (3rd sg. aor. pass. ind. of βάλλω) **εἰς τὴν θάλασσαν** (loc.), **καὶ** (result, "and then, and so" [BDAG 495a]) **ἐγένετο** (3rd sg. aor. mid. ind. of γίνομαι) **τὸ τρίτον** (subst., subj. nom.) **τῆς θαλάσσης** (part. gen.) **αἷμα** (pred. nom.)

Use of the OT: This judgment is similar to the first plague, which turned the water in the Nile to blood (Exod 7:14–25) but there are no lexical connections beyond αἷμα. In an oracle against Babylon in Jer 28:25 LXX (51:25 EVV), Jeremiah prophesies that God is against Babylon (ἰδοὺ ἐγὼ πρὸς σέ), the destroying mountain which destroys all the earth (τὸ ὄρος τὸ διεφθαρμένον τὸ διαφθεῖρον πᾶσαν τὴν γῆν), and he would make it like a burned over mountain (καὶ δώσω σε ὡς ὄρος ἐμπεπυρισμένον). This is a subtle allusion that perhaps gains strength when it is considered that the later judgment of Babylon would impact maritime trade (Rev 18:17–18) and will later be illustrated by a giant millstone thrown into the sea (18:21; cf. Jer 51:63–64). The same vb. is used for the destruction of the boats in 8:9 (διαφθείρω). The burning mountain in 8:8, however, is perhaps more likely explained by the description of rebellious angels as stars like burning mountains in 1 En. 18:13–16; 21:3. These backgrounds are not incompatible if the burning mountain is understood as the angel representing or associated with Babylon and the judgment in heaven paralleled or preceded the judgment of Babylon on earth.

8:9 καὶ ἀπέθανεν (3rd sg. aor. act. ind. of ἀποθνήσκω) **τὸ τρίτον** ("third," subst., subj. nom.) **τῶν κτισμάτων** (κτίσμα, -ατος, τό, "creature," part. gen.) **τῶν** (adjectivizer) **ἐν τῇ θαλάσσῃ** (loc.) **τὰ ἔχοντα** (nom. pl. neut. of pres. act. ptc. of ἔχω, subst., appos.) **ψυχὰς** (dir. obj.) **καὶ τὸ τρίτον** (subst., subj. nom.) **τῶν πλοίων** (πλοῖον, -ου, το, "ship," part. gen.) **διεφθάρησαν** (3rd pl. aor. pass. ind. of διαφθείρω, "destroy," pl. because of the part. gen. and not the subj. nom.).

The nom. neut. pl. ptc. τὰ ἔχοντα should be in the gen. case to match τῶν κτισμάτων but is probably functioning as a nom. neut. subj. of the vb. ἀπέθανεν in appos. to τὸ τρίτον (Moţ 118–19).

Use of the OT: Although lacking lexical connections, thematic connections exist to the statement in Exod 7:21 that οἱ ἰχθύες οἱ ἐν τῷ ποταμῷ ἐτελεύτησαν because of the Nile turning to blood.

---

c. The Third Trumpet (8:10–11)

8:10 Καὶ ὁ τρίτος ("third," attrib.) **ἄγγελος** (subj. nom.) **ἐσάλπισεν** (3rd sg. aor. act. ind. of σαλπίζω, "blow a trumpet"). **καὶ ἔπεσεν** (3rd sg. aor. act. ind. of πίπτω) **ἐκ τοῦ οὐρανοῦ** (source) **ἀστὴρ** (ἀστήρ, -έρος, ὁ, "star," subj. nom.) **μέγας** (attrib.) **καιόμενος** (nom. sg. masc. of pres. pass. ptc. of καίω, "burn," attrib.) **ὡς** (comp.) **λαμπὰς** (λαμπάς, -άδος, ἡ, "lamp, torch") **καὶ ἔπεσεν** (3rd sg. aor. act. ind. of πίπτω) **ἐπὶ τὸ τρίτον** (subst., loc.) **τῶν ποταμῶν** (ποταμός, -οῦ, ὁ, "river," part. gen.) **καὶ ἐπὶ τὰς πηγὰς** (πηγή, -ῆς, ἡ, "spring," loc.) **τῶν ὑδάτων** (gen. of content),

8:11 καὶ τὸ ὄνομα (subj. nom.) **τοῦ ἀστέρος** (ἀστήρ, -έρος, ὁ, "star," poss.) **λέγεται** (3rd sg. pres. pass. ind. of λέγω, gnomic pres.) **ὁ Ἄψινθος** (ἀψίνθος, -ου, τό, "wormwood," nom. of appellation), **καὶ ἐγένετο** (3rd sg. aor. mid. ind. of γίνομαι) **τὸ τρίτον** ("third," subst., subj. nom.) **τῶν ὑδάτων** (part. gen.) **εἰς ἄψινθον** (ἀψίνθιον, -ου, τό, "wormwood," the prep. phrase functions as a pred. nom. "the third became wormwood" [Wallace 47]) **καὶ πολλοὶ** (subst., subj. nom.) **τῶν ἀνθρώπων** (part. gen.) **ἀπέθανον** (3rd pl. aor. act. ind. of ἀποθνήσκω) **ἐκ τῶν ὑδάτων** (cause) **ὅτι** (causal) **ἐπικράνθησαν** (3rd pl. aor. pass. ind. of πικραίνω, "make bitter").

The effect of the third trumpet parallels the second trumpet but affects fresh water instead of salt water. The second trumpet features a great burning mountain being cast into the sea to turn a third of it to blood while the third trumpet features a great burning star falling from heaven to poison a third of fresh water. Ἄψινθος was well known as a bitter herb but it was not generally associated with death or poison (BDAG 161c).

Use of the OT: See 8:8 on the first Exodus plague. The ability of the extreme bitterness to cause death is likely inferred from descriptions of God's judgment in the OT as poisonous water. Jeremiah 9:14 LXX (9:15 EVV) contains God's threat to punish his people with poisonous water (καὶ ποτιῶ αὐτοὺς ὕδωρ χολῆς) while Jer 23:15 repeats the threat (ποτιῶ αὐτοὺς ὕδωρ πικρόν).

FOR FURTHER STUDY

35. The Seven Trumpets (8:6–11:19)

Paulien, J. *Decoding Revelation's Trumpets: Literary Allusions and the Interpretation of Revelation 8:7–12*. AUSDDS 11. Berrien Springs, MI: Andrews University Press, 1987.

Villiers, Pieter G. R. de. "The Eschatological Celebration of Salvation and the Prophetic Announcement of Judgment: The Message of Revelation 8:1–6 in the Light of Its Composition." *Neot* 41 (2007): 67–96.

d. The Fourth Trumpet (8:12–13)

8:12 Καὶ ὁ τέταρτος (τέταρτος, -η, -ον, "fourth," attrib.) **ἄγγελος** (subj. nom.) **ἐσάλπισεν** (3rd sg. aor. act. ind. σαλπίζω, "blow a trumpet"). **καὶ ἐπλήγη** (3rd sg. aor. pass. ind. πλήσσω, "strike," a sg. vb. with coord. sg. subjects) **τὸ τρίτον** ("third," subst., subj. nom.) **τοῦ ἡλίου** (ἥλιος, -ου, ὁ, "sun," part. gen.) **καὶ τὸ τρίτον** (subst., coord. subj. nom.) **τῆς σελήνης** (σελήνη, -ης, ἡ, "moon," part. gen.) **καὶ τὸ τρίτον** (subst., coord. subj. nom.) **τῶν ἀστέρων** (ἀστήρ, -έρος, ὁ, "star," part. gen.), **ἵνα** (result) **σκοτισθῇ** (3rd sg. aor. pass. subjunc. σκοτίζω, "darken") **τὸ τρίτον** (subst., subj. nom.) **αὐτῶν** (part. gen.) **καὶ ἡ ἡμέρα** (subj. nom.) **μὴ φάνῃ** (3rd sg. aor. act. subjunc. φαίνω, "shine") **τὸ τρίτον** (subst., dir. obj.) **αὐτῆς** (part. gen.) **καὶ ἡ νὺξ** (subj. nom. with implied φάνῃ) **ὁμοίως** (comp. adv., "likewise").

Use of the OT: The ninth Exodus plague consisted of complete darkness for three days (Exod 10:21–29). Apart from the general theme of the diminishment of light in the ninth plague, there are not explicit connections there to the fourth trumpet. Amos 8:9 associates God's judgment with the diminishment of light when he claims that the sun will set at midday (καὶ δύσεται ὁ ἥλιος μεσημβρίας) and the light will be darkened in the land in the day (καὶ συσκοτάσει ἐπὶ τῆς γῆς ἐν ἡμέρᾳ τὸ φῶς). For more on the diminishment of cosmic light, see Rev 6:12–13. Beale cites Jewish interpretations of the Exodus plagues that understand and apply them, at least partly, as a theological metaphor for spiritual darkness or ignorance (Beale 481–82; Wis 17; Philo, *On Dreams*, 1.114).

8:13 Καὶ εἶδον (1st sg. aor. act. ind. of ὁράω; καὶ εἶδον introduces a new vision, scene, figure, or activity [Aune[a] 338]), **καὶ ἤκουσα** (1st sg. aor. act. ind. of ἀκούω) **ἑνὸς** (functioning as an indef. art., "an") **ἀετοῦ** (ἀετός, -οῦ, ὁ, "eagle," sometimes vulture is meant [BDAG 22d], gen. dir. obj.) **πετομένου** (gen. sg. masc. of pres. mid. ptc. of πέτομαι, "fly," attrib.) **ἐν μεσουρανήματι** (μεσουράνημα, -ατος, τό, "zenith" [BDAG 635d], the point in the sky directly above the viewer, loc.) **λέγοντος** (gen. sg. masc. of pres. act. ptc. of λέγω, compl. in obj.-compl. gen. construction) **φωνῇ** (dat. of means) **μεγάλῃ** (attrib.), **Οὐαὶ οὐαὶ οὐαὶ** (interj., "pain"; as a subst. it can denote "a state of intense hardship or distress" or "woe" [BDAG 734c], the repetition provides emph.) **τοὺς κατοικοῦντας** (acc. pl. masc. of pres. act. ptc. of κατοικέω, "dwell," subst., acc. of reference but see below on the case) **ἐπὶ τῆς γῆς** (loc.) **ἐκ τῶν λοιπῶν** (attrib.) **φωνῶν** (gen. of cause) **τῆς σάλπιγγος** (σάλπιγξ, -ιγγος, ἡ, "trumpet," gen. of source, "sounds from the trumpet," or attrib. gen., "trumpet sounds") **τῶν τριῶν** (attrib.) **ἀγγέλων** (poss.) **τῶν μελλόντων** (gen. pl. masc. of pres. act. ptc. of μέλλω, "about to," attrib.) **σαλπίζειν** (pres. act. inf. of σαλπίζω, "blow a trumpet," compl. inf.).

Οὐαί is elsewhere in biblical literature followed by a dat. or a nom. as voc. to indicate the person or thing to whom pain is expressed (BDAG 734c); Rev 8:13 and 12:12 are apparently unique in using an acc. to indicate the group or location affected by the woe. Because the activity better fits an angel, the TR along with a few other mss read ἀγγέλου instead of ἀετοῦ, but א A 046 and most minuscules are decisive (Metzger 669). On John's consistent negative view of "the ones dwelling on the earth" see 3:10.

Use of the OT: An eagle, as a powerful predatory bird, is sometimes associated with warnings or pronouncements of judgment (Deut 28:49; Hos 8:1; Hab 1:8; Jer 4:13; Lam 4:19; Ezek 17:3), often to indicate the swiftness or inevitability of the pronounced judgment.

---

e. The Fifth Trumpet (9:1–12)

9:1 Καὶ ὁ πέμπτος (πέμπτος, -η, -ον, "fifth," attrib.) **ἄγγελος** (subj. nom.) **ἐσάλπισεν** (3rd sg. aor. act. ind. of σαλπίζω, "blow a trumpet")· **καὶ εἶδον** (1st sg. aor. act. ind. of ὁράω) **ἀστέρα** (ἀστήρ, -έρος, ὁ, "star," dir. obj.) **ἐκ τοῦ οὐρανοῦ** (source, adv. modifying the ptc.) **πεπτωκότα** (acc. sg. masc. of pf. act. ptc. of πίπτω, attrib.) **εἰς τὴν γῆν** (loc.), **καὶ ἐδόθη** (3rd sg. aor. pass. ind. of δίδωμι) **αὐτῷ** (indir. obj.) **ἡ κλεὶς** (κλείς, -ιδός, ἡ, "key," subj. nom.) **τοῦ φρέατος** (φρέαρ, -ατος, τό, "well, pit," obj. gen., "key to the pit") **τῆς** ("well-known" use of the art., "*the* abyss" assumes the hearers already knew about this realm, or monadic to indicate there is only one abyss) **ἀβύσσου** (ἄβυσσος, -ου, ἡ, "abyss," epex., "the shaft, that is, the abyss," or perhaps part. to indicate the shaft as the narrow opening to the broader demonic realm of the abyss)

The pf. πεπτωκότα does not highlight process but the stative result of a past action or event. The pf. would naturally refer back to the star that fell in 8:10 (or even the burning mountain of 8:8 which is connected with stars in 1 En. 18:13–16; 21:3) although the significance of such a connection is not obvious. The burning mountain in 8:8 was cast on the sea and the star in 8:10 fell on the rivers and springs, while the star which had fallen in 9:1 fell upon the land so it could just be that the pf. assumes a third star that brings judgment to a different sphere without narrating the fall of the star.

The star is certainly an angelic being who is empowered with the key to carry out an act of divine judgment, but this description does not explicitly indicate whether the star is an angel of God (Koester 456; Fanning 295) or a demonic being (Beale 491–92). It would seem natural to identify a fallen star with a demonic being through parallels with apocalyptic literature noted above and Isa 14:12; Luke 10:18. But there is perhaps a closer parallel in Revelation with the angel who has the key to the abyss in 20:1. The star in 9:1 should be distinguished from the destroyer of 9:11 who was presumably in the abyss with the demons.

Although various ancient writers conflate the abyss with the underworld, Hades, and fiery torment in various ways, Revelation seems to maintain careful distinctions (Koester 456–57): (1) the abyss is the spiritual demonic realm whose entrance is controlled by God (9:1–2, 11; 11:7; 17:8; 20:1, 3); (2) "under the earth" contains natural created beings who properly worship the creator (5:3, 13); (3) Hades is the holding place for the dead until the final judgment (1:18; 6:8; 20:13–14); and (4) the lake of fire is the realm of eternal punishment for the beasts, Satan, Death, Hades, and those whose names are not in the lamb's book of life (19:20; 20:10, 14, 15). The reference to the abyss in Luke 8:31 suggests that there were both demons active outside the abyss and demons imprisoned within the abyss.

9:2 καὶ ἤνοιξεν (3rd sg. aor. act. ind. of ἀνοίγω) **τὸ φρέαρ** (φρέαρ, -ατος, τό, "well, pit," dir. obj.) **τῆς ἀβύσσου** (ἄβυσσος, -ου, ἡ, "abyss," epex. or part.), **καὶ ἀνέβη** (3rd sg. aor. act. ind. of ἀναβαίνω) **καπνὸς** (καπνός, -οῦ, ὁ, "smoke," subj. nom.) **ἐκ τοῦ φρέατος** (φρέαρ, -ατος, τό, gen. of source) **ὡς** (comp.) **καπνὸς καμίνου** (κάμινος, -ου, ἡ, "furnace, oven," source) **μεγάλης** (attrib.), **καὶ ἐσκοτώθη** (3rd sg. aor. pass. ind. of σκοτόω, "darken," the sg. vb. is used with coord. sg. subjects) **ὁ ἥλιος** (ἥλιος, -ου, ὁ, "sun," subj. nom.) **καὶ ὁ ἀὴρ** (ἀήρ, -έρος, ὁ, "air," coord. subj. nom.) **ἐκ τοῦ καπνοῦ** (καπνός, -οῦ, ὁ, "smoke," causal) **τοῦ φρέατος** (source).

Use of the OT: Genesis 19:28, in describing the judgment of Sodom and Gomorrah, notes that the smoke of the land was ascending like the smoke of a furnace (καὶ ἰδοὺ ἀνέβαινεν φλὸξ τῆς γῆς ὡσεὶ ἀτμὶς καμίνου). A similar expression is used to describe the smoke on Sinai that accompanied God's descent in Exod 19:18 (καὶ ἀνέβαινεν ὁ καπνὸς ὡς καπνὸς καμίνου).

9:3 **καὶ ἐκ τοῦ καπνοῦ** (καπνός, -οῦ, ὁ, "smoke," source) **ἐξῆλθον** (3rd pl. aor. act. ind. of ἐξέρχομαι) **ἀκρίδες** (ἀκρίς, -ίδος, ἡ, "locust," subj. nom.) **εἰς τὴν γῆν** (loc.) **καὶ ἐδόθη** (3rd sg. aor. pass. ind. of δίδωμι) **αὐταῖς** (indir. obj.) **ἐξουσία** (subj. nom., here with a focus more on capability or capacity than on rightful or official authority [BDAG 352d–53a]) **ὡς** (comp.) **ἔχουσιν** (3rd pl. pres. act. ind. of ἔχω) **ἐξουσίαν** (dir. obj.) **οἱ σκορπίοι** (σκορπίος, -ου, ὁ, "scorpion," subj. nom.) **τῆς γῆς** (source, "from the earth," loc., "upon the earth," or subord., "over the earth").

Use of the OT: In Exod 10:12 God instructs Moses to stretch out his hand over the land of Egypt so that locusts rise up upon the land (ἀναβήτω ἀκρὶς ἐπὶ τὴν γῆν).

9:4 **καὶ** (adversative, "but") **ἐρρέθη** (3rd sg. aor. pass. ind. of λέγω) **αὐταῖς** (indir. obj.) **ἵνα** (content, introduces indir. speech, the cl. functions as subj. of ἐρρέθη) **μὴ ἀδικήσουσιν** (3rd pl. fut. act. ind. of ἀδικέω, "harm, damage," fut. in place of the subjunc.) **τὸν χόρτον** (χόρτος, -ου, ὁ, "grass," dir. obj.) **τῆς γῆς** (loc.) **οὐδὲ** (neg. conj., "neither . . . nor") **πᾶν** (attrib.) **χλωρὸν** (χλωρός, -ά, -όν, "pale green," subst., "green plant," coord. dir. obj.) **οὐδὲ πᾶν** (attrib., "any" [BDAG 782c]) **δένδρον** (δένδρον, -ου, τό, "tree," coord. dir. obj.), **εἰ μὴ** ("except") **τοὺς ἀνθρώπους** (dir. obj., ant. of οἵτινες) **οἵτινες** (indef. rel. pron., "whoever," sub. nom.) **οὐκ ἔχουσιν** (3rd pl. pres. act. ind. of ἔχω, narrative pres.) **τὴν** (anaphoric to 7:2) **σφραγῖδα** (σφραγίς, -ῖδος, ἡ, "seal," dir. obj.) **τοῦ θεοῦ** (source, poss., or subj. gen.) **ἐπὶ τῶν μετώπων** (μέτωπον, -ου, τό, "forehead," loc.).

The demonic oppression and violence of the fifth trumpet is explicitly directed toward those who do not have God's seal (Rev 9:4) while the demonic oppression and violence of the sixth trumpet is directed toward those who are engaged in idolatrous worship, murder, sexual immorality, and thefts (Rev 9:20–21). These two woes are not pictured as randomly afflicting everyone but are focused on people who lack God's seal and are actively engaged in evil activities.

There is no need to suggest that there was time for some grass to grow again between the burning up of all the green grass in the first trumpet and this prohibition against harming grass; it is better to recognize that apocalyptic visions are not generally concerned with such inconsistencies. Note a similar problem with the diminishment of a third of the stars in the fourth trumpet (8:12) after the sixth seal states that the stars of the heaven fell to the earth (6:13). Such inconsistencies are only difficult with an overly literalistic or rigid chronological reading of the visions.

Use of the OT: Exodus 10:15 states that the locusts covered the face of the land (καὶ ἐκάλυψεν τὴν ὄψιν τῆς γῆς) so that no green thing was left in the trees (οὐχ ὑπελείφθη χλωρὸν οὐδὲν ἐν τοῖς ξύλοις). In contrast, Rev 9:4 makes it clear that these locusts were not to harm any green thing (πᾶν χλωρὸν) or tree (οὐδὲ πᾶν δένδρον). Wisdom of Solomon 16:9 states the bites of the locusts and flies were fatal to the Egyptians (οὓς μὲν γὰρ ἀκρίδων καὶ μυιῶν ἀπέκτεινεν δήγματα). On Ezek 9:4 as background for God's seal, see Rev 7:3.

9:5 καὶ ἐδόθη (3rd sg. aor. pass. ind. of δίδωμι) **αὐτοῖς** (indir. obj.) **ἵνα** (content, the subord. cl. functions as the subj. of ἐδόθη) **μὴ ἀποκτείνωσιν** (3rd pl. pres. act. subjunc. of ἀποκτείνω) **αὐτούς** (dir. obj.), **ἀλλ'** (adversative) **ἵνα** (content, coord. with the prior ἵνα) **βασανισθήσονται** (3rd pl. fut. pass. ind. of βασανίζω, "subject to punitive judicial procedure, *torture*" or "subject to severe distress, *torment, harass*" [BDAG 168a], the fut. is used in place of subjunc.) **μῆνας** (μήν, -μηνός, ὁ, "month," acc. of time) **πέντε** ("five," attrib.), **καὶ ὁ βασανισμὸς** (βασανισμός, -οῦ, ὁ, "torment," subj. nom. of verbless cl.) **αὐτῶν** (subj. gen.) **ὡς** (comp. functions as pred. of verbless cl.) **βασανισμὸς σκορπίου** (σκορπίος, -ου, ὁ, "scorpion," subj. gen.) **ὅταν** (indef. temp. conj.) **παίσῃ** (3rd sg. aor. act. subjunc. of παίω, "sting, strike") **ἄνθρωπον** (dir. obj.).
9:6 καὶ ἐν ταῖς ἡμέραις (temp.) **ἐκείναις** (demon. pron., attrib.) **ζητήσουσιν** (3rd pl. fut. act. ind. of ζητέω, note the switch from aor. to fut. to mark a transition from recounting the vision to predicting the future response of people to the locusts) **οἱ ἄνθρωποι** (subj. nom.) **τὸν θάνατον** (dir. obj.) **καὶ οὐ μὴ** (emph. double neg.) **εὑρήσουσιν** (3rd pl. fut. act. ind. of εὑρίσκω, fut. instead of subj.) **αὐτόν** (dir. obj.), **καὶ ἐπιθυμήσουσιν** (3rd pl. fut. act. ind. of ἐπιθυμέω) **ἀποθανεῖν** (aor. act. inf. of ἀποθνήσκω, compl. inf.) **καὶ φεύγει** (3rd sg. pres. act. ind. of φεύγω, "flee," futuristic pres.) **ὁ θάνατος** (subj. nom., personification) **ἀπ' αὐτῶν** (separation).

Use of the OT: When Job is lamenting his birth, he asks why life is given to those with pain in the soul who desire death but do not obtain it (οἳ ὁμείρονται τοῦ θανάτου καὶ οὐ τυγχάνουσιν [Job 3:21]). When Jeremiah declares judgment on the sons of Judah, he proclaims that they will choose death over life (εἵλοντο τὸν θάνατον ἢ τὴν ζωήν) in God's judgment (Jer 8:3).

9:7 Καὶ τὰ ὁμοιώματα (ὁμοίωμα, -ατος, τό, "likeness," subj. nom. of verbless cl.) **τῶν ἀκρίδων** (ἀκρίς, -ίδος, ἡ, "locust," poss.) **ὅμοια** (ὅμοιος, -οία, -οιον, "like, similar," pred. adj. with implied copulative) **ἵπποις** (ἵππος, -ου, ὁ, "horse," compl. of ὅμοια) **ἡτοιμασμένοις** (dat. pl. masc. of pf. pass. ptc. of ἑτοιμάζω, "prepare," attrib.) **εἰς πόλεμον** (πόλεμος, -ου, ὁ, "battle," purpose), **καὶ ἐπὶ τὰς κεφαλὰς** (loc.) **αὐτῶν** (poss.) **ὡς** (comp., implied subj. and vb., "*there was something* like") **στέφανοι** (στέφανος, -ου, ὁ, "wreath, crown") **ὅμοιοι χρυσῷ** (χρυσός, -οῦ, ὁ, "gold," compl. of ὅμοιοι, attrib. with implied *crowns*), **καὶ τὰ πρόσωπα** (subj. nom. of verbless cl.) **αὐτῶν** (poss.) **ὡς** (comp., functions as pred. of verbless cl.) **πρόσωπα ἀνθρώπων** (poss.),

---

Use of the OT: The appearance of the locusts/soldiers in the Lord's terrible army in Joel 2:4 is like horses (ὡς ὅρασις ἵππων ἡ ὄψις αὐτῶν). These soldiers had been prepared for battle (Joel 2:5: παρατασσόμενος εἰς πόλεμον). When human armies are compared to locusts the emph. is on the large size of the army (Judg 6:5; 7:12; Jer 46:23; 51:14).

9:8 καὶ εἶχον (3rd pl. impf. act. ind. of ἔχω, the impf. provides offline information that does not advance the narrative) **τρίχας** (θρίξ, τριχός, ἡ, "hair," dir. obj.) **ὡς** (comp.) **τρίχας γυναικῶν** (poss.), **καὶ οἱ ὀδόντες** (ὀδούς, ὀδόντος, ὁ, "tooth," subj. nom.) **αὐτῶν** (poss.) **ὡς** (comp., compl. of ἦσαν) **λεόντων** (λέων, -οντος, ὁ, "lion," poss. of implied ὀδόντες) **ἦσαν** (3rd pl. impf. act. ind. of εἰμί),

---

Use of the OT: The locusts in Joel 1:6 have teeth like a lion (οἱ ὀδόντες αὐτοῦ ὀδόντες λέοντος).

9:9 καὶ εἶχον (3rd pl. impf. act. ind. of ἔχω) **θώρακας** (θώραξ, -ακος, ὁ, "breastplate," dir. obj.) **ὡς** (comp.) **θώρακας σιδηροῦς** (σιδηροῦς, -ᾶ, -οῦν, "made of iron," attrib.), **καὶ ἡ φωνὴ** (subj. nom. of verbless cl.) **τῶν πτερύγων** (πτέρυξ, -υγος, ἡ, "wing," source) **αὐτῶν** (poss.) **ὡς** (comp., functions as pred. with "was" implied) **φωνὴ ἁρμάτων** (ἅρμα, -ατος, τό, "chariot," source) **ἵππων** (ἵππος, -ου, ὁ, "horse," gen. of association, "with") **πολλῶν** (attrib.) **τρεχόντων** (gen. pl. masc. of pres. act. ptc. of τρέχω, "run," attrib. ptc.) **εἰς πόλεμον** (πόλεμος, -ου, ὁ, "battle," purpose),

---

Use of the OT: The sound of the locusts in Joel 2:5 is as chariots (ὡς φωνὴ ἁρμάτων).

9:10 καὶ ἔχουσιν (3rd pl. pres. act. ind. of ἔχω, narrative pres., the change to the pres. from the prior two impf. vbs. in 9:8, 9 could indicate a transition from background physical description to their leader and ability to harm [Math 121]; Fanning describes the switch to the pres. as a transition to a report or description mode [Fanning 299]) **οὐρὰς** (οὐρά, -ᾶς, ἡ, "tail," dir. obj.) **ὁμοίας** (ὅμοιος, -οία, -οιον, "like, similar," comp. adj.) **σκορπίοις** (σκορπίος, -ου, ὁ, "scorpion") **καὶ κέντρα** (κέντρον, -ου, τό, "sting," coord. dir. obj. of ἔχουσιν), **καὶ ἐν ταῖς οὐραῖς** (loc.) **αὐτῶν** (poss.) **ἡ ἐξουσία** (subj. nom. of verbless cl.) **αὐτῶν** (poss. or subj. gen.) **ἀδικῆσαι** (aor. act. inf. of ἀδικέω, "harm, damage," epex, inf.) **τοὺς ἀνθρώπους** (dir. obj.) **μῆνας** (μήν, μηνός, ὁ, "month," acc. of time) **πέντε** ("five," attrib.).

9:11 ἔχουσιν (3rd pl. pres. act. ind. of ἔχω, narrative pres., asyndeton) **ἐπ' αὐτῶν** (subord.) **βασιλέα** (dir. obj.) **τὸν** (possibly well-known or monadic) **ἄγγελον** (appos. to βασιλέα) **τῆς ἀβύσσου** (ἄβυσσος, -ου, ἡ, "abyss," gen. of subord.), **ὄνομα** (parenthetical nom. [Math 122] or subj. nom. of verbless cl.) **αὐτῷ** (poss. dat.) **Ἑβραϊστὶ** (adv. or dat. of reference, "in Hebrew/Aramaic") **Ἀβαδδών** (Ἀβαδδών, ὁ, indeclinable, "Abaddon," transliteration of the Hebrew word for "destruction" elsewhere used as a designation for the abyss but which is applied by John to the king of the abyss [Koester 461; BDAG 1b], appos. to ὄνομα or pred. nom. of verbless cl., "His name was Abaddon in Hebrew") **καὶ ἐν τῇ Ἑλληνικῇ** (Ἑλληνικός, -ή, -όν, "Greek," subst., dat. of reference) **ὄνομα** (dir. obj.) **ἔχει** (3rd sg. pres. act. ind. of ἔχω) **Ἀπολλύων** (Ἀπολλύων, -ονος, ὁ, "Apollyon, the Destroyer," given as a translation of the Hebrew, nom. of appellation in appos. to acc. ὄνομα).

The king over the abyss is likely Satan based on his description elsewhere in early Christianity and Second Temple Judaism as the prince of demons (Matt 9:34; 12:24; Mark 3:22; Luke 11:15; T. Sol. 2:9) or angel of Sheol (Mart. Ascen. Isa. 10:8; 11:19) but he could also be an intermediary demonic figure because Satan is not described as an ἄγγελος elsewhere in Revelation (Koester 461).

9:12 Ἡ (the art. nominalizes the interj.) **οὐαὶ** (as a subst. it denotes "a state of intense hardship or distress," or "woe" [BDAG 734c], subj. nom., ant. of ταῦτα at the end of the verse) **ἡ μία** (attrib., "first" [BDAG 293a]) **ἀπῆλθεν** (3rd sg. aor. act. ind. of ἀπέρχομαι)· **ἰδοὺ** (emph. interj.) **ἔρχεται** (3rd sg. pres. mid. ind. of ἔρχομαι, futuristic pres.) **ἔτι** (temp. adv., "still, yet") **δύο** (attrib.) **οὐαὶ** (subj. nom., the pl. subj. does not match the sg. vb.; the δύο οὐαὶ are being viewed as a sg. entity) **μετὰ ταῦτα** (subst., temp., "after these things," over one hundred minuscules use μετὰ ταῦτα to start 9:13 since John normally uses the prep. phrase to begin a cl. but he does occasionally use the expression to close a sentence [in 1:19; 4:1] and its placement with 9:12 has much stronger external support [Metzger 669–70]).

f. The Sixth Trumpet (9:13–21)

9:13 Καὶ ὁ ἕκτος ("sixth," attrib.) **ἄγγελος** (subj. nom.) **ἐσάλπισεν** (3rd sg. aor. act. ind. of σαλπίζω, "blow a trumpet")· **καὶ ἤκουσα** (1st sg. aor. act. ind. of ἀκούω) **φωνὴν** (dir. obj.) **μίαν** (attrib., functioning as indef. art., "a" [BDAG 292d]) **ἐκ τῶν [τεσσάρων]** ("four," attrib., regarding the inclusion of τεσσάρων, the external evidence is balanced and the internal evidence is inconclusive [Metzger 670]) **κεράτων** (κέρας, -ατος, τό, "horn," source) **τοῦ θυσιαστηρίου** (θυσιαστήριον, -ου, τό, "altar," part. gen.) **τοῦ χρυσοῦ** (χρυσοῦς, -ῆ, -οῦν, "golden," attrib.) **τοῦ ἐνώπιον τοῦ θεοῦ** (loc.),

---

Use of the OT: On the incense altar overlaid with gold in Exod 30:1–3, see on 8:3. Each reference to the θυσιαστήριον in Revelation likely refers to the same incense altar in the divine throne room/heavenly temple, which is associated with the prayer of God's people for justice and God's response in judgment.

9:14 λέγοντα (acc. sg. masc. of pres. act. ptc. of λέγω, compl. in obj.-compl. acc. construction, "I heard a voice speaking," the masc. ptc. is incongruous with the fem. φωνή but reflects a *constructio ad sensum*) **τῷ ἕκτῳ** ("sixth," attrib.) **ἀγγέλῳ** (indir. obj.), **ὁ ἔχων** (nom. sg. masc. of pres. act. ptc. of ἔχω, subst., appos., ἔχων is a solecism and should be dat. [τῷ ἔχοντι] to match τῷ ἕκτῳ ἀγγέλῳ unless it is taken as a parenthetical nom.) **τὴν σάλπιγγα** (σάλπιγξ, -ιγγος, ἡ, "trumpet," dir. obj.), **λῦσον** (2nd sg. aor. act. impv. of λύω) **τοὺς** (the well-known art., not in regard to the human hearers but to the sixth angel who is being addressed [Fanning 301]; not anaphoric to 7:1 as argued by Aune [Aune[b] 536–37]) **τέσσαρας** ("four," attrib.) **ἀγγέλους** (dir. obj.) **τοὺς δεδεμένους** (acc. pl. masc. of pf. pass. ptc. of δέω, "bind," attrib.) **ἐπὶ τῷ ποταμῷ** (ποταμός, -οῦ, ὁ, "river," loc.) **τῷ μεγάλῳ** (attrib.) **Εὐφράτῃ** (Εὐφράτης, -ου, ὁ, "Euphrates River," appos. to ποταμῷ).

Mention of the Euphrates provides a point of connection between the sixth trumpet and the sixth bowl judgment where the Euphrates dries up to allow the kings from the east to cross (16:12); this could suggest an overlap between the trumpets and bowls whereby they describe the same event with different details and perspectives (Beale 507).

Use of the OT: The Euphrates features prominently in the OT as the eastern boundary of the territory promised by God to Israel (Gen 15:18; Exod 23:31; Deut 1:7; 11:24; Josh 1:4) and a natural boundary crossed in times of invasion in the OT (Isa 8:7; 2 Kgs 23:29; 24:7; Jer 46:10) and in the contemporary conflict between Rome and Parthia.

9:15 καὶ ἐλύθησαν (3rd pl. aor. pass. ind. of λύω) **οἱ τέσσαρες** ("four," attrib.) **ἄγγελοι** (subj. nom.) **οἱ ἡτοιμασμένοι** (nom. pl. masc. of pf. pass. ptc. of ἑτοιμάζω, "prepare," attrib.) **εἰς τὴν** (the art. introduces a list in which each impers. element is a subset of the next [Wallace 286–87]) **ὥραν** (temp., Mathewson identifies it as "goal" [Math 124]) **καὶ ἡμέραν** (temp.), **καὶ μῆνα** (μήν, μηνός, ὁ, "month," temp.) **καὶ ἐνιαυτόν** (ἐνιαυτός, -οῦ, ὁ, "year," temp.) **ἵνα** (purpose) **ἀποκτείνωσιν** (3rd pl. pres. act. subjunc. of ἀποκτείνω) **τὸ τρίτον** ("third," subst., dir. obj.) **τῶν ἀνθρώπων** (part. gen.).

The four angels who are bound are likely demonic beings utilized by God to enact judgment similar to the four horsemen/four winds that are restrained for the right time (6:1–8; 7:1), the locusts held captive in the abyss until being released (9:2–3), and Satan being bound to restrict his deceiving activities (20:1–3; Koester 466; Beale 506). That their alignment is ambiguous (cf. the argument that they are holy angels in

Fanning 302) highlights a larger question regarding the relationship of God to demonic agents in Revelation. Cato Gulaker argues against the more common dualistic paradigm of cosmic conflict in Revelation and in favor of a more monistic understanding of Satan (and other demonic beings) as divine agents in Revelation (Gulaker, *Heavenly Adversary of Man*). From this monistic perspective, Gulaker argues that Satan is not God's adversary or anti-divine and there is no cosmic conflict. Satan is God's obedient servant or tool who is just doing his job in fulfillment of the satanic office. He is the main antagonist of human beings who tests and sifts humanity in service to God's plan, but he is not antagonistic toward God. In response, monism rightly stresses the titles for God, divine passives, and evident limitations on and control over evil characters in Revelation while dualism rightly highlights Satan's competing throne in 2:13; 13:2; 16:10, his attempt to destroy the Messiah in 12:4, his war with Michael and his angels in 12:7, his great wrath in 12:12, his hubris in competition for worship in Rev 13 and 18, his connection with the beasts who wage war against the Messiah in 19:19, his items of restraint in Rev 20:1–2, and his severe punishment in 20:10. It is evident that Revelation does not support a pure form of cosmological dualism or monism and it is better to recognize a blending of the two positions resisting tidy categorization; the evil forces in Revelation are evil and oppose God, his people, and humanity, but they are not outside of God's control and sovereignty.

9:16 καὶ ὁ ἀριθμὸς (ἀριθμός, -οῦ, ὁ, "number," subj. nom. of verbless cl.) **τῶν** (the art. is perhaps unexpected here; Fanning suggests it is appropriate due to the connection of the soldiers to the Euphrates and the well-known connection of the river with invading armies bringing divine judgment [Fanning 303]) **στρατευμάτων** (στράτευμα, -ατος, τό, "soldier," obj. gen.) **τοῦ ἱππικοῦ** (ἱππικός, -ή, -όν, "cavalry," attrib. gen.) **δισμυριάδες** (δισμυριάς, -άδος, ἡ, "double-myriad,") **μυριάδων** (see on 5:11, the expression indicates an uncountable or immense number), **ἤκουσα** (1st sg. aor. act. ind. of ἀκούω) **τὸν ἀριθμὸν** (ἀριθμός, -οῦ, ὁ, "number," dir. obj.) **αὐτῶν** (obj. gen.).

9:17 καὶ οὕτως (adv.) **εἶδον** (1st sg. aor. act. ind. of ὁράω) **τοὺς ἵππους** (ἵππος, -ου, ὁ, "horse," dir. obj.) **ἐν τῇ ὁράσει** (ὅρασις, -εως, ἡ, "vision," manner "or the context or circumstances in which he saw them: in a vision" [Math 126]) **καὶ τοὺς καθημένους** (acc. pl. masc. of pres. mid. ptc. of κάθημαι, subst., dir. obj.) **ἐπ' αὐτῶν** (loc.), **ἔχοντας** (acc. pl. masc. of pres. act. ptc. of ἔχω, attrib., the following cl. makes clear it is modifying ἵππους) **θώρακας** (θώραξ, -ακος, ὁ, "breastplate," dir. obj.) **πυρίνους** (πύρινος, -η, -ον, "fiery," attrib.) **καὶ ὑακινθίνους** (ὑακίνθινος, -ίνη, -ινον, "dark blue/red," attrib., coord.) **καὶ θειώδεις** (θειώδης, -ες, "sulfurous, yellow," attrib., coord.), **καὶ αἱ κεφαλαὶ** (subj. nom. of verbless cl.) **τῶν ἵππων** (ἵππος, -ου, ὁ, "horse," poss. [Wallace 84]) **ὡς** (comp. which functions as pred. nom.) **κεφαλαὶ λεόντων** (λέων, -οντος, ὁ, "lion," poss. or attrib. gen.), **καὶ ἐκ τῶν στομάτων** (source) **αὐτῶν** (poss.) **ἐκπορεύεται** (3rd sg. pres. mid. ind. of ἐκπορεύομαι, narrative pres., the sg. vb. is followed by three coord. sg. subjects) **πῦρ καὶ καπνὸς** (καπνός, -οῦ, ὁ, "smoke") **καὶ θεῖον** (θεῖον, -ου, τό, "sulfur").

Note the hearing-seeing literary technique by which what is seen by John interprets what he has heard (9:13, 17; cf. 5:5–6; 7:9; 21:9–10); in this case, there are not literal contradictions between what John heard and saw, but the horror of what he saw could not have been anticipated by the auditory report alone. Aune notes, "The

closest approximation to such a creature in antiquity is probably the Chimaera slain by the hero Bellerophon with the aid of Pegasus as described in Greek and Roman mythology. The Chimaera is consistently described as having the head of a lion, the tail of a dragon or serpent, and the body of a goat belching fire (*Iliad* 6.181–82; Hesiod, *Theogony* 319–24; Euripides, *Ion* 203–4; *Electra* 474–75; Apollodorus 2.3.1; Lucretius, *De rerum natura* 2.705; 5.905–7; Hyginus, *Fabulae* 57.2). The extensive iconographic tradition is extremely consistent, depicting the Chimaera as a lion with the head of a goat coming from the top middle of its body, with a long snake's body and head for a tail" (Aune[b] 539). The biggest difference between the Chimaera and the horsemen of the sixth trumpet is the goat head coming out of its body but the similarities in the description would have produced a fearful response through this association.
9:18 ἀπὸ (asyndeton) **τῶν τριῶν** (attrib.) **πληγῶν** (πληγή, -ῆς, ἡ, "plague," source) **τούτων** (attrib.) **ἀπεκτάνθησαν** (3rd pl. aor. pass. ind. of ἀποκτείνω, pl. vb. with sg. subj. according to the sense) **τὸ τρίτον** ("third," subst., subj. nom.) **τῶν ἀνθρώπων** (part. gen.), **ἐκ τοῦ πυρὸς** (source, cause, or means) **καὶ τοῦ καπνοῦ** (καπνός, -οῦ, ὁ, "smoke," coord.) **καὶ τοῦ θείου** (θεῖον, -ου, τό, "sulfur," coord.) **τοῦ ἐκπορευομένου** (gen. sg. neut. of pres. mid. ptc. of ἐκπορεύομαι, attrib., the ptc. is sg. but seems to modify each obj. of prep.) **ἐκ τῶν στομάτων** (source) **αὐτῶν** (poss.).

An interesting observation can be made by considering the use of πληγή in Revelation. It is used here and in 9:20 to characterize the judgment of the sixth trumpet. It is also used to describe all seven of the bowl judgments (15:1, 6, 8, 9; 16:9, 21; 21:9) and the judgment of Babylon (18:4, 8). Revelation 22:18 threatens that if anyone adds to the words of the book God will add the plagues described in the book to that person. This threat would seem to imply that any person throughout history could experience the plagues within history; an easily missed argument in favor of a symbolic interpretation of the trumpet and bowl judgments to indicate God's judgments within history, which culminate in the final judgment (Beale 1152). Fire and sulfur are elsewhere used in Revelation to describe eternal judgment (14:10, note the addition of smoke ascending in 14:11 and Gen 19:28 below) and the lake of fire (19:20; 20:10; 21:8); death by these means proleptically anticipates participation in the second death (21:8).

Use of the OT: God rained sulfur and fire down on Sodom and Gomorrah (Gen 19:24: καὶ κύριος ἔβρεξεν ἐπὶ Σοδομα καὶ Γομορρα θεῖον καὶ πῦρ παρὰ κυρίου ἐκ τοῦ οὐρανοῦ) and the next day Abraham observed the flame of the land ascending like the smoke of a furnace (19:28: ἀνέβαινεν φλὸξ τῆς γῆς ὡσεὶ ἀτμὶς καμίνου; note ἀτμίς instead of καπνός for smoke).

9:19 ἡ γὰρ (causal or explanatory) **ἐξουσία** (subj. nom.) **τῶν ἵππων** (ἵππος, -ου, ὁ, "horse," poss. or subj. gen.) **ἐν τῷ στόματι** (loc.) **αὐτῶν** (poss.) **ἐστιν** (3rd sg. pres. act. ind. of εἰμί) **καὶ ἐν ταῖς οὐραῖς** (οὐρά, -ᾶς, ἡ, "tail," coord. loc.) **αὐτῶν** (poss.), **αἱ γὰρ** (cause)

οὐραὶ (οὐρά, -ᾶς, ἡ, "tail," subj. nom. of verbless cl.) **αὐτῶν** (poss.) **ὅμοιαι** (ὅμοιος, -οία, -οιον, "like, similar," functions as pred. adj. with implied copulative) **ὄφεσιν** (ὄφις, -εως, ὁ, "serpent"), **ἔχουσαι** (nom. pl. fem. of pres. act. ptc. of ἔχω, attrib., modifying οὐραὶ) **κεφαλὰς** (dir. obj.) **καὶ ἐν αὐταῖς** (means) **ἀδικοῦσιν** (3rd pl. pres. act. ind. of ἀδικέω, "harm, damage," narrative pres.).

9:20 Καὶ οἱ λοιποὶ (subj. nom., ant. of οἵ) **τῶν ἀνθρώπων** (part. gen.), **οἳ** (subj. nom.) **οὐκ ἀπεκτάνθησαν** (3rd pl. aor. pass. ind. of ἀποκτείνω) **ἐν ταῖς πληγαῖς** (πληγή, -ῆς, ἡ, "plague, wound," means) **ταύταις** (attrib.), **οὐδὲ** (neg. conj., "and not, not even") **μετενόησαν** (3rd pl. aor. act. ind. of μετανοέω) **ἐκ τῶν ἔργων** (separation) **τῶν χειρῶν** (subj. gen.) **αὐτῶν** (poss.), **ἵνα** (result) **μὴ προσκυνήσουσιν** (3rd pl. fut. act. ind. of προσκυνέω, the fut. is used here in place of the subjunc.) **τὰ δαιμόνια** (dir. obj.) **καὶ τὰ εἴδωλα** (εἴδωλον, -ου, τό, "idol," coord. dir. obj., ant. of ἅ) **τὰ χρυσᾶ** (χρυσοῦς, -ῆ, -οῦν, "golden," attrib.) **καὶ τὰ ἀργυρᾶ** (ἀργυροῦς, -ᾶ, -οῦν, "made of silver," attrib., coord.) **καὶ τὰ χαλκᾶ** (χαλκοῦς, -ῆ, -οῦν, "made of bronze," attrib., coord.) **καὶ τὰ λίθινα** (λίθινος, -ίνη, -ον, "made of stone," attrib., coord.) **καὶ τὰ ξύλινα** (ξύλινος, -η, -ον, "wooden," attrib., coord.), **ἃ** (subj. nom. of δύνανται) **οὔτε** (adv. functioning as neg. correlative conj., "neither . . . nor") **βλέπειν** (pres. act. inf. of βλέπω, compl. inf., fronted for emph.) **δύνανται** (3rd pl. pres. mid. ind. of δύναμαι) **οὔτε ἀκούειν** (pres. act. inf. ἀκούω, coord. compl. inf.) **οὔτε περιπατεῖν** (pres. act. inf. of περιπατέω, coord. compl. inf.),

The motif of a refusal to repent occurs again in the bowl judgments of 16:9, 11. It is appropriate here because it parallels Pharaoh's hardened heart and refusal to repent in the face of the original Exodus plagues (Exod 4:21; 7:13, 22; 8:15, 19, 32; 9:2, 35). Aune and Beale conclude that the trumpet judgments are purely punitive and are not intended to produce repentance (Aune[b] 545; Beale 472–73, 517). Although this is true on the narrative level, this description of how survivors responded is not intended to be the model for John's hearers. Rhetorically, the narrated lack of repentance increases the perceived danger of failing to repent and thus strengthens the vision's persuasive impact.

Use of the OT: The connection of demons with idolatry is evident in Deut 32:17, which notes that the people sacrificed to demons and not to God (ἔθυσαν δαιμονίοις καὶ οὐ θεῷ). Paul also makes this connection in 1 Cor 10:19–20. The critique of idolatry in Ps 113:12 LXX (115:4 EVV) describes idols as silver and gold (τὰ εἴδωλα τῶν ἐθνῶν ἀργύριον καὶ χρυσίον), the works of the hands of men (ἔργα χειρῶν ἀνθρώπων), which are not able to speak, see, hear, smell, touch, or walk (113:13–15 LXX [115:5–7 EVV]). Isaiah 44:9–20 and Jer 10:1–5 contain a similar critique of the material out of which idols are made and their inability to do anything. In the LXX, Daniel confronts the king with the fact that he praised all the idols made by the hands of men (5:23: ᾑνέσατε πάντα τὰ εἴδωλα τὰ χειροποίητα τῶν ἀνθρώπων), while the Hebrew better matches Revelation by drawing attention to the fact that the idols were silver, gold, bronze, iron, wood, and stone and could not see, hear, or know.

9:21 καὶ οὐ μετενόησαν (3rd pl. aor. act. ind. of μετανοέω) **ἐκ τῶν φόνων** (φόνος, -ου, ὁ, "murder," separation) **αὐτῶν** (subj. gen.) **οὔτε ἐκ τῶν φαρμάκων** (φάρμακον, -ου, τό, "magic potion, charm," a hapax legomenon but related to nouns and vbs. for making potions, normally in connection to magic [BDAG 1050a], coord. separation) **αὐτῶν** (subj. gen.) **οὔτε ἐκ τῆς πορνείας** (πορνεία, -ας, ἡ, "sexual immorality," coord. separation) **αὐτῶν** (subj. gen.) **οὔτε ἐκ τῶν κλεμμάτων** (κλέμμα, -ατος, τό, "theft," coord. separation) **αὐτῶν** (subj. gen.).

Other vice lists occur in 21:8; 22:15 and cumulatively reflect general first-century Jewish and Christian morality; see Aune for many parallel references to the Ten Commandments, applications of the Ten Commandments, and early Christian vice lists (Aune[c] 1131).

FOR FURTHER STUDY

36. Magic

Aune, D. E. "Apocalypse of John and Greco-Roman Revelatory Magic." *NTS* 33 (1987): 481–501.

Thomas, R. L. *Magical Motifs in the Book of Revelation*. LNTS 416. London: T&T Clark, 2010.

37. Vivid Description

Stewart, A. E. "*Ekphrasis*, Fear, and Motivation in the Apocalypse of John." *BBR* 27 (2017): 227–40.

Whitaker, R. J. *Ekphrasis, Vision, and Persuasion in the Book of Revelation*. WUNT 2.410. Tübingen: Mohr Siebeck, 2015.

HOMILETICAL SUGGESTIONS

Regardless whether one takes the trumpet judgments as chronologically progressive or recapitulatory, similar points emerge.

The First Six Trumpet Judgments (8:7–9:21)

1. God will continue to judge unrepentant humanity (8:7–9:21).
2. God's people are protected from spiritual harm (9:4).
3. Many will remain unrepentant in the face of God's preliminary judgments within history (9:20–21).

3. John's Recommissioning (10:1–11)

The visions recounted in 10:1–11:14 function as an interlude or digression between the sounding of the sixth and seventh trumpet similar in function to the digression in chapter 7 between the sixth and seventh seals.

10:1 Καὶ εἶδον (1st sg. aor. act. ind. of ὁράω, καὶ εἶδον introduces a new vision, scene, figure, or activity [Aune[a] 338]) **ἄλλον** (attrib., "another" likely distinguishes this angel from the similar one in 5:2) **ἄγγελον** (dir. obj.) **ἰσχυρὸν** (ἰσχυρός, -ά, -όν, "strong," attrib.) **καταβαίνοντα** (acc. sg. masc. of pres. act. ptc. of καταβαίνω, compl. in obj.-compl. double acc. construction [Math 130], "I saw an angel descending") **ἐκ τοῦ οὐρανοῦ** (source) **περιβεβλημένον** (acc. sg. masc. of pf. pass. ptc. of περιβάλλω, "wrap, clothe," intensive pf., attrib.) **νεφέλην** (νεφέλη, -ης, ἡ, "cloud," dir. obj.), **καὶ ἡ ἶρις** (ἶρις, -ιδος, ἡ, "rainbow," subj. nom. of verbless cl.) **ἐπὶ τῆς κεφαλῆς** (loc.) **αὐτοῦ** (poss.) **καὶ τὸ πρόσωπον** (subj. nom. of verbless cl.) **αὐτοῦ** (poss.) **ὡς** (comp., this and the following comp. cl. function as predicates of verbless cls. [Math 130]) **ὁ ἥλιος** (ἥλιος, -ου, ὁ, "sun") **καὶ οἱ πόδες** (πούς, ποδός, ὁ, "foot," subj. nom., the comparison with a pillar indicates that πόδες here refers to the legs [BDAG 858c]) **αὐτοῦ** (poss.) **ὡς** (comp.) **στῦλοι** (στῦλος, -ου, ὁ, "pillar") **πυρός** (gen. of material, "consisting of," a subset of the attrib. gen.),

The details of the cloud (14:14), rainbow (4:3), face like the sun (1:16; 2:18), and legs like pillars of fire (1:15; 2:18), could indicate this ἄγγελος is the glorified Christ or the angel of the Lord (Beale 522–23), but ἄγγελος is not elsewhere applied to Jesus in Revelation and it is likely this is a unique and powerful angel.

10:2 καὶ ἔχων (nom. sg. masc. of pres. act. ptc. of ἔχω, could be functioning in parallel to the attrib. ptc. περιβεβλημένον in 10:1, but more likely is functioning as finite vb. [see below]) **ἐν τῇ χειρὶ** (loc.) **αὐτοῦ** (poss.) **βιβλαρίδιον** (βιβλαρίδιον, -ου, τό, "small scroll," dir. obj.) **ἠνεῳγμένον** (acc. sg. neut. of pf. pass. ptc. of ἀνοίγω, attrib.). **καὶ ἔθηκεν** (3rd sg. aor. act. ind. of τίθημι) **τὸν πόδα** (πούς, ποδός, ὁ, "foot," dir. obj.) **αὐτοῦ** (poss.) **τὸν δεξιὸν** (δεξιός, -ά, -όν, "right," attrib.) **ἐπὶ τῆς θαλάσσης** (loc.), **τὸν δὲ εὐώνυμον** (εὐώνυμος, -ον, "left," subst., dir. obj.) **ἐπὶ τῆς γῆς** (loc.),

The nom. ptc. ἔχων should be in the acc. case like καταβαίνοντα to match the acc. ἄλλον ἄγγελον in 10:1. Moţ suggests that since textual variants correct ἔχων into a finite vb. the problem lies in the use of a ptc. for a finite vb. instead of the use of the nom. in place of the acc. (Moţ 130), but switching to a finite vb. also solves the problem with the cases. The use of the diminutive βιβλαρίδιον could suggest a contrast between this scroll and the scroll of 5:1–9, which is designated βιβλίον, but this is not likely because the βιβλαρίδιον is also designated βιβλίον in 10:8. It is likely that the scroll of 10:2 is the same as the scroll of 5:1 (they are both associated with a mighty angel and allude to Ezek 2:9–10) but, whereas the scroll in 5:1 was sealed, it is open in 10:2. Bauckham makes a compelling case for the identification of the two scrolls (Bauckham 243–57).

10:3 καὶ ἔκραξεν (3rd sg. aor. act. ind. of κράζω) **φωνῇ** (means) **μεγάλῃ** (attrib.) **ὥσπερ** (comp.) **λέων** (λέων, -οντος, ὁ, "lion," subj. nom.) **μυκᾶται** (3rd sg. pres. mid. ind. of μυκάομαι, "roar," gnomic pres.). **καὶ ὅτε** (temp. subord. conj., "when") **ἔκραξεν** (3rd sg. aor. act. ind. of κράζω), **ἐλάλησαν** (3rd pl. aor. act. ind. of λαλέω) **αἱ** (it is not evident that these thunders would have been well known to the hearers and the art. is not anaphoric) **ἑπτὰ** ("seven," attrib.) **βρονταὶ** (βροντή, -ῆς, ἡ, "thunder," subj. nom.) **τὰς ἑαυτῶν** (refl. pron., gen. of source or subj. gen.) **φωνάς** (dir. obj.).

10:4 καὶ ὅτε (temp. subord. conj., although $\mathfrak{P}^{47}$ and א read ὅσα, the external evidence favors ὅτε) **ἐλάλησαν** (3rd pl. aor. act. ind. of λαλέω) **αἱ ἑπτὰ** ("seven," attrib.) **βρονταί** (βροντή, -ῆς, ἡ, "thunder," subj. nom.), **ἤμελλον** (1st sg. impf. act. ind. of μέλλω, "about to," a possible barbarism which should read ἔμελλον in the same way as the 3rd pl.

in Rev 3:2; John's use of ἤμελλον to distinguish between the 1st sg. and 3rd pl. is not unique and is parallel to examples in some papyri and inscriptions [Moț 101]) **γράφειν** (pres. act. inf. of γράφω, compl. inf.), **καὶ ἤκουσα** (1st sg. aor. act. ind. of ἀκούω) **φωνὴν** (dir. obj.) **ἐκ τοῦ οὐρανοῦ** (source) **λέγουσαν** (acc. sg. fem. of pres. act. ptc. of λέγω, attrib. ptc. or compl. of obj.-compl. double acc. construction, introduces dir. speech), **Σφράγισον** (2nd sg. aor. act. impv. of σφραγίζω, "seal") **ἃ** (headless rel. pron.; the cl. functions as dir. obj. of Σφράγισον, "which things") **ἐλάλησαν** (3rd pl. aor. act. ind. of λαλέω) **αἱ ἑπτὰ** (attrib.) **βρονταί** (subj. nom.), **καὶ μὴ αὐτὰ** (dir. obj.) **γράψῃς** (2nd sg. aor. act. subjunc. γράφω, of prohibition).

Use of the OT: In Lev 26:18–28 God warns of the punishments for disobedience with four sevenfold warnings. This could be the background for the four series of seven judgments in Revelation (seals, trumpets, thunders, and bowls). The goal of the punishments in Leviticus is to bring about repentance. Daniel was commanded to seal up the vision because there were still many days (8:26: πεφραγμένον τὸ ὅραμα, ἔτι γὰρ εἰς ἡμέρας πολλάς). He is later commanded to cover the commandments and seal the scroll until the time of completion (κάλυψον τὰ προστάγματα καὶ σφράγισαι τὸ βιβλίον ἕως καιροῦ συντελείας [12:4]; cf. Dan 12:9).

10:5 Καὶ ὁ ἄγγελος (subj. nom., ant. of ὅν), **ὃν** (dir. obj. of εἶδον) **εἶδον** (1st sg. aor. act. ind. of ὁράω) **ἑστῶτα** (acc. sg. masc. of pf. act. ptc. of ἵστημι, compl. in obj.-compl. double acc. construction) **ἐπὶ τῆς θαλάσσης** (loc.) **καὶ ἐπὶ τῆς γῆς** (coord. loc.), **ἦρεν** (3rd sg. aor. act. ind. of αἴρω) **τὴν χεῖρα** (dir. obj.) **αὐτοῦ** (poss.) **τὴν δεξιὰν** (δεξιός, -ά, -όν, "right," attrib.) **εἰς τὸν οὐρανὸν** (loc.)

Use of the OT: In Dan 12:7 the man clothed in linen is above the water of the river (ὃς ἦν ἐπάνω τοῦ ὕδατος τοῦ ποταμοῦ) when he lifts his right and left hands to heaven and swears by the God who lives into the age (ὕψωσε τὴν δεξιὰν καὶ τὴν ἀριστερὰν εἰς τὸν οὐρανὸν καὶ ὤμοσε τὸν ζῶντα εἰς τὸν αἰῶνα θεὸν) that it would be a time, times, and half a time characterized by the shattering of the holy people until the end. In contrast, the angel in Rev 10:6 swears that there will be no more delay (ὅτι χρόνος οὐκέτι ἔσται). Deuteronomy 32:40 describes God lifting up his right hand to heaven to swear by himself (ὅτι ἀρῶ εἰς τὸν οὐρανὸν τὴν χεῖρά μου καὶ ὀμοῦμαι τῇ δεξιᾷ μου καὶ ἐρῶ Ζῶ ἐγὼ εἰς τὸν αἰῶνα).

10:6 καὶ ὤμοσεν (3rd sg. aor. act. ind. of ὀμνύω, "swear an oath") **ἐν τῷ ζῶντι** (dat. sg. masc. of pres. act. ptc. of ζάω, subst., oath [Wallace 205], ant. of ὅς) **εἰς τοὺς αἰῶνας**

(measure) **τῶν αἰώνων** (emph. repetition of αἰών), **ὃς** (subj. nom.) **ἔκτισεν** (3rd sg. aor. act. ind. of κτίζω, "create") **τὸν οὐρανὸν** (dir. obj.) **καὶ τὰ** (substantivizer, dir. obj.) **ἐν αὐτῷ** (loc., "the things in it") **καὶ τὴν γῆν** (dir. obj.) **καὶ τὰ** (substantivizer, dir. obj.) **ἐν αὐτῇ** (loc.) **καὶ τὴν θάλασσαν** (dir. obj.) **καὶ τὰ** (substantivizer, dir. obj.) **ἐν αὐτῇ** (loc.), **ὅτι** (content, "that") **χρόνος** (subj. nom.) **οὐκέτι** (temp. neg. adv. functioning as pred. of ἔσται [Math 134], "no longer") **ἔσται** (3rd sg. fut. act. ind. of εἰμί, this expression idiomatically indicates that "the period of waiting will be up" [Math 134], it is not predicting the end of time as an abstract or philosophical entity [Fanning 315]),

Homoeoarcton and homoeoteleuton likely explain the omission of καὶ τὴν θάλασσαν . . . αὐτῇ in א* and A along with a few minuscules and versions (Metzger 671).

Use of the OT: In Gen 14:19 Melchizedek blesses Abram by the highest God who created the heaven and the earth (Εὐλογημένος Αβραμ τῷ θεῷ τῷ ὑψίστῳ, ὃς ἔκτισεν τὸν οὐρανὸν καὶ τὴν γῆν). In Abram's response he also describes the highest God as the creator of heaven and earth (14:22: ὃς ἔκτισεν τὸν οὐρανὸν καὶ τὴν γῆν). The rationale for keeping the Sabbath holy in Exod 20:11 is grounded in the fact that in six days God made the heaven and the earth and the sea and all the things in them (ἐν γὰρ ἓξ ἡμέραις ἐποίησεν κύριος τὸν οὐρανὸν καὶ τὴν γῆν καὶ τὴν θάλασσαν καὶ πάντα τὰ ἐν αὐτοῖς). In 2 Esd 19:6 (Neh 9:6 EVV) Ezra praises God because he made the heavens, the earth and all things as much as is in it (τὴν γῆν καὶ πάντα, ὅσα ἐστὶν ἐν αὐτῇ), and the seas and all the things in them (τὰς θαλάσσας καὶ πάντα τὰ ἐν αὐταῖς). The psalmist in Ps 145:6 LXX (146:6 EVV) praises God as the one who made heaven and the earth, the sea and all the things in them (τὸν ποιήσαντα τὸν οὐρανὸν καὶ τὴν γῆν, τὴν θάλασσαν καὶ πάντα τὰ ἐν αὐτοῖς).

10:7 ἀλλ' (adversative) **ἐν ταῖς ἡμέραις** (temp.) **τῆς φωνῆς** (descriptive gen.) **τοῦ ἑβδόμου** (ἕβδομος, -η, -ον, "seventh," attrib.) **ἀγγέλου** (subj. gen. or source), **ὅταν** (indef. temp. subord. conj., "when") **μέλλῃ** (3rd sg. pres. act. subjunc. of μέλλω) **σαλπίζειν** (pres. act. inf. of σαλπίζω, "blow a trumpet," compl. inf.), **καὶ** (temp., "then," Aune explains that "καί is translated 'then' because it follows a dependent cl. [protasis] and introduces an independent cl. [apodosis]" [Aune[b] 550]) **ἐτελέσθη** (3rd sg. aor. pass. ind. of τελέω, proleptic aor. [Wallace 564]) **τὸ μυστήριον** (μυστήριον, -ου, τό, "mystery, secret," subj. nom.) **τοῦ θεοῦ** (poss.), **ὡς** (manner) **εὐηγγέλισεν** (3rd sg. aor. act. ind. of εὐαγγελίζω) **τοὺς ἑαυτοῦ** (refl. pron., poss.) **δούλους** (dir. obj. functioning as indir. obj.) **τοὺς προφήτας** (appos.).

The solemnity of the oath and declaration seems to clearly establish the seventh trumpet as the end; this is confirmed by the content of the seventh trumpet itself (see on 11:15–19). This is a compelling argument against a strict chronologically progressive approach to the visions since the seventh trumpet is certainly not the end of John's visions of the events leading up to the end. Visions occurring after the seventh trumpet must then provide different details or perspectives on events leading up to the end described in the seventh trumpet.

In early Christianity, the mystery of God normally describes the fulfillment of OT prophecy in an unexpected manner (for the use of parables to explain the unexpected nature of the kingdom of God see Matt 13:11//Mark 4:11//Luke 8:10; for the unexpected inclusion of gentiles in God's plan and among God's people see Rom 11:25; Eph 3:3–9). In Revelation *μυστήριον* refers elsewhere to an element in the vision that requires further explanation (1:20; 17:5, 7). A comparison with the question posed in 6:10 (How long?) and the answer given there is important (*καὶ ἐρρέθη αὐτοῖς ἵνα ἀναπαύσονται ἔτι χρόνον μικρόν*). The angel's oath in 10:6–7 seems to be a direct and more specific answer to the question of 6:10; God will bring judgment and vindicate his oppressed people when the seventh trumpet sounds. There is no reason to restrict the prophets mentioned here to OT or NT prophets. John clearly builds upon the OT prophets and acknowledges the existence of NT prophets who shared a similar function, authority, and message. John saw more continuity than discontinuity between the two groups of prophets.

Use of the OT: Daniel confesses that they did not listen to God's servants the prophets (*οὐκ ἠκούσαμεν τῶν παίδων σου τῶν προφητῶν* [Dan 9:6]; cf. Dan 6:10) who spoke about and against their kings, masters, and fathers and to every nation upon the earth (*ἃ ἐλάλησαν . . . ἐπὶ τοὺς βασιλεῖς ἡμῶν καὶ δυνάστας ἡμῶν καὶ πατέρας ἡμῶν καὶ παντὶ ἔθνει ἐπὶ τῆς γῆς* [Dan 9:6]; cf. Dan 9:10). Amos 3:7 declares that God does not do a deed unless he reveals his instruction to his servants the prophets (*διότι οὐ μὴ ποιήσῃ κύριος ὁ θεὸς πρᾶγμα, ἐὰν μὴ ἀποκαλύψῃ παιδείαν αὐτοῦ πρὸς τοὺς δούλους αὐτοῦ τοὺς προφήτας*). Zechariah 1:6 connects God's words with what he commanded by his Spirit to his servants the prophets (*πλὴν τοὺς λόγους μου καὶ τὰ νόμιμά μου δέχεσθε, ὅσα ἐγὼ ἐντέλλομαι ἐν πνεύματί μου τοῖς δούλοις μου τοῖς προφήταις*).

10:8 Καὶ ἡ φωνὴ (subj. nom. of verbless cl. or nom. abs., ant. of *ἥν*) **ἣν** (dir. obj.) **ἤκουσα** (1st sg. aor. act. ind. of *ἀκούω*) **ἐκ τοῦ οὐρανοῦ** (source) **πάλιν** (additive adv.) **λαλοῦσαν** (acc. sg. fem. of pres. act. ptc. of λαλέω, compl. of obj.-compl. double acc. construction with *ἥν* [Math 136]), **μετ' ἐμοῦ** (association) **καὶ λέγουσαν** (acc. sg. fem. of pres. act. ptc. of λέγω, syntactically coord. with the prior ptc. and drawing its case from *ἥν*) **Ὕπαγε** (2nd sg. pres. act. impv. of ὑπάγω) **λάβε** (2nd sg. aor. act. impv. of λαμβάνω) **τὸ βιβλίον** (βιβλίον, -ου, τό, "scroll," dir. obj.) **τὸ ἠνεῳγμένον** (acc. sg. neut. of pf. pass. ptc. of *ἀνοίγω*, attrib.) **ἐν τῇ χειρὶ** (loc.) **τοῦ ἀγγέλου** (poss.) **τοῦ ἑστῶτος** (gen. sg. masc. of pf. act. ptc. of *ἵστημι*, attrib.) **ἐπὶ τῆς θαλάσσης** (loc.) **καὶ ἐπὶ τῆς γῆς** (coord. loc.).

Use of the OT: John's experience of eating the scroll parallels that of Ezekiel, who was commanded to open his mouth and eat what was given to him (2:8: *χάνε τὸ στόμα σου καὶ φάγε ἃ ἐγὼ δίδωμί σοι*). Ezekiel's scroll was written on the back and front with lamentation, mourning and woe (2:10: *γεγραμμένα ἦν τὰ ὄπισθεν καὶ τὰ ἔμπροσθεν, καὶ ἐγέγραπτο εἰς αὐτὴν θρῆνος καὶ μέλος καὶ οὐαί*). This detail connects this scroll with the scroll of Rev 5:1. Ezekiel's scroll was sweet as honey in his mouth (3:3: *καὶ ἐγένετο ἐν τῷ στόματί μου ὡς μέλι γλυκάζον*) while John's scroll was sweet as honey in the mouth, but it embittered his stomach (see 10:10). Bitterness can be observed in Ezek 3:14, but it is not a direct response to eating the scroll and the word for bitterness is omitted from the LXX.

10:9 ***καὶ ἀπῆλθα*** (1st sg. aor. act. ind. of ἀπέρχομαι, this could be considered a barbarism, which should read ἀπῆλθον, but is simply the use of 1st aor. endings on a 2nd aor. vb. The use of 1st aor. terminations on 2nd aor. vbs. was not uncommon in the first century with many more examples in the second century [Moţ 102–3]) **πρὸς τὸν ἄγγελον** (loc.) **λέγων** (nom. sg. masc. of pres. act. ptc. of λέγω, manner) ***αὐτῷ*** (indir. obj.) **δοῦναί** (aor. act. inf. of δίδωμι, ind. speech) ***μοι*** (indir. obj.) **τὸ βιβλαρίδιον** (βιβλαρίδιον, -ου, τό, "small scroll," dir. obj.). ***καὶ*** **λέγει** (3rd sg. pres. act. ind. of λέγω, narrative pres.) ***μοι*** (indir. obj.), **λάβε** (2nd sg. aor. act. impv. of λαμβάνω) ***καὶ κατάφαγε*** (2nd sg. aor. act. impv. of κατεσθίω, "consume, devour," likely intensified by the prep., "eat entirely") ***αὐτό*** (dir. obj.), ***καὶ*** **πικρανεῖ** (3rd sg. fut. act. ind. of πικραίνω, "make bitter") ***σου*** (poss., fronted for emph.) **τὴν κοιλίαν** (κοιλία, -ας, ἡ, "stomach," dir. obj.), ***ἀλλ'*** (adversative) ***ἐν τῷ στόματί*** (loc.) ***σου*** (poss.) ***ἔσται*** (3rd sg. fut. act. ind. of εἰμί) ***γλυκὺ*** (γλυκύς, -εῖα, -ύ, "sweet," pred. adj.) ***ὡς*** (comp.) ***μέλι*** (μέλι, -ιτος, τό, "honey").
10:10 ***καὶ ἔλαβον*** (1st sg. aor. act. ind. of λαμβάνω) **τὸ βιβλαρίδιον** (βιβλαρίδιον, -ου, τό, "small scroll," dir. obj., ℵ 046 1854 *al* read βιβλίον while A C P *al* and βιβλίδιον in 𝔓[47] seem to more strongly support βιβλαρίδιον [Metzger 671]) ***ἐκ τῆς χειρὸς*** (source or separation) **τοῦ ἀγγέλου** (poss.) ***καὶ κατέφαγον*** (1st sg. aor. act. ind. of κατεσθίω, "consume, devour") ***αὐτό*** (dir. obj.), ***καὶ ἦν ἐν τῷ στόματί*** (loc.) ***μου*** (poss.) ***ὡς*** (the comp. functions as a pred. adj.) ***μέλι*** (μέλι, -ιτος, τό, "honey") ***γλυκὺ*** (γλυκύς, -εῖα, -ύ, "sweet," attrib.) ***καὶ ὅτε*** (temp. subord. conj.) ***ἔφαγον*** (1st sg. aor. act. ind. of ἐσθίω) ***αὐτό*** (dir. obj.), ***ἐπικράνθη*** (3rd sg. aor. pass. ind. of πικραίνω, "make bitter") ***ἡ κοιλία*** (κοιλία, -ας, ἡ, "stomach," subj. nom.) ***μου*** (poss.).

It is likely that the scroll is sweet to the taste because it is God's message but bitter because of the harsh judgment. Revelation does not explicitly provide an explanation for this.
10:11 ***καὶ λέγουσίν*** (3rd pl. pres. act. ind. of λέγω, narrative pres., the switch to pl. is prob. impers., "it was said to me" [Math 138]) ***μοι*** (indir. obj.), **δεῖ** (3rd sg. pres. act. ind., impers.) ***σε*** (acc. subj. of inf. προφητεῦσαι) **πάλιν** (additive adv., "again," building upon the original commission to "write" in 1:11, 19) **προφητεῦσαι** (aor. act. inf. of προφητεύω, "prophesy," compl. inf.) ***ἐπὶ*** **λαοῖς** (either disadvantage, "against,"

or reference, "about") **καὶ ἔθνεσιν** (coord.) **καὶ γλώσσαις** (γλῶσσα, -ης, ἡ, "tongue, language," coord.) **καὶ βασιλεῦσιν** (coord.) **πολλοῖς** (attrib., likely referring to each item in the list).

On peoples, nations, tongues, and kings, see 5:9.

Use of the OT: When God commissions Jeremiah and puts his words in Jeremiah's mouth, he appoints him over nations and kings (1:10: κατέστακά σε σήμερον ἐπὶ ἔθνη καὶ βασιλείας). God later commands Jeremiah to prophesy these words against them (32:30 LXX [25:30 EVV]: σὺ προφητεύσεις ἐπ' αὐτοὺς τοὺς λόγους τούτους).

---

4. The Temple (11:1–2)

The interlude continues with a vision of the temple and two witnesses. Although there are many variations, the main interpretive decision regards whether this interlude (1) describes a literal rebuilt temple in the past that was destroyed by the Romans (preterism); (2) a literal rebuilt temple in the future and two specific literal prophetic individuals who minister right before Jesus's return (Fanning 326–38; Thomas 2:80–89); or most likely (3) symbolic imagery of the temple and two witnesses who describe God's protection of his people throughout history, their prophetic witnessing ministry, their opposition, and their eventual victory and vindication (Beale 557–76; Koester 484–97).

11:1 Καὶ ἐδόθη (3rd sg. aor. pass. ind. of δίδωμι) **μοι** (indir. obj.) **κάλαμος** (κάλαμος, -ου, ὁ, "measuring rod [reed]" [BDAG 502c], subj. nom.) **ὅμοιος** (ὅμοιος, -οία, -οιον, "like, similar") **ῥάβδῳ** (ῥάβδος, -ου, ἡ, "rod, staff, scepter," compl. of ὅμοιος), **λέγων** (nom. sg. masc. of pres. act. ptc. of λέγω, manner, the subject of this speaking is not indicated and it is not clear when the dir. speech ends; this awkwardness is somewhat alleviated by the inclusion of καὶ εἱστήκει ὁ ἄγγελος before λέγων in א[2] 046 1854 2329 2351 [Metzger 671]), **Ἔγειρε** (2nd sg. pres. act. impv. of ἐγείρω) **καὶ μέτρησον** (2nd sg. aor. act. impv. of μετρέω, "measure") **τὸν ναὸν** (ναός, -οῦ, ὁ, "temple," dir. obj.) **τοῦ θεοῦ** (poss.) **καὶ** (likely coord. but possibly epex.) **τὸ θυσιαστήριον** (θυσιαστήριον, -ου, τό, "altar," dir. obj.) **καὶ τοὺς προσκυνοῦντας** (acc. pl. masc. of pres. act. ptc. of προσκυνέω, subst., coord. dir. obj.) **ἐν αὐτῷ** (loc., the ant. could be either θυσιαστήριον or ναός but logically ναός).

Use of the OT: The man like glistening bronze in Ezek 40:3 also has a measuring rod [reed] (κάλαμος μέτρου) with which to measure dimensions of the rebuilt temple. Zechariah witnesses a man with a measuring cord (σχοινίον γεωμετρικόν) who was commanded to measure Jerusalem (2:5–6 LXX [2:1–2

EVV]: Διαμετρῆσαι τὴν Ιερουσαλημ) as an indication of its abundant restoration. In 2 Sam 8:2, David uses a rope to measure the people to be killed and the ones to be spared (καὶ διεμέτρησεν αὐτοὺς ἐν σχοινίοις). In Lam 2:8, measurement is used to indicate how God measured the city for destruction: he stretched out the measure (ἐξέτεινεν μέτρον). The symbolic act of measuring could indicate preservation and protection or destruction.

11:2 καὶ (adversative [Aune[b] 578]) **τὴν αὐλὴν** (dir. obj. of ἔκβαλε, fronted for emph.) **τὴν** (adjectivizer) **ἔξωθεν** (spatial adv., "outside," א and around thirty-five minuscules change the adv. to ἔσωθεν [Metzger 671]) **τοῦ ναοῦ** (ναός, -οῦ, ὁ, "temple," part. gen.) **ἔκβαλε** (2nd sg. aor. act. impv. of ἐκβάλλω) **ἔξωθεν καὶ μὴ αὐτὴν** (dir. obj.) **μετρήσῃς** (2nd sg. aor. act. subjunc. of μετρέω, "measure," prohibition), **ὅτι** (causal) **ἐδόθη** (3rd sg. aor. pass. ind. of δίδωμι) **τοῖς ἔθνεσιν** (indir. obj.), **καὶ τὴν πόλιν** (dir. obj.) **τὴν ἁγίαν** (attrib.) **πατήσουσιν** (3rd pl. fut. act. ind. of πατέω) **μῆνας** (acc. of time) **τεσσεράκοντα** ("forty") **[καὶ] δύο**.

The outer court is related to the holy city, perhaps through metonymy. The outer court is not measured because it has been given to the nations who will trample the city for forty-two months. In Luke 21:24, Jesus prophesies that Jerusalem would be trampled by the gentiles until the times of the gentiles might be fulfilled (Ἰερουσαλὴμ ἔσται πατουμένη ὑπὸ ἐθνῶν, ἄχρι οὗ πληρωθῶσιν καιροὶ ἐθνῶν); in Luke the "times of the gentiles" spans the distance between the destruction of the temple in AD 70 and Jesus's return. A symbolic interpretation of the temple in 11:2 is suggested by the following points (Beale 557–71; Bauckham 273–83; Koester 484–86). In early Christianity the temple is regularly understood as God's people in whom God dwells by his Spirit (1 Cor 3:16–17; 6:19; 2 Cor 6:16; Eph 2:20–22; 1 Pet 2:4–10); this connection of people to temple is also evident in Rev 3:12 and hinted at by the lack of a temple in Rev 21:22. The use of a lampstand as an image for the churches associates God's people with temple furnishings. The command to measure the temple *and* its worshippers ties the temple to people (cf. 1 Pet 2:5). A literal temple would mean the revival of the OT sacrificial system—a future development not anticipated by any NT documents (cf. Heb 10:1–12). The Apocalypse never uses ναός to indicate a literal temple and John clearly applies Ezekiel 40–48 to the new Jerusalem and new creation (see on 21:9–22:5). A symbolic understanding of 11:1–2 would suggest that the measuring is a symbol for the spiritual protection of God's people (parallel to God's seal in 7:1–8, the protection of the two witnesses in 11:5, the protection of the woman in the wilderness in 12:13–16, and the names written in the book of life in 13:8; 17:8) while the trampling indicates their physical vulnerability to persecution (parallel to how God's people are killed in 6:9–11 and go through tribulation in 7:14, the two witnesses are overcome and slain in 11:7, the woman's children are harmed in 12:17, and the saints are taken captive and killed in 13:10, 15).

Revelation never mentions a seven-year period of tribulation. Instead, the visions mention a three-and-a-half-year period of persecution five different times: 11:2 (forty-two months), 11:3 (1,260 days); 12:6 (1,260 days), 12:14 (time, times, and half a time); 13:5 (forty-two months). This three-and-a-half-year period in Revelation is characterized by persecution during which God's people must bear faithful witness no matter what the cost. It is described as the period of time in which the holy city is trampled, the two witnesses prophesy, the woman is protected in the wilderness, and the beast is allowed to exercise authority and make war on the saints. This period begins with Jesus's ascension and enthronement (see on 12:5–6) and culminates with Christ's return (note specifically the defeat of the beast at Jesus's return in 17:14; 19:11–21 and parallel accounts in 6:17; 11:17–18; 14:14–20).

Use of the OT: Isaiah 63:18 laments that enemies have trampled God's sanctuary (οἱ ὑπεναντίοι ἡμῶν κατεπάτησαν τὸ ἁγίασμά σου). Zechariah 12:3 LXX differs from the MT in describing Jerusalem as a stone being trampled by all the nations; everyone trampling it will mock it and all the nations of the earth will be gathered against it (θήσομαι τὴν Ιερουσαλημ λίθον καταπατούμενον πᾶσιν τοῖς ἔθνεσιν, πᾶς ὁ καταπατῶν αὐτὴν ἐμπαίζων ἐμπαίξεται, καὶ ἐπισυναχθήσονται ἐπ' αὐτὴν πάντα τὰ ἔθνη τῆς γῆς). The three-and-a-half-year period of persecution against God's people in the end times with particular focus on the temple is drawn from Daniel (Dan 7:25; 9:27; 12:7, 11–12). Interpreters have also drawn connections to Elijah's three-and-a-half-year judgment of drought (1 Kgs 18:1; Luke 4:25; Jas 5:17) and the way the Israelites had forty-two encampments during their years in the wilderness (Num 33:5–49; compare the wilderness setting of Rev 12:6 and 12).

FOR FURTHER STUDY

38. Temple (11:1–2)

Briggs, R. A. *Jewish Temple Imagery in the Book of Revelation*. StBibLit 10. New York: Lang, 1999.

Dalrymple, R. "The Use of Καί in Revelation 11:1 and the Implications for the Identification of the Temple, the Altar, and the Worshipers." *Bib* 87 (2006): 387–94.

Giblin, C. H. "Revelation 11:1–13: Its Form, Function and Contextual Integration." *NTS* 30 (1984): 433–59.

Jauhiainen, M. "The Measuring of the Sanctuary Reconsidered (Rev 11,1–2)." *Bib* 83 (2002): 507–26.

Stevenson, G. *Power and Place: Temple and Identity in the Book of Revelation*. BZNW 107. Berlin: de Gruyter, 2001.

5. The Two Witnesses (11:3–14)

Mathewson argues that the pres. and fut. tenses of 11:3–10 describe the witnesses and their activities while the aor. tense forms in 11:11–13 function to resume the narrative from 1a (Math 142). Fanning describes the customary presents as typical for John's "report mode" (Fanning 331).

11:3 καὶ δώσω (1st sg. fut. act. ind. of δίδωμι, the lack of dir. obj. should be filled with an implied ἐξουσίαν as is explicit in 2:26; 6:8; 9:3; 13:2, 4, 5, 7 [Fanning 331]) **τοῖς** (they are def. because of the following poss. pron. μου [Fanning 331]) **δυσὶν** ("two," attrib.) **μάρτυσίν** (μάρτυς, -υρος, ὁ, "witness," indir. obj.) **μου** (poss., "my," or obj. gen. "about me") **καὶ** (Aune argues for a consecutive function equivalent to a purpose cl., "so that" [Aune[b] 579]) **προφητεύσουσιν** (3rd pl. fut. act. ind. of προφητεύω, "prophesy") **ἡμέρας** (acc. of time) **χιλίας** ("one thousand," attrib.) **διακοσίας** ("two hundred") **ἑξήκοντα** ("sixty") **περιβεβλημένοι** (nom. pl. masc. of pf. pass. ptc. of περιβάλλω, "wrap, clothe," manner; the nom. prob. matches the implied subj. of προφητεύσουσιν [Moț 121]) **σάκκους** (σάκκος, -ου, ὁ, "sackcloth, a course cloth made of animal [goat or camel] hair" [BDAG 910d], dir. obj.).

Sackcloth is associated with mourning (Gen 37:34; Jer 4:8) and repentance (Jonah 3:5–10; Matt 11:21). The witnesses' clothing suggests a message of judgment and call for repentance.

11:4 οὗτοί (subj. nom.) **εἰσιν** (3rd pl. pres. act. ind. of εἰμί) **αἱ** (likely well-known in a nod to Zech 4:3) **δύο** (attrib.) **ἐλαῖαι** (ἐλαία, -ας, ἡ, "olive tree," pred. nom.) **καὶ αἱ** (likely well known) **δύο** (attrib.) **λυχνίαι** (λυχνία, -ας, ἡ, "lampstand," coord. pred. nom.) **αἱ** (art. which, despite discord in gender, would seem to go with ἑστῶτες; the fem. art. matches the olive trees and lampstands while the masc. ptc. matches the demon. pron. οὗτοί) **ἐνώπιον τοῦ κυρίου** (loc.) **τῆς γῆς** (gen. of subord.) **ἑστῶτες** (nom. pl. masc. of pf. act. ptc. of ἵστημι, attrib.).

The two witnesses (cf. the need for two witnesses in Deut 19:15; Matt 18:16 and the two olive trees in Zech 4:3) likely represent the people of God throughout the entire church age based on the parallel descriptions of the beast overcoming and killing the saints in Rev 11:7; 13:7, the explicit identification of lampstands as churches in Rev 1:20, and the description of believers as witnesses throughout the Apocalypse (Rev 6:9; 12:11, 17; 19:10; 20:4). See below on the significance of olive trees.

Use of the OT: Zechariah receives a vision of one lampstand with seven lamps with seven wicks each. The lampstand is flanked by two olive trees (Zech 4:3: δύο ἐλαῖαι), which are identified as the two anointed ones who stand beside the Lord of the whole earth (4:14: οἱ δύο υἱοὶ τῆς πιότητος παρεστήκασιν τῷ κυρίῳ πάσης τῆς γῆς). In Zechariah, these two anointed ones seem to indicate Zerubbabel, the governor and Davidic heir, and Joshua the high priest, who are promised God's favor and empowerment through God's Spirit to rebuild the temple. The allusion could then point to the kingly and priestly identity of God's people (corporately represented by two witnesses) in this vision (cf. 1:6; 5:10).

11:5 καὶ εἴ (introduces 1st class cond. cl.) **τις** (indef. pron., subj. nom.) **αὐτοὺς** (dir. obj. of ἀδικῆσαι) **θέλει** (3rd sg. pres. act. ind. of θέλω) **ἀδικῆσαι** (aor. act. inf. of ἀδικέω, "harm, damage," compl. inf.) **πῦρ** (subj. nom. of apod.) **ἐκπορεύεται** (3rd sg. pres. mid. ind. of ἐκπορεύομαι) **ἐκ τοῦ στόματος** (source, distributive sg. modified by a pl. gen. [Math 143–44]) **αὐτῶν** (poss.) **καὶ κατεσθίει** (3rd sg. pres. act. ind. of κατεσθίω, "consume, devour," coord.) **τοὺς ἐχθροὺς** (ἐχθρός, -ά, -όν, "hostile," subst. used for "enemy," dir. obj.) **αὐτῶν** (relationship). **καὶ εἴ** (see below) **τις** (subj. nom.) **θελήσῃ** (3rd sg. aor. act. subjunc. of θέλω) **αὐτοὺς** (dir. obj.) **ἀδικῆσαι** (aor. act. inf. of ἀδικέω, compl. inf.), **οὕτως** (manner) **δεῖ** (3rd sg. pres. act. ind. of δεῖ) **αὐτὸν** (acc. subj. of inf.) **ἀποκτανθῆναι** (aor. pass. inf. of ἀποκτείνω, compl. inf.).

The second cond. cl. provides emph. The use of εἰ suggests a 1st class cond. cl. while the use of the subjunc. mood more strongly indicates a 3rd class cond. cl. In Koine Greek, the nuanced distinction between εἰ and ἐάν could be blurred and there are examples of εἰ being used in 3rd class cond. cl. in the papyri and elsewhere (Aune[b] 579, 614). The subjunc. mood introduces a greater degree of possibility and uncertainty.

Use of the OT: In Jer 5:14, God tells Jeremiah that he will make his words a fire that would consume the people (ἰδοὺ ἐγὼ δέδωκα τοὺς λόγους μου εἰς τὸ στόμα σου πῦρ καὶ τὸν λαὸν τοῦτον ξύλα, καὶ καταφάγεται αὐτούς). If this allusion is intentional, it would suggest that the fire from the mouths of the two witnesses indicates God's message and should not be understood as literal fire. Fire from heaven consumes Elijah's adversaries in 4 Kgdms 1:10 (2 Kgs 1:10 EVV; καὶ κατέβη πῦρ ἐκ τοῦ οὐρανοῦ καὶ κατέφαγεν αὐτὸν καὶ τοὺς πεντήκοντα αὐτοῦ). This could suggest a typological connection between Elijah and the two witnesses. David's song of deliverance in 2 Kgdms 22:9 (2 Sam 22:9 EVV) describes how fire came from God's mouth (καὶ πῦρ ἐκ στόματος αὐτοῦ κατέδεται) in a poetic description of his deliverance from Saul. Similarly, Ps 96:3 LXX (97:3 EVV) declares of Yahweh that πῦρ ἐναντίον αὐτοῦ προπορεύσεται καὶ φλογιεῖ κύκλῳ τοὺς ἐχθροὺς αὐτοῦ. Fourth Ezra 13:25–39 describes the Messiah as destroying Israel's enemies by fire proceeding from his mouth, which is interpreted as the law.

11:6 οὗτοι (subj. nom.) **ἔχουσιν** (3rd pl. pres. act. ind. of ἔχω) **τὴν ἐξουσίαν** (dir. obj.) **κλεῖσαι** (aor. act. inf. of κλείω, "shut," epex. inf.) **τὸν οὐρανόν** (dir. obj.), **ἵνα** (purpose or result; the difference lies in the degree of intentionality) **μὴ ὑετὸς** (ὑετός, -οῦ, ὁ, "rain," subj. nom.) **βρέχῃ** (3rd sg. pres. act. subjunc. of βρέχω, "rain") **τὰς ἡμέρας** (acc. of time) **τῆς προφητείας** ("the days when they prophesied" [Math 145]) **αὐτῶν** (subj. gen.) **καὶ ἐξουσίαν** (dir. obj.) **ἔχουσιν** (3rd pl. pres. act. ind. of ἔχω) **ἐπὶ τῶν ὑδάτων** (subord.) **στρέφειν** (pres. act. inf. of στρέφω, "turn," epex. inf.) **αὐτὰ** (dir. obj.) **εἰς αἷμα** (goal [Math 145]) **καὶ πατάξαι** (aor. act. inf. of πατάσσω, "strike," coord. epex. inf.) **τὴν γῆν**

(dir. obj.) **ἐν πάσῃ** (attrib.) **πληγῇ** (πληγή, -ῆς, ἡ, "plague, wound," means) **ὁσάκις** (temp. adv., "as often as, whenever") **ἐὰν θελήσωσιν** (3rd pl. aor. act. subjunc. of θέλω).

The explicit typology between the two witnesses and Elijah and Moses does not require that the two witnesses be Elijah and Moses, but rather that there is a typological connection between their identity, function, and/or activity (note also the Jeremiah typology in 11:5 and the Jesus typology in 11:8; the life and ministry of the two witnesses is a pastiche of Jesus, Elijah, Moses, and Jeremiah). The turning of water to blood parallels the second trumpet judgment (8:8) and the second and third bowl judgments (16:3–6).

Use of the OT: In 3 Kgdms 17:1 (1 Kgs 17:1 EVV) Elijah tells Ahab there would be a drought controlled by his word (εἰ ἔσται τὰ ἔτη ταῦτα δρόσος καὶ ὑετὸς ὅτι εἰ μὴ διὰ στόματος λόγου μου). This strengthens the parallel between the ministry of the two witnesses and Elijah. The drought lasts three and a half years (Luke 4:25; Jas 5:17). The first Egyptian plague involves Moses turning the water of the Nile to blood in Exod 7:17, 19–20 (7:20: καὶ μετέβαλεν πᾶν τὸ ὕδωρ τὸ ἐν τῷ ποταμῷ εἰς αἷμα), which parallels the activity of the two witnesses. In 1 Kgdms 4:8 (1 Sam 4:8 EVV) the Philistines lament that the gods who struck the Egyptians with every sort of plague were afflicting them (οὗτοι οἱ θεοὶ οἱ πατάξαντες τὴν Αἴγυπτον ἐν πάσῃ πληγῇ καὶ ἐν τῇ ἐρήμῳ).

11:7 καὶ ὅταν (temp. subord. conj.) **τελέσωσιν** (3rd pl. aor. act. subjunc. of τελέω, subjunc. because of ὅταν) **τὴν μαρτυρίαν** (dir. obj.) **αὐτῶν** (subj. gen.), **τὸ θηρίον** (θηρίον, -ου, τό, "animal, beast," subj. nom.) **τὸ ἀναβαῖνον** (nom. sg. neut. of pres. act. ptc. of ἀναβαίνω, attrib.) **ἐκ τῆς ἀβύσσου** (ἄβυσσος, -ου, ἡ, "abyss," source) **ποιήσει** (3rd sg. fut. act. ind. of ποιέω) **μετ' αὐτῶν** (association with the contextual nuance of disadvantage, "against") **πόλεμον** (πόλεμος, -ου, ὁ, "battle," dir. obj.) **καὶ νικήσει** (3rd sg. fut. act. ind. of νικάω, "overcome, conquer," coord.) **αὐτοὺς** (dir. obj.) **καὶ ἀποκτενεῖ** (3rd sg. fut. act. ind. of ἀποκτείνω, coord.) **αὐτούς** (dir. obj.).

The ascent of the beast from the abyss parallels its ascent from the sea in 13:1. Parallel to 11:7, the beast in 13:7 makes war with and overcomes the saints; these intratextual connections support the interpretation of the two witnesses as the saints of 13:7. The visions are repetitive and not chronologically sequential and Revelation 13 provides more details regarding this cryptic and brief account in 11:7. Parallel visions in Revelation are not identical but provide different details and perspectives on the same sequence of events. The beast in 17:8 is described as being about to ascend from the abyss (μέλλει ἀναβαίνειν ἐκ τῆς ἀβύσσου).

Use of the OT: Daniel 7:3 describes the ascent of four beasts from the sea (*καὶ τέσσαρα θηρία ἀνέβαινον ἐκ τῆς θαλάσσης*). Daniel 7:7 describes the fourth beast as devouring and pounding (*ἐσθίον καὶ κοπανίζον*). Daniel 7:21 describes the other horn of the fourth beast as making war with the saints and putting them to flight (*τὸ κέρας ἐκεῖνο πόλεμον συνιστάμενον πρὸς τοὺς ἁγίους καὶ τροπούμενον αὐτοὺς*).

11:8 καὶ τὸ πτῶμα (*πτῶμα, -ατος, τό*, "body, corpse," subj. nom., distributive sg. with pl. gen.) **αὐτῶν** (poss.) **ἐπὶ τῆς πλατείας** (*πλατεῖα, -ας, ἡ*, "street," loc.) **τῆς πόλεως** (part. gen., ant. of *ἥτις*) **τῆς μεγάλης** (attrib.), **ἥτις** (subj. nom.) **καλεῖται** (3rd sg. pres. pass. ind. of *καλέω*, gnomic) **πνευματικῶς** (adv., manner, "spiritually, symbolically") **Σόδομα** ("Sodom," pred. nom. with pass. of *καλέω* [Wallace 40]) **καὶ Αἴγυπτος** ("Egypt," pred. nom. with pass. of *καλέω*, coord.), **ὅπου** (adv. of place, "where") **καὶ** (adv., "also") **ὁ κύριος** (subj. nom.) **αὐτῶν** (gen. of subord. or poss. gen.) **ἐσταυρώθη** (3rd sg. aor. pass. ind. of *σταυρόω*, "crucify").

The great city in Revelation is consistently Babylon (16:19; 17:18; 18:10, 16, 18, 19, 21), described here symbolically as Sodom, Egypt, and Jerusalem (where their lord also was crucified). The typological trajectory evident in the career of the witnesses and Jesus further support a corporate understanding of the witnesses. In Revelation, God's people are to overcome as Jesus overcame (through faithfulness to death, 3:21). They will bear witness as he did (1:5), engage in miraculous prophetic ministry (11:4–6), be killed in the same place (11:8), remain dead for a similar period of time (11:9), come back to life (11:11), and ascend to heaven in a cloud (11:12; cf. Acts 1:9). The lamb's blood enables his followers to overcome (7:14; 12:11) and they follow the lamb wherever he goes (14:4). The point of this Jesus typology is not to establish literal connections at each point but to make the broader point regarding the need for faithful witness to the point of death, which will be followed by resurrection and supernatural vindication by God.

Use of the OT: Isaiah addresses his message to God's people, whom he describes as the rulers of Sodom and people of Gomorrah (1:10: *Ἀκούσατε λόγον κυρίου, ἄρχοντες Σοδομων, προσέχετε νόμον θεοῦ, λαὸς Γομορρας*) and who proclaim their sin like Sodom (3:9: *τὴν δὲ ἁμαρτίαν αὐτῶν ὡς Σοδομων ἀνήγγειλαν*). Jeremiah similarly describes Jerusalem as having become like Sodom and Gomorrah (23:14: *ἐγενήθησάν μοι πάντες ὡς Σοδομα καὶ οἱ κατοικοῦντες αὐτὴν ὥσπερ Γομορρα*). Ezekiel joins Isaiah and Jeremiah in describing Jerusalem as Sodom (16:46–56).

11:9 καὶ βλέπουσιν (3rd pl. pres. act. ind. of βλέπω) **ἐκ τῶν λαῶν** (this and the following gens. are part. with an assumed subj. nom. τίνες) **καὶ φυλῶν** (φυλή, -ῆς, ἡ, "tribe, nation," coord.) **καὶ γλωσσῶν** (γλῶσσα, -ης, ἡ, "tongue, language," coord.) **καὶ ἐθνῶν** (coord.) **τὸ πτῶμα** (πτῶμα, -ατος, τό, "body, corpse," dir. obj., distributive sg. with pl. gen.) **αὐτῶν** (poss.) **ἡμέρας** (acc. of time) **τρεῖς** (attrib.) **καὶ ἥμισυ** (ἥμισυς, -εια, -υ, "half," attrib.) **καὶ τὰ πτώματα** (acc. subj. of inf. τεθῆναι) **αὐτῶν** (poss.) **οὐκ ἀφίουσιν** (3rd pl. pres. act. ind. of ἀφίημι, narrative pres., impers. sub. is the implied τίνες at the start of the verse) **τεθῆναι** (aor. pass. inf. of τίθημι, compl. inf.; Wallace notes that it "is possible to treat compl. inf. as dir. obj. inf." [Wallace 599]) **εἰς μνῆμα** (μνῆμα, -ατος, τό, "tomb," loc.).

The refusal to bury the dead constituted a significant and intentional act to shame the defeated witnesses (cf. Jer 16:4). On peoples, tribes, tongues, and nations, see 5:9.

11:10 καὶ οἱ κατοικοῦντες (nom. pl. masc. of pres. act. ptc. of κατοικέω, "dwell," subst., subj. nom.) **ἐπὶ τῆς γῆς** (loc.) **χαίρουσιν** (3rd pl. pres. act. ind. of χαίρω) **ἐπ' αὐτοῖς** (causal) **καὶ εὐφραίνονται** (3rd pl. pres. mid. ind. of εὐφραίνω, "be glad") **καὶ δῶρα** (δῶρον, -ου, τό, "gift," dir. obj.) **πέμψουσιν** (3rd pl. fut. act. ind. of πέμπω) **ἀλλήλοις** (indir. obj., reciprocal pron.), **ὅτι** (cause) **οὗτοι** (attrib.) **οἱ δύο** (attrib.) **προφῆται** (subj. nom.) **ἐβασάνισαν** (3rd pl. aor. act. ind. of βασανίζω, "torture") **τοὺς κατοικοῦντας** (acc. pl. masc. of pres. act. ptc. of κατοικέω, "dwell," subst., dir. obj.) **ἐπὶ τῆς γῆς** (loc.).

On John's consistent negative view of "the ones dwelling on the earth," see 3:10.

11:11 καὶ μετὰ (with acc., "after") **τὰς** (anaphoric to 11:9) **τρεῖς** (attrib.) **ἡμέρας** (time) **καὶ ἥμισυ** (ἥμισυς, -εια, -υ, "half," attrib.) **πνεῦμα** (subj. nom.) **ζωῆς** (gen. of production, "produced by," or attrib. gen., "living") **ἐκ τοῦ θεοῦ** (source) **εἰσῆλθεν** (3rd sg. aor. act. ind. of εἰσέρχομαι, the aor. tense resumes the main narrative after pres. and fut. tenses were primarily used to describe the nature and activity of the two witnesses [Math 149]) **ἐν αὐτοῖς** (loc., note the interchangeability of ἐν and εἰς [prefixed to the prior vb.] which is not uncommon in Koine Greek), **καὶ ἔστησαν** (3rd pl. aor. act. ind. of ἵστημι) **ἐπὶ τοὺς πόδας** (loc.) **αὐτῶν** (poss.), **καὶ φόβος** (subj. nom.) **μέγας** (attrib.) **ἐπέπεσεν** (3rd sg. aor. act. ind. of ἐπιπίπτω) **ἐπὶ τοὺς θεωροῦντας** (acc. pl. masc. of pres. act. ptc. of θεωρέω, subst., loc.) **αὐτούς** (dir. obj.).

Use of the OT: In Ezekiel's vision of dry bones, the spirit of life enters and brings life to the corpses (καὶ εἰσῆλθεν εἰς αὐτοὺς τὸ πνεῦμα, καὶ ἔζησαν καὶ ἔστησαν ἐπὶ τῶν ποδῶν αὐτῶν [37:10]; 37:5 describes the spirit as πνεῦμα ζωῆς). This allusion likely supports a corporate understanding of the two witnesses since the spirit of life in Ezekiel brought life to the dry bones of the whole house of Israel.

11:12 καὶ ἤκουσαν (3rd pl. aor. act. ind. of ἀκούω, 𝔓[47] ℵ 046 and many minuscules read ἤκουσα, which is the easier reading because it occurs elsewhere twenty-four times in Revelation; the external evidence favors ἤκουσαν [Metzger 672]) **φωνῆς** (gen. dir.

obj.) **μεγάλης** (attrib.) **ἐκ τοῦ οὐρανοῦ** (source) **λεγούσης** (gen. sg. fem. of pres. act. ptc. of λέγω, compl. in obj.-compl. double gen. construction) **αὐτοῖς** (indir. obj.), **Ἀνάβατε** (2nd pl. aor. act. impv. of ἀναβαίνω) **ὧδε** (adv. of place). **καὶ ἀνέβησαν** (3rd pl. aor. act. ind. of ἀναβαίνω) **εἰς τὸν οὐρανὸν** (loc.) **ἐν τῇ νεφέλῃ** (νεφέλη, -ης, ἡ, "cloud," loc. or means), **καὶ ἐθεώρησαν** (3rd pl. aor. act. ind. of θεωρέω) **αὐτοὺς** (dir. obj.) **οἱ ἐχθροὶ** (subj. nom.) **αὐτῶν** (relationship).

Use of the OT: The end of the two witnesses continues the parallel with Elijah, who went up to heaven in a whirlwind (4 Kgdms 2:11 [2 Kgs 2:11 EVV]: καὶ ἀνελήμφθη Ηλιου ἐν συσσεισμῷ ὡς εἰς τὸν οὐρανόν).

11:13 Καὶ ἐν ἐκείνῃ (attrib.) **τῇ ὥρᾳ** (temp.) **ἐγένετο** (3rd sg. aor. mid. ind. of γίνομαι) **σεισμὸς** (σεισμός, -οῦ, ὁ, "earthquake," subj. nom., "an earthquake happened") **μέγας** (attrib.) **καὶ τὸ δέκατον** (δέκατος, -η, -ον, "tenth," subst., subj. nom.) **τῆς πόλεως** (part. gen.) **ἔπεσεν** (3rd sg. aor. act. ind. of πίπτω) **καὶ ἀπεκτάνθησαν** (3rd pl. aor. pass. ind. of ἀποκτείνω) **ἐν τῷ σεισμῷ** (means) **ὀνόματα** (subj. nom.) **ἀνθρώπων** (poss.) **χιλιάδες** (χιλιάς, -άδος, ἡ, "thousand," attrib., modifying ὀνόματα) **ἑπτὰ** ("seven") **καὶ οἱ λοιποὶ** (subst. adj., subj. nom.) **ἔμφοβοι** (ἔμφοβος, -ον, "terrified," pred. adj.) **ἐγένοντο** (3rd pl. aor. mid. ind. of γίνομαι) **καὶ ἔδωκαν** (3rd pl. aor. act. ind. of δίδωμι, coord.) **δόξαν** (dir. obj.) **τῷ θεῷ** (indir. obj.) **τοῦ οὐρανοῦ** (subord. or loc.).

The response of the οἱ λοιποί seems to mirror the response commanded in the eternal Gospel in 14:7 to Φοβήθητε τὸν θεὸν καὶ δότε αὐτῷ δόξαν. The response of οἱ λοιποί is a positive response to the message of God's witnesses combined with God's judgment; this could provide an implicit contrast with the response elicited by God's judgments alone in 9:20–21; 16:9, 11 although there is no indication in Revelation that the failure to repent in the face of God's judgments indicates any deficiency or lack of intended efficacy. God's judgments are just (16:5–7) regardless of whether or not they result in the repentance of the ones punished.

The vision of the two witnesses seems to end on a positive note that matches other indications that many from the nations will be saved. Revelation 7:9 describes an uncountable multitude of the saved. In 21:24 the nations will walk by the light of the new Jerusalem and bring their glory into it, and in 22:2 the leaves of the tree of life will be for the healing of the nations. These visions do not suggest universalism, but they are more hopeful than might be expected in light of the lengthy descriptions of God's judgments.

Use of the OT: The earthquake imagery seems to allude to the judgment of Gog in Ezek 38:19–20 (ἐν τῇ ἡμέρᾳ ἐκείνῃ ἔσται σεισμὸς μέγας ἐπὶ γῆς Ισραηλ, καὶ σεισθήσονται ἀπὸ προσώπου κυρίου . . . καὶ πᾶν τεῖχος ἐπὶ τὴν γῆν πεσεῖται). In

Elijah's ministry, the number 7,000 indicates the faithful remnant (1 Kgs 19:18) so the death of 7,000 in judgment reverses the Elijah typology.

11:14 Ἡ οὐαὶ (as a subst. it denotes "a state of intense hardship or distress" or "woe" [BDAG 734c], subj. nom.) **ἡ δευτέρα** ("second," attrib.) **ἀπῆλθεν** (3rd sg. aor. act. ind. of ἀπέρχομαι). **ἰδοὺ** (interj.) **ἡ οὐαὶ** (subj. nom.) **ἡ τρίτη** ("third," attrib.) **ἔρχεται** (3rd sg. pres. mid. ind. of ἔρχομαι) **ταχύ** (ταχύς, -εῖα, -ύ, "soon, quickly," temp. adv.).

The reference to the completion of the second woe builds upon the numbered list of woes in 8:13 and 9:12 and indicates that the interlude of 10:1–11:14 is associated with the sixth trumpet. The vision of the two witnesses likely culminates at the same point as the end of the sixth trumpet and blowing of the seventh trumpet with the establishment of God's kingdom on the earth and the final judgment (11:15–18). This terminus is supported by the occurrence in judgment of the great eschatological earthquake, which occurs at parallel moments right before the end in 6:12; 8:5; 11:19; 16:18.

FOR FURTHER STUDY

39. Witness

Peters, O. K. *The Mandate of the Church in the Apocalypse of John*. StBibLit 77. New York: Lang, 2005.

Dalrymple, R. "These Are the Ones . . . (Rev 7)." *Bib* 86 (2005): 396–406.

6. The Seventh Trumpet Judgment (11:15–19)

11:15 Καὶ ὁ ἕβδομος (ἕβδομος, -η, -ον, "seventh," attrib.) **ἄγγελος** (subj. nom.) **ἐσάλπισεν** (3rd sg. aor. act. ind. of σαλπίζω, "blow a trumpet"). **καὶ ἐγένοντο** (3rd pl. aor. mid. ind. of γίνομαι) **φωναὶ** (subj. nom.) **μεγάλαι** (attrib.) **ἐν τῷ οὐρανῷ** (loc.) **λέγοντες** (nom. pl. masc. of pres. act. ptc. of λέγω, manner, the masc. ptc. does not match the fem. subj. but likely reflects the implied source of the voice as a *constructio ad sensum*), **Ἐγένετο** (3rd sg. aor. mid. ind. of γίνομαι, the aor. is likely not proleptic but rather points to "an event that has just taken place, but which also overlaps with present time" [Math 152]) **ἡ βασιλεία** (subj. nom.) **τοῦ κόσμου** (subord. or obj. gen.) **τοῦ κυρίου** (poss. modifying an implied pred. nom. βασιλεία, "the kingdom of the world became *the kingdom* of our Lord," ant. of αὐτοῦ) **ἡμῶν** (subord.) **καὶ τοῦ Χριστοῦ** (coord. poss.) **αὐτοῦ** (relationship), **καὶ βασιλεύσει** (3rd sg. fut. act. ind. of βασιλεύω, the sg. vb. is used with a compound subj., suggesting a unity of the Lord and his Messiah) **εἰς τοὺς αἰῶνας** (measure) **τῶν αἰώνων** (emph. repetition of αἰών).

Use of the OT: The Song of the Sea ends in Exod 15:18 with the proclamation that κύριος βασιλεύων τὸν αἰῶνα καὶ ἐπ' αἰῶνα καὶ ἔτι. Psalm 9:37 LXX (10:16 EVV) celebrates the fact that βασιλεύσει κύριος εἰς τὸν αἰῶνα καὶ εἰς τὸν αἰῶνα τοῦ αἰῶνος. Psalm 21:29 LXX (22:28 EVV) declares ὅτι τοῦ κυρίου ἡ βασιλεία, καὶ αὐτὸς δεσπόζει τῶν ἐθνῶν. In the interpretation of the stone in Nebuchadnezzar's dream, Daniel explains στήσει ὁ θεὸς τοῦ οὐρανοῦ βασιλείαν ἄλλην, ἥτις ἔσται εἰς τοὺς αἰῶνας (Dan 2:44). In Dan 7:14, the Son of Man is given an everlasting kingdom: καὶ ἡ ἐξουσία αὐτοῦ ἐξουσία αἰώνιος, ἥτις οὐ μὴ ἀρθῇ, καὶ ἡ βασιλεία αὐτοῦ, ἥτις οὐ μὴ φθαρῇ. Zechariah 14:9 prophesies a day when ἔσται κύριος εἰς βασιλέα ἐπὶ πᾶσαν τὴν γῆν.

11:16 καὶ οἱ (anaphoric to 4:4) **εἴκοσι** ("twenty") **τέσσαρες** ("four") **πρεσβύτεροι** (subj. nom.) [**οἱ**] (modifies the ptc. following the prep. phrase) **ἐνώπιον τοῦ θεοῦ** (loc.) **καθήμενοι** (nom. pl. masc. of pres. mid. ptc. of κάθημαι, attrib. modifying πρεσβύτεροι) **ἐπὶ τοὺς θρόνους** (loc.) **αὐτῶν** (poss.) **ἔπεσαν** (3rd pl. aor. act. ind. of πίπτω) **ἐπὶ τὰ πρόσωπα** (loc.) **αὐτῶν** (poss.) **καὶ προσεκύνησαν** (3rd pl. aor. act. ind. of προσκυνέω, coord.) **τῷ θεῷ** (dat. dir. obj.)
11:17 λέγοντες (nom. pl. masc. of pres. act. ptc. of λέγω, manner), **Εὐχαριστοῦμέν** (1st pl. pres. act. ind. of εὐχαριστέω, "give thanks") **σοι** (indir. obj.), **κύριε** (voc.) **ὁ θεὸς** (appos., the switch from the voc. to the nom. is common in the LXX and classical Greek; θεός and παντοκράτωρ are nom. of address; this same expression occurs in 15:3; 16:7) **ὁ παντοκράτωρ** (παντοκράτωρ, -ορος, ὁ, "almighty," appos.), **ὁ ὢν** (nom. sg. masc. of pres. act. ptc. of εἰμί, subst.) **καὶ ὁ** (substantivizer) **ἦν** (3rd sg. impf. act. ind. of εἰμί, see on 1:4, but note here that the third element of the expression is missing; this is prob. explained by the fact that at this point in the narrative God has come to his creation [note the aor. Ἐγένετο in 11:15]), **ὅτι** (causal, 𝔓[47] ℵ* C 2344 read καὶ ὅτι, but this does not fit John's style while 051 1006 and the TR read ὁ ἐρχόμενος ὅτι; ὅτι by itself has the best external support and best explains the emergence of the other readings [Metzger 672]) **εἴληφας** (2nd sg. pf. act. ind. of λαμβάνω, aoristic) **τὴν δύναμίν** (dir. obj.) **σου** (poss.) **τὴν μεγάλην** (attrib. adj.) **καὶ ἐβασίλευσας** (2nd sg. aor. act. ind. of βασιλεύω, prob. with ingressive nuance).

Use of the OT: Amos 3:13 describes God as κύριος ὁ θεὸς ὁ παντοκράτωρ. Amos 4:13 describes this as God's name: κύριος ὁ θεὸς ὁ παντοκράτωρ ὄνομα αὐτῷ. See Rev 1:4 on Exod 3:14.

11:18 καὶ τὰ ἔθνη (subj. nom.) **ὠργίσθησαν** (3rd pl. aor. pass. ind. of ὀργίζω, "be angry," the pass. form seems to lack pass. meaning and should prob. be taken as mid. [Math 154], the neut. pl. subj. would lead us to expect a sg. vb. but in Revelation neut. pl. subjects that refer to personal beings often take pl. vbs. [Math 154]), **καὶ ἦλθεν** (3rd sg. aor. act. ind. of ἔρχομαι, a sg. vb. is used with two subjects: ὀργή and καιρός) **ἡ ὀργή** (ὀργή, -ῆς, ἡ, "anger, wrath," subj. nom.) **σου** (subj. gen.) **καὶ ὁ καιρὸς** (coord. subj. nom.) **τῶν**

νεκρῶν (the acc. is expected as the subject of the following inf.; as a gen., it is prob. poss.) **κριθῆναι** (aor. pass. inf. of κρίνω, epex.) **καὶ δοῦναι** (aor. act. inf. of δίδωμι, epex., coord.) **τὸν μισθὸν** (μισθός, -οῦ, ὁ, "wages, reward," dir. obj.) **τοῖς δούλοις** (indir. obj.) **σου** (poss.) **τοῖς προφήταις** (appos. to δούλοις) **καὶ τοῖς ἁγίοις** (subst. adj., coord. indir. obj.) **καὶ** (if this is coord. it provides a third group but it is more likely epex. and further describes the first two groups) **τοῖς φοβουμένοις** (dat. pl. masc. of pres. mid. ptc. of φοβέω, subst., indir. obj.) **τὸ ὄνομά** (dir. obj.) **σου** (poss.), **τοὺς μικροὺς** (subst. adj., appos., the case incongruity may reflect an allusion to Ps 113:21 LXX [115:13 EVV] [Math 154], the incongruity is fixed by the use of dats. in ℵ P 046 and most minuscules [Metzger 672]) **καὶ τοὺς μεγάλους** (subst. adj., appos.), **καὶ διαφθεῖραι** (aor. act. inf. of διαφθείρω, "destroy," epex., the three coord. epex. infs. further explain and clarify καιρός: it is time to be judged, to give, and to destroy) **τοὺς διαφθείροντας** (acc. pl. masc. of pres. act. ptc. of διαφθείρω, subst., dir. obj.) **τὴν γῆν** (dir. obj.).

The closing line of 11:18 is important for highlighting the target of God's judgments, which are not indiscriminately inflicted on human beings, as some of the apocalyptic descriptions would suggest, but are targeted at the ones destroying the earth. This should not be limited to ecological harm but taken as broadly referring to those whose allegiance lies with the beasts and Babylon (note how 19:2 claims that Babylon ἔφθειρεν τὴν γῆν ἐν τῇ πορνείᾳ αὐτῆς and below on Jer 28:25 LXX). There will be no innocent recipients of God's judgment.

The seventh trumpet celebrates that the kingdom of the world has become the kingdom of God and the Messiah. It celebrates the established reign of God on earth, the wrath of God that has come, and the coming of the time of final judgment. These descriptions are not anticipatory, but descriptive of the reality and content of the seventh trumpet (recall 10:6–7). The seventh trumpet declares that the final judgment has taken place although it is not narrated in full until 20:11–15. This is a strong argument for some degree of repetition and overlap in the visions, since the following visions in Revelation 12–20 further narrate events that lead up to the end that is described in the seventh trumpet.

Use of the OT: Although Ps 2:1 LXX translates the rage of the nations as ἐφρύαξαν ἔθνη, an allusion to Ps 2:1 can be discerned in John's ἔθνη ὠργίσθησαν. Psalm 45:7 LXX (46:6 EVV) describes the nations as ἐταράχθησαν. In an oracle against Babylon in Jer 28:25 LXX (51:25 EVV), Jeremiah prophesies that God is against Babylon (ἰδοὺ ἐγὼ πρὸς σέ), the destroying mountain which destroys all the earth (τὸ ὄρος τὸ διεφθαρμένον τὸ διαφθεῖρον πᾶσαν τὴν γῆν). On the expression "your servants the prophets," see on 10:7. Psalm 113:21 LXX (115:13 EVV) declares εὐλόγησεν τοὺς φοβουμένους τὸν κύριον, τοὺς μικροὺς μετὰ τῶν μεγάλων.

11:19 **καὶ ἠνοίγη** (3rd sg. aor. pass. ind. of ἀνοίγω) **ὁ ναὸς** (ναός, -οῦ, ὁ, "temple," subj. nom.) **τοῦ θεοῦ** (poss.) **ὁ** (adjectivizer, 𝔓[47] ℵ P 046 051 and most minuscules lack the art. [Metzger 672–73]) **ἐν τῷ οὐρανῷ** (loc.) **καὶ ὤφθη** (3rd sg. aor. pass. ind. of ὁράω) **ἡ κιβωτὸς** (κιβωτός, -οῦ, ἡ, "ark, chest," subj. nom.) **τῆς διαθήκης** (διαθήκη, -ης, ἡ, "covenant," descriptive gen.) **αὐτοῦ** (poss., either modifying "ark" or "covenant," Aune makes the case that it modifies the entire expression [Aune[b] 677]) **ἐν τῷ ναῷ** (loc.) **αὐτοῦ** (poss.), **καὶ ἐγένοντο** (3rd pl. aor. mid. ind. of γίνομαι) **ἀστραπαὶ** (ἀστραπή, -ῆς, ἡ, "lightning," subj. nom.) **καὶ φωναὶ** (coord. subj. nom.) **καὶ βρονταὶ** (βροντή, -ῆς, ἡ, "thunder," coord. subj. nom.) **καὶ σεισμὸς** (σεισμός, -οῦ, ὁ, "earthquake," coord. subj. nom.) **καὶ χάλαζα** (χάλαζα, -ης, ἡ, "hail," coord. subj. nom.) **μεγάλη** (attrib.).

Hebrews 8:5 describes how the human tabernacle was constructed according to a heavenly pattern (cf. Acts 7:44; Exod 25:9, 40; 26:30). Revelation 11:19, however, is the only reference in the Bible to a heavenly ark of the covenant (Fanning 343). The appearance of the ark at this point is enigmatic. It is properly associated with the blowing of trumpets in the judgment of Jericho (Beale 619) and contextually is associated here with the judgment of oppressive powers (Koester 541).

Use of the OT: Third Kingdoms 8:1 (1 Kgs 8:1 EVV) describes Solomon's transport of the ark of the covenant (τὴν κιβωτὸν διαθήκης κυρίου) to the completed temple (cf. 2 Chr 5:7). Exodus 9:24 describes the seventh plague of hail as ἡ δὲ χάλαζα πολλὴ σφόδρα σφόδρα, ἥτις τοιαύτη οὐ γέγονεν ἐν Αἰγύπτῳ ἀφ' οὗ γεγένηται ἐπ' αὐτῆς ἔθνος. On the allusion to the Sinai theophany in Exod 19:16–19, see on 4:5.

HOMILETICAL SUGGESTIONS

John's recommissioning along with the vision of the temple and the two witnesses provide a digression between the sixth and seventh trumpets to slow down the narrative (making the reader experience and feel the delay) as well as interpret the time of the delay before the end.

Faithfulness to the End (10:1–11:19)

1. John is recommissioned for prophetic service (10:1–11).
2. God's people are protected, empowered, opposed, and victorious (11:1–12).
3. God's victory will come at last to bring final salvation and judgment (11:15–19).

D. AN OVERVIEW AND INTERPRETATION OF HISTORY (12:1–14:20)

These three chapters are closely linked. They begin with visions of Jesus's birth and enthronement in heaven (12:5), which results in the decisive defeat of Satan and his expulsion from heaven (12:7–12). Satan tries to destroy God's people (12:13, 17) by empowering two beasts (13:1–18). Chapter 14 contrasts those who take the beast's mark with those who have God's seal and overcome (14:1–13) before providing a vision of the harvest of the earth (14:14–20), which has strong intratextual parallels to Jesus's coming more fully narrated in 19:11–21. The visions in Revelation 12–14 thus provide a visionary overview of history from Jesus's resurrection until Jesus's return that provides rhetorical motivation through describing the different end results of those who are faithful to Jesus and those who give their allegiance to the beast.

1. The Cause of Conflict: The Woman, the Dragon, and the Seed (12:1–17)

Chapter 12 is easily divided into three parts based on the content. Verses 1–6 introduce the main characters (12:1–4) and the key events: the dragon wants to destroy the child (12:4), the child is born and enthroned (12:5), and the woman is protected by God for 1,260 days (12:6). Verses 7–12 describe a war in heaven caused by the enthronement of the child (12:7). The war results in the expulsion of the dragon from heaven, which is linked to a celebration of the coming rule of God and his Messiah (12:10). In a clear articulation of inaugurated eschatology, the salvation and kingdom secured by and for the Messiah through his enthronement in heaven is not yet fully realized on earth and the dragon has a little time left to try to harm God's people (12:12). The third section in verses 13–17 picks up the story of the woman who is protected in the wilderness for 1,260 days by describing how the dragon tries but is unable to harm her (12:13–16). The dragon then turns his attention to those whom he could harm: the rest of her seed, the people of God on earth who were faithfully overcoming through keeping the commandments of God and holding to the testimony of Jesus (12:17). The vision does not end with chapter 12 but transitions in 12:17–13:1 to show how the dragon is linked to the beast arising from the sea. The beast is then empowered in chapter 13 to execute the war begun against God's people by the dragon in 12:17.

a. The Woman and the Dragon (12:1–6)

12:1 Καὶ σημεῖον (subj. nom.) **μέγα** (attrib.) **ὤφθη** (3rd sg. aor. pass. ind. of ὁράω) **ἐν τῷ οὐρανῷ** (loc.), **γυνὴ** (appos. to σημεῖον) **περιβεβλημένη** (nom. sg. fem. of pf. pass. ptc. of περιβάλλω, "wrap, clothe," attrib.) **τὸν ἥλιον** (ἥλιος, -ου, ὁ, "sun," dir. obj.), **καὶ ἡ σελήνη** (σελήνη, -ης, ἡ, "moon," subj. nom. of verbless cl.) **ὑποκάτω** (prep., "below, under") **τῶν ποδῶν** (loc.) **αὐτῆς** (poss.) **καὶ ἐπὶ τῆς κεφαλῆς** (loc.) **αὐτῆς** (poss.) **στέφανος** (στέφανος, -ου, ὁ, "wreath," indicating honor or victory, subj. nom. of verbless cl.) **ἀστέρων** (ἀστήρ, -έρος, ὁ, "star," gen. of material) **δώδεκα** ("twelve," attrib.),

This is the first occurrence of σημεῖον in Revelation, although the cognate vb. σημαίνω is used to describe the means of communication of the book in 1:1 from Jesus through his angel to John to God's servants. Both the noun and the vb. in 1:1 indicate symbolic communication through visual symbols. Σημεῖον also occurs in 12:3

to describe the dragon and 15:1 to describe the seven angels with seven plagues. The noun is also used to indicate miracles presented by demonic beings as signs of power in order to deceive (Rev 13:13, 14; 16:14; 19:20).

The woman is likely a transtemporal symbol for God's united people throughout history that would have mainly consisted of Jews before Jesus's birth and the multiethnic messianic community of both Jews and gentiles following his resurrection ("the people of God both before and after Jesus's birth" [Koester 542]). The woman should also probably be identified with the bride of the Lamb (19:6–9; 20:7–9; cf. Eph 5:22–32); the bride is explicitly contrasted with the prostitute Babylon in Revelation 17–19. The sun, moon, and wreath of twelve stars indicate the woman's fundamental Israelite identity (see below on Gen 37:9), but this is not an identity in which gentile believers in Jesus could not identify and enter into (see comments on 7:8). God's people in Revelation are consistently described with Jewish characteristics while also being from every tribe, tongue, and nation. Revelation celebrates a Jewish salvation accomplished by the Jewish Messiah in fulfillment of God's promises of restoration to Israel in the Jewish Scriptures into which gentiles could freely participate and identify through allegiance to Jesus. The identification of the woman as both Israel and the transnational messianic community is not a contradiction but a result of the outworking of God's plan in salvation history.

Use of the OT: Joseph's dream in Gen 37:9 describes the sun, moon, and eleven stars bowing down to him. See 12:2 for passages in which Israel is described as a woman in labor suffering birth pains.

12:2 καὶ ἐν γαστρὶ (γαστήρ, -τρός, ἡ, "belly," loc.) **ἔχουσα** (nom. sg. fem. of pres. act. ptc. of ἔχω, functioning as finite vb., the idiom "having in the womb" indicates pregnancy), **καὶ κράζει** (3rd sg. pres. act. ind. of κράζω, narrative pres.) **ὠδίνουσα** (nom. sg. fem. of pres. act. ptc. of ὠδίνω, "have birth pains," manner or cause) **καὶ βασανιζομένη** (nom. sg. fem. of pres. pass. ptc. of βασανίζω, "torment," manner or cause) **τεκεῖν** (aor. act. inf. of τίκτω, "give birth," prob. purpose).

Use of the OT: The imagery of Israel as a pregnant woman experiencing birth pains in anticipation of God's salvation occurs throughout the prophets (Isa 26:17–18; note the curious removal of negation in Isa 26:18 LXX in which Israel's labor and delivery would produce a spirit of salvation upon the earth). Isaiah 66:7–12 describes the suddenness of God's deliverance and restoration as birth before labor or birth pains. In Mic 4:10, God's people are called to experience the birth pains of exile with courage because restoration would come (ὤδινε καὶ ἀνδρίζου καὶ ἔγγιζε, θύγατερ Σιων, ὡς τίκτουσα). Jeremiah 4:31 describes

Jerusalem under God's judgment as crying out as a woman in labor with her firstborn (φωνὴν ὡς ὠδινούσης ἤκουσα, τοῦ στεναγμοῦ σου ὡς πρωτςτοκούσης).

12:3 καὶ ὤφθη (3rd sg. aor. pass. ind. of ὁράω) **ἄλλο** (attrib.) **σημεῖον** (subj. nom.) **ἐν τῷ οὐρανῷ** (loc.), **καὶ ἰδοὺ** (emph. interj.) **δράκων** (δράκων, -οντος, ὁ, "dragon, serpent," subj. nom. of verbless cl.) **μέγας** (attrib.) **πυρρὸς** (πυρρός, -ά, -όν, "fiery red," attrib.) **ἔχων** (nom. sg. masc. pres. act. ptc. ἔχω, attrib.) **κεφαλὰς** (dir. obj.) **ἑπτὰ** ("seven," attrib.) **καὶ κέρατα** (κέρας, -ατος, τό, "horn," dir. obj.) **δέκα** ("ten," attrib.) **καὶ ἐπὶ τὰς κεφαλὰς** (loc.) **αὐτοῦ** (poss.) **ἑπτὰ** (attrib.) **διαδήματα** (διάδημα, -ατος, τό, "crown," "royal headband," or "a symbol of royalty" [BDAG 227d], dir. obj.),

Διαδήματα occurs three times in Revelation: the dragon and beast both wear seven crowns (12:3; 13:1) while the rider on the white horse who defeats the beasts wears διαδήματα πολλά (19:12). The διαδήματα suggest an explicit contrast between the dragon and the beast on the one hand and the lamb regarding who is the rightful ruler of the world. On the difference between διάδημα and στέφανος, see 2:10.

Use of the OT: The dragon's ten horns match the description of the fourth beast in Dan 7:7 (εἶχε δὲ κέρατα δέκα).

12:4 καὶ ἡ οὐρὰ (οὐρά, -ᾶς, ἡ, "tail," subj. nom.) **αὐτοῦ** (poss.) **σύρει** (3rd sg. pres. act. ind. of σύρω, "drag away," narrative pres.) **τὸ τρίτον** ("third," subst., dir. obj.) **τῶν ἀστέρων** (ἀστήρ, -έρος, ὁ, "star," part. gen.) **τοῦ οὐρανοῦ** (descriptive gen. or loc.) **καὶ ἔβαλεν** (3rd sg. aor. act. ind. of βάλλω) **αὐτοὺς** (dir. obj.) **εἰς τὴν γῆν** (loc.). **καὶ ὁ** (anaphoric to v. 3) **δράκων** (δράκων, -οντος, ὁ, "dragon, serpent," subj. nom.) **ἕστηκεν** (3rd sg. pf. act. ind. of ἵστημι) **ἐνώπιον τῆς** (anaphoric to v. 1) **γυναικὸς** (loc.) **τῆς μελλούσης** (gen. sg. fem. of pres. act. ptc. of μέλλω, "about to," attrib.) **τεκεῖν** (aor. act. inf. of τίκτω, "give birth," compl. inf.), **ἵνα** (purpose) **ὅταν** (indef. temp. conj.) **τέκῃ** (3rd sg. aor. act. subjunc. of τίκτω) **τὸ τέκνον** (dir. obj.) **αὐτῆς** (relationship) **καταφάγῃ** (3rd sg. aor. act. subjunc. of κατεσθίω, "consume, devour"; the dir. obj. is implied from the temp. subord. cl. to be τέκνον).

The common connection of stars with angels in apocalyptic literature and of fallen angels with fallen stars could suggest that this is a picture of Satan's rebellion against God in which he was joined by rebellious supernatural beings. The imagery could also simply suggest an assault upon heaven by the dragon (Koester 545). This latter conclusion is strengthened by Dan 8:10 MT (see below). Many combat myths circulated in ancient cultures that narrate the conflict between a hero and an adversary or a primordial struggle between diving beings with the antagonist often pictured as a monster, serpent, or dragon. Parallels with Revelation 12 are often drawn with the Apollo-Leto-Python, Isis-Osiris-Horus-Typhon, or Damkina-Marduk-Tiamat myths; the cosmic-conflict motif in Jewish apocalyptic literature often functions to explain the presence of evil and suffering in the world (Aune[b] 667–74). There is no doubt that John's various hearers throughout Asia Minor would have thought of such comparisons, but it seems that John himself is more directly influenced by the OT, particularly the protoeuangelion in Gen 3:15, which anticipates future conflict between a serpent, the woman, and the seed of the woman (*καὶ ἔχθραν θήσω ἀνὰ μέσον σου καὶ ἀνὰ μέσον τῆς γυναικὸς καὶ ἀνὰ μέσον τοῦ σπέρματός σου καὶ ἀνὰ μέσον τοῦ σπέρματος αὐτῆς*). This seems to be confirmed by John's characterization of the dragon as *ὁ ὄφις ὁ ἀρχαῖος* in 12:9.

Use of the OT: The little horn that grew on the goat in the vision in Dan 8:10 MT becomes great to the stars of heaven and casts down and tramples (some) from them. Contrary to the use of the *hiphil* and *qal* in the MT, the subj. and meaning are changed with pass. vbs. in the LXX: the little horn was struck to the earth by/from the stars and was trampled by them (*καὶ ὑψώθη ἕως τῶν ἀστέρων τοῦ οὐρανοῦ, καὶ ἐρράχθη ἐπὶ τὴν γῆν ἀπὸ τῶν ἀστέρων καὶ ἀπὸ αὐτῶν κατεπατήθη*). John seems not to follow the LXX in 12:4 but perhaps in 12:9 to describe how Satan was cast to the earth.

12:5 καὶ ἔτεκεν (3rd sg. aor. act. ind. of *τίκτω*, "give birth") **υἱὸν** (dir. obj., ant. of *ὅς*) **ἄρσεν** (*ἄρσην, -εν*, neut., "male," attrib. with incongruity in gender or subst. in appos.; 12:13 contains the masc. *ἄρσενα* and Beale suggests the incongruous neut. here signals an allusion to Isa 66:7 [Beale 640–41]), **ὃς** (subj. nom.) **μέλλει** (3rd sg. pres. act. ind. of *μέλλω*) **ποιμαίνειν** (pres. act. inf. of *ποιμαίνω*, "shepherd, rule," compl. inf.) **πάντα** (attrib.) **τὰ ἔθνη** (dir. obj.) **ἐν ῥάβδῳ** (*ῥάβδος, -ου, ἡ*, "rod, staff, scepter," means) **σιδηρᾷ** (*σιδηροῦς, -ᾶ, -οῦν*, "made of iron," attrib.). **καὶ ἡρπάσθη** (3rd sg. aor. pass. ind. of *ἁρπάζω*, "grab, seize by force," with the purpose of removing and/or controlling" [L&N 18.4]) **τὸ τέκνον** (subj. nom.) **αὐτῆς** (relationship) **πρὸς τὸν θεὸν** (loc.) **καὶ πρὸς τὸν** (anaphoric to 4:2) **θρόνον** (loc.) **αὐτοῦ** (poss.).

John does not focus on Jesus's ministry or death here (see for this 1:5–6; 5:9–10; 7:14; 12:11) but rather on his enthronement and the resultant consequences in the following verses.

Use of the OT: Psalm 2:9 provides God's speech to his appointed king regarding his rule of the nations (*ἔθνη*) and the ends of the earth (*πέρατα τῆς γῆς*): *ποιμανεῖς αὐτοὺς ἐν ῥάβδῳ σιδηρᾷ*. John clearly presents this son as the one who will fulfill God's declaration in Psalm 2; the allusion to Psalm 2 also connects the son in Rev 12:5 with the rider in 19:15. The phrase *ἔτεκεν υἱόν* is similar to the famous prophecy in Isa 7:14 regarding a virgin who *τέξεται υἱόν*. John does not highlight his name as *Εμμανουηλ* or explicitly present the woman as a virgin, although such could perhaps be implied by her heavenly description. In light of 3:21, the explicit mention of the throne here suggests an echo of Ps 109:1 LXX (110:1 EVV): Εἶπεν ὁ κύριος τῷ κυρίῳ μου Κάθου ἐκ δεξιῶν μου. The prophecy of restoration in Isa 66:7 celebrates that πρὶν ἢ τὴν ὠδίνουσαν τεκεῖν, πρὶν ἐλθεῖν τὸν πόνον τῶν ὠδίνων, ἐξέφυγεν καὶ ἔτεκεν ἄρσεν. John's allusion to Isa 66:7 narrows down the corporate focus from the birth of a nation to the individual birth of the nation's Messiah.

12:6 καὶ ἡ (anaphoric to 12:1) **γυνὴ** (subj. nom.) **ἔφυγεν** (3rd sg. aor. act. ind. of φεύγω, "flee") **εἰς τὴν ἔρημον** (ἔρημος, -ον, "wilderness, desert," loc.), **ὅπου** (loc. conj. functions like a rel. pron., "where") **ἔχει** (3rd sg. pres. act. ind. of ἔχω, narrative pres.) **ἐκεῖ** (loc. adv., "there," redundant for emph.) **τόπον** (dir. obj.) **ἡτοιμασμένον** (acc. sg. masc. of pf. pass. ptc. of ἑτοιμάζω, "prepare," attrib.) **ἀπὸ τοῦ θεοῦ** (source implying agency), **ἵνα** (purpose) **ἐκεῖ** (loc. adv.) **τρέφωσιν** (3rd pl. pres. act. subjunc. of τρέφω, "nourish," the pl. subj. is not identified and could indicate an impers. vb. which could be translated as pass. [Math 160]) **αὐτὴν** (dir. obj.) **ἡμέρας** (temp.) **χιλίας** ("thousand," attrib.) **διακοσίας** ("two hundred") **ἑξήκοντα** ("sixty").

The narrative progression from v. 5 to v. 6 suggests that the three-and-a-half-year period in Revelation begins with Jesus's ascension and enthronement; there is no indication of a long gap in time (Koester 547, 562; Beale 567; and many others; contra Fanning who argues the sequence of the vision is elliptical [353] and fragmented [351] at this point but such conclusions do not obviously come from the vision but from a system that is imposed from outside the text). On the time period see 11:2.

FOR FURTHER STUDY

40. The Use of the Psalms in Revelation

Moyise, S. "The Psalms in the Book of Revelation." Pages 231–46 in *The Psalms in the New Testament*. Edited by S. Moyise and M. J. J. Menken. London: T&T Clark, 2004.

b. War in Heaven (12:7–12)

12:7 Καὶ ἐγένετο (3rd sg. aor. mid. ind. of γίνομαι) **πόλεμος** (πόλεμος, -ου, ὁ, "battle," subj. nom.) **ἐν τῷ οὐρανῷ** (loc.), **ὁ** (well-known use of the art. suggesting that John expected his hearers to know about Michael) **Μιχαὴλ** ("Michael," nom. subj. of inf. [see below]) **καὶ οἱ ἄγγελοι** (coord. subj. nom.) **αὐτοῦ** (poss.) **τοῦ πολεμῆσαι** (aor. act. inf., see below) **μετὰ τοῦ** (anaphoric to 12:3) **δράκοντος** (assoc. with the nuance here of disadvantage, "against"). **καὶ ὁ** (anaphoric) **δράκων** (δράκων, -οντος, ὁ, "dragon, serpent," subj. nom.) **ἐπολέμησεν** (3rd sg. aor. act. ind. of πολεμέω, "fight, make war," the sg. vb. with a compound subj. draws its number from the first or more prominent subj.) **καὶ οἱ ἄγγελοι** (coord. subj. nom.) **αὐτοῦ** (poss.),

Although it is possible to take the war and expulsion of Satan as a description of a primordial fall or a future event linked with Jesus's second coming, it is most natural in the narrative flow of the vision to take the war in heaven and its outcome as describing the immediate consequences of Jesus's death, resurrection, and enthronement as described in 12:5 (Koester 547; Beale 652).

Michael was well-known in early Christianity as the archangel tasked with protecting Israel (Dan 10:13; 12:1; Jude 9); he also features prominently in foundational Second Temple Jewish literature (1 En. 20:5; 24:6 [the chief angel]; 40:9). This is the only appearance of Michael in Revelation, and it would suggest that he is a powerful and leading figure in the angelic hierarchy assumed by John.

The use of the nom. case ὁ Μιχαὴλ καὶ οἱ ἄγγελοι is irregular as the subject of the articular inf. τοῦ πολεμῆσαι. The solecism has multiple possible explanations. It could be a Hebraism related to the common Heb. construction of a subj. plus an inf. with a לְ prefix. If so, the construction implies necessity: "Michael and his angels had to make war" (Beale 654). This Hebrew idiom, however, is not always translated in the LXX with an articular inf., and an explanation that does not depend on Semitic influence is possible (Moţ 125). It is possible that there is ellipsis and a vb. of arising or coming is implied before ὁ Μιχαὴλ. This would result in an inf. of purpose or result (i.e., Michael *came* to fight against). Assuming ellipsis in 12:4, the expression would function similarly to 12:17 (ἀπῆλθεν ποιῆσαι πόλεμον). Without assuming ellipsis, the inf. most naturally seems to be functioning as an independent inf. in the predicate slot (Porter, *Verbal Aspect in the Greek of the New Testament*, 377), but that does not explain the use of the nom. as subj. of the inf. It is perhaps significant that this is the only use of the articular inf. in the critical text, although weakly supported variants of an articular inf. appear in 4:11; 5:3; 9:6, 10; 12:2; 14:15 (Thompson 62). The solecism here is most likely explained by the influence of Semitic syntax (Thompson 60–63). The fact that John clearly knows how to communicate the same idea more properly with an anar. inf. (see ποιῆσαι πόλεμον in 12:17; 13:7; 19:19; πολεμῆσαι in 13:4) strengthens Beale's suggestion that the articular inf. in 12:7 signals an allusion to τοῦ πολεμῆσαι in Dan 10:20 (Theod.; Beale 654). Michael's significant role in fighting the prince of Persia and the prince of Greece in Dan 10 parallels his war against the dragon in Revelation 12, and John hints at this connection with the articular inf.

Use of the OT: Daniel 10:13, 21 describes the activity of Michael who aided the man clothed in linen (Dan 10:5) against the prince of the kingdom of Persia (10:13: Μιχαηλ εἷς τῶν ἀρχόντων τῶν πρώτων ἐπῆλθε βοηθῆσαί μοι). Michael will also help fight against the prince of Greece (10:21: καὶ οὐθεὶς ἦν ὁ βοηθῶν μετ' ἐμοῦ ὑπὲρ τούτων ἀλλ' ἢ Μιχαηλ ὁ ἄγγελος). Daniel 12:1 declares that Michael will arise at a future time of great tribulation, which would be followed by the deliverance of everyone written in the book (καὶ κατὰ τὴν ὥραν ἐκείνην παρελεύσεται Μιχαηλ ὁ ἄγγελος ὁ μέγας ὁ ἑστηκὼς ἐπὶ τοὺς υἱοὺς τοῦ λαοῦ σου, ἐκείνη ἡ ἡμέρα θλίψεως, οἵα οὐκ ἐγενήθη ἀφ' οὗ ἐγενήθησαν ἕως τῆς ἡμέρας ἐκείνης, καὶ ἐν ἐκείνῃ τῇ ἡμέρᾳ ὑψωθήσεται πᾶς ὁ λαός, ὃς ἂν εὑρεθῇ ἐγγεγραμμένος ἐν τῷ βιβλίῳ). Jude 9 describes a conflict between Michael and the devil over the body of Moses.

12:8 καὶ οὐκ ἴσχυσεν (3rd sg. aor. act. ind. of ἰσχύω, "be strong") **οὐδὲ** ("nor") **τόπος** (subj. nom.) **εὑρέθη** (3rd sg. aor. pass. ind. of εὑρίσκω) **αὐτῶν** (advantage, "place for them," or poss., "their place") **ἔτι** (temp. adv., "again, still") **ἐν τῷ οὐρανῷ** (loc.).
12:9 καὶ ἐβλήθη (3rd sg. aor. pass. ind. of βάλλω) **ὁ** (anaphoric to 12:3) **δράκων** (δράκων, -οντος, ὁ, "dragon, serpent," subj. nom.) **ὁ μέγας** (attrib.), **ὁ ὄφις** (ὄφις, -εως, ὁ, "serpent," appos.) **ὁ ἀρχαῖος** (ἀρχαῖος, -αία, -αῖον, "ancient," attrib.), **ὁ καλούμενος** (nom. sg. masc. of pres. pass. ptc. of καλέω, subst. in appos. or attrib.) **Διάβολος** (διάβολος, -ον, "slanderer, adversary, devil," pred. nom. with pass. καλέω [Wallace 40]) **καὶ ὁ Σατανᾶς** (σατανᾶς, -ᾶ, ὁ, "Satan, enemy, adversary," coord. pred. nom. with pass. καλέω), **ὁ πλανῶν** (nom. sg. masc. of pres. act. ptc. of πλανάω, "deceive," subst. in appos. or attrib.) **τὴν οἰκουμένην** (dir. obj.) **ὅλην** (attrib.), **ἐβλήθη** (3rd sg. aor. pass. ind. of βάλλω, resumptive of the first vb. in 12:9) **εἰς τὴν γῆν** (loc.), **καὶ οἱ ἄγγελοι** (subj. nom.) **αὐτοῦ** (poss.) **μετ' αὐτοῦ** (association) **ἐβλήθησαν** (3rd pl. aor. pass. ind. of βάλλω).

Because of Jesus's death, resurrection, and enthronement the dragon is cast out from the highest spiritual realm connected to the divine throne room and heavenly temple to the lowest spiritual realm that exists parallel to the created material world. Jesus claims that he saw Satan fall like lightning from heaven (Luke 10:18: Ἐθεώρουν τὸν Σατανᾶν ὡς ἀστραπὴν ἐκ τοῦ οὐρανοῦ πεσόντα) and the ruler of the world would be cast out (John 12:31: νῦν ὁ ἄρχων τοῦ κόσμου τούτου ἐκβληθήσεται ἔξω). Satan is consistently connected with deception and temptation in early Christianity (Matt 4:1; John 8:44; 1 Cor 7:5; 2 Cor 11:14) and in Rev 16:13–14; 20:3, 7.

Use of the OT: Both διάβολος and σατάν are used to translate שָׂטָן (Heb., "adversary") and are generally used as syn. in early Christianity. First Chronicles 21:1 describes how the διάβολος incited David to take the census (Καὶ ἔστη διάβολος ἐν τῷ Ισραηλ καὶ ἐπέσεισεν τὸν Δαυιδ τοῦ ἀριθμῆσαι τὸν Ισραηλ). The διάβολος also features prominently in Job (1:6, 7, 9, 12, 2:1, 2, 3, 4, 6, 7). In Zech 3:1, the διάβολος accuses Joshua in the heavenly courtroom (καὶ ὁ διάβολος εἱστήκει ἐκ δεξιῶν αὐτοῦ τοῦ ἀντικεῖσθαι αὐτῷ). The Wisdom of Solomon claims that the devil brought death into the world by envy, and those being part of that (one) experience it (2:24: φθόνῳ δὲ διαβόλου θάνατος εἰσῆλθεν εἰς τὸν κόσμον, πειράζουσιν δὲ αὐτὸν οἱ τῆς ἐκείνου μερίδος ὄντες). Numbers 22:22 describes the angel of the Lord as a שָׂטָן against Balaam (translated with a vb. in the LXX: καὶ ἀνέστη ὁ ἄγγελος τοῦ θεοῦ ἐνδιαβάλλειν αὐτόν). In Isaiah's taunt against the king of Babylon he describes him as having fallen from heaven and being crushed into the earth (14:12: πῶς ἐξέπεσεν ἐκ τοῦ οὐρανοῦ ὁ ἑωσφόρος ὁ πρωὶ ἀνατέλλων; συνετρίβη εἰς τὴν γῆν ὁ ἀποστέλλων πρὸς πάντα τὰ ἔθνη). John's reference to ὁ ὄφις ὁ ἀρχαῖος seems to be a clear allusion to the ὄφις throughout Genesis 3.

12:10 καὶ ἤκουσα (1st sg. aor. act. ind. of ἀκούω) **φωνὴν** (dir. obj.) **μεγάλην** (attrib.) **ἐν τῷ οὐρανῷ** (loc.) **λέγουσαν** (acc. sg. fem. of pres. act. ptc. of λέγω, compl. in obj.-compl.

double acc. construction), Ἄρτι (temp. adv., "now") ἐγένετο (3rd sg. aor. mid. ind. of γίνομαι, the sg. vb. is used with compound subjects, the adv. indicates immediate past) **ἡ σωτηρία** (subj. nom.) **καὶ ἡ δύναμις** (coord. subj. nom.) **καὶ ἡ βασιλεία** (coord. subj. nom.) **τοῦ θεοῦ** (subj. gen.) **ἡμῶν** (subord.) **καὶ ἡ ἐξουσία** (coord. subj. nom.) **τοῦ Χριστοῦ** (subj. gen.) **αὐτοῦ** (relationship), **ὅτι** (causal) **ἐβλήθη** (3rd sg. aor. pass. ind. of βάλλω) **ὁ κατήγωρ** (κατήγωρ, -ορος, ὁ, "accuser," subj. nom., all mss except A read κατήγορος instead of the hapax legomenon κατήγωρ [Metzger 673]) **τῶν ἀδελφῶν** (obj. gen.) **ἡμῶν** (relationship), **ὁ κατηγορῶν** (nom. sg. masc. of pres. act. ptc. of κατηγορέω, "accuse" or "bring serious charges or accusations against someone, with the possible connotation of a legal or court context" [L&N 33.427], subst. in appos. to κατήγωρ or attrib.) **αὐτοὺς** (dir. obj.) **ἐνώπιον τοῦ θεοῦ** (loc.) **ἡμῶν** (subord.) **ἡμέρας** (gen. of time) **καὶ νυκτός** (gen. of time).

In Revelation, βασιλεία describes: (1) the present hostile kingdom of the world (11:15), the beast (16:10), the ten horns (17:12, 17) and Babylon (17:18) who reject God's rule; and (2) the present kingdom formed by Jesus consisting of the churches, God's people (1:6, 9; 5:10). These contrasting kingdoms exist in opposition to each other on earth in an asymmetrical relationship of oppressor and oppressed (note the dragon's wrath and activity in 12:12, 17). The seventh trumpet declares that God's final victory will see the kingdom of the world become the kingdom of the Lord and his Messiah. The kingdom inaugurated in 12:10 is announced in heaven, but it is a consequence of Jesus's enthronement and is interpreted as the casting down of the accuser. This event describes the moment in heaven when Jesus makes his people a kingdom on earth (1:6, 9; 5:10).

This casting down of Satan is interpreted in the vision as ending his ability to bring accusations against God's people in the divine council. This theological visionary interpretation of the defeat of Satan parallels Paul's celebration in Rom 8:33–34 (τίς ἐγκαλέσει κατὰ ἐκλεκτῶν θεοῦ; θεὸς ὁ δικαιῶν· τίς ὁ κατακρινῶν;).

Use of the OT: Both Job 1:9–11 and Zech 3:1 describe the διάβολος accusing human beings in the divine council or heavenly court.

12:11 καὶ αὐτοὶ (subj. nom.) **ἐνίκησαν** (3rd pl. aor. act. ind. of νικάω, "overcome, conquer") **αὐτὸν** (dir. obj.) **διὰ τὸ αἷμα** (causal) **τοῦ ἀρνίου** (ἀρνίον, -ου, τό, "lamb," poss. or source) **καὶ διὰ τὸν λόγον** (coord. causal) **τῆς μαρτυρίας** (subj. gen., "the message that their testimony communicates" [Fanning 358] or epex.) **αὐτῶν** (subj. gen.) **καὶ οὐκ ἠγάπησαν** (3rd pl. aor. act. ind. of ἀγαπάω) **τὴν ψυχὴν** (dir. obj., distributive sg. with pl. gen. modifier) **αὐτῶν** (poss.) **ἄχρι** ("until," takes a gen. obj.) **θανάτου** (extent with ἄχρι).

The "they" refers to God's people (not Michael and his angels) who suffered (12:17; 3:7) but participate in heaven's defeat of Satan by also overcoming him on earth. The aor. ἐνίκησαν produces a similar effect as the vision of 7:9 in which those coming out of the tribulation are pictured as having won the victory and are standing and worshipping before the throne. Information on how the believers in the intermediate state overcame the dragon provides instruction and direction for those who are still in the middle of the same conflict. Every overcomer, from the past to the future, will overcome the dragon in this way. There is no indication that every overcomer had to die for their faith, but that they should be willing to do so if necessary (note that all the churches are expected and called to overcome in Revelation 2–3, and the distinction between captivity and the sword in 13:10 assumes not all will die by the sword). The participation of God's people in the victory over the dragon is attributed to the blood of the Lamb (Jesus's sacrificial death; 1:5; 7:14) and to the faith expressed in their witness/testimony to the point of death (12:11; cf. 2:10). The fact that they would need to be faithful until death anticipates the upcoming description of the war of the dragon (12:17) and beast (13:7) against God's people.

12:12 διὰ τοῦτο (causal, the ant. is 12:10–11) **εὐφραίνεσθε** (2nd pl. pres. mid. impv. of εὐφραίνω, "celebrate"), [οἱ] **οὐρανοὶ** (nom. for voc.) ***καὶ οἱ ἐν αὐτοῖς*** (loc.) ***σκηνοῦντες*** (nom. pl. masc. of pres. act. ptc. of σκηνόω, "live in a tent, dwell," subst., nom. for voc.). **οὐαὶ** (interj., as a subst. it can denote "a state of intense hardship or distress" or "woe" [BDAG 734c], asyndeton) **τὴν γῆν** (dir. obj. of verbless cl., on the case see 8:13) **καὶ τὴν θάλασσαν** (coord. dir. obj. of verbless cl.), **ὅτι** (causal) **κατέβη** (3rd sg. aor. act. ind. of καταβαίνω) **ὁ διάβολος** (διάβολος, -ον, "slanderer, adversary, devil," subj. nom.) **πρὸς ὑμᾶς** (loc.) **ἔχων** (nom. sg. masc. of pres. act. ptc. of ἔχω, manner) **θυμὸν** (θυμός, -οῦ, ὁ, "anger," dir. obj.) **μέγαν** (attrib.), **εἰδὼς** (nom. sg. masc. of pf. act. ptc. of οἶδα, cause or manner) **ὅτι** (content) **ὀλίγον** (ὀλίγος, -η, -ον, "small, short, little," attrib.) **καιρὸν** (dir. obj.) **ἔχει** (3rd sg. pres. act. ind. of ἔχω).

The saints and God are described as dwelling in the heavenly tabernacle in 7:15; 13:6; 21:3. The devil's "short time" is described elsewhere in Revelation as a three-and-a-half-year period (see on 11:2 and 12:6). The dragon's wrath is directed at the woman (12:13, 17) but physically carried out through a war against her vulnerable seed (12:17).

Use of the OT: The heavens are called to rejoice in Deut 32:43 (εὐφράνθητε, οὐρανοί); 1 Chr 16:31 (εὐφρανθήτω ὁ οὐρανός); Ps 95:11 LXX (96:11 EVV) (εὐφραινέσθωσαν οἱ οὐρανοί); Isa 44:23 (εὐφράνθητε, οὐρανοί); 45:8 (εὐφρανθήτω ὁ οὐρανὸς ἄνωθεν); 49:13 (εὐφραίνεσθε, οὐρανοί). The call for heaven to rejoice is consistently linked with expectation of or celebration for God's judgments or actions on behalf of his people.

---

c. Divine Protection for the Woman (12:13–17)

The narrative of the woman's flight and protection in the wilderness signifies God's divine protection of his people (12:13–16). It communicates the same idea of divine protection as the sealing of the 144,000 (7:3), the measuring of the temple (11:1), and the miraculous defensive ministry of the two witnesses (11:5).

12:13 Καὶ ὅτε (temp. subord. conj., "when") **εἶδεν** (3rd sg. aor. act. ind. of ὁράω) **ὁ** (anaphoric to 12:3) **δράκων** (δράκων, -οντος, ὁ, "dragon, serpent," subj. nom.) **ὅτι** (content) **ἐβλήθη** (3rd sg. aor. pass. ind. of βάλλω) **εἰς τὴν γῆν** (loc.), **ἐδίωξεν** (3rd sg. aor. act. ind. of διώκω) **τὴν** (anaphoric to 12:1) **γυναῖκα** (dir. obj., ant. of ἥτις) **ἥτις** (subj. nom.) **ἔτεκεν** (3rd sg. aor. act. ind. of τίκτω, "give birth") **τὸν** (anaphoric to 12:5) **ἄρσενα** (ἄρσην, -εν, "male," subst., dir. obj.).
12:14 καὶ ἐδόθησαν (3rd pl. aor. pass. ind. of δίδωμι) **τῇ** (anaphoric to 12:1) **γυναικὶ** (indir. obj.) **αἱ δύο** ("two," attrib.) **πτέρυγες** (πτέρυξ, -υγος, ἡ, "wing," subj. nom.) **τοῦ** (generic, "an" [Wallace 228]) **ἀετοῦ** (ἀετός, -οῦ, ὁ, "eagle," poss.) **τοῦ μεγάλου** (attrib.), **ἵνα** (purpose) **πέτηται** (3rd sg. pres. mid. subjunc. of πέτομαι, "fly") **εἰς τὴν ἔρημον** (ἔρημος, -ον, "wilderness, desert," loc.) **εἰς τὸν τόπον** (loc.) **αὐτῆς** (poss.), **ὅπου** (loc. adv. functions as rel. pron., "where") **τρέφεται** (3rd sg. pres. pass. ind. of τρέφω, "nourish") **ἐκεῖ** (loc. adv., "there," redundant for emph.) **καιρὸν** (temp.) **καὶ καιροὺς καὶ ἥμισυ** (ἥμισυς, -εια, -υ, "half," attrib.) **καιροῦ** (part. gen.) **ἀπὸ προσώπου** (separation) **τοῦ ὄφεως** (ὄφις, -εως, ὁ, "serpent," poss.).

The woman is protected during the same period that the temple is being trampled (11:2), the two witnesses are fulfilling their prophetic ministry (11:3), and the beast is overcoming God's people (13:5–7). Drawing from Daniel (see below), the "time" is one year, the "times" are two years, and the "half a time" is half a year.

Use of the OT: Flight to the desert is associated with protection and nourishment in Elijah's life (1 Kgs 17:1–7), and the wilderness also functions this way to some degree for Hagar, Moses, and David. In light of Exodus parallels in the trumpet and bowl judgments, it would be possible to see the wilderness as a place of deliverance and protection from Egypt; this connection is strengthened by the allusion to Exod 19:4 in which God declares that he lifted Israel up on the wings of eagles (ἀνέλαβον ὑμᾶς ὡσεὶ ἐπὶ πτερύγων ἀετῶν) and brought them to himself (καὶ προσηγαγόμην ὑμᾶς πρὸς ἐμαυτόν).

Daniel 7:25 describes how God's people will be given into the hands of the final horn/king of the fourth beast (ἕως καιροῦ καὶ καιρῶν καὶ ἕως ἡμίσους καιροῦ). Daniel 12:7 similarly uses this expression to indicate the period of time that would conclude the shattering of the power of the holy people (εἰς καιρὸν καὶ καιροὺς καὶ ἥμισυ καιροῦ ἡ συντέλεια χειρῶν ἀφέσεως λαοῦ ἁγίου, καὶ συντελεσθήσεται πάντα ταῦτα).

12:15 καὶ ἔβαλεν (3rd sg. aor. act. ind. of βάλλω) **ὁ ὄφις** (ὄφις, -εως, ὁ, "serpent," subj. nom.) **ἐκ τοῦ στόματος** (source) **αὐτοῦ** (poss.) **ὀπίσω** (prep. with gen. obj., "behind, after") **τῆς** (anaphoric to 12:1) **γυναικὸς** (loc. with ὀπίσω) **ὕδωρ** (dir. obj. of ἔβαλεν) **ὡς** (comp.) **ποταμόν** (ποταμός, -οῦ, ὁ, "river"), **ἵνα** (purpose) **αὐτὴν** (dir. obj., fronted for emph.) **ποταμοφόρητον** (ποταμοφόρητος, -ον, "swept away by a river," pred. double acc., "he might make her *to be* swept away") **ποιήσῃ** (3rd sg. aor. act. subjunc. of ποιέω).

12:16 καὶ ἐβοήθησεν (3rd sg. aor. act. ind. of βοηθέω, "help, aid") **ἡ γῆ** (subj. nom.) **τῇ γυναικὶ** (dat. dir. obj.) **καὶ ἤνοιξεν** (3rd sg. aor. act. ind. of ἀνοίγω) **ἡ γῆ** (subj. nom.) **τὸ στόμα** (dir. obj.) **αὐτῆς** (poss.) **καὶ κατέπιεν** (3rd sg. aor. act. ind. of καταπίνω, "swallow") **τὸν ποταμὸν** (ποταμός, -οῦ, ὁ, "river," dir. obj., ant. of ὅν) **ὃν** (dir. obj.) **ἔβαλεν** (3rd sg. aor. act. ind. of βάλλω) **ὁ** (anaphoric to 12:3) **δράκων** (δράκων, -οντος, ὁ, "dragon, serpent," subj. nom.) **ἐκ τοῦ στόματος** (source) **αὐτοῦ** (poss.).

12:17 καὶ ὠργίσθη (3rd sg. aor. pass. ind. of ὀργίζω, "be angry") **ὁ** (anaphoric to 12:3) **δράκων** (δράκων, -οντος, ὁ, "dragon, serpent," subj. nom.) **ἐπὶ τῇ γυναικὶ** (causal) **καὶ ἀπῆλθεν** (3rd sg. aor. act. ind. of ἀπέρχομαι) **ποιῆσαι** (aor. act. inf. of ποιέω, purpose) **πόλεμον** (πόλεμος, -ου, ὁ, "battle," dir. obj.) **μετὰ τῶν λοιπῶν** (λοιπός, -ή, -όν, "left, remaining," subst., association with the contextual nuance of disadvantage, "against") **τοῦ σπέρματος** (σπέρμα, -ατος, τό, "seed, offspring," part. gen.) **αὐτῆς** (relationship) **τῶν τηρούντων** (gen. pl. masc. of pres. act. ptc. of τηρέω, attrib.) **τὰς ἐντολὰς** (dir. obj.) **τοῦ θεοῦ** (source) **καὶ ἐχόντων** (gen. pl. masc. of pres. act. ptc. of ἔχω, attrib.) **τὴν μαρτυρίαν** (dir. obj.) **Ἰησοῦ** (likely obj. gen., "testimony about Jesus," but possibly subj. gen., "Jesus's testimony"; possibly a description of the book of Revelation itself).

The rest of the woman's seed are generically described as Christians (both Jew and gentile): they keep God's commands (14:12; cf. τηρέω in 1:3; 2:26; 3:3, 8, 10; 16:15; 22:7, 22) and hold to the witness of Jesus (12:11; cf. μαρτυρία in 1:2, 9; 6:9; 11:7; 19:10; 20:4). The description of them as τῶν λοιπῶν links them back to the firstborn male child of 12:4–5 and τοῦ σπέρματος alludes to the seed of the woman who would be in conflict with the serpent in Gen 3:15. Paul likewise alludes to the seed of Gen 3:15 to refer singularly to Jesus (Gal 3:16) and corporately to God's people (Rom 16:20, note that the recipients of Romans included both Jewish and gentile Christians so Paul does not strictly apply Gen 3:15 to Jewish Christians).

Use of the OT: The other horn of the fourth beast in Dan 7:21 would make war with the holy ones (τὸ κέρας ἐκεῖνο πόλεμον συνιστάμενον πρὸς τοὺς ἁγίους καὶ τροπούμενον αὐτούς). With Rev 12:17–18 it becomes evident that the beast's activity in 11:7 and 13:7 is an extension of the dragon's war against God's people.

HOMILETICAL SUGGESTIONS

Several important points highlight how the combination of woman, seed, and ancient serpent connect this vision back to the protoeuangelion of Gen 3:15. Revelation 12:6 is crucial in showing that for John the symbolic three-and-a-half-year period begins with Jesus's ascension and enthronement. The middle section celebrating victory in heaven corresponds to this enthronement (12:7–12). The final section of the vision shows how God's people are divinely protected while remaining physically vulnerable to the dragon's attacks.

Understanding the Present Time (12:1–17)

1. Jesus has been enthroned (12:1–6).
2. The enemy has been decisively defeated (12:7–12).
3. God's people must expect opposition (12:13–17).

2. The Present and Future Conflict: Two Beasts (12:18–13:18)

a. The Beast out of the Sea (12:18–13:10)

12:18 καὶ ἐστάθη (3rd sg. aor. pass. ind. of ἵστημι, the pass. functions as mid., the subj. is the δράκων from 12:17, but 051 1006 1611 1841 2053 2329 *Byz* [P 046] read ἐστάθην to make John the 1st subj. in coord. with εἶδον in 13:1; the weight of 𝔓[47] א A C support ἐστάθη) **ἐπὶ τὴν ἄμμον** (ἄμμος, -ου, ἡ, "sand," loc.) **τῆς θαλάσσης** (descriptive gen.).
13:1 Καὶ εἶδον (1st sg. aor. act. ind. of ὁράω; introduces a new vision, scene, figure, or activity [Aune[a] 338]) **ἐκ τῆς θαλάσσης** (source) **θηρίον** (θηρίον, -ου, τό, "animal, beast," dir. obj.) **ἀναβαῖνον** (acc. sg. neut. of pres. act. ptc. of ἀναβαίνω, compl. in obj.-compl. double acc. construction), **ἔχον** (acc. sg. neut. of pres. act. ptc. of ἔχω, attrib.) **κέρατα** (κέρας, -ατος, τό, "horn," dir. obj.) **δέκα** ("ten," attrib.) **καὶ κεφαλὰς** (coord. dir. obj.) **ἑπτὰ** ("seven," attrib.) **καὶ ἐπὶ τῶν κεράτων** (loc.) **αὐτοῦ** (poss.) **δέκα** (attrib.) **διαδήματα** (διάδημα, -ατος, τό, "crown," dir. obj.) **καὶ ἐπὶ τὰς κεφαλὰς** (loc.) **αὐτοῦ** (poss.) **ὀνόμα[τα]** (dir. obj., both the external and internal evidence seems evenly divided between ὄνομα and ὀνόματα) **βλασφημίας** (βλασφημία, -ας, ἡ, "slander, blasphemy," attrib. gen.).

The description of the beast ascending from the abyss in 11:7 parallels this account of the beast ascending from the sea. The seven heads and ten horns identify this beast with the beast in Rev 17:3 and reveal a family resemblance with the dragon in 12:3. The ten horns are identified in 17:12 as ten kings. The description of blasphemous names on the beast's heads is physically illustrated by Roman imperial coins, which almost always had an image of the face of the emperor on the front surrounded by various titles and acclamations, some of which would have been perceived by Jews and Christians as blasphemous or offensive such as variations of *divvs* (Latin: "divine"). The reverse of imperial coins generally featured a deity to physically illustrate the close connection between the emperor and the gods. In Daniel, the four beasts represent kingdoms, and most interpreters argue that that the first hearers would have identified this beast with the Roman Empire. This original historical identification does not preclude the possibility that the beast is transtemporal (Beale 685–86) or that various historical instantiations of the beast typologically foreshadow the final fulfillment of Daniel's prophecy right before Christ's return (Fanning 371).

Use of the OT: Daniel 7:3 describes the ascent of four beasts from the sea (καὶ τέσσαρα θηρία ἀνέβαινον ἐκ τῆς θαλάσσης). The beast's ten horns match the description of the fourth beast in Dan 7:7 (εἶχε δὲ κέρατα δέκα) and are later identified in Dan 7:24 as ten kings (καὶ τὰ δέκα κέρατα τῆς βασιλείας, δέκα

> βασιλεῖς στήσονται). The fourth beast's eleventh horn/king speaks words against the Highest (7:25: καὶ ῥήματα εἰς τὸν ὕψιστον λαλήσει).

13:2 καὶ τὸ (anaphoric to 13:1) **θηρίον** (θηρίον, -ου, τό, "animal, beast," subj. nom., ant. of ὅ) **ὃ** (dir. obj.) **εἶδον** (1st sg. aor. act. ind. of ὁράω) **ἦν** (3rd sg. impf. act. ind. of εἰμί) **ὅμοιον** (ὅμοιος, -οία, -οιον, "like, similar," pred. adj.) **παρδάλει** (πάρδαλις, -εως, ἡ, "leopard," compl. of ὅμοιον) **καὶ οἱ πόδες** (subj. nom. of verbless cl.) **αὐτοῦ** (poss.) **ὡς** (comp.) **ἄρκου** (ἄρκος, -ου, ὁ, ἡ, "bear") **καὶ τὸ στόμα** (subj. nom. of verbless cl.) **αὐτοῦ** (poss.) **ὡς** (comp.) **στόμα λέοντος** (λέων, -οντος, ὁ, "lion," poss.). **καὶ ἔδωκεν** (3rd sg. aor. act. ind. of δίδωμι) **αὐτῷ** (indir. obj.) **ὁ δράκων** (δράκων, -οντος, ὁ, "dragon, serpent," subj. nom.) **τὴν δύναμιν** (dir. obj.) **αὐτοῦ** (poss.) **καὶ τὸν θρόνον** (dir. obj.) **αὐτοῦ** (poss.) **καὶ ἐξουσίαν** (dir. obj.) **μεγάλην** (attrib.).

> **Use of the OT**: Daniel 7:4–6 describe Daniel's four beasts. John's singular beast draws elements from each of the four Danielic beasts. Beale suggests that Revelation's amalgamation of Daniel's four beasts points to the temporal transcendency of the beast that would exist throughout history, just as Daniel's four beasts spanned several centuries, and the sea monster imagery was applied in the OT to various nations across the centuries (Beale 685–86).

13:3 καὶ μίαν (dir. obj. of verbless cl.; the acc. μίαν suggests an unwritten εἶδον [Moț 153]) **ἐκ τῶν κεφαλῶν** (part. gen.) **αὐτοῦ** (poss.) **ὡς** (comp.) **ἐσφαγμένην** (acc. sg. fem. of pf. pass. ptc. of σφάζω, "slaughter," subst. ptc.) **εἰς θάνατον** (extent), **καὶ ἡ πληγὴ** (πληγή, -ῆς, ἡ, "plague, wound," subj. nom.) **τοῦ θανάτου** (descriptive gen.) **αὐτοῦ** (poss.) **ἐθεραπεύθη** (3rd sg. aor. pass. ind. of θεραπεύω, "heal"). **καὶ ἐθαυμάσθη** (3rd sg. aor. pass. ind. of θαυμάζω, "be astonished," the pass. functions as mid.) **ὅλη** (attrib.) **ἡ γῆ** (subj. nom.) **ὀπίσω** (prep. which takes a gen. obj., "behind, after") **τοῦ θηρίου** (θηρίον, -ου, τό, "animal, beast," loc., lit. "behind the beast" with a figurative extension to indicate following the beast's leadership [L&N 36.35])

The parallel description of the lamb in 5:6 (ὡς ἐσφαγμένον) provides intentional contrast and suggests that the comp. ὡς is not hypothetical; the beast is presented as having been slain, not as *if* it had been slain (Math 171). The wound and recovery are highlighted through repetition in 13:12, 14 and is utilized to convince or deceive human beings to worship the dragon and beast instead of God and the lamb. This parallelism between the beast and the lamb is part of the larger theme of satanic imitation of divine reality (note how the second beast has two horns like a lamb in Rev 13:11). The first hearers would have likely thought of the devastating events of AD 69 during which many people thought the Roman Empire was at its end but which resulted in complete recovery under Vespasian's rule. This historical explanation is possible, but the detail that the beast was wounded and healed might also reflect the continued existence of evil even after Jesus's enthronement and the casting down of Satan from the divine throne room. Evil has been decisively defeated but continues with the appearance of life and power for a time. Revelation 17:8 similarly describes how the inhabitants of the earth will marvel to see the beast.

13:4 καὶ προσεκύνησαν (3rd pl. aor. act. ind. of προσκυνέω, the pl. vb. refers to the sg. subj. γῆ in 13:3 as a *constructio ad sensum* related to the "whole world") **τῷ δράκοντι** (δράκων, -οντος, ὁ, "dragon, serpent," dat. dir. obj.), **ὅτι** (causal) **ἔδωκεν** (3rd sg. aor. act. ind. of δίδωμι) **τὴν ἐξουσίαν** (dir. obj.) **τῷ θηρίῳ** (θηρίον, -ου, τό, "animal, beast," indir. obj.), **καὶ προσεκύνησαν** (3rd pl. aor. act. ind. of προσκυνέω, coord. vb.) **τῷ θηρίῳ** (dat. dir. obj.) **λέγοντες** (nom. pl. masc. of pres. act. ptc. of λέγω, manner), **Τίς** (interr. pron., subj. nom. of verbless cl.) **ὅμοιος** (ὅμοιος, -οία, -οιον, "like, similar," pred. adj.) **τῷ θηρίῳ** (compl. of ὅμοιος) **καὶ τίς** (interr. pron., subj. nom.) **δύναται** (3rd sg. pres. mid. ind. of δύναμαι) **πολεμῆσαι** (aor. act. inf. of πολεμέω, "fight, make war," compl. inf.) **μετ' αὐτοῦ** (association with the contextual nuance of disadvantage, "against");

The worship of the dragon and beast by the whole world stands in explicit contrast with the universal worship ascribed to God and the lamb throughout Revelation (particularly in chapters 4 and 5). God's rule is rejected on earth as human beings wrongly direct their worship. Worship in Revelation reflects and expresses allegiance and faith. The question posed at the end of 13:4 is directly answered in 17:13–14 and 19:19–20 when the lamb defeats the beast and his allied kings.

Use of the OT: The question "Who is like?" is regularly used in contexts of worship of the true God: Exod 15:11 (τίς ὅμοιός σοι ἐν θεοῖς, κύριε; τίς ὅμοιός σοι . . . ;); Ps 88:7 LXX (89:6 EVV) (τίς ὁμοιωθήσεται τῷ κυρίῳ ἐν υἱοῖς θεοῦ;); Isa 46:5 (τίνι με ὡμοιώσατε;).

13:5 Καὶ ἐδόθη (3rd sg. aor. pass. ind. of δίδωμι, pass. without a stated agent are likely best understood as divine passives, see 6:2) **αὐτῷ** (indir. obj.) **στόμα** (subj. nom.) **λαλοῦν** (nom. sg. neut. of pres. act. ptc. of λαλέω, attrib.) **μεγάλα** (subst. adj., dir. obj.) **καὶ βλασφημίας** (βλασφημία, -ας, ἡ, "slander, blasphemy," dir. obj.) **καὶ ἐδόθη** (3rd sg. aor. pass. ind. of δίδωμι) **αὐτῷ** (indir. obj.) **ἐξουσία** (subj. nom.) **ποιῆσαι** (aor. act. inf. of ποιέω, epex., note the lack of dir. obj.; ποιέω can function with the acc. of time to indicate a general action or activity, "to be active in some way" [BDAG 841c]) **μῆνας** (μήν, -μηνός, ὁ, "month," temp. acc.) **τεσσεράκοντα** ("forty," attrib.) **[καὶ] δύο** ("two").

The reference to forty-two months matches and parallels the time for the trampling of the holy city in 11:2, the activity of the two witnesses (11:3), and the protection of the woman in the wilderness (12:6, 14).

Patristic interpreters regularly make various connections between the beast of Revelation 13, the man of lawlessness of 2 Thess 2:3–12, the antichrist(s) of 1 and 2 John (1 John 2:18, 22; 4:18; 2 John 7), and the fourth beast or little horn of Dan

7:8 (Barn. 4:1–5; Did. 16:3–4; Irenaeus, *Against Heresies* 5.28.2; Justin, *Dialogue with Trypho* 32; 110; Hippolytus, *De antichristo* 49 [Fanning 372]), but this is somewhat overstated and there is no consistent combination of these passages, although Hippolytus comes closest to such an interpretive synthesis. Barnabas 4:1–5 exhorts hearers to resist the work of lawlessness but grounds this primarily in 1 Enoch and Dan 7:24. Didache 16:3–4 primarily draws from the Olivet Discourse and 2 Thessalonians 2 to predict an increase of false prophets and deceivers, lawlessness, hatred, persecution, and betrayal before the appearance of the one who deceives the world by presenting himself as the Son of God and working signs and wonders. Irenaeus, *Against Heresies* 5.28.2, combines the eschatological antagonist from Revelation 13 with 2 Thessalonians 2. Justin, *Dialogue with Trypho* 32 discusses Daniel 7 while chapter 110 mainly seems to reflect on 2 Thessalonians 2. John recognizes the widespread belief in a future antichrist figure (1 John 2:18) but focuses more on many antichrists who are already active in the present time (1 John 2:22; 2 John 7) and suggests that the spirit of the antichrist that they had heard was coming was now already in the world (1 John 4:3). Paul anticipates a future individual figure and specific future rebellion although the mystery of lawlessness was already at work in the world (2 Thess 2:7). Preterist and futurist interpreters can perhaps find common ground in recognizing the beast of Revelation 13, like the antichrist(s) in 1–2 John, as already being present in the world and throughout history, while still coming to a focused point in the final period of time right before Jesus's return.

Use of the OT: The little horn of the Danielic fourth beast has a mouth speaking great things (7:8: στόμα λαλοῦν μεγάλα; cf. Dan. 7:20, 25). The king of Dan 11:36 will exalt himself above every god and speak extraordinary things against the God of gods (ὑψωθήσεται ἐπὶ πάντα θεὸν καὶ ἐπὶ τὸν θεὸν τῶν θεῶν ἔξαλλα λαλήσει).

13:6 καὶ ἤνοιξεν (3rd sg. aor. act. ind. of ἀνοίγω) **τὸ στόμα** (dir. obj.) **αὐτοῦ** (poss.) **εἰς βλασφημίας** (βλασφημία, -ας, ἡ, "slander, blasphemy," purpose) **πρὸς τὸν θεὸν** (disadvantage, "against") **βλασφημῆσαι** (aor. act. inf. of βλασφημέω, "revile, blaspheme," epex.) **τὸ ὄνομα** (dir. obj.) **αὐτοῦ** (poss.) **καὶ τὴν σκηνὴν** (σκηνή, -ῆς, ἡ, "tent," dir. obj.) **αὐτοῦ** (poss.), **τοὺς** (the art. modifies the following ptc.) **ἐν τῷ οὐρανῷ** (loc.) **σκηνοῦντας** (acc. pl. masc. of pres. act. ptc. of σκηνόω, "live in a tent, dwell," subst. ptc. in appos. to σκηνήν, 𝔓[47] lacks σκηνοῦντας while א P 046* 051 205 209 2053 add καί before τούς to smooth out the syntax [Metzger 674]).
13:7 καὶ ἐδόθη (3rd sg. aor. pass. ind. of δίδωμι) **αὐτῷ** (indir. obj.) **ποιῆσαι** (aor. act. inf. of ποιέω, subst. inf., subj. of ἐδόθη, "to make war was given") **πόλεμον** (πόλεμος, ου, ὁ, "battle," dir. obj.) **μετὰ τῶν ἁγίων** (association with the contextual nuance of disadvantage, "against") **καὶ νικῆσαι** (aor. act. inf. of νικάω, "overcome, conquer," subst. inf., compound subj. of ἐδόθη) **αὐτούς** (dir. obj.), **καὶ ἐδόθη** (3rd sg. aor. pass. ind. of δίδωμι)

αὐτῷ (indir. obj.) **ἐξουσία** (subj. nom.) **ἐπὶ πᾶσαν** (attrib.) **φυλὴν** (φυλή, -ῆς, ἡ, "tribe, nation," this and the following acc. nouns are subord.) **καὶ λαὸν καὶ γλῶσσαν** (γλῶσσα, -ης, ἡ, "tongue, language") **καὶ ἔθνος**.

Several mss lack the entire phrase καὶ ἐδόθη αὐτῷ ποιῆσαι πόλεμον μετὰ τῶν ἁγίων καὶ νικῆσαι αὐτούς (𝔓[47] A C P and about fifty minuscules). This is likely due to homoeoarcton with the repetition of καὶ ἐδόθη (Metzger 674). The war made against God's people parallels the description in 11:7 and 12:17. On every tribe, people, tongue, and nation see 5:9.

Use of the OT: Daniel 7:7 describes the fourth beast as devouring and pounding (ἐσθίον καὶ κοπανίζον). Daniel 7:8 describes the little horn as making war with the saints (ἐποίει πόλεμον πρὸς τοὺς ἁγίους). Daniel 7:21 describes the other horn of the fourth beast as making war with the saints and putting them to flight (τὸ κέρας ἐκεῖνο πόλεμον συνιστάμενον πρὸς τοὺς ἁγίους καὶ τροπούμενον αὐτούς).

13:8 καὶ προσκυνήσουσιν (3rd pl. fut. act. ind. of προσκυνέω, note the shift from aor. to fut.) **αὐτὸν** (dir. obj., likely referring to the neut. θηρίον with a masc. pron. as a *constructio ad sensum*) **πάντες** (attrib.) **οἱ κατοικοῦντες** (nom. pl. masc. of pres. act. ptc. of κατοικέω, "dwell," subst., subj. nom., ant. of the sg. οὗ) **ἐπὶ τῆς γῆς** (loc.), **οὗ** (poss. with ὄνομα) **οὐ γέγραπται** (3rd sg. pf. pass. ind. of γράφω) **τὸ ὄνομα** (subj. nom.) **αὐτοῦ** (poss., redundant with οὗ) **ἐν τῷ βιβλίῳ** (βιβλίον, -ου, τό, "scroll," loc.) **τῆς ζωῆς** (descriptive gen.) **τοῦ ἀρνίου** (ἀρνίον, -ου, τό, "lamb," poss.) **τοῦ ἐσφαγμένου** (gen. sg. neut. of pf. pass. ptc. of σφάζω, "slaughter," attrib., recalling 5:6) **ἀπὸ καταβολῆς** (καταβολή, -ῆς, ἡ, "foundation," temp., the prep. phrase could modify ἐσφαγμένου as the nearest ant. or γέγραπται; the parallel expression in 17:8 strongly points to γέγραπται as the ant.; the names were written from the foundation of the world in the lamb's book of life) **κόσμου** (obj. gen.).

The book of life appears elsewhere in Rev 3:5; 17:8; 20:12, 15; 21:27. The slain lamb recalls 5:6, 12. John 1:29 describes Jesus as ὁ ἀμνὸς τοῦ θεοῦ ὁ αἴρων τὴν ἁμαρτίαν τοῦ κόσμου. On John's consistent negative view of "the ones dwelling on the earth," see 3:10.

Use of the OT: On the book of life, see 3:5. The reference to the slain lamb alludes to the πρόβατον ἐπὶ σφαγήν in Isa 53:7.

13:9 Εἴ (introduces 1st class cond. cl.) **τις** (subj. nom.) **ἔχει** (3rd sg. pres. act. ind. of ἔχω, gnomic) **οὖς** (οὖς, ὠτός, τό, "ear," dir. obj.) **ἀκουσάτω** (3rd sg. aor. act. impv. of ἀκούω, apod., the impv. mood sets 13:9–10 apart from the surrounding context as a motivational or hortatory parenthetical aside).

The call to hear links these visions of the beast back to the proclamations to the seven churches (Rev 2–3), which each end with a similar call. This suggests that the visions of the beast along with the seven proclamations were meant to be applied to the first hearers and, by extension, all Christian hearers throughout history.

13:10 εἴ (introduces 1st class cond. cl.) **τις** (subj. nom. of verbless cl.) **εἰς αἰχμαλωσίαν** (αἰχμαλωσία, -ας, ἡ, "captivity," loc. or goal [Math 175]), **εἰς αἰχμαλωσίαν** (loc.) **ὑπάγει** (3rd sg. pres. act. ind. of ὑπάγω, apod., gnomic pres.). **εἴ** (introduces 1st class cond. cl.) **τις** (subj. nom. of verbless cl.) **ἐν μαχαίρῃ** (μάχαιρα, -ης, ἡ, "sword," means) **ἀποκτανθῆναι** (aor. pass. inf. of ἀποκτείνω, pred. of implied copulative vb.) **αὐτὸν** (acc. subj. of inf.) **ἐν μαχαίρῃ** (means) **ἀποκτανθῆναι** (aor. pass. inf. of ἀποκτείνω, compl. inf. with implicit vb. as the apod.). **Ὧδέ** (adv. often indicating spatial proximity, "here," used to suggest logical proximity or relevance, "in this"; idiomatically, "this calls for endurance" or "here is [an opportunity for] endurance" [BDAG 1101d], cf. 14:12) **ἐστιν** (3rd sg. pres. act. ind. of εἰμί) **ἡ ὑπομονὴ** (ὑπομονή, -ῆς, ἡ, "endurance," pred. nom.) **καὶ ἡ πίστις** (coord. pred. nom.) **τῶν ἁγίων** (subj. gen.).

The cryptic reading εἰς αιχμαλωσίαν, εἰς αἰχμαλωσίαν ὑπάγει only occurs in A vg[ww, st] but likely best explains the other variants that generally seek to clarify or improve it (Metzger 674–75). In the second half of the verse, many variants occur with ἀποκτανθῆναι, αὐτόν (A); these variants often read the act. ἀποκτενεῖ instead of the pass. to introduce the idea of retributive justice in line with Matt 26:52. With the active ἀποκτενεῖ it is the one who kills with the sword who will be killed.

Use of the OT: When Jeremiah announces judgment against God's people, he proclaims that Ὅσοι εἰς θάνατον, εἰς θάνατον, καὶ ὅσοι εἰς μάχαιραν, εἰς μάχαιραν, καὶ ὅσοι εἰς λιμόν, εἰς λιμόν, καὶ ὅσοι εἰς αἰχμαλωσίαν, εἰς αἰχμαλωσίαν (Jer 15:2). Regarding Egypt, he later declare οὓς εἰς θάνατον, εἰς θάνατον, καὶ οὓς εἰς ἀποικισμόν, εἰς ἀποικισμόν, καὶ οὕς εἰς ῥομφαίαν, εἰς ῥομφαίαν (Jer 50:11 LXX [43:11 EVV]).

FOR FURTHER STUDY

41. The Beast and Emperor Worship (13:1–18)

Frey, J. "The Relevance of the Roman Imperial Cult for the Book of Revelation: Exegetical and Hermeneutical Reflections on the Relation between the Seven Letters and the Visionary Main Part of the Book." Pages 231–55 in *The New Testament and Early Christian Literature in Greco-Roman Context: Studies in Honor of David E. Aune*. Edited by John Fotopoulos. NovTSup 122. Leiden: Brill, 2006.

*Friesen, S. J. *Imperial Cults and the Apocalypse of John: Reading Revelation in the Ruins*. Oxford: Oxford University Press, 2001.

———. "Myth and Symbolic Resistance in Revelation 13." *JBL* 123 (2004): 281–313.

Harland, P. A. "Honouring the Emperor or Assailing the Beast: Participation in Civic Life among Associations (Jewish, Christian and Other) in Asia Minor and the Apocalypse of John." *JSNT* 22 (2000): 99–121.

Naylor, M. P. *Complexity and Creativity: John's Presentation of Jesus in the Book of Revelation*. Gorgias Biblical Studies 69. Piscataway, NJ: Gorgias, 2018.

42. The Social Setting of Revelation

DeSilva, D. A. "The Revelation to John: A Case Study in Apocalyptic Propaganda and the Maintenance of Sectarian Identity." *Sociological Analysis* 53 (1992): 375–95.

———. "The Social Setting of the Apocalypse of John: Conflicts within, Fears without." *WTJ* 54 (1992): 273–302.

*Friesen, S. "Satan's Throne, Imperial Cults and the Social Settings of Revelation." *JSNT* 27 (2005): 351–73.

Rowland, C. "The Apocalypse: Sensitivity and Outsiders." Pages 401–17 in *Sensitivity towards Outsiders: Exploring the Dynamic Relationship between Mission and Ethics in the New Testament and Early Christianity*. Edited by J. Kok, T. Nicklas, D. T. Roth, and C. M. Hays. WUNT 364. Tübingen: Mohr Siebeck, 2014.

Slater, T. B. "On the Social Setting of the Revelation." *NTS* 44 (1998): 232–56.

b. The Beast out of the Land (13:11–18)

Mathewson argues that the concentration of pres. tense verbal forms in 13:11–18, in contrast to the preponderance of aor. tenses in 13:1–8, sets this section apart as more prominent, perhaps highlighting it as particularly relevant to the original hearers (Math 178).

13:11 Καὶ εἶδον (1st sg. aor. act. ind. of ὁράω; *καὶ εἶδον* introduces a new vision, scene, figure, or activity [Aune[a] 338]) **ἄλλο** (attrib.) **θηρίον** (θηρίον, -ου, τό, "animal, beast," dir. obj.) **ἀναβαῖνον** (acc. sg. neut. of pres. act. ptc. of ἀναβαίνω, compl. in obj.-compl. double acc. construction) **ἐκ τῆς γῆς** (source), **καὶ εἶχεν** (3rd sg. impf. act. ind. of ἔχω, impf. provides offline background information) **κέρατα** (κέρας, -ατος, τό, "horn," dir. obj.) **δύο** ("two," attrib.) **ὅμοια** (ὅμοιος, -οία, -οιον, "like, similar," comp. adj.) **ἀρνίῳ** (ἀρνίον, -ου, τό, "lamb," compl. of ὅμοια) **καὶ ἐλάλει** (3rd sg. impf. act. ind. of λαλέω) **ὡς** (manner) **δράκων** (δράκων, -οντος, ὁ, "dragon, serpent").

The second beast is later described as the false prophet (16:13; 19:20; 20:10). The physical similarity to a lamb continues the theme of demonic counterfeit and deception (see 13:3).

13:12 καὶ τὴν ἐξουσίαν (dir. obj. fronted for emph.) **τοῦ πρώτου** ("first," attrib.) **θηρίου** (θηρίον, -ου, τό, "animal, beast," subj. gen.) **πᾶσαν** (attrib. modifying ἐξουσίαν) **ποιεῖ** (3rd sg. pres. act. ind. of ποιέω, narrative pres.) **ἐνώπιον αὐτοῦ** (although ἐνώπιον is often loc., it can be used to indicate the authority behind or beneficiary of an action [BDAG 342d]), **καὶ ποιεῖ** (3rd sg. pres. act. ind. of ποιέω, narrative pres.) **τὴν γῆν** (dir. obj.) **καὶ τοὺς ἐν αὐτῇ** (loc.) **κατοικοῦντας** (acc. pl. masc. of pres. act. ptc. of κατοικέω, "dwell," subst., coord. dir. obj.) **ἵνα** (Mathewson prob. rightly argues that this introduces a content cl. as the compl. of ποιεῖ in a causal construction: "he causes the earth to worship" [Math 179]; this occurs also in 3:9; 13:16–17; the idiomatic combination of ποιέω + ἵνα could also express causation, "make [to] cause [someone] to" or "bring it about that" [BDAG 840b–c]) **προσκυνήσουσιν** (3rd pl. fut. act. ind. προσκυνέω, fut. for subjunc.) **τὸ θηρίον** (θηρίον, ου, τό, "animal, beast," dir. obj., ant. of οὗ) **τὸ πρῶτον** (attrib.), **οὗ** (poss. with πληγὴ) **ἐθεραπεύθη** (3rd sg. aor. pass. ind. of θεραπεύω, "heal") **ἡ πληγὴ** (πληγή, -ῆς, ἡ, "wound," subj. nom.) **τοῦ θανάτου** (descriptive gen.) **αὐτοῦ** (poss., redundant with the poss. οὗ).

On John's consistent negative view of "the ones dwelling on the earth" see 3:10.

13:13 καὶ ποιεῖ (3rd sg. pres. act. ind. of ποιέω, narrative pres.) **σημεῖα** (dir. obj.) **μεγάλα** (attrib.), **ἵνα** (epex.) **καὶ** (adv., "also, even") **πῦρ** (acc. subj. of inf.) **ποιῇ** (3rd sg. pres. act. subjunc. of ποιέω) **ἐκ τοῦ οὐρανοῦ** (source) **καταβαίνειν** (pres. act. inf. of καταβαίνω, compl. inf.) **εἰς τὴν γῆν** (loc.) **ἐνώπιον τῶν ἀνθρώπων** (loc.),

Jesus prophesies in Matt 24:24 that false christs and prophets would do great signs and wonders to deceive (δώσουσιν σημεῖα μεγάλα καὶ τέρατα ὥστε πλανῆσαι). Paul teaches in 2 Thess 2:9 that the coming of the lawless one would happen by the activity of Satan with power, false signs, and wonders (οὗ ἐστιν ἡ παρουσία κατ' ἐνέργειαν τοῦ Σατανᾶ ἐν πάσῃ δυνάμει καὶ σημείοις καὶ τέρασιν ψεύδους). The falseness of these signs does not require the wonders to be tricks but could rather refer to real demonically empowered miracles which are false in that they are not from God. Luke describes several instances of magicians using magic to deceive people (Acts 8:9; 13:6). The demonic spirits in 16:14 perform signs (ποιοῦντα σημεῖα) to assemble the kings of the earth to support the dragon, beast, and false prophet.

The authentic function of fire from heaven as a demonstration of true divine approval, power, and protection (see below regarding Elijah and Rev 11:5) strengthens the theme of satanic counterfeit imitation.

Use of the OT: The contest between Elijah and the prophets of Baal centered on the ability to call down fire from heaven (1 Kgs 18:20–40). Elijah later calls down fire to destroy soldiers sent by Ahaziah (2 Kgs 1:10, 12). James and John likely had Elijah's miracle in mind when they expressed the desire to destroy a Samaritan village with fire in Luke 9:54. The magicians of Egypt also produced a parallel miracle by turning staffs to snakes (Exod 7:12).

13:14 καὶ πλανᾷ (3rd sg. pres. act. ind. of πλανάω, "deceive" narrative pres.) **τοὺς κατοικοῦντας** (acc. pl. masc. of pres. act. ptc. of κατοικέω, "dwell," subst., dir. obj.) **ἐπὶ τῆς γῆς** (loc.) **διὰ τὰ σημεῖα** (causal, ant. of ἅ) **ἃ** (subj. nom.) **ἐδόθη** (3rd sg. aor. pass. ind. δίδωμι, sg. vb. with neut. pl. subj.) **αὐτῷ** (indir. obj.) **ποιῆσαι** (aor. act. inf. ποιέω, purpose) **ἐνώπιον τοῦ θηρίου** (θηρίον, -ου, τό, "animal, beast," loc.), **λέγων** (nom. sg. masc. of pres. act. ptc. of λέγω, attendant circumstance, this is another use of the masc. with the neut. θηρίον as a *constructio ad sensum*) **τοῖς κατοικοῦσιν** (dat. pl. masc.

of pres. act. ptc. of κατοικέω, subst., indir. obj.) **ἐπὶ τῆς γῆς** (loc.) **ποιῆσαι** (aor. act. inf. of ποιέω, ind. speech) **εἰκόνα** (εἰκών, -όνος, ἡ, "image," dir. obj.) **τῷ θηρίῳ** (a gen. is expected here as in 13:15 but the dat. would indicate advantage, "for," ant. of ὅς), **ὃς** (subj. nom., the masc. rel. pron. with a neut. ant. points to the masc. gender of the beast) **ἔχει** (3rd sg. pres. act. ind. ἔχω) **τὴν πληγὴν** (πληγή, -ῆς, ἡ, "plague, wound," dir. obj.) **τῆς μαχαίρης** (μάχαιρα, -ης, ἡ, "sword," source or cause) **καὶ ἔζησεν** (3rd sg. aor. act. ind. of ζάω, prob. ingressive).

On John's consistent negative view of "the ones dwelling on the earth" see 3:10. The original hearers would have likely understood the second beast to represent those who promoted the ruler cult within the cities of Asia Minor.

Use of the OT: Deuteronomy 13:2–4 warns of prophets using fulfilled signs or wonders to entice the people to worship other gods and describes such a scenario as a test from God.

13:15 καὶ ἐδόθη (3rd sg. aor. pass. ind. δίδωμι) **αὐτῷ** (indir. obj.) **δοῦναι** (aor. act. inf. δίδωμι, subst., subj., "to give was given to him") **πνεῦμα** (dir. obj.) **τῇ** (anaphoric to 13:14) **εἰκόνι** (εἰκών, -όνος, ἡ, "image," indir. obj.) **τοῦ θηρίου** (θηρίον, -ου, τό, "animal, beast," the use of the gen. following εἰκών does not easily fit in a category and could vaguely be labeled descriptive for lack of a clearer category or perhaps as a kind of obj. gen.; Mathewson notes that it "indicates the form or likeness that the image represents or reflects" [Math 181]), **ἵνα** (purpose) **καὶ** (adv., "even, also") **λαλήσῃ** (3rd sg. aor. act. subjunc. of λαλέω) **ἡ** (anaphoric to 13:14) **εἰκὼν** (εἰκών, -όνος, ἡ, "image," subj. nom.) **τοῦ θηρίου** (obj. gen.) **καὶ ποιήσῃ** (3rd sg. aor. act. subjunc. of ποιέω) **[ἵνα]** (introduces content cl. as compl. to causative ποιήσῃ [Math 181], evidence for the presence or absence of ἵνα is evenly balanced [Metzger 675–76]) **ὅσοι** (subj. nom. of προσκυνήσωσιν, the comp. cl. introduced by ὅσοι functions as the subj. of ἀποκτανθῶσιν) **ἐὰν** (introduces indefiniteness or generality to the subj. [BDAG 729b]) **μὴ προσκυνήσωσιν** (3rd pl. aor. act. subjunc. προσκυνέω) **τῇ εἰκόνι** (dat. dir. obj.) **τοῦ θηρίου** (obj. gen.) **ἀποκτανθῶσιν** (3rd pl. aor. pass. subjunc. of ἀποκτείνω).

There is no indication here that the miracle is faked or a hoax; John's recounting of the vision suggests sorcery and demonically empowered miracles. Enforced worship of the image of the emperor is historically illustrated in a letter from Pliny the Younger to Emperor Trajan regarding the persecution of Christians at the beginning of the second century in Pontus and Bithynia whereby Christians could avoid persecution and death by reviling the name of Christ, repeating an invocation of the gods, and offering wine and incense to the statue of the emperor (Pliny, *Letters*, 10.96–97). Revelation here symbolically and prophetically predicts events in the near future of the communities addressed; this does not preclude the possibility it may be referring to events in the distant future, but it does not require it.

Use of the OT: Daniel 3:6 describes how Nebuchadnezzar declared that anyone who would not worship his image would be killed (καὶ πᾶς, ὃς ἂν μὴ πεσὼν προσκυνήσῃ, ἐμβαλοῦσιν αὐτὸν εἰς τὴν κάμινον τοῦ πυρὸς τὴν καιομένην).

13:16 καὶ ποιεῖ (3rd sg. pres. act. ind. of ποιέω, narrative pres.) **πάντας** (dir. obj.; each of the following three pairs of acc. subst. adjs. and nouns function in appos. to πάντας to indicate that the "all" is inclusive of the furthest extents of class, social, and economic status), **τοὺς μικροὺς** (subst.) **καὶ τοὺς μεγάλους** (subst.), **καὶ τοὺς πλουσίους** (πλούσιος, -ία, -ιον, "wealthy," subst.) **καὶ τοὺς πτωχούς** (πτωχός, -ή, -όν, "poor," subst.) **καὶ τοὺς ἐλευθέρους** (ἐλεύθερος, -έρα, -ον, "free," subst.) **καὶ τοὺς δούλους, ἵνα** (introduces a content cl. as compl. to causative ποιεῖ [Math 182]; the idiomatic combination of ποιέω + ἵνα could express causation, "make [to] cause [someone] to" of "bring it about that" [BDAG 840b–c]) **δῶσιν** (3rd pl. aor. act. subjunc. of δίδωμι, prob. impers. pl.) **αὐτοῖς** (indir. obj.) **χάραγμα** (χάραγμα, -ατος, τό, "mark," dir. obj.) **ἐπὶ τῆς χειρὸς** (loc., the distributive sg. is used with a pl. pron.) **αὐτῶν** (poss.) **τῆς δεξιᾶς** (attrib.) **ἢ** (disjunctive conj., "or") **ἐπὶ τὸ μέτωπον** (μέτωπον, -ου, τό, "forehead," loc., the distributive sg. is used with a pl. pron.) **αὐτῶν** (poss.).

The mark of the beast occurs in Rev 14:9, 11; 16:2; 19:20; 20:4 and is always associated with worship of the beast. In the visions of Revelation, the beast's mark is another instance of counterfeit imitation. It parallels God's divine seal (7:2; 9:4), which is the divine name (14:1; 22:4). The point seems to be that all of humanity will be marked or sealed to indicate ownership and allegiance expressed through worship.

13:17 καὶ (missing in א* C and some minuscules) **ἵνα** (coord. with ἵνα cl. in 13:16) **μή τις** (subj. nom.) **δύνηται** (3rd sg. pres. mid. subjunc. of δύναμαι) **ἀγοράσαι** (aor. act. inf. of ἀγοράζω, "buy," compl. inf.) **ἢ** (disjunctive, "or") **πωλῆσαι** (aor. act. inf. of πωλέω, "sell," compl. inf.) **εἰ μὴ** ("except") **ὁ ἔχων** (nom. sg. masc. of pres. act. ptc. of ἔχω, subst., subj. nom. of verbless cl.) **τὸ χάραγμα** (χάραγμα, -ατος, τό, "mark," dir. obj.) **τὸ ὄνομα** (appos. to χάραγμα, "the mark, that is, the name") **τοῦ θηρίου** (θηρίον, -ου, τό, "animal, beast," poss.) **ἢ** (disjunctive) **τὸν ἀριθμὸν** (ἀριθμός, -οῦ, ὁ, "number," appos. to χάραγμα) **τοῦ ὀνόματος** (prob. gen. of production, "the number which is produced by the name") **αὐτοῦ** (poss.).

The original hearers of Revelation would likely have understood the economic costs of faithfulness to refer to the way that participation in trade guilds (and the public life of the city more generally) required participation in idolatry through the emperor cult or some other cultic deity (Koester 595; see 13:1 for a possible connection with imperial coinage). Participation in the economic life of the ancient city would have been very difficult for conscientious Christians even apart from the threat of death (recall Antipas in 2:13 and Pliny, *Letters* 10.96–97).

13:18 Ὧδε (adv. often indicating spatial proximity, "here," used to suggest logical proximity or relevance, "in this"; it could also be understood to function as subj. of ἐστίν; idiomatically, "this calls for discernment" [BDAG 1101d], cf. 17:9) **ἡ σοφία** (σοφία, -ας, ἡ, "wisdom," pred. nom.) **ἐστίν** (3rd sg. pres. act. ind. of εἰμί). **ὁ ἔχων**

(nom. sg. masc. of pres. act. ptc. of ἔχω, subst., subj. nom.) **νοῦν** (νοῦς, νοός, νοΐ, νοῦν, ὁ, "understanding," dir. obj.) **ψηφισάτω** (3rd sg. aor. act. impv. of ψηφίζω, "count, calculate, interpret") **τὸν ἀριθμὸν** (ἀριθμός, -οῦ, ὁ, "number," dir. obj.) **τοῦ θηρίου** (θηρίον, -ου, τό, "animal, beast," poss.), **ἀριθμὸς** (pred. nom.) **γὰρ** (causal) **ἀνθρώπου** (possibly attrib. referring to generic humanity, "a human number," or more likely poss. to refer to a specific person, "the number of a man") **ἐστίν** (3rd sg. pres. act. ind. of εἰμί), **καὶ ὁ ἀριθμὸς** (subj. nom., of verbless cl.) **αὐτοῦ** (poss.) **ἑξακόσιοι** ("six hundred," pred. adj. of implied linking vb.) **ἑξήκοντα** ("sixty") **ἕξ** ("six").

Six hundred and sixty six is strongly supported in the mss, but some read δέκα ἕξ (616; C vg^{ms} mss$^{acc.\ to\ Irenaeus}$ Caesarius), τεσσαράκοντα ἕξ (646; it^{ar}), or ἑξήκοντα πέντε (665; 2344).

The call to calculate the number points toward the practice of gematria whereby the numerical value of the letters in a name (A = 1, B = 2, etc.) could be added up to create the number of a name. Many names have been proposed throughout history, but the most likely option comes from the way that "Nero Caesar" equals 666 when transliterated from Greek into Hebrew. This would seem to make sense of the way that the mark of the beast is 616 in some ancient mss of Revelation; 616 is the result of transliterating "Nero Caesar" from Latin (instead of Greek) to Hebrew (see Aune^{b} 770–73; Koester 597–99 for more detailed discussion). It seems evident that some, if not many, early Christians viewed the number as a reference to Nero, although Nero likely died decades before John wrote Revelation. Many people in the decades following Nero's death believed that Nero was not really dead and would return to wage war against Rome at the head of an army from Parthia, Rome's main rival in the East, in the first century (Bauckham 407–23). Nero is the likely answer not because John thought he was still alive (Koester 571), but because he was the most infamous tyrant and persecutor of Christians in the first century. He is traditionally associated with the execution of both Peter and Paul in Rome, and he brutally killed many Christians after blaming a devastating fire in Rome upon them. Nero was thus the symbolic and typological figurehead for the dragon's use of the beast to wage war against the children of the woman. Future persecutors, including the final persecutor, will follow Nero's lead in the trajectory initially set by Antiochus Epiphanes.

FOR FURTHER STUDY

43. The Mark of the Beast (13:16–18)

Gumerlock, F. X. "Nero Antichrist: Patristic Evidence for the Use of Nero's Naming in Calculating the Number of the Beast (Rev 13:18)." *WTJ* 68 (2006): 347–60.

Koester, C. R. "The Number of the Beast in Revelation 13 in Light of Papyri, Graffiti, and Inscriptions." *Journal of Early Christian History* 6 (2016): 1–21.

Williams, P. J. "P115 and the Number of the Beast." *TynBul* 58 (2007): 151–53.

HOMILETICAL SUGGESTIONS

The vision of the two beasts in Revelation 13 shows how the dragon, in seeking to carry out his wrath from 12:17, recruits and empowers two beasts to harm God's people. From the perspective of the first-century hearers, the first beast represents the Roman imperial power employed to persecute God's people, while the second beast reflects local provincial and pagan religious leaders seeking to promote and enforce worship of the first beast. The key verse for application is 13:10, which exhorts God's people to faithful perseverance no matter what the cost.

How to Overcome the Beasts (12:18–13:18)

1. Understand the source of opposition (12:18–13:8).
2. Understand the way to overcome (13:9–10).
3. Understand the strategies of demonic deception (13:11–18).

3. Victory in the Conflict: The 144,000 on Mount Zion (14:1–5)

Chapter 14 can be divided into three sections that each begin with Καὶ εἶδον: 14:1–5, 6–13, 14–20. All three sections, in different ways, portray the outcome of the two paths set before the hearers of Revelation; they will either overcome with faithfulness to God or join the inhabitants of the earth in their allegiance to the beast. The path to overcome involves suffering and possibly death in the present time but eternal vindication and rest, while the path of compromise would avoid suffering for their faith in the present time but would result in eternal judgment. The final vision of God's judgment in 14:19–20 uses imagery picked up again with Jesus's return in 19:15, suggesting that these visions provide parallel pictures of the same final event.

14:1 Καὶ εἶδον (1st sg. aor. act. ind. of ὁράω; καὶ εἶδον introduces a new vision, scene, figure, or activity [Aune[a] 338]), **καὶ ἰδοὺ** (emph. interj.) **τὸ** (anaphoric to 5:6, the art. is lacking in 𝔓[47] P 051 and the TR [Metzger 677]) **ἀρνίον** (ἀρνίον, -ου, τό, "lamb," subj. nom. of verbless cl.) **ἑστὸς** (nom. sg. neut. of pf. act. ptc. of ἵστημι, attrib. ptc. or ptc. functioning as finite vb.) **ἐπὶ τὸ ὄρος** (loc.) **Σιὼν** (appos.) **καὶ μετ' αὐτοῦ** (association) **ἑκατὸν** ("hundred," the number functions as the indeclinable subst. subj. of verbless cl. coord. with ἀρνίον) **τεσσεράκοντα** ("forty") **τέσσαρες** ("four") **χιλιάδες** ("thousand") **ἔχουσαι** (nom. pl. fem. of pres. act. ptc. of ἔχω, attrib.) **τὸ ὄνομα** (dir. obj.) **αὐτοῦ** (poss.) **καὶ τὸ ὄνομα** (dir. obj.) **τοῦ πατρὸς** (poss.) **αὐτοῦ** (relationship) **γεγραμμένον** (acc. sg. neut. of pf. pass. ptc. of γράφω, attrib., the sg. ptc. modifying two names could suggest that John treated the names as a unity [Math 185]) **ἐπὶ τῶν μετώπων** (μέτωπον, -ου, τό, "forehead," loc.) **αὐτῶν** (poss.).

Both the timing (present/millennium/new creation) and location (earth/heaven) of this vision is disputed with conflicting evidence and arguments. The decisive observation seems to be how 14:1–5 parallels other visions of God's people in Revelation as in victory and rest (6:9–11; 7:9–17; 14:13; 15:2–4; possibly 20:4–6; cf. 19:1–9). These parallel visions do not provide identical details but generally describe the intermediate state which, as in 7:9–17, transitions seamlessly into a description of the final state. The explicit reference to the 144,000 connects this group with 7:4 and provides the additional information that the seal of God is the name of God and the lamb written on their foreheads. This detail demonstrates the explicit contrast between the seal/name of God and the mark/name of the beast in the immediately prior verses. Revelation 22:4 describes all of God's people with his name on their foreheads, suggesting that the 144,000 symbolically describes all of God's people. This observation is not determinative, however, since the 144,000 could still represent a subset of the full number of redeemed humanity even if all have God's name written on their foreheads in the end. Revelation 3:12 promises the overcomers in Philadelphia that they would be made pillars in God's temple and would have God's name and the name of God's city written on them.

Use of the OT: For Ezek 9:4, see on 7:3. In Ps 2:6 God declares that he has established his king *ἐπὶ Σιων ὄρος τὸ ἅγιον αὐτοῦ* (cf. 4 Ezra 13:32–38 on the connection of the Messiah to restored Mount Zion). Several passages refer to eschatological Zion (Isa 2:2–5; 30:19–21 [with "a teacher"]; 52:7–10; 59:18–20 [a redeemer will come to Zion]; Zech 8:2–22 [God will dwell in Zion]; Heb 12:18–24 [with an element of realized eschatology; note the pf. tense of *προσεληλύθατε* in Heb 12:22]). The high priest wore a golden plate on his *μέτωπον* saying "Holy to the Lord" (Exod 28:36: *Ἁγίασμα κυρίου*)

14:2 καὶ ἤκουσα (1st sg. aor. act. ind. of *ἀκούω*) **φωνὴν** (dir. obj.) **ἐκ τοῦ οὐρανοῦ** (source) **ὡς** (comp.) **φωνὴν ὑδάτων** (source or subj. gen.) **πολλῶν** (attrib.) **καὶ ὡς** (comp.) **φωνὴν βροντῆς** (*βροντή, -ῆς, ἡ*, "thunder," source or subj. gen.) **μεγάλης** (attrib.), **καὶ ἡ φωνὴ** (subj. nom. of verbless cl., ant. of *ἥν*) **ἣν** (dir. obj.) **ἤκουσα** (1st sg. aor. act. ind. of *ἀκούω*) **ὡς** (comp.) **κιθαρῳδῶν** (*κιθαρῳδός, -οῦ, ὁ*, "lyre-player") **κιθαριζόντων** (gen. pl. masc. of pres. act. ptc. of *κιθαρίζω*, "play a lyre," attrib.) **ἐν ταῖς κιθάραις** (*κιθάρα, -ας, ἡ*, "lyre," means) **αὐτῶν** (poss.).

Jesus's voice in 1:15 is *ὡς φωνὴ ὑδάτων πολλῶν*. The voice of the great crowd in 19:6 is *ὡς φωνὴν ὑδάτων πολλῶν*. The twenty-four elders in 5:8 have lyres but the closer parallel is with the overcomers in 15:2 who have lyres and sing.

Use of the OT: Ezekiel states that the wings of the living creatures sound like the sound of many waters (1:24: *ὡς φωνὴν ὕδατος πολλοῦ*). The sound of God's coming in Ezek 43:2 is like the sound of many waters (MT and EVV; the LXX, on the other hand, translates this as the sound of the encampment being like the sound of many doublings/repetitions [*φωνὴ τῆς παρεμβολῆς ὡς φωνὴ διπλασιαζόντων πολλῶν*]).

14:3 καὶ ᾄδουσιν (3rd pl. pres. act. ind. of ᾄδω, "sing," narrative pres.) [**ὡς**] (the comp. phrase functions as dir. obj., evidence for the presence or absence of ὡς is evenly balanced) **ᾠδὴν** (ᾠδή, -ῆς, ἡ, "song") **καινὴν** (attrib.) **ἐνώπιον τοῦ** (anaphoric to 4:2) **θρόνου** (loc.) **καὶ ἐνώπιον τῶν** (anaphoric to 4:6) **τεσσάρων** ("four," attrib.) **ζῴων** (ζῷον, -ου, τό, "animal, living thing," loc.) **καὶ τῶν** (anaphoric to 4:4) **πρεσβυτέρων** (loc., the prep. ἐνώπιον is not repeated), **καὶ οὐδεὶς** (subj. nom.) **ἐδύνατο** (3rd sg. impf. mid. ind. of δύναμαι) **μαθεῖν** (aor. act. inf. of μανθάνω, "learn," compl. inf.) **τὴν ᾠδὴν** (dir. obj.) **εἰ μὴ** ("except") **αἱ** (anaphoric to 14:1) **ἑκατὸν** ("hundred," indeclinable, but the art. indicates it is nom. fem. pl., subj. nom. of verbless cl.) **τεσσεράκοντα** ("forty") **τέσσαρες** ("four") **χιλιάδες** ("thousand"), **οἱ ἠγορασμένοι** (nom. pl. masc. pf. pass. ptc. ἀγοράζω, "buy," subst. ptc. in appos. or attrib. ptc., the masc. gender is incongruous with the fem. number but points to the masc. gender indicated in 14:4) **ἀπὸ τῆς γῆς** (separation).

In Rev 5:9, the four living creatures and twenty-four elders ᾄδουσιν ᾠδὴν καινήν.

Use of the OT: The psalmist commands God's people to sing to God a new song (Ps 32:3 LXX [33:3 EVV] ᾄσατε αὐτῷ ᾆσμα καινόν; cf. Ps 95:1 LXX [96:1 EVV]; Ps 97:1 LXX [98:1 EVV]; Ps 149:1). God put a new song (ᾆσμα καινόν) in David's mouth (Ps 39:4 LXX [40:3 EVV]) and he declares that he will sing a new song to God (Ps 143:9 LXX [144:9 EVV]: ᾠδὴν καινὴν ᾄσομαί σοι). Isaiah commands the hearer to sing to the Lord a new song (42:10: Ὑμνήσατε τῷ κυρίῳ ὕμνον καινόν). New songs indicate fresh praise of God.

14:4 οὗτοί (subj. nom.) **εἰσιν** (3rd pl. pres. act. ind. of εἰμί) **οἳ** (subj. nom.; the headless rel. cl. functions as pred. compl.) **μετὰ γυναικῶν** (association) **οὐκ ἐμολύνθησαν** (3rd pl. aor. pass. ind. of μολύνω, "defile, make dirty"), **παρθένοι** (παρθένος, -ου, ἡ, "virgin," pred. nom.) **γάρ** (explanatory) **εἰσιν** (3rd pl. pres. act. ind. of εἰμί), **οὗτοι** (prob. sub. of εἰσιν, "these, the ones who follow, are virgins," [Koester 611]) **οἱ ἀκολουθοῦντες** (nom. pl. masc. of pres. act. ptc. of ἀκολουθέω, attrib.) **τῷ ἀρνίῳ** (ἀρνίον, -ου, τό, "lamb," dat. dir. obj.) **ὅπου** (adv., "where") **ἂν** (adds an element of indefiniteness, "-ever") **ὑπάγῃ** (3rd sg. pres. act. subjunc. of ὑπάγω). **οὗτοι** (subj. nom.) **ἠγοράσθησαν** (3rd pl. aor. pass. ind. of ἀγοράζω, "buy") **ἀπὸ τῶν ἀνθρώπων** (separation) **ἀπαρχὴ** (ἀπαρχή, -ῆς, ἡ, "firstfruits," appos. to οὗτοι) **τῷ θεῷ** (advantage, "for") **καὶ τῷ** (anaphoric to 5:6) **ἀρνίῳ** (advantage),

The 144,000 are described with masculine imagery (not being defiled with women), feminine imagery (παρθένος was only very rarely applied to males in antiquity), and harvest imagery (Koester 610–11). The masculine imagery of not being defiled by women likely develops the image of God's people engaged in holy war in which sexual abstinence was required for a time (Deut 23:9–11; 1 Sam 21:5 [Bauckham 229–32]; see on 2:14 for how sexual purity is generally used in Revelation to describe religious fidelity). The feminine imagery points forward to the picture of God's people as the pure bride of Christ (19:7–8; 21:9, cf. Paul's goal in 2 Cor 11:2 to παρθένον ἁγνὴν παραστῆσαι τῷ Χριστῷ). The imagery of firstfruits points forward to the grain harvest in 14:14–16 and could be taken to distinguish the 144,000 as a group of Jewish believers from the rest of God's people (Fanning 391) or to indicate the totality of believers throughout history (Beale 742–43; Koester 619; see Jer 2:3 below, although the normal idea of firstfruits would suggest the first subset of the later larger harvest as in Rom 16:5; 1 Cor 15:23; 16:15; 2 Thess 2:13). Ἀκολουθέω is used with frequency in the Gospels to indicate discipleship.

Use of the OT: Israel is collectively called by God a virgin in Jer 38:4, 21 LXX (31:4, 21 EVV) (παρθένος Ισραηλ) in an oracle of restoration leading up to the promise of a new covenant. The description of Israel as a virgin occurs also in 4 Kgdms 19:21 (2 Kgs 19:21 EVV) (παρθένος θυγάτηρ Σιων), Lam 2:13 (παρθένος θύγατερ Σιων), Amos 5:2 (παρθένος τοῦ Ισραηλ). Jeremiah 2:3 describes the nation of Israel as the beginning of God's harvest (τῷ κυρίῳ ἀρχὴ γενημάτων αὐτοῦ); this example uses the metaphor of firstfruits to describe the whole nation and not just a subset of the whole. An allusion to Jer 2:3 is particularly likely because Jeremiah also moves from bridal imagery with attention to how Israel followed God (τοῦ ἐξακολουθῆσαί σε τῷ ἁγίῳ Ισραηλ [Jer 2:2]) to harvest imagery in Jer 2:3.

14:5 καὶ ἐν τῷ στόματι (loc., distributive sg. with pl. pron.) **αὐτῶν** (poss.) **οὐχ εὑρέθη** (3rd sg. aor. pass. ind. of εὑρίσκω) **ψεῦδος** (ψεῦδος, -ους, τό, "lie," subj. nom.), **ἄμωμοί** (ἄμωμος, -ον, "blameless," pred. adj., several mss add γάρ to make this last cl. less abrupt in parallel to its use in 14:4 [𝔓[47] ℵ 046 and the TR among others] but it is not likely that it would have been removed if original [Metzger 677]) **εἰσιν** (3rd pl. pres. act. ind. of εἰμί).

Truth and deception are significant themes in Revelation and God's people who will access the new Jerusalem will tell the truth (21:8, 27; 22:15). This is the only occurrence of ἄμωμος in Revelation and it is contextually connected with truth but probably refers more broadly to moral blamelessness.

Use of the OT: David declares blessedness over the man in whose mouth there is not deceit (Ps 31:2 LXX [32:2 EVV]: οὐδὲ ἔστιν ἐν τῷ στόματι αὐτοῦ δόλος). Deceit is not found in the mouth of the suffering servant in Isa 53:9 (οὐδὲ εὑρέθη δόλος ἐν τῷ στόματι αὐτοῦ). Deceitfulness will not be found in the mouth of the one who participates in Israel's restoration in Zeph 3:13 (οὐ μὴ εὑρεθῇ ἐν τῷ στόματι αὐτῶν γλῶσσα δολία). John differs from each of these texts in his use of the syn. ψεῦδος; this could suggest that John had the Hebrew in mind and chose a different Greek word to communicate the idiomatic Hebraic expression.

---

4. The Call to Choose Sides: Four Proclamations (14:6–13)

a. The Eternal Gospel (14:6–7)

14:6 Καὶ εἶδον (1st sg. aor. act. ind. of ὁράω; καὶ εἶδον introduces a new vision, scene, figure, or activity [Aune[a] 338]) **ἄλλον** (attrib., it is likely that ἄλλον is missing in 𝔓[47] ℵ* 046 and most minuscules because no individual angel has appeared since 11:15 [Metzger 678]) **ἄγγελον** (dir. obj.) **πετόμενον** (acc. sg. masc. of pres. mid. ptc. of πέτομαι, "fly," compl. in obj.-compl. double acc. construction) **ἐν μεσουρανήματι** (μεσουράνημα, -ατος, τό, "zenith" [BDAG 635d], the point in the sky directly above the viewer, loc.), **ἔχοντα** (acc. sg. masc. of pres. act. ptc. of ἔχω, attrib.) **εὐαγγέλιον** (dir. obj.) **αἰώνιον** (attrib.) **εὐαγγελίσαι** (aor. act. inf. εὐαγγελίζω, purpose inf.) **ἐπὶ τοὺς καθημένους** (acc. pl. masc. of pres. mid. ptc. of κάθημαι, subst., with ἐπί the acc. here functions similar to an indir. obj. and indicates "to whom," "for whom," or "about whom" [BDAG 366b]) **ἐπὶ τῆς γῆς** (loc.) **καὶ** (epex.) **ἐπὶ πᾶν** (attrib.) **ἔθνος** (this and the following nouns function as καθημένους above) **καὶ φυλὴν** (φυλή, -ῆς, ἡ, "tribe") **καὶ γλῶσσαν** (γλῶσσα, -ης, ἡ, "tongue, language") **καὶ λαόν**,

This is the only place in Revelation where John refers to humanity as "the ones sitting on the earth." This could be seen as synonymous with his normal expression for those who ultimately refuse to repent (see 3:10 on "the ones dwelling on the earth"), but it is more likely a softened way to describe human beings as existing in the middle and who must choose between Jesus and the beast. This is strengthened by the connection with the more neutral fourfold formula of every nation, tribe, tongue, and people (see 5:9).

Use of the OT: Jeremiah announces that God is summoning a sword against the ones dwelling on the earth (Jer 32:29 LXX [25:29 EVV]: μάχαιραν ἐγὼ καλῶ ἐπὶ τοὺς καθημένους ἐπὶ τῆς γῆς).

14:7 λέγων (nom. sg. masc. of pres. act. ptc. of λέγω, manner, see below on the case) **ἐν φωνῇ** (means) **μεγάλῃ** (attrib.), **Φοβήθητε** (2nd pl. aor. pass. impv. of φοβέω, pass. functions as mid.) **τὸν θεὸν** (dir. obj.) **καὶ δότε** (2nd pl. aor. act. impv. of δίδωμι) **αὐτῷ** (indir. obj.) **δόξαν** (dir. obj.), **ὅτι** (causal) **ἦλθεν** (3rd sg. aor. act. ind. of ἔρχομαι) **ἡ ὥρα** (subj. nom.) **τῆς κρίσεως** (κρίσις, -εως, ἡ, "judgment," descriptive gen.) **αὐτοῦ** (subj. gen.), **καὶ προσκυνήσατε** (2nd pl. aor. act. impv. of προσκυνέω) **τῷ ποιήσαντι** (dat. sg. masc. of aor. act. ptc. of ποιέω, subst., dat. dir. obj.) **τὸν οὐρανὸν** (this and the following nouns are coord. dir. obj.) **καὶ τὴν γῆν καὶ θάλασσαν** (the art. is missing from these final two nouns because they are a subset of the prior noun γῆν [Wallace 287]) **καὶ πηγὰς** (πηγή, -ῆς, ἡ, "spring") **ὑδάτων** (gen. of content or product).

The nom. ptc. λέγων should be in the acc. case like πετόμενον and ἔχοντα to match the acc. ant. ἄγγελον. Some scribes solved the problem by deleting λέγων in 14:7 (ℵ) or changing it to the acc. case λέγοντα (𝔓[47], 051). The use of the nom. ptc. λέγων parallels the proper use of the nom. with a nom. ant. in 14:8 and 14:9 so it is possible that 14:7 anticipates the following syntax (Moţ 130).

Fear and worship reflect the saving response of humanity to God throughout Revelation (11:13, 18; 15:4; 19:5) and the hymns of worship regularly guide the hearer to give God glory (1:6; 4:9, 11; 5:12, 13; 7:12; 19:1, 7) while the unrepentant refuse to give God glory (16:9).

Use of the OT: King Darius commanded all the nations, regions, and languages (τοῖς ἔθνεσι καὶ χώραις καὶ γλώσσαις) who dwelt in the all the earth (τοῖς οἰκοῦσιν ἐν πάσῃ τῇ γῇ) to tremble (זוע) and fear (דחל) before God (Dan 6:27 [6:26 EVV], note how the response is changed from fear in the MT to worship in the LXX: ἔστωσαν προσκυνοῦντες καὶ λατρεύοντες τῷ θεῷ). Exodus 20:11 describes how the Lord made the heaven and the earth and the sea and all the things in them (ἐποίησεν κύριος τὸν οὐρανὸν καὶ τὴν γῆν καὶ τὴν θάλασσαν καὶ πάντα τὰ ἐν αὐτοῖς). The psalmist also celebrates God as τὸν ποιήσαντα τὸν οὐρανὸν καὶ τὴν γῆν, τὴν θάλασσαν καὶ πάντα τὰ ἐν αὐτοῖς (Ps 145:6 LXX [146:6 EVV]).

---

b. The Fall of Babylon (14:8)

14:8 Καὶ ἄλλος (attrib.) **ἄγγελος** (subj. nom.) **δεύτερος** ("second," subst., "a second one," appos., the reading ἄγγελος δεύτερος in א[2] C P 051 205 209 1611 2053 2344 best explains the other readings that change the word order or drop either ἄγγελος or δεύτερος [Metzger 678]) **ἠκολούθησεν** (3rd sg. aor. act. ind. of ἀκολουθέω) **λέγων** (nom. sg. masc. of pres. act. ptc. of λέγω, manner), **Ἔπεσεν** (3rd sg. aor. act. ind. of πίπτω, proleptic aor.; "It is also possible that the aor. could be taken as pres. referring from the standpoint of the angelic pronouncement of judgment: it refers to the verdict of judgment by the angel given in advance of the execution of the verdict" [Math 192]) **ἔπεσεν** (repetition for emph.) **Βαβυλὼν** ("Babylon," the subj. nom. of the prior vb. but following for emph., "It fell! It fell! Great Babylon," ant. of ἥ) **ἡ μεγάλη** (attrib.) **ἣ** (subj. nom.) **ἐκ τοῦ οἴνου** (οἶνος, -ου, ὁ, "wine," source, the prep. phrase functions as dir. obj. of the following vb. πεπότικεν) **τοῦ θυμοῦ** (θυμός, -οῦ, ὁ, "strong passion, anger," epex., if this were referring to God it would indicate anger but since the source is Babylon it indicates strong passion) **τῆς πορνείας** (πορνεία, -ας, ἡ, "sexual immorality," descriptive or attrib. gen.) **αὐτῆς** (subj. gen.) **πεπότικεν** (3rd sg. pf. act. ind. of ποτίζω, "cause to drink") **πάντα** (attrib.) **τὰ ἔθνη** (dir. obj.).

This first reference to Babylon in Revelation anticipates the fuller visions in Revelation 17–18. In particular 18:2 announces Ἔπεσεν ἔπεσεν Βαβυλὼν ἡ μεγάλη and 17:2 states μεθ' ἧς ἐπόρνευσαν οἱ βασιλεῖς τῆς γῆς καὶ ἐμεθύσθησαν οἱ κατοικοῦντες τὴν γῆν ἐκ τοῦ οἴνου τῆς πορνείας αὐτῆς (cf. 18:3).

Use of the OT: The oracle against Babylon in Isa 21:9 announces πέπτωκεν Βαβυλών. Jeremiah has a similar message but further describes how Babylon was a golden cup in the hand of the Lord, which makes all the world drunk (Jer 28:7 LXX [51:7 EVV]: ποτήριον χρυσοῦν Βαβυλὼν ἐν χειρὶ κυρίου μεθύσκον πᾶσαν τὴν γῆν). Jeremiah 28:8 LXX (51:8 EVV) declares that Babylon fell suddenly and was shattered (καὶ ἄφνω ἔπεσεν Βαβυλὼν καὶ συνετρίβη). Psalm 74:9 LXX (75:8 EVV) describes how all the sinners of the earth will drink (πίονται πάντες οἱ ἁμαρτωλοὶ τῆς γῆς) a cup of unmixed wine in the hand of the Lord (ποτήριον ἐν χειρὶ κυρίου οἴνου ἀκράτου). Isaiah 14:3–22 contains a significant oracle against Babylon.

---

c. The Suffering of Beast Worshippers (14:9–12)

14:9 Καὶ ἄλλος (attrib.) **ἄγγελος** (subj. nom.) **τρίτος** ("third," subst., appos., "a third one") **ἠκολούθησεν** (3rd sg. aor. act. ind. of ἀκολουθέω) **αὐτοῖς** (dat. dir. obj.) **λέγων** (nom. sg. masc. of pres. act. ptc. of λέγω, manner) **ἐν φωνῇ** (means) **μεγάλῃ** (attrib.), **Εἴ** (introduces 1st class cond. cl.) **τις** (subj. nom.) **προσκυνεῖ** (3rd sg. pres. act. ind. of προσκυνέω) **τὸ θηρίον** (θηρίον, -ου, τό, "animal, beast," dir. obj.) **καὶ τὴν εἰκόνα** (εἰκών, -όνος, ἡ, "image," coord. dir. obj.) **αὐτοῦ** (obj. gen.) **καὶ λαμβάνει** (3rd sg. pres. act. ind. of λαμβάνω) **χάραγμα** (χάραγμα, -ατος, τό, "mark," dir. obj.) **ἐπὶ τοῦ μετώπου** (μέτωπον, -ου, τό, "forehead," loc.) **αὐτοῦ** (poss.) **ἢ** (disjunctive) **ἐπὶ τὴν χεῖρα** (loc.) **αὐτοῦ** (poss.),

On the mark of the beast, see 13:17.

14:10 καὶ (adv., "even, also") **αὐτὸς** (subj. nom.) **πίεται** (3rd sg. fut. mid. ind. of πίνω, the apod. of the cond. cl. started in 14:9) **ἐκ τοῦ οἴνου** (οἶνος, -ου, ὁ, "wine," source) **τοῦ θυμοῦ** (θυμός, οῦ, ὁ, "strong passion, anger," epex., in contrast to θυμός in 14:8, here the focus is on anger) **τοῦ θεοῦ** (subj. gen.) **τοῦ κεκερασμένου** (gen. sg. masc. of pf. pass. ptc. of κεράννυμι, "mix," attrib.) **ἀκράτου** (ἄκρατος, -ον, "unmixed, undiluted," attrib.) **ἐν τῷ ποτηρίῳ** (ποτήριον, -ου, τό, "cup," loc.) **τῆς ὀργῆς** (ὀργή, -ῆς, ἡ, "anger," gen. of content) **αὐτοῦ** (subj. gen.) **καὶ βασανισθήσεται** (3rd sg. fut. pass. ind. βασανίζω, "torture") **ἐν πυρὶ** (means) **καὶ θείῳ** (θεῖον, -ου, τό, "sulfur," coord. means) **ἐνώπιον ἀγγέλων** (loc.) **ἁγίων** (attrib.) **καὶ ἐνώπιον τοῦ** (anaphroic to 5:6) **ἀρνίου** (ἀρνίον, -ου, τό, "lamb," loc.).

The cup of God's wrath is also mentioned in 16:19 and could be seen as parallel to the bowls of wrath in 15:7. Elsewhere in Revelation, fire and sulfur is connected with the lake of fire (19:20; 20:10; 21:8).

Use of the OT: The cup of God's wrath is a common metaphor for judgment in the OT (Isa 51:17, 22; Jer 25:15; Ps 75:8). Genesis 19:24 describes God's judgment of Sodom and Gomorrah with sulfur and fire (θεῖον καὶ πῦρ; cf. 3 Macc 2:5). David prays in Ps 10:6 LXX (11:6 EVV) that God would rain fire and sulfur upon sinners (πῦρ καὶ θεῖον). Ezekiel 38:22 prophesies that God will rain hailstones, fire, and sulfur upon Gog and his hoards (πῦρ καὶ θεῖον). On the use of fire and sulfur in Isa 30:27–33, see on 19:20.

14:11 καὶ ὁ καπνὸς (καπνός, -οῦ, ὁ, "smoke," subj. nom.) **τοῦ βασανισμοῦ** (βασανισμός, -οῦ, ὁ, "torture," source) **αὐτῶν** (obj. gen.) **εἰς αἰῶνας** (measure) **αἰώνων** (emph. repetition of αἰών) **ἀναβαίνει** (3rd sg. pres. act. ind. of ἀναβαίνω, futuristic pres.), **καὶ οὐκ ἔχουσιν** (3rd pl. pres. act. ind. of ἔχω, futuristic pres., apod. of cond. cl.) **ἀνάπαυσιν** (ἀνάπαυσις, -εως, ἡ, "rest," dir. obj.) **ἡμέρας** (gen. of time) **καὶ νυκτὸς** (gen. of time) **οἱ προσκυνοῦντες** (nom. pl. masc. of pres. act. ptc. of προσκυνέω, subst., subj. nom.) **τὸ θηρίον** (θηρίον, -ου, τό, "animal, beast," dir. obj.) **καὶ τὴν εἰκόνα** (εἰκών, -όνος, ἡ, "image," dir. obj.) **αὐτοῦ** (obj. gen.) **καὶ** (coordinates the cond. cl. with the subst. ptc. προσκυνοῦντες as compound subjects of ἔχουσιν) **εἴ** (introduces 1st class cond. cl.) **τις** (subj. nom.) **λαμβάνει** (3rd sg. pres. act. ind. of λαμβάνω) **τὸ χάραγμα** (χάραγμα, -ατος, τό, "mark," dir. obj.) **τοῦ ὀνόματος** (epex., "the mark, that is, his name") **αὐτοῦ** (poss.).

Βασανισμός is elsewhere in Revelation associated with the locusts in the fifth trumpet (9:5) and the judgment of Babylon (18:7, 10, 15). Descriptions of eternal punishment are widespread in early Christianity (Matt 25:41, 46; Mark 9:43–48; 2 Thess 1:9; Heb 6:2; Jude vv. 6–7).

Use of the OT: Several parallels are evident to the description of cosmic upheaval in God's judgment of Edom in Isa 34:9–10. The land will be turned to sulfur (καὶ ἡ γῆ αὐτῆς εἰς θεῖον) that night and day will not be extinguished into the eternal time (νυκτὸς καὶ ἡμέρας καὶ οὐ σβεσθήσεται εἰς τὸν αἰῶνα χρόνον) with the smoke going up (καὶ ἀναβήσεται ὁ καπνὸς αὐτῆς ἄνω).

14:12 Ὧδε (asyndeton, adv. often indicating spatial proximity, "here," used to suggest logical proximity or relevance, "in this"; functions as subj.; idiomatically, "this calls for endurance" or "here is [an opportunity for] endurance" [BDAG 1101d], cf. 13:10) **ἡ ὑπομονὴ** (ὑπομονή, -ῆς, ἡ, "endurance," pred. nom.) **τῶν ἁγίων** (subj. gen.) **ἐστίν, οἱ τηροῦντες** (nom. pl. masc. of pres. act. ptc. of τηρέω, subst., appos.) **τὰς ἐντολὰς** (ἐντολή, -ῆς, ἡ, "command," dir. obj.) **τοῦ θεοῦ** (subj. gen.) **καὶ τὴν πίστιν** (dir. obj.) **Ἰησοῦ** (obj. gen., faith in Jesus or faithfulness to Jesus).

This verse summarizes the rhetorical goal of the visionary description of judgment; it is intended to motivate God's people to endure (cf. 13:10). The description of the saints as keeping the commandments of God and faith in Jesus parallels the description of the seed of the woman targeted by the dragon in 12:17 (τῶν τηρούντων τὰς ἐντολὰς τοῦ θεοῦ καὶ ἐχόντων τὴν μαρτυρίαν Ἰησοῦ).

The nom. ptc. τηροῦντες should be in the gen. case (τῶν τηρούντων) to match its ant. τῶν ἁγίων; some mss contain this correction (א, 1006, 1611, 1841). It could be explained instead as the pred. nom. of the copulative ἐστίν: the perseverance of the saints is the ones who keep (i.e., the saints who persevere are the ones who keep [Moţ 119]).

d. The Blessedness of God's People (14:13)

14:13 Καὶ ἤκουσα (1st sg. aor. act. ind. of ἀκούω) **φωνῆς** (gen. dir. obj.) **ἐκ τοῦ οὐρανοῦ** (source) **λεγούσης** (gen. sg. fem. of pres. act. ptc. of λέγω, compl. in obj.-compl. double gen. construction), **Γράψον** (2nd sg. aor. act. impv. of γράφω)· **μακάριοι** (μακάριος, -ία, -ιον, "blessed, happy," pred. nom. of verbless cl.) **οἱ νεκροὶ** (subj. nom. of verbless cl.) **οἱ ἐν κυρίῳ** (loc.) **ἀποθνῄσκοντες** (nom. pl. masc. of pres. act. ptc. of ἀποθνῄσκω, attrib.) **ἀπ' ἄρτι** (temp. adv. functioning as obj. of prep., the phrase could be seen to exclude those who died earlier; Beale argues it refers to the redemptive work of Christ [Beale 769]). **ναί** (affirmative interj., missing in 𝔓[47] ℵ* and a few minuscules but strongly supported by most mss and in line with John's style in 1:7; 16:7; 22:20 [Metzger 678–79]), **λέγει** (3rd sg. pres. act. ind. of λέγω) **τὸ πνεῦμα** (subj. nom.), **ἵνα** (the logic seems to require a causal cl., which is made explicit by ὅτι in 𝔓[47], but it could be a content cl. describing the content of the blessing or the content of the Spirit's speech, "the Spirit says *that* they will rest," or, perhaps most naturally, a purpose or result cl., "*they die* that they might rest") **ἀναπαήσονται** (3rd pl. fut. pass. ind. of ἀναπαύω, "rest," fut. for subjunc., prob. pass. for mid.) **ἐκ τῶν κόπων** (κόπος, -ου, ὁ, "work, trouble," separation) **αὐτῶν** (subj. gen.), **τὰ γὰρ** (explanatory) **ἔργα** (subj. nom.) **αὐτῶν** (subj. gen.) **ἀκολουθεῖ** (3rd sg. pres. act. ind. of ἀκολουθέω, futuristic pres.) **μετ' αὐτῶν** (association).

John is commanded to write at various points (1:11, 19; 2:1, 8, 12, 18; 3:1, 7, 14; 19:9; 21:5). This is the second of the seven macarisms (1:3; 16:15; 19:9; 20:6; 22:7, 14). Hebrews 4:10 describes entrance into God's rest as resting from one's works.

5. The End of Conflict: Two Harvests (14:14–20)

Interpreters are divided on whether the grain and grape harvests are both descriptions of judgment or whether the first describes salvation while the second describes judgment. The arguments are fairly evenly balanced but the literary context of chapter 14, which is focused on describing the two contrasting end results of allegiance to the beast verses the lamb, favors seeing the grain harvest as a positive picture of salvation (see further arguments in Bauckham 289–96).

a. The Grain Harvest (14:14–16)

14:14 Καὶ εἶδον (καὶ εἶδον introduces a new vision, scene, figure, or activity [Aune[a] 338]), **καὶ ἰδοὺ** (emph. interj.) **νεφέλη** (νεφέλη, -ης, ἡ, "cloud," subj. nom. of verbless cl.) **λευκή** (λευκός, -ή, -όν, "white, bright," attrib.), **καὶ ἐπὶ τὴν νεφέλην** (loc.) **καθήμενον** (acc. sg. masc. of pres. mid. ptc. of κάθημαι, subst., dir. obj. of verbless cl. with implied εἶδον) **ὅμοιον** (ὅμοιος, -οία, -οιον, "like, similar," comp. adj.) **υἱὸν** (compl. of ὅμοιον) **ἀνθρώπου** (relationship, "son of man," or attrib., "human son"), **ἔχων** (nom. sg. masc. of pres. act. ptc. of ἔχω, prob. attrib. but see below) **ἐπὶ τῆς κεφαλῆς** (loc.) **αὐτοῦ** (poss.) **στέφανον** (στέφανος, -ου, ὁ, "wreath, crown," dir. obj.) **χρυσοῦν** (χρυσοῦς, -ῆ,

-οῦν, "golden," attrib.) **καὶ ἐν τῇ χειρὶ** (loc.) **αὐτοῦ** (poss.) **δρέπανον** (δρέπανον, -ου, τό, "sickle," dir. obj.) **ὀξύ** (ὀξύς, -εῖα, -ύ, "sharp," attrib.).

The nom. ptc. ἔχων should be acc. to match its ant. 𝔓[47] solves the problem by reading εχοντα while ℵ*, with a variant spelling, reads εχοτα. The parallel with 1:13 would suggest that the figure like the Son of Man is Jesus.

Use of the OT: Daniel 7:13 describes a vision of one like a son of man coming with the clouds of heaven (ἐπὶ τῶν νεφελῶν τοῦ οὐρανοῦ ὡς υἱὸς ἀνθρώπου ἤρχετο).

14:15 καὶ ἄλλος (attrib.) **ἄγγελος** (subj. nom.) **ἐξῆλθεν** (3rd sg. aor. act. ind. of ἐξέρχομαι) **ἐκ τοῦ ναοῦ** (ναός, -οῦ, ὁ, "temple," source) **κράζων** (nom. sg. masc. of pres. act. ptc. of κράζω, manner) **ἐν φωνῇ** (means) **μεγάλῃ** (attrib.) **τῷ καθημένῳ** (dat. sg. masc. of pres. mid. ptc. of κάθημαι, subst., indir. obj.) **ἐπὶ τῆς νεφέλης** (νεφέλη, -ης, ἡ, "cloud," loc.), Πέμψον (2nd sg. aor. act. impv. of πέμπω) **τὸ δρέπανόν** (δρέπανον, -ου, τό, "sickle," dir. obj.) **σου** (poss.) **καὶ θέρισον** (2nd sg. aor. act. impv. of θερίζω, "reap," coord.), **ὅτι** (causal) **ἦλθεν** (3rd sg. aor. act. ind. of ἔρχομαι) **ἡ ὥρα** (subj. nom.) **θερίσαι** (aor. act. inf. of θερίζω, epex.), **ὅτι** (causal) **ἐξηράνθη** (3rd sg. aor. pass. ind. of ξηραίνω, "become dry, be ripe") **ὁ θερισμὸς** (θερισμός, -οῦ, ὁ, "harvest," subj. nom.) **τῆς γῆς** (obj. gen.).

Use of the OT: On Joel 4:13 LXX [3:13 EVV], see on 14:19.

14:16 καὶ ἔβαλεν (3rd sg. aor. act. ind. of βάλλω) **ὁ καθήμενος** (nom. sg. masc. of pres. mid. ptc. of κάθημαι, subst., subj. nom.) **ἐπὶ τῆς νεφέλης** (νεφέλη, -ης, ἡ, "cloud," loc.) **τὸ δρέπανον** (δρέπανον, -ου, τό, "sickle," dir. obj. of ἔβαλεν) **αὐτοῦ** (poss.) **ἐπὶ τὴν γῆν** (loc.) **καὶ ἐθερίσθη** (3rd sg. aor. pass. ind. of θερίζω, "reap") **ἡ γῆ** (subj. nom.).

b. The Grape Harvest (14:17–20)

14:17 Καὶ **ἄλλος** (attrib.) **ἄγγελος** (subj. nom.) **ἐξῆλθεν** (3rd sg. aor. act. ind. ἐξέρχομαι) **ἐκ τοῦ ναοῦ** (ναός, -οῦ, ὁ, "temple," source) **τοῦ** (adjectivizer) **ἐν τῷ οὐρανῷ** (loc.) **ἔχων** (nom. sg. masc. pres. act. ptc. ἔχω, manner) **καὶ** (adv., "also") **αὐτὸς** (redundant pron. for emph., "also he") **δρέπανον** (δρέπανον, -ου, τό, "sickle," dir. obj.) **ὀξύ** (ὀξύς, -εῖα, -ύ, "sharp," attrib.).

14:18 Καὶ ἄλλος (attrib.) **ἄγγελος** (subj. nom.) [**ἐξῆλθεν**] (3rd sg. aor. act. ind. of ἐξέρχομαι, missing in 𝔓[47] A 1611 2053 and some versions) **ἐκ τοῦ θυσιαστηρίου** (θυσιαστήριον, -ου, τό, "altar," source) [ὁ] **ἔχων** (nom. sg. masc. of pres. act. ptc. of ἔχω, attrib.) **ἐξουσίαν** (dir. obj.) **ἐπὶ τοῦ πυρός** (subord.), **καὶ ἐφώνησεν** (3rd sg. aor. act. ind. of φωνέω) **φωνῇ**

(means) **μεγάλῃ** (attrib.) **τῷ ἔχοντι** (dat. sg. masc. of pres. act. ptc. of ἔχω, subst., indir. obj.) **τὸ** (anaphroic to 14:17) **δρέπανον** (δρέπανον, -ου, τό, "sickle," dir. obj.) **τὸ ὀξὺ** (ὀξύς, -εῖα, -ύ, "sharp," attrib.) **λέγων** (nom. sg. masc. of pres. act. ptc. of λέγω, manner), **Πέμψον** (2nd sg. aor. act. impv. of πέμπω) **σου** (poss., fronted for emph.) **τὸ** (anaphoric to 14:17) **δρέπανον** (dir. obj.) **τὸ ὀξὺ** (attrib.) **καὶ τρύγησον** (2nd sg. aor. act. impv. of τρυγάω, "harvest grapes") **τοὺς βότρυας** (βότρυς, -υος, ὁ, "cluster of grapes," dir. obj.) **τῆς ἀμπέλου** (ἄμπελος, -ου, ἡ, "vine," source or separation) **τῆς γῆς** (appos.), **ὅτι** (causal) **ἤκμασαν** (3rd pl. aor. act. ind. of ἀκμάζω, "be ripe") **αἱ σταφυλαὶ** (σταφυλή, -ῆς, ἡ, "grapes," subj. nom.) **αὐτῆς** (poss.).

The reference to the altar links this judgment to the prayers of the souls under the altar for justice in 6:9.

14:19 καὶ ἔβαλεν (3rd sg. aor. act. ind. of βάλλω) **ὁ ἄγγελος** (subj. nom.) **τὸ δρέπανον** (δρέπανον, -ου, τό, "sickle," dir. obj.) **αὐτοῦ** (poss.) **εἰς τὴν γῆν** (loc.) **καὶ ἐτρύγησεν** (3rd sg. aor. act. ind. of τρυγάω, "harvest grapes") **τὴν ἄμπελον** (ἄμπελος, -ου, ἡ, "vine," dir. obj.) **τῆς γῆς** (appos.) **καὶ ἔβαλεν** (3rd sg. aor. act. ind. of βάλλω) **εἰς τὴν ληνὸν** (ληνός, -οῦ, ἡ, "winepress," loc.) **τοῦ θυμοῦ** (θυμός, -οῦ, ὁ, "strong passion, anger," content) **τοῦ θεοῦ** (subj. gen.) **τὸν μέγαν** (attrib. which does not match θεοῦ in case or ληνὸν in gender; proximity suggests that it modifies θεοῦ but the case connection would favor ληνὸν, "the great winepress"; Beale suggests the incongruous gender points to an allusion to Isa 63:2 [Beale 779–80]).

Use of the OT: Joel 4:13 LXX (3:13 EVV) describes God's judgment of the nations as both harvesting with a sickle and treading the winepress: ἐξαποστείλατε δρέπανα, ὅτι παρέστηκεν τρύγητος, εἰσπορεύεσθε πατεῖτε, διότι πλήρης ἡ ληνός, ὑπερεκχεῖται τὰ ὑπολήνια, ὅτι πεπλήθυνται τὰ κακὰ αὐτῶν. This could suggest both a grain and a grape harvest as parallel images of judgment, but the LXX translates קָצִיר (harvest) with τρύγητος (vintage), which could suggest that only a vintage is in view in Joel 4:13 LXX.

This allusion to Joel 4:13 is part of a number of allusions in Revelation to Joel 3:3–4:21 LXX (2:30–3:21 EVV), which describes the judgment of the nations leading to the restoration of Jerusalem.

The day of the Lord would be accompanied by the diminishment of cosmic light.	Rev 6:12, 17
Joel 3:4 (2:31 EVV): ὁ ἥλιος μεταστραφήσεται εἰς σκότος καὶ ἡ σελήνη εἰς αἷμα πρὶν ἐλθεῖν ἡμέραν κυρίου τὴν μεγάλην	
Joel 4:15 (3:15 EVV): ὁ ἥλιος καὶ ἡ σελήνη συσκοτάσουσιν, καὶ οἱ ἀστέρες δύσουσιν φέγγος αὐτῶν	
Joel 4:16 (3:16 EVV): καὶ σεισθήσεται ὁ οὐρανὸς καὶ ἡ γῆ	
Joel 4:14 (3:14 EVV): ἐγγὺς ἡμέρα κυρίου	

God will gather the nations and enter into judgment with them. Joel 4:2 (3:2 EVV): *συνάξω πάντα τὰ ἔθνη . . . διακριθήσομαι πρὸς αὐτοὺς*	Rev 16:14, 16; 19:19; 20:8
This judgment will lead to God dwelling in Zion, a restoration of Jerusalem in which it will be holy. Joel 4:17 (3:17 EVV): *ὁ κατασκηνῶν ἐν Σιων ἐν ὄρει ἁγίῳ μου, καὶ ἔσται Ιερουσαλημ πόλις ἁγία*	Rev 21:3, 10
Strangers will not pass through restored Jerusalem. Joel 4:17 (3:17 EVV): *καὶ ἀλλογενεῖς οὐ διελεύσονται δι᾽ αὐτῆς οὐκέτι*	Rev 21:27; 22:15
A spring of water that will come out of the house of the Lord to water the land. Joel 4:18 (3:18 EVV): *καὶ πηγὴ ἐξ οἴκου κυρίου ἐξελεύσεται καὶ ποτιεῖ τὸν χειμάρρουν τῶν σχοίνων*	Rev 7:17; 21:6
God will judge the nations because they shed innocent blood. Joel 4:19 (3:19 EVV): *ἐξέχεαν αἷμα δίκαιον ἐν τῇ γῇ*	Rev 16:6; 17:6; 18:24
God will avenge their blood. Joel 4:21 (3:21 EVV): *καὶ ἐκδικήσω τὸ αἷμα αὐτῶν καὶ οὐ μὴ ἀθῳώσω*	Rev 6:10; 19:2

The book of Joel ends similarly to the final vision of Revelation with a prophecy that God would dwell in Zion (Joel 4:21: *κύριος κατασκηνώσει ἐν Σιων*). As in Revelation, Joel blends battle imagery with judicial action when describing God's judgment of the nations (*πόλεμος* [4:9]; *συνάγω* [4:11]; *καθιῶ τοῦ διακρῖναι πάντα τὰ ἔθνη κυκλόθεν* [4:12]; *δίκη* [4:14]).

This network of allusions throughout the different visions in Revelation to Joel 3:3–4:21 LXX suggests that the vision of judgment in Rev 14:17–20 is parallel in meaning to the day of the Lord in the sixth seal, the gathering of the nations in the sixth bowl judgment, the judgment of Babylon, the trampling of the vintage at Jesus's return, and the gathering of the nations for battle after the millennium, because John alludes in all of these visions within Revelation to this prophetic oracle in Joel.

14:20 καὶ ἐπατήθη (3rd sg. aor. pass. ind. of *πατέω*) **ἡ ληνὸς** (*ληνός, -οῦ, ἡ*, "winepress," subj. nom.) **ἔξωθεν** (improper prep., "from outside") **τῆς πόλεως** (loc.) **καὶ ἐξῆλθεν** (3rd sg. aor. act. ind. of *ἐξέρχομαι*) **αἷμα** (subj. nom.) **ἐκ τῆς ληνοῦ** (source) **ἄχρι τῶν χαλινῶν** (*χαλινός, -οῦ, ὁ*, "bridle," extent) **τῶν ἵππων** (*ἵππος, -ου, ὁ*, "horse," poss.) **ἀπὸ σταδίων** (*στάδιον, -ου, τό*, a measurement of distance of about 192 meters or one-eighth of a mile [BDAG 940b], separation) **χιλίων** ("thousand," attrib.) **ἑξακοσίων** ("six hundred," attrib., a few mss read 1,606, 1,200, or 1,500 stadia [Metzger 679]).

One thousand and six hundred stadia would literally be about two hundred miles but the distance likely indicates the unimaginably vast effects of this judgment. The imagery of treading the winepress of the wrath of God is directly paralleled in the description of Jesus's coming in 19:15 (αὐτὸς πατεῖ τὴν ληνὸν τοῦ οἴνου τοῦ θυμοῦ τῆς ὀργῆς τοῦ θεοῦ τοῦ παντοκράτορος), which suggests that the grape harvest of 14:17–20 is also a visionary description of the judgment that will accompany Jesus's return.

Use of the OT: For Joel 4:13 LXX (3:13 EVV), see 14:19. Lamentations 1:15 laments God's judgment of Jerusalem: ληνὸν ἐπάτησεν κύριος παρθένῳ θυγατρὶ Ιουδα. The image of trampling the winepress is also central in Isa 63:3 (see 19:13).

HOMILETICAL SUGGESTIONS

Chapter 14 provides visions of final victory (14:1–5), exhortations to respond to the gospel and overcome the beasts (14:6–13), and visions of final salvation and judgment (14:14–20).

What You Need to Know to Overcome (14:1–20)

1. God's sealed people will be victorious through suffering and death (14:1–5).
2. Final victory is worth present suffering (14:6–13).
3. Jesus's coming will bring full and final salvation and judgment (14:14–20).

E. THE SEVEN BOWL JUDGMENTS (15:1–16:21)

Chapters 15 and 16 conclude the three (four with thunders) series of seven judgment cycles. The introduction to the bowl judgments in 15:1–8 utilizes a similar interlocking structure to 8:1–5, wherein John introduces the seven angels with seven bowls in 15:1 but then uses 15:2–4 to conclude the prior topic of those who overcame the beast before returning to the seven bowls in 15:5. In 8:2 the seven trumpet judgments are introduced, but 8:3–5 concludes the seventh seal judgment before returning to the seven trumpets in 8:6. This suggests a literary connection between the sets of seven, but it does not seem to favor telescoping over recapitulation or chronological progression.

1. Introduction of Seven Bowls (15:1)

15:1 Καὶ εἶδον (1st sg. aor. act. ind. of ὁράω; καὶ εἶδον introduces a new vision, scene, figure, or activity [Aune[a] 338]) **ἄλλο** (attrib.) **σημεῖον** (dir. obj.) **ἐν τῷ οὐρανῷ** (loc.) **μέγα** (attrib. modifying σημεῖον) **καὶ θαυμαστόν** (θαυμαστός, -ή, -όν, "marvelous," coord. attrib.), **ἀγγέλους** (appos. to σημεῖον) **ἑπτὰ** ("seven," attrib.) **ἔχοντας** (acc. pl. masc. of pres. act. ptc. of ἔχω, attrib.) **πληγὰς** (πληγή, -ῆς, ἡ, "plague," dir. obj.) **ἑπτὰ** (attrib.) **τὰς ἐσχάτας** (ἔσχατος, -η, -ον, "last," attrib.), **ὅτι** (causal) **ἐν αὐταῖς** (means) **ἐτελέσθη** (3rd sg. aor. pass. ind. of τελέω, proleptic) **ὁ θυμὸς** (θυμός, -οῦ, ὁ, "strong passion, anger," subj. nom.) **τοῦ θεοῦ** (subj. gen.).

On πληγή in Revelation to possibly describe judgments poured out throughout history see 9:18; the description of them here as "the last" would indicate that the seven bowls represent the final such judgments in history before the second coming.

Use of the OT: God warns the Hebrew people in Lev 26:21 that he will add to them seven plagues for/according to their sins (προσθήσω ὑμῖν πληγὰς ἑπτὰ κατὰ τὰς ἁμαρτίας ὑμῶν).

---

2. The Song of Moses and the Lamb (15:2–4)

The vision in 15:2–4 parallels other visions in Revelation of God's people in victory and rest (6:9–11; 7:9–17; 14:1–5, 13; 15:2–4; possibly 20:4–6; cf. 19:1–9). These parallel visions do not provide identical details but generally describe the intermediate state of believers between death and resurrection who are conscious and actively praying, resting, or worshiping in the divine throne room.

15:2 Καὶ εἶδον (1st sg. aor. act. ind. of ὁράω; καὶ εἶδον introduces a new vision, scene, figure, or activity [Aune[a] 338]) **ὡς** (the comp. cl. functions as dir. obj.) **θάλασσαν ὑαλίνην** (ὑάλινος, -η, -ον, "made of glass," attrib.) **μεμιγμένην** (acc. sg. fem. of pf. pass. ptc. of μίγνυμι, "mix," attrib.) **πυρὶ** (association) **καὶ τοὺς νικῶντας** (acc. pl. masc. of pres. act. ptc. of νικάω, "overcome, conquer," subst., dir. obj. coordinated with the comp. cl. as the obj. of John's seeing) **ἐκ τοῦ θηρίου** (θηρίον, -ου, τό, "animal, beast," this and the following two gens. are separation, "from," or subord., "over" [BDAG 296b suggests this is a possible Latinism]) **καὶ ἐκ τῆς εἰκόνος** (εἰκών, -όνος, ἡ, "image") **αὐτοῦ** (obj. gen.) **καὶ ἐκ τοῦ ἀριθμοῦ** (ἀριθμός, -οῦ, ὁ, "number") **τοῦ ὀνόματος** (appos.) **αὐτοῦ** (poss.) **ἑστῶτας** (acc. pl. masc. of pf. act. ptc. of ἵστημι, compl. of an obj.-compl. double acc. construction) **ἐπὶ** (both "on" or "beside" are possible; the sea seems to indicate the solid floor of the divine throne room through which events on earth could be viewed) **τὴν θάλασσαν** (loc.) **τὴν ὑαλίνην** (attrib.) **ἔχοντας** (acc. pl. masc. of pres. act. ptc. of ἔχω, manner) **κιθάρας** (κιθάρα, -ας, ἡ, "lyre," dir. obj.) **τοῦ θεοῦ** (source).

On overcoming as a primary image for both the necessary human response and the final result of salvation see 2:5, 7; 3:5. Here, God's people are pictured as overcoming the beast in contrast to how the vision in 13:7 showed the beast overcoming God's people. God's people overcome by being overcome—by being faithful to the point of death (12:11).

Use of the OT: A stream of fire comes out from before the throne of fiery flames in Dan 7:9–10 (ὁ θρόνος ὡσεὶ φλὸξ πυρός, καὶ ἐξεπορεύετο κατὰ πρόσωπον αὐτοῦ ποταμὸς πυρός).

15:3 καὶ ᾄδουσιν (3rd pl. pres. act. ind. ᾄδω, "sing," narrative pres.) **τὴν ᾠδὴν** (ᾠδή, -ῆς, ἡ, "song," cognate dir. obj.) **Μωϋσέως** ("Moses," subj. gen.) **τοῦ δούλου** (appos.) **τοῦ θεοῦ** (poss.) **καὶ** (epex., it is one song and not two different songs) **τὴν ᾠδὴν** (coord. dir. obj.) **τοῦ ἀρνίου** (ἀρνίον, -ου, τό, "lamb," prob. obj. gen., "song about the lamb") **λέγοντες** (manner), **Μεγάλα** (pred. adj. of verbless cl.) **καὶ θαυμαστὰ** (θαυμαστός, -ή, -όν, "marvelous," coord. pred. adj.) **τὰ ἔργα** (subj. nom. of verbless cl.) **σου** (subj. gen.), **κύριε** (voc.) **ὁ θεὸς** (appos., nom. of address, the switch from the voc. to the nom. is common in the LXX and classical Greek) **ὁ παντοκράτωρ** (παντοκράτωρ, -ορος, ὁ, "almighty," appos., nom. of address)· **δίκαιαι** (pred. adj. of verbless cl.) **καὶ ἀληθιναὶ** (ἀληθινός, -ή, -όν, "true," coord. pred. adj.) **αἱ ὁδοί** (subj. nom. of verbless cl.) **σου** (poss.), **ὁ βασιλεὺς** (nom. of address) **τῶν ἐθνῶν** (subord., the external evidence seems balanced between ἐθνῶν [$\aleph^1$ A P 046 051 and most minuscules] and αἰώνων [$\mathfrak{P}^{47}$ ℵ* C 94 469 1006 1611 1841 2040 2065 2073[mg] 2076 2254 2258 2344[vid] 2432] while the context perhaps better supports ἐθνῶν; the reading of ἁγίων in the TR has very little Greek ms support [Metzger 679–80])

God is described elsewhere in Revelation as the Lord God Almighty (1:8; 4:8; 11:17; 16:7; 19:6; 21:22; cf. 16:14; 19:15). The justness and truth of God's actions in judgment are proclaimed throughout Revelation (16:5–7; 19:2); God's judgments are not vindictive or arbitrary but are the perfect expression of divine justice against evil (11:18).

Use of the OT: The song of Moses and the lamb draws from many songs of worship and praise in the OT. Exodus 15:1 describes how Moses and the sons of Israel sang a song to God (ᾖσεν Μωυσῆς καὶ οἱ υἱοὶ Ισραηλ τὴν ᾠδὴν ταύτην τῷ θεῷ). The song praises God for being marvelous in glories, doing wonders (Exod 15:11: θαυμαστὸς ἐν δόξαις, ποιῶν τέρατα). The Song of Moses in Deuteronomy includes the expression θεός, ἀληθινὰ τὰ ἔργα αὐτοῦ, καὶ πᾶσαι αἱ ὁδοὶ αὐτοῦ κρίσεις, θεὸς πιστός, καὶ οὐκ ἔστιν ἀδικία, δίκαιος καὶ ὅσιος κύριος (Deut 32:4). Psalm 144:17 LXX (145:17 EVV) proclaims δίκαιος κύριος ἐν πάσαις ταῖς ὁδοῖς αὐτοῦ καὶ ὅσιος ἐν πᾶσιν τοῖς ἔργοις αὐτοῦ. Psalm 91:6 LXX (92:5 EVV) declares how God's works were magnified/made great (ὡς ἐμεγαλύνθη τὰ ἔργα σου) while Ps 110:2 LXX (111:2 EVV) proclaims μεγάλα τὰ ἔργα κυρίου. The description of God as the Lord God Almighty (κύριος ὁ θεὸς ὁ παντοκράτωρ) is found in Amos 3:13; 4:13.

15:4 τίς (interr. pron., subj. nom.) **οὐ μὴ** (emph. neg.) **φοβηθῇ** (3rd sg. aor. pass. subjunc. of φοβέω, pass. as mid.), **κύριε** (voc.), **καὶ δοξάσει** (3rd sg. fut. act. ind. of δοξάζω, fut. for subjunc.) **τὸ ὄνομά** (dir. obj.) **σου** (poss.); **ὅτι** (causal) **μόνος** (attrib. adj.) **ὅσιος** (ὅσιος, -ία, -ον, "holy," pred. adj. of verbless cl., "*you are* the only holy one"), **ὅτι** (causal, coord. with the prior ὅτι cl.) **πάντα** (attrib.) **τὰ ἔθνη** (subj. nom.) **ἥξουσιν** (3rd pl. fut. act. ind. of ἥκω, "come") **καὶ προσκυνήσουσιν** (3rd pl. fut. act. ind. of προσκυνέω) **ἐνώπιόν σου** (loc.), **ὅτι** (causal, likely coord. with the prior two ὅτι cls.) **τὰ δικαιώματά** (δικαίωμα, -ατος, τό, "righteous deed," subj. nom.) **σου** (subj. gen.) **ἐφανερώθησαν** (3rd pl. aor. pass. ind. of φανερόω, "reveal").

The rhetorical question serves as a counterpart to the eternal gospel proclaimed in 14:7; the proper response of humanity to God is fear and worship.

Use of the OT: Jeremiah 10:6–7 is missing in the LXX but asks the rhetorical question, "Who should not fear you, King of the nations?" (Jer 10:7; CSB). Psalm 85:9–10 LXX (86:9 EVV) states that all the nations, as many as you made, will come and will worship before you, Lord and will glorify your name because you are great and doing marvelous things, you are the only great God (πάντα τὰ ἔθνη, ὅσα ἐποίησας, ἥξουσιν καὶ προσκυνήσουσιν ἐνώπιόν σου, κύριε, καὶ δοξάσουσιν τὸ ὄνομά σου, ὅτι μέγας εἶ σὺ καὶ ποιῶν θαυμάσια, σὺ εἶ ὁ θεὸς μόνος ὁ μέγας). In Mal 1:11 God declares that his name has been glorified among the nations (τὸ ὄνομά μου δεδόξασται ἐν τοῖς ἔθνεσιν). Isaiah 2:2 prophesies that in the latter days all the nations will come to the mountain of the Lord (καὶ ἥξουσιν ἐπ' αὐτὸ πάντα τὰ ἔθνη). Isaiah 60:3 prophesies that nations and kings will come to the light of restored Israel (καὶ πορεύσονται βασιλεῖς τῷ φωτί σου καὶ ἔθνη τῇ λαμπρότητί σου). Near the conclusion of the book, Isaiah prophesies that all flesh will come to worship before God in Jerusalem (66:23: ἥξει πᾶσα σὰρξ ἐνώπιόν μου προσκυνῆσαι ἐν Ιερουσαλημ). Jeremiah likewise prophesies that the nations will come from the ends of the earth in repentance in the restoration of Israel (16:19: πρὸς σὲ ἔθνη ἥξουσιν ἀπ' ἐσχάτου τῆς γῆς). The song of the overcomers in Rev 15:4 celebrates this theme from throughout the Hebrew prophets of the nations turning to God in worship.

---

3. The Seven Bowls (15:5–16:21)

a. Preparation for the Seven Bowls (15:5–8)

15:5 Καὶ μετὰ ταῦτα (temp., subst., "after these things") **εἶδον** (1st sg. aor. act. ind. of ὁράω, καὶ εἶδον introduces a new vision, scene, figure, or activity [Aune[a] 338]), **καὶ ἠνοίγη** (3rd sg. aor. pass. ind. of ἀνοίγω) **ὁ ναὸς** (ναός, -οῦ, ὁ, "temple," subj. nom.) **τῆς σκηνῆς** (σκηνή, -ῆς, ἡ, "tent," appos., "the temple, that is, the tent") **τοῦ μαρτυρίου** (descriptive gen.) **ἐν τῷ οὐρανῷ** (loc.),

The seventh trumpet concluded with the temple being opened (11:19).

Use of OT: The "tent of meeting/testimony" (σκηνή τοῦ μαρτυρίου) is described throughout the Pentateuch (see Exod 27:21; 37:19 LXX [38:21 EVV]; 40:34; Num 1:50; cf. Acts 7:44).

15:6 καὶ ἐξῆλθον (3rd pl. aor. act. ind. of ἐξέρχομαι) **οἱ** (anaphoric to 15:1) **ἑπτὰ** ("seven," attrib.) **ἄγγελοι** (subj. nom.) **[οἱ] ἔχοντες** (nom. pl. masc. of pres. act. ptc. of ἔχω, attrib.) **τὰς** (anaphoric to 15:1) **ἑπτὰ** (attrib.) **πληγὰς** (πληγή, -ῆς, ἡ, "plague, wound," dir. obj.) **ἐκ τοῦ ναοῦ** (ναός, -οῦ, ὁ, "temple," source or separation) **ἐνδεδυμένοι** (nom. pl. masc. of pf. mid. ptc. of ἐνδύω, "dress, clothe," manner) **λίνον** (λίνον, -ου, τό, "linen," dir. obj., several important mss read λίθον ["stone," A C 2053 vg *al*] perhaps with reference to Ezek 28:13, but λίθον, unlike λίνον, does not make sense with the adj. καθαρὸν [Metzger 680]) **καθαρὸν** (καθαρός, -ά, -όν, "pure," attrib.) **λαμπρὸν** (λαμπρός, -ά, -όν, "bright," attrib.) **καὶ περιεζωσμένοι** (nom. pl. masc. of pf. mid. ptc. of περιζώννυμι, "gird, tie around," coord. manner) **περὶ τὰ στήθη** (στῆθος, -ους, τό, "chest," loc.) **ζώνας** (ζώνη, -ης, ἡ, "belt, sash," dir. obj.) **χρυσᾶς** (χρυσοῦς, -ῆ, -οῦν, "golden," attrib.).

Use of the OT: On the seven plagues, see Rev 15:1 on Lev 26:21.

15:7 καὶ ἓν (subj. nom.) **ἐκ τῶν** (anaphoric to 4:6) **τεσσάρων** ("four," attrib.) **ζῴων** (ζῷον, -ου, τό, "animal, living thing," part. gen.) **ἔδωκεν** (3rd sg. aor. act. ind. of δίδωμι) **τοῖς** (anaphoric to 15:1) **ἑπτὰ** ("seven," attrib.) **ἀγγέλοις** (indir. obj.) **ἑπτὰ** (attrib.) **φιάλας** (φιάλη, -ης, ἡ, "bowl," dir. obj.) **χρυσᾶς** (χρυσοῦς, -ῆ, -οῦν, "golden," attrib.) **γεμούσας** (acc. pl. fem. of pres. act. ptc. of γέμω, "be full," attrib.) **τοῦ θυμοῦ** (θυμός, -οῦ, ὁ, "strong passion, anger," gen. of content) **τοῦ θεοῦ** (subj. gen.) **τοῦ ζῶντος** (gen. sg. masc. of pres. act. ptc. of ζάω, attrib.) **εἰς τοὺς αἰῶνας** (measure) **τῶν αἰώνων** (emph. repetition of αἰών).

Although using different lexemes, the ἑπτὰ φιάλας seem to connect conceptually with the ποτήριον in 14:10 (τῷ ποτηρίῳ τῆς ὀργῆς αὐτοῦ) and 16:19 (τὸ ποτήριον τοῦ οἴνου τοῦ θυμοῦ τῆς ὀργῆς αὐτοῦ).

Use of the OT: On the cup of wrath, see 14:10.

15:8 καὶ ἐγεμίσθη (3rd sg. aor. pass. ind. of γεμίζω, "fill") **ὁ ναὸς** (ναός, -οῦ, ὁ, "temple," subj. nom.) **καπνοῦ** (καπνός, -οῦ, ὁ, "smoke," gen. of content) **ἐκ τῆς δόξης** (source) **τοῦ θεοῦ** (poss.) **καὶ ἐκ τῆς δυνάμεως** (coord. source) **αὐτοῦ** (subj. gen.), **καὶ οὐδεὶς** (subj. nom.) **ἐδύνατο** (3rd sg. impf. mid. ind. of δύναμαι) **εἰσελθεῖν** (aor. act. inf. of εἰσέρχομαι, compl. inf.) **εἰς τὸν ναὸν** (loc.) **ἄχρι** (temp. subord. conj. of extent, "until") **τελεσθῶσιν** (3rd pl. aor. pass. subjunc. of τελέω) **αἱ** (anaphoric to 15:1) **ἑπτὰ** ("seven," attrib.) **πληγαὶ** (πληγή, -ῆς, ἡ, "plague," subj. nom.) **τῶν** (anaphoric to 15:1) **ἑπτὰ** (attrib.) **ἀγγέλων** (source or poss.).

Use of the OT: The book of Exodus concludes in 40:34–35 with an account of the cloud covering the tent of meeting (ἐκάλυψεν ἡ νεφέλη τὴν σκηνὴν τοῦ μαρτυρίου) and the glory of the Lord filling the tabernacle (καὶ δόξης κυρίου ἐπλήσθη ἡ σκηνή) so that Moses was not able to enter because of the cloud and the glory (καὶ οὐκ ἠδυνάσθη Μωυσῆς εἰσελθεῖν εἰς τὴν σκηνὴν τοῦ μαρτυρίου). In Isa 6:4 the temple is filled with smoke (καὶ ὁ οἶκος ἐπλήσθη καπνοῦ) after the seraphim proclaim that all the earth is full (πλήρης) of God's glory (Isa 6:3). When the ark is brought to the temple in 3 Kgdms 8:10–11 (1 Kgs 8:10–11 EVV) a cloud fills the house (ἡ νεφέλη ἔπλησεν τὸν οἶκον [3 Kgdms 8:10]) so that the priests are unable to minister because of the glory of the Lord filling the house (καὶ οὐκ ἠδύναντο οἱ ἱερεῖς στῆναι λειτουργεῖν ἀπὸ προσώπου τῆς νεφέλης, ὅτι ἔπλησεν δόξα κυρίου τὸν οἶκον [3 Kgdms 8:11]; cf. 2 Chr 5:13–14). Ezekiel sees a vision of the future temple filled by the glory of the Lord (44:4: πλήρης δόξης ὁ οἶκος κυρίου). The smoke in Rev 15:8 prevents any other heavenly activity until God's judgments are completed.

---

b. The First Bowl (16:1–2)

Unlike the seven seals and seven trumpets, there is no lengthy break between the sixth and seventh bowl judgments. Instead, a few brief pauses are used to reflect on the justice of the judgments or on the refusal of those who oppose God to repent. The seven bowl judgments are modeled on the Exodus plagues and five have direct parallels with the trumpet judgments. The bowl judgments involve intensification over prior judgments.

Trumpets	Bowls
2nd: one-third of the sea turned to blood and one-third of the creatures in it die.	2nd: Sea turned to blood and all the creatures in it die.
3rd: one-third of the fresh water is embittered.	3rd: fresh water turned to blood.
4th: one-third of light darkened.	5th: darkness on earth.
6th: troops gathered at the Euphrates.	6th: kings and armies come from across the Euphrates.
7th: lighting, earthquake, and hail.	7th: lightning, earthquake, and hail.

16:1 Καὶ ἤκουσα (1st sg. aor. act. ind. of ἀκούω) **μεγάλης** (attrib.) **φωνῆς** (gen. dir. obj.) **ἐκ τοῦ ναοῦ** (ναός, -οῦ, ὁ, "temple," source, the prep. phrase is missing in 046 and in about ninety minuscules and replaced by ἐκ τοῦ οὐρανοῦ in a handful of mss [Metzger 680]) **λεγούσης** (gen. sg. fem. of pres. act. ptc. of λέγω, compl. of an obj.-compl. double gen. construction) **τοῖς** (anaphoric to 15:1) **ἑπτὰ** ("seven," attrib.) **ἀγγέλοις** (indir. obj.), **Ὑπάγετε** (2nd pl. pres. act. impv. of ὑπάγω) **καὶ ἐκχέετε** (2nd pl. pres. act. impv. of ἐκχέω, "pour out") **τὰς** (anaphoric to 15:7) **ἑπτὰ** (attrib.) **φιάλας** (φιάλη, -ης, ἡ, "bowl," dir. obj.) **τοῦ θυμοῦ** (θυμός, -οῦ, ὁ, "strong passion, anger," gen. of content) **τοῦ θεοῦ** (subj. gen.) **εἰς τὴν γῆν** (loc.).

Use of the OT: Regarding the voice from the temple announcing judgment, see Isa 66:6 (φωνὴ κραυγῆς ἐκ πόλεως, φωνὴ ἐκ ναοῦ, φωνὴ κυρίου ἀνταποδιδόντος ἀνταπόδοσιν τοῖς ἀντικειμένοις). On the pouring out of wrath (the combination of ἐκχέω and θυμός), see Ps 68:25 LXX (69:24 EVV); Zeph 3:8; Jer 10:25; Lam 2:4; 4:11; Ezek 7:5; 9:8; 14:19; 20:8, 13, 21; 22:22, 31; 30:15; 36:18; Sir 36:6; 39:28 (There is a notable concentration of this idiom in Ezekiel).

16:2 Καὶ ἀπῆλθεν (3rd sg. aor. act. ind. of ἀπέρχομαι) **ὁ πρῶτος** (subst., subj. nom.) **καὶ ἐξέχεεν** (3rd sg. aor. act. ind. of ἐκχέω, "pour out") **τὴν φιάλην** (φιάλη, -ης, ἡ, "bowl," dir. obj.) **αὐτοῦ** (poss.) **εἰς τὴν γῆν** (loc.), **καὶ ἐγένετο** (3rd sg. aor. mid. ind. of γίνομαι) **ἕλκος** (ἕλκος, -ους, τό, "sore, abscess, ulcer" [BDAG 317d], subj. nom., collective sg. [Math 210]) **κακὸν** (κακός, -ή, -όν, "bad, evil," attrib.) **καὶ πονηρὸν** (coord. attrib.) **ἐπὶ**

τοὺς ἀνθρώπους (loc.) **τοὺς ἔχοντας** (acc. pl. masc. of pres. act. ptc. of ἔχω, attrib.) **τὸ χάραγμα** (χάραγμα, -ατος, τό, "mark," dir. obj.) **τοῦ θηρίου** (θηρίον, -ου, τό, "beast," poss.) **καὶ** (epex.) **τοὺς προσκυνοῦντας** (acc. pl. masc. of pres. act. ptc. of προσκυνέω, subst.) **τῇ εἰκόνι** (εἰκών, -όνος, ἡ, "image," dat. dir. obj.) **αὐτοῦ** (obj. gen.).

The bowl judgments are explicitly directed against those who have the beast's mark and worship the beast's image.

Use of the OT: Exodus 9:10 describes the plague of boils in the sixth plague against Egypt (καὶ ἐγένετο ἕλκη). The curses for covenant faithlessness in Deut 28:35 include the warning that the Lord will strike with wicked boils (πατάξαι σε κύριος ἐν ἕλκει πονηρῷ).

---

c. The Second Bowl (16:3)

16:3 Καὶ ὁ δεύτερος ("second," subst., subj. nom.) **ἐξέχεεν** (3rd sg. aor. act. ind. of ἐκχέω, "pour out") **τὴν φιάλην** (φιάλη, -ης, ἡ, "bowl," dir. obj.) **αὐτοῦ** (poss.) **εἰς τὴν θάλασσαν** (loc.), **καὶ ἐγένετο** (3rd sg. aor. mid. ind. of γίνομαι) **αἷμα** (pred. nom., "it became blood," or subj. nom., "blood happened/became") **ὡς** (comp.) **νεκροῦ** (subst., source), **καὶ πᾶσα** (attrib.) **ψυχὴ** (subj. nom.) **ζωῆς** (attrib. gen., "living soul") **ἀπέθανεν** (3rd sg. aor. act. ind. of ἀποθνῄσκω) **τὰ** (substantivizer, appos. to ψυχή) **ἐν τῇ θαλάσσῃ** (loc.).

Use of the OT: Exodus 7:17–21 describes the first plague in which Moses strikes the Nile and it turns to blood (7:17: καὶ μεταβαλεῖ εἰς αἷμα), with the result that the fish in the Nile die (7:18: καὶ οἱ ἰχθύες οἱ ἐν τῷ ποταμῷ τελευτήσουσιν). The second bowl in Revelation focuses on the sea, while the first plague in Exodus targets the water in the river (ποταμός), although this is expanded in Exod 7:19 to canals, ponds, and pools.

---

d. The Third Bowl (16:4–7)

16:4 Καὶ ὁ τρίτος ("third," subst., subj. nom.) **ἐξέχεεν** (3rd sg. aor. act. ind. of ἐκχέω, "pour out") **τὴν φιάλην** (φιάλη, -ης, ἡ, "bowl," dir. obj.) **αὐτοῦ** (poss.) **εἰς τοὺς ποταμοὺς** (ποταμός, -οῦ, ὁ, "river," loc.) **καὶ τὰς πηγὰς** (πηγή, -ῆς, ἡ, "spring," coord. loc.) **τῶν ὑδάτων** (gen. of content), **καὶ ἐγένετο** (3rd sg. aor. mid. ind. of γίνομαι, the sg. is used with coord. pl. subjects, this is smoothed over by the pl. ἐγένοντο in 𝔓[47] A 1006 1854 2053 *al* [Metzger 681]) **αἷμα** (pred. nom.).

Use of the OT: See 16:3 on the first plague in Exod 7:17–24. Psalm 77:44 LXX (78:44 EVV) celebrates God's judgment of the Egyptians by recalling how he turned their rivers and rain waters to blood (μετέστρεψεν εἰς αἷμα τοὺς ποταμοὺς αὐτῶν καὶ τὰ ὀμβρήματα αὐτῶν) in order that they could not drink (ὅπως μὴ πίωσιν).

16:5 καὶ ἤκουσα (1st sg. aor. act. ind. of ἀκούω) **τοῦ ἀγγέλου** (gen. dir. obj.) **τῶν ὑδάτων** (subord.) **λέγοντος** (gen. sg. masc. of pres. act. ptc. of λέγω, compl. in obj.-compl. double gen. construction), **Δίκαιος** (pred. adj.) **εἶ** (2nd sg. pres. act. ind. of εἰμί), **ὁ ὢν** (nom. sg. masc. of pres. act. ptc. of εἰμί, see 1:4, subst., appos. to subj. contained in εἶ, "you, the one who is . . . are righteous") **καὶ ὁ** (substantivizer) **ἦν** (3rd sg. impf. act. ind. of εἰμί), **ὁ ὅσιος** (ὅσιος, -ία, -ον, "holy," subst., appos. to ὤν), **ὅτι** (causal) **ταῦτα** (dir. obj.) **ἔκρινας** (2nd sg. aor. act. ind. of κρίνω),

---

Use of the OT: The declaration that "you are righteous" echoes Pss 118:137 LXX (119:137 EVV) (Δίκαιος εἶ, κύριε); 144:17 LXX (145:17 EVV) (δίκαιος κύριος ἐν πάσαις ταῖς ὁδοῖς αὐτοῦ καὶ ὅσιος ἐν πᾶσιν τοῖς ἔργοις αὐτοῦ); and Deut 32:4 (θεὸς πιστός, καὶ οὐκ ἔστιν ἀδικία, δίκαιος καὶ ὅσιος κύριος). On Exod 3:14, see Rev 1:4.

16:6 ὅτι (causal, poss. coord. with the cl. in 16:5 or more prob. connected to [δ]έδωκας and fronted for emph.) **αἷμα** (dir. obj.) **ἁγίων** (poss.) **καὶ προφητῶν** (coord. poss.) **ἐξέχεαν** (3rd pl. aor. act. ind. of ἐκχέω, "pour out") **καὶ αἷμα** (dir. obj.) **αὐτοῖς** (indir. obj.) **[δ]έδωκας** (2nd sg. pf. act. ind. of δίδωμι) **πιεῖν** (aor. act. inf. of πίνω, purpose), **ἄξιοί** (ἄξιος, -ία, -ον, "worthy," pred. adj.) **εἰσιν** (3rd pl. pres. act. ind. of εἰμί).

Use of the OT: Psalm 78:3 LXX (79:3 EVV) laments that the nations have poured out the blood of God's servants like water around Jerusalem (ἐξέχεαν τὸ αἷμα αὐτῶν ὡς ὕδωρ κύκλῳ Ιερουσαλημ). In Isa 49:26, God promises that in Israel's restoration he will make the ones oppressing them eat their own flesh, drink their own blood like new wine, and get drunk (καὶ φάγονται οἱ θλίψαντές σε τὰς σάρκας αὐτῶν καὶ πίονται ὡς οἶνον νέον τὸ αἷμα αὐτῶν καὶ μεθυσθήσονται).

16:7 καὶ ἤκουσα (1st sg. aor. act. ind. of ἀκούω) **τοῦ θυσιαστηρίου** (θυσιαστήριον, -ου, τό, "altar," gen. dir. obj.) **λέγοντος** (gen. sg. masc. of pres. act. ptc. of λέγω, compl. in obj.-compl. double gen. construction), **Ναί** (particle of affirmation) **κύριε** (voc.) **ὁ θεὸς** (nom. of address in appos.; the switch from the voc. to the nom. is common in the LXX and classical Greek) **ὁ παντοκράτωρ** (παντοκράτωρ, -ορος, ὁ, "almighty," nom. of address in appos.), **ἀληθιναὶ** (ἀληθινός, -ή, -όν, "true," pred. adj. of verbless cl.) **καὶ δίκαιαι** (coord. pred. adj.) **αἱ κρίσεις** (subj. nom.) **σου** (subj. gen.).

Revelation 19:2 praises God ὅτι ἀληθιναὶ καὶ δίκαιαι αἱ κρίσεις αὐτοῦ. The overcomers in 15:3 also declare δίκαιαι καὶ ἀληθιναὶ αἱ ὁδοί σου. The reference to the altar, blood, and the attention to the justice of God's judgments intratextually connects the third bowl judgment back to the prayer of the souls under the altar for God to avenge their blood in 6:10.

Use of the OT: On the expression κύριε ὁ θεὸς ὁ παντοκράτωρ, see on 1:8. Psalm 18:10 LXX (19:9 EVV) declares that the judgments of the Lord are true (τὰ κρίματα κυρίου ἀληθινά), while Ps 118:137 LXX (119:137 EVV) states that God's judgment is upright (καὶ εὐθὴς ἡ κρίσις σου). On God being true and righteous see on 15:3. Daniel 3:27 LXX contains a prayer from the midst of the fiery furnace in the middle of a long section missing from the MT: ὅτι δίκαιος εἶ ἐπὶ πᾶσιν, οἷς ἐποίησας ἡμῖν, καὶ πάντα τὰ ἔργα σου ἀληθινά, καὶ αἱ ὁδοί σου εὐθεῖαι, καὶ πᾶσαι αἱ κρίσεις σου ἀληθιναί.

---

e. The Fourth Bowl (16:8–9)

16:8 Καὶ ὁ τέταρτος ("fourth," subst., subj. nom.) **ἐξέχεεν** (3rd sg. aor. act. ind. of ἐκχέω, "pour out") **τὴν φιάλην** (φιάλη, -ης, ἡ, "bowl," dir. obj.) **αὐτοῦ** (poss.) **ἐπὶ τὸν ἥλιον** (ἥλιος, -ου, ὁ, "sun," loc.), **καὶ ἐδόθη** (3rd sg. aor. pass. ind. of δίδωμι) **αὐτῷ** (indir. obj.) **καυματίσαι** (aor. act. inf. of καυματίζω, "burn, scorch," subst. inf. functioning as subj., "to burn was given to it") **τοὺς ἀνθρώπους** (dir. obj.) **ἐν πυρί** (means).
16:9 καὶ ἐκαυματίσθησαν (3rd pl. aor. pass. ind. of καυματίζω, "burn, scorch") **οἱ ἄνθρωποι** (subj. nom.) **καῦμα** (καῦμα, -ατος, τό, "heat," cognate acc., "men were scorched a great scorching heat") **μέγα** (attrib.) **καὶ ἐβλασφήμησαν** (3rd pl. aor. act. ind. of βλασφημέω, "revile, blaspheme") **τὸ ὄνομα** (dir. obj.) **τοῦ θεοῦ** (poss.) **τοῦ ἔχοντος** (gen. sg. masc. of pres. act. ptc. of ἔχω, attrib.) **τὴν ἐξουσίαν** (dir. obj.) **ἐπὶ τὰς πληγὰς** (πληγή, -ῆς, ἡ, "plague," subord.) **ταύτας** (attrib.) **καὶ οὐ μετενόησαν** (3rd pl. aor. act. ind. of μετανοέω, "repent," coord.) **δοῦναι** (aor. act. inf. of δίδωμι, result) **αὐτῷ** (indir. obj.) **δόξαν** (dir. obj.).

The recipients of judgment do not repent in 9:20–21 or 16:11 and even blaspheme God in 16:11, 21. The fourth bowl judgment is the opposite of the promise made regarding those who come out of the great tribulation in 7:16 that neither the sun nor any scorching heat would fall upon them (οὐδὲ μὴ πέσῃ ἐπ᾽ αὐτοὺς ὁ ἥλιος οὐδὲ πᾶν καῦμα).

f. The Fifth Bowl (16:10–11)

16:10 Καὶ ὁ πέμπτος ("fifth," subst., subj. nom.) **ἐξέχεεν** (3rd sg. aor. act. ind. of ἐκχέω, "pour out") **τὴν φιάλην** (φιάλη, -ης, ἡ, "bowl," dir. obj.) **αὐτοῦ** (poss.) **ἐπὶ τὸν θρόνον** (loc.) **τοῦ θηρίου** (θηρίον, -ου, τό, "beast," poss.), **καὶ ἐγένετο** (3rd sg. aor. mid. ind. of γίνομαι) **ἡ βασιλεία** (subj. nom.) **αὐτοῦ** (poss.) **ἐσκοτωμένη** (nom. sg. fem. of pf. mid. ptc. of σκοτόω, "darken," functions as pred. adj. [Math 215] or periph. with γίνομαι instead of the normal εἰμί to highlight becoming instead of being [Fanning 418–19]), **καὶ ἐμασῶντο** (3rd pl. impf. mid. ind. of μασάομαι, "bite, chew") **τὰς γλώσσας** (dir. obj.) **αὐτῶν** (poss.) **ἐκ τοῦ πόνου** (πόνος, -ου, ὁ, "pain," causal),

Pergamum is identified as the location of Satan's throne in 2:13, which is given to the beast by the dragon in 13:2.

Use of the OT: The ninth plague against Egypt in Exod 10:21 brings darkness upon the land (γενηθήτω σκότος ἐπὶ γῆν Αἰγύπτου) that could be felt/touched (ψηλαφητὸν σκότος) although it does not associate this darkness with πόνος. See Rev 6:12 for OT passages that employ the motif of cosmic darkness in the judgment of the day of the Lord.

16:11 καὶ ἐβλασφήμησαν (3rd pl. aor. act. ind. of βλασφημέω, "revile, blaspheme") **τὸν θεὸν** (dir. obj.) **τοῦ οὐρανοῦ** (gen. of subord.) **ἐκ τῶν πόνων** (πόνος, -ου, ὁ, "pain," causal) **αὐτῶν** (poss.) **καὶ ἐκ τῶν ἑλκῶν** (ἕλκος, -ους, τό, "sore, abscess, ulcer" [BDAG 317d], causal, recalling the first bowl in 16:2) **αὐτῶν** (poss.) **καὶ οὐ μετενόησαν** (3rd pl. aor. act. ind. of μετανοέω, "repent") **ἐκ τῶν ἔργων** (separation) **αὐτῶν** (subj. gen.).

Their "works" are elsewhere detailed in the vice lists of 9:20–21; 21:8; 22:15. The blasphemy from human beings opposed to God parallels the blasphemy directed from the beast to God in 13:1, 5–6. For both saints and unbelievers, the followers mirror the attitude and actions of their leader whose name they bear.

g. The Sixth Bowl (16:12–16)

16:12 Καὶ ὁ ἕκτος ("sixth," subst., subj. nom.) **ἐξέχεεν** (3rd sg. aor. act. ind. of ἐκχέω, "pour out") **τὴν φιάλην** (φιάλη, -ης, ἡ, "bowl," dir. obj.) **αὐτοῦ** (poss.) **ἐπὶ τὸν ποταμὸν** (ποταμός, -οῦ, ὁ, "river," loc.) **τὸν μέγαν** (attrib.) **τὸν Εὐφράτην** ("Euphrates," appos. to ποταμὸν), **καὶ ἐξηράνθη** (3rd sg. aor. pass. ind. of ξηραίνω, "become dry") **τὸ ὕδωρ** (subj. nom.) **αὐτοῦ** (poss.), **ἵνα** (purpose) **ἑτοιμασθῇ** (3rd sg. aor. pass. subjunc. of ἑτοιμάζω, "prepare") **ἡ ὁδὸς** (subj. nom.) **τῶν βασιλέων** (advantage, "for") **τῶν** (adjectivizer) **ἀπὸ ἀνατολῆς** (ἀνατολή, ῆς, ἡ, "rising," source) **ἡλίου** (ἥλιος, -ου, ὁ, "sun," subj. gen.).

The Euphrates also featured prominently in the sixth trumpet judgment (9:14).

Use of the OT: Isaiah 11:15 describes the desolation of the sea of Egypt (καὶ ἐρημώσει κύριος τὴν θάλασσαν Αἰγύπτου) so that God's people could return to the land with sandals (i.e., on foot). Isaiah 44:27 proclaims God's ability to dry up the rivers to enable his people to return from exile (ὁ λέγων τῇ ἀβύσσῳ Ἐρημωθήσῃ, καὶ τοὺς ποταμούς σου ξηρανῶ). The oracle against Babylon in Jer 28:36 LXX (51:36 EVV) declares that God will desolate her sea and dry up her spring (καὶ ἐρημώσω τὴν θάλασσαν αὐτῆς καὶ ξηρανῶ τὴν πηγὴν αὐτῆς). The Euphrates features prominently in the OT as the eastern boundary of the territory promised by God to Israel (Gen 15:18; Exod 23:31; Deut 1:7; 11:24; Josh 1:4) and a natural boundary crossed in times of invasion in the OT (Isa 8:7; 2 Kgs 23:29; 24:7; Jer 46:10) and in the contemporary conflict between Rome and Parthia.

16:13 Καὶ εἶδον (1st sg. aor. act. ind. of ὁράω; καὶ εἶδον introduces a new vision, scene, figure, or activity [Aune[a] 338]) **ἐκ τοῦ στόματος** (source) **τοῦ δράκοντος** (δράκων, -οντος, ὁ, "dragon, serpent," poss.) **καὶ ἐκ τοῦ στόματος** (coord., source) **τοῦ θηρίου** (θηρίον, -ου, τό, "beast," poss.) **καὶ ἐκ τοῦ στόματος** (coord., source) **τοῦ ψευδοπροφήτου** (ψευδοπροφήτης, -ου, ὁ, "false prophet," poss.) **πνεύματα** (dir. obj. of εἶδον) **τρία** ("three," attrib.) **ἀκάθαρτα** (ἀκάθαρτος, -ον, "unclean," attrib.) **ὡς** (comp.) **βάτραχοι** (βάτραχος, -ου, ὁ, "frog")

The combined presence of the dragon, beast, and false prophet is noteworthy. All three evil agents are featured in the sixth bowl judgment as deceiving and gathering human beings to oppose God and his people. The bowl judgments portray this as a single final event culminating in the end (Γέγονεν of 16:17). Later visions separate the beast and false prophet from the dragon in two separate battle visions (19:11–21; 20:7–10); these are either overlapping visionary descriptions of one final event associated with Christ's return (amillennial) or multiple (at least two) final battles separated by 1,000 years (premillennial). The second beast is here described as the false prophet, a designation maintained in subsequent references (19:20; 20:10).

A symbolic interpretation of the bowl judgments is suggested by the three demonic spirits like frogs; the frog plague was literal in the original Exodus narratives but in Revelation they are not literal frogs (Beale 832). John uses the nom. βάτραχοι after the comp. ὡς instead of the usual dat. (βατράχοις). This is likely not a Semitism but rather characteristic of John's elliptical style with comparisons (see 6:1; Moţ 122–23).

16:14 εἰσὶν (3rd pl. pres. act. ind. of εἰμί) **γὰρ** (explanatory) **πνεύματα** (pred. nom., ant. of ἅ) **δαιμονίων** (δαιμόνιον, -ου, τό, "demon," attrib. or epex.) **ποιοῦντα** (nom. pl. neut. of pres. act. ptc. of ποιέω, attrib. modifying πνεύματα) **σημεῖα** (dir. obj.), **ἃ** (subj. nom., neut. pl. with sg. vb.) **ἐκπορεύεται** (3rd sg. pres. mid. ind. of ἐκπορεύομαι) **ἐπὶ τοὺς βασιλεῖς** (loc.) **τῆς οἰκουμένης** (οἰκουμένη, -ης, ἡ, "world," subord.) **ὅλης** (attrib.) **συναγαγεῖν** (aor. act. inf. of συνάγω, purpose) **αὐτοὺς** (dir. obj.) **εἰς τὸν πόλεμον** (πόλεμος, -ου, ὁ, "battle," loc.) **τῆς ἡμέρας** (descriptive) **τῆς μεγάλης** (attrib.) **τοῦ θεοῦ** (poss.) **τοῦ**

παντοκράτορος (παντοκράτωρ, -ορος, ὁ, "almighty," appos., "God, the almighty one," or attrib. gen., "the almighty God").

The kings mentioned here are likely equivalent to the kings from the east in 16:12 and parallel to the ten kings allied with the beast in 17:12–18 and those involved in the final battle of 19:19–21 and possibly 20:7 (depending upon the adoption of an amillennial or premillennial perspective). The great day of God recalls OT prophecies of the day of the Lord and intratextually connects back to the great day of their wrath in the sixth seal (6:17).

Use of the OT: The gathering of the nations for war most closely parallels Zech 14:2 (καὶ ἐπισυνάξω πάντα τὰ ἔθνη ἐπὶ Ιερουσαλημ εἰς πόλεμον). It is important, however, to note that all five uses of συνάγω in Revelation occur in contexts filled with multiple other allusions to Ezekiel 38–39 (Rev 16:14, 16; 19:17, 19; 20:8), and the Gog oracles of Ezekiel also feature the gathering of the nations for war (Ezek 38:4: καὶ συνάξω σε, 7: οἱ συνηγμένοι μετὰ σοῦ, 13: συνήγαγες συναγωγήν σου, 15: συναγωγὴ μεγάλη). See 14:19 on the gathering of the nations for judgment in Joel 4:2 LXX (3:2 EVV) (συνάξω πάντα τὰ ἔθνη . . . διακριθήσομαι πρὸς αὐτούς). The "battle" in Rev 16:14 relates to the great future conflict anticipated in Ezekiel 38–39, Joel 3, and Zechariah 12, 14, among other places.

16:15 Ἰδοὺ (emph. interj.) **ἔρχομαι** (1st sg. pres. mid. ind. of ἔρχομαι) **ὡς** (manner) **κλέπτης** (κλέπτης, -ου, ὁ, "thief"). **μακάριος** (μακάριος, -ία, -ιον, "blessed," pred. adj. of verbless cl.) **ὁ γρηγορῶν** (nom. sg. masc. of pres. act. ptc. of γρηγορέω, "be awake, be alert," subst., subj. nom.) **καὶ τηρῶν** (nom. sg. masc. of pres. act. ptc. of τηρέω, subst., coord. subj. nom.) **τὰ ἱμάτια** (dir. obj.) **αὐτοῦ** (poss.), **ἵνα** (purpose) **μὴ γυμνὸς** (γυμνός, -ή, -όν, "naked," adj. functioning as adv. of manner [Math 218]) **περιπατῇ** (3rd sg. pres. act. subjunc. of περιπατέω) **καὶ βλέπωσιν** (3rd pl. pres. act. subjunc. of βλέπω, the subj. is a generic "they") **τὴν ἀσχημοσύνην** (ἀσχημοσύνη, -ης, ἡ, "shame," dir. obj.) **αὐτοῦ** (poss.).

This abrupt parenthesis pauses the narration of the bowl visions to directly exhort and motivate the hearer to respond to the visions appropriately (cf. 13:10; 14:12). The visions of the future were not given to satisfy intellectual curiosity but to motivate God's people to overcome. Jesus's statement that Ἰδοὺ ἔρχομαι ὡς κλέπτης alludes to Jesus's teaching in the Gospels regarding the Son of Man coming as a thief (Matt 24:43–44; Luke 12:39 –40) and early Christian expectation (1 Thess 5:2, 4; 2 Pet 3:10). The comparison points to the unexpected nature of his coming (see on Rev 3:3). It is not possible to know the exact timing so God's people must always be prepared and must live in constant expectation. This is the third macarism in Revelation.

16:16 καὶ συνήγαγεν (3rd sg. aor. act. ind. of συνάγω, the subj. is the neut. pl. πνεύματα in 16:14) **αὐτοὺς** (dir. obj.) **εἰς τὸν τόπον** (loc.) **τὸν καλούμενον** (acc. sg. masc. of pres. pass. ptc. of καλέω, attrib.) **Ἑβραϊστὶ** ("Hebrew" or "Aramaic," reference) **Ἁρμαγεδών**

("Armageddon," transliteration from Heb., "mountain of Megiddo," dir. obj., the spelling varies widely in the mss: Ἁρμαγεδών, Μαγεδδών, Αρμεγηδων, Ἀρμαγεδῶ, Αρμαγεδον, Αρμαγεδωμ, Μαγεδωδ, Μαγιδων, and Μακεδδων, among others [Metzger 681]).

The problem with taking Ἁρμαγεδών as the mountain of Megiddo is that there is no such mountain; Megiddo was a plain that featured many battles in Israel's history due to its strategic location between Egypt and Syria. It is likely that John has combined the reference to Megiddo from the description of God's victory over hostile nations in Zech 12:11 with the mountains featured in the Gog and Magog oracles in Ezek 38:8–21; 39:2, 4, 17 (Koester 660). The location Armageddon indicates the defeat of those opposed to God (Koester 668). Through the transcription of the Heb. letter *'ayin* for the Greek letter *gamma*, Ἁρμαγεδών could refer to the mountain of assembly mentioned as the place where the king of Babylon sought to exalt himself like the Most High in Isa 14:13 (בְּהַר־מוֹעֵד, see the sources listed below in For Further Study 44 [Armageddon]).

Use of the OT: The Song of Deborah and Barak in Judg 5:19 describes the battle as having taken place by the waters of Megiddo (ἐπὶ ὕδατος Μαγεδδω). Ahaziah died in Megiddo in 4 Kgdms 9:27 (2 Kgs 9:27 EVV) (καὶ ἔφυγεν εἰς Μαγεδδων καὶ ἀπέθανεν ἐκεῖ). Pharaoh Neco killed Josiah at Megiddo in 4 Kgdms 23:29 (2 Kgs 23:29 EVV) (καὶ ἐθανάτωσεν αὐτὸν Νεχαω ἐν Μαγεδδω). The reference to mourning for Hadad-rimmon in the plain of Megiddo in Zech 12:11 likely refers to mourning for Josiah's death.

---

h. The Seventh Bowl (16:17–21)

16:17 Καὶ ὁ ἕβδομος ("seventh," subst., subj. nom.) **ἐξέχεεν** (3rd sg. aor. act. ind. of ἐκχέω, "pour out") **τὴν φιάλην** (φιάλη, -ης, ἡ, "bowl," dir. obj.) **αὐτοῦ** (poss.) **ἐπὶ τὸν ἀέρα** (ἀήρ, -έρος, ὁ, "air," loc.), **καὶ ἐξῆλθεν** (3rd sg. aor. act. ind. of ἐξέρχομαι) **φωνὴ** (subj. nom.) **μεγάλη** (attrib.) **ἐκ τοῦ ναοῦ** (ναός, -οῦ, ὁ, "temple," source) **ἀπὸ τοῦ** (anaphoric to 4:2) **θρόνου** (ἀπό provides the more specific source, א reads ναοῦ τοῦ θεοῦ while various mss add τοῦ οὐρανοῦ and/or τοῦ θεοῦ [Metzger 681]) **λέγουσα** (nom. sg. fem. of pres. act. ptc. of λέγω, manner), **Γέγονεν** (3rd sg. pf. act. ind. of γίνομαι).

The declaration Γέγονεν matches God's declaration in 21:6 (καὶ εἶπέν μοι Γέγοναν). This would suggest that even though the battle is not here narrated, the seventh bowl brings us to the end of the battle and the inauguration of God's new creation. The intervening visions between 16:17 and 20:10 bring us back in time and fill in additional details leading up to the final conflict.

Use of the OT: Isaiah 66:6 describes the sound of the Lord coming from the temple giving recompense to the adversaries (φωνὴ ἐκ ναοῦ, φωνὴ κυρίου ἀνταποδιδόντος ἀνταπόδοσιν τοῖς ἀντικειμένοις).

16:18 καὶ ἐγένοντο (3rd pl. aor. mid. ind. of γίνομαι) **ἀστραπαὶ** (ἀστραπή, -ῆς, ἡ, "lightning," subj. nom.) **καὶ φωναὶ** (coord. subj. nom.) **καὶ βρονταὶ** (βροντή, -ῆς, ἡ, "thunder," coord. subj. nom.) **καὶ σεισμὸς** (σεισμός, -οῦ, ὁ, "earthquake," subj. nom., ant. of οἷος) **ἐγένετο** (3rd sg. aor. mid. ind. of γίνομαι) **μέγας** (attrib.), **οἷος** (correlative pron., "such as") **οὐκ ἐγένετο** (3rd sg. aor. mid. ind. of γίνομαι) **ἀφ' οὗ** (headless rel. pron. indicating temp. extent, "from which/when") **ἄνθρωπος** (subj. nom.) **ἐγένετο** (3rd sg. aor. mid. ind. of γίνομαι) **ἐπὶ τῆς γῆς** (loc.) **τηλικοῦτος** (τηλικοῦτος, -αύτη, -οῦτο, "so great," attrib.) **σεισμὸς** (subj. nom. of verbless cl.) **οὕτως** (adv., "thus, likewise," or indicating high degree, "so") **μέγας** (adj. compl. of οὕτως).

The great eschatological earthquake is described in parallel visions at the sixth and seventh seal judgments (6:12; 8:5), the vindication of the two witnesses (11:13), and the seventh trumpet (11:19). The earthquake described in the seventh bowl judgment is the final and most descriptive reference to the great eschatological earthquake in Revelation.

Use of the OT: On the allusion to the Sinai theophany in Exod 19:16–19, see Rev 4:5. The earthquake imagery in the following passages is similar to the Sinai theophany in Exod 19:18 but is poetically expanded in anticipation of God's future actions (Pss 68:8; 77:17–18; 114:4, 6–7; Isa 64:2; Hab 3:6, 7, 10; cf. 1 En. 1:3–9; As. Mos. 10:1–7). Daniel describes a future tribulation οἵα οὐκ ἐγενήθη ἀφ' οὗ ἐγενήθησαν ἕως τῆς ἡμέρας ἐκείνης (Dan 12:1).

16:19 καὶ ἐγένετο (3rd sg. aor. mid. ind. of γίνομαι) **ἡ πόλις** (subj. nom.) **ἡ μεγάλη** (attrib.) **εἰς** (the prep. phrase functions as pred. compl. of ἐγένετο) **τρία** ("three," attrib.) **μέρη καὶ αἱ πόλεις** (subj. nom.) **τῶν ἐθνῶν** (poss.) **ἔπεσαν** (3rd pl. aor. act. ind. of πίπτω). **καὶ Βαβυλὼν** ("Babylon," subj. nom.) **ἡ μεγάλη** (attrib.) **ἐμνήσθη** (3rd sg. aor. pass. ind. of μιμνήσκομαι, "remember") **ἐνώπιον τοῦ θεοῦ** (loc.) **δοῦναι** (aor. act. inf. of δίδωμι, purpose) **αὐτῇ** (indir. obj.) **τὸ ποτήριον** (ποτήριον, -ου, τό, "cup," dir. obj.) **τοῦ οἴνου** (οἶνος, -ου, ὁ, "wine," content) **τοῦ θυμοῦ** (θυμός, -οῦ, ὁ, "strong passion, anger," appos., "the wine, that is, the fury") **τῆς ὀργῆς** (ὀργή, -ῆς, ἡ, "anger, wrath," syn. gen. for emph., attrib.) **αὐτοῦ** (subj. gen.).

The reference to Babylon prepares the reader for the detailed visions of the judgment of Babylon in 17:1–19:10. The great city consistently points to Babylon in Revelation (17:18; 18:10, 16, 18, 21); in John's visionary world the great city encompasses the world system in opposition to God and has characteristics of Babylon, Rome, Jerusalem, Sodom, and Egypt (Koester 668; Beale 843). These upcoming visions do not advance the narrative but provide details and perspective on what it means that God remembered Babylon in the seventh bowl judgment. The combination of θυμός and ὀργή is redundant but functions as a "superlative of divine indignation" (Moţ 213).

Use of the OT: On the cup of wrath, see 14:10.

16:20 **καὶ πᾶσα** (attrib.) **νῆσος** (νῆσος, -ου, ἡ, "island," subj. nom.) **ἔφυγεν** (3rd sg. aor. act. ind. of φεύγω, "flee") **καὶ ὄρη** (subj. nom.) **οὐχ εὑρέθησαν** (3rd pl. aor. pass. ind. εὑρίσκω).

The cosmic upheaval described in this verse parallels the mountains and islands moving in Rev 6:14 in response to a great earthquake (καὶ πᾶν ὄρος καὶ νῆσος ἐκ τῶν τόπων αὐτῶν ἐκινήθησαν) and the earth and heaven fleeing before the final judgment in 20:11 (οὗ ἀπὸ τοῦ προσώπου ἔφυγεν ἡ γῆ καὶ ὁ οὐρανὸς καὶ τόπος οὐχ εὑρέθη αὐτοῖς). This parallelism in cosmic upheaval supports a cyclical or spiral approach to understanding the chronology of the visions of judgment in Revelation under the assumption that this cosmic upheaval does not happen multiple times but only once at the end.

16:21 **καὶ χάλαζα** (χάλαζα, -ης, ἡ, "hail," subj. nom.) **μεγάλη** (attrib.) **ὡς** (comp.) **ταλαντιαία** (ταλαντιαῖος, -α, -ον, "weight of a talent," about 100 pounds [BDAG 988c]) **καταβαίνει** (3rd sg. pres. act. ind. of καταβαίνω, narrative pres.) **ἐκ τοῦ οὐρανοῦ** (source) **ἐπὶ τοὺς ἀνθρώπους** (loc.), **καὶ ἐβλασφήμησαν** (3rd pl. aor. act. ind. of βλασφημέω, "revile, blaspheme") **οἱ ἄνθρωποι** (subj. nom.) **τὸν θεὸν** (dir. obj.) **ἐκ τῆς πληγῆς** (πληγή, -ῆς, ἡ, "plague," causal) **τῆς χαλάζης**, (appos.), **ὅτι** (causal) **μεγάλη** (pred. adj.) **ἐστὶν** (3rd sg. pres. act. ind. of εἰμί) **ἡ πληγὴ** (subj. nom.) **αὐτῆς** (poss.) **σφόδρα** (adv., "very, extreme," modifying the pred. adj. μεγάλη, "extremely great").

Use of the OT: Exodus 9:24 describes the seventh plague of hail as ἡ δὲ χάλαζα πολλὴ σφόδρα σφόδρα, ἥτις τοιαύτη οὐ γέγονεν ἐν Αἰγύπτῳ ἀφ᾽ οὗ γεγένηται ἐπ᾽ αὐτῆς ἔθνος. The sixth and seventh bowl judgments closely parallel descriptions of the Gog-Magog episode from Ezekiel 38–39. Ezekiel's vision describes a deceptive gathering of global forces to fight against God's people (Ezek 38:2–7, 15). The battle in Ezekiel involves God's use of an earthquake and the demolishment of mountains, hail, and fiery brimstone (Ezek 38:19–22).

FOR FURTHER STUDY

44. Armageddon (16:16)

Kline, M. G. "Har Magedon: The End of the Millennium." *JETS* 39 (1996): 207–22.
Loasby, R. E., "'Har-Magedon' according to the Hebrew in the Setting of the Seven Last Plagues of Revelation 16." *AUSS* 27 (1989): 129–32.

HOMILETICAL SUGGESTIONS

The bowl judgments largely repeat and intensify the scenes of judgment seen with the seals and trumpets. The themes particularly emphasized in the bowl judgments include the need for God's people to persevere (16:15), the justice of God's judgments (16:5–6), and the refusal of the recipients of judgment to repent (16:8, 11).

Responding to God's Judgment (15:1–16:21)

1. We should respond to God's just judgment with worship (15:1–8; 16:5–7).
2. Many will refuse to repent in the face of God's judgments (16:9, 11, 21).
3. We must respond to God's judgment with faithful perseverance (16:15).

IV. In the Spirit in the Wilderness (17:1–21:8)

Babylon's judgment was announced in 14:8, and in the seventh bowl judgment of 16:19 it is said that God remembered Babylon the Great to include her in judgment. Two entire chapters are dedicated to narrating and reflecting on God's judgment of Babylon. Structurally, Babylon is explicitly contrasted with the bride of the Lamb; the contrasting visions are both introduced by one of the seven angels having the seven bowls who move John in the Spirit to a new location to show him a woman (17:1–3 and 21:9–10). These women represent the broader contrasting communities with whom John's hearers must identify; they will either be a part of Babylon and share in her judgment (18:4) or become a part of the bride of the Lamb. Revelation 19:1–9 serves as the hinge of this contrast in which heaven celebrates God's judgment of Babylon (19:1–5) and the marriage of the Lamb (19:6–9).

A. BABYLON THE GREAT (17:1–18:24)

The Babylon visions serve as the structural hinge in John's introduction of the spiritual opponents and his visionary descriptions of their defeat. The visions in Revelation introduce the adversaries of God's people in a certain order and narrates their judgment in reverse order. Death and Hades are introduced in Rev 1:18 and 6:8, the dragon comes in 12:3, the beasts in 13:1, 11 (apart from the brief preview in Rev 11:7), and Babylon the Great in 14:8. The four central adversaries are described together in the sixth and seventh bowl judgments (the dragon, the beast, the false prophet, and Babylon; 16:13, 19). John then narrates the judgment of the main foes in reverse order: Babylon the Great in Revelation 17–18, the beasts in 19:20, the dragon in 20:10, and death and Hades in 20:14. From an amillennial perspective, the actual judgment of these adversaries takes place at Jesus's return and the final judgment, but the defeat of each one is described in its own vision, that is, they are all defeated at the second coming but John receives separate visions for each to provide unique perspectives on the conflict and its conclusion. A premillennial approach highlights the differences in the accounts of the various battles and judgments to argue for distinct battles before and after the millennium.

1. Vision of Babylon and the Beast (17:1–14)

Mathewson observes that 17:1–6 mainly employs ptcs. to describe the woman and the beast while 17:7–18 primarily utilizes pres. and fut. forms to describe what the characters actually do (Math 228).

17:1 Καὶ ἦλθεν (3rd sg. aor. act. ind. of ἔρχομαι) **εἷς** (subj. nom.) **ἐκ τῶν ἑπτὰ** ("seven," attrib.) **ἀγγέλων** (part. gen.) **τῶν ἐχόντων** (gen. pl. masc. of pres. act. ptc. of ἔχω, attrib.) **τὰς ἑπτὰ** (attrib.) **φιάλας** (φιάλη, -ης, ἡ, "bowl," dir. obj.) **καὶ ἐλάλησεν** (3rd sg. aor. act. ind. of λαλέω) **μετ' ἐμοῦ** (association) **λέγων** (nom. sg. masc. of pres. act. ptc. of λέγω, manner), **Δεῦρο** (spatial adv. "here," often used as a command, "*come* here!"), **δείξω** (1st sg. fut. act. ind. of δείκνυμι, "show," Wallace suggests this is a hortatory subjunc., "let me show" [Wallace 465]) **σοι** (indir. obj.) **τὸ κρίμα** (κρίμα, -ατος, τό, "judgment," dir. obj.) **τῆς πόρνης** (πόρνη, -ης, ἡ, "prostitute," obj. gen., ant. of ἧς in 17:2) **τῆς μεγάλης** (attrib., prob. superl. for positive adj., "greatest" [Fanning 436]) **τῆς καθημένης** (gen. sg. fem. of pres. mid. ptc. of κάθημαι, attrib.) **ἐπὶ ὑδάτων** (loc.) **πολλῶν** (attrib.),

The fact that the angel who speaks with John was one from the seven bowl judgments strengthens the connection of Revelation 17–18 with the seventh bowl judgment. The symbolism of many waters is interpreted in 17:15 as peoples, multitudes, nations, and languages.

Use of the OT: Jeremiah describes the inhabitants of Babylon as the ones dwelling by many waters (51:13 EVV; 28:13 LXX: κατασκηνοῦντας ἐφ' ὕδασι πολλοῖς). Isaiah accuses Jerusalem of being a prostitute (1:21: Πῶς ἐγένετο πόρνη πόλις πιστὴ Σιων). This critique is echoed in Jeremiah (3:3: ὄψις πόρνης ἐγένετό σοι) and Ezekiel (see the lengthy sections in Ezek 16 and 23) and also extended to other nations (Tyre in Isa 23:16 [πόρνη ἐπιλελησμένη] and Nineveh in Nah 3:4 [ἀπὸ πλήθους πορνείας. πόρνη καλή] who sells nations in her sexual immorality [ἡ πωλοῦσα ἔθνη ἐν τῇ πορνείᾳ αὐτῆς]). Sexual immorality is regularly used by OT authors to describe idolatry: 2 Kgs 9:22 (significantly associated with Jezebel); 1 Chr 5:25 regarding the half-tribe of Manasseh who committed sexual immorality after the gods of the peoples of the land (ἐπόρνευσαν ὀπίσω θεῶν λαῶν τῆς γῆς); Ps 72:27 LXX (73:27 EVV), which declares God's judgment of those who are sexually unfaithful to him (τὸν πορνεύοντα ἀπὸ σοῦ); Jer 3:6, which explicitly describes idolatrous practices as sexual immorality (ἐπορεύθησαν ἐπὶ πᾶν ὄρος ὑψηλὸν καὶ ὑποκάτω παντὸς ξύλου ἀλσώδους καὶ ἐπόρνευσαν ἐκεῖ).

17:2 μεθ' ἧς (association) **ἐπόρνευσαν** (3rd pl. aor. act. ind. of πορνεύω, "commit sexual immorality") **οἱ βασιλεῖς** (subj. nom.) **τῆς γῆς** (subord.) **καὶ ἐμεθύσθησαν** (3rd pl. aor. pass. ind. of μεθύσκω, "make intoxicated") **οἱ κατοικοῦντες** (nom. pl. masc. of pres. act. ptc. of κατοικέω, "dwell," subst., subj. nom.) **τὴν γῆν** (dir. obj.) **ἐκ τοῦ οἴνου** (οἶνος, -ου, ὁ, "wine," means) **τῆς πορνείας** (πορνεία, -ας, ἡ, "sexual immorality," appos., "the wine, that is, her immorality") **αὐτῆς** (subj. gen.)

The description of the prostitute picks up on the brief oracle concerning Babylon in 14:8. In 14:8 it is stated that she caused all the nations to drink the wine of the passion of her sexual immorality while 18:3 uses the pf. tense to declare that all the nations have drunk the wine of the passion of her sexual immorality. See 3:10 on John's consistent negative view of "the ones dwelling on the earth."

Use of the OT: Isaiah prophesies that Tyre will prostitute herself with the kingdoms of the world (23:17) to provide wages holy to the Lord to supply food and clothing to God's people in their restoration (23:18). The negative connotation of prostitution alongside the positive result likely led the LXX translators to replace the imagery of prostitution with trade (ἐμπόριον). John seems to keep the two ideas connected with prostitution indicating oppressive trade/economic activities (as evident in Rev 18) alongside religious compromise through idolatry (the normal indication of πορνεία in Revelation). Jeremiah 28:7 LXX (51:7 EVV) describes Babylon as a golden cup in the hand of the Lord that made all the earth drunk (ποτήριον χρυσοῦν Βαβυλὼν ἐν χειρὶ κυρίου μεθύσκον πᾶσαν τὴν γῆν). The nations drank from her wine, and because of this they were shaken (ἀπὸ τοῦ οἴνου αὐτῆς ἐπίοσαν ἔθνη, διὰ τοῦτο ἐσαλεύθησαν).

17:3 καὶ ἀπήνεγκέν (3rd sg. aor. act. ind. of ἀποφέρω, "carry away") **με** (dir. obj.) **εἰς ἔρημον** (ἔρημος, -ον, "wilderness, desert," loc.) **ἐν πνεύματι** (loc. or manner, see 1:10). **καὶ εἶδον** (1st sg. aor. act. ind. of ὁράω, καὶ εἶδον introduces a new vision, scene, figure, or activity [Aune[a] 338]) **γυναῖκα** (dir. obj.) **καθημένην** (acc. sg. fem. of pres. mid. ptc. of κάθημαι, compl. in obj.-compl. double acc. construction) **ἐπὶ θηρίον** (θηρίον, -ου, τό, "beast," loc.) **κόκκινον** (κόκκινος, -η, -ον, "red," attrib.), **γέμον[τα]** (acc. pl. neut. of pres. act. ptc. of γέμω, "be full," attrib., poss. pl. which would be incongruous with the sg. θηρίον, but more likely acc. masc. sg. which is incongruous with the neut. θηρίον but consistent with how John elsewhere uses masc. ptcs. to modify the beast and represent it as personal and masc.) **ὀνόματα** (dir. obj. functioning in place of an expected gen. of content which John uses everywhere else except here and 17:4) **βλασφημίας** (βλασφημία, -ας, ἡ, "slander, blasphemy," attrib.), **ἔχων** (nom. sg. masc. of pres. act. ptc. of ἔχω, attrib., the masc. ptc. ἔχων [in A] should be neut. to match θηρίον; it is possible the earliest text had an acc. based on the masc. acc. ἔχοντα in א, P, 2053 and the neut. acc. ἔχον in many minuscules) **κεφαλὰς** (dir. obj.) **ἑπτὰ** ("seven," attrib.) **καὶ κέρατα** (κέρας, -ατος, τό, "horn," coord. dir. obj.) **δέκα** ("ten," attrib.).

The description of the beast as full of blasphemous names and having seven heads and ten horns connects this beast with the beast of 13:1.

17:4 καὶ ἡ (anaphoric to 17:3) **γυνὴ** (subj. nom.) **ἦν** (3rd sg. impf. act. ind. of εἰμί) **περιβεβλημένη** (nom. sg. fem. of pf. pass. ptc. of περιβάλλω, "wrap, clothe," periph.) **πορφυροῦν** (πορφυροῦς, -ᾶ, -οῦν, "purple," subst., dir. obj.) **καὶ κόκκινον** (κόκκινος, -η, -ον, "red," subst., coord. dir. obj.) **καὶ κεχρυσωμένη** (nom. sg. fem. of pf. pass. ptc. of χρυσόω, "make golden," coord. periph.) **χρυσίῳ** (χρυσίον, -ου, τό, "gold," cognate dat., means) **καὶ λίθῳ** (coord. means) **τιμίῳ** (τίμιος, -α, -ον, "valuable," attrib.) **καὶ μαργαρίταις** (μαργαρίτης, -ου, ὁ, "pearl," coord. means), **ἔχουσα** (nom. sg. fem. of pres. act. ptc. of ἔχω, manner) **ποτήριον** (ποτήριον, -ου, τό, "cup," dir. obj.) **χρυσοῦν** (attrib.) **ἐν τῇ χειρὶ** (loc.) **αὐτῆς** (poss.) **γέμον** (acc. sg. neut. of pres. act. ptc. of γέμω, "be full," attrib. modifying ποτήριον) **βδελυγμάτων** (βδέλυγμα, -ατος, τό, "defilement, abomination," content) **καὶ τὰ ἀκάθαρτα** (ἀκάθαρτος, -ον, "unclean," subst. adj., acc. of content or dir. obj., see below) **τῆς πορνείας** (πορνεία, -ας, ἡ, "sexual immorality," source) **αὐτῆς** (subj. gen., some mss read τῆς γῆς instead of αὐτῆς [2030 2053 2062 2329 *Byz*] while א conflates the two with αὐτῆς καὶ τῆς γῆς [Metzger 681–82])

Revelation 18:16 describes the city as being clothed with fine linen, purple, and scarlet, adorned with gold, jewels, and pearls; this description clearly connects the prostitute of 17:4 with the city of Revelation 18. The prostitute's luxurious clothing contrasts with the pure and bright linen of the Lamb's bride, which is the righteous deeds of the saints (19:8).

The use of καί to coordinate two different cases, the gen. βδελυγμάτων and acc. ἀκάθαρτα, is unexpected. Moţ suggests that this irregularity could be explained by γέμω being active in form but pass. in meaning ("be full"), as the act. voice requires an acc. obj. while the pass. meaning would take the gen. (Moţ 155–56). "The literary translation would be 'being full *of* abominations and filled *with* the unclean things of her fornication'" (Moţ 156).

Use of the OT: The lament over the king of Tyre in Ezek 28:13 notes that he was covered with every precious stone (πᾶν λίθον χρηστὸν ἐνδέδεσαι). For Jer 51:7, see Rev 17:2.

17:5 καὶ ἐπὶ τὸ μέτωπον (μέτωπον, -ου, τό, "forehead," loc.) **αὐτῆς** (poss.) **ὄνομα** (subj. nom. of verbless cl.) **γεγραμμένον** (nom. sg. neut. of pf. pass. ptc. of γράφω, attrib.), **μυστήριον** (μυστήριον, -ου, τό, "mystery, secret," appos., likely an introduction to the title and not part of the title), **Βαβυλὼν** ("Babylon," appellation or appos.) **ἡ μεγάλη** (attrib.), **ἡ** (par excellence [Fanning 439]) **μήτηρ** (μήτηρ, -τρός, ἡ, "mother," appos.) **τῶν πορνῶν** (πόρνη, -ης, ἡ, "prostitute," relationship or subord.) **καὶ τῶν βδελυγμάτων** (βδέλυγμα, -ατος, τό, "defilement, abomination," relationship involving personification or subord.) **τῆς γῆς** (loc. or attrib. gen.).
17:6 καὶ εἶδον (1st sg. aor. act. ind. of ὁράω; καὶ εἶδον introduces a new vision, scene, figure, or activity [Aune[a] 338]) **τὴν** (anaphoric to 17:3) **γυναῖκα** (dir. obj.) **μεθύουσαν** (acc. sg. fem. of pres. act. ptc. of μεθύω, "be intoxicated," compl. in obj.-compl. double acc. construction) **ἐκ τοῦ αἵματος** (source) **τῶν ἁγίων** (source) **καὶ ἐκ τοῦ αἵματος** (coord. source) **τῶν μαρτύρων** (μάρτυς, -υρος, ὁ, "witness," source) **Ἰησοῦ** (obj. gen.). **Καὶ ἐθαύμασα** (1st sg. aor. act. ind. of θαυμάζω, "marvel," Louw and Nida note, "whether the reaction is favorable or unfavorable depends on the context" [L&N 25.213]) **ἰδὼν** (nom. sg. masc. of aor. act. ptc. of ὁράω, temp.) **αὐτὴν** (dir. obj. of ἰδών) **θαῦμα** (θαῦμα, -ατος, τό, "marvel," cognate acc., dir. obj. of ἐθαύμασα) **μέγα** (attrib.).

The imagery of being drunk with the blood of the saints connects to 18:24 (καὶ ἐν αὐτῇ αἷμα προφητῶν καὶ ἁγίων εὑρέθη καὶ πάντων τῶν ἐσφαγμένων ἐπὶ τῆς γῆς) and 19:2 (καὶ ἐξεδίκησεν τὸ αἷμα τῶν δούλων αὐτοῦ ἐκ χειρὸς αὐτῆς).
17:7 καὶ εἶπέν (3rd sg. aor. act. ind. of λέγω) **μοι** (indir. obj.) **ὁ ἄγγελος** (subj. nom.), **Διὰ τί** (causal indef. pron., "Because of what?" or simply "Why?") **ἐθαύμασας** (2nd sg. aor. act. ind. of θαυμάζω, "marvel"); **ἐγὼ** (subj. nom.) **ἐρῶ** (1st sg. fut. act. ind. of λέγω) **σοι** (indir. obj.) **τὸ μυστήριον** (μυστήριον, -ου, τό, "mystery, secret," dir. obj.) **τῆς** (anaphoric to 17:3) **γυναικὸς** (appos.) **καὶ τοῦ** (anaphoric to 17:3) **θηρίου** (θηρίον, -ου, τό, "beast," coord. appos.) **τοῦ βαστάζοντος** (gen. sg. neut. of pres. act. ptc. of βαστάζω, "bear, endure," attrib.) **αὐτὴν** (dir. obj.) **τοῦ ἔχοντος** (gen. sg. neut. of pres. act. ptc. of ἔχω, attrib.) **τὰς ἑπτὰ** ("seven," attrib.) **κεφαλὰς** (dir. obj.) **καὶ τὰ δέκα** ("ten," attrib.) **κέρατα** (κέρας, -ατος, τό, "horn," coord. dir. obj.).
17:8 τὸ θηρίον (θηρίον, -ου, τό, "beast," asyndeton, subj. nom., ant. of ὅ) **ὃ** (dir. obj.) **εἶδες** (2nd sg. aor. act. ind. of ὁράω) **ἦν** (3rd sg. impf. act. ind. of εἰμί) **καὶ οὐκ ἔστιν** (3rd sg. pres. act. ind. of εἰμί) **καὶ μέλλει** (3rd sg. pres. act. ind. of μέλλω, "about to") **ἀναβαίνειν** (pres. act. inf. of ἀναβαίνω, compl. inf.) **ἐκ τῆς ἀβύσσου** (ἄβυσσος, -ου, ἡ, "abyss," source) **καὶ εἰς ἀπώλειαν** (ἀπώλεια, -ας, ἡ, "destruction," loc.) **ὑπάγει** (3rd sg. pres. act. ind. of ὑπάγω, futuristic pres., an easier reading with the compl. inf. ὑπάγειν is found in א 051 205 209 1006 1841 1854 2030 2329 2344[vid] *Byz*), **καὶ θαυμασθήσονται** (3rd pl. fut. pass. ind. of θαυμάζω, "marvel," pass. for mid.) **οἱ κατοικοῦντες** (nom. pl. masc. of pres. act. ptc. of κατοικέω, "dwell," subst., subj. nom., ant. of ὧν) **ἐπὶ τῆς γῆς**

(loc.), **ὧν** (poss. with ὄνομα) **οὐ γέγραπται** (3rd sg. pf. pass. ind. of γράφω) **τὸ ὄνομα** (subj. nom.) **ἐπὶ τὸ βιβλίον** (βιβλίον, -ου, τό, "scroll," loc.) **τῆς ζωῆς** (descriptive) **ἀπὸ καταβολῆς** (καταβολή, -ῆς, ἡ, "foundation," temp., extent of time) **κόσμου** (κόσμος, -ου, ὁ, "world," obj. gen.), **βλεπόντων** (gen. pl. masc. of pres. act. ptc. of βλέπω, temp. ptc., "when seeing") **τὸ θηρίον** (θηρίον, -ου, τό, "beast," dir. obj.) **ὅτι** (causal) **ἦν** (3rd sg. impf. act. ind. of εἰμί) **καὶ οὐκ ἔστιν** (3rd sg. pres. act. ind. of εἰμί) **καὶ παρέσται** (3rd sg. fut. mid. ind. of πάρειμι, "be present, arrive")

At first glance it seems that the gen. ptc. βλεπόντων is a solecism because it does not match the nom. ant. οἱ κατοικοῦντες. This is technically true, but John seems to grammatically connect the ptc. to the rel. pron. ὧν. This simply indicates attraction to the nearest ant. and should not be seen as indicating a distinction among the inhabitants of the earth between those whose names are and are not written in the book of life (contra Moţ 136). For John, οἱ κατοικοῦντες ἐπὶ τῆς γῆς are always viewed negatively and this group should be distinguished from the nations who are caught in the middle: some from the nations will be deceived and lost but others will also be saved.

The threefold description of the beast as "was and is not and is about to ascend out of the abyss and go into destruction" is a parody of the divine name in 1:4, 8; 4:8. This builds on the theme of satanic imitation and counterfeiting of divine reality noted in chapter 13. Unlike the coming of God and Christ, which will result in the establishment of an eternal kingdom, the coming of the beast will result in his destruction. Futurist interpreters highlight the fact that the beast currently is not, but this makes too much of a rhetorical detail supplied for parody since the three-and-a-half-year period of the beast's reign with support of the dragon commences with Jesus's ascension and enthronement (see on 12:5–6).

The beast in 11:7 arose from the abyss (τὸ θηρίον τὸ ἀναβαῖνον ἐκ τῆς ἀβύσσου), and the beast in 13:1 arose from the sea (Καὶ εἶδον ἐκ τῆς θαλάσσης θηρίον ἀναβαῖνον). The various visions of the beast in Revelation 11, 13, 16, and 17 should not be read as different time periods but as parallel descriptions of the beast's war against God's people that concludes in 19:20. Each account of the beast and its activities provides different details and perspectives, but they do not seem to represent different events. On John's consistent negative view of "the ones dwelling on the earth," see 3:10.

The reference to names being written in the book of life parallels 13:8, but 17:8 clarifies that the lamb was not slain from the foundation of the world but that names were written in the book from the foundation of the world. The book of life appears elsewhere in Rev 3:5; 13:8; 20:12, 15; 21:27. See 3:5 on the need to distinguish between assurance of salvation and eternal security in the promise that the names of the overcomers would not be blotted from the book.

Use of the OT: On the book of life, see 3:5. The four beasts in Dan 7:3 rise out of the sea (καὶ τέσσαρα θηρία ἀνέβαινον ἐκ τῆς θαλάσσης).

17:9 ὧδε (adv. often indicating spatial proximity, "here," used to suggest logical proximity or relevance, "in this," functions as subj. of verbless cl.; idiomatically, "this calls for discernment" [BDAG 1101d], cf. 13:18) **ὁ νοῦς** (νοῦς, νοός, νοΐ, νοῦν, ὁ, "mind," pred. nom. of verbless cl.) **ὁ ἔχων** (nom. sg. masc. of pres. act. ptc. of ἔχω, attrib.) **σοφίαν** (σοφία, -ας, ἡ, "wisdom," dir. obj.). **αἱ ἑπτὰ** ("seven," attrib.) **κεφαλαὶ** (subj. nom.) **ἑπτὰ** (attrib.) **ὄρη** (pred. nom.) **εἰσίν** (3rd pl. pres. act. ind. of εἰμί), **ὅπου** (subord. spatial conj., "where") **ἡ** (anaphoric to 17:3) **γυνὴ** (subj. nom.) **κάθηται** (3rd sg. pres. mid. ind. of κάθημαι, narrative pres.) **ἐπ' αὐτῶν** (loc., redundant with ὅπου for emph.). **καὶ βασιλεῖς** (pred. nom.) **ἑπτά** (attrib.) **εἰσιν** (3rd pl. pres. act. ind. of εἰμί)

The identification of the seven heads as seven mountains makes the identification of Babylon with Rome certain since Rome was commonly and traditionally described as the city on seven hills (Aune[c] 944–45). This does not limit Babylon to Rome but indicates that Rome was the first-century embodiment and expression of Babylon through its promotion of idolatry (both polytheism and emperor worship), its persecution of God's faithful people, and its economic exploitation (Koester 683–84; Beale 888; Fanning 440–41 describes the relationship of Rome to the end-times expression of godless and oppressive influence through typology). There are also indications throughout Revelation 13 and 17 that the beast represented the Roman Empire or Roman imperial power focused in the emperor. It is not necessary to try to make precise differentiations between Babylon and the beast; in the vision they are closely linked (Babylon rides the beast) while also distinct (note the destruction of Babylon by the beast in 17:16). Both Babylon and the beast engage in deception and the persecution of God's people, but the picture of the beast generally focuses more on ruling power and efficient and ruthless political and militaristic domination, while Babylon generally focuses on the seduction of idolatry, excessive and oppressive economic luxury, and self-sufficiency. Both Babylon and the beast would have been rightly associated by the original hearers with Rome, the Roman Empire, and the emperor while remaining bigger than these historical embodiments; they transtemporally include the nations, rulers, and world systems throughout history that culminate and intensify in their opposition to God and God's people right before Jesus's return.

17:10 οἱ (substantivizer) **πέντε** ("five," subst., subj. nom.) **ἔπεσαν** (3rd pl. aor. act. ind. of πίπτω), **ὁ** (substantivizer) **εἷς** ("one," subst., subj. nom.) **ἔστιν** (3rd sg. pres. act. ind. of εἰμί), **ὁ** (substantivizer) **ἄλλος** (subst., subj. nom.) **οὔπω** (neg. adv., "not yet") **ἦλθεν** (3rd sg. aor. act. ind. of ἔρχομαι), **καὶ ὅταν** (indef. temp. subord. conj., "whenever") **ἔλθῃ** (3rd sg. aor. act. subjunc. ἔρχομαι) **ὀλίγον** (ὀλίγος, -η, -ον, "small, short, few," temp. adv. acc., "briefly") **αὐτὸν** (acc. subj. of inf. μεῖναι) **δεῖ** (3rd sg. impers. pres. act. ind. of δεῖ) **μεῖναι** (aor. act. ind. of μένω, compl.).

Attempts to identify the heads with historic emperors have been unsuccessful. If the sixth emperor was Domitian (AD 81–96), then the eighth would be Trajan, but that would make the first emperor Galba (AD 68–69) or Gaius (AD 37–41, assuming the short reigns of Galba, Otho, and Vitellius are not counted). Neither Galba nor Gaius, however, was the first emperor. If the sixth emperor were Nero (AD 54–68), there would not have been five prior emperors although the dictator Julius Caesar (49–44 BC) could possibly be thought of as filling that role since his actions set in motion the dissolution of the republic; the eighth emperor would then be the short-lived and insignificant Otho (AD 69). Aune is likely correct to suggest that "the number seven may simply be a schematic representation for the complete number of Roman emperors (who were generally called 'kings' in the eastern provinces)" (Aune[c] 961).

The fact that one of the heads currently "is" superficially contradicts the description of the beast in 17:8 as "is not," but apocalyptic visions do not require logical consistency and to expect such consistency leads to faulty interpretations. The point of Rev 17:10 seems to be that the beast had existed for a while now but was nearing the end of its existence: "five down and two to go."

17:11 καὶ τὸ θηρίον (θηρίον, -ου, τό, "beast," subj. nom., ant. of ὅ) **ὃ** (subj. nom.) **ἦν** (3rd sg. impf. act. ind. of εἰμί) **καὶ οὐκ ἔστιν** (3rd sg. pres. act. ind. of εἰμί) **καὶ** (adv., "also") **αὐτὸς** (subj. nom., emph., the masc. pron. with the neut. ant. points to the human identity of the θηρίον) **ὄγδοός** ("eighth," subst., pred. adj.) **ἐστιν καὶ ἐκ τῶν ἑπτά** ("seven," subst., part. or source) **ἐστιν, καὶ εἰς ἀπώλειαν** (ἀπώλεια, -ας, ἡ, "destruction," goal) **ὑπάγει** (3rd sg. pres. act. ind. of ὑπάγω, futuristic pres.).

The beast as a whole is described in the vision as an eighth head of the beast; this is logically impossible in a literal way but probably points to the ultimate intensification of the beast in its fullness right before Jesus's return. The idea that the seven, even eight, heads represent oppressive rulers throughout history is strengthened by recognizing a Hebrew poetic device that has been labeled "graded numerical sayings" (Bauckham 405; Beale 877–78). Proverbs 6:16, Eccl 11:2, and Mic 5:5 demonstrate graded numerical sayings that parallel how an eighth king is added to the seven even though it seems quite forced and does not naturally arise from the original symbol of a beast with seven heads. The point is not the literal number eight but that seven, even eight, brings a sense of fullness, completion, and finality to the symbol.

17:12 καὶ τὰ δέκα ("ten," attrib.) **κέρατα** (κέρας, -ατος, τό, "horn," subj. nom., ant. of ἅ) **ἃ** (dir. obj.) **εἶδες** (2nd sg. aor. act. ind. of ὁράω) **δέκα** (attrib.) **βασιλεῖς** (pred. nom., ant. of οἵτινες) **εἰσιν** (3rd pl. pres. act. ind. of εἰμί), **οἵτινες** (subj. nom.) **βασιλείαν** (dir. obj.) **οὔπω** (neg. adv., "not yet") **ἔλαβον** (3rd pl. aor. act. ind. of λαμβάνω), **ἀλλ'** (adversative) **ἐξουσίαν** (dir. obj.) **ὡς** (manner) **βασιλεῖς** (compl.) **μίαν** (attrib.) **ὥραν** (acc. of time) **λαμβάνουσιν** (3rd pl. pres. act. ind. of λαμβάνω, futuristic pres.) **μετὰ τοῦ θηρίου** (θηρίον, -ου, τό, "beast," association).

The Roman emperors regularly extended their power and influence through client kings (such as King Herod) who were expected to provide military support when called upon. It is likely that these "ten" kings are equal to or a subset of the kings of the earth gathered by the beast to execute his war against God's people (16:12, 14; 19:19–21 and possibly 20:7). The time period of "one hour" matches the length of time necessary for Babylon's judgment in 18:10, 17, 19 (Koester 692).

Use of the OT: On the ten horns and Dan 7:24, see 12:3.

17:13 οὗτοι (subj. nom.) **μίαν** ("one," attrib.) **γνώμην** (γνώμη, -ης, ἡ, "mind," dir. obj.) **ἔχουσιν** (3rd pl. pres. act. ind. of ἔχω) **καὶ τὴν δύναμιν** (dir. obj.) **καὶ ἐξουσίαν** (coord. dir. obj.) **αὐτῶν** (poss.) **τῷ θηρίῳ** (θηρίον, -ου, τό, "beast," indir. obj.) **διδόασιν** (3rd pl. pres. act. ind. of δίδωμι, futuristic pres.).
17:14 οὗτοι (subj. nom.) **μετὰ τοῦ ἀρνίου** (ἀρνίον, -ου, τό, "lamb," disadvantage, "against") **πολεμήσουσιν** (3rd pl. fut. act. ind. of πολεμέω, "fight, make war") **καὶ τὸ ἀρνίον** (subj. nom.) **νικήσει** (3rd sg. fut. act. ind. of νικάω, "overcome, conquer") **αὐτούς** (dir. obj.), **ὅτι** (causal) **κύριος** (pred. nom.) **κυρίων** (gen. of subord.) **ἐστὶν** (3rd sg. pres. act. ind. of εἰμί) **καὶ βασιλεὺς** (pred. nom.) **βασιλέων** (subord.) **καὶ οἱ** (substantivizer, subj. nom. of verbless cl.) **μετ' αὐτοῦ** (association) **κλητοὶ** (κλητός, -ή, -όν, "called," pred. adj.) **καὶ ἐκλεκτοὶ** (ἐκλεκτός, -ή, -όν, "chosen," coord. pred. adj.) **καὶ πιστοί** (coord. pred. adj.).

Revelation 19:16 describes the rider as βασιλεὺς βασιλέων καὶ κύριος κυρίων. Paul describes God in a similar way in 1 Tim 6:15 (ὁ βασιλεὺς τῶν βασιλευόντων καὶ κύριος τῶν κυριευόντων). The brief war recounted here anticipates the fuller visionary description in 19:11–21.

Use of the OT: Deuteronomy 10:17 describes God as God of gods and Lord of lords (ὁ γὰρ κύριος ὁ θεὸς ὑμῶν, οὗτος θεὸς τῶν θεῶν καὶ κύριος τῶν κυρίων). King Nebuchadnezzar acknowledges that Daniel's god is the God of gods and Lord of kings (2:47: ἐστὶν ὁ θεὸς ὑμῶν θεὸς τῶν θεῶν καὶ κύριος τῶν βασιλέων). God is described as the King of kings in 2 Macc 13:4 (ὁ βασιλεὺς τῶν βασιλέων; cf. 3 Macc 5:35; 1 En. 9:4).

---

2. Destruction of Babylon (17:15–18)

17:15 Καὶ λέγει (3rd sg. pres. act. ind. of λέγω, narrative pres.) **μοι** (indir. obj.), **Τὰ ὕδατα** (subj. nom. of εἰσὶν, ant. of ἅ) **ἃ** (dir. obj.) **εἶδες** (2nd sg. aor. act. ind. of ὁράω) **οὗ** (adv., "where," functions as subord. conj.) **ἡ πόρνη** (πόρνη, -ης, ἡ, "prostitute," subj. nom.) **κάθηται** (3rd sg. pres. mid. ind. of κάθημαι), **λαοὶ** (pred. nom.) **καὶ ὄχλοι** (coord. pred. nom.) **εἰσὶν** (3rd pl. pres. act. ind. of εἰμί) **καὶ ἔθνη** (coord. pred. nom.) **καὶ γλῶσσαι** (γλῶσσα, -ης, ἡ, "tongue, language," coord. pred. nom.).

On peoples, crowds, nations, and tongues, see 5:9.
17:16 καὶ τὰ δέκα ("ten," attrib.) **κέρατα** (κέρας, -ατος, τό, "horn," nom. abs., a "topic construction" resumed by οὗτοι below [Math 234], ant. of ἅ) **ἃ** (dir. obj.) **εἶδες** (2nd sg. aor. act. ind. of ὁράω) **καὶ τὸ θηρίον** (θηρίον, -ου, τό, "beast," nom. abs.) **οὗτοι** (subj. nom., the masc. gender is incongruous with its neut. ant. to highlight the personhood of the horns and beast) **μισήσουσιν** (3rd pl. fut. act. ind. of μισέω, "hate") **τὴν πόρνην** (πόρνη, -ης, ἡ, "prostitute," dir. obj.) **καὶ ἠρημωμένην** (acc. sg. fem. of pf. pass. ptc. of ἐρημόω, "make desolate," compl. in obj.-compl. double acc. construction, "they will make her *to be* desolated") **ποιήσουσιν** (3rd pl. fut. act. ind. of ποιέω) **αὐτὴν** (dir. obj.) **καὶ γυμνὴν** (γυμνός, -ή, -όν, "naked," coord. with ἠρημωμένην, "desolated and naked")

καὶ τὰς σάρκας (dir. obj.) **αὐτῆς** (poss.) **φάγονται** (3rd pl. fut. mid. ind. of ἐσθίω) **καὶ αὐτὴν** (dir. obj.) **κατακαύσουσιν** (3rd pl. fut. act. ind. of κατακαίω, "burn up, consume") **ἐν πυρί** (means).

John briefly moves us back in time to before the lamb conquers the beast at the second coming in 17:14 to describe how evil turns on itself and self-destructs. God's preliminary judgment of them involves something akin to a civil war among the principal adversaries. The Roman Empire came very close to self-destructing through civil war in the famous year of the four emperors (AD 69), and the first hearers would have likely looked back at those events as a model for understanding how God's judgment would cause the adversaries to turn on themselves.

Use of the OT: Leviticus 21:9 commands that a daughter of a priest who is profaned through sexual immorality/prostitution (ἐὰν βεβηλωθῇ τοῦ ἐκπορνεῦσαι) must be burned with fire (ἐπὶ πυρὸς κατακαυθήσεται). Ezekiel 38:21 notes that God will defeat Gog, in part, by turning the sword of a man against his brother.

17:17 ὁ γὰρ (causal) **θεὸς** (subj. nom.) **ἔδωκεν** (3rd sg. aor. act. ind. of δίδωμι) **εἰς τὰς καρδίας** (loc.) **αὐτῶν** (poss.) **ποιῆσαι** (aor. act. inf. of ποιέω, subst. inf., dir. obj., "God gave to do") **τὴν γνώμην** (γνώμη, -ης, ἡ, "mind," dir. obj. of ποιῆσαι) **αὐτοῦ** (subj. gen.) **καὶ ποιῆσαι** (aor. act. inf. of ποιέω, coord. subst. inf., dir. obj. of ἔδωκεν) **μίαν** ("one," attrib.) **γνώμην** (dir. obj. of ποιῆσαι) **καὶ δοῦναι** (aor. act. inf. of δίδωμι, coord. subst. inf. dir. obj. of ἔδωκεν) **τὴν βασιλείαν** (dir. obj.) **αὐτῶν** (poss.) **τῷ θηρίῳ** (θηρίον, -ου, τό, "beast," indir. obj.) **ἄχρι** (subord. conj. of temp. extent, "until") **τελεσθήσονται** (3rd pl. fut. pass. ind. of τελέω, fut. in place of subjunc.) **οἱ λόγοι** (subj. nom.) **τοῦ θεοῦ** (subj. gen.).

For all the wrath and power of spiritual and physical forces opposing God and his people, such forces are ultimately powerless to oppose his purposes.

17:18 καὶ ἡ (anaphoric to 17:3) **γυνὴ** (subj. nom., ant. of ἥν) **ἣν** (dir. obj.) **εἶδες** (2nd sg. aor. act. ind. of ὁράω) **ἔστιν** (3rd sg. pres. act. ind. of εἰμί) **ἡ πόλις** (pred. nom.) **ἡ μεγάλη** (attrib.) **ἡ ἔχουσα** (nom. sg. fem. of pres. act. ptc. of ἔχω, attrib.) **βασιλείαν** (dir. obj.) **ἐπὶ τῶν βασιλέων** (subord.) **τῆς γῆς** (loc. or subord.).

The imagery used to describe the destruction of Babylon the Great is quite graphic and severe, but it is important to remember that she is not a real person: she is a symbolic representative of a cultural, religious, and economic system opposed to God and his people. Revelation 18:8 describes the judgment of the city by fire (καὶ ἐν πυρὶ κατακαυθήσεται). The judgment of the woman in 17:16 figuratively points to the judgment of the great city Babylon.

FOR FURTHER STUDY

45. Divine Violence

Barr, D. "Violence in the Apocalypse of John." Pages 291–306 in *OHR*.
Bauckham, R. "Judgment in the Book of Revelation." Pages 55–79 in *The Book of Revelation: Currents in British Research on the Apocalypse*. Edited by G. V. Allen, I. Paul, and S. P. Woodman. WUNT 2.411. Tübingen: Mohr Siebeck, 2015.
Decock, P. "Images of War and Creation: Of Violence and Non-Violence in the Revelation of John." Pages 185–200 in *Coping with Violence in the New Testament*. Edited by P. G. R. de Villiers and J. W. van Henten. Leiden: Brill, 2012.
Harris, D. M. "John and Punishment: Did He Delight in Violence?" Pages 68–86 in S&B.
———. "Understanding Images of Violence in the Book of Revelation." Pages 148–64 in *Encountering Violence in the Bible*. Edited by M. Zehnder and H. Hagelia. The Bible in the Modern World 55. Sheffield: Sheffield Phoenix, 2013.
Skaggs, R., and T. Doyle. "Violence in the Apocalypse of John." *CurBR* 5 (2007): 220–34.
Streett, M. *Here Comes the Judge: Violent Pacifism in the Book of Revelation*. LNTS 462. London T&T Clark, 2012.

3. Mourning over Babylon's Fall (18:1–24)

Revelation 18 does not directly narrate the destruction of Babylon but features several voices commenting upon, lamenting over, or celebrating God's judgment of her.

18:1 Μετὰ ταῦτα (subst., temp., "after these things") **εἶδον** (1st sg. aor. act. ind. of ὁράω; εἶδον introduces a new vision, scene, figure, or activity [Aune[a] 338]) **ἄλλον** (attrib.) **ἄγγελον** (dir. obj.) **καταβαίνοντα** (acc. sg. masc. of pres. act. ptc. of καταβαίνω, compl. in obj.-compl. double acc. construction) **ἐκ τοῦ οὐρανοῦ** (source) **ἔχοντα** (acc. sg. masc. of pres. act. ptc. of ἔχω, attrib. or manner) **ἐξουσίαν** (dir. obj.) **μεγάλην** (attrib.), **καὶ ἡ γῆ** (subj. nom.) **ἐφωτίσθη** (3rd sg. aor. pass. ind. of φωτίζω, "give light, enlighten") **ἐκ τῆς δόξης** (means) **αὐτοῦ** (subj. gen.).

18:2 καὶ ἔκραξεν (3rd sg. aor. act. ind. of κράζω) **ἐν ἰσχυρᾷ** (ἰσχυρός, -ά, -όν, "strong," attrib.) **φωνῇ** (means) **λέγων** (nom. sg. masc. of pres. act. ptc. of λέγω, manner), **Ἔπεσεν** (3rd sg. aor. act. ind. of πίπτω) **ἔπεσεν** (repetition for emph.) **Βαβυλὼν** ("Babylon," subj. nom., "It fell! It fell! Great Babylon") **ἡ μεγάλη** (attrib.), **καὶ ἐγένετο** (3rd sg. aor. mid. ind. of γίνομαι) **κατοικητήριον** (κατοικητήριον, -ου, τό, "dwelling," pred. nom.) **δαιμονίων** (δαιμόνιον, -ου, τό, "demon," subj. gen.) **καὶ φυλακὴ** (φυλακή, -ῆς, ἡ, "prison, haunt" [BDAG 1067d], coord. pred. nom.) **παντὸς** ("every kind of, all sorts of" [BDAG 784c], attrib.) **πνεύματος** (obj. gen.) **ἀκαθάρτου** (ἀκάθαρτος, -ον, "unclean," attrib.) **καὶ φυλακὴ** (coord. pred. nom.) **παντὸς** ("every kind of," attrib.) **ὀρνέου** (ὄρνεον, -ου, τό, "bird," obj. gen.) **ἀκαθάρτου** (attrib.) [**καὶ φυλακὴ** (coord. pred. nom.) **παντὸς** ("every kind of," attrib.) **θηρίου** (θηρίον, -ου, τό, "animal, beast," obj. gen.) **ἀκαθάρτου** (attrib. adj.)] **καὶ μεμισημένου** (gen. sg. neut. of pf. pass. ptc. of μισέω, "hate," attrib., modifying ὀρνέου or θηρίου depending upon the textual variant),

The announcement of the fall of Babylon parallels 14:8. There is variation in the mss in the order of the three phrases which start with καὶ φυλακή, but they are likely original based on the allusion to Isa 13:21 and 34:11 although the final phrase (καὶ φυλακὴ παντὸς θηρίου ἀκαθάρτου) is missing in ℵ 2053 2080 vg *al* (Metzger 682–83).

Use of the OT: On announcements of the fall of Babylon in Isa 21:9 and Jer 51:8, see Rev 14:8. The oracle against Babylon in Isa 13:21 prophesies that beasts will rest there (καὶ ἀναπαύσονται ἐκεῖ θηρία) and demons will dance there (καὶ δαιμόνια ἐκεῖ ὀρχήσονται; cf. Jer 50:39). Isaiah 34:11 describes the judgment of Edom, which would entail various wild animals dwelling in it (καὶ κατοικήσουσιν ἐν αὐτῇ). Baruch 4:35 similarly prophecies that Babylon will be inhabited by demons for much time (καὶ κατοικηθήσεται ὑπὸ δαιμονίων τὸν πλείονα χρόνον).

18:3 ὅτι (causal) **ἐκ τοῦ οἴνου** (οἶνος, -ου, ὁ, "wine," source) **τοῦ θυμοῦ** (θυμός, -οῦ, ὁ, "strong passion," appos.) **τῆς πορνείας** (πορνεία, -ας, ἡ, "sexual immorality," descriptive or attrib.) **αὐτῆς** (subj. gen.) **πέπωκαν** (3rd pl. pf. act. ind. of πίνω, see below). **πάντα** (attrib.) **τὰ ἔθνη** (subj. nom.) **καὶ οἱ βασιλεῖς** (subj. nom.) **τῆς γῆς** (subord.) **μετ' αὐτῆς** (association) **ἐπόρνευσαν** (3rd pl. aor. act. ind. of πορνεύω, "commit sexual immorality") **καὶ οἱ ἔμποροι** (ἔμπορος, -ου, ὁ, "merchant," coord. subj. nom.) **τῆς γῆς** (loc.) **ἐκ τῆς δυνάμεως** (source or means) **τοῦ στρήνους** (στρῆνος, -ους, τό, "luxury, sensuality," descriptive gen.) **αὐτῆς** (poss.) **ἐπλούτησαν** (3rd pl. aor. act. ind. πλουτέω, "prosper, be wealthy," likely ingressive).

The imagery of sexual immorality parallels the description in 17:2, and the description of her luxury recalls her clothing in 17:4. Πέπωκαν is a possible barbarism and the 3rd pl. pf. act. ind. should read πεπώκασιν. John's assimilation of the pf. endings with the aor. anticipates later developments in the Greek language (Moţ 99). The external evidence strongly supports a vb. for falling (πέπτωκαν in A C 69 2031 or πεπτώκασιν in ℵ 046 and about fifty minuscules) but the context seems to require a vb. for drinking as in P 051 1006 2329 and various versions (cf. 14:8; Metzger 683). The string of gens. led to a variation in the order in some mss (τοῦ θυμοῦ τοῦ οἴνου τῆς πορνείας in P 051 and about ninety minuscules) and the omission of one of the gens. (τοῦ θυμοῦ τῆς πορνείας in A 1611 2053 and τοῦ οἴνου τῆς πορνείας in 792 1854 2070[comm] [Metzger 683]).

Use of the OT: On Isa 23:17, see 17:2. On Jer 51:7, see 14:8. Nahum 3:4 similarly describes economic exploitation as sexual immorality.

18:4 Καὶ ἤκουσα (1st sg. aor. act. ind. of ἀκούω) **ἄλλην** (attrib.) **φωνὴν** (dir. obj.) **ἐκ τοῦ οὐρανοῦ** (source) **λέγουσαν** (acc. sg. fem. of pres. act. ptc. of λέγω, compl. in obj.-compl. double acc. construction), **Ἐξέλθατε** (2nd pl. aor. act. impv. of ἐξέρχομαι, the pl. vb. commands the sg. λαός as a *constructio ad sensum*) **ὁ λαός** (nom. of address) **μου** (poss.) **ἐξ αὐτῆς** (separation) **ἵνα** (purpose) **μὴ συγκοινωνήσητε** (2nd pl. aor. act. subjunc. of συγκοινωνέω, "share, participate") **ταῖς ἁμαρτίαις** (functions as dat. dir. obj. of the thing shared) **αὐτῆς** (subj. gen.), **καὶ ἐκ τῶν πληγῶν** (πληγή, -ῆς, ἡ, "plague," part.) **αὐτῆς** (obj. gen.) **ἵνα** (purpose) **μὴ λάβητε** (2nd pl. aor. act. subjunc. of λαμβάνω),

The imperative directed at God's people highlights the rhetorical and motivational purpose of the vision of judgment (more direct than 13:10; 14:12; and 16:15 and similar to the warnings contained in the seven proclamations of Rev 2–3). Paul uses similar logic from Isa 52:11 (see below) in his exhortation in 2 Cor 6:17 for God's people to come out of their midst and not touch any unclean thing (διὸ ἐξέλθατε ἐκ μέσου αὐτῶν καὶ ἀφορίσθητε, λέγει κύριος, καὶ ἀκαθάρτου μὴ ἅπτεσθε· κἀγὼ εἰσδέξομαι ὑμᾶς).

Use of the OT: Isaiah 48:20 commands God's people to come out of Babylon and flee from Chaldea (Ἔξελθε ἐκ Βαβυλῶνος φεύγων ἀπὸ τῶν Χαλδαίων) as a celebration that the Lord had rescued his servant Jacob (λέγετε Ἐρρύσατο κύριος τὸν δοῦλον αὐτοῦ Ιακωβ). Similarly, Isa 52:11 emphatically commands the hearer to depart and go out from there (ἀπόστητε ἀπόστητε ἐξέλθατε ἐκεῖθεν), to not touch the unclean (καὶ ἀκαθάρτου μὴ ἅπτεσθε), to go out from her midst (ἐξέλθατε ἐκ μέσου αὐτῆς), and to be separate (ἀφορίσθητε). Jeremiah 27:8 LXX (50:8 EVV) similarly commands the hearer to be estranged out of the midst of Babylon and from the land of the Chaldeans and to go out (ἀπαλλοτριώθητε ἐκ μέσου Βαβυλῶνος καὶ ἀπὸ γῆς Χαλδαίων καὶ ἐξέλθατε). Jeremiah 28:6 LXX (51:6 EVV) gives the command to flee out of the midst of Babylon (φεύγετε ἐκ μέσου Βαβυλῶνος) and for each person to save their soul (καὶ ἀνασῴζετε ἕκαστος τὴν ψυχὴν αὐτοῦ) and not be cast away in her injustice (καὶ μὴ ἀπορριφῆτε ἐν τῇ ἀδικίᾳ αὐτῆς) because the time of her punishment is from the Lord (ὅτι καιρὸς ἐκδικήσεως αὐτῆς ἐστιν παρὰ κυρίου) and he will repay repayment to her (ἀνταπόδομα αὐτὸς ἀνταποδίδωσιν αὐτῇ). Jeremiah 28:9 LXX (51:9 EVV) employs a hortatory subj. to urge the hearer: let us abandon her (ἐγκαταλίπωμεν αὐτήν) and let us go out, each into his land (καὶ ἀπέλθωμεν ἕκαστος εἰς τὴν γῆν αὐτοῦ), because her judgment has drawn near into heaven (ὅτι ἤγγισεν εἰς οὐρανὸν τὸ κρίμα αὐτῆς) and has raised up until the stars (ἐξῆρεν ἕως τῶν ἄστρων). The LXX is missing Jer 51:45 MT, which states, "Come out from among her, my people! Save your lives, each of you, from the Lord's burning anger!" (CSB). The commands in Jer 27:8; 28:6, 9 LXX; and Jer 51:45 MT are similar to Revelation in that the separation is commanded in order to avoid being caught up in God's judgment of her.

18:5 ὅτι (causal, connected to the impv. ἐξέλθατε in 18:4) **ἐκολλήθησαν** (3rd pl. aor. pass. ind. of κολλάω, "bind, unite with," pass. for mid.) **αὐτῆς** (subj. gen., fronted for emph.)

αἱ ἁμαρτίαι (subj. nom.) **ἄχρι τοῦ οὐρανοῦ** (extent, "as far as heaven") **καὶ ἐμνημόνευσεν** (3rd sg. aor. act. ind. of μνημονεύω, "remember") **ὁ θεὸς** (subj. nom.) **τὰ ἀδικήματα** (ἀδίκημα, -ατος, τό, "crime, misdeed, unrighteous act," dir. obj.) **αὐτῆς** (subj. gen.).

God's punitive remembrance of Babylon also features in 16:19. This is the only occurrence in Revelation of injustice or unjust acts (ἀδίκημα) as a contrast to God's justice (15:3; 16:5, 7; 19:2).

Use of the OT: God's remembrance is elsewhere connected to judgment (Ps 108:14 LXX [109:14 EVV]; Hos 9:9). Genesis 18:20 describes the sins of Sodom and Gomorrah as exceedingly great (καὶ αἱ ἁμαρτίαι αὐτῶν μεγάλαι σφόδρα). On Babylon's judgment being piled up to heaven, see 18:4 for Jer 28:9 LXX (51:9 EVV).

18:6 ἀπόδοτε (2nd pl. aor. act. impv. of ἀποδίδωμι) **αὐτῇ** (indir. obj.) **ὡς** (comp.) **καὶ** (adv., "also") **αὐτὴ** (subj. nom.) **ἀπέδωκεν** (3rd sg. aor. act. ind. of ἀποδίδωμι) **καὶ διπλώσατε** (2nd pl. aor. act. impv. of διπλόω, "double") **τὰ διπλᾶ** (διπλοῦς, -ῆ, -οῦν, "double," cognate acc., dir. obj.) **κατὰ τὰ ἔργα** (correspondence or standard, "according to works") **αὐτῆς** (subj. gen.), **ἐν τῷ ποτηρίῳ** (ποτήριον, -ου, τό, "cup," loc., ant. of ᾧ) **ᾧ** (dir. obj., the case is dat. because of attraction to its ant.) **ἐκέρασεν** (3rd sg. aor. act. ind. of κεράννυμι, "mix substances," normally liquids [L&N 63.9]) **κεράσατε** (2nd pl. aor. act. impv. of κεράννυμι) **αὐτῇ** (advantage/disadvantage, "for her") **διπλοῦν** (dir. obj.),

The command to repay Babylon could be directed toward implicit angelic agents of judgment, but the literary context would suggest it is given to God's people as in 18:4 or perhaps even the beast and ten kings of 17:17. If the command is directed to God's people it anticipates the later vision of Jesus's return accompanied by the armies of heaven (17:14; 19:14) and is not a call for violent vengeance in the present time. In Revelation, God's people do not overcome with physical violence but by faithfulness to death (12:11), and the violence they are said to inflict is related to their prophetic witness and speech (11:5). Based on the OT passages below, Paul expresses a similar conviction regarding God's justice in 2 Thess 1:6: "since it is just according to God to repay affliction to those who afflict you" (εἴπερ δίκαιον παρὰ θεῷ ἀνταποδοῦναι τοῖς θλίβουσιν ὑμᾶς θλῖψιν).

The idiomatic expression "double the double" (διπλώσατε τὰ διπλᾶ) could point to a punishment that does exceed the crime to highlight the seriousness of the sin and deter others (Exod 22:4, 7, 9; possibly Jer 16:18; 17:18; cf. Exod 22:1; 2 Sam 12:6 [Fanning 461]). Doubling could also hyperbolically describe the fullness of something (possibly 2 Kgs 2:9; Isa 61:7; Zech 9:12; 1 Tim 5:17). Finally, instead of an asymmetrically excessive punishment, the call for double punishment could express "reduplication or equivalency" (Math 242) through the production of a duplicate (Beale 901) in accordance with the claims in 18:5 and 18:7 of correspondence between the actions and the punishment (possibly Gen 43:15; Jer 16:18; 17:18; Matt 23:15). Correspondence fits better with indications elsewhere in Revelation of symmetry in judgment that fits the crime (11:18; 16:6) and in the justness of God's judgments (15:3; 16 5, 7; 19:2).

Use of the OT: The imprecatory Psalm against Babylon declares blessedness over the one who will repay to you your repayment, which you repaid to us (Ps 136:8 LXX [137:8 EVV]: *μακάριος ὃς ἀνταποδώσει σοι τὸ ἀνταπόδομά σου, ὃ ἀνταπέδωκας ἡμῖν*). Jeremiah 27:15 LXX (50:15 EVV) calls upon God to take vengeance upon her (*ἐκδικεῖτε ἐπ' αὐτήν*); just as she did, do to her (*καθὼς ἐποίησεν, ποιήσατε αὐτῇ*). Jeremiah 27:29 LXX (50:29 EVV) similarly commands: repay her according to her works (*ἀνταπόδοτε αὐτῇ κατὰ τὰ ἔργα αὐτῆς*) and do to her in accordance with all things, as much as she did (*κατὰ πάντα ὅσα ἐποίησεν ποιήσατε αὐτῇ*).

18:7 *ὅσα* (correlative, "as much as, to the degree that," topic construction resumed by *τοσοῦτον* [Math 242]) ***ἐδόξασεν*** (3rd sg. aor. act. ind. of *δοξάζω*) ***αὐτὴν*** (refl. dir. obj., "herself") ***καὶ ἐστρηνίασεν*** (3rd sg. aor. act. ind. of *στρηνιάω*, "live in luxury or sensuality"), ***τοσοῦτον*** (*τοσοῦτος, -αύτη, -οῦτον*, "so much," attrib., modifying *βασανισμὸν*) ***δότε*** (2nd pl. aor. act. impv. of *δίδωμι*) ***αὐτῇ*** (indir. obj.) ***βασανισμὸν*** (*βασανισμός, -οῦ, ὁ*, "torture, torment," dir. obj.) ***καὶ πένθος*** (*πένθος, -ους, τό*, "mourning, sorrow," coord. dir. obj.). ***ὅτι*** (causal) ***ἐν τῇ καρδίᾳ*** (loc.) ***αὐτῆς*** (poss.) ***λέγει*** (3rd sg. pres. act. ind. of *λέγω*) ***ὅτι*** (content) ***Κάθημαι*** (1st sg. pres. mid. ind. of *κάθημαι*) ***βασίλισσα*** ("queen," compl. of an assumed *ὡς*, "I sit like a queen") ***καὶ χήρα*** (*χήρα, -ας, ἡ*, "widow," pred. nom.) ***οὐκ εἰμὶ*** (1st sg. pres. act. ind. *εἰμί*) ***καὶ πένθος*** (acc. dir. obj.) ***οὐ μὴ*** (emph. neg.) ***ἴδω*** (1st sg. aor. act. subjunc. of *ὁράω*).

Use of the OT: John seems to clearly allude here to the imputed speech of Babylon in Isa 47:7–9:

> And you said, into the age I will be ruling [*καὶ εἶπας Εἰς τὸν αἰῶνα ἔσομαι ἄρχουσα*], you did not understand these things in your heart nor remember the last things [*οὐκ ἐνόησας ταῦτα ἐν τῇ καρδίᾳ σου οὐδὲ ἐμνήσθης τὰ ἔσχατα*]. Now hear these things, the delicate one [*νῦν δὲ ἄκουσον ταῦτα, ἡ τρυφερά*], the one sitting confidently [*ἡ καθημένη πεποιθυῖα*], the one saying in her heart, I am, and there is not another [*ἡ λέγουσα ἐν τῇ καρδίᾳ αὐτῆς Ἐγώ εἰμι, καὶ οὐκ ἔστιν ἑτέρα*], I am not sitting as a widow and will not know bereavement [*οὐ καθιῶ χήρα οὐδὲ γνώσομαι ὀρφανείαν*]. Now these two things will come suddenly upon you in one day [*νῦν δὲ ἥξει ἐξαίφνης ἐπὶ σὲ τὰ δύο ταῦτα ἐν μιᾷ ἡμέρᾳ*], widowhood and childlessness will come suddenly upon you [*χηρεία*

καὶ ἀτεκνία ἥξει ἐξαίφνης ἐπὶ σὲ] in your sorcery in the exceeding strength of your enchanters [ἐν τῇ φαρμακείᾳ σου ἐν τῇ ἰσχύι τῶν ἐπαοιδῶν σου σφόδρα].

18:8 διὰ τοῦτο (causal, the ant. is the arrogant and self-sufficient claim made in 18:7) **ἐν μιᾷ** ("one," attrib.) **ἡμέρᾳ** (temp.) **ἥξουσιν** (3rd pl. fut. act. ind. of ἥκω, "come") **αἱ πληγαὶ** (πληγή, -ῆς, ἡ, "plague," subj. nom.) **αὐτῆς** (obj. gen.), **θάνατος** (appos.) **καὶ πένθος** (πένθος, -ους, τό, "mourning, sorrow," coord. appos.) **καὶ λιμός** (λιμός, -οῦ, ὁ, "hunger," coord. appos.), **καὶ ἐν πυρὶ** (means) **κατακαυθήσεται** (3rd sg. fut. pass. ind. of κατακαίω, "burn up, consume"), **ὅτι** (causal) **ἰσχυρὸς** (ἰσχυρός, -ά, -όν, "strong," pred. adj. of verbless cl.) **κύριος** (subj. nom. of verbless cl.) **ὁ θεὸς** (appos.) **ὁ κρίνας** (nom. sg. masc. of aor. act. ptc. of κρίνω, attrib. or subst. in appos.) **αὐτήν** (dir. obj.).

Use of the OT: See 18:7 on Isa 47:7–9 in 18:7–8. The oracle against Babylon in Jer 27:34 LXX (50:34 EVV) proclaims that the one redeeming them is strong, the Lord Almighty is his name (ὁ λυτρούμενος αὐτοὺς ἰσχυρός, κύριος παντοκράτωρ ὄνομα αὐτῷ), he will judge judgment against his adversaries (κρίσιν κρινεῖ πρὸς τοὺς ἀντιδίκους αὐτοῦ).

18:9 Καὶ κλαύσουσιν (3rd pl. fut. act. ind. of κλαίω, "weep") **καὶ κόψονται** (3rd pl. fut. mid. ind. of κόπτω, "cut, beat [mourn greatly]") **ἐπ' αὐτὴν** (figuratively spatial to indicate "feelings directed toward someone" [BDAG 366c]) **οἱ βασιλεῖς** (subj. nom.) **τῆς γῆς** (subord.) **οἱ μετ' αὐτῆς** (association) **πορνεύσαντες** (nom. pl. masc. of aor. act. ptc. of πορνεύω, "commit sexual immorality," attrib.) **καὶ στρηνιάσαντες** (nom. pl. masc. of aor. act. ptc. of στρηνιάω, "live in luxury or sensuality," coord. attrib.), **ὅταν** (indef. temp. subord. conj., "when") **βλέπωσιν** (3rd pl. pres. act. subjunc. of βλέπω) **τὸν καπνὸν** (καπνός, -οῦ, ὁ, "smoke," dir. obj.) **τῆς πυρώσεως** (πύρωσις, -εως, ἡ, "burning," source) **αὐτῆς** (obj. gen.),

---

Use of the OT: The prophecy against Tyre in Ezek 26:16 includes the prediction that all the rulers out of the nations of the sea will come down from their thrones (καταβήσονται ἀπὸ τῶν θρόνων αὐτῶν πάντες οἱ ἄρχοντες ἐκ τῶν ἐθνῶν τῆς θαλάσσης) and will fear their destruction and groan over the city (καὶ φοβηθήσονται τὴν ἀπώλειαν αὐτῶν καὶ στενάξουσιν ἐπὶ σέ). The lament over Tyre in Ezekiel 27 provides the background to various parts of Revelation 18:

> Your wealth, merchandise, and goods, your sailors and captains, those who repair your leaks, those who barter for your goods, and all the warriors on board, with all the other people within you, sink into the heart of the sea on

> the day of your downfall. The countryside shakes at the sound of your sailors' cries. All the oarsmen disembark from their ships. The sailors and all the captains of the sea stand on the shore. Because of you, they raise their voices and cry out bitterly. They throw dust on their heads; they roll in ashes. They shave their heads because of you and wrap themselves in sackcloth. They weep over you with deep anguish and bitter mourning. In their wailing they lament for you, mourning over you: Who was like Tyre, silenced in the middle of the sea? When your merchandise was unloaded from the seas, you satisfied many peoples. You enriched the kings of the earth with your abundant wealth and goods. Now you are wrecked by the sea in the depths of the waters; your goods and the people within you have gone down. All the inhabitants of the coasts and islands are appalled at you. Their kings shudder with fear; their faces are contorted. Those who trade among the peoples scoff at you; you have become an object of horror and will never exist again. (Ezek 27:27–36 CSB)

18:10 ἀπὸ μακρόθεν (adv. functioning as obj. of prep., "far away," separation, "from a distance") **ἑστηκότες** (nom. pl. masc. of pf. act. ptc. of ἵστημι, manner, modifies the coord. main vbs. in 18:9) **διὰ τὸν φόβον** (causal) **τοῦ βασανισμοῦ** (βασανισμός, -οῦ, ὁ, "torture, torment," obj. gen.) **αὐτῆς** (obj. gen.) **λέγοντες** (nom. pl. masc. of pres. act. ptc. of λέγω, manner), **Οὐαὶ οὐαί** (interj., "woe," repeated for emph.), **ἡ πόλις** (nom. of address) **ἡ μεγάλη** (attrib.), **Βαβυλὼν** ("Babylon," appos. to πόλις) **ἡ πόλις** (appos.) **ἡ ἰσχυρά** (ἰσχυρός, -ά, -όν, "strong," attrib.), **ὅτι** (causal, explaining the woes) **μιᾷ** ("one," attrib.) **ὥρᾳ** (temp.) **ἦλθεν** (3rd sg. aor. act. ind. of ἔρχομαι) **ἡ κρίσις** (subj. nom.) **σου** (obj. gen.).

> **Use of the OT:** Building on Ezek 26:16 in Rev 18:9, Ezek 26:17–18 describes how people will take up a lament over Tyre and mourn her destruction. The words of the lament in 18:10 reflect Nebuchadnezzar's boast in Dan 4:30 when he asks, "Is this not Babylon the great" (Αὕτη ἐστὶ Βαβυλὼν ἡ μεγάλη)?

18:11 Καὶ οἱ ἔμποροι (ἔμπορος, -ου, ὁ, "merchant," subj. nom.) **τῆς γῆς** (loc.) **κλαίουσιν** (3rd pl. pres. act. ind. of κλαίω, "weep," futuristic pres.) **καὶ πενθοῦσιν** (3rd pl. pres. act. ind. of πενθέω, "mourn," coord. futuristic pres.) **ἐπ' αὐτήν** (figuratively spatial to indicate "feelings directed toward someone" [BDAG 366c]), **ὅτι** (causal) **τὸν γόμον** (γόμος, -ου, ὁ, "cargo," dir. obj. fronted for emph.) **αὐτῶν** (poss.) **οὐδεὶς** (subj. nom.) **ἀγοράζει** (3rd sg. pres. act. ind. of ἀγοράζω, "buy") **οὐκέτι** (neg. adv., "no longer")

Use of the OT: On Ezek 27:36, see 18:9.

18:12 γόμον (γόμος, -ου, ὁ, "cargo," appos. to γόμον in 18:11) **χρυσοῦ** (χρυσός, -οῦ, ὁ, "gold," this and the following gens. indicate the content of the cargo) **καὶ ἀργύρου** (ἄργυρος, -ου, ὁ, "silver") **καὶ λίθου τιμίου** (τίμιος, -α, -ον, "valuable," attrib.) **καὶ μαργαριτῶν** (μαργαρίτης, -ου, ὁ, "pearl") **καὶ βυσσίνου** (βύσσινος, -η, -ον, "fine linen," subst.) **καὶ πορφύρας** (πορφύρα, -ας, ἡ, "purple cloth") **καὶ σιρικοῦ** (σιρικός, -ή, -όν, "silk," subst.) **καὶ κοκκίνου** (κόκκινος, -η, -ον, "red," subst.), **καὶ πᾶν** (attrib.) **ξύλον** (ξύλον, -ου, τό, "wood," on the switch to acc., see 18:13, the acc. nouns in the list are coord. with γόμον while the gen. nouns give the content of the cargo) **θύϊνον** (θύϊνος, -η, -ον, "from a citron tree," attrib.) **καὶ πᾶν** (attrib.) **σκεῦος** (σκεῦος, -ους, τό, "object, vessel") **ἐλεφάντινον** (ἐλεφάντινος, -η, -ον, "made of ivory," attrib.) **καὶ πᾶν** (attrib.) **σκεῦος ἐκ ξύλου** (material, a few mss read λίθου [A 106 1841] to better match what follows [Metzger 684]) **τιμιωτάτου** (superl. adj. from τίμιος, "most valuable," prob. functioning as elative adj., "very valuable") **καὶ χαλκοῦ** (χαλκός, -οῦ, ὁ, "bronze," gen. of material) **καὶ σιδήρου** (σίδηρος, -ου, ὁ, "iron," gen. of material) **καὶ μαρμάρου** (μάρμαρος, -ου, ὁ, "marble," gen. of material),

---

Use of the OT: The list of cargo is similar to that of Tyre in Ezek 27:12 (silver, [gold in LXX], iron, tin, lead), 27:13 (human beings [ψυχαῖς ἀνθρώπων] and vessels of bronze [σκεύη χαλκᾶ]), and 27:22 (spices, precious stones, and gold).

18:13 καὶ κιννάμωμον (κιννάμωμον, -ου, τό, "cinnamon") **καὶ ἄμωμον** (ἄμωμον, -ου, τό, "amomum spice") **καὶ θυμιάματα** (θυμίαμα, -ατος, τό, "incense") **καὶ μύρον** (μύρον, -ου, τό, "perfume") **καὶ λίβανον** (λίβανος, -ου, ὁ, "frankincense") **καὶ οἶνον** (οἶνος, -ου, ὁ, "wine") **καὶ ἔλαιον** (ἔλαιον, -ου, τό, "olive oil") **καὶ σεμίδαλιν** (σεμίδαλις, -εως, ἡ, "fine flour") **καὶ σῖτον** (σῖτος, -ου, ὁ, "wheat") **καὶ κτήνη** (κτῆνος, -ους, τό, "domesticated animal") **καὶ πρόβατα** (πρόβατον, -ου, τό, "sheep"), **καὶ ἵππων** (ἵππος, -ου, ὁ, "horse," see below on the switch to gen. nouns) **καὶ ῥεδῶν** (ῥέδη, -ης, ἡ, "carriage") **καὶ σωμάτων, καὶ** (coord. or epex., "that is") **ψυχὰς ἀνθρώπων** (attrib. gen., "human souls").

The list of trade goods seems to alternate back and forth between acc. and gen. arbitrarily. "This kind of structure is used when, to continue the sentence in a uniform manner, some important thought may be lost, or when the writing becomes heavy and obscure" (Moţ 140).

18:14 καὶ ἡ ὀπώρα (ὀπώρα, -ας, ἡ, "fruit," subj. nom.) **σου** (poss.) **τῆς ἐπιθυμίας** (ἐπιθυμία, -ας, ἡ, "desire," appos. to ὀπώρα) **τῆς ψυχῆς** (subj. gen.) **ἀπῆλθεν** (3rd sg. aor. act. ind. of ἀπέρχομαι) **ἀπὸ σοῦ** (separation), **καὶ πάντα** (attrib.) **τὰ λιπαρὰ** (λιπαρός, -ά, -όν, "luxury," subst., subj. nom., "luxurious things") **καὶ τὰ λαμπρὰ** (λαμπρός, -ά,

-όν, "bright," subst., subj. nom., "bright things") **ἀπώλετο** (3rd sg. aor. mid. ind. of ἀπόλλυμι) **ἀπὸ σοῦ** (separation) **καὶ οὐκέτι** (neg. adv., "no longer") **οὐ μὴ** (emph. neg. heightened even more by οὐκέτι) **αὐτὰ** (dir. obj.) **εὑρήσουσιν** (3rd pl. fut. act. ind. of εὑρίσκω, fut. for subjunc., the pl. subj. is the ἔμποροι of 18:11 or it is an impers. vb. which could be translated as pass. [Math 249]).

18:15 οἱ ἔμποροι (ἔμπορος, -ου, ὁ, "merchant," subj. nom., asyndeton) **τούτων** (obj. gen., the ant. of the demon. pron. is prob. the list of cargo in 18:13–14) **οἱ πλουτήσαντες** (nom. pl. masc. of aor. act. ptc. of πλουτέω, "prosper, be wealthy," attrib.) **ἀπ' αὐτῆς** (source) **ἀπὸ μακρόθεν** (adv. functioning as obj. of prep., "far away," separation, "from a distance") **στήσονται** (3rd pl. fut. mid. ind. of ἵστημι) **διὰ τὸν φόβον** (causal) **τοῦ βασανισμοῦ** (βασανισμός, -οῦ, ὁ, "torture," obj. gen.) **αὐτῆς** (obj. gen.) **κλαίοντες** (nom. pl. masc. of pres. act. ptc. of κλαίω, "weep," manner) **καὶ πενθοῦντες** (nom. pl. masc. of pres. act. ptc. of πενθέω, "mourn," coord. manner)

Use of the OT: On Ezek 27:36, see 18:9.

18:16 λέγοντες (nom. pl. masc. of pres. act. ptc. of λέγω, manner), **Οὐαὶ οὐαί** (interj., "woe," repetition for emph.), **ἡ πόλις** (nom. of address or pred. nom. of verbless cl., "woe *be to* the city") **ἡ μεγάλη** (attrib.), **ἡ περιβεβλημένη** (nom. sg. fem. of pf. pass. ptc. of περιβάλλω, "wrap, clothe," attrib.) **βύσσινον** (βύσσινος, -η, -ον, "fine linen," subst., dir. obj.) **καὶ πορφυροῦν** (πορφυροῦς, -ᾶ, -οῦν, "purple," subst., coord. dir. obj.) **καὶ κόκκινον** (κόκκινος, -η, -ον, "red," subst., coord. dir. obj.) **καὶ κεχρυσωμένη** (nom. sg. fem. of pf. pass. ptc. of χρυσόω, "make golden," attrib., coord. with περιβεβλημένη) **[ἐν] χρυσίῳ** (χρυσίον, -ου, τό, "gold," cognate dat., means) **καὶ λίθῳ** (coord. means) **τιμίῳ** (τίμιος, -α, -ον, "valuable," attrib.) **καὶ μαργαρίτῃ** (μαργαρίτης, -ου, ὁ, "pearl," coord. means),

The prostitute in 17:4 is similarly clothed with purple, scarlet, gold, jewels, and pearls.

Use of the OT: On Ezek 28:13, see 17:4.

18:17 ὅτι (causal) **μιᾷ** ("one," attrib.) **ὥρᾳ** (temp.) **ἠρημώθη** (3rd sg. aor. pass. ind. of ἐρημόω, "make desolate") **ὁ τοσοῦτος** (τοσοῦτος, -αύτη, -οῦτον, "so much," attrib.) **πλοῦτος** (πλοῦτος, -ου, ὁ, "wealth," subj. nom.). **Καὶ πᾶς** (attrib.) **κυβερνήτης** (κυβερνήτης, -ου, ὁ, "shipmaster," subj. nom.) **καὶ πᾶς** (attrib.) **ὁ ἐπὶ τόπον** (loc., this unusual expression led to improvements in several mss such as ἐπὶ τῶν πλοίων [boats] in P 051 and about 100 minuscules, ἐπὶ πόντον [sea] in 469 582 2076* 2254, ὁ ἐπὶ τῶν πλοίων ἐπὶ τόπον in syr^{ph}, and ὁ ἐπὶ τὸν ποταμὸν [river] in 2053 2062 [Metzger 684]) **πλέων** (nom. sg.

masc. of pres. act. ptc. of πλέω, "sail," subst., coord. subj. nom.) **καὶ ναῦται** (ναύτης, -ου, ὁ, "sailor," coord. subj. nom.) **καὶ ὅσοι** ("as many as," subst., coord. subj. nom.) **τὴν θάλασσαν** (dir. obj.) **ἐργάζονται** (3rd pl. pres. mid. ind. of ἐργάζομαι, "work"), **ἀπὸ μακρόθεν** (adv. functioning as obj. of prep., "far away," separation, "from a distance") **ἔστησαν** (3rd pl. aor. act. ind. of ἵστημι)

The vb. ἐρημόω is applied to Babylon pictured as a woman in 17:16 and Babylon pictured as a city in 18:17, 19.

Use of the OT: On Ezek 27:27–29, see 18:9.

18:18 καὶ ἔκραζον (3rd pl. impf. act. ind. of κράζω, the switch to the impf. perhaps anticipates the transition in 18:20 [Math 251]) **βλέποντες** (nom. pl. masc. of pres. act. ptc. of βλέπω, temp., "while seeing") **τὸν καπνὸν** (καπνός, -οῦ, ὁ, "smoke," dir. obj.) **τῆς πυρώσεως** (πύρωσις, -εως, ἡ, "burning," source) **αὐτῆς** (obj. gen.) **λέγοντες** (nom. pl. masc. of pres. act. ptc. of λέγω, manner), **Τίς** (interr. pron., subj. nom. of verbless cl., "Who *is* like") **ὁμοία** (ὅμοιος, -οία, -οιον, "like, similar," pred. adj. of verbless cl.) **τῇ πόλει** (compl. of ὁμοία) **τῇ μεγάλῃ** (attrib.);

Use of the OT: On Ezek 27:32, see 18:9.

18:19 καὶ ἔβαλον (3rd pl. aor. act. ind. of βάλλω) **χοῦν** (χοῦς, χοός, "dust," dir. obj.) **ἐπὶ τὰς κεφαλὰς** (loc.) **αὐτῶν** (poss.) **καὶ ἔκραζον** (3rd pl. impf. act. ind. of κράζω) **κλαίοντες** (nom. pl. masc. of pres. act. ptc. of κλαίω, "weep," manner) **καὶ πενθοῦντες** (nom. pl. masc. of pres. act. ptc. of πενθέω, "mourn," coord. manner) **λέγοντες** (nom. pl. masc. of pres. act. ptc. of λέγω, coord. manner), **Οὐαὶ οὐαί** (interj., "woe," repetition for emph.), **ἡ πόλις** (pred. nom. of verbless cl., "woe *be to* the city," or nom. of address, ant. of ᾗ) **ἡ μεγάλη** (attrib.), **ἐν ᾗ** (means) **ἐπλούτησαν** (3rd pl. aor. act. ind. of πλουτέω, "prosper, be wealthy") **πάντες** (attrib.) **οἱ ἔχοντες** (nom. pl. masc. of pres. act. ptc. of ἔχω, subst., subj. nom.) **τὰ πλοῖα** (πλοῖον, -ου, τό, "ship," dir. obj.) **ἐν τῇ θαλάσσῃ** (loc.) **ἐκ τῆς τιμιότητος** (τιμιότης, -ητος, ἡ, "wealth," source) **αὐτῆς** (poss.), **ὅτι** (causal) **μιᾷ** ("one," attrib.) **ὥρᾳ** (temp.) **ἠρημώθη** (3rd sg. aor. pass. ind. of ἐρημόω, "make desolate").

Use of the OT: On Ezek 27:30–34, see 18:9.

18:20 Εὐφραίνου (2nd sg. pres. pass. impv. of εὐφραίνω, "celebrate"; the switch in mood signals a transition; sg. vb. with coord. subjects) **ἐπ' αὐτῇ** (causal), **οὐρανὲ** (voc. of address) **καὶ οἱ ἅγιοι** (ἅγιος, -ία, -ον, "holy," coord. nom. of address) **καὶ οἱ ἀπόστολοι** (coord. nom. of address) **καὶ οἱ προφῆται** (coord. nom. of address), **ὅτι** (causal) **ἔκρινεν** (3rd sg. aor. act. ind. of κρίνω) **ὁ θεὸς** (subj. nom.) **τὸ κρίμα** (κρίμα, -ατος, τό, "judgment," cognate acc., dir. obj.) **ὑμῶν** (obj. gen., "a judgment for/against you") **ἐξ αὐτῆς** (the meaning here is difficult; Mathewson following Louw and Nida, connects this prep. phrase with κρίμα to indicate source, producing something like "God judged the judgment from her against you" with the meaning being "God condemned her for what she did to you" [L&N 90.16, Math 252] or "God has pronounced on her the judgment she wished to impose on you" [BDAG 567b]; it is also possible for the expression to read "God has pronounced judgment for you against her" [BDAG 567b]).

The heavens are called to rejoice in 12:12 (εὐφραίνεσθε, [οἱ] οὐρανοί) at the ejection of the devil from heaven.

Use of the OT: The Song of Moses in Deut 32:43 similarly calls upon the heavens to rejoice (εὐφράνθητε, οὐρανοί, ἅμα αὐτῷ). The sons of God are called upon to worship him (καὶ προσκυνησάτωσαν αὐτῷ πάντες υἱοὶ θεοῦ) and the nations are commanded to celebrate with God's people (εὐφράνθητε, ἔθνη, μετὰ τοῦ λαοῦ αὐτοῦ [Deut 32:43]; this line is lacking in the MT). The reason for this celebration is that God has avenged the blood of his sons (ὅτι τὸ αἷμα τῶν υἱῶν αὐτοῦ ἐκδικᾶται). The song then celebrates the hope that he will avenge and repay justice to the enemies and the ones who hate (καὶ ἐκδικήσει καὶ ἀνταποδώσει δίκην τοῖς ἐχθροῖς καὶ τοῖς μισοῦσιν). Psalm 95:11 LXX (96:1 EVV) calls upon the heavens to celebrate (εὐφραινέσθωσαν οἱ οὐρανοί). Isaiah 44:23 calls upon the heavens to celebrate because God had shown mercy upon Israel (εὐφράνθητε, οὐρανοί, ὅτι ἠλέησεν ὁ θεὸς τὸν Ισραηλ). Isaiah 49:13 similarly calls upon the heavens to celebrate because God has shown mercy on his people and comforted the humble of his people (εὐφραίνεσθε, οὐρανοί . . . ὅτι ἠλέησεν ὁ θεὸς τὸν λαὸν αὐτοῦ καὶ τοὺς ταπεινοὺς τοῦ λαοῦ αὐτοῦ παρεκάλεσεν). Jeremiah 51:48 is missing in the LXX but states, "Heaven and earth and everything in them will shout for joy over Babylon, because the destroyers from the north will come against her" (CSB).

18:21 Καὶ ἦρεν (3rd sg. aor. act. ind. of αἴρω) **εἷς** ("one," functioning as indef. art., "a") **ἄγγελος** (subj. nom.) **ἰσχυρὸς** (ἰσχυρός, -ά, -όν, "strong," attrib.) **λίθον** (dir. obj.) **ὡς** (comp.) **μύλινον** (μύλινος, -η, -ον, "from a mill," subst.) **μέγαν** (attrib.) **καὶ ἔβαλεν** (3rd sg. aor. act. ind. of βάλλω, coord.) **εἰς τὴν θάλασσαν** (loc.) **λέγων** (nom. sg. masc. of pres. act. ptc. of λέγω, manner), **Οὕτως** (manner) **ὁρμήματι** (ὅρμημα, -ατος, τό, "violent rush," manner) **βληθήσεται** (3rd sg. fut. pass. ind. βάλλω) **Βαβυλὼν** ("Babylon," subj. nom.) **ἡ μεγάλη** (attrib.) **πόλις** (appos.) **καὶ οὐ μὴ** (emph. neg.) **εὑρεθῇ** (3rd sg. aor.

pass. subjunc. of εὑρίσκω) **ἔτι** (adv. indicating "extension of time up to and beyond an expected point" [L&N 67.128]; "still, yet, anymore").

Use of the OT: Jeremiah commands Seraiah to read the oracle against Babylon when he arrives in Babylon and then tie a stone to the book and cast it into the Euphrates as a sign that Babylon would sink to rise no more (Jer 28:63–64 LXX [51:63–64 EVV]). The prophecy against Tyre in Ezekiel 26 concludes with God's claim that he would give destruction and Tyre would not exist into the age (26:21: ἀπώλειάν σε δώσω, καὶ οὐχ ὑπάρξεις ἔτι εἰς τὸν αἰῶνα).

18:22 καὶ φωνὴ (subj. nom.) **κιθαρῳδῶν** (κιθαρῳδός, -οῦ, ὁ, "lyre player," subj. gen.) **καὶ μουσικῶν** (μουσικός, -ή, -όν, "musician," coord. subj. gen.) **καὶ αὐλητῶν** (αὐλητής, -οῦ, ὁ, "flute player," coord. subj. gen.) **καὶ σαλπιστῶν** (σαλπιστής, -οῦ, ὁ, "trumpet player," coord. subj. gen.) **οὐ μὴ** (emph. neg.) **ἀκουσθῇ** (3rd sg. aor. pass. subjunc. of ἀκούω) **ἐν σοὶ** (loc.) **ἔτι** (adv., extension of time), **καὶ πᾶς** (attrib.) **τεχνίτης** (τεχνίτης, -ου, ὁ, "craftsman," subj. nom.) **πάσης** (attrib.) **τέχνης** (τέχνη, -ης, ἡ, "skill, craft," obj. gen., "The absence of πάσης τέχνης in א A cop[bo] is prob. accidental; the words are adequately attested by C P 046 051 most minuscules it[gig] vg syr[h] cop[sa] *al*, and are in harmony with the author's style, but would scarcely have been inserted by copyists" [Metzger 684]) **οὐ μὴ** (emph. neg.) **εὑρεθῇ** (3rd sg. aor. pass. subjunc. of εὑρίσκω) **ἐν σοὶ** (loc.) **ἔτι** (adv., extension of time), **καὶ φωνὴ** (subj. nom.) **μύλου** (μύλος, -ου, ὁ, "mill stone," subj. gen.) **οὐ μὴ** (emph. neg.) **ἀκουσθῇ** (3rd sg. aor. pass. subjunc. of ἀκούω) **ἐν σοὶ** (loc.) **ἔτι** (adv., extension of time),

---

Use of the OT: The oracle against the whole earth in Isa 24:8 declares, "The joyful tambourines have ceased. The noise of the jubilant has stopped. The joyful lyre has ceased [πέπαυται φωνὴ κιθάρας]" (CSB). The prophecy against Tyre in Ezek 26:13 claims that God will stop the music of their songs (καὶ καταλύσει τὸ πλῆθος τῶν μουσικῶν σου), and the sound of their lyres would not be heard any more (καὶ ἡ φωνὴ τῶν ψαλτηρίων σου οὐ μὴ ἀκουσθῇ ἔτι).

18:23 καὶ φῶς (subj. nom.) **λύχνου** (λύχνος, -ου, ὁ, "lamp," subj. gen.) **οὐ μὴ** (emph. neg.) **φάνῃ** (3rd sg. aor. act. subjunc. of φαίνω, "shine") **ἐν σοὶ** (loc.) **ἔτι** (adv., extension of time), **καὶ φωνὴ** (subj. nom.) **νυμφίου** (νυμφίος, -ου, ὁ, "bridegroom," subj. gen.) **καὶ νύμφης** (νύμφη, -ης, ἡ, "bride," coord. subj. gen.) **οὐ μὴ** (emph. neg.) **ἀκουσθῇ** (3rd sg. aor. pass. subjunc. of ἀκούω) **ἐν σοὶ** (loc.) **ἔτι** (adv., extension of time) **ὅτι** (causal) **οἱ ἔμποροί** (ἔμπορος, -ου, ὁ, "merchant," subj. nom.) **σου** (poss.) **ἦσαν** (3rd pl. impf. act. ind. of εἰμί) **οἱ μεγιστᾶνες** (μεγιστάν, -ᾶνος, ὁ, "important person," pred. nom.) **τῆς γῆς**

(subord.), **ὅτι** (coord. causal cl.) **ἐν τῇ φαρμακείᾳ** (φαρμακεία, -ας, ἡ, "magic," means) **σου** (subj. gen.) **ἐπλανήθησαν** (3rd pl. aor. pass. ind. of πλανάω, "deceive," pl. vb. with neut. pl. personal subj.) **πάντα** (attrib.) **τὰ ἔθνη** (subj. nom.),

---

Use of the OT: Jeremiah 7:34 prophesies judgment against Jerusalem: God will silence the voice of the bridegroom and bride (φωνὴν νυμφίου καὶ φωνὴν νύμφης; cf. Jer 16:9; 25:10). Jeremiah 25:10 adds the grinding of the millstones and light of the lamp (ὀσμὴν μύρου καὶ φῶς λύχνου) to what will be destroyed from them in judgment. The oracle against Tyre in Isa 23:8 describes her merchants as glorious, the rulers of the earth (οἱ ἔμποροι αὐτῆς ἔνδοξοι, ἄρχοντες τῆς γῆς). For Isa 47:9, see 18:7.

18:24 καὶ (coord. the two vbs., ἐπλανήθησαν and εὑρέθη) **ἐν αὐτῇ** (loc.) **αἷμα** (subj. nom.) **προφητῶν** (source) **καὶ ἁγίων** (coord. source) **εὑρέθη** (3rd sg. aor. pass. ind. of εὑρίσκω) **καὶ πάντων** (attrib.) **τῶν ἐσφαγμένων** (gen. pl. masc. of pf. pass. ptc. of σφάζω, "slaughter," subst., coord. source) **ἐπὶ τῆς γῆς** (loc.).

This verse provides a key reason for Babylon's judgment; not only is Babylon responsible for the slaughter of God's people as in 6:10; 17:6; 19:2, she also is responsible for the blood of all the ones slain on the earth. This suggests that Babylon encompasses more than any specific individual historical city in Revelation's visionary world.

Use of the OT: Jeremiah 28:49 LXX (51:49 EVV) claims that the wounded of all the earth will fall in Babylon (καὶ ἐν Βαβυλῶνι πεσοῦνται τραυματίαι πάσης τῆς γῆς). This differs from the Jer 51:49 MT, which could be translated, "Babylon must fall because of the slain of Israel, even as the slain of all the earth fell because of Babylon" (CSB). Ezekiel 24:6–7 describes Jerusalem as the bloody city (πόλις αἱμάτων) because the blood caused by her is in her midst (ὅτι αἷμα αὐτῆς ἐν μέσῳ αὐτῆς ἐστιν). This shedding of blood roused God's wrath to vengeance (24:8: τοῦ ἀναβῆναι θυμὸν εἰς ἐκδίκησιν ἐκδικηθῆναι).

FOR FURTHER STUDY

46. Revelation as Anti-Empire

Bauckham, R. "The Economic Critique of Rome in Revelation 18." Pages 47–90 in *Images of Empire*. Edited by L. Alexander. Sheffield: JSOT Press, 1991.

Callahan, A. D. "Apocalypse as Critique of Political Economy: Some Notes on Revelation 18." *HBT* 21 (1999): 46–65.

Collins, A. Y. "The Political Perspective of the Revelation to John." *JBL* 96 (1977): 241–56.

———. "Revelation 18: Taunt-Song or Dirge?" Pages 185–204 in *L'Apocalypse johannique dans le Nouveau Testament*. Edited by J. Lambrecht. BETL 53. Leuven: Leuven University Press, 1980.

Kraybill, J. N. *Imperial Cult and Commerce in John's Apocalypse*. JSNTSup 132. Sheffield: Sheffield Academic Press, 1996.

Perry, P. S. "Critiquing the Excess of Empire: A *Synkrisis* of John of Patmos and Dio of Prusa." *JSNT* 29 (2007): 473–96.

HOMILETICAL SUGGESTIONS

Chapters 17–18 focus on the judgment of Babylon. She represents the demonically empowered world system, the great city, behind the persecution of both Christians (17:6; 18:24) and all human beings (18:13, 24), economic oppression (18:1–24), and religious deception characterized by sexual immorality throughout Revelation (17:2, 4, 8; 18:23). Her judgment reveals that God can and will use evil actors to judge evil actors (17:17). Jesus's power, lordship, and victory are a key theme (17:14). The key moment of exhortation comes in 18:4 as God's people are called to separate themselves from Babylon to avoid participating in her sins and sharing in her judgments.

It is important to note the literary structure of these visions in Revelation 17–20. From an amillennial perspective they largely overlap in time and meaning, but each one focuses on a different aspect of the opposition against God and his people: chapters 17–18 describe God's judgment of Babylon, chapter 19 focuses on Jesus's judgment of the beasts, and chapter 20 focuses on God's judgment of the devil. The separate visions do not require three different battles in history but rather provide literary closure to each opponent within a dedicated visionary scene. The premillennial approach differs in seeing the defeat of the beasts and the devil as two different events separated by the millennium.

The Judgment of Babylon (17:1–18:24)

1. Babylon's crimes are evident and her judgment deserved (17:1–6; 18:1–24).
2. Jesus will overcome (17:14).
3. God's people must renounce Babylon's sins (18:4).

B. FINAL VICTORY (19:1–21:8)

Revelation 19:1–9 functions as a transition to conclude the destruction of Babylon (19:1–5) and highlight Babylon's counterpart, the bride of the Lamb (19:6–9), in anticipation of Jesus's return. This is followed by visions of Jesus's return and the defeat of the beasts (19:11–21), the millenium (20:1–6), the defeat of Satan (20:7–10), the final judgment (20:11–15), and the new creation (21:1–8).

1. The Coming of the Lamb (19:1–21)

a. The Wedding of the Lamb (19:1–9)

19:1 Μετὰ ταῦτα (subst., temp.) **ἤκουσα** (1st sg. aor. act. ind. of ἀκούω) **ὡς** (comp. cl. functions as dir. obj.) **φωνὴν** (compl.) **μεγάλην** (attrib.) **ὄχλου** (subj. gen.) **πολλοῦ** (attrib.) **ἐν τῷ οὐρανῷ** (loc.) **λεγόντων** (gen. pl. masc. of pres. act. ptc. of λέγω, compl. in obj.-compl. double gen. construction, on the case, see 1:11), **Ἀλληλουϊά** ("hallelujah," interj.) **ἡ σωτηρία** (subj. nom. of verbless cl.) **καὶ ἡ δόξα** (coord. subj. nom.) **καὶ ἡ δύναμις** (coord. subj. nom.) **τοῦ θεοῦ** (poss., "salvation *is* God's") **ἡμῶν** (subord.),

Hallelujah only occurs here in Revelation (19:1, 3, 4, 6). It is a common expression of praise in the Psalms which utilizes a 2nd pl. impv. to command the hearer to "praise Yah[weh]" (הַלְלוּיָהּ). The expression calls upon God's people to join in joyful praise directed toward God. In transliterated Greek liturgical use, the impv. nature of the expression gives way to its function as an interj. and declaration of praise to God. Tobit 13:18 describes how all the streets in the rebuilt Jerusalem will say ἀλληλουϊά.

19:2 ὅτι (causal) **ἀληθιναὶ** (ἀληθινός, -ή, -όν, "true," pred. adj. of verbless cl.) **καὶ δίκαιαι** (coord. pred. adj.) **αἱ κρίσεις** (subj. nom. of verbless cl.) **αὐτοῦ** (subj. gen.) **ὅτι** (causal, either coord. with or subord. to the prior ὅτι cl.) **ἔκρινεν** (3rd sg. aor. act. ind. of κρίνω) **τὴν πόρνην** (πόρνη, -ης, ἡ, "prostitute," dir. obj., ant. of ἥτις) **τὴν μεγάλην** (attrib.) **ἥτις** (subj. nom.) **ἔφθειρεν** (3rd sg. impf. act. ind. of φθείρω, "corrupt," the impf. here provides "supporting or explanatory material" [Math 257]) **τὴν γῆν** (dir. obj.) **ἐν τῇ πορνείᾳ** (πορνεία, -ας, ἡ, "sexual immorality," means) **αὐτῆς** (subj. gen.), **καὶ ἐξεδίκησεν** (3rd sg. aor. act. ind. of ἐκδικέω, "give justice, avenge, punish") **τὸ αἷμα** (dir. obj.) **τῶν δούλων** (poss.) **αὐτοῦ** (poss.) **ἐκ χειρὸς** (means, "blood *shed* by her hand," [Math 257]) **αὐτῆς** (poss.).

Babylon is here charged with corrupting (ἔφθειρεν) the earth. This recalls the celebration in the seventh trumpet judgment that the time had come for God to destroy the ones destroying the earth (Rev 11:18; καὶ διαφθεῖραι τοὺς διαφθείροντας τὴν γῆν). The judgment of Babylon is presented as God's explicit answer to the prayers of the souls under the altar for justice in 6:10 (Ἕως πότε, ὁ δεσπότης ὁ ἅγιος καὶ ἀληθινός, οὐ κρίνεις καὶ ἐκδικεῖς τὸ αἷμα ἡμῶν ἐκ τῶν κατοικούντων ἐπὶ τῆς γῆς;). For the combination of truth and justice, see 15:3; 16:7.

Use of the OT: This hymn of praise reflects many OT passages. On the truth and justice of God's judgments in Pss 19:9; 119:137, see 16:7. On the avenging of blood in Deut 32:43; 2 Kgs 9:7; Ps 79:10, see 6:10.

19:3 καὶ δεύτερον (adv., "a second time") **εἴρηκαν** (3rd pl. pf. act. ind. of λέγω, εἴρηκαν could be seen as a barbarism and should read εἰρήκασιν, but John's assimilation of the pf. endings with the aor. anticipates later developments in the Greek language [Moţ 99]), **Ἀλληλουϊά** ("hallelujah," interj.) **καὶ** (prob. adv., "indeed" [Math 258]) **ὁ καπνὸς** (καπνός, -οῦ, ὁ, "smoke," subj. nom.) **αὐτῆς** (source) **ἀναβαίνει** (3rd sg. pres. act. ind. of ἀναβαίνω) **εἰς τοὺς αἰῶνας** (measure) **τῶν αἰώνων** (emph. repetition of αἰών).

The smoke of Babylon's judgment ascends into the ages of ages just as the smoke of the torment of those who worship the beast in 14:11 (ὁ καπνὸς τοῦ βασανισμοῦ αὐτῶν εἰς αἰῶνας αἰώνων ἀναβαίνει).

Use of the OT: In the oracle against Edom in Isa 34:10, it states that the burning of her land will not be quenched night and day into the eternal time (νυκτὸς καὶ ἡμέρας καὶ οὐ σβεσθήσεται εἰς τὸν αἰῶνα χρόνον) and the smoke from her will ascend upward (καὶ ἀναβήσεται ὁ καπνὸς αὐτῆς ἄνω).

19:4 καὶ ἔπεσαν (3rd pl. aor. act. ind. of πίπτω) **οἱ** (anaphoric to 4:4) **πρεσβύτεροι** (subj. nom.) **οἱ εἴκοσι** ("twenty," attrib.) **τέσσαρες** ("four") **καὶ τὰ** (anaphoric to 4:6) **τέσσαρα** (attrib.) **ζῷα** (ζῷον, -ου, τό, "living thing," coord. subj. nom.) **καὶ προσεκύνησαν** (3rd pl. aor. act. ind. of προσκυνέω) **τῷ θεῷ** (dat. dir. obj.) **τῷ** (anaphoric to 4:2) **καθημένῳ** (dat. sg. masc. of pres. mid. ptc. of κάθημαι, attrib.) **ἐπὶ τῷ** (anaphoric to 4:2) **θρόνῳ** (loc.) **λέγοντες** (nom. pl. masc. of pres. act. ptc. of λέγω, manner), **Ἀμὴν** (interj.) **Ἀλληλουϊά** ("hallelujah," interj.).

Use of the OT: For the background of God sitting on his throne, see 4:2.

19:5 Καὶ φωνὴ (subj. nom.) **ἀπὸ τοῦ** (anaphoric to 4:2) **θρόνου** (source) **ἐξῆλθεν** (3rd sg. aor. act. ind. of ἐξέρχομαι) **λέγουσα** (nom. sg. fem. of pres. act. ptc. of λέγω, manner), **Αἰνεῖτε** (2nd pl. pres. act. impv. of αἰνέω) **τῷ θεῷ** (dat. dir. obj.) **ἡμῶν** (subord.) **πάντες** (attrib.) **οἱ δοῦλοι** (nom. of address) **αὐτοῦ** (poss.) [**καὶ**] (epex., the ms evidence is evenly balanced between inclusion or omission) **οἱ φοβούμενοι** (nom. pl. masc. of pres. mid. ptc. of φοβέω, subst., appos. to δοῦλοι, without the καί it would be attrib.) **αὐτόν** (dir. obj.), **οἱ μικροὶ** (appos.) **καὶ οἱ μεγάλοι** (coord. appos.).

The command to praise God (Αἰνεῖτε τῷ θεῷ) gives the Gk. translation for the transliterated Heb. expression Ἀλληλουϊά. Revelation 11:18 also uses the expression "the small and the great" to describe the broad class and social diversity of God's people.

Use of the OT: Psalm 21:24 LXX (22:23 EVV) commands the ones fearing the Lord to praise him (Οἱ φοβούμενοι κύριον, αἰνέσατε αὐτόν). Psalm 133:1 LXX (134:1 EVV) commands all the servants of the Lord to bless the Lord (εὐλογεῖτε τὸν κύριον, πάντες οἱ δοῦλοι κυρίου). Psalm 134:1 LXX (135:1 EVV) commands servants to praise the name of the Lord and praise the Lord (Αἰνεῖτε τὸ ὄνομα κυρίου, αἰνεῖτε, δοῦλοι, κύριον). Psalm 113:21 LXX (115:13 EVV) declares εὐλόγησεν τοὺς φοβουμένους τὸν κύριον, τοὺς μικροὺς μετὰ τῶν μεγάλων.

19:6 καὶ ἤκουσα (1st sg. aor. act. ind. of ἀκούω) **ὡς** (comp., these three comp. phrases function as the dir. obj. of ἤκουσα) **φωνὴν** (compl.) **ὄχλου** (subj. gen.) **πολλοῦ** (attrib.) **καὶ ὡς** (comp.) **φωνὴν ὑδάτων** (subj. gen.) **πολλῶν** (attrib.) **καὶ ὡς** (comp.) **φωνὴν βροντῶν** (βροντή, -ῆς, ἡ, "thunder," subj. gen.) **ἰσχυρῶν** (ἰσχυρός, -ά, -όν, "strong," attrib.) **λεγόντων** (gen. pl. masc. of pres. act. ptc. of λέγω, compl. in obj.-compl. double gen. construction with the acc. φωνὴν [Math 259]; on the case, see 1:11), **Ἀλληλουϊά** ("hallelujah," interj.), **ὅτι** (causal) **ἐβασίλευσεν** (3rd sg. aor. act. ind. of βασιλεύω, "rule," inceptive aor.) **κύριος** (subj. nom.) **ὁ θεὸς** (appos.) **[ἡμῶν]** (subord. or relationship, the ms. evidence is evenly balanced, and a decision is uncertain) **ὁ παντοκράτωρ** (παντοκράτωρ, -ορος, ὁ, "almighty," appos.).

Use of the OT: On the voice of many waters in Ezek 1:24; 43:2, see 1:15. On the statement that the Lord reigns, see 11:15.

19:7 χαίρωμεν (1st pl. pres. act. subjunc. of χαίρω, hortatory) **καὶ ἀγαλλιῶμεν** (1st pl. pres. act. subjunc. of ἀγαλλιάω, "rejoice," coord. hortatory) **καὶ δώσωμεν** (1st pl. aor. act. subjunc. of δίδωμι, coord. hortatory, the variant reading δῶμεν in א* 046 051 and most minuscules is the regular aor. act. subjunc. form; in contrast, δώσομεν [fut.] in א[2] A 2053 *al* would be unlikely following two hortatory subjuncs. [Metzger 685]) **τὴν δόξαν** (dir. obj.) **αὐτῷ** (indir. obj.), **ὅτι** (causal) **ἦλθεν** (3rd sg. aor. act. ind. of ἔρχομαι, dramatic aor. [Wallace 564]) **ὁ γάμος** (γάμος, -ου, ὁ, "wedding," subj. nom.) **τοῦ ἀρνίου** (ἀρνίον, -ου, τό, "lamb," subj. gen.) **καὶ ἡ γυνὴ** (subj. nom.) **αὐτοῦ** (relationship) **ἡτοίμασεν** (3rd sg. aor. act. ind. of ἑτοιμάζω, "prepare") **ἑαυτὴν** (refl. dir. obj.)

The three hortatory subjuncs. are climactic in calling the hearers to join in the cosmic worship being described.

Use of the OT: The royal wedding in Psalm 45 is likely in the background (Aune[c] 1046).

19:8 καὶ ἐδόθη (3rd sg. aor. pass. ind. of δίδωμι) **αὐτῇ** (indir. obj.) **ἵνα** (content, the subord. cl. functions as subj. of ἐδόθη) **περιβάληται** (3rd sg. aor. mid. subjunc. of περιβάλλω, "wrap, clothe") **βύσσινον** (βύσσινος, -η, -ον, "fine linen," subst., dir. obj.) **λαμπρὸν** (λαμπρός, -ά, -όν, "bright," attrib.) **καθαρόν** (καθαρός, -ά, -όν, "clean," attrib.)· **τὸ γὰρ** (explanatory) **βύσσινον** (subst., subj. nom.) **τὰ δικαιώματα** (δικαίωμα, -ατος, τό, "righteous deed," pred. nom.) **τῶν ἁγίων** (subj. gen.) **ἐστίν** (3rd sg. pres. act. ind. of εἰμί).

The act. (from 19:7) and pass. combine to express the mystery of divine sovereignty and human responsibility: the bride prepared herself, and it was given to her to clothe herself with the garments, which were the righteous deeds of the saints. The apocalyptic imagery is not consistent or precise; the bride is likely connected to the woman of chapter 12 who, in the vision, is both distinct from and closely connected to the rest of her seed (12:17). The bride here has a similar relationship to those invited to the wedding in 19:9. The bride is clothed with the actions of the saints and is described as a city in 21:10. Understanding the bride as the people of God is a natural development of OT descriptions of Israel as Yahweh's wife (Isa 50:1; 54:5–6; Jer 3:20; Hos 2:16–20), a connection applied to the church by Paul in Eph 5:22–33.

Use of the OT: Isaiah 61:10 prophesies the restoration of Zion with the claim that God had clothed Zion with a garment of salvation (ἐνέδυσεν γάρ με ἱμάτιον σωτηρίου) and covered her with a tunic of celebration (καὶ χιτῶνα εὐφροσύνης) as a bridegroom prepares himself and as a bride adorns herself with jewels (ὡς νύμφην κατεκόσμησέν με κόσμῳ).

19:9 Καὶ λέγει (3rd sg. pres. act. ind. of λέγω, narrative pres.) **μοι** (indir. obj.), **Γράψον** (2nd sg. aor. act. impv. of γράφω)· **Μακάριοι** (μακάριος, -ία, -ιον, "blessed," pred. adj. of verbless cl.) **οἱ** (goes with κεκλημένοι) **εἰς τὸ δεῖπνον** (δεῖπνον, -ου, τό, "dinner, feast," loc.) **τοῦ γάμου** (γάμος, -ου, ὁ, "wedding," attrib. gen.) **τοῦ ἀρνίου** (ἀρνίον, -ου, τό, "lamb," subj. gen.) **κεκλημένοι** (nom. pl. masc. of pf. pass. ptc. of καλέω, subst., subj. nom. of verbless cl.). **καὶ λέγει** (narrative pres.) **μοι** (indir. obj.), **Οὗτοι** (subj. nom.) **οἱ λόγοι** (pred. nom.) **ἀληθινοὶ** (ἀληθινός, -ή, -όν, "true," attrib.) **τοῦ θεοῦ** (source) **εἰσιν** (3rd pl. pres. act. ind. of εἰμί).

This statement regarding the supper of the wedding of the Lamb parallels Jesus's parable of the wedding feast in Matt 22:2–3 and the great banquet in Luke 14:15.

b. Worshipping the Angel (19:10)

19:10 καὶ ἔπεσα (1st sg. aor. act. ind. of πίπτω) **ἔμπροσθεν** (adv., "before") **τῶν ποδῶν** (loc.) **αὐτοῦ** (poss.) **προσκυνῆσαι** (aor. act. inf. of προσκυνέω, purpose) **αὐτῷ** (dat. dir. obj.). **καὶ λέγει** (3rd sg. pres. act. ind. of λέγω, narrative pres.) **μοι** (indir. obj.), **Ὅρα** (2nd sg. pres. act. impv. of ὁράω, idiomatic expression of prohibition) **μή· σύνδουλός** (σύνδουλος, -ου, ὁ, "fellow-servant," pred. nom.) **σού** (association [Wallace 129]) **εἰμι** (1st sg. pres. act. ind. of εἰμί) **καὶ τῶν ἀδελφῶν** (association) **σου** (relationship) **τῶν ἐχόντων** (gen. pl. masc. of pres. act. ptc. of ἔχω, attrib.) **τὴν μαρτυρίαν** (dir. obj.) **Ἰησοῦ** (obj. gen.)· **τῷ θεῷ** (dat. dir. obj., fronted for emph.) **προσκύνησον** (2nd sg. aor. act. impv. of προσκυνέω). **ἡ γὰρ** (explanatory) **μαρτυρία** (subj. nom.) **Ἰησοῦ** (obj. gen.) **ἐστιν** (3rd sg. pres. act. ind. of εἰμί) **τὸ πνεῦμα** (pred. nom.) **τῆς προφητείας** (attrib. gen., "prophetic," or gen. of product, "which produces prophecy").

John's actions and the angel's rebuke parallel the way that Peter rebukes Cornelius for falling at his feet to worship him in Acts 10:24–26. John repeats this misplaced action in Rev 22:8–9; the repeated action thus concludes the main section on Babylon's judgment and the main vision of the bride (21:9–22:5). The final expression is notoriously difficult to interpret (ἡ γὰρ μαρτυρία Ἰησοῦ ἐστιν τὸ πνεῦμα τῆς προφητείας). The testimony to Jesus could refer to the book of Revelation itself (see on 1:2; cf. 22:18, 20), and "spirit of prophecy" likely indicates that "God's Spirit communicates the prophecy" (Koester 732). More generally, it could indicate that testimony to Jesus is (reflects or represents) the Spirit who inspires God's prophets (Fanning 485).

FOR FURTHER STUDY

47. Angel Veneration (19:10; 22:8–9)

Stuckenbruck, L. T. *Angel Veneration and Christology: A Study in Early Judaism and in the Christology of the Apocalypse of John*. WUNT 2.70. Tübingen: Mohr Siebeck, 1995.

c. The Rider on a White Horse (19:11–16)

This is a clear description of the return of Christ, but its features do not match other traditions associated with Jesus's return in early Christianity (Aune[c] 1046); it is a description uniquely appropriate for Revelation. It is important to note that many traditional features are included in earlier parallel visions. Note the cosmic upheaval of the sixth seal and day of the Lord (6:12–17); the two witnesses that ascend to heaven in a cloud (11:12); the seven trumpets that are sounded and culminate in the establishment of the Messiah's kingdom on earth (11:15); the one like a son of man sitting on a cloud in the grain harvest (14:14); the intentional reference to Jesus coming like a thief in the sixth bowl judgment (16:15); and the messianic banquet (19:9).

The attempt to structure 19:11–21:8 around seven visions introduced by καὶ εἶδον (19:11, 17, 19; 20:1, 4, 11; 21:1) seems forced since the expression also occurs in

20:12; 21:2. Mathewson argues that the high concentration of pres. and pf. tense forms to describe the rider in Rev 19:11–16 suggests this section "functions as a peak in the discourse" (Math 264).

19:11 Καὶ εἶδον (1st sg. aor. act. ind. of ὁράω, καὶ εἶδον introduces a new vision, scene, figure, or activity [Aune[a] 338]) **τὸν οὐρανὸν** (dir. obj.) **ἠνεῳγμένον** (acc. sg. masc. of pf. pass. ptc. of ἀνοίγω, compl. in obj.-compl. double acc. construction), **καὶ ἰδοὺ** (emph. interj.) **ἵππος** (ἵππος, -ου, ὁ, "horse," subj. nom. of verbless cl.) **λευκὸς** (λευκός, -ή, -όν, "white, bright," attrib.) **καὶ ὁ καθήμενος** (nom. sg. masc. of pres. mid. ptc. of κάθημαι, subst., coord. subj. nom. of verbless cl.) **ἐπ' αὐτὸν** (loc.) **[καλούμενος]** (nom. sg. masc. of pres. pass. ptc. of καλέω, attrib., several important mss lack καλούμενος [A P 051 1 2042 2081 *al*] while א includes it after πιστός) **πιστὸς** (pred. adj. with pass. καλέω [Wallace 40]) **καὶ ἀληθινός** (ἀληθινός, -ή, -όν, "true," coord. pred. adj. with pass. καλέω), **καὶ ἐν δικαιοσύνῃ** (manner) **κρίνει** (3rd sg. pres. act. ind. of κρίνω, narrative pres.) **καὶ πολεμεῖ** (3rd sg. pres. act. ind. of πολεμέω, "fight, make war," coord. narrative pres.).

Although John had earlier seen θύρα ἠνεῳγμένη ἐν τῷ οὐρανῷ (Rev 4:1) and the opening of books, seals, and the heavenly temple among other things, this is the first and only reference to heaven being opened. The pred. adjs. ascribed to the rider parallel the titular expression ὁ μάρτυς ὁ πιστὸς καὶ ἀληθινός applied to Jesus in Rev 3:14. The combination of δικαιοσύνῃ and κρίνω indicates the judicial nature of the war, while the prior adjs. and prep. phrase describe the character of the warrior judge: he is faithful, true, and just. Such attributes would characterize his judicial warfare.

Use of the OT: Psalm 95:13 LXX (96:13 EVV) gives the reason for calling the heavens and earth to rejoice with joy: God comes to judge the earth and the inhabited world with righteousness and the peoples by his truth (ὅτι ἔρχεται κρῖναι τὴν γῆν, κρινεῖ τὴν οἰκουμένην ἐν δικαιοσύνῃ καὶ λαοὺς ἐν τῇ ἀληθείᾳ αὐτοῦ). The celebratory praise in Psalm 95 LXX leading up to this announcement shares many motifs and words with the praise in Rev 19:1–10 (σωτήριον, δόξα, κύριος, αἰνετός, προσκυνέω, Ὁ κύριος ἐβασίλευσεν, κρίνω, ἀγαλλιάω, χαίρω) suggesting that Psalm 95 LXX was influential in the entire movement from Rev 19:1–11. Isaiah 11:4 prophesies that the righteous branch will judge the poor with righteousness (the LXX replaces "with righteousness" with κρίσιν). Ezekiel begins his visions by stating ἠνοίχθησαν οἱ οὐρανοί, καὶ εἶδον ὁράσεις θεοῦ (1:1). The opened heaven reveals God to Ezekiel while it reveals the rider to John.

19:12 οἱ δὲ ὀφθαλμοὶ (subj. nom. of verbless cl.) **αὐτοῦ** (poss.) **[ὡς]** (comp., the comp. phrase functions as the pred. compl.; the ms. evidence is evenly balanced for and against ὡς) **φλὸξ** (φλόξ, φλογός, ἡ, "flame") **πυρός** (attrib.), **καὶ ἐπὶ τὴν κεφαλὴν** (loc.) **αὐτοῦ** (poss.) **διαδήματα** (διάδημα, -ατος, τό, "crown," subj. nom. of verbless cl.) **πολλά** (attrib.), **ἔχων** (nom. sg. masc. of pres. act. ptc. of ἔχω, likely modifies ὁ καθήμενος in the prior verse, but it could be functioning as a finite vb. [Math 265]) **ὄνομα** (dir. obj., ant. of ὅ) **γεγραμμένον** (acc. sg. neut. of pf. pass. ptc. of γράφω, attrib.) **ὃ** (dir. obj.) **οὐδεὶς** (subj. nom.) **οἶδεν** (3rd sg. pf. act. ind. of οἶδα) **εἰ μὴ** ("if not, except") **αὐτός** (prob. refl., but possibly functions as the subj. nom. of the implied vb. οἶδεν [Math 266]: "No one knows except he [knows]"),

Δέ generally indicates a new or distinct development (Runge 31); in this case that would be a transition to the physical description of the rider (Math 265). The absence of ὡς in P 046 051 and about 170 minuscules is the harder reading, and its presence in A, roughly twenty minuscules, and most ancient versions is likely due to scribal assimilation to both John's normal style and the identical expression in Rev 1:14 (Metzger 686). The many crowns suggest what is stated explicitly in Rev 19:16; he is Βασιλεὺς βασιλέων καὶ κύριος κυρίων. A name that nobody knows is promised to the overcomer in 2:17.

Use of the OT: On the eyes like flaming fire in Dan 10:6, see 1:14.

19:13 καὶ περιβεβλημένος (nom. sg. masc. of pf. pass. ptc. of περιβάλλω, "wrap, clothe," likely modifies ὁ καθήμενος in 19:11, but it could be functioning as a finite vb.) **ἱμάτιον** (dir. obj.) **βεβαμμένον** (acc. sg. neut. of pf. pass. ptc. of βάπτω, "dip," attrib., several mss replace βάπτω with a vb. for sprinkling [ἐρραντισμένον in 172 256 792 1006 1341 1778 1862 2017 2018 2040 2065 2070; ῥεραντισμένον in P 2019 2321 2329; ἐρραμμένον in 2053 2062; ῥεραμμένον in 105 1611; περιρεραμμένον in א* or περιρεραντισμένον in א^{2} [Metzger 686–87]) **αἵματι** (loc.), **καὶ κέκληται** (3rd sg. pf. pass. ind. of καλέω) **τὸ ὄνομα** (subj. nom.) **αὐτοῦ** (poss.) **ὁ λόγος** (pred. nom. with pass. καλέω [Wallace 40]) **τοῦ θεοῦ** (source).

His name being the word of God reflects the introduction to John's Gospel in John 1:1, 14, although a parallel with Wis 18:15, which describes God's all-powerful word from heaven (ὁ παντοδύναμός σου λόγος ἀπ' οὐρανῶν ἐκ θρόνων) as a severe warrior (ἀπότομος πολεμιστὴς) with a sharp sword (ξίφος ὀξὺ) who will bring death to the first-born, better fits the context (Fanning 487).

Use of the OT: It is common for commentators to observe that the robes are stained with blood before the battle begins and conclude that it is the rider's own blood, shed as the slain lamb (Koester 755). The cluster of allusions to Psalm 2 in Rev 19:15, 19, along with the most likely direct allusion, Isa 63:1–6, however, makes this interpretation unlikely.

> Who is this coming from Edom in crimson-stained garments [ἱματίων] from Bozrah—this one who is splendid in his apparel, striding in his formidable might? It is I, proclaiming vindication, powerful to save [ἐγὼ διαλέγομαι

δικαιοσύνην καὶ κρίσιν σωτηρίου].” Why are your clothes red, and your garments like one who treads a winepress [ληνοῦ]? I trampled the winepress alone, and no one from the nations was with me. I trampled them in my anger [κατεπάτησα αὐτοὺς ἐν θυμῷ] and ground them underfoot in my fury; their blood spattered my garments, and all my clothes were stained. For I planned the day of vengeance, and the year of my redemption came. I looked, but there was no one to help, and I was amazed that no one assisted; so my arm accomplished victory for me, and my wrath assisted me. I crushed nations in my anger [κατεπάτησα αὐτοὺς τῇ ὀργῇ]; I made them drunk with my wrath and poured out their blood on the ground. (Isa 63:1–6 CSB)

In addition to the stained garments and the connection to righteousness and judgment (see Rev 19:11), the motif of trampling the winepress is explicitly mentioned in Rev 19:15 (αὐτὸς πατεῖ τὴν ληνὸν τοῦ οἴνου τοῦ θυμοῦ τῆς ὀργῆς τοῦ θεοῦ τοῦ παντοκράτορος). The prebattle stains on the garments in Rev 19:13 more likely relates to the fact that the garments start as stained in Isa 63:1 and the trampling of the winepress was already recounted in Rev 14:19–20 (καὶ ἔβαλεν εἰς τὴν ληνὸν τοῦ θυμοῦ τοῦ θεοῦ τὸν μέγαν. καὶ ἐπατήθη ἡ ληνὸς ἔξωθεν τῆς πόλεως καὶ ἐξῆλθεν αἷμα ἐκ τῆς ληνοῦ).

19:14 καὶ τὰ στρατεύματα (στράτευμα, -ατος, τό, “military, soldiers,” subj. nom.) **[τὰ]** (adjectivizer) **ἐν τῷ οὐρανῷ** (loc.) **ἠκολούθει** (3rd sg. impf. act. ind. of ἀκολουθέω, the impf. provides background information and does not advance the narrative) **αὐτῷ** (dat. dir. obj.) **ἐφ’ ἵπποις** (ἵππος, -ου, ὁ, “horse,” loc.) **λευκοῖς** (λευκός, -ή, -όν, “white, bright,” attrib.), **ἐνδεδυμένοι** (nom. pl. masc. of pf. mid. ptc. of ἐνδύω, “dress, clothe,” manner, the masc. ptc. describes the neut. στρατεύματα as a *constructio ad sensum*) **βύσσινον** (βύσσινος, -η, -ον, “fine linen,” subst., dir. obj.) **λευκὸν** (attrib.) **καθαρόν** (καθαρός, -ά, -όν, “pure,” attrib.).

The clothing of the soldiers parallels the clothing of the bride in 19:8 (βύσσινον λαμπρὸν καθαρόν). The vision does not explicitly indicate whether these soldiers include overcomers in the intermediate state with the angelic forces. There is no support here for Christians taking up physical weapons to try to establish the kingdom of God in anticipation of Jesus’s return.

Use of the OT: Zechariah 14:5 includes all the holy ones with God (καὶ πάντες οἱ ἅγιοι μετ’ αὐτοῦ) when he comes to fight against the nations destroying Jerusalem. The OT prophetic motif of nations arrayed against Jerusalem leads premillennial interpreters to assume that the battle in 19:11–21 is against Jerusalem (Fanning 490), but no such indication of location appears in the vision itself and, ironically, can best be inferred by merging this battle with the later battle that references the beloved city in 20:9.

19:15 καὶ ἐκ τοῦ στόματος (source) **αὐτοῦ** (poss.) **ἐκπορεύεται** (3rd sg. pres. mid. ind. of ἐκπορεύομαι) **ῥομφαία** (ῥομφαία, -ας, ἡ, "sword," subj. nom.) **ὀξεῖα** (ὀξύς, -εῖα, -ύ, "sharp," attrib.), **ἵνα** (purpose) **ἐν αὐτῇ** (means) **πατάξῃ** (3rd sg. aor. act. subjunc. of πατάσσω, "strike") **τὰ ἔθνη** (dir. obj.), **καὶ αὐτὸς** (subj. nom.) **ποιμανεῖ** (3rd sg. fut. act. ind. of ποιμαίνω, "shepherd, rule") **αὐτοὺς** (dir. obj., masc. pron. has a neut. ant. [ἔθνη] as a *constructio ad sensum*) **ἐν ῥάβδῳ** (ῥάβδος, -ου, ἡ, "rod, staff, scepter," means) **σιδηρᾷ** (σιδηροῦς, -ᾶ, -οῦν, "made of iron," attrib.), **καὶ αὐτὸς** (subj. nom.) **πατεῖ** (3rd sg. pres. act. ind. of πατέω, narrative pres.) **τὴν ληνὸν** (ληνός, -οῦ, ἡ, "winepress," dir. obj.) **τοῦ οἴνου** (οἶνος, -ου, ὁ, "wine," content) **τοῦ θυμοῦ** (θυμός, -οῦ, ὁ, "strong passion, anger," appos.) **τῆς ὀργῆς** (ὀργή, -ῆς, ἡ, "anger, wrath," appos. or attrib.) **τοῦ θεοῦ** (subj. gen.) **τοῦ παντοκράτορος** (παντοκράτωρ, -ορος, ὁ, "almighty," appos.),

---

Use of the OT: On the sword, see 1:16. On Ps 2:9, see 12:5. On the winepress, see 14:15, 20; 19:13. The combination of θεός and παντοκράτωρ is found in Amos 3:13 and 4:13 LXX.

19:16 καὶ ἔχει (3rd sg. pres. act. ind. of ἔχω, narrative pres.) **ἐπὶ τὸ ἱμάτιον** (loc.) **καὶ** (epex.) **ἐπὶ τὸν μηρὸν** (μηρός, -οῦ, ὁ, "thigh, leg," loc.) **αὐτοῦ** (poss.) **ὄνομα** (dir. obj.) **γεγραμμένον** (acc. sg. neut. of pf. pass. ptc. of γράφω, attrib.)· **Βασιλεὺς** (titular nom.) **βασιλέων** (subord.) **καὶ κύριος** (titular) **κυρίων** (subord.).

The location of the name is likely explained by the need for the name to be visible to people on foot.

Use of the OT: On the designation King of kings and Lord of lords, see 17:14.

---

d. The Final Defeat of the Two Beasts (19:17–21)

19:17 Καὶ εἶδον (1st sg. aor. act. ind. of ὁράω, καὶ εἶδον introduces a new vision, scene, figure, or activity [Aune[a] 338]) **ἕνα** ("one," attrib., prob. functioning as an indef. art., "an") **ἄγγελον** (dir. obj.) **ἑστῶτα** (acc. sg. masc. of pf. act. ptc. of ἵστημι, compl. in obj.-compl. double acc. construction) **ἐν τῷ ἡλίῳ** (ἥλιος, -ου, ὁ, "sun," loc.) **καὶ ἔκραξεν** (3rd sg. aor. act. ind. of κράζω) [**ἐν**] **φωνῇ** (means) **μεγάλῃ** (attrib.) **λέγων** (nom. sg. masc. of pres. act. ptc. of λέγω, manner) **πᾶσιν** (attrib.) **τοῖς ὀρνέοις** (ὄρνεον, -ου, τό, "bird," indir. obj.) **τοῖς πετομένοις** (dat. pl. neut. of pres. mid. ptc. of πέτομαι, "fly," attrib.) **ἐν μεσουρανήματι** (μεσουράνημα, -ατος, τό, "zenith" [BDAG 635d], the point in the sky directly above the viewer, loc.), **Δεῦτε** (spatial adv. often used as impv. "*come* here!")

συνάχθητε (2nd pl. aor. pass. impv. of συνάγω, pass. for mid.) **εἰς τὸ δεῖπνον** (δεῖπνον, -ου, τό, "dinner, feast," loc.) **τὸ μέγα** (attrib.) **τοῦ θεοῦ** (source or poss.)

This dinner and these invitees are explicitly contrasted with the marriage supper of the Lamb (19:9).

Use of the OT: See 19:18.

19:18 ἵνα (purpose) **φάγητε** (2nd pl. aor. act. subjunc. of ἐσθίω) **σάρκας** (dir. obj.) **βασιλέων** (poss.) **καὶ σάρκας** (dir. obj.) **χιλιάρχων** (χιλίαρχος, -ου, ὁ, "military unit, military commander," poss.) **καὶ σάρκας** (dir. obj.) **ἰσχυρῶν** (ἰσχυρός, -ά, -όν, "strong," subst., poss.) **καὶ σάρκας** (dir. obj.) **ἵππων** (ἵππος, -ου, ὁ, "horse," poss.) **καὶ τῶν καθημένων** (gen. pl. masc. of pres. mid. ptc. of κάθημαι, subst., poss.) **ἐπ' αὐτῶν** (loc.) **καὶ σάρκας** (dir. obj.) **πάντων** (attrib.) **ἐλευθέρων** (ἐλεύθερος, -έρα, -ον, "free," subst., poss.) **τε καὶ** ("both . . . and") **δούλων** (poss.) **καὶ μικρῶν** (subst., poss.) **καὶ μεγάλων** (subst., poss.).

Use of the OT: There is a large cluster of allusions connecting Rev 19:17–18 with Ezek 39:17–20 (cf. Ezek 39:4). This involves both exact lexical matches along with a large number of synonyms (noted by italics), which suggests use of a Hebrew text or perhaps loose paraphrasing from memory. This correspondence suggests that John saw the rider's victory over the beasts and the kings of the earth as parallel to Ezekiel's prophecy of God's defeat of Gog, although Ezekiel does not mention a messianic figure in this context.

Rev 19:17–18: Καὶ εἶδον ἕνα ἄγγελον ἑστῶτα ἐν τῷ ἡλίῳ καὶ ἔκραξεν [ἐν] φωνῇ μεγάλῃ **λέγων πᾶσιν** τοῖς **ὀρνέοις** τοῖς **πετομένοις** ἐν μεσουρανήματι· *Δεῦτε* **συνάχθητε** εἰς τὸ *δεῖπνον* τὸ **μέγα** τοῦ θεοῦ ἵνα **φάγητε** *σάρκας βασιλέων* καὶ σάρκας *χιλιάρχων* καὶ σάρκας ἰσχυρῶν καὶ σάρκας **ἵππων** καὶ τῶν καθημένων ἐπ' αὐτῶν καὶ σάρκας πάντων ἐλευθέρων τε καὶ δούλων καὶ μικρῶν καὶ μεγάλων	Ezek 39:17–20: καὶ σύ, υἱὲ ἀνθρώπου, εἰπόν Τάδε λέγει κύριος **Εἰπὸν παντὶ ὀρνέῳ πετεινῷ** καὶ πρὸς πάντα τὰ θηρία τοῦ πεδίου **Συνάχθητε** καὶ *ἔρχεσθε*, **συνάχθητε** ἀπὸ πάντων τῶν περικύκλῳ ἐπὶ τὴν *θυσίαν* μου, ἣν τέθυκα ὑμῖν, *θυσίαν* **μεγάλην** ἐπὶ τὰ ὄρη Ισραηλ, καὶ **φάγεσθε** *κρέα* καὶ πίεσθε αἷμα. *κρέα γιγάντων* **φάγεσθε** καὶ αἷμα *ἀρχόντων* τῆς γῆς πίεσθε, κριοὺς καὶ μόσχους καὶ τράγους, καὶ οἱ μόσχοι ἐστεατωμένοι πάντες. καὶ **φάγεσθε** στέαρ εἰς πλησμονὴν καὶ πίεσθε αἷμα εἰς μέθην ἀπὸ τῆς θυσίας μου, ἧς ἔθυσα ὑμῖν. καὶ ἐμπλησθήσεσθε ἐπὶ τῆς *τραπέζης* μου **ἵππον** καὶ *ἀναβάτην*, γίγαντα καὶ πάντα ἄνδρα πολεμιστήν, λέγει κύριος.

19:19 Καὶ εἶδον (1st sg. aor. act. ind. of ὁράω, καὶ εἶδον introduces a new vision, scene, figure, or activity [Aune[a] 338]) **τὸ θηρίον** (θηρίον, -ου, τό, "beast," dir. obj.) **καὶ τοὺς βασιλεῖς** (coord. dir. obj.) **τῆς γῆς** (subord.) **καὶ τὰ στρατεύματα** (στράτευμα, -ατος, τό, "military, soldiers," coord. dir. obj.) **αὐτῶν** (poss.) **συνηγμένα** (acc. pl. neut. of pf. pass. ptc. of συνάγω, compl. in obj.-compl. double acc. construction) **ποιῆσαι** (aor. act. inf. of ποιέω, purpose) **τὸν πόλεμον** (πόλεμος, -ου, ὁ, "battle," dir. obj.) **μετὰ τοῦ καθημένου** (gen. sg. masc. of pres. mid. ptc. of κάθημαι, subst., association with the contextual nuance of disadvantage, "against") **ἐπὶ τοῦ ἵππου** (ἵππος, -ου, ὁ, "horse," loc.) **καὶ μετὰ τοῦ στρατεύματος** (association) **αὐτοῦ** (poss.).

Although Revelation repeatedly uses the language of warfare, it lacks any narrative of actual battle; there are no details that would require a future physical conflict. The visions of Revelation could be fulfilled by a future physical battle, but the apocalyptic visions do not require such a battle and could be fulfilled in various ways through global persecution or spiritual conflict (Koester 764).

Use of the OT: Psalm 2:2 notes how οἱ βασιλεῖς τῆς γῆς were gathered (συνήχθησαν) κατὰ (against) τοῦ κυρίου καὶ κατὰ τοῦ χριστοῦ αὐτοῦ. Note the allusion to Ps 2:9 in Rev 19:15 above. The irony is that the kings in Rev 19:19 have completely failed to heed the instructions to kings in Ps 2:10–12: "So now, kings [βασιλεῖς], be wise; receive instruction, you judges of the earth. Serve the Lord with reverential awe and rejoice with trembling. Pay homage to the Son or he will be angry and you perish in your rebellion, for his anger may ignite at any moment. All who take refuge in him are happy" (CSB).

19:20 καὶ ἐπιάσθη (3rd sg. aor. pass. ind. of πιάζω, "seize, hold," sg. vb. with compound subj. focuses on the first or most important subj. listed) **τὸ θηρίον** (θηρίον, -ου, τό, "beast," subj. nom.) **καὶ μετ' αὐτοῦ** (association) **ὁ ψευδοπροφήτης** (ψευδοπροφήτης, -ου, ὁ, "false prophet," coord. subj. nom.) **ὁ ποιήσας** (nom. sg. masc. of aor. act. ptc. of ποιέω, attrib.) **τὰ σημεῖα** (dir. obj., ant. of οἷς) **ἐνώπιον αὐτοῦ** (loc. or "by the authority of, on behalf of" [BDAG 342d]), **ἐν οἷς** (means) **ἐπλάνησεν** (3rd sg. aor. act. ind. of πλανάω, "deceive") **τοὺς λαβόντας** (acc. pl. masc. of aor. act. ptc. of λαμβάνω, subst., dir. obj.) **τὸ χάραγμα** (χάραγμα, -ατος, τό, "mark," dir. obj.) **τοῦ θηρίου** (θηρίον, -ου, τό, poss. or source) **καὶ τοὺς προσκυνοῦντας** (acc. pl. masc. of pres. act. ptc. of προσκυνέω, subst., dir. obj.) **τῇ εἰκόνι** (εἰκών, -όνος, ἡ, "image," dat. dir. obj.) **αὐτοῦ** (obj. gen.)· **ζῶντες** (nom. pl. masc. pres. act. ptc. ζάω, manner) **ἐβλήθησαν** (3rd pl. aor. pass. ind. βάλλω) **οἱ** (substantivizer) **δύο** ("two," subst.) **εἰς τὴν λίμνην** (λίμνη, -ης, ἡ, "lake," loc.)

τοῦ πυρὸς (content or attrib. gen.) **τῆς καιομένης** (gen. sg. fem. of pres. mid. ptc. of καίω, "burn," attrib.) **ἐν θείῳ** (θεῖον, -ου, τό, "sulfur," association or means).

See 9:1 on the distinctions between the abyss, Hades, and the lake of fire in Revelation. "The participle καιομένης is in gender agreement with λίμνην, and in case concord with πυρὸς. Though late and not original, the emendations of the scribes suggest that 19:20 contains a case, not a gender problem" (Moţ 140). "John started the accord with the correct gender, thinking of τὴν λίμνην, and ended up with an unexpected case, thinking of τοῦ πυρὸς" (Moţ 141). Jesus commands the goats to go to the eternal fire prepared for the devil and his angels in Matt 25:41 (Πορεύεσθε ἀπ' ἐμοῦ [οἱ] κατηραμένοι εἰς τὸ πῦρ τὸ αἰώνιον τὸ ἡτοιμασμένον τῷ διαβόλῳ καὶ τοῖς ἀγγέλοις αὐτοῦ).

Use of the OT: Isaiah 30:27–32 does not mention a lake (λίμνη) but describes God's judgment of Assyria and her king with particular attention to verbal judgment, fire, sulfur, and a "burning place" (Topheth):

> Behold, the name of the LORD comes from afar,
> burning with his anger [καιόμενος ὁ θυμός], and in thick rising smoke;
>
> his lips are full of fury,
> and his tongue is like a devouring fire;
>
> his breath is like an overflowing stream
> that reaches up to the neck;
>
> to sift the nations with the sieve of destruction,
> and to place on the jaws of the peoples a bridle that leads astray . . .

And the LORD will cause his majestic voice to be heard and the descending blow of his arm to be seen, in furious anger and a flame of devouring fire [μετὰ θυμοῦ καὶ ὀργῆς καὶ φλογὸς κατεσθιούσης], with a cloudburst and storm and hailstones [χάλαζα]. The Assyrians will be terror-stricken at the voice of the LORD, when he strikes with his rod. [The Hebrew for "rod" (שֵׁבֶט) matches the rod in Ps 2:9, which was alluded to in Rev 19:15; this link-word between the two OT passages is obscured by the LXX translation: ᾗ ἂν πατάξῃ αὐτούς] And every stroke of the appointed staff that the Lord lays on them will be to the sound of tambourines and lyres. Battling with brandished arm, he will fight with them. For a burning place has long been prepared [this reference to a burning place could connect to John's lake of fire but the Heb. is difficult (תָּפְתֶּה; prob. Topheth from 2 Kgs 23:10) and the LXX omits the word perhaps because of uncertainty regarding how to translate it]; indeed, for the king it is made ready, its pyre made deep and wide, with fire and wood in abundance [πῦρ καὶ ξύλα πολλά]; the breath of the LORD, like a stream of sulfur, kindles it [ὁ θυμὸς κυρίου ὡς φάραγξ ὑπὸ θείου [sulfur] καιομένη]. (Isa 30:27–33 ESV)

For additional OT passages that employ sulfur in contexts of judgment, see 14:10.

19:21 καὶ οἱ λοιποὶ (λοιπός, -ή, -όν, "left, rest," subst., subj. nom.) **ἀπεκτάνθησαν** (3rd pl. aor. pass. ind. of ἀποκτείνω) **ἐν τῇ ῥομφαίᾳ** (ῥομφαία, -ας, ἡ, "sword," means) **τοῦ καθημένου** (gen. sg. masc. of pres. mid. ptc. of κάθημαι, subst., poss. or source) **ἐπὶ τοῦ ἵππου** (ἵππος, -ου, ὁ, "horse," loc.) **τῇ ἐξελθούσῃ** (dat. sg. fem. of aor. act. ptc. of ἐξέρχομαι, attrib.) **ἐκ τοῦ στόματος** (source) **αὐτοῦ** (poss.), **καὶ πάντα** (attrib.) **τὰ ὄρνεα** (ὄρνεον, -ου, τό, "bird," subj. nom.) **ἐχορτάσθησαν** (3rd pl. aor. pass. ind. of χορτάζω, "feed, fill," pl. vb. with neut. pl. subj.) **ἐκ τῶν σαρκῶν** (source) **αὐτῶν** (poss.).

Use of the OT: See 19:18.

HOMILETICAL SUGGESTIONS

Revelation 19 begins with heaven's worship and praise from God's people elicited by his just actions against Babylon (19:1–10). The vision of Jesus's coming focuses on his victory over the two beasts (19:11–21). The chapter juxtaposes the marriage supper of the Lamb with the supper of judgment in order to motivate the hearer to choose to be a part of the proper supper.

Jesus Comes at Last! (19:1–21)

1. Heaven's worship invites a human response (19:1–5).
2. The bride is prepared for the marriage supper (19:6–10).
3. Jesus brings salvation and judgment (19:11–21).

2. The Millennium (20:1–6)

The millennial debate does not particularly hinge on grammar or syntax and involves broader hermeneutical discussions. The following points support a premillennial position. First, the description of Satan's binding in Rev 20:2–3 is not presented as partial, and it is hard to construe it as such within the vision itself. Second, the language of resurrection (ζάω; ἀνάστασις) is explicitly contrasted with the later general resurrection (20:5) and most naturally points to a physical, bodily resurrection (20:4–5) (In support of premillennialism, see Fanning 508–14).

The following points support an amillennial interpretation. First, other early Christian texts present Satan as bound, restrained, or hindered because of the Christ event (Matt 12:29; Mark 3:27; Luke 10:17–19; John 12:31–33; Col 2:15; 2 Thess 2:6–12; Heb 2:14). These bindings do not restrict all of Satan's activities (2 Pet 2:4; Jude v. 6) but demonstrate Jesus's ultimate power over him. Second, apocalyptic literature invites and requires a symbolic approach to interpretation (Rev 1:1; σημαίνω). Third, apart from this single apocalyptic text (Rev 20:4–5) the rest of Christian Scripture points forward to a single future resurrection of believers and unbelievers prior to eschatological judgment and reward (Isa 26:19–21; Dan 12:2; John 5:28–29; Acts 24:15; 2 Thess 1:7–10). Fourth, the millennial vision naturally parallels visions earlier in Revelation of believers in victory and rest in the intermediate state (6:9–11; 7:9–17; 14:1–5, 13; 15:2–4; cf. 19:1–9). Fifth, John's reliance on the Gog and Magog oracles in Ezekiel to describe both the battle against the beast before the millennium and the battle against the dragon after the millennium suggests that the two different visions describe the same final event. Sixth, a literal interpretation raises a host of unnecessary questions and problems. Why is Satan bound only to be released? Who are the deceived nations at the end of the millennium? Whom do the saints rule? How does it work for resurrected people to live amid unresurrected people in the old, untransformed creation? Why are the nations protected from Satan's deception right after they had just been deceived, judged, and destroyed by Christ? Why is it necessary for the nations to be deceived and destroyed twice? (in support of amillennialism, see Beale 972–1021).

The attempt to compare the millennium with the temporary messianic kingdom in Jewish apocalyptic writings is on the right track but must not miss how the earliest Christians transformed this expectation of a temporary messianic kingdom in light of the messiah's enthronement at God's right hand into inaugurated eschatology (see Stewart, "Temporary Messianic Kingdom").

20:1 Καὶ εἶδον (1st sg. aor. act. ind.of ὁράω, καὶ εἶδον introduces a new vision, scene, figure, or activity [Aune[a] 338]) **ἄγγελον** (dir. obj.) **καταβαίνοντα** (acc. sg. masc. of pres. act. ptc. of καταβαίνω, compl. in obj.-compl. double acc. construction) **ἐκ τοῦ οὐρανοῦ** (source) **ἔχοντα** (acc. sg. masc. of pres. act. ptc. of ἔχω, attrib.) **τὴν κλεῖν** (κλείς, κλειδός, ἡ, "key," dir. obj.) **τῆς ἀβύσσου** (ἄβυσσος, -ου, ἡ, "abyss," obj. gen.) **καὶ ἅλυσιν** (ἅλυσις, -εως, ἡ, "chain," coord. dir. obj.) **μεγάλην** (attrib.) **ἐπὶ τὴν χεῖρα** (loc.) **αὐτοῦ** (poss.).

The key to the abyss had earlier been given to a fallen star to release demonic tormentors (9:1).

20:2 καὶ ἐκράτησεν (3rd sg. aor. act. ind. of κρατέω, "hold, seize") **τὸν δράκοντα** (δράκων, -οντος, ὁ, "dragon, serpent," dir. obj., ant. of ὅς), **ὁ ὄφις** (ὄφις, -εως, ὁ, "serpent," appos., the incongruous use of the nom. likely indicates a title; several mss [A 1678 1778 2080] read the acc. τὸν ὄφιν τὸν ἀρχαῖον to fix the problem [Metzger 678]) **ὁ ἀρχαῖος** (ἀρχαῖος, -αία, -αῖον, "ancient," attrib.), **ὅς** (subj. nom.) **ἐστιν** (3rd sg. pres. act. ind. of εἰμί) **Διάβολος** (διάβολος, -ον, "slanderer, adversary, devil," pred. nom.) **καὶ ὁ Σατανᾶς** (σατανᾶς, ᾶ, ὁ, "Satan," coord. pred. nom.), **καὶ ἔδησεν** (3rd sg. aor. act. ind. of δέω, "bind") **αὐτὸν** (dir. obj.) **χίλια** ("thousand," attrib.) **ἔτη** (ἔτος, -ους, τό, "year," temp.)

The string of noms. are functioning in appos. to the acc. τὸν δράκοντα and should thus be in the acc. case. The lack of agreement likely indicates that the noms. are titles or quotations functioning as if they were proper names. The discord places emph. on the noms. (Wallace 62). The names and titles unambiguously connect this figure to the character in 12:9.

20:3 καὶ ἔβαλεν (3rd sg. aor. act. ind. of βάλλω) **αὐτὸν** (dir. obj.) **εἰς τὴν ἄβυσσον** (ἄβυσσος, -ου, ἡ, "abyss," loc.) **καὶ ἔκλεισεν** (3rd sg. aor. act. ind. of κλείω, "shut") **καὶ ἐσφράγισεν** (3rd sg. aor. act. ind. of σφραγίζω, "seal") **ἐπάνω** (prep., "above, over") **αὐτοῦ** (loc. with ἐπάνω), **ἵνα** (purpose) **μὴ πλανήσῃ** (3rd sg. aor. act. subjunc. of πλανάω, "deceive") **ἔτι** (adv., extension of time) **τὰ ἔθνη** (dir. obj.) **ἄχρι** (subord. conj. indicating extension of time, "until") **τελεσθῇ** (3rd sg. aor. pass. subjunc. of τελέω) **τὰ** (anaphoric to 20:2) **χίλια** ("thousand," attrib.) **ἔτη** (ἔτος, -ους, τό, "year," subj. nom.). **μετὰ ταῦτα** (subst., temp.) **δεῖ** (3rd sg. pres. act. ind. impers., "it is necessary") **λυθῆναι** (aor. pass. inf. of λύω, compl.) **αὐτὸν** (acc. subj. of inf.) **μικρὸν** (μικρός, -ά, -όν, "small, little," attrib.) **χρόνον** (χρόνος, -ου, ὁ, "time, period," temp.).

Revelation is entirely unique in suggesting that the devil would be bound and then temporarily released before the end (Koester 771). There are significant similarities between 20:1–6 and 12:7–11 (Beale 992), which suggests that the two visions could be describing the same sequence of events with different emphases and perspectives, not with pedantic copying. Alternatively, if the visions are sequential, the career of Satan in Revelation consists of a series of defeats that result in him being cast from one location to another (from heaven to earth at Jesus's enthronement in heaven [12:7–11], from earth to the abyss after Jesus's return [20:1–3], from the abyss to earth to the lake of fire after the 1,000 years [20:10]).

Most, but not all, numbers in Revelation are symbolic, but there is no definitive argument to settle the debate regarding the 1,000 years. The abyss has been mentioned previously in 9:1–2, 11; 11:7; 17:8. Peter describes how God did not spare angels who sinned but handed them over to be kept in Tartarus in gloomy chains until judgment (2 Pet 2:4: Εἰ γὰρ ὁ θεὸς ἀγγέλων ἁμαρτησάντων οὐκ ἐφείσατο ἀλλὰ σειραῖς ζόφου ταρταρώσας παρέδωκεν εἰς κρίσιν τηρουμένους). Jude 6 describes how God has kept rebellious angels in bonds until the judgment of the great day (εἰς κρίσιν μεγάλης ἡμέρας δεσμοῖς).

20:4 Καὶ εἶδον (1st sg. aor. act. ind. of ὁράω, καὶ εἶδον introduces a new vision, scene, figure, or activity [Aune[a] 338]) **θρόνους** (dir. obj.) **καὶ ἐκάθισαν** (3rd pl. aor. act. ind. of καθίζω, "sit," the subj. is not explicit) **ἐπ' αὐτοὺς** (loc.) **καὶ κρίμα** (κρίμα, -ατος, τό, "judgment," subj. nom.) **ἐδόθη** (3rd sg. aor. pass. ind. of δίδωμι) **αὐτοῖς** (indir. obj. indicating their authority to judge or dat. of advantage indicating a positive verdict, "judgment was given for them or on their behalf"; the allusion to Dan 7:22 noted below supports the dat. of advantage), **καὶ** (likely epex. to further explain the identity of the αὐτοῖς or coord. to describe the souls as a separate group from those on the thrones) **τὰς ψυχὰς** (dir. obj. of εἶδον, ant. of οἵτινες) **τῶν πεπελεκισμένων** (gen. pl. masc. of pf. pass. ptc. of πελεκίζω, "behead," subst., poss.) **διὰ τὴν μαρτυρίαν** (causal) **Ἰησοῦ** (obj. gen.) **καὶ διὰ τὸν λόγον** (coord. causal) **τοῦ θεοῦ** (subj. or obj. gen.) **καὶ** (likely epex. pointing to a single group despite incongruity [*constructio ad sensum*] between the masc. οἵτινες and the fem. ψυχάς) **οἵτινες** (subj. nom.) **οὐ προσεκύνησαν** (3rd pl. aor. act. ind. of προσκυνέω) **τὸ θηρίον** (θηρίον, -ου, τό, "beast," dir. obj.) **οὐδὲ τὴν εἰκόνα** (εἰκών, -όνος, ἡ, "image," coord. dir. obj.) **αὐτοῦ** (obj. gen.) **καὶ οὐκ ἔλαβον** (3rd pl. aor. act. ind. of λαμβάνω) **τὸ χάραγμα** (χάραγμα, -ατος, τό, "mark," dir. obj.) **ἐπὶ τὸ μέτωπον** (μέτωπον, -ου, τό, "forehead," loc., distributive noun with pl. pron.) **καὶ ἐπὶ τὴν χεῖρα**

(loc., distributive noun with pl. pron.) **αὐτῶν** (poss.). **καὶ ἔζησαν** (3rd pl. aor. act. ind. of ζάω, ingressive) **καὶ ἐβασίλευσαν** (3rd pl. aor. act. ind. of βασιλεύω, "rule," ingressive) **μετὰ τοῦ Χριστοῦ** (association) **χίλια** ("thousand," attrib.) **ἔτη** (ἔτος, -ους, τό, "year," temp.).

The references to disembodied souls (ψυχή) and the cause of their death (διὰ τὴν μαρτυρίαν Ἰησοῦ καὶ διὰ τὸν λόγον τοῦ θεοῦ) make a strong connection back to the souls under the altar in 6:9 who are here equated with the Christians who resisted the beasts. They had cried out to God for justice and are now pictured as vindicated either through an additional visionary description of the rest they were promised in the intermediate state (amillennial), or through public earthly vindication in resurrected bodies (premillennial). There is no clear indication in 20:4–6 regarding the location of the vision (earth or heaven), although the presence of the thrones would suggest the divine council and heavenly throne room as in Daniel 7 and elsewhere in Revelation.

In addition to Rev 20:6 below, the vb. βασιλεύω applied to God's people is also found in 5:10, where it anticipates future reigning, and 22:5 with reference to eternal reigning in God's new creation. The present existence of God's people as a kingdom (βασιλεία) is expressed in Rev 1:6, 9; 5:10 with dependence on Exod 19:6. Jesus promises his disciples in Luke 22:28 that they would sit on thrones judging the twelve tribes of Israel. Paul seems to pick up on this saying of Jesus in 1 Cor 6:2 but expands it from the disciples to the saints and from the twelve tribes of Israel to the world (ἢ οὐκ οἴδατε ὅτι οἱ ἅγιοι τὸν κόσμον κρινοῦσιν). Revelation does not mention Israel in this vision, and it seems to be in line with the Pauline expansion of the Jesus tradition.

Premillennial approaches tend to view the millennium as the fulfillment of various promises in the OT regarding Israel's restoration, the transformation of the earth, and the reign of the Messiah from Jerusalem (Fanning 509–10), but Rev 20:4–6 does not mention the fulfillment of these things: "[r]ather, the vision of the new creation, which paraphrases Isaiah, Ezekiel, and other texts, makes it clear that the new creation is where Revelation expects the prophetic hopes to be realized. . . . The millennium does not have this role in Revelation" (Koester 749).

Use of the OT: Daniel 7:9 states that thrones were put (θρόνοι ἐτέθησαν); this points to the divine court/council. Daniel 7:22 describes how the ancient of days gave judgment for the saints of the highest (καὶ τὴν κρίσιν ἔδωκε τοῖς ἁγίοις τοῦ ὑψίστου) and the time was given (καὶ ὁ καιρὸς ἐδόθη) and the holy ones held fast the kingdom (καὶ τὸ βασίλειον κατέσχον οἱ ἅγιοι). The vision in Daniel 7 concludes in 7:27 by describing how God gave the kingdom and the authority and their majesty and the rule of all the ones reigning under the heaven to the holy people of the Most High (καὶ τὴν βασιλείαν καὶ τὴν ἐξουσίαν καὶ τὴν μεγαλειότητα αὐτῶν καὶ τὴν ἀρχὴν πασῶν τῶν ὑπὸ τὸν οὐρανὸν βασιλειῶν ἔδωκε λαῷ ἁγίῳ ὑψίστου) to rule an eternal kingdom (βασιλεῦσαι βασιλείαν αἰώνιον), and all the authorities will be subjected to him and they will obey him (καὶ πᾶσαι αἱ ἐξουσίαι αὐτῷ ὑποταγήσονται καὶ πειθαρχήσουσιν αὐτῷ).

The vb. ἔζησαν alludes to the identical form of the vb. in Ezek 37:10 (other allusions to Ezekiel 37 include Ezek 37:3 in Rev 7:13–14; Ezek 37:5, 10 in Rev 11:11; Ezek 37:27 in Rev 7:15; 21:3). This suggests that John viewed the Ezekiel 37 prophecy as finding fulfillment in the intermediate state in Rev 7:13–15; the vindication of the two witnesses in Rev 11:11; the millennium in Rev 20:4–5; and the new creation in Rev 21:3.

20:5 οἱ λοιποὶ (λοιπός, -ή, -όν, "left, rest," subst., subj. nom.) **τῶν νεκρῶν** (part. gen.) **οὐκ ἔζησαν** (3rd pl. aor. act. ind. of ζάω, ingressive) **ἄχρι** (temp. subord. conj., extent, "until") **τελεσθῇ** (3rd sg. aor. pass. subjunc. of τελέω) **τὰ χίλια** ("thousand," attrib.) **ἔτη** (ἔτος, -ους, τό, "year," subj. nom.). **αὕτη** (subj. nom. of verbless cl., the ant. is 20:4) **ἡ ἀνάστασις** (ἀνάστασις, -εως, ἡ, "resurrection," pred. nom. of verbless cl.) **ἡ πρώτη** ("first," attrib.). This verse anticipates the final judgment scene in 20:11–15.
20:6 μακάριος (μακάριος, -ία, -ιον, "blessed, happy," pred. adj. of verbless cl.) **καὶ ἅγιος** (coord. pred. adj.) **ὁ ἔχων** (nom. sg. masc. of pres. act. ptc. of ἔχω, subst., subj. nom. of verbless cl.) **μέρος** (μέρος, -ους, τό, "part," dir. obj.) **ἐν τῇ ἀναστάσει** (ἀνάστασις, -εως, ἡ, "resurrection," with μέρος ἐν this functions as something like a part. dat., the resurrection is the whole of which μέρος is a share/part) **τῇ πρώτῃ** ("first," attrib.)· **ἐπὶ τούτων** (subord., the pl. pron. has a sg. ant. [ἔχων] as a *constructio ad sensum*) **ὁ δεύτερος** ("second," attrib.) **θάνατος** (subj. nom.) **οὐκ ἔχει** (3rd sg. pres. act. ind. of ἔχω) **ἐξουσίαν** (dir. obj.), **ἀλλ'** (adversative) **ἔσονται** (3rd pl. fut. mid. ind. of εἰμί) **ἱερεῖς** (ἱερεύς, -έως, ὁ, "priest," pred. nom.) **τοῦ θεοῦ** (poss.) **καὶ τοῦ Χριστοῦ** (coord. poss.) **καὶ βασιλεύσουσιν** (3rd pl. fut. act. ind. of βασιλεύω, "rule, reign") **μετ' αὐτοῦ** (association) **[τὰ]** (the manuscript evidence is evenly balanced on the inclusion or omission of the art.) **χίλια** ("thousand," attrib.) **ἔτη** (ἔτος, -ους, τό, "year," temp.).

This is the fifth macarism in Revelation. The second death is identified in 20:14 as the lake of fire. The reference builds upon the promise that the one who conquers will not be harmed by the second death (2:11). The description of God's people as ἱερεῖς connects back to Rev 1:6; 5:10 with dependence on Exod 19:6 and Isa 61:6 (ὑμεῖς δὲ ἱερεῖς κυρίου κληθήσεσθε). It also matches the liturgical service in the heavenly temple during the intermediate state pictured in 7:15. These observations (along with comments in 20:4) suggest that the millennial vision describes the positive fate of all of God's people and not just a particular subset.

FOR FURTHER STUDY

48. The Millennium (20:1–6)

*Beale, G. K. "The Millennium in Revelation 20:1–10: An Amillennial Perspective." *CTR* 11 (2013): 29–62.

Blaising, C. A. "Premillennialism: A Progressive Dispensational View." *CTR* 11 (2013): 63–70.

Blomberg, C. L. "Why I Am a Historic Premillennialist." *CTR* 11 (2013): 71–87.

Bock, D. L., ed. *Three Views on the Millennium and Beyond*. Counterpoints. Grand Rapids: Zondervan, 1999.
Gentry, K. L. "The Postmillennial Vision of Christian Eschatology." *CTR* 11 (2013): 89–101.
Giblin, C. H. "The Millennium (Rev 20.4–6) as Heaven." *NTS* 45 (1999): 553–70.
Mathewson, D. L. "A Re-Examination of the Millennium in Rev 20:1–6: Consummation and Recapitulation." *JETS* 44 (2001): 237–51.
Poythress, V. S. "Genre and Hermeneutics in Rev 20:1–6." *JETS* 36 (1993): 41–54.
*Schnabel, E. J. "The Viability of Premillennialism and the Text of Revelation." *JETS* 64 (2021): 785–95.

3. Satan's Final Defeat (20:7–10)

20:7 Καὶ ὅταν (temp. subord. conj.) **τελεσθῇ** (3rd sg. aor. pass. subjunc. of τελέω) **τὰ χίλια** ("thousand," attrib.) **ἔτη** (ἔτος, -ους, τό, "year," subj. nom.), **λυθήσεται** (3rd sg. fut. pass. ind. of λύω) **ὁ Σατανᾶς** (σατανᾶς, ᾶ, ὁ, subj. nom.) **ἐκ τῆς φυλακῆς** (φυλακή, -ῆς, ἡ, "prison," separation) **αὐτοῦ** (obj. gen.)
20:8 καὶ ἐξελεύσεται (3rd sg. fut. mid. ind. of ἐξέρχομαι) **πλανῆσαι** (aor. act. inf. of πλανάω, "deceive," purpose) **τὰ ἔθνη** (dir. obj., ant. of ὧν) **τὰ** (adjectivizer) **ἐν ταῖς τέσσαρσιν** ("four," attrib.) **γωνίαις** (γωνία, -ας, ἡ, "corner," loc.) **τῆς γῆς** (part. gen.), **τὸν Γὼγ** ("Gog," appos. to ἔθνη) **καὶ Μαγώγ** ("Magog," appos. to ἔθνη), **συναγαγεῖν** (aor. act. inf. of συνάγω, purpose) **αὐτοὺς** (dir. obj.) **εἰς τὸν πόλεμον** (πόλεμος, -ου, ὁ, "battle," purpose), **ὧν** (poss.) **ὁ ἀριθμὸς** (ἀριθμός, -οῦ, ὁ, "number," subj. nom. of verbless cl.) **αὐτῶν** (obj. gen., redundant with ὧν for emph.) **ὡς** (comp.) **ἡ ἄμμος** (ἄμμος, -ου, ἡ, "sand") **τῆς θαλάσσης** (poss.).

Use of the OT: Ezekiel 7:2 describes the end that has come upon the four wings/edges of the earth (τὸ πέρας ἥκει ἐπὶ τὰς τέσσαρας πτέρυγας τῆς γῆς). John's reference to Gog and Magog clearly signals an allusion to Ezek 38:2 and the Gog from the Magog oracles in Ezekiel 38–39. This parallels the clear allusion to the Gog and Magog oracles in the battle recounted in 19:17–18.

20:9 καὶ ἀνέβησαν (3rd pl. aor. act. ind. of ἀναβαίνω) **ἐπὶ τὸ πλάτος** (πλάτος, -ους, τό, "width," loc.) **τῆς γῆς** (part. gen.) **καὶ ἐκύκλευσαν** (3rd pl. aor. act. ind. of κυκλεύω, "surround") **τὴν παρεμβολὴν** (παρεμβολή, -ῆς, ἡ, "military camp," dir. obj.) **τῶν ἁγίων** (poss.) **καὶ** (epex., "even, that is") **τὴν πόλιν** (dir. obj.) **τὴν ἠγαπημένην** (acc. sg. fem. of pf. pass. ptc. of ἀγαπάω, attrib.), **καὶ κατέβη** (3rd sg. aor. act. ind. of καταβαίνω) **πῦρ** (subj. nom.) **ἐκ τοῦ οὐρανοῦ** (source, a large number of mss add ἀπὸ τοῦ θεοῦ either before or after ἐκ τοῦ οὐρανοῦ but this is likely an addition influenced by 21:2, 10 [Metzger 687–88]) **καὶ κατέφαγεν** (3rd sg. aor. act. ind. of κατεσθίω, "consume, devour") **αὐτούς** (dir. obj., the masc. pron. is incongruous with its neut. ant. ἔθνη as a *constructio ad sensum*).

The encampment of the saints is further described as the beloved city, a likely allusion to Jerusalem (Pss 78:68; 87:2). This, however, does not require Jerusalem as a literal location since in Revelation it could also refer collectively to God's people (note how the bride is shown to be a city in 21:10; cf. 11:2).

Use of the OT: Gog's army "goes up" (ἀναβαίνω) in Ezek 38:9, 11, 16. The expression καὶ κατέβη πῦρ ἐκ τοῦ οὐρανοῦ καὶ κατέφαγεν αὐτὸν καὶ τοὺς πεντήκοντα αὐτοῦ occurs in 4 Kgdms 1:10, 12 (2 Kgs 1:10, 12 EVV) when fire comes down from heaven to consume two separate groups, each consisting of a captain and fifty men, who had been sent to capture Elijah. The use of fire to destroy Gog in Ezek 38:22; 39:6 is important to note because of the reference to Gog and Magog in Rev 20:8. Fire frequently occurs in contexts of judgment; the most important of which for Revelation probably include Gen 19:24; 1 Kgs 18:38; 4 Ezra 13:10–11, 37–38. Elsewhere in Revelation fire destroys Babylon (18:8–9) and the enemies of the two witnesses (11:5). Fire is also produced by the second beast to deceive (13:13) and occurs throughout the trumpet and bowl judgments.

20:10 καὶ ὁ διάβολος (διάβολος, -ον, "slanderer, adversary, devil," subj. nom.) **ὁ πλανῶν** (nom. sg. masc. of pres. act. ptc. of πλανάω, "deceive," attrib.) **αὐτοὺς** (dir. obj.) **ἐβλήθη** (3rd sg. aor. pass. ind. of βάλλω) **εἰς τὴν λίμνην** (λίμνη, -ης, ἡ, "lake," loc.) **τοῦ πυρὸς** (content) **καὶ θείου** (θεῖον, -ου, τό, "sulfur," coord. content) **ὅπου** (loc. subord. conj., "where") **καὶ** (adv., "also") **τὸ θηρίον** (θηρίον, -ου, τό, "beast," subj. nom. of verbless cl.) **καὶ ὁ ψευδοπροφήτης** (ψευδοπροφήτης, -ου, ὁ, "false prophet," coord. subj. nom.), **καὶ βασανισθήσονται** (3rd pl. fut. pass. ind. of βασανίζω, "torture") **ἡμέρας** (temp.) **καὶ νυκτὸς** (temp.) **εἰς τοὺς αἰῶνας** (measure) **τῶν αἰώνων** (emph. repetition of αἰών).

Use of the OT: On the lake of fire and sulfur, see 19:20 on Isa 30:33. On the use of fire and sulfur for judgment, see 14:10.

---

4. The Final Judgment (20:11–15)

20:11 Καὶ εἶδον (1st sg. aor. act. ind. of ὁράω, καὶ εἶδον introduces a new vision, scene, figure, or activity [Aune[a] 338]) **θρόνον** (dir. obj., the lack of an anaphoric art. is noteworthy since John uses it so consistently; this could suggest that this throne differs from the one in 4:2 but this point should prob. not be pushed) **μέγαν** (attrib.) **λευκὸν** (λευκός, -ή, -όν, "white, bright," attrib.) **καὶ τὸν** (anaphoric to 4:2) **καθήμενον** (acc. sg.

masc. of pres. mid. ptc. of κάθημαι, subst., dir. obj., ant. of οὗ) **ἐπ' αὐτόν** (loc.), **οὗ** (poss.) **ἀπὸ τοῦ προσώπου** (separation) **ἔφυγεν** (3rd sg. aor. act. ind. of φεύγω, "flee," the sg. vb. is used with a compound subj.) **ἡ γῆ** (subj. nom.) **καὶ ὁ οὐρανὸς** (coord. subj. nom.) **καὶ τόπος** (subj. nom.) **οὐχ εὑρέθη** (3rd sg. aor. pass. ind. of εὑρίσκω) **αὐτοῖς** (advantage, "for").

The cosmic upheaval mirrors similar descriptions of the day of the Lord in the fifth seal (6:14) and the seventh bowl judgment (16:20). The seventh trumpet section also clearly describes the judgment of the dead (11:18).

Use of the OT: Psalm 113:3–4 LXX (114:3–4 EVV) describes how before the presence of God the sea fled (ἡ θάλασσα εἶδεν καὶ ἔφυγεν), the Jordan turned back (ὁ Ιορδάνης ἐστράφη εἰς τὰ ὀπίσω), and the mountains skipped like rams and the hills like the lambs of the sheep (τὰ ὄρη ἐσκίρτησαν ὡσεὶ κριοὶ καὶ οἱ βουνοὶ ὡς ἀρνία προβάτων). Verse 7 goes on to declare that the earth was shaken from the face of the Lord (ἀπὸ προσώπου κυρίου ἐσαλεύθη ἡ γῆ).

20:12 καὶ εἶδον (1st sg. aor. act. ind. of ὁράω, καὶ εἶδον introduces a new vision, scene, figure, or activity [Aune[a] 338]) **τοὺς νεκρούς** (dir. obj.), **τοὺς μεγάλους** (subst., appos.) **καὶ τοὺς μικρούς** (μικρός, -ά, -όν, "small," subst., appos.), **ἑστῶτας** (acc. pl. masc. of pf. act. ptc. of ἵστημι, compl. in obj.-compl. double acc. construction) **ἐνώπιον τοῦ** (anaphoric to 20:11) **θρόνου** (loc.). **καὶ βιβλία** (βιβλίον, -ου, τό, "scroll," subj. nom.) **ἠνοίχθησαν** (3rd pl. aor. pass. ind. of ἀνοίγω), **καὶ ἄλλο** (attrib.) **βιβλίον** (βιβλίον, -ου, τό, subj. nom., ant. of ὅ) **ἠνοίχθη** (3rd sg. aor. pass. ind. of ἀνοίγω), **ὅ** (subj. nom.) **ἐστιν** (3rd sg. pres. act. ind. of εἰμί) **τῆς ζωῆς** (descriptive gen. with implied pred. nom. βιβλίον), **καὶ ἐκρίθησαν** (3rd pl. aor. pass. ind. of κρίνω) **οἱ νεκροὶ** (subj. nom.) **ἐκ τῶν γεγραμμένων** (gen. pl. neut. of pf. pass. ptc. of γράφω, subst., causal) **ἐν τοῖς βιβλίοις** (loc.) **κατὰ τὰ ἔργα** (standard, "in accordance with") **αὐτῶν** (subj. gen.).

The books reveal the works of those who are judged and demonstrate that God's judgment is based on evidence; it is not capricious or arbitrary (Koester 791). The book of life is determinative, but the books are not viewed in the vision as conflicting; both verdicts converge on each person. Jesus makes it clear that he will judge his people based on their works (2:23), while it is also true that only the lamb's blood frees us from our sins (1:5), purifies us (7:14), and enables us to overcome (12:11). "Overcoming" in Revelation does not pit justification against sanctification as if they were in conflict.

The book of life is elsewhere mentioned in 3:5; 13:8; 17:8; 20:15; 21:27 with OT precedent in Exod 32:32 and Isa 4:3 and NT parallels in Luke 10:20; Phil 4:3; Heb 12:23. The description of the final judgment in Matt 25:31–46 provides important background in the teaching of Jesus and would suggest that this judgment includes both the saved and the damned (Beale 1032; Koester 791). This vision could also be interpreted as a judgment of just the lost, which results in the second death (Fanning

518) because judgment was already passed on all the overcomers in 20:4, which resulted in their participation in the first resurrection.

Use of the OT: On the book of life, see 3:5. Daniel 7:9–10 provides background to the final judgment vision in 20:11–12. God established a court of judgment and books were opened (καὶ κριτήριον ἐκάθισε καὶ βίβλοι ἠνεῴχθησαν).

20:13 καὶ ἔδωκεν (3rd sg. aor. act. ind. of δίδωμι) **ἡ θάλασσα** (subj. nom.) **τοὺς νεκροὺς** (dir. obj.) **τοὺς** (adjectivizer) **ἐν αὐτῇ** (loc.) **καὶ ὁ θάνατος** (subj. nom.) **καὶ ὁ ᾅδης** (ᾅδης, -ου, ὁ, "Hades," coord. subj. nom.) **ἔδωκαν** (3rd pl. aor. act. ind. of δίδωμι) **τοὺς νεκροὺς** (dir. obj.) **τοὺς** (adjectivizer) **ἐν αὐτοῖς** (loc.), **καὶ ἐκρίθησαν** (3rd pl. aor. pass. ind. of κρίνω, pl. vb. with distributive sg. subj.) **ἕκαστος** (subj. nom.) **κατὰ τὰ ἔργα** (standard) **αὐτῶν** (subj. gen.).

Use of the OT: On judgment according to works, see 2:23.

20:14 καὶ ὁ θάνατος (subj. nom.) **καὶ ὁ ᾅδης** (ᾅδης, -ου, ὁ, "Hades," coord. subj. nom.) **ἐβλήθησαν** (3rd pl. aor. pass. ind. of βάλλω) **εἰς τὴν λίμνην** (λίμνη, -ης, ἡ, "lake," loc.) **τοῦ πυρός** (content). **οὗτος** (subj. nom.) **ὁ θάνατος** (pred. nom.) **ὁ δεύτερός** (δεύτερος, -α, -ον, "second," attrib.) **ἐστιν** (3rd sg. pres. act. ind. of εἰμί), **ἡ λίμνη** (appos. to οὗτος) **τοῦ πυρός** (content).

See death and Hades in 1:18; 6:8. In 1 Cor 15:26 Paul describes death as the last enemy to be defeated before Jesus hands the kingdom over to the Father (ἔσχατος ἐχθρὸς καταργεῖται ὁ θάνατος).

20:15 καὶ εἴ (introduces 1st class cond. cl.) **τις** (subj. nom.) **οὐχ εὑρέθη** (3rd sg. aor. pass. ind. of εὑρίσκω) **ἐν τῇ βίβλῳ** (βίβλος, -ου, ἡ, "scroll," loc.) **τῆς ζωῆς** (descriptive) **γεγραμμένος** (nom. sg. masc. of pf. pass. ptc. of γράφω, pred. nom. of pass. εὑρέθη, "anyone not found written"), **ἐβλήθη** (3rd sg. aor. pass. ind. of βάλλω) **εἰς τὴν λίμνην** (λίμνη, -ης, ἡ, "lake," loc.) **τοῦ πυρός** (content).

John is not unique or excessive in his vision of eternal punishment; it parallels Jesus's teaching (Matt 5:22; 18:9; 25:41, 46; Mark 9:43; Luke 16:23–24).

Use of the OT: On the book of life, see 3:5. On the lake of fire, see 19:20.

FOR FURTHER STUDY

49. The Final Judgment (20:11–15)

Glasson, T. F. "The Last Judgment in Rev. 20 and Related Writings." *NTS* 28 (1982): 528–39.

Lambrecht, J. "Final Judgments and Ultimate Blessings: The Climactic Visions of Revelation 20,11–21,8." *Bib* 81 (2000): 362–85.

HOMILETICAL SUGGESTIONS

Revelation 20 divides easily into three main sections: the millennium (20:1–6), the defeat of Satan (20:7–10), the final judgment (20:11–15).

The Final Judgment: Where Is Your Name Written? (20:1–15)

1. God will vindicate and reward his persecuted people (20:1–6).
2. Satan will be defeated finally and forever (20:7–10).
3. The final judgment will conclude human history and begin God's new creation (20:11–15).

5. New Creation (21:1–8)

The following chiastic structure can be observed in 21:1–5a.

"(A) New heavens and earth (1a–b)
  (B) The sea is no more (1c)
    (C) The holy city, the new Jerusalem (v. 2)
    (C′) The dwelling of God with his people (v. 3)
  (B′) Suffering and crying are no more (4)
(A′) New creation (5a)" (Math 283)

21:1 Καὶ εἶδον (1st sg. aor. act. ind. of ὁράω, καὶ εἶδον introduces a new vision, scene, figure, or activity [Aune[a] 338]) **οὐρανὸν** (dir. obj.) **καινὸν** (attrib.). **καὶ γῆν** (coord. dir. obj.) **καινήν** (attrib.) **ὁ γὰρ** (explanatory) **πρῶτος** ("first," attrib.) **οὐρανὸς** (subj. nom.) **καὶ ἡ πρώτη** (attrib.) **γῆ** (coord. subj. nom.) **ἀπῆλθαν** (3rd pl. aor. act. ind. of ἀπέρχομαι; ἀπῆλθαν could be considered a barbarism, but it is simply the use of first aor. endings on a second aor. vb.; the 3rd pl. aor. act. ind. should read ἀπῆλθον) **καὶ ἡ θάλασσα** (subj. nom.) **οὐκ ἔστιν** (3rd sg. pres. act. ind. of εἰμί) **ἔτι** (temp. adv., "extension of time up to and beyond an expected point 'still, yet'" [L&N 67.128]).

The new heaven and earth should not be understood as a different planet somewhere else but the transformation of the current world following Revelation's narrative of decreation in judgment leading to the recreation of the world (cf. Heb 12:26–27; 2 Pet 3:10–13). The new creation reflects points of both continuity and discontinuity with the current creation. New creation represents "God's faithfulness to creation, not his abandonment of it" (Koester 83). The sea was widely seen in antiquity as a symbol and source of evil, chaos, danger, and disorder (note the beast from the sea in

12:18–13:1, the seat of the prostitute in 17:1, and the connection of the sea to death in 20:13). In 2 Pet 3:13, Peter comforts his hearers with the reminder that we are waiting for new heavens and a new earth according to his promise in which righteousness dwells (καινοὺς δὲ οὐρανοὺς καὶ γῆν καινὴν κατὰ τὸ ἐπάγγελμα αὐτοῦ προσδοκῶμεν, ἐν οἷς δικαιοσύνη κατοικεῖ).

Use of the OT: Isaiah 65:17 declares that there will be a new heaven and new earth (ἔσται γὰρ ὁ οὐρανὸς καινὸς καὶ ἡ γῆ καινή), and no one will certainly remember the former things (καὶ οὐ μὴ μνησθῶσιν τῶν προτέρων) nor will such things be remembered in their hearts (οὐδ᾽ οὐ μὴ ἐπέλθῃ αὐτῶν ἐπὶ τὴν καρδίαν). In Isa 66:22, God promises that the way he has made the new heaven and new earth to endure before him (ὃν τρόπον γὰρ ὁ οὐρανὸς καινὸς καὶ ἡ γῆ καινή, ἃ ἐγὼ ποιῶ, μένει ἐνώπιόν μου) is the same way the seed and name of the people will be established (λέγει κύριος, οὕτως στήσεται τὸ σπέρμα ὑμῶν καὶ τὸ ὄνομα ὑμῶν).

21:2 καὶ τὴν πόλιν (dir. obj.) **τὴν ἁγίαν** (attrib.) **Ἰερουσαλὴμ** (appos. to πόλιν) **καινὴν** (attrib.) **εἶδον** (1st sg. aor. act. ind. of ὁράω) **καταβαίνουσαν** (acc. sg. fem. of pres. act. ptc. of καταβαίνω, compl. in obj.-compl. double acc. construction) **ἐκ τοῦ οὐρανοῦ** (source) **ἀπὸ τοῦ θεοῦ** (source, with attention on "the originator of the action" [BDAG 106d]) **ἡτοιμασμένην** (acc. sg. fem. of pf. pass. ptc. of ἑτοιμάζω, "prepare," attrib. to πόλιν) **ὡς** (comp.) **νύμφην** (νύμφη, -ης, ἡ, "bride") **κεκοσμημένην** (acc. sg. fem. of pf. pass. ptc. of κοσμέω, "adorn," attrib.) **τῷ ἀνδρὶ** (advantage, "for") **αὐτῆς** (relationship).

Hebrews 11:10 states that Abraham was looking forward to a city having foundations whose architect and builder was God, while Heb 11:16 notes that God prepared a city for all those who died in faith.

Use of the OT: Isaiah 52:1 (cf. Joel 3:16) calls Jerusalem the holy city (Ιερουσαλημ πόλις ἡ ἁγία) and calls on her to no longer allow the uncircumcised and unclean to pass through (οὐκέτι προστεθήσεται διελθεῖν διὰ σοῦ ἀπερίτμητος καὶ ἀκάθαρτος). In the future restoration, God's people declare in Isa 61:10 that he has clothed them with a garment of salvation (ἐνέδυσεν γάρ με ἱμάτιον σωτηρίου) and a tunic of celebration (καὶ χιτῶνα εὐφροσύνης; "of righteousness" in the MT) and has adorned them with ornamentation as a bride (ὡς νύμφην κατεκόσμησέν με κόσμῳ). Jeremiah 3:17 speaks of a future time when "they will call Jerusalem 'the throne of the Lord'" (καλέσουσιν τὴν Ιερουσαλημ Θρόνος κυρίου). See 19:8 on Israel as Yahweh's wife.

21:3 καὶ ἤκουσα (1st sg. aor. act. ind. of ἀκούω) **φωνῆς** (gen. dir. obj.) **μεγάλης** (attrib.) **ἐκ τοῦ** (anaphoric to 4:2 or 20:11) **θρόνου** (source, P 046 along with most minuscules and versions read οὐρανοῦ to match 21:2 contra θρόνου in א A 94 and many church fathers [Metzger 688]) **λεγούσης** (gen. sg. fem. of pres. act. ptc. of λέγω, compl. in obj.-compl. double gen. construction), **Ἰδοὺ** (emph. interj.) **ἡ σκηνὴ** (σκηνή, -ῆς, ἡ, "tent," subj. nom. of verbless cl.) **τοῦ θεοῦ** (poss.) **μετὰ τῶν ἀνθρώπων** (association), **καὶ σκηνώσει** (3rd sg. fut. act. ind. of σκηνόω, "live in a tent, dwell") **μετ' αὐτῶν** (association), **καὶ αὐτοὶ** (subj. nom.) **λαοὶ** (pred. nom.) **αὐτοῦ** (relationship) **ἔσονται** (3rd pl. fut. mid. ind. of εἰμί), **καὶ αὐτὸς** (intensive) **ὁ θεὸς** (subj. nom.) **μετ' αὐτῶν** (association, functions as pred. compl.) **ἔσται** (3rd sg. fut. mid. ind. of εἰμί) [**αὐτῶν** (subord.) **θεός** (appos. to θεὸς for emph., or suggests an implied ὡς, "as their God"; א *Byz* omit αὐτῶν θεός)],

The vision describes a removal of the division between the physical creation and God's heavenly realm. In the new creation the earthly and heavenly will be blended, and God will dwell directly with his people.

Use of the OT: The covenantal promise is foundational for OT theology. Revelation presents this vision as the final and definitive fulfillment of this recurring promise.

- Leviticus 26:11–12 concludes the blessing that will be upon those who keep God's commands with the promise that ἐμπεριπατήσω ἐν ὑμῖν καὶ ἔσομαι ὑμῶν θεός, καὶ ὑμεῖς ἔσεσθέ μου λαός.
- Ezekiel 37:27 concludes a prophecy of the unification and restoration of Israel under David with the promise that ἔσται ἡ κατασκήνωσίς μου ἐν αὐτοῖς, καὶ ἔσομαι αὐτοῖς θεός, καὶ αὐτοί μου ἔσονται λαός.
- Jeremiah 24:7 concludes a promise to restore the Babylonian exiles to the land with καὶ δώσω αὐτοῖς καρδίαν τοῦ εἰδέναι αὐτοὺς ἐμὲ ὅτι ἐγώ εἰμι κύριος, καὶ ἔσονταί μοι εἰς λαόν, καὶ ἐγὼ ἔσομαι αὐτοῖς εἰς θεόν, ὅτι ἐπιστραφήσονται ἐπ' ἐμὲ ἐξ ὅλης τῆς καρδίας αὐτῶν.
- Jeremiah 30:22 states, "And you shall be my people, and I will be your God" (וִהְיִיתֶם לִי לְעָם וְאָנֹכִי אֶהְיֶה לָכֶם לֵאלֹהִים [the verse is omitted in the LXX]). The oracle (Jeremiah 37 LXX) concerns the restoration of Israel and Judah to their land from captivity (Jer 30:3, 10); a day of distress (30:7); the future rule of David their king (30:9) who would approach God (30:21); the repayment of enemies with *lex talionis* (30:16); the rebuilding of Zion (30:18); celebration (30:19); the storm, wrath, whirling tempest, and fierce anger of God against the wicked to accomplish his intentions (30:23–24); and the occurrence of these things in the "latter days" (30:24).
- Jeremiah 31:1 states ἔσομαι εἰς θεὸν τῷ γένει Ισραηλ, καὶ αὐτοὶ ἔσονταί μοι εἰς λαόν (38:1 LXX), while 31:33 states ἔσομαι αὐτοῖς εἰς θεόν, καὶ αὐτοὶ ἔσονταί μοι εἰς λαόν (38:33 LXX). Jeremiah 31 (38 LXX) focuses on the restoration of Israel from exile to the land, the rebuilding of Jerusalem, the celebration

over God's salvation, and the new covenant that God will establish with the houses of Israel and Judah.

- Jeremiah 32:38 promises similarly that *ἔσονταί μοι εἰς λαόν, καὶ ἐγὼ ἔσομαι αὐτοῖς εἰς θεόν* (39:38 LXX). This reassurance comes alongside promises to restore God's people from exile, make an everlasting covenant with them, bring them back to Jerusalem, and plant them in the land (Jer 32:36–44).
- For parts of the covenant formula of promise, see Ezek 11:20; 14:11; 34:30–31; 36:28; 37:23, 27–28; Zech 2:11, 14; 8:8; 13:9; Jub. 1:17, 29; cf. 2 Sam 7:14 and Ps 89:26–29 in Rev 21:7.

John indicates that this covenantal promise will be ultimately and finally fulfilled in God's new creation. The most distinctive thing to note regarding John's utilization of this well-known covenant formula is that he uniquely expands the recipients to "peoples," thus universalizing or expanding the ethnic particularity of the promise central to each of these foundational OT texts. This point is clouded by textual variation in which E and P along with most minuscules and versions read *λαός* in line with the OT promises. *Λαοί* is found in א A 046 2053 as well as a few minuscules it[ar] Irenaeus[lat] (Metzger 688). Significant for how we understand the future fulfillment of land promises in the Hebrew prophets, John applies the promises about restoration in the land to the resurrection life of God's people in God's new creation.

21:4 καὶ ἐξαλείψει (3rd sg. fut. act. ind. of ἐξαλείφω, "wipe away") **πᾶν** (attrib.) **δάκρυον** (δάκρυον, -ου, τό, "tear," dir. obj.) **ἐκ τῶν ὀφθαλμῶν** (separation) **αὐτῶν** (poss.), **καὶ ὁ θάνατος** (subj. nom.) **οὐκ ἔσται** (3rd sg. fut. mid. ind. of εἰμί) **ἔτι** (adv., extension of time) **οὔτε πένθος** (πένθος, -ους, τό, "mourning, sorrow," coord. subj. nom.) **οὔτε κραυγὴ** (κραυγή, -ῆς, ἡ, "weeping, shout," coord. subj. nom.) **οὔτε πόνος** (πόνος, -ου, ὁ, "pain," coord. subj. nom.) **οὐκ ἔσται ἔτι** (adv., extension of time), [**ὅτι**] (causal, the internal and external evidence seems evenly balanced on the inclusion or omission of ὅτι) **τὰ πρῶτα** (πρῶτος, -η, -ον, "first," subst., subj. nom.) **ἀπῆλθαν** (3rd pl. aor. act. ind. of ἀπέρχομαι, similar to Rev 21:1, ἀπῆλθαν instead of ἀπῆλθον reflects 1st aor. endings on a 2nd aor. vb.; unusual use of pl. vb. with neut. pl. impers. subj.).

This recalls the promise in Rev 7:17 that ἐξαλείψει ὁ θεὸς πᾶν δάκρυον ἐκ τῶν ὀφθαλμῶν αὐτῶν.

Use of the OT: Isaiah 25:8 states *ἀφεῖλεν ὁ θεὸς πᾶν δάκρυον ἀπὸ παντὸς προσώπου* right after stating "He will swallow up death forever" (ESV; בִּלַּע הַמָּוֶת לָנֶצַח). The vision of the return of God's people to Zion in Isaiah 35 brings together many themes found in Revelation, including God's people seeing his glory (*καὶ ὁ λαός μου ὄψεται τὴν δόξαν κυρίου καὶ τὸ ὕψος τοῦ θεοῦ* [35:2]; cf. Rev 21:23; 22:4), God's judicial recompense (*ὁ θεὸς ἡμῶν κρίσιν ἀνταποδίδωσιν καὶ ἀνταποδώσει* [35:4]; cf. Rev 14:7; 16:7; 18:6, 10; 19:2;

22:12), God coming to save his people (αὐτὸς ἥξει καὶ σώσει ἡμᾶς [35:4]; cf. with ἔρχομαι for בוא throughout Revelation), the availability of springs of water for the thirsty (εἰς τὴν διψῶσαν γῆν πηγὴ ὕδατος ἔσται [35:7]; Rev 7:16–17; 21:6; 22:17), the path of holiness from which the unclean will be excluded (ἐκεῖ ἔσται ὁδὸς καθαρὰ καὶ ὁδὸς ἁγία κληθήσεται, καὶ οὐ μὴ παρέλθῃ ἐκεῖ ἀκάθαρτος, οὐδὲ ἔσται ἐκεῖ ὁδὸς ἀκάθαρτος [35:8]; cf. Rev 21:27), the description of eternal celebration, praise, and joy (εὐφροσύνη αἰώνιος ὑπὲρ κεφαλῆς αὐτῶν, ἐπὶ γὰρ κεφαλῆς αὐτῶν αἴνεσις καὶ ἀγαλλίαμα [35:10]; cf. Rev 18:20; 19:5, 7), and the fleeing away of pain, sorrow, and sighing (ἀπέδρα ὀδύνη καὶ λύπη καὶ στεναγμός [35:10]; cf. Rev 21:4). Isaiah 35 thus serves a foundational role for many of the visions of future restoration in Revelation. In Isa 65:19, God declares that he will rejoice over Jerusalem and celebrate over his people (καὶ ἀγαλλιάσομαι ἐπὶ Ιερουσαλημ καὶ εὐφρανθήσομαι ἐπὶ τῷ λαῷ μου) and no longer will the voices of weeping or crying be heard in her (καὶ οὐκέτι μὴ ἀκουσθῇ ἐν αὐτῇ φωνὴ κλαυθμοῦ οὐδὲ φωνὴ κραυγῆς).

21:5 Καὶ εἶπεν (3rd sg. aor. act. ind. of λέγω) **ὁ** (anaphoric to 4:2) **καθήμενος** (nom. sg. masc. of pres. mid. ptc. of κάθημαι, subst. subj. nom.) **ἐπὶ τῷ** (anaphoric to 4:2 or 20:11) **θρόνῳ** (loc.), **Ἰδοὺ** (emph. interj.) **καινὰ** (pred. adj. compl. in an obj.-compl. double acc. construction, "I am making all things *to become* new," fronted for emph.) **ποιῶ** (1st sg. pres. act. ind. of ποιέω) **πάντα** (subst., dir. obj.) **καὶ λέγει** (3rd sg. pres. act. ind. of λέγω, narrative pres.), **Γράψον** (2nd sg. aor. act. impv. of γράφω), **ὅτι** (content to communicate the content of what John is commanded to write or causal to communicate the cause for the command to write) **οὗτοι** (attrib.) **οἱ λόγοι** (subj. nom.) **πιστοὶ** (pred. adj.) **καὶ ἀληθινοί** (ἀληθινός, -ή, -όν, "true," coord. pred. adj.) **εἰσιν** (3rd pl. pres. act. ind. of εἰμί).

God speaks here in the first person as in 1:8. In 2 Cor 5:17, Paul teaches that if anyone is in Christ, that person is a new creation (εἴ τις ἐν Χριστῷ, καινὴ κτίσις); the old things passed away, behold new things have come into being (τὰ ἀρχαῖα παρῆλθεν, ἰδοὺ γέγονεν καινά). Paul declares here an individual (τις) inaugurated experience of God's new creation that anticipates the full restoration of creation described by John in this vision.

Use of the OT: For God sitting on his throne, see 4:2.

21:6 καὶ εἶπέν (3rd sg. aor. act. ind. of λέγω) **μοι** (indir. obj.), **Γέγοναν** (a possible barbarism; the 3rd per. pl. pf. act. ind. should read γεγόνασιν; John's assimilation of the pf. endings with the aor. anticipates later developments in the Gk. language [Moț 99], the pf. tense stresses the stative aspect of the new creation). **ἐγώ** (subj. nom.) **[εἰμι] τὸ**

Ἄλφα (pred. nom.) **καὶ τὸ Ὦ** (coord. pred. nom.), **ἡ ἀρχὴ** (ἀρχή, -ῆς, ἡ, "beginning," appos.) **καὶ τὸ τέλος** (coord. appos.). **ἐγὼ** (subj. nom.) **τῷ διψῶντι** (dat. sg. masc. of pres. act. ptc. of διψάω, "thirst," subst., indir. obj.) **δώσω** (1st sg. fut. act. ind. of δίδωμι) **ἐκ τῆς πηγῆς** (πηγή, -ῆς, ἡ, "spring," source) **τοῦ ὕδατος** (content or product) **τῆς ζωῆς** (attrib., "living/moving water") **δωρεάν** (adv. acc., manner, "freely").

Revelation 22:17 turns this promise to the one who thirsts into an invitation. Jesus calls the one who thirsts to come to him and drink in John 7:37 (Ἐάν τις διψᾷ ἐρχέσθω πρός με καὶ πινέτω).

Use of the OT: On the divine self-designation as the beginning and the end, see 1:8. Isaiah 55:1 commands the one who is thirsting to come upon water (Οἱ διψῶντες, πορεύεσθε ἐφ' ὕδωρ) and, those who do not have silver (καὶ ὅσοι μὴ ἔχετε ἀργύριον), to come and purchase a drink without silver and price (βαδίσαντες ἀγοράσατε καὶ πίετε ἄνευ ἀργυρίου καὶ τιμῆς). David declares to God in Ps 35:10 LXX (36:9 EVV) that the fountain of life is with God (παρὰ σοὶ πηγὴ ζωῆς). In Jer 2:13 God describes himself as the fountain of living water (πηγὴν ὕδατος ζωῆς) that his people abandoned.

21:7 ὁ νικῶν (nom. sg. masc. of pres. act. ptc. of νικάω, "overcome, conquer," subst., subj. nom.) **κληρονομήσει** (3rd sg. fut. act. ind. of κληρονομέω, "inherit") **ταῦτα** (dir. obj., the ant. is prob. 21:1–6) **καὶ ἔσομαι** (1st sg. fut. mid. ind. of εἰμί) **αὐτῷ** (poss. dat.) **θεὸς** (pred. nom.) **καὶ αὐτὸς** (subj. nom.) **ἔσται** (3rd sg. fut. mid. ind. of εἰμί) **μοι** (poss. dat.) **υἱός** (pred. nom.).

This final promise to the one who overcomes sums up the promise made at the end of each of the seven proclamations in Revelation 2–3.

Use of the OT: This language reflects the promise by God to David regarding his heir in 2 Kgdms 7:14 (2 Sam 7:14 EVV) (ἐγὼ ἔσομαι αὐτῷ εἰς πατέρα, καὶ αὐτὸς ἔσται μοι εἰς υἱόν). It parallels the covenant promise discussed in 21:3. Here in Revelation, the promise is extended beyond the Davidic heir to everyone who overcomes.

21:8 τοῖς δὲ (adversative) **δειλοῖς** (δειλός, -ή, -όν, "cowardly," subst., dat. of reference, "in regard to," the coord. dat. pls. function as a topic construction which are grammatically unconnected to the main cl. and are resumed by αὐτῶν below) **καὶ ἀπίστοις** (ἄπιστος, -ον, "without faith," subst.) **καὶ ἐβδελυγμένοις** (dat. pl. masc. of pf. pass. ptc. of βδελύσσομαι, "detest," subst.) **καὶ φονεῦσιν** (φονεύς, -έως, ὁ, "murderer") **καὶ πόρνοις** (πόρνος, -ου, ὁ, "sexually immoral person") **καὶ φαρμάκοις** (φάρμακος, -ου, ὁ, "sorcerer") **καὶ εἰδωλολάτραις** (εἰδωλολάτρης, -ου, ὁ, "idolater") **καὶ πᾶσιν** (attrib.) **τοῖς ψευδέσιν** (ψευδής, -ές, "false, lie," subst.) **τὸ μέρος** (subj. nom. of verbless cl.) **αὐτῶν** (poss., constitutes the dat. pls. above) **ἐν τῇ λίμνῃ** (λίμνη, -ης, ἡ, "lake," loc., ant. of ὅ) **τῇ καιομένῃ** (dat. sg. fem. of pres. pass. ptc. of καίω, "burn," attrib.) **πυρὶ** (means) **καὶ θείῳ** (θεῖον, -ου, τό, "sulfur," coord. means), **ὅ** (subj. nom., the neut. gender is incongruent with the fem. λίμνη and may take μέρος as its ant.) **ἐστιν** (3rd sg. pres. act. ind. of εἰμί) **ὁ θάνατος** (pred. nom.) **ὁ δεύτερος** (δεύτερος, -α, -ον, "second," attrib.).

Vice lists elsewhere do not front cowardice and faithlessness, but these seem to be particular dangers to John's hearers in light of an expected, imminent increase in persecution. The inclusion of a vice list of those who are excluded in the middle of visions of the new creation emphasize the pervasive hortatory force of John's visions. Other vice lists occur in 9:20–21; 22:15. On the second death, see 2:11; 20:6, 14; 21:8.

Use of the OT: On the lake burning with fire and sulfur, see 14:10; 19:20.

FOR FURTHER STUDY

50. New Jerusalem (21:1–22:5)

Gundry, R. H. "The New Jerusalem: People as Place, Not Place for People." *NovT* 29 (1987): 254–64.

Lee, P. *The New Jerusalem in the Book of Revelation: A Study of Revelation 21–22 in the Light of its Background in Jewish Tradition*. WUNT 2.129. Tübingen: Mohr Siebeck, 2001.

Mathewson, D. *A New Heaven and a New Earth: The Meaning and Function of the Old Testament in Revelation 21:1–22:5*. JSNTSup 238. Sheffield, UK: Sheffield Academic Press, 2001.

Rand, J. A. du. "The Imagery of the Heavenly Jerusalem (Revelation 21:9–22:5)." *Neot* 22 (1988): 65–86.

*Tõniste, K. *The Ending of the Canon: A Canonical and Intertextual Reading of Revelation 21–22*. LNTS 526. London: T&T Clark, 2016.

51. The Use of Isaiah in Revelation

Fekkes, J. "'His Bride Has Prepared Herself': Revelation 19–21 and Isaian Nuptial Imagery." *JBL* 109 (1990): 269–87.

———. *Isaiah and the Prophetic Traditions in the Book of Revelation: Visionary Antecedents and Their Developments*. JSNTSup 93. Sheffield: Sheffield Academic Press, 1994.

*Mathewson, D. "Isaiah in Revelation." Pages 189–210 in *Isaiah in the New Testament*. Edited by S. Moyise and M. J. J. Menken. London: T&T Clark, 2005.

V. In the Spirit on a High Mountain (21:9–22:5)

21:9 Καὶ ἦλθεν (3rd sg. aor. act. ind. of ἔρχομαι) **εἷς** ("one," subj. nom.) **ἐκ τῶν** (anaphoric to 15:1) **ἑπτὰ** ("seven," attrib.) **ἀγγέλων** (part. gen.) **τῶν ἐχόντων** (gen. pl. masc. of pres. act. ptc. of ἔχω, attrib., narrative pres.) **τὰς** (anaphoric to 15:7) **ἑπτὰ** (attrib.) **φιάλας** (φιάλη, -ης, ἡ, "bowl," dir. obj.) **τῶν γεμόντων** (gen. pl. fem. of pres. act. ptc. of γέμω, "be full," attrib.) **τῶν** (anaphoric to 15:1) **ἑπτὰ** (attrib.) **πληγῶν** (πληγή, -ῆς, ἡ, "plague," content) **τῶν ἐσχάτων** (ἔσχατος, -η, -ον, "last," attrib.) **καὶ ἐλάλησεν** (3rd sg. aor. act. ind. of λαλέω) **μετ' ἐμοῦ** (association) **λέγων** (nom. sg. masc. of pres. act. ptc. of λέγω, manner), **Δεῦρο** (spatial adv. "here," often used as a command, "*come* here!"), **δείξω** (1st sg. fut. act. ind. of δείκνυμι, "show," Wallace suggests this is a hortatory subjunc., "let me show" [Wallace 465]) **σοι** (indir. obj.) **τὴν νύμφην** (νύμφη, -ης, ἡ, "bride," dir. obj.) **τὴν γυναῖκα** (appos.) **τοῦ ἀρνίου** (ἀρνίον, -ου, τό, "lamb," relationship).

The introductory material explicitly contrasts the lamb's bride with the prostitute in 17:1–3; the bride is also intratextually connected with the woman in the wilderness (12:1) and the people of God (19:8). This vision focuses on the bride/new Jerusalem as the dwelling place of God with humanity in his new creation. Both people and place are reflected in the new Jerusalem imagery. The gen. ptc. τῶν γεμόντων should be in the acc. case to modify τὰς φιάλας. Moţ argues this is a genuine grammatical irregularity without an evident explanation (Moţ 145) while Mathewson suggests it may be influenced by the following genitives (Math 290).

21:10 καὶ ἀπήνεγκέν (3rd sg. aor. act. ind. of ἀποφέρω, "take away") **με** (dir. obj.) **ἐν πνεύματι** (manner) **ἐπὶ ὄρος** (loc.) **μέγα** (attrib.) **καὶ ὑψηλόν** (ὑψηλός, -ή, -όν, "high," coord. attrib.), **καὶ ἔδειξέν** (3rd sg. aor. act. ind. of δείκνυμι, "show) **μοι** (indir. obj.) **τὴν πόλιν** (dir. obj.) **τὴν ἁγίαν** (attrib.) **Ἰερουσαλὴμ** (appos.) **καταβαίνουσαν** (acc. sg. fem. of pres. act. ptc. of καταβαίνω, compl. of obj.-compl. double acc. construction) **ἐκ τοῦ οὐρανοῦ** (source) **ἀπὸ τοῦ θεοῦ** (source, with attention on "the originator of the action" [BDAG 106d])

This is an example of the hearing-seeing literary technique employed elsewhere by John whereby what he sees interprets what he hears and vice versa, but the juxtaposition of what he sees and hears is unexpected, paradoxical, or seemingly contradictory. This hearing-seeing literary technique is particularly noteworthy at 1:12; 5:5–6; 7:2–9; 21:9–10.

Use of the OT: Ezekiel 40:2 describes how God moved Ezekiel in visions to the land of Israel and put him on an exceedingly high mountain (καὶ ἔθηκέν με ἐπ' ὄρους ὑψηλοῦ σφόδρα) to see the city and temple. This allusion prepares the hearer for a series of significant allusions to Ezekiel 40–48 in the following description of the new Jerusalem, which suggests that John understood the vision of Rev 21:9–22:5 to be an interpretation and application of Ezekiel 40–48. The following chart is from Alexander E. Stewart ("Future of Israel," 572–73; ESV is used for the English).

Revelation 21:9–22:5	Ezekiel 40–48
"And he carried me away in the Spirit to a great, high mountain [ἐπὶ ὄρος μέγα καὶ ὑψηλόν], and showed me the holy city Jerusalem coming down out of heaven from God" (21:10)	"In visions of God he brought me to the land of Israel, and set me down on a very high mountain [ἐπ' ὄρους ὑψηλοῦ σφόδρα], on which was a structure like a city to the south" (40:2)
"having the glory of God [τὴν δόξαν τοῦ θεοῦ], its radiance like a most rare jewel, like a jasper, clear as crystal" (21:11)	"[T]he glory of the God (δόξα θεοῦ) of Israel was coming from the east . . . and the earth shone with his glory. . . . As the glory of the Lord entered the temple by the gate facing east, the Spirit lifted me up and brought me into the inner court; and behold, the glory of the Lord filled the temple" (43:2–5)
"It had a great, high wall, with twelve gates, and at the gates twelve angels, and on the gates the names of the twelve tribes of the sons of Israel were inscribed [ὀνόματα ἐπιγεγραμμένα, ἅ ἐστιν (τὰ ὀνόματα) τῶν δώδεκα φυλῶν υἱῶν Ἰσραήλ] on the east three gates [ἀπὸ ἀνατολῆς πυλῶνες τρεῖς], on the north three gates [ἀπὸ βορρᾶ πυλῶνες τρεῖς], on the south three gates [ἀπὸ νότου πυλῶνες τρεῖς], and on the west three gates [ἀπὸ δυσμῶν πυλῶνες τρεῖς]" (21:12–13)	"These shall be the exits of the city: On the north side . . . three gates [πύλαι τρεῖς πρὸς βορρᾶν], the gate of Reuben, the gate of Judah, and the gate of Levi, the gates of the city being named after the tribes of Israel [καὶ αἱ πύλαι τῆς πόλεως ἐπ' ὀνόμασιν φυλῶν τοῦ Ισραηλ]. On the east side . . . three gates [πρὸς ἀνατολὰς . . . καὶ πύλαι τρεῖς], the gate of Joseph, the gate of Benjamin, and the gate of Dan. On the south side . . . three gates [πρὸς νότον . . . καὶ πύλαι τρεῖς], the gate of Simeon, the gate of Issachar, and the gate of Zebulun. On the west side . . . three gates [πρὸς θάλασσαν . . . καὶ πύλαι τρεῖς], the gate of Gad, the gate of Asher, and the gate of Naphtali" (48:30–34; cf. 40:5–6; 42:15–20)
"And the one who spoke with me had a measuring rod [μέτρον κάλαμον] of gold to measure the city and its gates [πυλῶνας] and walls [τεῖχος]" (21:15)	"[T]here was a man whose appearance was like bronze, with a linen cord and a measuring reed [κάλαμος μέτρου] in his hand. . . . So he measured the thickness of the wall [τὸ προτείχισμα]. . . . Then he went into the gateway facing east . . . and measured the threshold of the gate [τῆς πύλης]" (40:3, 5–6)
"The city lies foursquare, its length [μῆκος] the same as its width [πλάτος]. And he measured the city with his rod, 12,000 stadia. Its length and width and height are equal" (21:16)	The city (48:16–17), temple (45:2), and most holy place (41:4) would be foursquare. The language of length [μῆκος] and width [πλάτος] comes from 48:8–13.

"He also measured its wall [ἐμέτρησεν τὸ τεῖχος αὐτῆς], 144 cubits by human measurement, which is also an angel's measurement" (21:17)	"Then he measured the wall [διεμέτρησεν τὸν τοῖχον] of the temple" (41:5) "So he measured the thickness of the wall [διεμέτρησεν τὸ προτείχισμα]" (40:5)
"And the city has no need of sun or moon to shine on it, for the glory of God gives it light, and its lamp is the Lamb [ἡ γὰρ δόξα τοῦ θεοῦ ἐφώτισεν αὐτήν, καὶ ὁ λύχνος αὐτῆς τὸ ἀρνίον]" (21:23)	"[A]nd the earth shone with his glory [ἡ γῆ ἐξέλαμπεν ὡς φέγγος ἀπὸ τῆς δόξης κυκλόθεν]" (43:2; cf. Isa 60:9)
"Then the angel showed me the river of the water of life, bright as crystal, flowing [ποταμὸν ὕδατος ζωῆς λαμπρὸν ὡς κρύσταλλον, ἐκπορευόμενον] from the throne of God and of the Lamb through the middle of the street of the city" (22:1–2a).	"[A]nd behold, water was issuing [ὕδωρ ἐξεπορεύετο] from below the threshold of the temple toward the east . . . so everything will live [ζήσεται] where the river goes" (47:1, 9).
"also, on either side of the river [τοῦ ποταμοῦ ἐντεῦθεν καὶ ἐκεῖθεν], the tree of life with its twelve kinds of fruit, yielding its fruit each month [κατὰ μῆνα ἕκαστον ἀποδιδοῦν τὸν καρπὸν αὐτοῦ]. The leaves [τὰ φύλλα] of the tree were for the healing [εἰς θεραπείαν] of the nations" (Rev 22:2)	"And on the banks, on both sides of the river [ἐπὶ τοῦ ποταμοῦ ἀναβήσεται ἐπὶ τοῦ χείλους αὐτοῦ ἔνθεν καὶ ἔνθεν], there will grow all kinds of trees for food. Their leaves will not wither, nor their fruit fail, but they will bear fresh fruit every month [לְחֳדָשָׁיו; missing in LXX], because the water for them flows from the sanctuary. Their fruit will be for food, and their leaves [ἀνάβασις αὐτῶν; וְעָלֵהוּ] for healing [εἰς ὑγίειαν]" (47:12).

As will be noted below, the main difference is the lack of a temple in John's vision (21:22), which is compensated for by the addition of height to the dimensions of the city to make it a cube (22:16) reflective of the holy of holies in 1 Kgs 6:20. The entire city, which encompasses the known world, is presented in John's vision as the holy of holy in which God dwells.

21:11 ἔχουσαν (acc. sg. fem. of pres. act. ptc. of ἔχω, manner) **τὴν δόξαν** (dir. obj.) **τοῦ θεοῦ** (descriptive), **ὁ φωστὴρ** (φωστήρ, -ῆρος, ὁ, "radiance," subj. nom. of verbless cl.) **αὐτῆς** (subj. gen.) **ὅμοιος** (ὅμοιος, -οία, -οιον, "like, similar," comp. adj. functioning as pred. compl. of implied linking vb.) **λίθῳ** (compl. of ὅμοιος) **τιμιωτάτῳ** (τίμιος, -α, -ον, "valuable," attrib.) **ὡς** (comp.) **λίθῳ ἰάσπιδι** (ἴασπις, -ιδος, ἡ, "jasper," the noun seems to function here as attrib. adj.) **κρυσταλλίζοντι** (dat. sg. masc. of pres. act. ptc. of κρυσταλλίζω, "shine like crystal," attrib.).

The mention of ἴασπις recalls the description of God's appearance and splendor in 4:3; the city reflects God's glory.

Use of the OT: Isaiah 60:1–2 promises the future glory of Israel.

Arise, shine, for your light has come [Φωτίζου φωτίζου, Ιερουσαλημ, ἥκει γάρ σου τὸ φῶς], and the glory of the LORD shines over you [καὶ ἡ δόξα κυρίου ἐπὶ σὲ ἀνατέταλκεν]. For look, darkness will cover the earth [ἰδοὺ σκότος καὶ γνόφος καλύψει γῆν], . . . but the LORD will shine over you [ἐπὶ δὲ σὲ φανήσεται κύριος], and his glory will appear over you [καὶ ἡ δόξα αὐτοῦ ἐπὶ σὲ ὀφθήσεται]."

21:12 ἔχουσα (nom. sg. fem. of pres. act. ptc. of ἔχω, the switch to the nom. case suggests attraction to φωστήρ in 21:11 and not πόλιν in 21:10, alternatively, the ptc. could function as finite vb.) **τεῖχος** (τεῖχος, -ους, τό, "wall," dir. obj.) **μέγα** (attrib.) **καὶ ὑψηλόν** (ὑψηλός, -ή, -όν, "high," coord. attrib.), **ἔχουσα** (parallel to the ptc. starting 21:12) **πυλῶνας** (πυλών, -ῶνος, ὁ, "gateway," dir. obj.) **δώδεκα** ("twelve," attrib.) **καὶ ἐπὶ τοῖς πυλῶσιν** (loc., the matching number of angels and names suggests a distributed correspondence of one angel and name upon each gate) **ἀγγέλους** (dir. obj. coord. with πυλῶνας) **δώδεκα** (attrib.) **καὶ ὀνόματα** (ant. of ἅ, the third coord. dir. obj. of ἔχουσα, "having gates, angels, names") **ἐπιγεγραμμένα** (acc. pl. neut. of pf. pass. ptc. of ἐπιγράφω, attrib.), **ἅ** (subj. nom., neut. pl. subj. with sg. vb.) **ἐστιν** (3rd sg. pres. act. ind. of εἰμί) [**τὰ ὀνόματα**] (dir. obj., the internal and external evidence seems evenly balanced on the inclusion or omission of ὀνόματα) **τῶν δώδεκα** (attrib.) **φυλῶν** (φυλή, -ῆς, ἡ, "tribe," poss.) **υἱῶν** (appos.) **Ἰσραήλ** (relationship)

Use of the OT: Exodus 28:21 describes how the breastpiece for the high priest would have twelve stones with the names of the twelve sons of Israel according to their names (καὶ οἱ λίθοι ἔστωσαν ἐκ τῶν ὀνομάτων τῶν υἱῶν Ισραηλ δέκα δύο κατὰ τὰ ὀνόματα αὐτῶν). For Ezek 48:30–35, see on 21:10.

21:13 ἀπὸ ἀνατολῆς (ἀνατολή, -ῆς, ἡ, "east," source) **πυλῶνες** (πυλών, -ῶνος, ὁ, "gateway," subj. nom. of verbless cl.) **τρεῖς** ("three," attrib.) **καὶ ἀπὸ βορρᾶ** (βορρᾶς, -ᾶ, ὁ, "north," source) **πυλῶνες** (subj. nom. of verbless cl.) **τρεῖς καὶ ἀπὸ νότου** (νότος, -ου, ὁ, "south [wind]," source) **πυλῶνες** (subj. nom. of verbless cl.) **τρεῖς καὶ ἀπὸ δυσμῶν** (δυσμή, -ῆς, ἡ, "west," source) **πυλῶνες** (subj. nom. of verbless cl.) **τρεῖς**.

21:14 καὶ τὸ τεῖχος (τεῖχος, -ους, τό, "wall," subj. nom.) **τῆς πόλεως** (part. gen.) **ἔχων** (nom. sg. masc. of pres. act. ptc. of ἔχω, functions as finite vb. although incongruous in gender) **θεμελίους** (θεμέλιος, -ου, ὁ, "foundation," dir. obj.) **δώδεκα** ("twelve," attrib.) **καὶ ἐπ' αὐτῶν** (loc.) **δώδεκα** (attrib.) **ὀνόματα** (dir. obj.) **τῶν δώδεκα** (attrib.) **ἀποστόλων** (poss.) **τοῦ ἀρνίου** (ἀρνίον, -ου, τό, "lamb," poss.).

21:15 Καὶ ὁ λαλῶν (nom. sg. masc. of pres. act. ptc. of λαλέω, subst., subj. nom.) **μετ' ἐμοῦ** (association) **εἶχεν** (3rd sg. impf. act. ind. of ἔχω, the impf. tense provides background information and does not advance the main narrative) **μέτρον** (μέτρον, -ου, τό, "measure," dir. obj.) **κάλαμον** (κάλαμος, -ου, ὁ, "measuring rod [reed]," appos.) **χρυσοῦν** (χρυσοῦς, -ῆ, -οῦν, "golden," attrib.), **ἵνα** (purpose) **μετρήσῃ** (3rd sg. aor. act. subjunc. of μετρέω, "measure") **τὴν πόλιν** (dir. obj.) **καὶ τοὺς πυλῶνας** (πυλών, -ῶνος, ὁ, "gateway," coord. dir. obj.) **αὐτῆς** (poss.) **καὶ τὸ τεῖχος** (τεῖχος, -ους, τό, "wall," coord. dir. obj.) **αὐτῆς** (part. gen.).

Use of the OT: For Ezek 40:3, 5, see 21:10.

21:16 καὶ ἡ πόλις (subj. nom.) **τετράγωνος** (τετράγωνος, -ον, "four-sided," functions as pred. adj.) **κεῖται** (3rd sg. pres. mid. ind. of κεῖμαι, "recline, be set, be appointed") **καὶ τὸ μῆκος** (μῆκος, -ους, τό, "length," subj. nom. of verbless cl.) **αὐτῆς** (poss.) **ὅσον** (ὅσος, -η, -ον, "as great, long," correlative adj. functioning as pred. adj. of verbless cl.) **[καὶ] τὸ πλάτος** (πλάτος, -ους, τό, "width"). **καὶ ἐμέτρησεν** (3rd sg. aor. act. ind. of μετρέω, "measure") **τὴν πόλιν** (dir. obj.) **τῷ καλάμῳ** (κάλαμος, -ου, ὁ, "measuring rod [reed]," means) **ἐπὶ σταδίων** (στάδιον, ου, τό, measurement of distance of about 192 meters or one-eighth of a mile [BDAG 940a]) **δώδεκα** ("twelve," attrib.) **χιλιάδων** (χιλιάς, -άδος, ἡ, "thousand"), **τὸ μῆκος** (the three sg. neut. subjs. have a sg. vb.) **καὶ τὸ πλάτος καὶ τὸ ὕψος** (ὕψος, -ους, τό, "height") **αὐτῆς** (poss.) **ἴσα** (ἴσος, -η, -ον, "equal," pred. adj.) **ἐστίν** (3rd sg. pres. act. ind. of εἰμί).

Its dimensions (12,000 stadia or 1,500 miles in each direction) are such that it covered more or less the entire known world. The addition of height is an important detail because it produces a cube; this presents the new Jerusalem as the holy of holies (1 Kgs 6:20), which descends down from heaven to earth.

Use of the OT: For Ezek 48:16, 17, see 21:10.

21:17 καὶ ἐμέτρησεν (3rd sg. aor. act. ind. of μετρέω, "measure") **τὸ τεῖχος** (τεῖχος, -ους, τό, "wall," dir. obj.) **αὐτῆς** (poss.) **ἑκατὸν** ("hundred," attrib.) **τεσσεράκοντα** ("forty") **τεσσάρων** ("four") **πηχῶν** (πῆχυς, -εως, ὁ, "cubit," the gen. provides the length measured, Mathewson identifies it as a gen. of content [Math 293]) **μέτρον** (μέτρον, -ου, τό, "measure," pred. nom. of verbless cl., ant. of ὅ) **ἀνθρώπου** (attrib., "human"), **ὅ** (subj. nom.) **ἐστιν** (3rd sg. pres. act. ind. of εἰμί) **ἀγγέλου** (attrib. gen. with implied pred. adj. μέτρον).

21:18 καὶ ἡ ἐνδώμησις (ἐνδώμησις, -εως, ἡ, "construction material," subj. nom. of verbless cl.) **τοῦ τείχους** (τεῖχος, -ους, τό, "wall," the gen. "seems to indicate the material out

of which the wall is constructed" [Math 294]) **αὐτῆς** (part. gen.) **ἴασπις** (ἴασπις, -ιδος, ἡ, "jasper," pred. nom. of verbless cl.) **καὶ ἡ πόλις** (subj. nom. of verbless cl.) **χρυσίον** (χρυσίον, -ου, τό, "gold," pred. nom.) **καθαρὸν** (καθαρός, -ά, -όν, "pure," attrib.) **ὅμοιον** (ὅμοιος, -οία, -οιον, "like, similar," comp. adj.) **ὑάλῳ** (ὕαλος, -ου, ἡ, "crystal," compl.) **καθαρῷ** (attrib.).
21:19 οἱ θεμέλιοι (θεμέλιος, -ου, ὁ, "foundation," subj. nom. of verbless cl.) **τοῦ τείχους** (τεῖχος, -ους, τό, "wall," part. gen.) **τῆς πόλεως** (part. gen.) **παντὶ** (attrib.) **λίθῳ** (means) **τιμίῳ** (τίμιος, -α, -ον, "valuable," attrib.) **κεκοσμημένοι** (nom. pl. masc. of pf. pass. ptc. of κοσμέω, "adorn," functions as finite vb.)· **ὁ θεμέλιος** (subj. nom. of verbless cl.) **ὁ πρῶτος** ("first," attrib.) **ἴασπις** (ἴασπις, -ιδος, ἡ, "jasper, reddish-brown stone," pred. nom. of verbless cl.), **ὁ δεύτερος** ("second," subst. adj., each of the twelve foundations are described similarly with a subst. adj. as the subj. nom. of a verbless cl. and the stone as the pred. nom.) **σάπφιρος** (σάπφιρος, -ου, ἡ, "sapphire, blue stone"), **ὁ τρίτος** ("third") **χαλκηδών** (χαλκηδών, -όνος, ὁ, "onyx, black stone"), **ὁ τέταρτος** ("fourth") **σμάραγδος** (σμάραγδος, -ου, ὁ, "emerald, green stone"),

---

Use of the OT: Jeremiah 31:38–40 (38:38–40 LXX) contains a promise regarding the rebuilding of Jerusalem with attention to the gates, sacredness of the land (ἁγίασμα τῷ κυρίῳ), and the security of the city (οὐκέτι οὐ μὴ ἐκλίπῃ καὶ οὐ μὴ καθαιρεθῇ ἕως τοῦ αἰῶνος). Jeremiah 38:39 LXX has a phrase not contained in the MT: περικυκλωθήσεται κύκλῳ ἐξ ἐκλεκτῶν λίθων, "It will be encircled all around with chosen [select, picked out] stones." Jeremiah, unlike John, does not list the chosen stones, but it is a similar idea. The prophecy of restoration in Isa 54:11–12 describes how the foundations, bulwarks, and gates will be made out of various precious stones. John draws from oracles about the rebuilding of Jerusalem to describe the new Jerusalem, placing the fulfillment of these prophecies in the new creation.

21:20 ὁ πέμπτος ("fifth") **σαρδόνυξ** (σαρδόνυξ, -υχος, ὁ, "sardonyx, striped stone"), **ὁ ἕκτος** ("sixth") **σάρδιον** (σάρδιον, -ου, τό, "carnelian, red stone"), **ὁ ἕβδομος** ("seventh") **χρυσόλιθος** (χρυσόλιθος, -ου, ὁ, "yellow stone"), **ὁ ὄγδοος** ("eighth") **βήρυλλος** (βήρυλλος, -ου, ὁ, ἡ, "beryl, green stone"), **ὁ ἔνατος** ("ninth") **τοπάζιον** (τοπάζιον, -ου, τό, "topaz, blue or yellow stone"), **ὁ δέκατος** ("tenth") **χρυσόπρασος** (χρυσόπρασος, -ου, ὁ, "green stone"), **ὁ ἑνδέκατος** ("eleventh") **ὑάκινθος** (ὑάκινθος, -ου, ὁ, "hyacinth, blue stone"), **ὁ δωδέκατος** ("twelve") **ἀμέθυστος** (ἀμέθυστος, -ου, ἡ, "amethyst, red stone"),

The mention of σάρδιον recalls the description of God's appearance and splendor in 4:3

21:21 καὶ οἱ δώδεκα ("twelve," attrib.) **πυλῶνες** (πυλών, -ῶνος, ὁ, "gateway," subj. nom. of verbless cl.) **δώδεκα** (attrib.) **μαργαρῖται** (μαργαρίτης, -ου, ὁ, "pearl," pred. nom.), **ἀνὰ** (distributive adv., "each") **εἷς** (subj. nom., "one") **ἕκαστος** (attrib. adj., redundant with ἀνά) **τῶν πυλώνων** (part. gen.) **ἦν** (3rd sg. impf. act. ind. of εἰμί) **ἐξ ἑνὸς** ("one," attrib.) **μαργαρίτου** (material, the prep. phrase functions as pred. copulative). **καὶ ἡ πλατεῖα** (πλατεῖα, -ας, ἡ, "road," likely indicating the main street of the city or public square, subj. nom. of verbless cl.) **τῆς πόλεως** (part. gen.) **χρυσίον** (χρυσίον, -ου, τό, "gold," pred. nom.) **καθαρὸν** (καθαρός, -ά, -όν, "pure," attrib.) **ὡς** (comp.) **ὕαλος** (ὕαλος, -ου, ἡ, "crystal, glass") **διαυγής** (διαυγής, -ές, "transparent," attrib.).

The massive pearls contrast and exceed the pearls used to adorn Babylon (17:4; 18:12, 16).

21:22 Καὶ ναὸν (ναός, -οῦ, ὁ, "temple," dir. obj., fronted for emph.) **οὐκ εἶδον** (1st sg. aor. act. ind. of ὁράω) **ἐν αὐτῇ** (loc.), **ὁ γὰρ** (causal) **κύριος** (subj. nom.) **ὁ θεὸς** (appos.) **ὁ παντοκράτωρ** (παντοκράτωρ, -ορος, ὁ, "almighty," appos.) **ναὸς** (pred. nom.) **αὐτῆς** (poss.) **ἐστιν** (3rd sg. pres. act. ind. of εἰμί, sg. vb. with compound subj. draws its number from the first subj.) **καὶ τὸ ἀρνίον** (ἀρνίον, -ου, τό, "lamb," coord. subj. nom. with κύριος).

The explicit acknowledgment that the city has no temple indirectly strengthens the case for John's use of Ezekiel 40–48 since it is a divergent detail requiring explanation. The vision, very unusually, describes God and the lamb as the temple (cf. Isa 8:14; John 2:19–21) although the broader point is that no temple is needed because God is directly dwelling in the entire city, which is now sacred space.

21:23 καὶ ἡ πόλις (subj. nom.) **οὐ χρείαν** (χρεία, -ας, ἡ, "need," dir. obj.) **ἔχει** (3rd sg. pres. act. ind. of ἔχω, narrative pres.) **τοῦ ἡλίου** (ἥλιος, -ου, ὁ, "sun," obj. gen. with χρείαν) **οὐδὲ** (neg. disjunctive conj.) **τῆς σελήνης** (σελήνη, -ης, ἡ, "moon," obj. gen. with χρείαν) **ἵνα** (introduces content cl. in appos. to χρείαν) **φαίνωσιν** (3rd pl. pres. act. subjunc. of φαίνω, "shine") **αὐτῇ** (loc.), **ἡ γὰρ** (causal) **δόξα** (subj. nom.) **τοῦ θεοῦ** (poss. or subj. gen.) **ἐφώτισεν** (3rd sg. aor. act. ind. of φωτίζω, "give light, enlighten") **αὐτήν** (dir. obj.), **καὶ ὁ λύχνος** (λύχνος, -ου, ὁ, "lamp," subj. nom. of verbless cl.) **αὐτῆς** (obj. gen.) **τὸ ἀρνίον** (ἀρνίον, -ου, τό, "lamb," pred. nom.).

Use of the OT: Isaiah 60:19 promises that the sun will not be a light for the day (καὶ οὐκ ἔσται σοι ὁ ἥλιος εἰς φῶς ἡμέρας), nor will the rising of the moon enlighten the night (οὐδὲ ἀνατολὴ σελήνης φωτιεῖ σοι τὴν νύκτα), but the Lord will be an eternal light for the people and God their glory (ἀλλ' ἔσται σοι κύριος φῶς αἰώνιον καὶ ὁ θεὸς δόξα σου). Isaiah 60:20 goes on to explain that the sun will not set on them (οὐ γὰρ δύσεται ὁ ἥλιός σοι), and the moon will not forsake them (καὶ ἡ σελήνη σοι οὐκ ἐκλείψει), for the Lord will be an eternal light to them (ἔσται γὰρ κύριός σοι φῶς αἰώνιον), and the days of their grief will be complete (καὶ ἀναπληρωθήσονται αἱ ἡμέραι τοῦ πένθους σου).

21:24 καὶ περιπατήσουσιν (3rd pl. fut. act. ind. of περιπατέω, pl. vb. with neut. pl. subj.) **τὰ ἔθνη** (subj. nom.) **διὰ τοῦ φωτὸς** (φῶς, φωτός, τό, "light," means or loc.) **αὐτῆς** (subj. gen.), **καὶ οἱ βασιλεῖς** (subj. nom.) **τῆς γῆς** (subord.) **φέρουσιν** (3rd pl. pres. act. ind. of φέρω, futuristic) **τὴν δόξαν** (dir. obj.) **αὐτῶν** (poss.) **εἰς αὐτήν** (loc.),

---

Use of the OT: The oracle concerning Cush in Isa 18:7 prophesies that they will carry up gifts to the Lord of Hosts (*ἐν τῷ καιρῷ ἐκείνῳ ἀνενεχθήσεται δῶρα κυρίῳ σαβαωθ*) into the place where the name of the Lord of Hosts is called upon, Mount Zion (*εἰς τὸν τόπον, οὗ τὸ ὄνομα κυρίου σαβαωθ ἐπεκλήθη, ὄρος Σιων*). Isaiah 60:3 prophesies that in the restoration of Israel the kings will come to its light and the nations to its brightness (*καὶ πορεύσονται βασιλεῖς τῷ φωτί σου καὶ ἔθνη τῇ λαμπρότητί σου*). Isaiah 60:5 builds on the theme: "then you will see and be afraid and be amazed in the heart [*τότε ὄψῃ καὶ φοβηθήσῃ καὶ ἐκστήσῃ τῇ καρδίᾳ*], because he will turn into you the wealth of the sea and the nations and the peoples [*ὅτι μεταβαλεῖ εἰς σὲ πλοῦτος θαλάσσης καὶ ἐθνῶν καὶ λαῶν*]." In Pss. Sol. 17:31 in the time of the future king, the son of David, the nations will come from the ends of the earth to see his glory (*ἔρχεσθαι ἔθνη ἀπ' ἄκρου τῆς γῆς ἰδεῖν τὴν δόξαν αὐτοῦ*) bearing gifts, that is, her (Jerusalem's) weak sons (*φέροντες δῶρα τοὺς ἐξησθενηκότας υἱοὺς αὐτῆς*) to see the glory of the Lord with which God glorified her (*ἰδεῖν τὴν δόξαν κυρίου, ἣν ἐδόξασεν αὐτὴν ὁ θεός*).

21:25 καὶ οἱ πυλῶνες (πυλών, -ῶνος, ὁ, "gateway," subj. nom.) **αὐτῆς** (part. gen.) **οὐ μὴ** (emph. neg.) **κλεισθῶσιν** (3rd pl. aor. pass. subjunc. of κλείω, "shut") **ἡμέρας** (temp.), **νὺξ** (subj. nom.) **γὰρ** (causal) **οὐκ ἔσται** (3rd sg. fut. mid. ind. of εἰμί) **ἐκεῖ** (spatial adv., "there"),

Revelation 22:5 reiterates the claim that night will no longer exist.

Use of the OT: Isaiah 60:11 prophesies that in God's restoration, the gates will be opened always (*καὶ ἀνοιχθήσονται αἱ πύλαι σου διὰ παντός*), by day and by night they will not be shut (*ἡμέρας καὶ νυκτὸς οὐ κλεισθήσονται*) to bring in to you (Jerusalem) the power of the nations and the kings leading (*εἰσαγαγεῖν πρὸς σὲ δύναμιν ἐθνῶν καὶ βασιλεῖς ἀγομένους*). Zechariah 14:17 warns that as many as do not go up out of all the tribes of the earth into Jerusalem to worship the King, the Lord Almighty, these things (lack of rain in the MT) also will be added to those ones (*καὶ ἔσται ὅσοι ἐὰν μὴ ἀναβῶσιν ἐκ πασῶν τῶν φυλῶν τῆς γῆς εἰς Ιερουσαλημ τοῦ προσκυνῆσαι τῷ βασιλεῖ κυρίῳ παντοκράτορι, καὶ οὗτοι ἐκείνοις προστεθήσονται*).

21:26 καὶ οἴσουσιν (3rd pl. fut. act. ind. of φέρω, the subj. could be impers. or it repeats the action of the βασιλεῖς in 21:24; the allusion to Isa 60:11 could point to the nations as the subj. [Math 299]) **τὴν δόξαν** (dir. obj.) **καὶ τὴν τιμὴν** (τιμή, -ῆς, ἡ, "honor," coord. dir. obj.) **τῶν ἐθνῶν** (source) **εἰς αὐτήν** (loc.).

Use of the OT: Psalm 71:10–11 LXX (72:10–11 EVV) prays concerning Solomon that the kings of Tarshish and the islands will bear gifts (*βασιλεῖς Θαρσις καὶ αἱ νῆσοι δῶρα προσοίσουσιν*), the kings of the Arabs and Seba will bring gifts (*βασιλεῖς Ἀράβων καὶ Σαβα δῶρα προσάξουσιν*), all the kings will worship him (*καὶ προσκυνήσουσιν αὐτῷ πάντες οἱ βασιλεῖς*), and all the nations will serve him (*πάντα τὰ ἔθνη δουλεύσουσιν αὐτῷ*). For other OT background passages, see 21:25 and 3:9.

21:27 καὶ (adversative) **οὐ μὴ** (emph. neg.) **εἰσέλθῃ** (3rd sg. aor. act. subjunc. of εἰσέρχομαι, the sg. vb. is used with a compound subj.) **εἰς αὐτὴν** (loc.) **πᾶν** (attrib.) **κοινὸν** (κοινός, -ή, -όν, "common," subst., subj. nom.) **καὶ** [**ὁ**] **ποιῶν** (nom. sg. masc. of pres. act. ptc. of ποιέω, subst., coord. subj. nom.) **βδέλυγμα** (βδέλυγμα, -ατος, τό, "defilement, abomination," dir. obj.) **καὶ ψεῦδος** (ψεῦδος, -ους, τό, "falsehood, lie," coord. dir. obj.) **εἰ μὴ** ("if not, except") **οἱ γεγραμμένοι** (nom. pl. masc. of pf. pass. ptc. of γράφω, subst., subj. nom.) **ἐν τῷ βιβλίῳ** (βιβλίον, -ου, τό, "scroll," loc.) **τῆς ζωῆς** (descriptive) **τοῦ ἀρνίου** (ἀρνίον, -ου, τό, "lamb," poss.).

Nothing common or defiled can enter because the entire city is sacred space filled with God's presence. The book of life functions here like a list of citizens. Revelation 22:15 describes how the dogs will be excluded from the city. In 1 Cor 6:9–10, Paul stresses that the unrighteous will not inherit the kingdom of God.

Use of the OT: Isaiah 52:1 prophesies that a day will come when the uncircumcised and unclean will no longer go through Jerusalem (*οὐκέτι προστεθήσεται διελθεῖν διὰ σοῦ ἀπερίτμητος καὶ ἀκάθαρτος*). Nahum 2:1 LXX states that in the future the adversaries will no longer go through Judah (*διότι οὐ μὴ προσθήσωσιν ἔτι τοῦ διελθεῖν διὰ σοῦ εἰς παλαίωσιν*). On the book of life, see 3:5.

22:1 Καὶ ἔδειξέν (3rd sg. aor. act. ind. of δείκνυμι, "show") **μοι** (indir. obj.) **ποταμὸν** (ποταμός, -οῦ, ὁ, "river," dir. obj.) **ὕδατος** (content) **ζωῆς** (attrib.) **λαμπρὸν** (λαμπρός, -ά, -όν, "bright, transparent," attrib. to ποταμὸν) **ὡς** (comp.) **κρύσταλλον** (κρύσταλλος, -ου, ὁ, "crystal"), **ἐκπορευόμενον** (acc. sg. masc. of pres. mid. ptc. of ἐκπορεύομαι, attrib. to ποταμὸν) **ἐκ τοῦ** (anaphoric to 4:2) **θρόνου** (source) **τοῦ θεοῦ** (poss.) **καὶ τοῦ** (anaphoric to 5:6) **ἀρνίου** (ἀρνίον, -ου, τό, "lamb," poss.).

Use of the OT: For Ezek 47:1, see 21:10. For Joel 3:18, see 14:19. Zechariah 14:8 promises that in that day the water of life will go out of Jerusalem (*καὶ ἐν τῇ ἡμέρᾳ ἐκείνῃ ἐξελεύσεται ὕδωρ ζῶν ἐξ Ιερουσαλημ*), half of it into the first sea and half of it into the last sea (τὸ ἥμισυ αὐτοῦ εἰς τὴν θάλασσαν τὴν πρώτην καὶ τὸ ἥμισυ αὐτοῦ εἰς τὴν θάλασσαν τὴν ἐσχάτην).

22:2 ἐν μέσῳ (loc., this could connect back to ἐκπορευόμενον in 22:1; the river proceeds from the throne and flows in the middle of the main street of the city) **τῆς πλατείας** (πλατεῖα, -ας, ἡ, "road," part. gen.) **αὐτῆς** (part. gen.) **καὶ τοῦ ποταμοῦ** (ποταμός, -οῦ, ὁ, "river," part. gen., presumably coord. with πλατείας, "in the midst of the street and the river") **ἐντεῦθεν** (adv., "from here") **καὶ ἐκεῖθεν** (adv., "from there," this idiomatically expresses the idea of "both sides of") **ξύλον** (ξύλον, -ου, τό, "tree," subj. nom. of verbless cl., the tree is sg. but it seems to be distributive since it grows on both sides of the river and seems to be indicated by ἕκαστον below) **ζωῆς** (descriptive or gen. of product) **ποιοῦν** (nom. sg. neut. of pres. act. ptc. of ποιέω, attrib.) **καρποὺς** (καρπός, -οῦ, ὁ, "fruit, harvest," dir. obj., the idea is twelve crops or harvests and not twelve different kinds of fruit) **δώδεκα** ("twelve," attrib.), **κατὰ** (correspondence, "according to") **μῆνα** (μήν, μηνός, ὁ, "month") **ἕκαστον** (nom. neut. sg. to match ξύλον above, likely subst. adj., "each one," it could be attrib. with μῆνα, "each month," but there is incongruity in gender) **ἀποδιδοῦν** (nom. sg. neut. of pres. act. ptc. of ἀποδίδωμι, prob. functions as finite vb. with ἕκαστον, "each one gives its fruit according to the month") **τὸν καρπὸν** (dir. obj.) **αὐτοῦ** (source), **καὶ τὰ φύλλα** (φύλλον, -ου, τό, "leaf," subj. nom. of verbless cl.) **τοῦ ξύλου** (part. gen.) **εἰς θεραπείαν** (θεραπεία, -ας, ἡ, "healing," purpose) **τῶν ἐθνῶν** (obj. gen.).

The picture seems to be of a river in the middle of the main street of the city with the tree of life growing on both sides of it. The general impression is more important than a specific visualization of the details.

Use of the OT: Genesis 2:9 describes the tree of life in the midst of the garden (τὸ ξύλον τῆς ζωῆς ἐν μέσῳ τῷ παραδείσῳ). Genesis 3:22 describes how God sent Adam out of the garden to prevent him from eating from the tree of life. For Ezek 47:12, see 21:10.

22:3 καὶ πᾶν (attrib.) **κατάθεμα** (κατάθεμα, -ατος, τό, "accursed thing," subj. nom.) **οὐκ ἔσται** (3rd sg. fut. mid. ind. of εἰμί) **ἔτι** (adv., extension of time). **καὶ ὁ** (anaphoric to 4:2; this is the last mention of God's throne) **θρόνος** (subj. nom.) **τοῦ θεοῦ** (poss.) **καὶ τοῦ** (anaphoric to 5:6) **ἀρνίου** (ἀρνίον, -ου, τό, "lamb," poss.) **ἐν αὐτῇ** (loc.) **ἔσται, καὶ οἱ δοῦλοι** (subj. nom.) **αὐτοῦ** (poss., the sg. pron. is used in 22:3, 4 in an ambiguous way that seemingly has both God and the lamb as an ant.; a single ant. can be arbitrarily chosen or the two potential ants. could be viewed as a unity in anticipation of later trinitarian reflection) **λατρεύσουσιν** (3rd pl. fut. act. ind. of λατρεύω, "worship, serve") **αὐτῷ** (dat. dir. obj.)

This is a continuation of the worship (λατρεύω) of God that began in the intermediate state (7:15).

Use of the OT: Zechariah 14:11 promises that the people will dwell in Jerusalem (κατοικήσουσιν ἐν αὐτῇ), and the curse will not be any more (καὶ οὐκ ἔσται ἀνάθεμα ἔτι) and Jerusalem will dwell confidently (καὶ κατοικήσει Ιερουσαλημ πεποιθότως). There is not a direct lexical connection to the curse of Gen 3:17, which uses the syn. ἐπικατάρατος, but a thematic connection cannot be ruled out because of allusions in the nearby verses to Genesis 3.

22:4 καὶ ὄψονται (3rd pl. fut. mid. ind. of ὁράω) **τὸ πρόσωπον** (dir. obj.) **αὐτοῦ** (poss.), **καὶ τὸ ὄνομα** (subj. nom. of verbless cl.) **αὐτοῦ** (poss.) **ἐπὶ τῶν μετώπων** (μέτωπον, -ου, τό, "forehead," loc.) **αὐτῶν** (poss.).

Revelation 3:12 promises that the overcomer will never leave the temple of God. God's seal was also placed on the foreheads of the 144,000 (7:4), which was identified in 14:1 as his name. This vision anticipates God's name on the forehead of all of God's servants. It was widely understood that humans could not look upon God (John 1:18; 1 John 4:12) but this will not be the case in the new creation. Jesus promises in Matt 5:8 that the pure in heart are blessed because they would see God (μακάριοι οἱ καθαροὶ τῇ καρδίᾳ, ὅτι αὐτοὶ τὸν θεὸν ὄψονται).

Use of the OT: David prays in Ps 16:15 LXX (17:15 EVV) to see God's face in righteousness (ἐγὼ δὲ ἐν δικαιοσύνῃ ὀφθήσομαι τῷ προσώπῳ σου) and says he will be satisfied when seeing God's glory (χορτασθήσομαι ἐν τῷ ὀφθῆναι τὴν δόξαν σου). The sons of Korah in Ps 41:3 LXX (42:2 EVV) ask when one might come and see the face of God (πότε ἥξω καὶ ὀφθήσομαι τῷ προσώπῳ τοῦ θεοῦ;).

22:5 καὶ νὺξ (subj. nom.) **οὐκ ἔσται** (3rd sg. fut. mid. ind. of εἰμί) **ἔτι** (adv., extension of time) **καὶ οὐκ ἔχουσιν** (3rd pl. pres. act. ind. of ἔχω, futuristic) **χρείαν** (χρεία, -ας, ἡ, "need," dir. obj.) **φωτὸς** (φῶς, φωτός, τό, "light," obj. gen.) **λύχνου** (λύχνος, -ου, ὁ, "lamp," source) **καὶ φωτὸς** (obj. gen. with χρείαν) **ἡλίου** (ἥλιος, -ου, ὁ, "sun," source), **ὅτι** (causal) **κύριος** (subj. nom.) **ὁ θεὸς** (appos.) **φωτίσει** (3rd sg. fut. act. ind. of φωτίζω, "give light, enlighten") **ἐπ' αὐτούς** (loc.), **καὶ βασιλεύσουσιν** (3rd pl. fut. act. ind. of βασιλεύω, "rule, reign") **εἰς τοὺς αἰῶνας** (measure) **τῶν αἰώνων** (emph. repetition of αἰών).

This conclusion of the vision stresses the point made in Rev 1:6, 9; 5:10; 20:6 regarding God's people as a kingdom who will reign and rule. This concluding statement describes humanity fulfilling the creation mandate from Gen 1:26–28 to rule and reign on earth as God's representative image bearers. Revelation describes how sin and death are overcome to enable God's people to fulfill this original purpose.

Use of the OT: Zechariah 14:7 promises that there will be a day (ἔσται μίαν ἡμέραν), which is known to the Lord (καὶ ἡ ἡμέρα ἐκείνη γνωστὴ τῷ κυρίῳ), where there will be no day and no night (καὶ οὐχ ἡμέρα καὶ οὐ νύξ), and in the evening it will be light (καὶ πρὸς ἑσπέραν ἔσται φῶς). For Isa 60:19–20, see Rev 21:23. Daniel 7:18 promises that the saints of the Most High will receive the kingdom and will hold fast to the kingdom until the age and until the age of the ages (καὶ παραλήψονται τὴν βασιλείαν ἅγιοι ὑψίστου καὶ καθέξουσι τὴν βασιλείαν ἕως τοῦ αἰῶνος καὶ ἕως τοῦ αἰῶνος τῶν αἰώνων). Daniel 7 concludes its vision by stating that God gave the kingdom, authority, majesty, and the rule of all the kings under the heaven to the holy people of the Most High (7:27: καὶ τὴν βασιλείαν καὶ τὴν ἐξουσίαν καὶ τὴν μεγαλειότητα αὐτῶν καὶ τὴν ἀρχὴν πασῶν τῶν ὑπὸ τὸν οὐρανὸν βασιλειῶν ἔδωκε λαῷ ἁγίῳ ὑψίστου) so as to rule an eternal kingdom (βασιλεῦσαι βασιλείαν αἰώνιον), and all the authorities will be subject to them and will obey them (καὶ πᾶσαι αἱ ἐξουσίαι αὐτῷ ὑποταγήσονται καὶ πειθαρχήσουσιν αὐτῷ).

FOR FURTHER STUDY

52. The Use of Ezekiel in Revelation

Bøe, S. *Gog and Magog: Ezekiel 38–39 as Pre-Text for Revelation 19, 17–21 and 20, 7–10*. WUNT 2.135. Tübingen: Mohr Siebeck, 2001.

Kowalski, B. "Transformation of Ezekiel in John's Revelation." Pages 279–311 in *Transforming Visions: Transformations of Text, Traditions, and Theology in Ezekiel*. Edited by W. A. Tooman and M. A. Lyons. Cambridge: Clarke, 2010.

Ruiz, J. P. *Ezekiel in the Apocalypse: The Transformation of Prophetic Language in Revelation 16,17–19,10*. Europäische Hochschulschriften Series 23, Theologie 376. Frankfurt am Main: Lang, 1989.

53. Salvation of the Nations

Bauckham, R. *The Climax of Prophecy: Studies on the Book of Revelation*. Edinburgh: T&T Clark, 1993. (see esp. 238–337)

Herms, R. *An Apocalypse for the Church and for the World: The Narrative Function of Universal Language in the Book of Revelation*. BZNW 143. Berlin: de Gruyter, 2006.

McNicol, A. J. *The Conversion of the Nations in Revelation*. LNTS 438. London: T&T Clark, 2011.

Mathewson, D. "The Destiny of the Nations in Revelation 21:1–22:5: A Reconsideration." *TynBul* 53 (2002): 121–42.

*Morales, J. *Christ, Shepherd of the Nations: The Nations as Narrative Character and Audience in John's Apocalypse*. LNTS 577. London: Bloomsbury, 2017.

54. Mission

*Osborne, G. "The Mission to the Nations in the Book of Revelation." Pages 347–67 in *New Testament Theology in Light of the Church's Mission: Essays in Honor of I. Howard Marshall*. Edited by J. C. Laansma, G. Osborne, and R. van Neste. Eugene, OR: Cascade, 2014.

Schnabel, E. J. "Early Christian Mission and Christian Identity in the Context of the Ethnic, Social, and Political Affiliations in Revelation." Pages 369–86 in *New Testament Theology in Light of the Church's Mission: Essays in Honor of I. Howard Marshall*. Edited by J. C. Laansma, G. Osborne, and R. van Neste. Eugene, OR: Cascade, 2014.

55. The Use of Genesis in Revelation

Moyise, S. "Genesis in Revelation." Pages 166–79 in *Genesis in the New Testament*. Edited by S. Moyise and M. J. J. Menken. LNTS 466. London: T&T Clark, 2014.

VI. Epilogue (22:6–21)

A. TRANSITIONAL CONCLUSION (22:6–9)

22:6 Καὶ εἶπέν (3rd sg. aor. act. ind.of λέγω) **μοι** (indir. obj.), **Οὗτοι** (attrib., the ant. could be the entire book, the vision starting at 4:1, or the vision starting at 21:1 or 21:9) **οἱ λόγοι** (subj. nom. of verbless cl.) **πιστοὶ** (pred. adj.) **καὶ ἀληθινοί** (ἀληθινός, -ή, -όν, "true," coord. pred. adj.), **καὶ ὁ κύριος** (subj. nom.) **ὁ θεὸς** (appos.) **τῶν πνευμάτων** (subord.) **τῶν προφητῶν** (poss.) **ἀπέστειλεν** (3rd sg. aor. act. ind. of ἀποστέλλω) **τὸν ἄγγελον** (dir. obj.) **αὐτοῦ** (poss.) **δεῖξαι** (aor. act. inf. of δείκνυμι, "show," purpose) **τοῖς δούλοις** (indir. obj.) **αὐτοῦ** (poss.) **ἃ** (headless rel. cl. functions as dir. obj. of δεῖξαι) **δεῖ γενέσθαι** (aor. mid. inf. of γίνομαι, compl. inf.) **ἐν τάχει** (τάχος, -ους, τό, "quickness," adv. use of prep. phrase).

The chain of revelatory communication outlined here parallels what was stated in Rev 1:1.

Use of the OT: Daniel 2:28–29 speaks of God as the one who reveals what is necessary to happen in the last days (ἃ δεῖ γενέσθαι ἐπ' ἐσχάτων τῶν ἡμερῶν). Daniel proceeds to claim that in Nebuchadnezzar's dream God signified to him the things that will be in the last days (2:45: ὁ θεὸς ὁ μέγας ἐσήμανε τῷ βασιλεῖ τὰ ἐσόμενα ἐπ' ἐσχάτων τῶν ἡμερῶν).

22:7 καὶ ἰδοὺ (emph. interj.) **ἔρχομαι** (1st sg. pres. mid. ind. of ἔρχομαι) **ταχύ** (ταχύς, -εῖα, -ύ, "soon, quickly," adv.). **μακάριος** (μακάριος, -ία, -ιον, "blessed, happy," pred. adj. of verbless cl.) **ὁ τηρῶν** (nom. sg. masc. of pres. act. ptc. of τηρέω, subst., subj. nom. of verbless cl.) **τοὺς λόγους** (dir. obj.) **τῆς προφητείας** (epex.) **τοῦ βιβλίου** (βιβλίον, -ου, τό, "scroll," poss.) **τούτου** (attrib.).

Note the switch to first-person divine speech. Jesus's imminent coming is also predicted in 2:16; 3:11; 22:12, 20. Revelation 2:16 seems to refer to Jesus coming within history to bring judgment before the climactic second coming. On the call to "keep" the words of the book, see 1:3.

22:8 Κἀγὼ (crasis, "I also, even I, and I," subj. nom.) **Ἰωάννης** ("John," appos.) **ὁ ἀκούων** (nom. sg. masc. of pres. act. ptc. of ἀκούω, subst., appos., narrative pres.) **καὶ βλέπων** (nom. sg. masc. of pres. act. ptc. of βλέπω, coord. subst. appos., narrative pres.) **ταῦτα** (dir. obj., the ant. is the entire book or the final vision in 21:9–22:5). **καὶ ὅτε** (temp. subord. conj.) **ἤκουσα** (1st sg. aor. act. ind. of ἀκούω) **καὶ ἔβλεψα** (1st sg. aor. act. ind. of βλέπω, coord.), **ἔπεσα** (1st sg. aor. act. ind. of πίπτω) **προσκυνῆσαι** (aor. act. inf. of προσκυνέω, purpose) **ἔμπροσθεν** ("before") **τῶν ποδῶν** (loc.) **τοῦ ἀγγέλου** (poss.) **τοῦ δεικνύοντός** (gen. sg. masc. of pres. act. ptc. of δείκνυμι, "show," attrib., narrative pres.) **μοι** (indir. obj.) **ταῦτα** (dir. obj.).

This narrative parallels Rev 19:10 and has similar components to Acts 10:25–26.

22:9 καὶ λέγει (3rd sg. pres. act. ind. of λέγω, narrative pres.) **μοι** (indir. obj.), **Ὅρα** (2nd sg. pres. act. impv. of ὁράω, idiomatic expression of prohibition) **μή· σύνδουλός** (σύνδουλος, -ου, ὁ, "fellow-servant," pred. nom.) **σού** (association [Wallace 128]) **εἰμι**

(1st sg. pres. act. ind. of εἰμί) **καὶ τῶν ἀδελφῶν** (coord. association) **σου** (relationship) **τῶν προφητῶν** (appos.) **καὶ** (epex. or coord. to indicate a new group) **τῶν τηρούντων** (gen. pl. masc. of pres. act. ptc. of τηρέω, subst., association) **τοὺς λόγους** (dir. obj.) **τοῦ βιβλίου** (βιβλίον, -ου, τό, "scroll," part. or poss.) **τούτου** (attrib.)· **τῷ θεῷ** (dat. dir. obj.) **προσκύνησον** (2nd sg. aor. act. impv. of προσκυνέω).

B. CONCLUDING EXHORTATIONS (22:10–21)

22:10 καὶ λέγει (3rd sg. pres. act. ind. of λέγω, narrative pres.) **μοι** (indir. obj.), **Μὴ σφραγίσῃς** (2nd sg. aor. act. subjunc. of σφραγίζω, "seal," prohibition) **τοὺς λόγους** (dir. obj.) **τῆς προφητείας** (προφητεία, -ας, ἡ, "prophecy," epex.) **τοῦ βιβλίου** (βιβλίον, -ου, τό, "scroll," part. or poss.) **τούτου** (attrib.), **ὁ καιρὸς** (subj. nom.) **γὰρ** (causal) **ἐγγύς** (adv., "near," functions as pred. compl.) **ἐστιν** (3rd sg. pres. act. ind. of εἰμί).

Use of the OT: Daniel 12:4 contains the exact opposite command: κάλυψον τὰ προστάγματα καὶ σφράγισαι τὸ βιβλίον ἕως καιροῦ συντελείας. This parallel would suggest that John saw Daniel's time of completion to be very near. It also suggests that John viewed his work of prophecy as similar in kind and authority to that of Daniel. The command for Daniel to "cover" (καλύπτω) the words could also have influenced John's choice to begin Revelation with a noun of uncovering (1:1: ἀποκάλυψις).

22:11 ὁ ἀδικῶν (nom. sg. masc. of pres. act. ptc. of ἀδικέω, "act unjustly, damage," subst., subj. nom.) **ἀδικησάτω** (3rd sg. aor. act. impv. of ἀδικέω) **ἔτι** (adv., extension of time, "still, yet") **καὶ ὁ ῥυπαρὸς** (ῥυπαρός, -ά, -όν, "unclean," subst., subj. nom.) **ῥυπανθήτω** (3rd sg. aor. pass. impv. of ῥυπαίνω, "defile," this is the only occurrence of this vb. in Greek literature [Koester 841]), **ἔτι καὶ ὁ δίκαιος** (subst., subj. nom.) **δικαιοσύνην** (dir. obj.) **ποιησάτω** (3rd sg. aor. act. impv. of ποιέω) **ἔτι καὶ ὁ ἅγιος** (subst., subj. nom.) **ἁγιασθήτω** (3rd sg. aor. pass. impv. of ἁγιάζω, "be holy") **ἔτι**.

The use of impvs. should not be taken as deterministic or as indicating that repentance was not possible or desired, but as a rhetorical strategy to motivate the hearer to be one who responds properly.

Use of the OT: Ezekiel 3:27 similarly uses 3rd pers. impvs. to make a similar point: let the one hearing hear and the one disobeying disobey (ἀκούων ἀκουέτω, καὶ ὁ ἀπειθῶν ἀπειθείτω). Daniel 12:10 states that the sinners will sin and all the sinners will certainly not understand (καὶ ἁμάρτωσιν οἱ ἁμαρτωλοί, καὶ οὐ μὴ διανοηθῶσι πάντες οἱ ἁμαρτωλοί).

22:12 Ἰδοὺ (emph. interj.) **ἔρχομαι** (1st sg. pres. mid. ind. of ἔρχομαι, futuristic) **ταχύ** (ταχύς, -εῖα, -ύ, "soon, quickly," functions adv.), **καὶ ὁ μισθός** (μισθός, -οῦ, ὁ, "wages, reward," subj. nom. of verbless cl.) **μου** (subj. gen.) **μετ' ἐμοῦ** (association) **ἀποδοῦναι** (aor. act. inf. of ἀποδίδωμι, purpose) **ἑκάστῳ** (indir. obj.) **ὡς** (correspondence providing a standard, prob. synonymous with κατὰ τὰ ἔργα in 2:23) **τὸ ἔργον** (subj. nom.) **ἐστὶν** (3rd sg. pres. act. ind. of εἰμί) **αὐτοῦ** (subj. gen. with ἔργον).

On Jesus coming soon, see 2:16; 3:11; 22:7, 20. Jesus participates with God in repaying to each according to one's work (20:12).

Use of the OT: Isaiah 40:10 states, "Behold the Lord comes with strength [ἰδοὺ κύριος μετὰ ἰσχύος ἔρχεται] and the arm with power [καὶ ὁ βραχίων μετὰ κυριείας], behold, his reward is with him and the work before him [ἰδοὺ ὁ μισθὸς αὐτοῦ μετ' αὐτοῦ καὶ τὸ ἔργον ἐναντίον αὐτοῦ]." Isaiah 62:11 similarly claims, "Behold, the savior comes to you having his own reward and the work before his face" (Ἰδού σοι ὁ σωτὴρ παραγίνεται ἔχων τὸν ἑαυτοῦ μισθὸν καὶ τὸ ἔργον πρὸ προσώπου αὐτοῦ). On judgment according to works, see 2:23.

22:13 ἐγὼ (subj. nom. of verbless cl.) **τὸ Ἄλφα** (pred. nom.) **καὶ τὸ Ὦ** (coord. pred. nom.), **ὁ πρῶτος** ("first," subst., appos.) **καὶ ὁ ἔσχατος** (ἔσχατος, -η, -ον, "last," subst., appos.), **ἡ ἀρχὴ** (ἀρχή, -ῆς, ἡ, "beginning, ruler," appos.) **καὶ τὸ τέλος** (appos.).

On God's self-designation as the Alpha and Omega, the first and last, the beginning and end, see 1:8; 21:6. Here it is Jesus who makes this claim.

22:14 Μακάριοι (μακάριος, -ία, -ιον, "blessed, happy," pred. adj. of verbless cl.) **οἱ πλύνοντες** (nom. pl. masc. of pres. act. ptc. of πλύνω, "wash," subst., subj. nom. of verbless cl.) **τὰς στολὰς** (στολή, -ῆς, ἡ, "robe," dir. obj.) **αὐτῶν** (poss.), **ἵνα** (introduces content cl. which is epex. with Μακάριοι, or result) **ἔσται** (3rd sg. fut. mid. ind. of εἰμί) **ἡ ἐξουσία** (subj. nom.) **αὐτῶν** (subj. gen.) **ἐπὶ τὸ ξύλον** (ξύλον, -ου, τό, "tree," subord.) **τῆς ζωῆς** (product, "the tree that produces life") **καὶ τοῖς πυλῶσιν** (πυλών, -ῶνος, ὁ, "gateway," means) **εἰσέλθωσιν** (3rd pl. aor. act. subjunc. of εἰσέρχομαι) **εἰς τὴν πόλιν** (loc.).

The phrase πλύνοντες τὰς στολὰς αὐτῶν has strong support in א A along with some minuscules and versions while 046, most minuscules, and the TR reads ποιοῦντες τὰς ἐντολὰς αὐτου, which intratextually parallels 12:17; 14:12.

Use of the OT: On the tree of life in Gen 2:9, 3:22, and Ezek 47:12, see 22:2.

22:15 ἔξω (adv. of place, "outside," functions as pred. compl. of verbless cl.) **οἱ κύνες** (κύων, κυνός, ὁ, "dog," each nom. in this list is a coord. subj. nom. of a verbless cl.) **καὶ οἱ φάρμακοι** (φάρμακος, -ου, ὁ, "sorcerer") **καὶ οἱ πόρνοι** (πόρνος, -ου, ὁ, "sexually immoral person") **καὶ οἱ φονεῖς** (φονεύς, -έως, ὁ, "murderer") **καὶ οἱ εἰδωλολάτραι** (εἰδωλολάτρης, -ου, ὁ, "idolater") **καὶ πᾶς** (attrib.) **φιλῶν** (nom. sg. masc. of pres. act.

ptc. of φιλέω, "love," subst.) **καὶ ποιῶν** (nom. sg. masc. of pres. act. ptc. of ποιέω, coord. subst.) **ψεῦδος** (ψεῦδος, -ους, τό, "falsehood, lie," dir. obj.).

Revelation 21:8, 27 also describes those who will be excluded from the new Jerusalem. The label "dogs" is unique here; it is generally pejorative but could more specifically relate to male prostitutes as in Deut 23:18 (Aune[c] 1222–23). Paul makes a similar claim in 1 Cor 6:9–10 that the unrighteous will not inherit the kingdom of God.

22:16 Ἐγὼ (subj. nom.) **Ἰησοῦς** (appos.) **ἔπεμψα** (1st sg. aor. act. ind. of πέμπω) **τὸν ἄγγελόν** (dir. obj.) **μου** (poss.) **μαρτυρῆσαι** (aor. act. inf. of μαρτυρέω, "testify, bear witness," purpose) **ὑμῖν** (indir. obj., the pl. points beyond just John) **ταῦτα** (dir. obj., the ant. may be the whole book) **ἐπὶ ταῖς ἐκκλησίαις** (advantage, "for the churches"). **ἐγώ** (subj. nom.) **εἰμι** (1st sg. pres. act. ind. of εἰμί) **ἡ ῥίζα** (ῥίζα, -ης, ἡ, "root," pred. nom.) **καὶ τὸ γένος** (γένος, -ους, τό, "descendent," coord. pred. nom.) **Δαυίδ** ("David," relationship or source), **ὁ ἀστὴρ** (ἀστήρ, -έρος, ὁ, "star," appos.) **ὁ λαμπρὸς** (λαμπρός, -ά, -όν, "bright," attrib.) **ὁ πρωϊνός** (πρωϊνός, -ή, -όν, "morning," attrib.).

Revelation 5:5 describes Jesus as ὁ λέων ὁ ἐκ τῆς φυλῆς Ἰούδα and ἡ ῥίζα Δαυίδ. In Rom 1:3, Paul describes Jesus as the one who came out of the seed of David according to the flesh (τοῦ γενομένου ἐκ σπέρματος Δαυὶδ κατὰ σάρκα). In Rev 2:28, Jesus promises to give the τὸν ἀστέρα τὸν πρωϊνόν to the one who overcomes.

Use of the OT: Isaiah 11:1 promises that a staff will come out of the root of Jesse (Καὶ ἐξελεύσεται ῥάβδος ἐκ τῆς ῥίζης Ιεσσαι) and a blossom out of the root will go up (καὶ ἄνθος ἐκ τῆς ῥίζης ἀναβήσεται). Isaiah 11:10 further claims that in that day the root of Jesse will rise up to rule the nations (Καὶ ἔσται ἐν τῇ ἡμέρᾳ ἐκείνῃ ἡ ῥίζα τοῦ Ιεσσαι καὶ ὁ ἀνιστάμενος ἄρχειν ἐθνῶν), and on him the nations will hope and his repose will be honor (ἐπ' αὐτῷ ἔθνη ἐλπιοῦσιν, καὶ ἔσται ἡ ἀνάπαυσις αὐτοῦ τιμή). Balaam's final oracle in Num 24:17 prophesies that a star will arise out of Jacob (ἀνατελεῖ ἄστρον ἐξ Ιακωβ).

22:17 Καὶ ("both") **τὸ πνεῦμα** (subj. nom.) **καὶ ἡ νύμφη** (νύμφη, -ης, ἡ, "bride," coord. subj. nom.) **λέγουσιν** (3rd pl. pres. act. ind. of λέγω), **Ἔρχου** (2nd sg. pres. mid. impv. of ἔρχομαι). **καὶ ὁ ἀκούων** (nom. sg. masc. of pres. act. ptc. of ἀκούω, subst., subj. nom.) **εἰπάτω** (3rd sg. aor. act. impv. of λέγω), **Ἔρχου. καὶ ὁ διψῶν** (nom. sg. masc. pres. act. ptc. διψάω, "thirst," subst., subj. nom.) **ἐρχέσθω** (3rd sg. pres. mid. impv. ἔρχομαι), **ὁ θέλων** (nom. sg. masc. of pres. act. ptc. of θέλω, subst. subj. nom.) **λαβέτω** (3rd sg. aor. act. impv. of λαμβάνω) **ὕδωρ** (dir. obj.) **ζωῆς** (attrib.) **δωρεάν** (adv. acc. of manner, "freely").

Use of the OT: On living water, see 21:6.

22:18 **Μαρτυρῶ** (1st sg. pres. act. ind. of *μαρτυρέω*, "testify, bear witness") **ἐγὼ** (subj. nom., the "I" is not explicit and is likely John or Jesus; the distinction is prob. not important since John prophetically speaks for Jesus in the first person in Revelation [cf. chapters 2–3]) **παντὶ** (attrib.) **τῷ ἀκούοντι** (dat. sg. masc. of pres. act. ptc. of *ἀκούω*, subst., indir. obj.) **τοὺς λόγους** (dir. obj.) **τῆς προφητείας** (*προφητεία, -ας, ἡ*, "prophecy," attrib., "the prophetic words," or epex., "the words, that is, the prophecy") **τοῦ βιβλίου** (*βιβλίον, -ου, τό*, "scroll," part. or poss.) **τούτου** (attrib.)· **ἐάν** (introduces 3rd class cond. cl.) **τις** (subj. nom.) **ἐπιθῇ** (3rd sg. aor. act. subjunc. of *ἐπιτίθημι*) **ἐπ' αὐτά** (indicates "addition to what already exists" [L&N 89.101]), **ἐπιθήσει** (3rd sg. fut. act. ind. of *ἐπιτίθημι*) **ὁ θεὸς** (subj. nom.) **ἐπ' αὐτὸν** (addition) **τὰς πληγὰς** (*πληγή, -ῆς, ἡ*, "plague," dir. obj.) **τὰς γεγραμμένας** (acc. pl. fem. of pf. pass. ptc. of *γράφω*, attrib.) **ἐν τῷ βιβλίῳ** (loc.) **τούτῳ** (attrib.),

---

Use of the OT: Deuteronomy 4:2 similarly orders the people not to add to the words that Moses commands them (*οὐ προσθήσετε πρὸς τὸ ῥῆμα, ὃ ἐγὼ ἐντέλλομαι ὑμῖν*), to not take away from them (*καὶ οὐκ ἀφελεῖτε ἀπ' αὐτοῦ*), and to keep the commandments of the Lord their God as much as Moses has commanded them (*φυλάσσεσθε τὰς ἐντολὰς κυρίου τοῦ θεοῦ ὑμῶν*). This is repeated in Deut 13:1 LXX (12:32 EVV): "Be careful to do everything I command you [*Πᾶν ῥῆμα, ὃ ἐγὼ ἐντέλλομαί σοι σήμερον, τοῦτο φυλάξῃ ποιεῖν;*] do not add anything to it or take anything away from it [*οὐ προσθήσεις ἐπ' αὐτὸ οὐδὲ ἀφελεῖς ἀπ' αὐτοῦ*]" [CSB].

22:19 **καὶ ἐάν** (introduces 3rd class cond. cl.) **τις** (subj. nom.) **ἀφέλῃ** (3rd sg. aor. act. subjunc. of *ἀφαιρέω*, "remove") **ἀπὸ τῶν λόγων** (separation) **τοῦ βιβλίου** (*βιβλίον, -ου, τό*, "scroll," part. or poss.) **τῆς προφητείας** (*προφητεία, -ας, ἡ*, "prophecy," content) **ταύτης** (attrib.), **ἀφελεῖ** (3rd sg. fut. act. ind. of *ἀφαιρέω*) **ὁ θεὸς** (subj. nom.) **τὸ μέρος** (*μέρος, -ους, τό*, "portion," dir. obj.) **αὐτοῦ** (poss.) **ἀπὸ τοῦ ξύλου** (*ξύλον, -ου, τό*, "tree," part. gen., the whole of which *μέρος* is a part, the TR reads *ἀπὸ βίβλου* based on Erasmus's translation of the Latin Vulgate with no support in any Gk. ms [Metzger 690]) **τῆς ζωῆς** (product) **καὶ ἐκ τῆς πόλεως** (part. with *μέρος*) **τῆς ἁγίας** (attrib.) **τῶν γεγραμμένων** (gen. pl. neut. of pf. pass. ptc. of *γράφω*, attrib., the pl. ptc. modifies the coord. gen. examples of the things written, *ἀπὸ τοῦ ξύλου* and *ἐκ τῆς πόλεως*) **ἐν τῷ βιβλίῳ** (loc.) **τούτῳ** (attrib.).

The warning against altering the text applies to the book of Revelation and not the entire canon; by extension, it could also function as a warning "not to falsify the scroll's message by one's teaching or manner of life" (Koester 844).

Use of the OT: On the tree of life, see on 21:10; 22:2.

22:20 Λέγει (3rd sg. pres. act. ind. of λέγω) **ὁ μαρτυρῶν** (nom. sg. masc. of pres. act. ptc. of μαρτυρέω, "testify, bear witness," subst. subj. nom.) **ταῦτα** (dir. obj., the ant. is likely the whole book of Revelation), **Ναί** (interj. of positive affirmation, "yes, indeed"), **ἔρχομαι** (1st sg. pres. mid. ind. of ἔρχομαι) **ταχύ** (ταχύς, -εῖα, -ύ, "soon, quickly," functions adv.), **Ἀμήν** (interj.), **ἔρχου** (2nd sg. pres. mid. impv. of ἔρχομαι) **κύριε** (voc.) **Ἰησοῦ** (appos.).

The promise of a swift coming is also found in 2:16; 3:11; 22:7, 12.

22:21 Ἡ χάρις (subj. nom. of verbless cl.) **τοῦ κυρίου** (source) **Ἰησοῦ** (appos.) **μετὰ πάντων** (association).

The text above follows A, but there is a great deal of textual variation in this final verse. Most minuscules add Χριστοῦ after Ἰησοῦ; ὑμῶν is added after πάντων in 296 and the TR; ἡμῶν is added after πάντων in 2050; τῶν ἁγίων replaces πάντων in א 2329 and is added after πάντων in 051[supp] 205 209 1006 1841 1611 1854 2030 2062 2377 *Byz* (this is congruent with the regular use of ἅγιος to describe God's people in Revelation); and ἀμήν concludes the book in א 046 051 and most minuscules but is missing in A 1006 2065[txt] 2432 and several versions (Metzger 690–91).

FOR FURTHER STUDY

56. The Use of Deuteronomy in Revelation

Tilly, M. "Deuteronomy in Revelation." Pages 169–88 in *Deuteronomy in the New Testament*. Edited by S. Moyise and M. J. J. Menken. LNTS 358. London: T&T Clark, 2007.

HOMILETICAL SUGGESTIONS

The final two visions provide overlapping descriptions of God's new creation (21:1–22:5) and the epilogue reviews many of the motivational themes of the book (22:6–21). God's new creation focuses on the theme of God's direct presence with his people (21:3, 22–23; 22:4), the removal of all sources of evil, chaos, and pain (21:4), and the security of God's people (21:12–25). The visions function to provide comfort (21:4), motivation (21:7; 22:7, 14), warning (21:8, 27; 22:12, 15, 18–19), and invitation (21:6; 22:17).

God's New Creation (21:1–22:21)

1. Visions of God's new creation bring comfort.
2. Visions of God's new creation provide motivation.
3. Visions of God's new creation contain warnings.
4. Visions of God's new creation serve as an invitation.

Exegetical Outline

I. Prologue (1:1–8)
   A. Title and Blessing (1:1–3)
   B. Epistolary Prescript (1:4–5c)
   C. Doxology (1:5d–6)
   D. Prophetic Oracles (1:7–8)

II. In the Spirit on Patmos (1:9–3:22)
   A. John's Vision and Commission (1:9–20)
      1. John's Commission (1:9–11)
      2. The Vision of Jesus (1:12–16)
      3. John's Commission Repeated (1:17–20)
   B. Proclamations to Seven Churches (2:1–3:22)
      1. Proclamation to Ephesus (2:1–7)
      2. Proclamation to Smyrna (2:8–11)
      3. Proclamation to Pergamum (2:12–17)
      4. Proclamation to Thyatira (2:18–29)
      5. Proclamation to Sardis (3:1–6)
      6. Proclamation to Philadelphia (3:7–13)
      7. Proclamation to Laodicea (3:14–22)

III. In the Spirit in Heaven (4:1–16:21)
   A. The Divine Throne Room (4:1–5:14)
      1. Worship of God (4:1–11)
      2. Enthronement of the Lamb (5:1–14)
   B. Opening the Seven Seals (6:1–8:5)
      1. The First Four Seals (6:1–8)
      2. The Fifth Seal (6:9–11)
      3. The Sixth Seal (6:12–17)
      4. The Sealing of 144,000 (7:1–8)

5. The Uncountable Multitude (7:9–17)
6. The Seventh Seal (8:1–5)

C. Seven Trumpet Judgments (8:6–11:19)

1. Preparation of the Seven Trumpets (8:6)
2. The First Six Trumpet Judgments (8:7–9:21)

a. The First Trumpet (8:7)
b. The Second Trumpet (8:8–9)
c. The Third Trumpet (8:10–11)
d. The Fourth Trumpet (8:12–13)
e. The Fifth Trumpet (9:1–12)
f. The Sixth Trumpet (9:13–21)

3. John's Recommissioning (10:1–11)
4. The Temple (11:1–2)
5. The Two Witnesses (11:3–14)
6. The Seventh Trumpet Judgment (11:15–19)

D. An Overview and Interpretation of History (12:1–14:20)

1. The Cause of Conflict: The Woman, Dragon, and Seed (12:1–17)

a. The Woman and Dragon (12:1–6)
b. War in Heaven (12:7–12)
c. Divine Protection for the Woman (12:13–17)

2. The Present and Future Conflict: Two Beasts (12:18–13:18)

a. The Beast out of the Sea (12:18–13:10)
b. The Beast out of the Land (13:11–18)

3. Victory in the Conflict: The 144,000 on Mount Zion (14:1–5)
4. The Call to Choose Sides: Four Proclamations (14:6–13)

a. The Eternal Gospel (14:6–7)
b. The Fall of Babylon (14:8)
c. The Suffering of Beast Worshippers (14:9–12)
d. The Blessedness of God's People (14:13)

5. The End of Conflict: Two Harvests (14:14–20)

a. The Grain Harvest (14:14–16)
b. The Grape Harvest (14:17–20)

E. The Seven Bowl Judgments (15:1–16:21)

1. Introduction of Seven Bowls (15:1)
2. The Song of Moses and the Lamb (15:2–4)
3. The Seven Bowls (15:5–16:21)

a. Preparation for the Seven Bowls (15:5–8)
b. The First Bowl (16:1–2)

c. The Second Bowl (16:3)
d. The Third Bowl (16:4–7)
e. The Fourth Bowl (16:8–9)
f. The Fifth Bowl (16:10–11)
g. The Sixth Bowl (16:12–16)
h. The Seventh Bowl (16:17–21)

IV. In the Spirit in the Wilderness (17:1–21:8)

A. Babylon the Great (17:1–18:24)

1. Vision of Babylon and the Beast (17:1–14)
2. Destruction of Babylon (17:15–18)
3. Mourning over Babylon's Fall (18:1–24)

B. Final Victory (19:1–21:8)

1. The Coming of the Lamb (19:1–21)

a. The Wedding of the Lamb (19:1–9)
b. Worshipping the Angel (19:10)
c. The Rider on a White Horse (19:11–16)
d. The Final Defeat of the Two Beasts (19:17–21)

2. The Millennium (20:1–6)
3. Satan's Final Defeat (20:7–10)
4. The Final Judgment (20:11–15)
5. New Creation (21:1–8)

V. In the Spirit on a High Mountain (21:9–22:5)

VI. Epilogue (22:6–21)

A. Transitional Conclusion (22:6–9)
B. Concluding Exhortations (22:10–21)

Grammar Index

Scripture Index